1978

SCIENCE,

FOLKLORE,

and

PHILOSOPHY

HARRY GIRVETZ

University of California, Santa Barbara

GEORGE GEIGER

Antioch College

HAROLD HANTZ

University of Arkansas

BERTRAM MORRIS

University of Colorado

SCIENCE, FOLKLORE, and PHILOSOPHY

Harper & Row, Publishers   *New York and London*

Contents

v

PART II   IMPACT OF THE NEW PHYSICS

PART III PHILOSOPHICAL RESPONSES TO DARWINISM

Preface

This book presents a special approach to philosophy. Even a skeptic may be persuaded that it is a fruitful one and, in any case, an effective way of making philosophy meaningful to readers who come to it for the first time. These, it is hoped, will not only be students, but also informed laymen—provided the greedy distractions of modern living leave them time for serious reading and meditation.

The work is divided into four parts preceded by a long introduction, setting forth the intent and plan of the authors, and followed by an epilogue. Although sharing a common conception of the guiding thesis of the work as a whole, each contributor has inevitably applied and interpreted this thesis in his own way. Uniformity in a work of collaboration could only be forced and artificial. Selected readings at the end of each chapter include references to paperback editions where these are available. The Introduction, Epilogue, and Part III are written by Harry Girvetz, Part I by Harold Hantz, Part II by Bertram Morris, and Part IV by George Geiger. Although each of the authors is responsible for his own material, each has benefited from the criticism and comments of the others.

The Introduction is intended primarily for instructors and readers with some philosophical background. Newcomers to philosophy need not avoid reading the Introduction in its proper order, but they may profit more if they return to it after having read the main body of the text.

H. G.

The unexamined life is not worth living.
PLATO, *Apology*

All men by nature desire to know.
ARISTOTLE, *Metaphysics*

Eppur si muove.
GALILEO (att.)

Introduction

Whatever philosophy may be today, it began as the pursuit of wisdom. In its theoretical aspect, wisdom meant possession of some unifying principle or principles by which to understand otherwise unrelated and isolated facts; in its practical aspect it meant insight into the meaning and direction of life. Implicit in this quest was a dissatisfaction with current explanations and prevailing orthodoxies and, with this, a critical attitude toward established authority. However, such dissatisfaction may come to rest in new orthodoxies which harden into new dogmas, and the critical spirit may languish and die. During much of the history of Western thought, and a good deal more of the history of Eastern thought, this has been true, for, in the absence of more precise tasks and more specific problems, it is unlikely that a generalized quest for wisdom (if in fact there ever was such) would ever have exceeded what Bertrand Russell has called the "isolated speculations of remarkable individuals." We would have reverie, mythology, cosmogonic poetry, homiletics, folk wisdom, imaginative insight, speculation—but probably not philosophy, not as we in the West have come to understand philosophy.

However, in the case of that part of world culture that traces its intellectual lineage to Greece, what began as a love of undifferentiated wisdom manifested itself also in the birth of the several sciences and thereby

1

created a problem that has presented philosophy with its major task from the time of the Ionians until the present day. Whether in the absence of science, we would have any philosophy—is debatable. Certainly the richness of philosophy—if not, in fact, the philosophic venture itself—is a result of the interaction of science with the prevailing system of beliefs. In general, the content of Western philosophy has been determined by its reactions to the methods and discoveries of science, and by the need to interpret these methods and discoveries and to relate the scientific enterprise as such to other human interests and undertakings. Sometimes the response has been to reject science, as did much of the romantic philosophy that flourished in the nineteenth century; sometimes philosophy has unreservedly embraced science, as did both historical and contemporary positivism; but its most prominent and significant role has been to bring about some kind of working relationship between science and so-called "common sense," and between science and those inherited beliefs which, for want of a better term, shall here be called "folklore." Thus, our assumption in the pages that follow is that philosophy is not in its main manifestations mere speculation, and that it has been infelicitously described as such—if by "speculation" we mean the attempt to interpret, to order, or to unify experience without reference to the discipline imposed by science.

It is not necessary to contend that speculation is mere irresponsible conjecture in order to argue that, unrestrained by science, the grandiose visions to which speculation gives rise are ultimately irrelevant to the solution of real problems, even though these visions may often exhibit the results of sustained reasoning, and, like poetry, afford an insight into the hopes and feelings of their authors. Traditionally, such speculation has been called "philosophy" because it represents a quest for understanding beyond what is yielded by our fragmentary everyday experience. No doubt, as one philosopher has observed, such speculative philosophy was born of exuberant overconfidence in the power of that same capacity for generalization which, more cautiously used, has provided the basis of science. But philosophy has another and, in our judgment, far more significant, role to play. If it were only speculative it would be an intellectual indulgence, and could justly be regarded by students as having no more than peripheral interest. On the contrary, philosophy has an urgent task to perform. It is not, as Aristotle once suggested, a mere "leisure-time recreation" to which men had recourse "when practically all the necessities of life were provided," although, no doubt, some freedom from the need to earn a living is essential. It is a response to specific needs, most especially those needs that are bred of the tensions produced by the advent of science in the culture of Europe.[1] To understand the nature of the problem thereby

[1] Some would contend that, because of the relative weakness of the scientific tradition in the Orient, its philosophy is so different from the philosophy of the West as to deserve

posed, and of the philosophical activity to which it leads, it is necessary to indicate more precisely what "folklore," "common sense," and "science" denote.

Anatomy of Conflict

Every group has a folklore; that is to say, a body of beliefs about itself and the world which reflects its wishes and aspirations, its habits of thought and its preconceptions. Folklore—to recall a well-known phrase— is concerned with the wonderful rather than the probable. Its origin is lost in obscurity. It is compounded of legend and myth, of custom, usage, and practice which are handed down from generation to generation without critical examination. In good time they became hallowed by tradition. The welfare of the group is regarded as bound up with their preservation. Elaborate rituals are evolved to consecrate them. A priesthood grows up to indoctrinate the young with the folklore and, should such a mischance arise, to protect it from the inroads of infidels. The folklore is precious, for it encompasses our vital fictions and cherished beliefs. Hence, society invokes sanctions against doubters and unbelievers. To challenge the folklore is to court the charge of heresy, or radicalism, and to invite excommunication, ostracism, even martyrdom.

All cultures, from the meanest to the most refined, have a folklore. This is as true of our own as of the culture of the aborigines. Those who have

---

a different name. It would be pointless to initiate a controversy which, however interesting, is essentially a side issue as far as this survey is concerned. Nevertheless, it is worthwhile obesrving that Hu Shih, in his *Chinese Renaissance*, describes the "highly developed scientific method in all its phases of operation" as one of the unique contributions of Western civilization to the world. F. S. C. Northrop, author of *The Meeting of East and West*, after noting Hu Shih's comment, goes on to say,

"Before the revolution of 1912 the ideology of the culture of China at, say, the end of the nineteenth century A.D. was for the most part identical with its ideology in 660 B.C. To be sure, Chinese historians draw distinctions seemingly analogous with those in the West between the Chinese medieval and the modern world. But these distinctions turn around the difference between Confucianism and Neo-Confucianism. They express differences no more deep going or radical than the difference between the Thomism of St. Thomas Aquinas and the contemporary Neo-Thomism of Professor Maritain. . . . the methodological reason why this is the case . . . is not unconnected with our previous observation that Oriental civilization never developed nor seriously pursued the theoretical hypothetical type of inquiry of the scientific methods of the West. Instead, as the leaders of Oriental thought continuously inform us, the Oriental mind has grounded its philosophical knowledge and its cultural values in the empirical methods of immediate apprehension or intuition and contemplation. What we apprehend with immediacy is what it is; it is not a postulated hypothesis indirectly verified and subject to change with further information. Thus, a culture whose values were grounded in such a methodology of philosophical knowledge would be expected to be devoid of the revolutionary reconstruction in philosophical theory and cultural ideals which characterize the West." "Evolution in its Relation to the Philosophy of Nature and the Philosophy of Culture," in *Evolutionary Thought in America*, ed. by Stow Persons (New York: Braziller, 1956), pp. 80–81.

learned to distinguish between fact and fiction, logic and illogic, often believe that in their own culture fact has triumphed over fiction and rationality has come to full flower, and they will therefore not fancy the term "folklore," which they reserve for the superstitions of savages and barbarians. Thus, the irony of a book entitled *The Folklore of Capitalism* finds its mark among those who regard the laws of capitalist economics as one with the laws of reason: Here is no body of wishful and unexamined beliefs—only logic working itself out in the market place. But we have our folklore, whether it be the assumption that free competition reigns in our economy and is an unmitigated good, or—in the noneconomic sphere —the notion (recently shaken) that Progress is automatic or that God has made man in His image. And we take the *content* of our folklore as seriously as others—as these examples are intended to suggest—however much we may scorn the name. Needless to say, no Russian counterpart of Thurman Arnold is even contemplating a "Folklore of Communism," although, in the land which purports to have enshrined science, dialectical materialism and the dictatorship of the proletariat are nothing if not folklore.

As Dewey has pointed out, it is not verisimilitude but emotional congeniality that determines the content of a folklore. Fidelity to fact is secondary, although, among literate peoples, some effort is made at plausibility, and superstition (which St. Thomas defined as the vice of excess in religion) is much less prominent. The beliefs that comprise a folklore are not thereby characterized invidiously; one does not properly disparage what is universal and inevitable and, in any case, satisfies some fundamental human need. But if, in the folklore, the control of ideas by facts is at a minimum, man must reckon in some measure with the world as it is, else he could not survive. He must show *common sense*; there must be, to recall Malinowski's useful distinction, a domain of the profane as well as of the sacred.[2]

It is difficult to draw a line between folklore and common sense. When the editors of a widely read magazine write, "So far as anyone

---

[2] "In every primitive community, studied by trustworthy and competent observers, there have been found two clearly distinguishable domains, the Sacred and the Profane; in other words, the domain of Magic and Religion and that of Science." *Magic, Science and Religion* (Garden City: Doubleday, 1955), pp. 17-18. Malinowski goes on: "On the one hand there are the traditional acts and observances, regarded by the natives as sacred, carried out with reverence and awe, hedged around with prohibitions and special rules of behavior. Such acts and observances are always associated with beliefs in supernatural forces, especially those of magic, or with ideas about beings, spirits, ghosts, dead ancestors, or gods. On the other hand, a moment's reflection is sufficient to show that no art or craft however primitive could have been invented or maintained, no organized form of hunting, fishing, tilling, or search for food could be carried out without the careful observation of natural process and a firm belief in its regularity, without the power of reasoning and without confidence in the power of reason; that is, without the rudiments of science."

knows there are only two ways to make men work: money or fear . . . the carrot or the stick," is this common sense or is it folklore? Is it folklore or common sense that virtue is rewarded and wickedness punished—even if not always, it would appear, in *this* world? And how shall we deal with the "self-evident" truth that "all men are created equal" or, for that matter with the "common sense" of Tom Paine's *Common Sense?*

Curiously, although folklore and common sense are identical in original meaning—one would be hard put to distinguish between the wisdom of the folk and the sense that is common—the terms are not used interchangeably, nor do the dictionaries define the one in terms of the other. By "common sense" we usually refer to that knowledge of matter of fact which is distinguished by its ubiquity, its inadvertency, and its rudimentary character. Careful definition and classification are strange to it. While most modern anthropologists are disposed to deny a prelogical stage in human development, it is fair to say that common sense is lacking in logical sophistication and innocent of the usages of mathematics (beyond simple counting and measurement) and the experimental method. It may therefore be called prescientific.[3] It relies on surface evidence and takes the world as it finds it. It dotes on the particular instance and its mainstay is the anecdotal argument. Common sense scorns theory and "theorists." (Therefore—as John Maynard Keynes remarked in another context—it invariably cherishes some defunct theory. All so-called practical men who shun theory are surreptitious theorists, just as those scientists who disparage or patronize philosophy are clandestine philosophers.) Common sense is primarily occupied with *means* rather than causes; that is to say, it is opportunistic and interested in what "pays off." Indeed, its quick dividends give comon sense such prestige as it enjoys, even if science has taught that neglect of causes is in the long run costly.

This is not to say that common sense does not embody a considerable store of reliable knowledge. Indeed, if this were not true the race would not have survived. Man has displayed marvelous ingenuity, even when lacking in what we now call science. But knowledge based on ordinary experi-

---

[3] Even Lévy-Bruhl, who, to the chagrin of his successors, described primitive mentality as "prelogical," indicated that he did not mean illogical or oblivious of considerations of consistency. Anthropologists like Melville Herskovits urge that, while nonliterate peoples may begin from different premises, they reason with as much consistency as literate peoples. [See Herskovits' *Man and His Works* (New York: Knopf, 1956), p. 73.] While primitive peoples may be characterized as "prescientific"—which is what Lévy-Bruhl meant in calling them "prelogical"—we are told that "the distinction between the prescientific and scientific mentality is not psychological but cultural, and does not reflect upon the inherent ability of a group of people to think logically." [David Bidney, *Theoretical Anthropology* (New York: Columbia, 1953), p. 158.] On the other hand, even though there is a logic or method in native ideology, "this does not obviate the radical and irreducible distinction between the category of the rational and scientific, on the one hand, and that of the irrational and mythical on the other." (*Ibid.*, p. 167.)

ence is bound to be incomplete, unsystematic, and strictly limited. Specifically, such knowledge rarely provides an explanation of why events occur as they do, and it tends to rely on loose and misleading analogies. Thus, in Professor Ernest Nagel's words:

. . . societies which have discovered the uses of the wheel usually know nothing of frictional forces, nor of any reasons why goods loaded on vehicles with wheels are easier to move than goods dragged on the ground. Many peoples have learned the advisability of manuring their agricultural fields, but only a few have concerned themselves with the reasons for so acting. The medicinal properties of herbs like the foxglove have been recognized for centuries, though usually no account was given of the grounds for their beneficent virtues. Moreover, when "common sense" does attempt to give explanations for its facts— as when the value of the foxglove as a cardiac stimulant is explained in terms of the similarity in shape of the flower and human heart—the explanations are frequently without critical tests of their relevance to the facts.[4]

There is a hard core of common sense that is the same everywhere and always: fire burns, water quenches thirst, colors characterize objects "out there," the world endures in the intervals when we are not aware of it, a bird in the hand is worth two in the bush, two plus two equals four (or perhaps only "more"), etc. On the other hand, the content of common sense may change; in primitive societies the proposition that organisms grow and physical objects do not, or that inanimate objects have no memory, may not be as obvious as it is to our common sense.

It might be supposed that the matter-of-fact knowledge represented by common sense would come into conflict with the folklore, but we may assume that the folklore has been more or less adjusted to the dictates of common sense from the outset and that, since the content of common sense is relatively static, such accommodations are likely to endure. Moreover, disparities are not likely to trouble the primitive mind, any more than they are likely to trouble the provincial mind in Euroamerican society. Should factual knowledge accumulate and disparities multiply, conflict may still be avoided as man's great talents for compartmentalization come into play. Some such relatively undisturbed state of affairs prevailed throughout the long history of man until, on the fringes of what was destined to become a remarkable civilization, an extraordinary development occurred—a development utterly boundless in its significance and consequences. Uniquely among men, the Greeks discovered the idea of science.

It is not necessary here to indicate the debt of the Greeks to their predecessors, notably the Babylonians and Egyptians,[5] nor to inquire other-

---

[4] Ernest Nagel, *The Structure of Science* (New York: Harcourt, Brace and World, 1961), pp. 3–4.

[5] Increasing credit has come to be given to the Minoan and Mycenean cultures of ancient Crete. Some would charge that the originality of Greece's contribution has been

wise into the origins of science. Some would say that, in a literal sense, the Greeks were cultural mutants. It was they who raised inquiry—in particular the quest for origins—above the level of mythopoeic thought.[6] It was they who substituted systematic, deliberate, self-conscious inquiry for random, inadvertent, trial-and-error learning. It was they who understood that particular experiences must be subsumed under general principles if knowledge is to be raised above simple rules of thumb. It was the Greeks who first freed inquiry from subservience to immediate ends and purposes, thereby releasing it from preoccupation with technology, and initiating the disinterested study of nature.

Thus began the remarkable, if uneven and long interrupted, march of science that was to usher in a new, radically different and wholly unprecedented era in the history of man. More significantly for the purpose of this survey, it was to set what has been the primary task for philosophy since the time of the Ionians. The advent of science meant that knowledge of matters of fact would inevitably reach proportions bringing it into active conflict with the folklore. It meant that collisions could no longer be avoided by a simple feat of compartmentalization. It meant that discrepancies would now become so glaring that they could no longer be ignored.

The advent of science meant also that a great gap would develop between the world as viewed by common sense and the world as scientists describe it. "We must be on our guard against that evil intruder 'common

exaggerated to the neglect of its debts to the Near East. The more conventional point of view, taken for granted here and associated with such great names as Cornford, is also supported by such students of preclassical antiquity as H. and H. A. Frankfort. The Frankforts stress that the absence in Ionian thought of personification, or of recourse to gods set it apart from the mythopoeic thought that preceded it. "The problem of understanding nature is moved . . . to a new plane. In the ancient Near East it had remained within the sphere of myth. The Milesian school of philosophers had moved it to the realm of the intellect in that they claimed the universe to be an intelligible whole." With "preposterous boldness" the Greeks "presumed that a single order underlies the chaos of our perception and furthermore that we are able to comprehend that order." *The Intellectual Adventure of Ancient Man* (Chicago: University of Chicago Press, (1950), pp. 377, 380–381, later published under the title, *Before Philosophy*.

[6] The Ionians did not look for origins to some ancestral divinity or progenitor. Instead, as the Frankforts note, they "asked for an immanent and *lasting* ground of existence . . . [a] 'sustaining principle' or 'first cause.' This change of viewpoint is breathtaking. . . . A cosmogonic myth is beyond discussion. It describes a sequence of sacred events, which one can either accept or reject. But no cosmogony can become part of a progressive and cumulative increase of knowledge . . . myth claims recognition by the faithful, not justification before the critical. But a sustaining principle or first cause must be comprehensible. . . . It does not pose the alternative of acceptance or rejection. It may be analyzed, modified, or corrected. In short, it is subject to intellectual judgment." (*Ibid.*, p. 376.)

On the other hand, Benjamin Farrington, an historian of science, argues that "progress in interpretation of the scientific writings of the older civilizations has gone far to abolish the claim of the Greeks to priority or to uniqueness in the creation of abstract theoretical science. . . ." *Greek Science* (London: Penguin Books, 1953), p. 16.

sense,' " a scientist recently declared in discussing the origins of galaxies and similar matters before the British Association for the Advancement of Science. His colleagues agreed. It is notorious that a vast chasm separates the microscopic and macroscopic worlds disclosed by modern science and the world of middle-sized objects to which common sense is accustomed. Whitehead reminds us, "We forget how strained and paradoxical is the view of nature which modern science imposes on our thoughts."[7] Science and the scientific method will be described in considerable detail in the pages which follow. It is enough to note here that the very absorption of science in abstraction, that same reliance on conceptual construction that gives it its distinctive character and special excellence, also removes it from the qualitative world of "uses and enjoyments" to which we are linked in everyday experience.

Finding ourselves in such a situation, even the most rational among us do not abandon our folklore or abjure common sense any more than we ignore the testimony of science. In one way or another we must reckon with all three. What we have, indeed, is no ordinary situation, but a predicament fraught with intolerable tension, a profound ambivalence from which only those who are ignorant, insensitive, or bigoted are exempt.[8] If gifted individuals, blinded by zeal—and there are zealots among scientists as well as among priests—or for whatever reason, are able in special cases to escape this ambivalence, society has not been able to escape it. Individually and collectively, men have sought to resolve the conflict by evolving a working relationship between science, on the one hand, and folklore and common sense on the other. *The history of philosophy in its most significant aspect is the effort of gifted thinkers to achieve such an accommodation. The reigning philosophies of any given era are usually those in which such a reconciliation has been achieved.*

It is for this reason that Dewey can urge that:

Philosophers are parts of history, caught in its movement—creators perhaps in some measure of its future—but also assuredly creatures of its past. . . . Take the history of philosophy from whatever angle and in whatever cross-section you please . . . and you find a load of traditions proceeding from an immemorial past. . . . The life of all thought is to effect a junction at some point of the new and the old, of deep-sunk customs and unconscious dispositions that are brought to the light of attention by some conflict with newly emerging directions of activity.[9]

---

[7] A. N. Whitehead, *Science and Modern World* (New York: Macmillan, 1925), p. 85.

[8] That is why Windelband, writing of the philosophy of the seventeenth century, can say: "All beginnings of modern philosophy have in common an impulsive opposition against 'Scholasticism' and at the same time a naïve lack of understanding for the common attitude of dependence upon some one of its traditions, which they nevertheless all occupy." W. Windelband, *History of Philosophy*, Tufts trans. (New York: Macmillan, 1923), p. 383.

[9] *Philosophy and Civilization* (New York: Minton, 1931), pp. 4–8.

An important complication must be noted. If the body of workaday knowledge that passes as common sense is comparatively fixed, this is not true of science. Consequently, every accommodation is unstable, so that the philosophy in which it is contained requires at the very least to be reconstructed and at the most to be superseded, as new knowledge flows from the scientific cornucopia. And, significantly, in this process much of the content of the regnant philosophy, although not strictly folklore as thus far defined, may well merge with the folklore; for, however timorously and suspiciously it may have been received at the outset, such a philosophy comes to represent established tradition, accepted opinion, prevailing orthodoxy—a precious and precarious balance of fact and belief not to be lightly discarded under the pressure of new facts. So the philosophy of Plato and Aristotle merged with the folklore of the Middle Ages; similarly Cartesianism became part of the folklore of the Enlightenment.

In what follows, the term "folklore" will be used in the broad sense to designate all these distinguishable factors; they will not be separately identified except as the context requires. Hence, "folklore," unless otherwise qualified, will designate all beliefs to which we commit ourselves uncritically, that is to say, without reckoning with the facts of science—beliefs to which we are predisposed because they reflect our wishes, were held by our fathers, and for one reason or other have become hallowed and habitual.

At this point a possible objection may be noted. It may be argued that strains and stresses provocative of philosophical activity are also brought about by the impact of technological innovations on the folklore, or by the contact of diverse cultures, and that exclusive emphasis on science slights these other factors. Perhaps so. However, as regards the first, it may be said that, unlike pure science, applied science is concerned with means and ends, that is, techniques and satisfactions. On the other hand, pure science, as a disclosure (even if only in a qualified and limited way) of the "nature of things," will come into conflict with the positions adopted in the traditional (or folkloric) account. Technological innovations obviously generate enormous strains, but these are of an order different from the tensions generated by pure science, and are of more interest to the sociologist and social reformer than to the philosopher. Japan, prior to World War II, could be an example of vast changes in technology not profoundly affecting the *Weltanschauung* because pure science was largely ignored.

Neither are the tensions produced by the contact of diverse cultures of the same order as those produced by pure science. When cultures meet, the consequence may be a conglomerate folklore rather than the kind of accommodation that is typically philosophical. To cite one example: The great fusion of Greek and Oriental cultures that took place in the eastern basin of the Mediterranean at the beginning of the Christian era, while it was featured by a great deal of reflection concerning the proper guidance of conduct, is not noted for evoking important or original philosophical activity.

However such issues are resolved, the tensions generated by the disclosures and methods of science have provided more than enough material to engross us—material surely of sufficient importance to justify the restriction here imposed.

There have been at least four occasions on which the discrepancies between science and folklore, as thus understood, might be described as climactic. Each of these occasions evoked a rich philosophical development which has set the period apart as one of great philosophical activity. In every case, no matter how the philosophers themselves may have estimated what they were doing, their work is best understood as an attempt to modify the folklore in such a way as to enable it to receive and absorb the new scientific material. In such circumstances the search for truth and meaning is more than undisciplined speculation or a wild leap of the imagination; it is contained and ordered by the requirements of a specific problem.

To introduce the student to philosophy by way of these predicaments will involve more historical considerations than are ordinarily included in an introduction to philosophy. But it is precisely this artificial divorce of introductions to philosophy from the history of philosophy which detaches philosophical concepts and standpoints from the cultural situations in which they were found meaningful and thereby renders them meaningless to the student. It is, indeed, more than this. It is the detachment of philosophy from what we have come to call *intellectual history* that gives it its appearance of remoteness and irrelevance. If the main objective of the intellectual historian is to relate ideas, including the ideas of the "thinkers" of a period, to the prevalent pattern of life in a given culture, then it may well substantially advance "introductions" to philosophy if they venture into intellectual history. If, in order to achieve such an approach, some of the material presented in conventional treatments that aspire to all-inclusiveness must necessarily be sacrificed, it is assumed that for the beginning student the material is expendable.[10]

The Greek Dawn

The first of the historic junctures to which reference has been made was produced by the appearance of the logical and mathematical sciences

---

[10] There is a curious convention about "introductions" whether to philosophy, sociology, economics, or whatever, which is that *everything* must be included. That some of the material will be uninteresting to the beginner, that the sheer profusion of material prevents him from pursuing any one topic to the point where his interest might be excited, that the panoramic view prevents him from discriminating between the burning and the dead issues, that the treatment in certain instances must be so superficial as to be useless or so brief that it has the liveliness of a lexicon—such considerations all too often yield to the passion for inclusiveness.

in ancient Greece.[11] The liberation of experience from the immediate and particular, which the Greeks initiated, involves the activities of abstracting and generalizing; and, so far as we know, they were the first to inquire systematically into the nature of these activities and thus to be led to a formulation of the principles underlying mathematics and logic. It is common to say that the Greeks used reason—which, of course, they did. But Locke's famous comment is worth paraphrasing: God was not so niggardly as to make man two-legged and leave it to Aristotle to make him rational. The predecessors of the Greeks also used reason, even if not so confidently and broadly. The significant point is not so much that the Greeks used reason, as that Greek thinkers were aware of it and made it an object of study.

But the exactions of logic are too much for ordinary common sense, as they are for any body of uncritically accepted beliefs. When, for example, we are forced to define what we mean by goodness and beauty and justice, and to accept the implications of our definitions or reject the definitions, when our most cherished beliefs are subjected to the test of consistency, the consequences may be iconoclastic. Common sense does not pause to define its terms, and, when goaded to do so, is likely to say with Cephalus in the *Republic* that justice is "to speak the truth and pay your debts," or with Euthyphro that piety is doing "as I am doing." When it encounters the rejoinder of Socrates that "I did not ask you to give me one or two or three examples of piety, but to explain the general idea which makes all pious things to be pious,"[12] it is likely to retreat in confusion—if not in anger.

One can trace, from the beginning, a growing awareness among the pre-Socratic philosophers of the failure of current beliefs to satisfy the requirements of reason. As Windelband points out, once the Greek cosmologists raise the question of what things *really* are, it is clear that reflective thought is challenging "the current, original, and naïve mode of thinking." It will be instructive to follow briefly Windelband's account here.

His [the individual's] philosophizing . . . even though he takes no account of this fact, grows out of the discrepancies between his experience and . . . the demands . . . of his understanding. . . . So strong has reflection become in itself that it not only proceeds to consequences which to the common thinking

---

[11] At this point it may be well to cite the caution of Professor Werner Jaeger:

It is hard to fix the point when rational thinking begins in Greece. The line should run through the Homeric epic. Yet it is hardly possible to separate 'mythical thinking' in the epic from the rational ideas with which it is interpenetrated. If we analyzed the epics from this point of view we should find that logic invaded mythology quite early, and began to transform it. There is no discontinuity between Ionian natural philosophy and the Homeric epics. W. Jaeger, *Paideia* (New York: Oxford, 1945), Vol. I, p. 151.

[12] *The Dialogues of Plato*, B. Jowett trans. (New York: Random House, 1937), Vol. 1, p. 387.

have become absolutely paradoxical, but also maintains expressly that it is itself the sole source of truth as opposed to opinions.

At first the nature of the requirements of thought or reason or under-standing is only vaguely grasped. But, with the Pythagorean assertion that knowledge consists in mathematical reasoning, we have "a great step in advance, inasmuch as there is here given for the first time a positive description of 'thought' as contrasted with 'perception' [i.e., common sense]."[13] The Eleatics supply another characteristic of thinking—namely, conformity to logical laws—so that the principle of contradiction comes, as with Zeno, to be employed with practical purpose. With the "men of science," the Sophists, this purpose not only becomes conscious and explicit, but is pursued with skeptical intent and completely iconoclastic consequences.

But philosophers do not permit the new science to culminate in dis-belief in the fifth century B.C. any more than in the time of Descartes. We must interpret the growth of Greek philosophy, observes Professor Werner Jaeger, "as the process by which the original religious conception of the universe, the conception implicit in the myth, was increasingly rationalized."[14] The folklore is not discarded. Greek folklore must be reconciled with Greek science and the task falls to philosophy. "The change from religion to philosophy was so great in form that their identity as to content is easily lost to view," writes John Dewey. "The form ceases to be that of the story told in imaginative and emotional style, and becomes that of rational discourse observing the canons of logic."[15]

The supreme accomplishment of this task falls to Plato and Aristotle who turn to the science of their day—not, as do the Sophists, to destroy established beliefs, but to render them more tenable. For Plato, the mathematical disciplines are the way to knowledge of the Good. Es-sentially, Plato's problem was to find certainty at a time when all the certitudes were threatened. If the growth of logic and mathematics was in part responsible for this state of affairs, mathematics and logic were also to provide the solution. By the Doctrine of Ideas and the one-sided dualism in which he involved it, Plato in effect brought to a culmination and climax the whole tendency of Greek philosophy to rationalize its folk-lore. Aristotle's problems and objectives were similar, save that he turned to logic, and to biology and the world of living organisms for his models instead of to mathematics, and he modified Platonism—especially Plato's dualism—to make it more acceptable to common sense. "If one looks at the foundations of the philosophies of Plato and Aristotle as an anthro-pologist looks at his material, that is, as cultural subject-matter, it is clear

13 W. Windelband, op. cit., pp. 58–59.
14 Jaeger, op. cit., p. 152.
15 The Quest for Certainty (New York: Minton, 1929), p. 14.

that these philosophies were systemizations in rational form of the content of Greek religious and artistic beliefs."[16] Thus, while Plato agrees with the Sophists that the prevalent notions of goodness and justice and beauty are inadequate, he retains the established notion that they do have a fixed and universal meaning. The spiritual heir of Pythagoras and Socrates seeks for goodness and justice and beauty that same stable, immutable character with which mathematics seemed to fix and order the otherwise transitory, deceptive world of sensory objects. That is why the famous dictum of the Sophist Protagoras, that man is the measure of all things, becomes with Plato, "The measure of all things is God."[17]

It becomes the task of those who would make philosophy comprehensible and meaningful to indicate in detail the nature of the problem presented to Plato and Aristotle as outlined above. Once the student knows *why* Plato had recourse to the Doctrine of Ideas as the basis on which to erect a metaphysic, he may be more disposed to explore what Platonic Idealism is. Here is the appropriate occasion for examining the nature of logical and mathematical reasoning; of rationalism and the distinction between rationalism and empiricism; of logical realism and the distinction between realism and nominalism; and of Plato's ethical perfectionism as contrasted to hedonism and ethical relativism. Here, too, one might deal with metaphysical idealism in general as well as with Plato's version of idealism and the distinction between Platonic idealism and materialism. In the course of such discussion, emphasis will properly have shifted—since a history of philosophy is not contemplated—from the historical context to the philosophical standpoints and distinctions themselves. But the historical—that is to say, the cultural situation that evoked the activities of Plato and Aristotle—need not be forgotten, and the historical question may well be posed by way of preparing the way for Part II: Why did Platonism and Aristotelianism prevail in the centuries which followed, while the materialists and the Sophists were relatively ignored? By virtue of what deep needs were Plato and Aristotle able to dominate the intellectual outlook of Europe for centuries after dusk had enveloped their own beloved Greece? Why, indeed, do they still strike responsive chords in a world largely hostile to that outlook?

The Seventeenth-Century Crisis

Another great crisis came to a climax in the seventeenth century, brought about this time by the advent of the physical sciences. The extraordinary development of celestial and terrestrial mechanics, from Copernicus to

---

[16] *Ibid.*, p. 16.
[17] *Laws,* 716c.

Newton, was made possible by assumptions, and led to conclusions, that were wholly alien to the medieval outlook. That outlook envisaged a universe narrowly circumscribed in space and time, with the earth at its center, and man as its focus. Hence, the world was to be understood teleologically and natural phenomena were to be explained in terms of final causes. With this conception of a purposefully ordered whole went a view of reality in which all things are differentiated by reference to the proportions of "form" and "matter" manifest in them into a series of levels ascending from the merely corporeal, through the orders of growing, living things, to the revolving and fixed spheres and, ultimately, at the summit, to pure spirituality or intellectuality. Each level of this hierarchy is characterized by a different degree of reality, as by a different degree of worth, so that in moving from lowest to highest one not only ascends the scale from the least real to the most real (*ens realissimum*) but from the base and corrupt to sheer perfection (*ens perfectissimum*). All striving, all movement, all change is the manifestation of a universal urge to achieve supreme reality and perfection, which is to say pure intellectuality, so that, in the epitomization of St. Thomas—who wedded these Aristotelian notions to the Christian theology and ethic—"the prime author and mover of the universe is intelligence."

It must follow that the task of science is to seek out the "reason" of things, their "meaning" or purpose. This can be discovered by a careful analysis of their nature or "essence" or "form," so that the main concern of medieval science is with types and definitions. In and of itself, a particular object has no meaning; it comes to be understood (both logically and axiologically) only when it is viewed as exemplifying the universal or class of which it is a member. Hence, medieval science is concerned primarily with classification, that is to say, with *what* an object is rather than with *how* it acts and reacts under different conditions. If definition and classification, however indispensable to clarity and understanding, do not add to what is already known, this is considered no shortcoming in the context of medieval science which regards the content of knowledge as finished and complete, needing only to be organized, elaborated, analyzed.

All of this is well known. Much of it should be qualified by reference to conflicting trends and tendencies such as—to cite a striking example—the nominalism of Occam. None of it can be omitted from an account of medieval folklore and the transformations that folklore was to undergo under the impact of seventeenth-century science.

When Copernicus substituted a heliocentric for a geocentric description of the solar system, he began the revolution that wiped out the spatial boundaries of the medieval world (Copernicus himself thought of the universe as a closed sphere of space) and relegated man to an insignificant planet in a boundless universe. The scientists who followed were virtually unanimous in rejecting the quest for final causes. Consistency with authority ceased to be the test of truth; modern science employed other criteria. Preoccupation with definition and classification, and hence with fixed essences, gave way to the observation of particular instances and the movements and changes in which they are involved. Concentration upon the qualitied aspects of reality—with all the limitations on expanding the horizons of knowledge that this imposes—was superseded by an approach to nature that went beyond objects as they present themselves to the senses, and viewed them in terms of the forces of which they are a product, and hence in respect of their quantitative variations. The use of mathematics was thus expanded beyond simple counting and measurement; mathematics became the language of science. The heavenly bodies, exposed at last by Galileo's crude telescope, lost their spiritual status, and the cosmic hierarchy was reduced to the dead level of a physical world ruled everywhere by the same impersonal laws. The contemplative ideal of knowledge had now to reckon with the Baconian ideal of control. Seventeenth-century science is not modern science—neither in its methods, nor in its content. But the conflict with folklore could hardly be more complete, as the trial of Galileo in 1616 attests.

The reconciliation of these diverse tendencies was achieved, as every student of philosophy knows, in the philosophy of Descartes. Not that he made converts of the orthodox. The Church, ignoring the Jansenists and yielding to the Jesuits, placed Descartes' works on the *Index Expurgatorius,* his teachings were banned at the University, and a royal command forbade an oration at his burial. But the "father of modern philosophy" provided a framework within which the discoveries of Kepler and Galileo and (after Descartes) Newton could subsist side by side with the heritage from the past; and, since this was what the great majority of thoughtful men—including churchmen—needed, Cartesianism became the reigning philosophy of Europe. "What seemed, to Descartes' contemporaries, an outstanding merit of his system," wrote Basil Willey, "was that although it represented a complete break with the scholastic tradition it left unchallenged the main fabric of the faith."[18]

Cartesianism is sometimes—perhaps often—presented as though it might as easily have appeared in the nineteenth or fifteenth as in the seventeenth century, and Cartesian dualism, as a kind of eternal alternative to monism and pluralism. To present it thus is to fail to see how it was an ingenious and extraordinarily satisfying solution to a specific problem.

Consider some of the ramifications of this solution. Descartes begins by employing the skeptical method so indispensable to science. But skepticism

[18] Basil Willey, *The Seventeenth Century Background* (New York: Doubleday, 1953), p. 92.

is disreputable—nor could Descartes have rescued skepticism for the uses of science by the mere circumspection that "The simple resolve to strip ones self of all opinions and beliefs formerly received is not to be regarded as an example that each man should follow . . ."[19] Descartes goes on to convert the fact that he doubts into the basis for a new argument— probably a powerful argument so far as his contemporaries were concerned —for the existence of God. Similarly, Descartes does not seek to free thinking from preoccupation with final causes by denying the presence of purpose in the universe; science is served just as well by the devout admonition that it is impertinent of us to suppose that we can know God's motives. Again, science must assume the regularity of the laws of nature, a requirement incompatible with the conventional notion that the Creator intervenes at appropriate junctures to alter the course of events. The problem is not solved by denying God's creative role; on the contrary, no one could have affirmed God's role more vigorously than Descartes. But, having created the world, a perfect deity does not need to intervene in its operations; thus, to imply that He changes His mind is to detract from His perfection.

However, Descartes' supreme achievement lies in the dualism by means of which he allocated nearly all of reality to the physical sciences and yet withheld from them that which is most distinctive of man. The vast universe and—with one major exception—everything in it is physical in character and completely understandable in mathematical terms. This is as true of the heavenly bodies as of the earth and it is as true of living things as of inanimate objects. Animal organisms—even man's body—are complicated mechanisms governed by the same laws that govern the vast machinery of the universe. This is what Descartes calls *res extensa*—extended things—or matter. Here is a kind of reality completely divested of all traits that do not lend themselves to mathematical treatment: There is no mind principle or consciousness permeating *res extensa*, no feeling, and none of the content of sensation, such as colors, odors and sounds— only pure spatiality (manifesting itself in shape, size, position, and motion). If Descartes had stopped here, he would have been expounding materialism, a position closely resembling the views of Thomas Hobbes, and he would have had just as little impact on the seventeenth century. But Descartes did not *deny* the existence of mind or consciousness, however much he constricted the area in which it operates; nor did he assert, as Hobbes often did, that the sensory content of experience is identical with bodily motions. Mind and its content are as real as material objects, only

---

[19] Descartes' triumph of circumspection deserves more extended quotation: ". . . I cannot in any way approve of those turbulent and unrestful spirits," he writes, "who, being called neither by birth nor fortune to the management of public affairs, never fail to have always in their minds some new reforms." And the reader is assured that the author would not publish his treatise if he thought it encouraged such folly. (*Discourse on Method*, Haldane and Ross, trans., Part II.)

they comprise a different *kind* of reality having nothing in common with matter, wholly disparate, underived from matter and irreducible to it.

Metaphysical dualism is thus to be seen as the device by means of which Cartesians deeded virtually all of reality to the physical sciences to be studied by the methods that were being used with such spectacular success, and yet conciliated tradition by preserving the separateness and difference of man as well as God. This was not too difficult since science —whatever its aspirations—had not yet acquired techniques for dealing with man. Cartesians even avoided completely outraging common sense (already reeling under the impact of the propositions that the earth is round, turns on its axis, and revolves about the sun) by accepting the reality of sense data even though, contrary to common sense, so-called "secondary qualities" were not imputed to physical objects. No wonder that, by the latter part of the seventeenth century, the victory of Cartesianism was complete.

The Galilean-Cartesian-Newtonian world view, as it has come to be known, precipitated all kinds of philosophical difficulties. It is at this point that newcomers to philosophy should be confronted with the mind-body problem and the problem of knowledge, as these were posed by Cartesianism. It is in such a context that the advent of phenomenalism and subjectivism can be made plausible. It is here that the student can be familiarized with mechanism and its implications and with how the superiority for science of the quantitative over the qualitative (Aristotelian) interpretation of nature culminated in philosophical materialism. Thus presented, these standpoints and tendencies lose their seeming abritrariness and are once more rooted in the needs from which they in fact emerged.

Evolution and Naturalism

A third great collision between science and folklore occurred with the triumph of the biological sciences—in particular with the appearance of Darwinism—in the nineteenth century. In the accepted view, the universe had been created at a given instant in time, and this beginning was considered relatively recent. Even Newton was a creationist and, although men like Kepler, Galileo, and Newton may have broken down the spatial boundaries of the medieval universe, they did not tamper with its temporal boundaries. If the "root metaphor" in terms of which men understand the universe is the Machine they will think more in terms of machinists (for example, God as the great Watchmaker) and acts of creation, and less in terms of slow growth through long spans of time. To this extent seventeenth-century science and the biblical account of creation were compatible.

Folklore also took for granted the unrelatedness, discreteness, and immutability of living species. Fixed in kind and number, the myriad species wear the same aspect as when they were brought into being "in the beginning." Here folklore accords with common sense: The casual observer does not see complex species deriving from simpler species and, while he is aware of biological sports, in his limited temporal perspective the striking thing about species is the fixity of their form.

Finally and most important, prevailing belief took for granted the discontinuity of man with the rest of nature, and was confirmed in this by the Cartesian bifurcation of reality which stressed the separateness and uniqueness of Mind.

It was against such a body of tradition that scientific evolutionism collided. Contrary to the folklore and to common sense, the evolutionary principle affirmed the variability of species, and with this the derivation of complex from simpler and ultimately from the simplest unicellular organisms. The geologists, Hutton and Lyell, had provided, in the principle of uniformitarianism, a basis for assuming the vast spans of time during which such changes might occur. What had been mere speculation or quasi-scientific surmise became, with Darwin, a richly evidenced hypothesis, which he climaxed by supplying a causal explanation of the origin of species in the notions of random variation and natural selection.

With this the last ramparts of the medieval folklore were leveled. Boundless space now stretched through endless time. Science was able to find a substitute for purposeful intervention in explaining the origin of species. Man took his place within the framework of nature from which the Cartesian system had still excluded him. Nature was no longer to be regarded as a closed system, finished and complete, but as eternally manifesting itself in fresh and novel ways.

The upshot has again been a rich philosophical activity which carries into our own time, having found its fullest expression only a few short decades ago. Some of this activity, the evolutionist philosophies of Herbert Spencer, John Fiske, and Ernst Haeckel, for example, has had only ephemeral consequences. The more enduring related philosophies, in which the requirements of both science and tradition are mirrored, have been pragmatism and a variety of naturalism increasingly known as "critical" naturalism. Pragmatism has properly perceived that evolutionary doctrine compels a reexamination of the cognitive relationship, which is now transformed from a miraculous and incomprehensible disclosure of ulterior objects to a function of the relationship between a complex organism and its environment. To say this, however, is not to reduce knowing to the techniques involved in making ordinary organic-environmental adjustments. Thanks to the use of tools and to communication—thanks, indeed, to the social nature of man—a new mode of interaction takes place, having a new order of consequences. Meanings and ideas supervene, and these are, when they occur, "characters of a new interaction of events; they are characters which in their incorporation with sentiency transform organic action, furnishing it with new properties."[20]

Similarly, assertion of man's derivation from, and continuity with, other organisms might culminate in a philosophy of conduct based on naked self-interest. But pragmatists—however much they may have rejected the moral absolutes and imperatives which the folklore is prone to invoke— have, unlike the logical positivists, refused to affirm the meaninglessness of moral predicates. On the contrary, few have argued more vehemently that moral judgments are significant, and that in being so, they represent a new order of event in nature. Finally, for pragmatists and critical naturalists, the *derivation* of man from simpler organisms does not imply his *identity* with them, any more than his chemical composition implies that he is *nothing but* a configuration of physical particles. Unlike the materialist, the critical naturalists eschew reductionism: The inclusion of man in the system of nature does not mean to them that he is despiritualized and degraded, or less noble and less free than he may happen to be. Nature manifests itself in many ways, of which the physical—however pervasive —is only one. If evolution teaches anything it is that nature is not a completed system; it is characterized by the appearance of novelty as well as by regularity and repetition, and such novelty, when it occurs and accumulates, requires generalizations that go beyond the vocabulary of physics. Organisms are such a novelty, as are "minded" organisms. Social institutions are still another form of novelty, as may be, finally, the appearance of "free" men capable of ethical deliberation and choice.

The issues to which a student may be directed in this context are, of course, manifold: What, for example, are the main theories concerning the cognitive relationship, and why does the "descent of man" compel their reexamination; what is "Nature," and what are the kinds of change in which it is involved; what is the difference between "critical" and "reductive" naturalism; how useful is the concept of "emergence"; can a naturalistic approach to man be reconciled with his "freedom"?

Today's Challenge

In our time, the success of the social sciences (which includes their liberation from flights of grandiose fancy, as well as from apologetics for the ruling class) has again led to tensions, all the more acute because the subject is man and his works. These tensions manifest themselves variously: positively, in waves of anti-intellectualism which recurrently sweep over those who labor in the vineyard of the social sciences; negatively, in the uneasiness and ambivalence with which the business com-

[20] John Dewey, *Experience and Nature* (Chicago: Open Court, 1926), p. 290.

munity regards its academic dependencies. Or, again, crudely, among the "irresponsibles" who found their hero in Senator Joseph McCarthy; suavely, by those who, like Dr. Russell Kirk, are worried about the American intellectual's becoming a "rootless Bohemian, a Jacobin, a presumptuous innovator, an alienated man . . ."[21]

The advent of the social sciences, better called the behavioral sciences, has meant, in the first place, a careful examination of the methods that must be employed by these sciences if they are to be fruitful, and, above all, an examination of the degree to which methods successfully employed in the natural sciences may be appropriated by the social sciences. Out of this has come, for example, an examination of the mechanistic-deductive method borrowed from the classical physics, and the genetic method borrowed from the life sciences, and a new insight into their possibilities and limitations. The maturing social sciences have become increasingly interested in their basic assumptions: Marx and Veblen have made social scientists keenly aware of the extent to which these are influenced by the economic interest; Mannheim and others who have pioneered in the sociology of knowledge have concentrated attention on the social matrix of ideas; Freud has called our attention to the role of the unconscious. In general there is a new understanding of the role of the rational, the nonrational (for example, habit, custom, impulse), and the irrational in conduct on both the individual and social levels.

The more fundamental insights recently gained by social science are admirably summarized by Mannheim in terms of three main tendencies: "first, the tendency toward the criticism of the collective-unconscious motivations in so far as they determine modern social thinking; second, the tendency toward the establishment of a new type of intellectual history which is able to interpret changes in ideas in relation to social-historical changes; and, third, the tendency toward the revision of our epistemology which up to now has not taken the social nature of thought sufficiently into account."[22]

Out of this has come a new understanding of ethnocentrism in both its nationalist and racist manifestations, a reexamination of the idea of Progress, a rejection of social Darwinism, a repudiation of the traditional approaches to criminality, including Benthamism as well as the pre-Benthamite disposition to "let the punishment fit the crime," a revaluation of incentives—especially the pecuniary incentive—in their bearing on initiative and work, etc.

In recent times one can find a surprising consensus among social or

---

[21] In an address before the Second National Conference on Spiritual Foundations. Dr. Kirk is author of *The Conservative Mind.*

[22] Karl Mannheim, *Ideology and Utopia,* L. Worth and E. Shils, trans. (New York: Harcourt, Brace and World, 1949), p. 45.

behavioral scientists concerning these and many other issues, as well as a considerable measure of confidence in their conclusions—conclusions which in most instances are not likely to be in accord with established doctrine. We do not yet know what philosophical activities the present impasse will evoke, although one may surmise that such activity may arrive at some more complete and adequate formulation of the role of value judgments in the social sciences and, per contra, the role of science in valuation, than we have yet had. It may well arrive at a formulation of the extent to which the individual as a reflective person and moral agent is a social derivative—a formulation which avoids the exaggerations of organicism and the vicious excesses of totalitarianism, as well as the blatant inadequacies of rugged individualism. New philosophical insights may enhance the role of religion: distinguishing it—as did Sir James Frazer—from magic, raising it above superstition, setting it apart from father imagery, freeing it from the subservience to ritual and tradition that characterizes most of its institutional manifestations, and bringing it into a new kind of relationship to science. Even science may be deflated when scientists make pretensions to omniscience.

Here surely is a springboard from which the student will more willingly plunge into the waters of philosophy, and range, one might expect, all the way from questions concerning the meaning of "objectivity" in science (especially social science) to a consideration of the "subconscious," to an examination of economic (and even libidinous) determinism, to an exploration of the meaning of God in human experience. Here, once again, by introducing the student to philosophy by way of a crisis—this one in his own time—we may avoid the gratuitous character that has haunted and even vitiated so much teaching in philosophy.

Two Views

In his famous lectures published under the title of *Pragmatism*, William James declared: "You want a system that will combine both things, the scientific loyalty to facts and willingness to take account of them . . . but also the old confidence in human values and the resultant spontaneity, whether of the religious or of the romantic type." And, he went on, "I offer the oddly named thing pragmatism as a philosophy that can satisfy both kinds of demand."[23] It is the point of view of the present approach to philosophy that the reigning philosophies of *every* period have satisfied "both kinds of demand," and that, whether deliberately or "subconsciously" (obviously the former in the case of pragmatism), this was what their authors intended them to accomplish. Accordingly, this account is in full and hearty accord with Professor Karl Popper when he says that *"We are*

23 New York: Longmans, Green, 1907, pp. 20, 33.

not students of subject matter but students of problems," and of problems, moreover, which *"arise outside philosophy."* He goes on, *"Genuine philosophical problems are always rooted in urgent problems outside philosophy, and they die if these roots decay."* Hence, says Professor Popper, philosophy has no method or techniques peculiar to it; what is peculiar to it is a "sensitiveness to problems, and a consuming passion for them."[24]

Accordingly, the present approach to philosophy is not in agreement with philosophical trends that have dominated Anglo-American thinking since the war. These, inspired prior to the war by Bertrand Russell, Ludwig Wittgenstein, and G. E. Moore, and manifesting themselves as "logical positivism" and "ordinary language" or "Oxford" philosophy (there are numerous other titles) will be explored in some detail in the last section of this volume. Their common feature is a rejection of traditional philosophy as hopelessly beset by linguistic confusion and, with this, a repudiation of the historic concerns of philosophy in favor of nearly exclusive preoccupation with language analysis and the problem of meaning. It is significant, however, that Russell has denounced the whole movement as sterile, and that Wittgenstein spectacularly abandoned the precepts set forth in his famous *Tractatus.* Wittgenstein, G. E. Moore, and J. L. Austin who, after Moore, was the prime mover of the so-called Oxford School, are dead. Significantly, the extraordinary influence of these men was limited to professional circles and the philosophical journals and, except for occasional denunciations from a handful of outsiders who took the pains to read them, their impact on our time has been negligible. The upshot of this partly therapeutic, partly escapist, preoccupation with meaning has been, as Professor Charles Frankel has pointed out, "a dialogue

---

[24] "The Nature of Philosophical Problems and Their Roots in Science," *The British Journal for the Philosophy of Science* (Vol. III, No. 10, Aug. 1952), pp. 124–156. (His italics.) On this basis Professor Popper condemns what he calls the *"prima facie* method of teaching philosophy." This method—it seems to him to be the only method—is that ". . . of giving the beginner (whom we take to be unaware of the history of mathematical, cosmological, and other ideas of science as well as of politics) the works of the great philosophers to read; say of Plato and Aristotle, Descartes and Leibniz, Locke, Berkeley, Hume, Kant, and Mill. What is the effect of such a course of reading? A new world of astonishingly subtle and vast *abstractions* opens itself to the reader, abstractions of an extremely high and difficult level. Thoughts and arguments are put before his mind which sometimes are not only hard to understand, but whose relevance remains obscure since he cannot find out what they may be relevant to. Yet the student knows that these are the great philosophers. . . . Thus he will make an effort to adjust. . . . He will attempt to speak their queer language, to match the tortuous spirals of their argumentation. . . . Some may learn these tricks in a superficial way, others . . . become . . . addicts. Yet I feel we ought to respect the man who, having made his effort, comes ultimately to what may be described as Wittgenstein's conclusion: 'I have learned the jargon . . . it is much ado about nothing . . . just a lot of nonsense.' " Popper declares this conclusion to be grossly mistaken, but decreed by this method of teaching philosophy.

between philosophers unbroken by reference to anything outside philosophy."

Philosophy will no doubt survive its recent detractors, and when it does history will record nothing more misleading and cavalier than their attempt to dispose of the entire past of philosophy as nonsense compounded of pseudo-problems and verbal puzzles, and limit its task to verbal analysis. It is the burden of this volume that philosophy is not—to borrow a phrase of Comte's—an inspiring historical ruin. However time and the critics of traditional philosophy dispose of its superficial manifestations, the deeper meaning of philosophy can be recaptured once we distinguish between what the great philosophers were really doing, and what they thought they were doing. For the most part they were unable to distinguish, lacking as most of them were in perspective and techniques of analysis.

What the great philosophers *thought* they were doing is interesting as a commentary on the aspirations of gifted men, on their vision, their vagaries, and their ingenuity in the art of architectonic. What they were really doing is, in the end, much more dramatic and meaningful, for they were coping with the dilemma of Western Man, perennially torn between his ancient need for the old and familiar and the exhilarating discovery of his potentialities for creative adventure. More than this, they were dealing with Western Man in his role as passenger—as none had been before him—between two worlds, the world of folklore and the world of fact, and, more recently, between the middle-sized world of common daily experience and the macroscopic and microscopic worlds that lie beyond. Most of us ride along, like all rootless commuters—reading our daily newspapers. But we shall not find the answers there. In the end we must turn to our philosophers.

P ART I

CLASSICAL BEGINNINGS

I have sought for myself.

HERACLITUS

. . . *the more acute and active minds, like that of Plato himself,
could no longer be content to accept, along with the conservative
citizen of the time, the old beliefs in the old way. The growth of
positive knowledge and of the critical, inquiring spirit undermined
these in their old form. The advantages in definiteness,
in accuracy, in verifiability were all on the side of the new knowledge.
Tradition was noble in aim and scope, but uncertain in foundation.
. . . What was to be done? Develop a method of rational
investigation and proof which should place the essential
elements of traditional belief upon an unshakable basis;
develop a method of thought and knowledge which while purifying
tradition should preserve its moral and social values unimpaired;
nay, by purifying them, add to their power and authority.*

JOHN DEWEY, *Reconstruction in Philosophy*

Aristotle aimed to understand Greece; he never forgot that aim.

J. H. RANDALL, JR., *Aristotle*

CHAPTER 1

Tragedy
and
Triumph

The trial of Socrates, like the trial of Christ, was a profoundly tragic moment in the stormy career of the human spirit. Plato tells the story in his *Apology*, one of the masterpieces of all time.

Socrates was charged with "investigating the things beneath the earth and in the heavens and making the weaker argument stronger and teaching others these same things." The accusation was also made that "he corrupts the youth and does not believe in the Gods the state believes in, but in other new spiritual beings." He had even denied, according to one of his accusers, that the sun and moon were gods: "He says that the sun is a stone, and the moon earth."[1]

What brought Socrates and his fellow Athenians to this tragic impasse? How could fifth-century Athens, the city we honor above all others, have destroyed one of its greatest and noblest citizens? Athens, in the year 399 B.C., when the trial took place, was a democracy; it had just emerged

[1] Plato, *The Apology*, H. N. Fowler, trans. (Cambridge: Harvard, 1947), pp. 75, 91, and 99.

from the rule of the infamous Thirty Tyrants. There may have been questions concerning the commitment of Socrates to the new regime, but they could hardly have been serious and, in point of fact, he had refused to ally himself with the now-discredited oligarchy.

True, Socrates had been, as he himself observed, a "gadfly," always arousing, reproaching, and exhorting those whom he encountered. If he was the center of a throng of admiring young disciples, he hardly enjoyed equal popularity with their elders, plagued as they were by the questions their sons learned from Socrates. Also, Socrates' address to the jury—a numerous jury of 501—no doubt goaded it to impose a harsh penalty. His words were hardly conciliatory:

If you should say to me . . . "Socrates, this time . . . we will let you go, on this condition, however, that you no longer spend your time in this investigation or in philosophy, and if you are caught doing so again you shall die"; if you should let me go on this condition which I have mentioned, I should say to you, "Men of Athens, I respect and love you, but I shall obey the god rather than you, and while I live and am able to continue, I shall never give up philosophy . . ."[2]

But none of this satisfactorily explains the bitterness of the encounter and the death penalty.

We find an important clue if we read *The Clouds*, where Aristophanes, Athens' brilliant and conservative comic poet, condemned the new "atheistic science" and lampooned "a certain Socrates" who taught that "Vortex reigns, and he has turned out Zeus."[3] The comment is significant, for not only Socrates but others in his day, notably the Sophists, were challenging the traditional religious beliefs.

In truth, before Socrates there had been one hundred and fifty years of conflict—conflict between radically new ideas relying on rules of proof and evidence, strange and suspect to solid citizens going about their everyday business, and old familiar modes of thought rooted in tradition and ratified by the Establishment. If we call the first science and the second folklore, each found a troubled spokesman and advocate in Socrates by whom the claims of each were recognized; and if the stalwarts who guarded the folklore felt themselves slighted and demanded punishment, this reaction has ever been their way. Socrates was not the first to incur their wrath; nor, as he himself noted, would he be the last.

If Socrates stands at the head of the Western philosophic tradition as its patron saint, its very fount and inspiration, it is because of his effort to reckon with the diverse tendencies of his era and somehow to reconcile them. The systematic accomplishment of this task fell to Plato and Aristotle, whose reconciliations not only were effective in their day but

---

[2] *Ibid*, pp. 107–109.
[3] B. B. Rogers, trans. (Cambridge: Harvard, 1960), p. 341.

also profoundly influenced Western thought for almost two thousand years. It will be the task of this section to record how this came about.

The record of Greek philosophy before Socrates is confused. We have only fragments of the pre-Socratic writings, which are often quoted by later philosophers, such as Plato and Aristotle, to illustrate points of view that they wish to support or to attack. Some fragments are found in compilations of philosophic opinions which were made centuries after the pre-Socratics lived. Rarely do we find their views sustained by extended arguments in their own words as we do with Plato and Aristotle. We are like archeologists engaged in piecing together the scattered fragments of Greek vases. They must sort and cement the fragments together, filling in the gaps with their own materials. We, too, need to sort and piece together; and our materials will sometimes be the interpretations of Plato or Aristotle or an ancient commentator. Sometimes they will be our own.

But this is not all. Science, philosophy, and sheer speculation, as understood now, were confusedly mingled in the years between 600 and 400 B.C. What has been called Greek science was often mere conjecture, and what has been called philosophy was in many cases mere speculation. Pythagoras and his followers could at one and the same time be laying the foundations of mathematics and indulging in fancy concerning the magical properties and potencies of numbers.

Nevertheless, we know enough to identify the strands of science and philosophy which, as claims to knowledge about the natural and social worlds, are distinguishable from, and run counter to, common sense and the folklore. In turning to them, our purpose is not that of the usual history of science or philosophy. We do not wish to examine early Greek science and philosophy in chronological detail, but rather to point to the key ideas which emerged to challenge the conventional wisdom.

The new ways of thinking and the new knowledge in science and philosophy developed first in the Greek colonies in Ionia on the eastern coast of the Mediterranean and in southern Italy. These new modes of thought expressed themselves in a remarkable growth of geometry, especially in the investigations of the Pythagoreans, and in speculation about the fundamental characteristics and development of the universe. The importance of these early investigations lies in their development of logical tools of analysis and their attempt to understand the constitution of the universe in naturalistic terms. It lies also in the extension of the method of logical analysis beyond mathematics to cherished social and moral ideals. What were the effects upon traditional religious beliefs, when the events of one's life and of the world were seen as natural occurrences and not the caprices of the gods? An answer to this question is essential to a proper understanding of Greek philosophy.

About the middle of the fifth-century B.C., Athens became the intellectual capital of Greece. This was the period of Athenian ascendancy in the political sphere, in material wealth, and in the arts. It was her Periclean Age, her Enlightenment, the period of her greatest glory. The citizens of Athens were rightfully proud of her achievements; and in this high noon, foreigners flocked to her to share in what glory they might, and to make a name for themselves if they could. It was a period of sophistication and urbanity, but it was also one of moral restlessness and intellectual uncertainty. Tradition was still respected, but it was being questioned by many young men and by teachers of uncertain reputation who also were often suspect as foreigners. These were the Sophists, who were interested in the new science and philosophy from Ionia and Italy and who used the new learning to attack the traditional religion, morals, laws, and customs. The guardians of the conventional wisdom were disturbed and dismayed. It will be our task to examine some of this criticism and the problems it bequeathed to subsequent philosophers.

As early Greek scientists and philosophers sought to understand occurrences in the universe in naturalistic terms, two related problems of cardinal importance emerged: (1) What are the fundamental substances and forces in nature in terms of which the great variety of things can be accounted for? Is not this wondrous fertility to be regarded as a manifestation of one substance or of several substances in combination? Is there not, after all, that which remains permanent amid all the changes around us? This search for the permanent in the changing became a dominant problem in Greek philosophy, and persisted through subsequent ages. (2) If there are a few substances and forces which account for the variety of things in nature, are they not more real than the things composed of them? To take a contemporary example for illustrative purposes, if water can be shown to be composed of molecules, which in turn are composed of atoms of hydrogen and oxygen, which in turn are made up of more fundamental particles, such as protons, electrons, and the like, are not these particles the true reality of nature since they are the ultimate substances of which the manifold variety of things in nature is composed? What is the true reality of nature? What merely seems to be real or only appears to be so? The distinction between appearance and reality was central in Greek philosophy. It, too, posed problems which have persisted ever since.

If the appearance-reality controversy strikes the reader as one which only closeted scientists and philosophers would argue about, the problem takes on a different hue and urgency when the frame of reference is transferred from science to the domain of religion and morals. What, for example, is the true reality of man? His flesh or his spirit? His body or his soul? What is the good or goods which are really or genuinely good for man? What is the good or goods which appear to be good for him but are not really so? It would be hard to argue that questions of this kind are mere matters of idle curiosity, since they involve ultimate com-mitments concerning what men ought to pursue in life. They are central in every Greek philosophy which reaches maturity. Greek philosophers begin with the conventional goods or ideals. They often end with them, but only after the ideals have been recast and clarified and placed upon a new foundation.

The most skillful accommodations between the new learning and the ancient wisdom were the philosophies of Plato and Aristotle. Plato saved and purified the traditional ideals against the attacks of the Sophists through his Doctrine of Ideas—perhaps the most influential single theory in Western philosophy—a standpoint which was modeled on the certainties of the new mathematics and logic. His philosophy is the classic expression of the ideal possibilities of life, and became the fountainhead of one of the main streams of Western thought, the philosophy of Idealism. Aristotle was the first great systematizer of logic. He was the father of biology and so encyclopedic was his scientific interest that he was possibly the last man in the West who came close to knowing all there was to know of the science of his day. Aristotle's learning did not lead him to disdain Greek traditions but rather to support them. He went beyond the Sophists in showing that the analysis of discourse did not necessarily lead to the disintegration of knowledge but rather could culminate in an ideal science which embodied certainty. The world of common sense was recaptured as the real world after some of the Sophists and scientist-philosophers had cast doubt upon its reality. The prevailing values of society were recast as the embodiment of what a reasonable Greek gentleman would do in the circumstances of the society in which he found himself. The tradi-tional religion must go, except for those conventional rituals to which a rational man could be expected to conform; but there is a divinity in nature which can excite the knowing man's natural piety. This divinity is found in nature's order, of which all things are a part, and in which they exist for the best.

To understand better the need for accommodation between the new science and the established belief, it is necessary to examine at the outset the Greek folklore and the Greek common-sense view of the world.

CHAPTER 2

The Greek Folklore

Role of the City-State

In the *Crito* of Plato we find Socrates in prison awaiting execution. Crito, an influential friend, has come to Socrates with the proposal that he and other friends will effect Socrates' escape from prison; they will spirit him away to another city where he can live out his life in exile. Will Socrates consent?

Socrates is as convinced as Crito that the sentence of death is unjust, but can he agree to the proposed escape? Would this be right? In order to answer the question, Socrates engages himself in an argument with the Laws of Athens. Socrates proposes that he play truant. In turn he answers for the Laws. The Laws ask Socrates whether a state can survive if the law is subverted any time anyone happens to disagree with a law or a judgment under it. Does Socrates really have any objection to the Laws? Did they not create him in providing laws for the marriage of his parents? "Has a philosopher like you," they continue, "failed to discover that our country is more to be valued and higher and holier far than mother or father or any ancestor, and more to be regarded in the eyes of the gods and of men of understanding?"[1] The Laws continue to press the point.

---

[1] *The Dialogues of Plato*, B. Jowett trans. (New York: Random House, 1937), Vol. 1, p. 435.

Socrates concedes he would be wrong in escaping and he rejects Crito's proposal. He is obedient to the judgment under the Laws at the cost of his life.

Whether this incident actually occurred in the life of Socrates is unknown. The dialogue may, after all, be only poetic license on the part of Plato, who was Socrates' worshipful disciple. But, as Aristotle suggested, poetry is more philosophic than history, and that Socrates or many another Greek might have shown this affection and even reverence for his city and its laws cannot be denied. Apart from the great issue it raises, the dialogue is an accurate, even if dramatic, rendering of the attitude that a Greek could feel toward his city-state.

It may be difficult for us now to understand this feeling of intimacy of a Greek for his city-state. So close was this tie that the full description of a man included his own name, that of his father, and that of his city. But what relevance has this to philosophy, after all? The relevance is that the institution of the city-state was intertwined with the political, social, economic, religious, and moral ideas of the Greeks; and it is essential to recognize the importance of the institution for an adequate understanding of the ideas. So powerful was its influence in the life of the Greeks that Gilbert Murray comments, "The real religion of the fifth century was . . . a devotion to the City itself."[2]

By modern standards the Greek city-states were diminutive indeed to assume the functions of sovereign powers. Small as they were, they were as jealous of their independence as today's states are of theirs. They were intensely competitive in political and economic affairs. Warfare was all too frequent among them, culminating in the tragic Peloponnesian War. In this welter of tiny, sovereign city-states, Greece failed to solve the political problems of unity and peace; but, in the often tumultuous climate of city-state political activity, there grew what we know as political theory and political philosophy. Aristotle wrote his *Politics,* having at hand 158 constitutions of Greek states reflecting a wide variety of political structures. The Greeks had achieved a high level of political sophistication by the time of Plato and Aristotle, the first two great political philosophers in the Western tradition.

The institution of the city-state, however, was far more important to the Greeks than simply a fertile ground for political experimentation. As the city-state gradually developed from earlier tribal organizations, it became the embodiment of the idea that law, not men, should rule. After the old tribal monarchies had disappeared, Greek city-states still knew, at times, what one-man rule could mean; but there is a nice story attributed to Thales, one of the first of the Greek philosophers, that the strangest thing he had ever seen in Greece was a tyrant growing old. The essential point is that the Greeks regarded themselves as free when they were

---

[2] *Five Stages of Greek Religion* (New York: Doubleday, 1955), p. 72.

governed by laws and not by the caprice of individual men. The long struggle for justice between the highborn and the lowborn, the rich and the poor, became in part a struggle for the rule of law. In these struggles the laws were gradually written down. Tradition and custom were made explicit, were codified, so that a man could point to his rights. In the dim past, tradition and custom had been hallowed by divine sanction; so now were the laws. Since the laws reflected the will of the gods, the laws should be obeyed. They protected a man and his country. They were holy in a very real sense, even holier than a man's family. They were the very foundation of the state. Thus, when Socrates refused to subvert the law, he refused to commit what to many Greeks was one of the worst of evils.

In a very real sense, the city-state was a man's home. So strong was the tie between the individual and his city-state that Plato went so far as to suggest that the city-state was a kind of oversized family. Thus, the city-state was a great deal more than an institution to protect life and property. The very laws themselves had an educative function; they enhanced or diminished the quality of goodness that citizens could achieve.

Similarly, Greek religion is incomprehensible without reference to the city-state. Each city had a protective deity; each dedicated a temple and festivals to that deity. One of the most elegant and renowned buildings in the world is such a temple, the Parthenon; one of the best-known religious festivals, the Panathenaea, is portrayed on its frieze. These festivals were at once a time for gaiety and worship; they contributed to a sense of oneness in the city.

It is against such a political and social background that those established beliefs of ancient Greece, which are here being called its "folklore," are to be regarded.

Greek Religion

Greek religion possessed no body of sacred writing as do the Jewish and Christian religions. It had no simple statement of doctrine; its priesthood provided no body of canonical writings. In fact, the priests did not function as religious teachers. Greek religion had poets, and it was they who exercised this function. Homer, Hesiod, lesser poets, the great writers of tragedy—these were the religious mentors of Greece.

When an American reads in *The Iliad* about the gay banqueting, philandering, and quarreling of the gods, he may well conclude that only a depraved people could have worshipped such depraved gods. No doubt the Greek gods would have been uncomfortable under the monastic vows of poverty, chastity, and obedience—but did they represent heavenly projections of the habits of a winebibbing, loose-living people? The evidence does not justify an affirmative answer, in spite of the fact that there are elements in the Greek religion uncongenial to, say, the ascetic strain in Christianity. There are criticisms, moreover, by Greeks themselves, of the religion found in Homer and other poets; and in the tragedies of Aeschylus, Sophocles, and Euripedes the religion undergoes significant transformations. Even so, before these later criticisms, Greek religion was anything but the creation of an undisciplined people.

What, then, were the gods like, and what were their relations with men? The Greek gods ruled not only the physical world but the inner life of man. In contrast to the worship of animals in some early religions, the Greek gods were anthropomorphic, that is, they possessed human forms and characteristics. Nature was governed by powers similar to man's own. There was, to be sure, a great difference between gods and men. For one thing, the gods were immortal. For another, they were of surpassing beauty, a beauty captured in sculpture indescribably wonderful. For still another, their strength was supreme; the gods were especially distinguished by their power, and a man could but hope such power would support him in his need. This superiority of the gods was worthy of awe, and awe can inspire the sense of the holy. But, as C. M. Bowra said, ". . . the Greek sense of the holy was based much less on a feeling of the goodness of the gods than on a devout respect for their incorruptible beauty and unfailing strength."[3]

Although the contrast between men and the gods was great, the humanizing of the gods is illustrated in the Greek practice with respect to sacrifice and prayer. The sacrifice was changed from "an act of expiation to an act of hospitality . . . [underlining the] . . . notion that the gods ultimately enjoyed the same pleasures as men and appreciated the same courtesies."[4] In prayer there was ". . . no confession of shortcomings, no promise of amendment, but simply an appeal for practical help. Such an appeal is valid only between friends, between men who have proved their devotion and gods who recognize and welcome it. If a man wishes to be helped by the gods, he must pay due attention to them, and then he may reap his reward."[5] In these attitudes it is obvious that there is little if any humility. A man could speak frankly to the gods. A sort of friendship did exist, even though the friendship was not between equals.

But friendship between men and the gods could also be like friendship among men in other ways. It was sometimes precarious. The gods could be offended; and when they were, they could be merciless. Moreover, suffering could be visited upon just men. How could this be? The Greeks

---

[3] *The Greek Experience* (New York: Mentor Books, 1959), p. 57.
[4] *Ibid.*, p. 59.
[5] *Ibid.*, p. 60.

were as fully aware as Job of the problem of a god or gods of power and the suffering of just men, and this became a major theme in Greek tragedy. Above all, a man must avoid *hubris*, a wanton pride or insolence. It was dangerous business to rival the skill or power of a god. Marsyus challenged Apollo to a contest on the flute, the winner to do what he wanted with the loser. Apollo won and promptly flayed Marsyus alive. This legend is by no means unique. The Greeks seemed especially to feel that too much success and happiness could bring disaster from the gods.

Because of the uncertainties of a man's relationship with the gods and the obvious precariousness of life, there was a note of melancholy in Greek religion. The Greek had no experience of salvation in his religion after which he could rest on the bosom of his Lord in the comforting assurance of a benign outcome. Except for a minority, in the mystery religions in the late classical period, the Greeks did not believe in immortality. In fact, in the heroic period, for men to claim immortality was blasphemy.[6] The gods were immortal; men were not. And what belief there might have been in a shadowy existence in Hades was poor comfort indeed. Many a Greek would have agreed with the ghost of the great Achilles when in *The Odyssey* it said, "My lord Odysseus . . . spare me your praise of Death. Put me on earth again, and I would rather be a serf in the house of some landless man, with little enough for himself to live on, than king of all these dead men that have done with life."[7]

The power of the gods could sustain or harm a man, but there was another power which profoundly influenced his life. This was Moira, Fate or Destiny. *Moira* means literally a "part," "portion," or "share"; with respect to the life of man it is that which is allotted him, that which is due him, that which he is fated to have. And what a man was fated to have, not even the gods could change. Zeus could not save his own son, Sarpedon, on the battlefield of Troy from fated death. No, the gods could not change Fate; in fact they also were subject to it. Hesiod says, "[Night] bare the Destinies and ruthless avenging Fates, Clotho and Lachesis and Atropos, who give men at their birth both evil and good to have, and they pursue the transgressions of men and of gods."[8] "Fate" in this quotation may suggest to us a predestined allotment of good or evil, but the idea of Fate is a difficult one in Greek religion, and it is probably inaccurate to think of Fate as consciously distributing favors or ills to mankind. Perhaps the interpretation of F. M. Cornford is as satisfactory as any: "[*Moira*] was not credited with foresight, purpose, design; these

---

[6] W. C. K. Guthrie, A *History of Greek Philosophy* (Cambridge at the University Press, 1962), Vol. I, p. 196.

[7] Homer, *The Odyssey*, E. N. Rieu trans. (Baltimore: Penguin, 1946), p. 184.

[8] *Theogony*, in Hugh G. Evelyn-White trans. *Hesiod, The Homeric Hymns and Homerica* (New York: Macmillan, 1914), p. 95.

belong to men and to the humanized Gods. *Moira* is the blind, automatic force which leaves their subordinate purposes and wills free play within their own legitimate spheres, but recoils in certain vengeance upon them the moment they cross their boundaries."⁹ Whatever problems of interpretation there may now be about the meaning of Fate in Homer and Hesiod, the idea of Fate suggested to the Greeks not so much that a man's number will come up on a given day—as some of us might conceive of Fate—but a definite limiting power on gods and men alike.

The religious beliefs here described, which centered in the mythology of the gods on Mount Olympus, became the civic religion in Greece. There were also nature religions concerned with fertility and death; but for our purposes, the Olympian religion is the important one.

In the tragedies of Aeschylus, Sophocles, and Euripides, the traditional religion underwent significant refinement. Interest centered, in play after play, on problems of man's suffering and destiny and his relations with the gods. In Aeschylus, for example, one of the persistent themes is that divine justice rules the world, a justice that is perfect. Why is it, then, that men, subject to the power of the gods, suffer? It is man's overweening pride which brings him to sorrow, and the evil deeds resulting from this pride must be punished.

To this familiar theme, however, Aeschylus adds a profoundly novel modification. He transforms justice from a matter of vengeance to one of reasonableness in the law court. In myths like the *Oresteia* it seemed that the expiation of one crime only led to another. Agamemnon sacrifices his daughter in order that his fleet might reach Troy. On his return his wife, Clytaemestra, kills him in part out of vengeance for the sacrifice of her daughter. Orestes, Agamemnon's and Clytaemestra's son, returns to kill his own mother to avenge his father's death. The Furies (representing the Fate that we have met before) pursue Orestes and demand his life. Then there is a dramatic turn in the ancient story. Is there no end to this bloodletting? Aeschylus asks. Orestes takes refuge at an altar of Athena in Athens, and an unusual trial of Orestes follows before a jury of Athenian citizens, with Athena presiding, the Furies the prosecution, and Apollo the defender. Orestes is absolved of his guilt, thus putting an end to the tradition of punishment by taking an eye for an eye. A new sense of justice has been molded. The problem of guilt is taken out of the context of vengeance and placed where persuasion, reasonableness, can triumph over the old law. This justice is more humane.

---

⁹ *From Religion to Philosophy* (New York: Harper Torchbooks, 1957), pp. 20–21.

One might argue that although this sense of justice is a vast improvement over the harsher ancient code, it still leaves unsolved the problem of the suffering of men at the hands of gods. After all, Orestes was ordered by Apollo to avenge the death of his father. What more does Aeschylus have to say? He did not state a solution. Perhaps there is none to this question that appears again and again in the great literature, poetic, religious, philosophical, in Greece and other cultures. But Aeschylus did say that through suffering men gain knowledge. At least they can, although some may not. A man in his suffering may cry out, "Why should this happen to me?" But when he has reached that level of understanding to ask, "Why should this not?" he may be only a little lower than the gods in his wisdom.

The theme of innocent suffering is also central in the plays of Sophocles; and although his works are considered to reflect the highest artistic skill of the three great writers of Greek tragedy, the problem reaches it climax in Euripides. Euripides was not popular in fifth-century Athens, and for this reason one might not accept him as a spokesman for the folklore. Yet in the next century his plays were seen far more than those of either Aeschylus or Sophocles. What he had to say on suffering and other religious questions reflected in part the interests of the Sophists and other philosophers. Ancient writers liked to call him the philosopher of the stage. He thus is something of a transition figure in Greek philosophy. Yet he did reflect the attitude of an increasing number of restless minds in the latter half of the fifth century and is appropriately discussed here.

In the *Heracles* Euripides goes so far as to challenge the notion that the suffering laid upon a man is the result of some flaw in his character such as excess of passion. The suffering of Heracles results simply from Hera's blind hatred, because he is the son of Zeus by a mortal woman. Heracles himself has done nothing to offend Hera; yet she makes him mad. During his madness he kills his wife and children.

When Heracles' sanity is restored, a remarkable exchange about the gods occurs between him and his close friend, Theseus. Heracles flatly asks, who could offer prayers to such a goddess as Hera?

Theseus responds:

> No other god is implicated here,
> except the wife of Zeus. Rightly you judge.
> My advice is this: be patient, suffer
> what you must, and do not yield to grief.
> Fate exempts no man; all men are flawed,
> and so the gods, unless the poets lie.
> Do not the gods commit adultery?
> Have they not cast their fathers into chains,
> in pursuit of power? Yet all the same,

> despite their crimes, they live upon Olympos
> How dare you then, mortal that you are,
> to protest your fate, when the gods do not?

Heracles continues:

> . . . I do not believe the gods commit
> adultery, or bind each other in chains.
> I never did believe it; I never shall;
> nor that one god is tyrant of the rest.
> If god is truly god, he is perfect,
> lacking nothing. These are poets' wretched lies.[10]

In this remarkable speech of Heracles, much of the traditional mythology is called into question. The stories are "poets' wretched lies." But even more, "If god is truly god, he is perfect"; if this be so, the entire mythology comes crashing down, as we shall find some of the philosophers quick to suggest.

The imagery and reality of the gods, and the relations of the gods to man as found in the traditional poetry of Homer and Hesiod were, in this fashion, seriously questioned in the tragedies of the late fifth century. It was still true that a man could be brought to trial on charges of impiety for questioning the traditional religion, as Socrates found. The tradition was still very much alive. But there was also no question that the restless minds of Euripides and such men as the Sophists and other philosophers were challenging the religious folklore and reconstructing it in the process.

Prevailing Ideals of Conduct

That the Greeks generally did not believe in immortality has been noted. Life, for them, was no preparation for a future estate, as it might be for the Christian. The idea of the reward of life eternal or the penalty of everlasting damnation decreed by a supernatural deity was not an operative force in their lives. Thus, the meaning and value of life must be found within the social and natural orders. Within this general frame of reference, specific elements of the Greek ideals of conduct will be examined.

The idea of *arete* or excellence is central in Greek writing concerned with the conduct of men, from Homer to Aristotle and beyond. *Arete* is a term of such broad significance in the Greek language that it can apply to the excellence of any activity or object. A Greek could speak of the excellence of a shoemaker or the shoes he made, the excellence of an athlete, or the excellence of a statue. As for morals, *arete* can have a specific meaning, such as courage, but it can also signify the overall excellence of a man's life. In this sense, *arete* refers to what a man should strive for, to make

---

10 Euripides, *Heracles*, William Arrowsmith, trans. in *The Complete Greek Tragedies* (Chicago: University of Chicago Press, 1959), Vol. III, pp. 332–333.

his life the best one possible. It is the end or purpose or goal of life. It is the ruling ideal of his existence.

In Homer, the source of so many of the Greek ideals, *arete* is the ideal of the great hero, such as Achilles. This heroic ideal is aristocratic; and although the ideal is later modified in many ways, the aristocratic note is never quite lost in the Greek philosophers.

What is the hero like? He is a man of great strength, courage, and superiority of mind. His manner is proud and courtly. He lives with a certain magnificence and liberality. His life is one of action in the performance of great deeds. He must strive, as Achilles' father urged him, ". . . always to be the best and to be distinguished above others."[11] His consuming passion is the desire for honor among his peers. Honor and the memory of his great deeds are his rewards. He could hope that his deeds might be recorded in memorable stories and poetry, which in their own way provide a kind of immortality.

Warfare was the soil in which the heroic ideal flourished. Hand-to-hand combat provided the dramatic conflict in which physical strength and courage could be tested. Homer describes the evils of war, but at the same time he is thrilled by it. In the Homeric age, the heroic ideal has its embodiment in the great warrior.

But the excellence of the hero consists not simply in physical strength and courage. Phoenix, who educated Achilles, reminds the great hero that he was to teach Achilles to be a speaker of words as well as a doer of deeds. The hero must be a warrior, but he should also excel in intelligence and possess a certain moral nobility. Odysseus is renowned for his wise counsel. The Greeks always maintained a high respect for intelligence and extended the idea of *arete* to something other than qualities important in warfare.

In the heroic ideal, the performance of great deeds is fundamentally for one's own gratification or out of duty to one's friends or family. Achilles sulks in his tent because of a feeling of personal insult, much to the misfortune of the Greek soldiers assembled before Troy, since he was their most able warrior. He returns to battle not out of a sense of duty to them but to avenge the death of his friend, Patroclus. The doing of great deeds was very much a personal, we might say self-centered, affair. One of the important transformations in the heoric ideal was the transference of this excellence of performance from the purpose of gratifying one's own sense of honor to the service of the city-state, a change which comes in part through an increasing concern for justice illustrated in the poetry of Hesiod.

The atmosphere of Hesiod's *Works and Days* contrasts sharply with that of Homer. Instead of moving among noble warriors in battle, we find

---

11 Homer, *Iliad,* XI, 784.

ourselves in the midst of peasants in the field. In place of praise of the hero in warfare, we find a cry against the highborn and an insistence upon justice for the lowborn.

The key word is *dike* or justice. In Hesiod, justice is elevated to the level of a goddess, daughter of Zeus, who sits beside her father and tells him of the evils that men do, in order that they may be righted. Justice is not simply a human claim, a demand of one individual or class upon another; it now possesses divine sanction. Men are enjoined by the will of Zeus to do justice; and if they suffer injustice, they can appeal to him for restitution.

But what has the demand for justice in Hesiod to do with *arete?* In the *Works and Days* Hesiod not only cries out for justice but also glorifies the work of the peasant as the good life. It is toil that brings *arete* or excellence of life. It is work, the hard work of the peasant that is the way of righteousness, the path of justice. To work hard is to be a good man, a just man. Quite obviously, a different sort of excellence from that of the hero in Homer is being eulogized. Thus "justice" has a double twist in Hesiod. It is identified with work but also with the notion of doing what is fair as an injunction of the gods. Hesiod lectures the nobility with his fable of the hawk and the nightingale: the hawk, having the nightingale in his talons, tells the weaker bird that the stronger can do anything it chooses with the weaker. When Hesiod chides in this fashion, he is not asking the nobles to go to work, although labor undoubtedly would have, to his way of thinking, improved them. He is rather telling them not to misuse their power. Work, *arete*, justice—all are mingled in Hesiod. It is important to note that *arete* and justice are wedded in some way, as we take a closer look at justice.

"Justice," *dike*, meant at first "due share." The increasing demands for justice, as reflected in the poetry of the seventh and sixth centuries B.C., were for justice in the sense of giving a man his due under the law. And giving a man his due under the law was obedience to the law. But the meaning of *dike* also developed to include the idea of equality, an extension of consummate importance. The initial equality before the law in disputes between individuals can become a demand for equality in many matters, public and private, such as equality of rights with respect to voting in the assembly and holding office. This sort of democratic equality came only after long, bitter struggles, not reaching its culmination until the Athenian democracy of the fifth century and available, even then, only to citizens.

The development of the idea of justice contributed to a change in the meaning of *arete* or excellence. Obedience to the law and equal treatment under the law are essential to justice; thus the man who lives accordingly, who is obedient to the law and undertakes to see that there is equal treatment for others is the just, the righteous man, the man of *arete*. Obviously, this *arete* is hardly the old heroic ideal; however, the *arete* of the warrior in the sense of courage is not forgotten. The warrior's *arete* now becomes subservient to justice. Instead of displaying courage for one's personal satisfaction, one lays his courage at the service of the city-state. The hero of the Homeric age in a moment of flaming action gave his life for personal honor; the man of *arete* will see it as his duty to give his life for the good of the city-state if need be.

Another aspect of *arete* is moderation in conduct. In our comments on Greek religion, it has been noted that a man must by all means avoid *hubris*, insolence or excessive pride, which leads to evils punishable by the gods or fate. A more positive way of asserting this attitude is found in the idea of prudence and moderation. A man ought to do that which is prudent, and the prudent act is the one done in moderation. Poets of the sixth century B.C. like Theognis and Solon could sing of moderation, and the concept comes to play a key role in the ethical writings of later philosophers.

If the notion of *arete* as excellence is central in Greek ideals of conduct, it may still be asked, "Did not the Greeks have any conception of virtue as an ideal?" It has been noted that the translation of *arete* is often "virtue"; and now, after focusing on the meaning of this key term as "excellence," we need to return to this question. If, for example, we today speak of courage as a virtue and a Greek spoke of it as an *arete*, we should both be talking about the same thing. Why not then simply translate *arete* as "virtue?" The translation is harmless if one very fundamental point is kept in mind. To us "virtue" can mean positive action, as in the case of courage. But "virtue" can also mean for us the fact of not doing something, as when we speak of a woman of virtue. The monastic life, which has meant dedication to the service of God through renunciation of much of the world, can for us be virtuous. Most Greeks could not have understood this sort of renunciation as virtue. Again, in the Christian tradition humility has been a virtue but pride one of the deadliest sins. The heroic ideal in Greece, even as transformed by her poets and philosophers, is the ideal of a proud man. Yes, in this discussion of Greek ideals we have been dealing with the general notion of virtue, and specific virtues like courage; and when the reader thinks of *arete*, he may consider this "virtue" if he prefers. But he should also remember that virtue is excellence of achievement, not renunciation or resignation.

Thus the important virtues for the Greeks were those of the courage of the warrior, initially a very personal thing which later was placed at the service of the city-state; justice as obedience to the laws of the state and concern for equality of rights; intelligence in the affairs of men; and temperance or moderation. Supported by his city-state and in turn supporting it, a man could hope to develop these virtues if he did not incur the enmity of the gods through insolence or overpowering passion. When they were achieved, he could be called a man of *arete*, excellence, or virtue. He was a good man.

The Universe in the Folklore

Although Greek religion and ideals of conduct were to be subjected to the scrunity of the philosophers—in terms of the tools of logical analysis and knowledge gained from a developing science in the sixth and fifth centuries B.C.—it was the traditional creation stories or cosmogonies which were first examined in the light of the new learning; hence, it is necessary to outline briefly the way the universe appeared in the folklore. One of the best known versions of the ancient myths is that of Hesiod's *Theogony*.

First of all Chaos came into being, and next broad-bosomed Earth, for all things a seat unshaken for ever, and Eros, fairest among the immortal gods, who looses the limbs and subdues the thought and wise counsel of all gods and of all men.

From Chaos were Born Erebus and black Night; and from Night in turn Bright Sky . . . and Day, whom Night conceived and bore in loving union with Erebus.

And Earth first gave birth to the starry Heaven, equal to herself, that he might cover her all round about, that there might be for the blessed gods a seat unshaken for ever.

And she bore the high Hills, the pleasant haunts of the goddess Nymphs who dwell in the wooded hills.

Also she bore the unharvested deep, with raging flood, the Sea . . . , without sweet rites of love.[12]

The story now changes profoundly. Heaven and Earth are married, and the first gods are born.

Certain matters of importance are to be noted here. In the first place, Heaven and Earth came into being before the gods did. The gods are of natural origin even though they then are deathless. This story is in profound contrast to "In the beginning God created the heavens and the earth." In the second place, although the language of the myth is anthropomorphic, the story reads more as if the forces at work were impersonal. It is only when Heaven and Earth are married that the personification becomes explicit for the birth of the gods. The cosmogony is beginning to lose its anthropomorphism, which it later does in the hands of the philosophers.

What, then, did the universe look like in the prevailing mythology?

---

[12] F. M. Cornford, *Principium Sapientiae: The Origins of Greek Philosophical Thought* (Cambridge at the University Press, 1952), p. 193.

The earth was conceived to be a circular plane, surrounded by a river, Oceanus. The "starry heaven" or sky was a concave surface of equal extent with the earth, seeming to rest on the earth but still in need of support of pillars, which Atlas upheld. Below the earth was Hades, the world of the dead. Between the earth and Hades was Erebus, a gloomy region which seemed to be a kind of passage between the two. Below Hades there was Tartarus, but in the later poets Tartarus became identified with Hades. This picture of the cosmos became traditional, as the account in Genesis became for Christianity.

It would, of course, be erroneous to assume that the Greeks knew nothing more about the earth than the account in Homer and Hesiod. In Homer the geography is admittedly primitive. He knew a zone which included a part of Greece, some of the Aegean islands, a portion of the coast of Asia Minor, Egypt, and Libya. By the sixth century B.C. there was a store of practical knowledge about geography considerably beyond that of the heroic age, enabling Anaximander, one of the Greek philosophers soon to be considered, to construct the first map of the known Western world. The importance of this common-sense knowledge cannot be minimized; but the speculation about the fundamental characteristics of the universe and about the course of the universe's development was the first great work of the early Greek philosophers.

Dramatic Turns in the Greek View of Life

In their plethora of city-states, the Greeks produced almost every type of political organization and gradually molded the idea that freedom consisted in obedience to law. In organized freedom, they held, men can achieve justice. Their religion provided gods which were not alien, evil powers, but were beings like man himself, except that the gods were immortal and were wiser, stronger, and more passionate. Notwithstanding the superiority of their gods, the Greeks were not abject before them. No priesthood was permitted to become the sole possessor and interpreter of religious truth. Unquestionably, the freedom of interpretation which prevailed was an important factor in permitting, perhaps even fostering, the growth of philosophy. The possibility of the good life was found here and now, in the cultivation of the specific excellences or virtues of courage, temperance, justice, and wisdom. When achieved, a man assuredly could be called a good man.

The Greeks were aware of the darker side of human nature, but, in this very awareness, it might be possible for a man to be moderate and temperate. They were sorely troubled over the question of why innocent men suffer, but as they explored this human predicament with candor, they found that in suffering, men can gain wisdom. In these explorations they illuminated one of the eternal perplexities of human existence.

The Greeks had, in short, achieved a remarkable perceptiveness in social organization, an incredible sophistication in the arts, and a relatively stable adjustment to the natural world around them and to the enigmatic forces in their own souls. What, then, disrupted this Greek view of life? Why did it not continue to satisfy the needs of men? One disrupting factor was war. The long Peloponnesian War at the end of the fifth century B.C., as so often happens with war, contributed to a social and political disintegration which disrupted prevailing values. The very foundation of the old society, the city-state—with its pre-eminent position in political, economic, social, and religious affairs—dissolved, before a century had passed, in the more alien and lonely soil of empire. To be sure, local customs and loyalties did not disappear over night. But when civic autonomy gives way to distant imperial control, civic virtue too changes. With the feeling that the seat of control is too distant or that the problems of the world are too vast for human powers, comes withdrawal to one's own garden or the flight to an escape religion; and so was it with the Greeks. When the Alexandrian empire and its successors supplanted the Greek city-state system, the folklore here described no longer satisfied the prevailing needs.

But forces much earlier and less obvious than those producing and following the Peloponnesian War—but powerful nonetheless—were at work which led to criticism and re-examination of the established view of life. These forces were the science and philosophy which budded around 600 B.C. and grew rapidly in the sixth and fifth centuries B.C. Their impact fell first upon the common-sense views of the world and then upon religion. By the end of the fifth century B.C., the critical acumen which developed in the new ways of thinking was turned upon every aspect of man's social and inner worlds. To the disturbing new science and philosophy we now turn.

Selected Readings

Bowra, C. M., *The Greek Experience*, New York: Mentor Books, 1959. (Paperback.)

Cornford, F. M., *From Religion to Philosophy: A Study in the Origins of Western Speculation*, New York: Harper Torchbooks, 1957. (Paperback.)

Guthrie, W. K. C., *In the Beginning, Some Greeks Views on the Origin of Life and the Early State*, Ithaca: Cornell, 1957.

Guthrie, W. K. C., *The Greeks and Their Gods*, Boston: Beacon Press, 1955. (Paperback.)

Jaeger, Werner, *Paideia, The Ideals of Greek Culture*, London: Oxford, 2nd ed., 1945, Vol. I.

Murray, Gilbert, *Five Stages of Greek Religion*, New York: Doubleday, 1955. (Paperback.)

CHAPTER 3

Early Greek Science
and
Early Greek Philosophy

Early Greek Science

Greek science and philosophy were born about 600 B.C. In the early years of philosophy and science in Greece, it was difficult to separate the two as we do now, for some of the first Greek philosophers were also some of the first Greek scientists. The separation of the ideas of the Pythagoreans, for example, such that some ideas are said to be scientific while others are philosophic, may seem quite arbitrary. Yet, even though the distinction between philosophy and science is blurred in the sixth century B.C., it is possible to see that the so-called Pythagorean theorem— "In right-angled triangles the square on the side subtending the right angle is equal to the squares on the sides containing the right angle"—is a different kind of knowledge from the Pythagorean claim that all things in nature are number. Thus, even in the early days two strands of thought are discernible.

At the outset, it is necessary to go beyond our general comments in the Introduction and consider what we mean by "science" in more precise detail. Indeed, in an important sense each of the four parts of this volume will contribute to the clarification of how "science" has been and is now understood. "Science" comes from the Latin word *scientia*, meaning simply "knowledge." But not *all* knowledge. Greek tragedy provides knowledge by illuminating the character of man. Shakespeare's plays afford a kind of knowledge concerning the human scene. It is fairly safe to say that science is not the whole of knowledge, but what kind of knowledge is it?

If we look at what scientists in the past have done, and what they today do, and read their comments on the way they work and the results of that work, we find at least this common element—that the knowledge called "science" is *knowledge arrived at by an identifiable method or methods.* It is this which gives science its character and validity. Whether there is just one method common to all the sciences from anthropology to zoology or whether the several sciences employ methods which have fundamental differences is a matter of debate among scientists and philosophers; this debate will be explored later. But there is rather general agreement that the scientific method or methods used in investigating the world undertake to achieve general statements about occurrences through careful observation and, if possible, through precisely controlled experiment. From such general statements or generalizations, consequences are deduced or predicted. These consequences or predictions are tested by further observations or experiments which verify or reject the predictions. This process—of generalization (or the formulation of hypotheses, as it may be called), deduction, verification—continues without end. As the body of knowledge in a specific area grows, there is often an effort to organize it into a deductive system. This creation of a system, however, usually comes only in a science that is subject to precise measurement and control, and capable of mathematical treatment.

Much of the general body of knowledge that is called "science" consists of the results of the methods just outlined. This body of knowledge changes, for the methods are self-corrective, in that what was conceived as a scientific truth at one time is found, under new hypotheses and more precise observations or experimental procedures, to be inadequate. The knowledge developed by the methods described in this general fashion is called *empirical* science and is illustrated in the Greek period by Aristotle's *Inquiries about Animals,* a substantial collection of data on the animal kingdom, in which he describes in detail the morphology or structural characteristics of many kinds of animals. Here Aristotle is making generalizations about classes of animals based upon accurate observation. This kind of scientific activity is illustrated today in any textbook of introductory zoology.

An early example of knowledge that is systematized in deductive form is provided by Archimedes' *On the Equilibrium of Planes.* From a set of seven postulates, such as "Equal weights at equal distances are in equilibrium, and equal weights at unequal distances are not in equilibrium but incline towards the weight which is at the greater distance," and certain propositions of Euclidean geometry, Archimedes deduces the law of the lever, which is, in his formulation, "Two magnitudes, whether commensurable or incommensurable, balance at distances reciprocally proportional to the magnitudes."[1] The postulate cited can be generalized from the observation of a simple balance, and the deduced proposition can be confirmed experimentally from the same instrument. The distinctive characteristic of this type of knowledge is that propositions which were originally based upon observation or experimentation are tied together in a system by formal logical and mathematical relations.

There is another kind of knowledge, closely related to the systematized knowledge of empirical science, which is also scientific but does not fit exactly into the empirical framework. Pure mathematics is a case in point, illustrated by geometry. "But," it may be asked, "can geometry be pure mathematics, when it developed out of problems of measuring the earth, as the name clearly indicates?" Geometry did originate out of such problems, but one need only look at Euclid's *Elements* to see that the subject has been lifted out of the context of surveying or engineering and placed at a high plane of abstraction. Turning to his definitions, we discover that:

1. A *point* is that which has no part.
2. A *line* is breadthless length. . . .
5. A surface is that which has length and breadth only.[2]

Clearly it would be futile to attempt to find or construct a physical point that has no part, or a physical line that has no breadth, or a physical surface that has no thickness. Points, lines, and surfaces are considered without reference to physical content; and the system of geometry becomes an investigation of logical relations among the definitions, axioms, and postulates laid down as the basis of the system.

That such a theoretical system as Euclidean geometry has application to the physical world is of course true, as the history of physics clearly shows. But a purely theoretical system can be developed independently of empirical application, and this sort of system is appropriately included in the use of the term "science." In summary, then, the term "science" is used here to signify any body of knowledge that answers our description of an empirical science or a purely theoretical science like geometry.

The sciences in Greece that made the first impact upon the folklore were mathematics, logic, and astronomy. Of these, mathematics—as the most highly developed—deserves first attention. We are not considering

---

[1] T. L. Heath, *The Works of Archimedes* (Cambridge at the University Press, 1897), pp. 189, 192.
[2] T. L. Heath, *The Thirteen Books of Euclid's Elements* (Cambridge at the University Press, 1908), Vol. I, p. 153.

Greek mathematics in the detail required of the historian of science; we wish to emphasize only two of its aspects: (1) its characteristic as a systematic science, and (2) the idea of proof.

The Babylonians and Egyptians had developed arithmetic and geometry for purposes of practical application, like the surveying of fields, and were capable of solving some kinds of theoretical problems; but it remained for the Greeks to raise these branches of mathematics to the level of a systematic science. They greatly advanced the study of mathematical relations when those relations themselves became an object of investigation. Furthermore, it was the Greeks, as far as we know, who developed to any degree the idea of proof, the heart of mathematics as a science.

The first Greek geometer of note was Thales of Miletus, who flourished about 600 B.C. Thales probably studied geometry in Egypt, but ancient sources credit him with the discovery of several geometrical theorems and, what is of particular note, a method of attack upon problems that was more general than that of earlier geometers. However, it was the Pythagoreans of the sixth and fifth centuries B.C. who achieved systematization in any real sense.

Since the greatest and most extensive work in Greek mathematics is Euclid's *Elements*, a monumental treatise of thirteen books, written about 300 B.C., we sometimes have the notion that Euclid sat down, wrote out twenty-three definitions, five postulates, and five common notions or axioms, and then proceeded to spin out of his head the thirteen books of proved propositions. Of course he did not. His was a magnificent systematization of much geometry already known, with the addition of his own original contributions. The initial labor was that of the Pythagoreans, who by the end of the fifth century B.C.—at least a hundred years before Euclid—had the knowledge of a substantial part of the work contained in Books I, II, IV, and VI, and part of that in VII of Euclid's *Elements*. This included such matters as:

. . . the properties of parallel lines, which they used for the purpose of establishing by a general proof the proposition that the sum of the three angles of any triangle is equal to two right angles. . . . They originated the subject of equivalent areas, the transformation of an area of one form into another of different form and, in particular, the whole method of *application of areas*, constituting a *geometrical algebra*, whereby they effected the equivalent of algebraical processes of addition, subtraction, multiplication, division, squaring, extraction of the square root, and finally the complete solution of the mixed quadratic equation $x^2 \pm px \pm q = 0$, so far as the roots are real. Expressed in terms of Euclid, this means the whole content of Book I, 35–48 and Book II. The method of *application of areas* is one of the most fundamental in the whole of later Greek geometry; it takes its place by the side of the powerful method of proportions; moreover, it is the starting point of Apollonius's theory of conics . . . Nor was the use of geometrical algebra for solving *numerical* problems unknown to the Pythagoreans; this is proved by the fact that the theorems of Euclid II, 9, 10 were invented for the purpose of finding successive integral solutions of the indeterminate equation $2x^2 - y^2 = \pm 1$.[3]

This quotation by no means exhausts the Pythagorean accomplishments; but we need not attend to further details except to note that they were aware of, in fact may have discovered, the five regular solids: the tetrahedron, the cube, the octahedron, the dodecahedron, and the icosahedron—figures found later in Plato's theory of nature.

The consequences of the Pythagorean achievement were manifold and important. In the first place, they set geometry winging on its way so that by 300 B.C. Euclid's remarkable *Elements* was possible. More important to us, however, is how this accomplishment took place. The Pythagoreans enlarged our knowledge of the properties of points, lines, and planes by developing the technique of *proof*. In this way they clearly made a systematized science of geometry, which in the mature form of Euclid became the model of *science as system* down to the modern era.

Proof is the heart of the matter. "Proof" means laying out or setting forth, step by step, the implications between one set of propositions—in the case of geometry: the definitions, axioms, and postulates—and another set—the theorems. Now the question arises, "Need proof be confined to mathematics?" To be sure, its most elegant and pure form was first constructed in an abstract realm of points, lines, and planes. But, with less rigidity and precision, men were quick to extend the technique to beliefs about the natural world, religion, politics, law, and other areas of human experience. A man could at least seek to determine the possible consequences of such beliefs, even if the aseptic purity of mathematics could not be attained. Anaximander, one of the early philosophers, could in effect ask, "If things in nature constantly come into existence and pass away, is it not necessary that there be an infinite source of material; otherwise will not the change in nature cease?" And Xenophanes will continue, "If there is an infinite source of all things, is this not God? And is there then just one god rather than the glorified projections of human hopes and fears which we call the gods?" The folklore will soon find itself in a perilous situation in the midst of questions like these. When men forget to remain among geometrical abstractions, and move on to analyze *objectively* their traditional beliefs about the world, the gods, and society, they may find it hard to keep these beliefs intact or at least unchanged. This questioning is precisely what happened in Greece with the emergence of objective habits of thought in the new science and philosophy.

---

[3] Sir Thomas Heath, *A History of Greek Mathematics* (Oxford at the Clarendon Press, 1921), Vol. I, pp. 166–167. All contemporary discussions of Greek mathematics are indebted to this classic work.

These habits of thought, moreover, can themselves become objects of study. When attention is focused on the techniques of proof and the ways of developing the consequences of propositions, *logic* is born. In fact, "logic" may be defined as the generalized study of proof. In Greek thought, logic reaches its culmination in Aristotle (see pp. 113 ff.); and, ever since, logic has remained one of the most important fields of philosophy.

There is another aspect of Pythagorean mathematics that had a powerful influence on Greek thought. The Pythagoreans were interested not only in geometry but also in theorizing about numbers. Again, the use of numbers in practical calculation for business transactions and other affairs of everyday life originated in the dim past, but the Pythagoreans initiated inquiry into the nature of numbers themselves. They undertook to define the unit and number. They classified numbers into odd and even, and made the distinction between prime and composite numbers. They developed a theory of proportion of commensurable quantities and they discovered the arithmetic, geometric, and harmonic means. Also, one of their most influential ideas was that of figured numbers.

Numbers were represented by dots in geometric patterns, as follows:

.   to represent 1

..   to represent 2

.·. to represent 3.   This is a triangular number.

::   to represent 4.   This is a square number.

:: ::   to represent 6.   This is an oblong number.

The system was generalized such that the successive additions of the odd integers could be represented by squares, as shown below.

$$1 + 3 + 5 = 9$$

The successive additions of even integers could be represented by oblongs.

$$2 + 4 + 6 = 12$$

The odd numbers were said to be limited, apparently because the form of the series was limited to that of a square while the even numbers were said to be unlimited since the geometrical representation of the series of even numbers could take the shape of various oblongs. The idea of the limited and the unlimited finds its way outside mathematics into philosophy. Later, its use both by the Pythagoreans (see pp. 61 ff.) and by Plato (see pp. 79 ff.) will be examined.

The geometrical representation of numbers meant a great deal more to the Pythagoreans, however, than what may appear to be a game; for things in nature—minerals and living things, too—exhibit geometrical patterns. Thus, it was argued, each kind of thing can be said to have a number. Needless to say, the leap from ideas about numbers to the pattern and structures of physical things is a long one; but it was to be one of the most fruitful ideas ever to strike man—that somehow mathematics is a key to nature. We have left the realm of pure mathematics to find ourselves in the world of empirical science and philosophy. How was the leap made? Could there be any evidence, anything more than a wild guess, that mathematics is the language of nature, as Galileo was to say in the seventeenth century?

One of the most persistent stories in the ancient literature attributes to Pythagoras or his followers the discovery of the mathematical ratios of three fundamental musical intervals: the octave, in the ratio of 1:2; the fifth, in the ratio of 3:2; and the fourth, in the ratio of 4:3. How the discovery was made is unknown. The intervals themselves were common enough, for they were the three concordant intervals of the Greek lyre. But noting the mathematical ratios was far from commonplace.

Many simple discoveries about nature, such as this, seem not at all extraordinary to later ages. But the notion is a little astonishing that something as evanescent as sound embodies mathematical relations. If this insubstantial thing does, then perhaps a substantial thing of nature—a stick or a stone—does also. And the Pythagoreans made precisely that intellectual leap to all things in nature. Assuredly, the empirical basis for the leap was extremely narrow. In our more empirically cautious age, we can only say that the generalization to all things was extravagant. It would receive further substantiation among the Greeks in the work of Archimedes, but extensive support would not come until the advent of modern science. Weak as the basis for the generalization was, the Pythagoreans were led to speculate upon its meaning and possible consequences. But before we examine these speculations (pp. 61 ff.), we may profitably turn from the world of sounds to the planets and the stars and take a look at Greek astronomy.

There is only a thin line between early Greek science and Greek folklore in the realm of astronomy. The reason is simple. There is more speculation than there are observational data, at least in the extant sources. But Greek astronomy of the sixth and fifth centuries B.C. has a quality which brings some of it close in spirit to science, and warrants attention even though the evidence for the speculation is meager; astronomy does not approach the level of sophistication achieved by the mathematics of these centuries.

In this period, one of the most important factors in Greek astronomy is its naturalistic character. The Greeks did not originate the study of heavenly bodies. Babylonia and Egypt have a long history of astronomical observations; but their astronomy was still, by the sixth century, closely tied to mythological and religious beliefs. It was primarily the province of priests. Although the Greeks in this period were inferior to the Babylonians and Egyptians in observing the heavenly bodies, their speculation about the origin of the sun, the moon, the earth and other planets, and the stars, as well as the movements of these bodies, was to a significant extent devoid of the mythological considerations of the Babylonians and Egyptians, not to mention those of Homer and Hesiod. Greek astronomers undertook to account both for the origin of the heavenly bodies and their movements by means of naturalistic explanations; that is to say, they argued that what occurred with respect to the heavenly bodies was the result of other occurrences in nature and not the actions of gods.

This step taken by the early Greek astronomers, the same to be taken by the early philosophers, was momentous. The scientific manner of thinking involves the notion of a *subject-object relationship*. We take such a relationship so much for granted that we forget that its prominence is recent and novel. "Subject-object" involves an "I-It" and not an "I-Thou" relationship, to use the apt terminology of H. and H. A. Frankfort; in the former case an object is something to be explained and understood, in the latter something to be "experienced emotionally in a dynamic reciprocal relationship."[4] Thus, when nature is regarded as a living "Thou," the terms in which it will be treated will be emotional and imaginative instead of intellectual; and the difference between these responses will not be distinguished and defined. In such a context, man's dealings with natural phenomena are akin to social intercourse, where we find such basic categories as friendship and hostility, cooperation and conflict, punishment and reward, and, embracing all of these, the histrionic act of role-taking on which all communication is based.

The world appears to primitive man neither inanimate nor empty but redundant with life; and life has individuality, in man and beast and plant, and in every phenomenon which confronts man—the thunderclap, the sudden shadow . . . the stone which . . . hurts him when he stumbles. . . . Any phenomenon may at any time face him, not as "It", but as "Thou." In this confrontation "Thou" reveals its individuality, its qualities, its will. "Thou" is not contemplated with intellectual detachment; it is experienced as life confronting life. . . .[5]

---

[4] *Before Philosophy* (Baltimore: Penguin, 1949), p. 14.
[5] *Ibid.*, p. 14.

Hence the central place of myth, the dramatic story in which fact and fiction mingle indistinguishably, in early man's dealings with the world. For myth is exactly that which deals not in impersonal entities to be described in prosaic generalization, but in living presences to be cajoled, importuned, propitiated, moved, and dramatized in poem and story. It is, of course, acknowledged that the predecessors of the Greeks addressed themselves to intellectual problems and asked the questions "why" and "how." But in their case "thought does not operate autonomously. The *whole* man confronts a living 'Thou' in nature; and the whole man—*emotional and imaginative* as well as intellectual—gives expression to the experience."[6]

When a phenomenon confronts us as "It" we regard it as an object to be investigated. We do not think of taking the role of an "It," or of using the supposed responses of an "It" to our actions or words as a guide to our future conduct. "It" is to be described, examined, analyzed, not communicated with. "It" is to be treated as a natural event or the manifestation of some material substance in nature. Although the mythopoeic manner of thinking lingered among them, the early men of science began the arduous task of depersonalizing nature's events, and disengaging themselves from those events in order that they might understand occurrences in terms of the internal mechanisms and forces of the events themselves.

The theories propounded by the early astronomers seem naïve now, but they had some ideas which were to be confirmed in later days and others of profound influence in the history of science and philosophy even though these ideas had to be abandoned in modern times. In the sixth century B.C. Anaximander maintained that the earth was the center of the universe, an idea which was finally to triumph in the astronomy of Ptolemy of the second century of our era—an astronomy which became the prevailing theory until the Copernican hypothesis of the sixteenth century. The Pythagoreans originated the ideas of the sphericity of the earth and its rotation on its axis.[7] They were interested in lunar and solar eclipses, and Thales predicted an eclipse of the sun in 585 B.C. The basis for the prediction was possibly data collected by Babylonian astronomers, but there is no reason to believe that Thales understood the cause of the eclipse. However, the nature of both lunar and solar eclipses was stated by the fifth century B.C.

One of the most important problems of Greek astronomy, and one which had significant historical consequences, was the study of the motion of the planets. By the fifth century B.C., the independent motion of the

---

[6] *Ibid.*, p. 14. (Our italics.)

[7] Copernicus in the sixteenth century refers through Cicero to the assumption of Hicetas of Syracuse, a Pythagorean, that the earth rotates on its axis. Cicero, *Academica*, II, 39, 123.

planets from west to east against the background of the so-called fixed stars had been recognized. It was not until the next century that Greek astronomers undertook to account for the irregularities of these planetary motions; but the birth of this problem is noteworthy, because it became central to theoretical astronomy. The complicated geocentric theory of Ptolemy undertook to answer the problem, and it was for this problem in particular that Copernicus in the sixteenth century sought a simpler solution than Ptolemy's." The solution that Copernicus found in the heliocentric theory was to revolutonize astronomy. It did a great deal more. It also revolutionized man's view of the universe. But the import of this scientific theory, with its attendant problems, will be explored later.

The significance of these early investigations and speculations in astronomy is that while Greek mythology had personified the heavenly bodies and spun marvelous tales about them, Greek astronomy—less poetically but more effectively—began to place the heavenly bodies in their natural settings and to ask hard questions about their origins, their relative positions, and their movements. Whatever answers were to be found had to be expected in terms of natural forces and not the actions of personified deities.

Small as these beginnings were, they embraced two further general hypotheses concerning nature, which were crucial for the development of both science and philosophy: that nature embodies order or orders; and that these orders are intelligible to man. Until there arises the suggestion of intelligible order which is objectively rooted in things themselves, the world is little more than a kaleidoscope of transient experiences, vivid and many-colored, subject to hidden forces, or manipulations by capricious gods.

To be sure, the dramatic achievements in geometry, the Pythagorean glimpse of mathematical order in physical events, and the first halting efforts to depersonalize the heavenly bodies did not put the mythology to flight in a day. After two hundred years, Socrates still found that the charge of teaching strange gods could bring fatal consequences to one so accused. But the gifted and fertile intellects, responsible for these slender beginnings in the sciences, put their new knowledge and new habits of thought to work in raising questions about the nature of the universe. The answers to these questions shook the foundations of the traditional religion, and provided in turn an intellectual framework for the more effective development of science. The early scientists were also the early philosophers, and to their philosophic investigations we now turn.

Early Greek Philosophy

The influence of the early science imparted a naturalistic temper to the philosophy of the same period. In fact, this temper is the most striking feature of the new philosophy. When we attend less to details of the various views, which are primarily of historical interest, and more to their general significance, we find their import in an attitude toward the world, an attitude which undertook, for example, to understand its fertility in terms not of myths concerning Demeter but of natural mechanisms. If all occurrences are the result of natural forces, the question is raised concerning the need for the gods, at least as the gods were popularly conceived. We shall illustrate how this turn in Greek thought came about.

Some of the early Greek philosophers wrote books *peri physeos, about nature*. Since, as a title, *About Nature* is obviously vague, we need to know what it was that the early Greek philosophers were writing or talking about when they referred to nature. Now the word *physis* is a work horse in Greek, as the word "nature" is in our own language, in having multiple meanings of importance. Some of the meanings of "nature" will be explored in other parts of this volume. Here, in passing, it may be noted that we can speak of "nature," meaning birds and trees and the earth and the sun and the stars, in short, the universe. We can use it to mean the character of something, or that which is fundamental to that thing, as when we speak of the nature of man. With only a slight shift in meaning, to one that is a little more abstract, we can speak of the nature of a problem. These illustrations hardly begin to exhaust the meaning of "nature." So it was with *physis*.

In writing about nature, the early Greeks were writing about nature in the comprehensive sense of the universe. They were initially concerned with two basic problems: (1) What is the most fundamental principle (*arche*) of nature, in the sense of what is it of which nature is ultimately composed or what is the ultimate substance or substances of nature? and (2) How did nature come to be what it is or how did nature or the universe develop into what it is? These questions were to breed a host of others, but it is to these two that we shall first attend.

What, then, is the nature of the universe, in the sense of the ultimate substance or substances of which all things are composed? The first answer of which there is any record was given by Thales. He has been called in ancient sources and modern the first Greek philosopher. His answer was that the ultimate substance of nature is water. All things come to be or are generated from water and ultimately perish into it. Why Thales selected water we do not know. Aristotle conjectured,[8] and is careful to point out that he is only conjecturing, that Thales selected water because the seeds and nutriment of living things are moist. The selection of water as the ultimate principle of all things, animate and inanimate, may now seem to us a little naïve, but the search for that which

---

[8] *Metaphysics*, 893b21 ff.

is constant in the manifold changes in nature and that from which the great variety of things in nature is derived is not naïve. Before we examine the significance of this notion, we need two further illustrations from the early Greeks.

Anaximander (611-545 B.C.), a younger contemporary of Thales and also a Milesian, likewise sought the ultimate principle of things; he found it to be the Infinite or the Boundless (*to apeiron*). His argument bears notice. The ultimate source of "all the heavens and the worlds in them"[9] must be infinite so that *becoming* (a term frequently used in Greek philosophy meaning anything, animate or inanimate, which comes into existence and perishes) might not fail. In other words, without an endless source the material of nature would be used up. The Infinite, moreover, has no characterization; otherwise, because of its infinitude, all things would have become one thing, that is, if Thales' water were the ultimate substance, all things would have become water. The ultimate substance cannot thus be characterized as any particular kind of substance that we know.

Whether Thales went beyond the question of the ultimate substance of which all things are composed is unknown, but Anaximander did take the step of asking how nature came to be what it is. Out of the Infinite, elemental substances are separated—the hot, the cold, the moist, and the dry. From these, Anaximander undertakes to account for the formation of the earth and the heavenly bodies. Details need not detain us, except to note that the earth and the heavenly bodies came into being through movements (we should be more inclined to say "forces") that are perfectly natural to the materials differentiated out of the Infinite. The actual description of the development of nature is crude, but nothing outside natural materials or forces is introduced to account for the development. The theory is speculative, unquestionably; it is also unquestionably naturalistic.

A third philosopher of Miletus, Anaximenes (flourished about 550 B.C.), who was perhaps a pupil of Anaximander, returned to an identifiable element, air, as the ultimate material substance of things. In this respect he may be less sophisticated than Anaximander, but he added a very important idea concerning the manner in which the variety of nature develops from one substance. The variety comes about, he argued, by the condensation or rarefaction of the air. By rarefaction air becomes fire, by condensation it becomes water, by further condensation earth and even stone. In this idea of Anaximenes an important principle, for the future of both philosophy and science, is found: that the variety in nature can be accounted for by variations in the quantity of some fundamental

---

[9] G. S. Kirk and J. E. Raven, *The Presocratic Philosophers* (Cambridge at the University Press, 1960), p. 106.

substance or substances. This principle is obviously related to the Pythagorean contention that all things are number. Although there is no evidence that Anaximenes was acquainted with the Pythagorean view, he should have known the work of Thales in mathematics. Later his idea became one of the foundation stones of the atomic theory.

From these slender beginnings in the reflections of three philosophers in Miletus, along with the development of mathematics and astronomy, were to grow two of the most important fields of Greek philosophy, *metaphysics* and *cosmology*. These fields are closely related; in fact they overlap so that it is sometimes hard to tell whether a given question or problem is metaphysical or cosmological, and tagging it one or the other is less important than the search for the answer. The fields may be loosely grouped together as *natural philosophy*. In view of the close ties between the two we shall not try to erect a wall between them.

Metaphysics is concerned with determining the fundamental and pervasive characteristics of existing things. When we say that something exists, what is it that we mean by "exists"? Thales had argued this to be water, Anaximander an infinite unspecified substance, Anaximenes air. As this sort of inquiry develops, there are those who insist there is not one ultimate substance but several or many. There are others who argue that not only material substances but other factors are also fundamental characteristics of existing things. For example, things are spatial and temporal as well as material. Thus, it is claimed, we must also understand the nature of space and time if we are to understand the basic principles of things. When we say something exists, do we allow for things to exist which are not material? Can, for example, an idea exist? a mind? a soul? A search for an ultimate substance of which the universe is composed generates a host of questions about the very nature of existence itself, such that Aristotle later formulated the questions like this: What does it mean to be? When we say that something exists, what is it that we mean by "exists"? And this sort of inquiry has continued to the present day as one of the important fields of philosophy.[10]

If we could determine the fundamental and pervasive characteristics of existing things, we could still ask, "How do things get to be the way they

---

[10] Our term "metaphysics" comes from a Latin translation of the Greek expression *ta meta ta physika*. The origin of the Greek expression is an historical accident. Andronicus of Rhodes published an edition of Aristotle's works in 70 B.C. He found several short works dealing with the common theme of what it means to be. In his edition he put them together; placed them after Aristotle's work, *The Physics*; and gave them the title, *ta meta ta physika*, which means literally, "the things after the physics." Hence, one of the most important words in the history of philosophy, Greek in origin and designating a subject about which most Greek philosophers had something to say, was not a creation of Greek philosophers at all.

There are those who prefer the term "ontology" to "metaphysics." "Ontology" is of Greek origin and means literally, "the study or theory of being." We shall understand "metaphysics" and "ontology" to designate the same kind of inquiry.

are? How did nature come to be what it is? What is the pattern or order of development of the universe?" This sort of question we can call "cosmo-logical," concerned with the order or pattern of development of the universe. Answers to these questions provide theories of that development. They may be elementary and crude, as they often were in early Greek philosophy and science; they may be sophisticated and complex, as one finds them in the hands of contemporary astronomers and philosophers. But the tradition of cosmological inquiry has persisted since the early Greek philosophers.

These early metaphysical and cosmological speculations had an immediate impact upon the traditional religion. We have noted already that in Hesiod the cosmology had begun to lose its anthropomorphism. This loss is virtually complete in the early Greek philosophers. The ultimate constituent material of their universe is an active, energetic substance, which is both the source of material and the energy from which all things come, even the gods. Anaximenes says that ". . . infinite air was the principle, from which the things that are becoming, and that are, and that shall be, and gods and things divine, all come into being and the rest from its products."[11] In Hesiod, too, the natural origin of the gods was noted, but in Anaximenes there is no marriage of heaven and earth for the birth of the gods. There is no personification of the materials or forces of nature in any way whatsoever. Nature has become depersonalized.

This sort of depersonalization of nature might easily go unnoticed in a philosophic work, but hardly the open attacks upon the traditional religion by Xenophanes. Like Thales, Anaximander, and Anaximenes, Xenophanes (570–470 b.c.) was an Ionian, and he is said to have heard Anaximander. He says of himself that he wandered about Greece for 67 years singing his poems. If he did, the audience for his views must have been considerable, and many listeners must have been shocked at his startling challenges to Homer, Hesiod, and the tradition. He had this to say, for example:

Homer and Hesiod have attributed to the gods everything that is a shame and reproach among men, stealing and adultery and deceiving each other. (*Fragment* 11.)

But mortals consider that the gods are born, and that they have clothes and speech and bodies like their own. (*Fragment* 14.)

The Ethiopians say that their gods are snub-nosed and black, the Thracians that theirs have light blue eyes and red hair. (*Fragment* 16.)

But if cattle and horses or lions had hands, or were able to draw with their hands and do the works that men can do, horses would draw the forms of the gods like horses, and cattle like cattle, and they would make their bodies such as they each had themselves. (*Fragment* 15.)[12]

---

[11] G. S. Kirk and J. E. Raven, *op. cit.*, pp. 144–145.
[12] *Ibid.*, pp. 168–169.

There are two striking criticisms of the traditional religion in these selections. The first is a complaint against the reputed immorality of the gods. We have already noted that Euripides later made precisely this criticism; we shall find it also in other philosophers. The second is against the anthropomorphism of religion, pointing to man's inveterate habit of creating his gods in his own image. The irony is sharp in the image of cattle fashioning their own bovine deities; and anticipates the quip of the eighteenth-century master ironist, Voltaire, when he said, "If God made us in His own image, we have more than reciprocated."

Was Xenophanes simply negative with respect to tradition? Did he have anything positive to replace the notions which he finds repugnant? He did in saying:

One god, greatest among gods and men, in no way similar to mortals either in body or in thought. (*Fragment* 23.)

Always he remains in the same place, moving not at all, nor is it fitting for him to go to different places at different times, but without toil he shakes all things by the thought of his mind. (*Fragment* 26.)

All of him sees, all thinks, and all hears. (*Fragment* 24.)[13]

Aristotle adds to these views that Xenophanes said that the one, that is, the universe, is god.[14]

Although Xenophanes' criticism of the traditional religion was strong, it did not lead him into atheism or moral lassitude. He would reform religious ideas, not destroy them. He still held to the divine, but his god embodied far more sophisticated notions than the gods of the received wisdom, a sophistication which reflects the depersonalization of nature in the philosophers and scientists. Xenophanes' god still sees, thinks, and hears, but he is in no way similar to mortals in body or in thought. He is ubiquitous and moves all things by his mind. If this god be a person, it is definitely not one in the human sense. Thus, there is an accommodation between the old views of the divine in nature and the new learning, by means of a conception of divinity that is less human, less personal, perhaps even less comforting, but more just, more profound, and more majestic. If men can see that the divine does not love and hate as they do, suggests Xenophanes, then perhaps Hesiod's *Dike*, Justice, who sits on the right hand of Zeus, can find her way more readily among the affairs of men. When men see that God is not a human politician, and that his rain must fall on the just and unjust alike, they themselves become a little more just and a little more like the divine. God or nature or perhaps more accurately, God or the order of nature, the supremely divine. Does it make much difference which term is used? This theme is to be sounded

---

13 *Ibid.*, pp. 169–170.
14 *Metaphysics*, 986b24.

by more than one Greek philosopher, culminating in the God of Aristotle's *Metaphysics* and caught up into one of the most magnificent and explicit of all such statements by Spinoza in the eighteenth century.

Number and Form, Keys to Nature and Goodness

The philosophers from Miletus had found the ultimate principle of the existence of things in a substance like air or water, and accounted for the great variety of things in nature by adding the notion of condensation or rarefaction of the substance. Are these principles adequate to account for the existence of things? The Pythagoreans did not think so; and their added insight into the principles of the existence of things warrants examination.

We have already seen the Pythagorean interest in number theory, noting, among other things, that the Pytharogeans classified numbers into odd and even and that they represented numbers geometrically. We have seen also that they discovered the mathematical ratios of three musical intervals—the octave, the fifth, and the fourth. We need to consider these ideas in more detail for the use to which they put them in metaphysical, cosmological, and even ethical inquiries.

From their study of number and their speculation about nature, the Pythagoreans came to say that the principles of number are the principles of everything.[15] What does this claim seem to mean and what is its significance?

The Pythagoreans undertook to find the principles upon which the natural number system is based, that is the numbers one, two, three, and so on, in terms of which we count. They found these principles to be the limited and the unlimited, the former being the fundamental principle of the odd numbers, the latter of the even. It is not very clear how they felt the limited and the unlimited accounted for the odd and even numbers except in terms of their idea of figured numbers. This theory with respect to the generation of numbers is admittedly obscure, but once the numbers were generated, their place in the existence of things is clearer. For, the Pythagoreans variously argued that things are numbers, or that things represent numbers, or that elements of numbers are elements of things.

But now, how could things *be* numbers? When the Pythagoreans discovered that the octave embodied the ratio 2:1, in a sense they could say that the octave *is* the mathematical ratio. Ask a physicist for a pitch today, and he will give you a vibration number. This of course is not quite true, but if we say that the frequency of middle C is 261.6, there is a sense in which a Pythagorean could claim, "Well, there you have it. Middle C

[15] Aristotle, *Metaphysics*, 985b26.

is 261.6." Of course we should say, "261.6 vibrations per second, not just 261.6." But the Pythagoreans were so enchanted with numbers that at times they seemed to say that it was sufficient to give the number of something, as if number were a kind of material of which things are composed. At other times, some could speak of things as representing numbers, as, that middle C is in some way a representation of the number 261.6. However uneasy we may now be with the notion that a thing is a number, the Pythagoreans were not; they went on to generalize the idea about musical intervals to the encompassing idea that all things are or embody numbers in some way.

Still another approach to the view that things are numbers was derived from a variant of the geometrical representation of numbers. The number two can be represented by two dots, .. ; but since two points determine a line, a person can argue conversely that two is the number of a line. If three dots, .'., can represent the number three, then three is the number of a triangle; and whatever is triangular has as its number three. Is the number three, then, just another name for whatever is triangular? Not at all. Since three points can determine a triangle, the number three determines or constitutes what is triangular. Put another way, the number three makes that which is triangular what it is and not something else. Whatever, then, embodies geometrical patterns or forms has a number. Even living things embody these forms, and thus have numbers determining the things to be what they are. Man is no exception.

Now, to say that there is a number for man begins to sound fanciful indeed. But is it quite out of reason? When a contemporary geneticist finds the number of chromosomes in the human germ plasm and then seeks the number of genes which determine human characteristics, is he not in a sense searching for man's number? We must beware of anachronisms and avoid reading into an early theory more than there is. It would, of course, be erroneous to say that the Pythagoreans anticipated modern genetic theory. But it would not be erroneous to say that the Pythagoreans hit upon one of the most fruitful ideas that has ever struck man: that there are numerical orders, patterns, forms which are as important in determining what a thing is as the materials of which it is composed. The Pythagoreans made numerical factors the sole important consideration for understanding the existence of things; and in so doing, they overstated their case. Perhaps they may be forgiven their enthusiasm, however, in view of the subsequent power of the idea for the development of both science and philosophy.

A further application of the notion that things are numbers is worth considering. The Pythagoreans were aware of the five regular solids: the tetrahedron, the cube, the octahedron, the dodecahedron, and the icosahedron. In the fifth century B.C., the theory had been advanced that the material substances of which nature is composed are four: earth, air, fire, and water. Some of the Pythagoreans went on to argue that the form or structure of each of the elements embodied one of the regular solids: earth, the cube; fire, the tetrahedron; air, the octahedron; and water, the icosahedron. This left the dodecahedron which, it was declared, the entire universe embodied as its shape. Thus, if the great variety of things—sticks and stones and so on—is composed of the four elements which have their form or structure determined by geometrical figures, and these in turn are the embodiment of number, once more it can be argued that in a fundamental sense all things are number.

The ancient Pythagoreans would truly be excited if they could see a contemporary periodic table of the elements, in which the elements are arranged according to their atomic number. "The more your theoretical physics and chemistry progress," they might comment, "the more things become numbers in your series of equations. Yes, you seem to be showing what we contended long ago—that all things are number." Again, it is not suggested that the Pythagoreans anticipated contemporary theoretical physics. But the Pythagoreans' insistence upon number as the key to the existence of things seems beautifully borne out by the development of modern physical science.

When the Pythagoreans said that all things are number, they meant not only that each thing in its existence embodies a number or has its existence determined by number but also that the universe hangs together in mathematical ratios. In grand style they combined their mathematical and musical theories to contend that the heavenly bodies constitute a "harmony of the spheres," as it was called.[16] So intriguing is this notion that Plato uses it in his Myth of Er in *The Republic*,[17] and Kepler—who discovered the three laws of planetary motion, a landmark in the development of modern astronomy (see p. 164)—undertakes in the year 1619 to show this coincidence of mathematics, music, and astronomy in his *The Harmonies of the World*.

The final meaning of "all things are number" may seem to be nonsense: for some Pythagoreans asserted that moral qualities also are numbers. For example, justice is a square number, the number four. There is no point in our pursuing this aspect of Pythagorean doctrine in detail since it would lead to a consideration of their religious and mystical beliefs, matters of historical interest but outside our theme.

The Pythagorean beliefs were a mixture of religious mysticism and

---

[16] For a detailed treatment see Sir Thomas Heath, *Aristarchus of Samos* (Oxford at the Clarendon Press, 1913), pp. 105–115.

[17] 616–617.

scientific and philosophic insights. Their achievements in geometry, their perception of mathematical order in nature, and their judgment that number is a fundamental key to the existence of things, seem not to have induced them to re-examine the Homeric religion. Their mysticism is not some sort of reconstruction of the traditional religion in the light of their science; it is rather an oriental import, not Greek in origin. A Plato will be needed to utilize effectively Pythagorean scientific ideas to modify and to buttress the folklore.

Nevertheless, there are justifiable reasons for indicating relationships between mathematics and morals in Pythagoreanism if not between mathematics and religion. The idea of moderation among the Greek ideals of conduct has already been noted. The Pythagoreans supported this ideal by means of their number theory. Although it seems fantastic to give specific numbers to moral qualities, it may not be fantastic to say that measure and order have something to do with that which is good, and the measureless and disorder with that which is evil. "The elements of number are the elements of all things" is another way of saying that all things are number, as we have seen. Thus, since the limit and the unlimited are the principles of number, they are also the principles of things; and among things, for the Pythagoreans, are good and evil. The limit is the ultimate principle of order and therefore, a Pythagorean could say, of that which is good; the unlimited is the ultimate principle of the disordered and of that which is evil. This notion of the ordered, the measured, as the essence of that which is good became central in many discussions in Greek ethics and is one way of interpreting and supporting the traditional ideal of moderation.

A second reason for mentioning mathematics and morals together is that one finds in Plato's *Republic* that mathematics is the heart of the education of the ruling class. This education is intended to make the rulers not only mathematicians but also good men and good rulers. Moreover, the study of mathematics becomes the preparation for grasping the ultimate moral idea, the Good. All this may seem strange; it is very strange indeed in our day and age, to say that the study of mathematics has anything to do with goodness or politics. Who would think of preparing congressmen for office by insisting that they study the calculus? Plato, at any rate, thought there was merit in the idea; and its seed is here in Pythagorean doctrine.

Permanence and Change, Appearance and Reality

In the preceding discussion of science and philosophy, there are two complementary themes hovering in the background which need to be brought forward for clarity and emphasis. They are the themes of permanence and change, and of appearance and reality.

In our treatment of Greek science and philosophy there has been repeated emphasis on their naturalistic temper, as involving objective analyses of ideas or events. This temper was illustrated in the Pythagorean examination of the relations among points, lines, and planes, and in the Ionian attempts to find a substance or substances which persisted throughout the changes in nature and to account for those changes in a purely mechanical operation like condensation or rarefaction of the substance. Again, there was the Pythagorean insistence that when the number of something or its internal numerical relations changed, the thing itself changed.

Quite clearly, in these efforts there is the search for the permanent underlying the panorama of change that is nature, a panorama of bewildering diversity. This search is no idle game, for if the substance or substances can be found and if nature's complexity is the result of variations of this substance or substances, then the bewilderment is reduced. Internal mechanisms begin to appear. Order emerges through the mist of former chaos. There can even be an elegant simplicity in the "heaven and earth, the sea, and all that in them is" if we but have the wit to see it. Is this not what a modern theoretical scientist like Einstein is doing when he undertakes to capture this order in his equations?

But "Nature loves to hide," observed Heraclitus (*c.* 530–470 B.C.), one of the later Ionians, and its ceaseless change may embrace disorder as well as order, indeterminacy as well as determinacy, as contemporary physicists like to point out (see p. 499). The search for the permanent as a substance or set of substances, or as a mathematical order has never been satisfied in the sense of being complete; perhaps it never can be. The history of science and philosophy is strewn with errors concerning the permanent within or behind the changing. Certainly the early Greeks, by comparison with the modern scientists or philosophers, had precious little data for determining the hidden substances and forces of nature. Of greater importance is what they added to the precious little. To it they added, they inaugurated, an approach to nature, a vision—for that is what *theoria,* from which we derive our word "theory," means—of nature as ordered process, with the order dependent upon some thing or some things which are permanent within the change itself. Nature may appear to be in continual flux, but there is a Logos, a rationale, an order to it which is the constancy within all. Nothing is more capricious than the weather, but even that is seasonal. Heraclitus saw all this clearly. His predecessors had caught the idea, even though they stated it naïvely in terms of a single substance or a simple process like condensation and rarefaction. The Pythagoreans introduced another dimension, that of number or numerical order as the permanent. Heraclitus' successors found answers of increasing complexity and sophistication—culminating, as we shall see, in the philosophies of Plato and Aristotle. But the search inaugurated by the Ionians is fundamentally the same problem which emerged as critical in Greek philosophy and which has persisted into the modern period.

The quest for the permanent within the changing led philosophers into a related problem: what is real in nature, over against what only appears to be so. In the Ionian philosophers, and in the Pythagoreans, the permanencies they found also turned out to be the most important factors in the existence of things in nature. A wooden table, Thales would say, is not really wooden but some sort of variant of water. For Anaximenes it is a condensation of air. For the Pythagorean a number. This is what the table really is—water, air, or number. It only appears to be wooden.

This distinction, between the reality and the appearance of things, may strike us as trivial or as a playful conundrum, but it is a distinction we employ constantly. We drive down the highway on a hot day and see water shimmering on the pavement. "But the pavement isn't really wet," we say. "It only appears to be so. We see a mirage." We write on the very solid, wooden table; but we say (if we know enough physics and chemistry) that the table isn't really solid—as it seems to our touch. It only appears to be so. It is really composed of molecules, which in turn are composed of atoms, which in turn are made up of ever so minute particles, which constitute the really real existence of the table. So the table is a sort of giant empty fraud. It isn't solid. Within each atom there are reaches of empty space. The table isn't what it appears to be at all. The real table, I cannot see or touch, And unless I am a nuclear physicist or chemist, I do not really know anything about the real table. And so it is with houses, automobiles, and mountains. I seem to live in a vast sea of appearances. What, then, is real in nature? What appearance?

We may now be, not playfully but genuinely, puzzled as to what is real in nature or what is appearance. As noted earlier, these questions assume particular urgency when we turn them upon man himself. What is man's true reality? His mind or his body? His spirit or his flesh? The appearance-reality disputes became serious in Greek philosophy and have continued to be so in the twentieth century.

We have already met this problem in the early Greek period, expressed in somewhat different language. A brief recapitulation is in order. Xenophanes obviously relegated the Homeric pantheon to the world of appearance. For him, the true divine reality was his one god identified with nature. He wished further to strip the mythological appearance from the reality of natural events. "What they [the many] call Iris [the rainbow], this too is cloud, purple and red and yellow to behold." "The rainbow a messenger of the gods? What could be more absurd?" he asks. "The rainbow is really a cloud."

The conflict between Xenophanes' reality and that of the Homeric religion is so obvious that the point need not be pressed. What may not be so obvious, or what may require further emphasis, is that the common-sense way of looking at things is challenged and that science as we know it presupposes precisely such a challenge. To the laborer in the field, who at the end of a hard day rests his weary frame in a wooden chair, probably his last concern in the world is whether the wood is really wood or whether it is condensed air, a number, or solidified water. Any of these suggestions would strike him as unbelievably absurd. Yet it is the intellect with the touch of wonder that fosters science and philosophy, the mind that is not satisfied with the superficial appearances of things and detects the unnoticed orders, the mind which directly challenges the common-sense views of the reality of things. Today, the world of the physicist is not the layman's world, subatomic particles are *not* billiard balls on a table. The contrast between science and common sense becomes greater the more sophisticated science becomes. That contrast was present, however, even in the early days of Greek science and philosophy.

Heraclitus, for example, was especially conscious of the contrast. He belabored the masses, and threw in Homer and Hesiod for good measure. One of the commonest of all follies, he contended, is taking things as they are. Men fasten on to what is stable; but all things flow, nothing abides. Even the most obdurate stone is in the process of change, however slow the process may be. Moreover, men seek peace; but whatever exists is the result of conflict, inner tension. Existence is a struggle not a repose. Thus, when the poets yearn for peace, they ask for death, nonexistence. When things cease to change, they cease to be, to exist. The reality of nature *is* its change. Stability, as popularly conceived, is a cosmic illusion. But, even in all this change, Heraclitus finds a stability, a permanence, which is the Logos or reason or law of the change. Few men—how very few he suggests—ever glimpse it. Thus the most real of all realities may be this Logos; but how remote it is from the realities of the common-sense world of chairs, tables, sticks, and stones!

There is an even subtler problem that arises out of the appearance-reality controversies, a problem concerning knowledge. If our everyday living world—the world of colors, sounds, odors—is but an appearance, where does this leave our sense experience as far as knowledge is concerned? We all know that a magician can trick our senses, but we seem to be able to depend on them pretty well for dealing with the world. Yet the clear implication of the Ionian and Pythagorean claims for reality leaves the senses in a position of doubtful reliability. Anaximander's Infinite is the ultimate reality. It cannot be seen, heard, or touched. Heraclitus' Logos obviously can be reached only through reason. The realities of the Pythagorean geometry are seen by the mind not the eyes. The question arises not only what is reality, but also what can we really know. If seeing is not believing, what is it, then, that we really can believe in?

The problems concerning the nature of knowledge, its origin, its extent, its validity, its reliability, its dependence upon the senses or the mind became an area of investigation in their own right, and acquired the inclusive name, *epistemology*, which means simply "theory of knowledge." In early Greek philosophy the problems were more implied by the appearance-reality controversies than clearly seen; however, the early philosophers began to glimpse them. Xenophanes was uneasy about man's capacity to know when he said,

No man knows, or ever will know, the truth about the gods and about everything I speak of: for even if one chanced to say the complete truth, yet oneself knows it not; but seeming [opinion] is wrought over all things. (*Fragment* 34.)[18]

Heraclitus remarked that the many talked as if each man had his own private reason, that is, as if each man were his own test of truth. Parmenides (born *c.* 515–510 B.C.), a vigorous opponent of Heraclitus concerning what is real in nature, nevertheless shared Heraclitus' dim view of the run of mankind and then went on to deny any validity whatsoever to the senses. But the problem did not become acute until the Sophists (to be considered in the next chapter) clearly and openly questioned whether men can know anything with any certainty by means of the senses or the mind.

The problems arising out of early Greek science and early Greek philosophy—concerning the permanent and the changing in nature, appearance and reality, and the status of knowledge—were sharpened in the investigations of such men as Zeno, (born *c.* 490–485 B.C.), Empedocles (flourished 450 B.C.), and Anaxagoras (fifth century B.C.). There was mounting tension between the ideas and ideals of the ancient religion and morality and those of the avant-garde in science and philosophy. This tension reached a crisis in Athens in the latter half of the fifth century B.C., when the new learning and critical thinking were turned, by these Sophists, upon many aspects of Greek life, religious, moral, legal, and social. Quite clearly, the ancient wisdom was endangered, and if it were to be retained in purified form to meet the criticism of the new intellectuals, a major reconstruction would be necessary. Because it was indeed a turning point in Greek thought, we must now look in some detail at the way the Sophists called tradition to account.

Selected Readings

Guthrie, W. K. C., A *History of Greek Philosophy*, Cambridge at the University Press, 1962, Vol. I.

Guthrie, W. K. C., *The Greek Philosophers from Thales to Aristotle*, New York: Harper Torchbooks, 1960.

Heath, Sir Thomas, *Greek Mathematics*, Oxford at the Clarendon Press, 1921, 2 vols.

Kirk, G. S. and J. E. Raven, *The Presocratic Philosophers*, Cambridge at the University Press, 1960.

Sarton, George, A *History of Science*, Cambridge: Harvard, 1952, Vol. I, Chs. VII, VIII.

[18] G. S. Kirk and J. E. Raven, *op. cit.*, p. 179.

CHAPTER 4

Man Is the Measure

For a century and a half Greek philosophers were primarily interested in metaphysical and cosmological problems. Mathematics and astronomy had led the philosophers to attend more to the nature of the universe and the gods than to the nature of man. The criticism of the folklore had been directed at its religious and mythopoeic content, and the challenge to common sense had dealt with the way men understand the objects of the everyday world around them. It was only on occasion that the prevailing ideals of conduct had been censured, as in Xenophanes when he chides his fellow Hellenes for their idolatry of athletics and their luxurious living.

In the latter half of the fifth century, however, Greek philosophy took a dramatic turn. "Man is the measure of all things," proclaimed Protagoras (c. 480–411 B.C.) the Sophist. Man, the measure of all things! With this astounding and even arrogant claim, man takes the center of the philosophic stage never to relinquish it again. To be sure, in Greek and subsequent thought there are numerous philosophers who roundly disagree with Protagoras. But the centrality of the human situation—or the human predicament, as many moderns would prefer—remains secure in philosophy. Even in the Middle Ages, when only God, and certainly not man, could be the measure of things, the philosophers would still insist that "the choir of heaven and the furniture of earth" were created as the setting for the drama of man's salvation. And when the development of modern science in the seventeenth century seems to shove man backstage in the philosophic theater, his removal from the center is only temporary; for, although the new science appears to be the absorbing interest of philosophers in that century, Spinoza can ask the hard question of what place man now holds in the vast, mechanistic world of science.

Why did this shift take place in Greek philosophy, from an absorption in a science of nature—with occasional shafts of criticism aimed at the established religion—to a primary concern for man's moral and social problems? The reasons are several, but two are especially prominent: (1) the ascendancy in the Greek world of the militant Athenian democracy after the Persian Wars, and (2) the abstract and internally conflicting character of philosophy itself.

After the periodic Persian invasions had ended with the great Greek victories at Salamis and Plataea, Sparta and Athens emerged as the two foremost city-states of Greece. The Persian threat did not end altogether with these victories, however, and Athens organized a naval alliance, called the Confederacy of Delos, which she transformed into an instrument of empire. By the middle of the fifth century B.C., Athens had become the richest and most powerful of all the Greek city-states. The interests of Athens and her allies on the one hand and Sparta and her allies on the other were in constant conflict. The eventual result was the devasting Peloponnesian War, which left Athens defeated and much of Greece prostrate.

Ironically, the very city-state, which became the seat of empire and at times dealt autocratically with her sister states, was for her own citizens almost as pure a democracy as could be devised and a citadel of individual freedom. At its most developed stage, Athenian democracy had three principal popular organs of government: the Council of Five Hundred, an administrative body; the Assembly; and the *Heliaea*, the law courts. Any citizen could sit in the Assembly. Members of the Council were selected annually by lot. The courts were large and were also selected by lot from an annual panel of 6,000 citizens. Thus the chances of the individual citizen's serving the state were considerable. Furthermore, in the law courts the parties to an action had to plead their own cause, since Athens did not permit a plea by legal counsel as does our judicial system. Litigation was common in Athens, the commercial center of the empire. Thus it was important, very important, for a citizen to know how to speak persuasively —to preserve his interests in court and to make his voice heard in government. For active, knowledgeable participation in the affairs of state, it would be hard to find a more literate citizenry than that of Athens in the latter half of the fifth century B.C.

And yet the traditional education had little relevance to this public and commercial life. Athenian youths were taught gymnastics and the arts of music and poetry. They learned to be cultivated gentlemen, at least those did who were well-to-do. But how useful were Homer and Hesoid as a defense in the law court, or in a rough-and-tumble debate in the Assembly concerning war or peace with Sparta, or in a policy decision in the Council? Now, if the traditional poetry failed to meet these needs, what did the new science and philosophy have to offer? There seemed precious little help here either. What did abstract geometry and speculation about the planets have to do with winning a lawsuit for damages? Could a legislator find any help or comfort in Anaximander's Infinite or Heraclitus' Logos? The philosophers' speculations about the universe seemed even more remote from practical life than the poetry of Homer and Hesiod. At least the poets celebrated the ancient virtues which the young must learn.

Not only was the new philosophy abstract and remote, but also it seemed to be a bundle of confusions and contradictions. The philosophers could not decide among themselves what was the ultimate composition of nature. Some said that everything in nature changes; others that change is an illusion. If this be what philosophy is, then let it be, the man in the street could argue. For what does this sort of philosophy have to do with the world in which most men live—the world of toil, argument, debate, intrigue, love, hate, public success, and personal failure? Philosophy, in truth, seemed to be of no use. Clearly, there was need for an education more relevant to Athens' modern world and for teachers to provide the necessary instruction. The new teachers who appeared to meet that need were the *Sophists*. What sort of education did they provide?

The heart of their education, in theory and in practice, was rhetoric, conceived as the art of persuasion. Among the Sophists there was no rigid doctrine as to the nature of that art. Protagoras and Gorgias (*c*. 483–*c*. 375 B.C.), the two most famous of the Sophists, held contrasting views. Protagoras emphasized logical structure and closely argued speeches. Gorgias preferred to persuade by flowery and elegant language. They gave their pupils model speeches to learn on a variety of topics. Sometimes a Sophist would write a speech for a litigant to memorize for his trial. Whatever different approaches for effective persuasion were used, the central aim was the practical one of influencing action—a victory in a law court, success in carrying or defeating a measure in the Assembly.

Although the intent of the Sophists in teaching rhetoric was quite practical and the intent achieved marked success, their studies of language contributed to the development of logic. The Sophists were among the first teachers and philosophers in the West to make a serious study of language, and philosophers have continued that study ever since. Indeed, many philosophers today insist that this is *the* function of philosophy. The Sophists investigated grammar, analyzing the parts of speech and determining correctness of style. Some were interested in careful distinctions among words of similar meaning. Although they made only a beginning, perhaps their major contribution to logic was the discrimination of some of the types of fallacious arguments. This undertaking was satirized by Plato and discredited by Aristotle, but these criticisms were far from impartial and based upon the uses to which this knowledge was put. The knowledge of even a few of the types of fallacious arguments common to everyday discourse was another step in the direction of a generalized study of proof.

In their teaching of rhetoric there is little doubt that the Sophists met an important social need and served a useful purpose, especially in the democratic city-states. It is true that since many Sophists asked money for their services, they were often considered, by the poor who could not afford them, somewhat as corporation lawyers are today. Moreover, elder citizens were dismayed by the glibness and skill in argument of the younger generation who readily took to the new learning. When these skills reinforced the usual impudence of youth, the younger generation could be insufferable indeed, as Aristophanes shows in *The Clouds*. But, on balance, from a distance of more than twenty centuries, we may say that the Sophists should generally be commended for meeting a need when others failed to do so. Who can deny that the art of persuasion is important when men live together? Why is it, then, that in antiquity and in the modern world the Sophists have acquired a bad name? For to be called a "sophist" or to be told that one's argument is nothing but "sophistry" is hardly a compliment today. Neither is it in Plato's dialogues. Why is this so?

Early in Greek history, "sophist" (*sophistes*) meant "master of a craft" or "wise one"; but by the end of the fifth century B.C., it could also mean "clever." It is not hard to see how this shift in meaning could have occurred. The teachers under consideration affected the name "Sophist." But when someone like Protagoras maintained that there are two sides to every question and showed how to argue accordingly, or how to attack and refute any proposition, or how to make the weaker argument the stronger, it is easy to understand why someone might say that Protagoras, and the other Sophists—if they did the same thing (and they did)—were more interested in being clever than wise; that is, if wisdom has anything to do with truth or goodness. Or, if the Sophists were masters of their craft, their craft seemed not a search for what is good or true in a situation but rather the cleverness to come out on top at any price. If this be wisdom, the critic could argue, it is certainly a different sort from that which won for Solon, one of Athens' greatest lawgivers, or Thales, renowned for his practical good sense and theoretical knowledge, the title of "Wise One [*sophistes*] of Greece."

But to convict the Sophist of being clever without an interest in truth or goodness may be a hasty judgment, or at least an oversimplified one. Our Anglo-American adversary system of law may be very close to what some of the Sophists were teaching. In a dispute over a contract, there *are* two sides to the question—the conflicting claims of the contending parties. In the extreme instance of murder, a man must be charged, provided with a defense, tried before a jury, and only then convicted *or* acquitted. There *are* two sides. In our system, the same lawyer may be counsel for the plaintiff in one case and for the defendant in another case of the same kind. He argues now on one side, later on the other. "What is *his* straight-line pursuit of truth or goodness?" the Sophist would ask. The truth or the goodness or the justice in these matters, he would contend, is achieved when the jurors come to a decision. What truth or goodness or justice would be irrespective of contention, argument, and decision, the Sophist would not claim to know. In fact, he would deny there is any such thing. Men are, he would insist, the measure of truth, goodness, and justice. How else could it be?

The claim that man is the measure of goodness, justice, and truth is at the core of the substantive teaching of the Sophists whenever they go beyond the technical aspects of argumentation. The meaning and consequences of this doctrine were so important for Greek and later philosophy that they need to be examined further.

One of the most obvious consequences is that man and not God, or men and not the gods are the source and the measure of moral standards. In fact, for Protagoras there was a question whether the gods existed at all.

About the gods, I am not able to know whether they exist or do not exist, nor what they are like in form; for the factors preventing knowledge are many: the obscurity of the subject, and the shortness of human life.[1]

In the light of this agnosticism, Protagoras would question divine sanction for the traditional ideals of the folklore or for the laws of the state. Justice may be fathered by Zeus, in Hesiod; but the more likely story, Protagoras and other Sophists would say, is that justice is the child of men in their customs and in the laws of their city-states. "Humanism" is a vague word, but insofar as it means that man is the source and justification for his standards of conduct, the Sophists were thoroughly humanistic. There is no question that there was a current of humanism in the Greek folklore too; but while the tradition utilized the gods for assistance in everyday affairs and to account for that which men could not explain, the Sophists rejected the gods either as active agents or principles of explanation.

A second aspect of the man-the-measure doctrine is the relativity of moral standards. It might be argued that even though man is the source and justification of his moral standards, these could be uniform and universal standards because human nature is a constant. Most of the Sophists rejected

---

[1] Kathleen Freeman, *Ancilla to the Pre-Socratic Philosophers* (*Fragment* 4), (Oxford: Blackwell, 1948), p. 126.

this possibility out of hand. They were too empirically minded to do otherwise. They were in fact the precursors of today's cultural anthropologists who, returning from their field studies, show us that moral codes vary in various cultures. The Sophists' criticism of prevailing claims to universality had the same impact on the folklore of their time as the cultural relativists have had today (see pp. 518–526). The Sophists had come from and had taught in too many city-states—with different customs, laws, and ideals of right and wrong—to accept the notion of universal moral standards, rules, or laws. There was one possible exception: some of them made the distinction between nature and laws or custom. They contended that man outside the confines of law and custom, man in a natural state is governed by only one law—that which is to his advantage. There is a kind of natural justice of self-preservation. This is universal. The minute that men enter group life, however, the customs and laws of the group or the city-state arise; and these not only are relative to the interests of the group but often run counter to natural law. Although Sophists might disagree among themselves as to whether there were universal natural laws of right and wrong, they were in agreement that the laws and customs of states are conventions determined by social utility. A city-state might invoke the gods or appeal to some principle inherent in human nature as justification for its laws. The real justification, the Sophists insisted, was what proved useful to the state.

The relativity and the social utility of moral standards were sometimes explained in terms of power. Thrasymachus (flourished *c.* 420 B.C.) argued that justice is the interest of the stronger. He contended that law is a function of the prevailing power in a state, which legislates for its own benefit. Justice, accordingly, is obedience to law which benefits the ruling power. In a democracy, the people will legislate what is beneficial to them; the monarch decrees what is to his advantage. Justice thus is relative to the distribution of power. Might not only can make right but is right.

If there were Athenians who were shocked at this bald assertion that justice is a function of power, all Thrasymachus had to do was to point to Athens' own foreign policy or the relations among the Greek city-states in general. He might remind the Athenians of their dealings with Melos, a small city-state that wished simply to remain neutral in the Peloponnesian War and maintained her right to do so under international justice. Justice, the Athenians contended in this instance, holds only among equals in power, not the weak and the strong. Athens, to its eternal shame, took the city, killed all the male captives, and sold the women and children into slavery. Thrasymachus might have asked, "Although men often talk loftily about justice, is not my view far more accurate as to what justice is when we look at the way the world wags?"

In his description of what justice is—as he finds it in societies and not as what it ought or is said to be—Thrasymachus is the father of an important, even if overdone, tendency in social science: namely, the *positivist* tradition which *describes* what in fact *is* the case and does not attempt to *prescribe* what *ought* to be. (See pp. 471–489). No doubt all men should seek justice without reference to what serves their personal power, justice defined in terms other than the will of the stronger. But if men are not doing so, this fact must honestly be reported. And to report such facts is to be "scientific."

Furthermore, was not Thrasymachus performing a great service in showing that prevailing laws often are not what they pretend to be, namely the embodiment of abstract justice, but rather a reflection of the will of the stronger? Is it not one of the tasks of social science to expose such rationalizations as these? Insofar as Thrasymachus was engaged in this task, he was laying the foundations of social science, even though no superstructure was to be built on them until much later. The trouble was, of course, that Thrasymachus, in the first blush of insight, went too far when he argued that justice could be nothing other than the interest of the stronger.

From another standpoint, one might ask whether it is quite fair to describe Thrasymachus as nothing more than one of the earliest defenders of *Realpolitik* or the might-makes-right doctrine in Western thought, as is frequently done. Obviously, he did urge that justice is a function of power. But when we look at his doctrine more closely, we find that he is also suggesting that justice cannot be dissociated from power. Talking about justice is one thing; making justice real in the social order is quite another. Thrasymachus is shown arguing to this effect in Plato's *Republic*. What good is it, anyway, simply to sit around and talk about justice? What is a right that is unenforceable? How can justice be divorced from law and power? If it is, it may be nothing more than words. Thomas Hobbes, an English philosopher of the seventeenth century, was to urge very much the same notion. Seen in this light the Thrasymachan doctrine has a very different cast.

The Sophists recognized that in statements like those of Thrasymachus about justice, they were going beyond the teaching of techniques of argumentation and debate; they were passing judgment upon men's morals and the quality of their lives. Protagoras said that a man who came to him would learn ". . . prudence in affairs private as well as public; . . . to order his own house in the best manner, and . . . to speak and act for the best in the affairs of the state."[2] "Prudence" to the Greeks meant sound, sensible judgment, one of the most important of the virtues in the tradition. Protagoras would develop this sort of solid capacity in men, for

---

[2] Plato, *Protagoras*, 318E, *The Dialogues of Plato*, B. Jowett trans. (New York: Random House, 1937), Vol. I, p. 90.

affairs public and private, and in this sense become a teacher of virtue. In fact, Protagoras and other Sophists came to be known as teachers not simply of prudence but of the virtues in general.

As teachers of virtue (*arete*), the Sophists were critics of the traditional morality. In their sophistication, they could smile at those who would derive moral standards from the traditional religion. In their urbanity, they could be disdainful of those who claimed to know eternal and universal virtue. Prudence in Miletus and in Athens need not be the same thing, as anyone could see who had lived in both cities. The Sophists found heroic virtue rather old-fashioned and a bit tiresome for their very modern world.

But the Sophists were also products of their culture, and in their teaching they abetted some of the traditional values. We have seen transformations in the Greek ideals, from heroic virtue to those virtues more congenial and appropriate to life in the city-state. These transformations had begun before the Sophists appeared; and those citizens who were concerned about achieving civic virtue—through excellence or competence in the affairs of their democratic, commercial world—provided a demand for those professing to assist in that achievement. As noted before, the Sophists undertook to meet this demand; and, insofar as they did help men to achieve this sort of civic virtue, they gave encouragement to and fostered prevailing ideals.

And what is so wrong with this kind of undertaking? Why have the Sophists been belabored for teaching prudence in affairs private and public, for helping a man to order his house in the best manner and for assisting him to speak and act for the best in the affairs of the state? To be sure, these were very secular values. That these were not heavenly virtues is clear enough. They had to do only with *oikonomia* (household management or economics), politics, international relations—mundane matters of which most of the business of living is made after all. Nothing very lofty, probably nothing very profound, but something very necessary if life in the city-state were to go on. Why should the Sophists be criticized for teaching these things? If they can be called philosophers, philosophy now would certainly be down to earth. It would be in the market place instead of among the stars. It would be concerned with the central and important problems of most men and not the rarefied interests of a few intellectuals who speculated about the nature of the universe. It would be concerned with man.

To indict the Sophists for their attempts to teach virtue appears callous, for the teaching of virtue would seem to be a noble enterprise. To assert that the concern of philosophy is with the forces of nature but not with the problems of human existence makes it hard to distinguish philosophy from natural science. In fact, Gorgias had undertaken to show what he considered to be the utter poverty of all earlier philosophy, for man or for anything else. In a work entitled, *On Not-Being or On Nature*, he bitterly satirized the traditional philosophical works on nature, which dealt with the basic characteristics of existence. After exhibiting the history of metaphysical inquiry as a chronicle of contradictions leading to the conclusion that nothing exists, Gorgias continues that if anything exists, it is incomprehensible, and even if it were comprehensible, it would be incommunicable. The tradition of philosophy, he insisted, is a dead end. Philosophy ought to be less pretentious, and turn to the affairs of men which possibly it could illuminate.

Where, then, did the Sophists go wrong? Or did they go wrong? Their concern for man and his moral problems is unimpeachable. With regard to their teaching virtue, however, there are certain problems. Protagoras would teach a man how to order his house in the *best* manner, and to speak and act for the *best* for the state. There is a small difficulty here, as Socrates is soon to say, for what does "best" mean? "Best" for Athens and "best" for Sparta did not seem to be the same "best." Furthermore, the "best" for one state or one family often was in flat contradiction with the "best" for another state or family. Is there not something wrong when "bests" can be contradictory? The "bests" may be explained as resulting from different social and economic conditions, but the explanation does not resolve the conflicts. Is there not a "best" for a man no matter what his family, or for a state no matter whether it is Athens, Sparta, or Miletus? This is the question that Socrates and Plato are to ask.

Furthermore, can the Sophists teach the "best," the virtues, as they profess to be able to do? Is virtue an academic subject? Can it be taught, in the sense in which mathematics can be taught? Or is virtue, goodness, something that a man's life acquires as he goes about his daily work in the market place, the law court, or the assembly, in short, in affairs public and private? Is it something which seeps into and gradually pervades a man's character, or is it learned like the multiplication table? One of the most persistent questions which Socrates raises in the Platonic dialogues is precisely the question: Can virtue be taught?

But, still, did the Sophists go wrong? Their moral relativity seemed to have the weight of anthropological and sociological evidence on its side. To be sure, this relativity could imply moral chaos if each man became the arbiter of his own moral standards; but the Sophists generally did not press their doctrine that far; they counted on the common sense of most men to find what was useful to the life of the community and to adhere to it. However, where virtue is concerned, such flexibility does not satisfy some men. It clearly troubled Socrates and Plato; and out of their reflections on the moral relativism of the Sophists, and out of the conflicting opinions of the early philosophers, they developed a philosophy of Idealism which is the fountainhead of one of the most important traditions in Western philosophy.

Selected Readings

Freeman, Kathleen, *Ancilla to the Pre-Socratic Philosophers*, Oxford: Blackwell, 1948.
Freeman, Kathleen, *The Pre-Socratic Philosophers*, Cambridge: Harvard, 2nd ed., 1959, pp. 341–423.
Gomperz, Theodor, *Greek Thinkers, A History of Ancient Philosophy*, New York: Scribner, 1901, Vol. I, pp. 412–496.
Jaeger, Werner, *Paideia: The Ideals of Greek Culture*, New York: Oxford, 2nd ed., 1945, Vol. I, pp. 286–331.
Untersteiner, Mario, *The Sophists*, Oxford: Blackwell, 1954.
Windelband, W., *History of Ancient Philosophy*, New York: Dover, 1956, pp. 108–123.

CHAPTER 5

Plato
and
Idealism

The Nature of Ideas or Forms

How might one begin to recover and refashion the ancient wisdom for the Greek world of the fourth century B.C.? Essentially, this was the question that Plato faced. To return to the traditional religion and morality was out of the question. Xenophanes, Euripides, and the Sophists had made it impossible for enlightened men to accept the anthropomorphism of the traditional religion. No stronger critic of the tradition can be found than Plato himself. He, too, finds the conventional morality inadequate, and he, too, objects to the stories about the immorality of the gods in Homer, Hesiod, and the other poets. In his ideal state, described in *The Republic*, he would purge myths of anything of this kind.[1] Or it might be more accurate to say that Plato would use the traditional myths, in purified form, to help cultivate the values which he would adopt on other grounds. The myths themselves were an unsatisfactory groundwork.

But what other foundation might be used for conserving the best of the past, and refashioning it in the light of new knowledge in science and

[1] See *The Republic*, pp. 377 ff., for an extended criticism.

philosophy? The Sophists had raised the issue of teaching virtue and made the claim that they could do that teaching. But the virtue that they taught turned out to be virtue relative to some time or place—how to be successful without troubling over the nature of the success or over the purposes of the ruling group. There seemed to be something wrong in making justice a whim of power or a matter of majority vote. Is there no firmer basis for justice and the other virtues than what people happen to think or feel at a given time and place? If virtue can be taught, does this not imply that it involves knowledge in some way? But what knowledge?

Even knowledge seemed to be in a precarious position if the Sophists' doctrine that man is the measure of things is true. The Sophists made the point that any man's knowledge of nature and of other men is based upon his sense experience. No two men have the same sense experiences; and thus when the Sophists argued that the basis for knowledge is never the same among men, the most that men can reply is that their knowledge is probable. At best, knowledge can be only relative for man; hence the knowledge involved in teaching virtue makes virtue no more secure than it was before.

But is all knowledge relative, as the Sophists say? It is this crucial question that Plato asks. What of the proofs in geometry? Is the proof that the interior angle sum of a triangle is equal to two right angles dependent upon Protagoras' thinking it so—as Protagoras would say—or not dependent upon any individual's thinking it so? Is it relevant just to Miletus, or Athens, or are Miletus and Athens irrelevant to it? Is there in mathematics an anchor for knowledge, however small it may seem at first, which will make at least some knowledge secure and certain? Clearly the notion is worth exploring; for the security, the certainty of knowledge is at stake. But even if this were so, what relevance would mathematics have for virtue? Socrates would urge that we should not be faint of heart but should pursue the matter. Did not the Pythagoreans suggest that mathematics had something to do with virtue, with being good? They may have been extravagant in giving numbers to the virtues; but the possibility that measure, order, harmony have something to do with virtue may be worth exploring. However, Socrates[2] and Plato would say we are not yet prepared for that step. It is necessary to return to mathematics.

There is a tale that over the entrance to Plato's school, the Academy, an inscription read, "Let no one destitute of geometry enter my doors." The story may be apocryphal, but it is symbolic of the importance of mathematics to Plato's philosophy. Plato was abreast of the best mathematics of his day, and geometry especially had advanced rapidly since the period of the Pythagoreans. Most of the content of Euclid's *Elements* was known by Plato's time, although the arrangement and methods in specific cases dif-

---

[2] Plato was a student of Socrates and usually used his teacher in the dialogues as a spokesman for his ideas so that, at many points, it is difficult to tell whether the ideas are Socrates' or Plato's.

fered from that of the classic work. To what philosophic use, then, did Plato put the knowledge available in mathematics?

It has been pointed out that geometry developed as a system of logical relations among definitions, axioms, and postulates. Points, lines, triangles, and other figures are defined without reference to a physical context. It can be said that the definition of a figure is the idea of the figure; for example, the definition of a triangle is the idea of a triangle. Now, when a plane triangle is defined as a plane figure bounded by three straight sides, the idea of a triangle is delimited without considerations of time, place, or materials. The idea is the same, whether "triangle" is being defined in Athens or Miletus, in the fourth century B.C. or the fourth century after Christ. The idea is the same whether a man is drawing a triangle in the sand or making one of wood. The idea is thus said to be *universal*: universal as to place, time, or material; universal in the sense that it is repeated in every particular instance of triangularity. The definition is the idea; if one prefers, one can say that the definition of a figure gives it its form; for example, the definition of a triangle gives or determines the form of a triangle.

Definition in geometry, as expressing the idea or determining the form of a figure possessing universal characteristics, provides perhaps the simplest illustration and the most direct introduction to Plato's famous *Doctrine of Ideas* or *Forms*—a doctrine central to his philosophy and to an understanding of much of the philosophy that followed. Plato uses the terms "Idea" and "Form" interchangeably; thus, his theory can be referred to either as his Doctrine of Ideas or Doctrine of Forms. Since the Ideas or Forms are universal in character, as described above, his theory has also been called a Doctrine of Universals.

The term "idea" has had a variety of meanings in the history of thought; and since its meaning in Plato is quite different from some common usages today, it will be helpful to describe this difference and then to illustrate Plato's Ideas further.[3] No assumption is made here of a fixed meaning of "idea" for all occasions today, but we often use the word to indicate a form of individual, personal thought or belief. For example, someone says, "I have an idea that it will snow today," meaning, "I think or I believe it will snow." Or someone asks, "Have you any idea how we can pay our bills next month?" in which the meaning seems to be, "Have you thought of a way of meeting the bills?" The reader can multiply instances endlessly, in which reference is made to some sort of personal, individual thought or belief. Again, no suggestion is made that this meaning is the only one for "idea" in current use. The suggestion is made, however, that this usage is common, and that we frequently think of "idea" in this individual, personal, and subjective sense.

To read this subjective meaning into a Platonic "Idea" is seriously to misread Plato. By "Idea" Plato means the *object* of thought, not a per-

---

[3] "Idea" will be capitalized when reference is made to Plato's particular meaning.

sonal act of thinking, *what* it is we are thinking about rather than the subjective process of thinking itself. The contrast is illustrated by distinguishing the landscape, which is the object of vision, from the act of seeing the landscape. An Idea is no more in our heads than the landscape is in our eyes. Thus, above all, it is important to remember that Plato's Ideas are *objective, not subjective.* "But," it may be asked, "more precisely, how are the Ideas objective, or what are the characteristics of the Ideas?" Further illustrations will be useful.

Let the reader draw a circle so: ◯ It is a very poor circle. Try it with string and crayon. Better, but still poor. Use a compass. Still better, but still imperfect; only an approximation, not a true circle. Use the most accurate instrument. What one achieves still falls short, is slightly flawed. Not every point on the circumference will be equidistant from the center. What is the true, the real circle? Clearly, the only *real* circle is no circle we can draw, no circle in space and time, that is, no particular perceived circular object, but the circle that is defined, the *idea* or *form* of a circle.

But what is the idea or definition of a circle? It is that without which a circle would not be what it is. It is that which is essential to it. It is its *essence*. But what is essential to the nature of being a circle? It is those traits which are universal to all circles, those which identify a particular circle as belonging to the *kind* or *class*, "circle," i.e., its *generic* traits.

To illustrate further the generic traits of an object in contrast with its individual characteristics, take a chair. Every chair in the room has certain characteristics by virtue of which we call it a chair, and not a table or a book. Also, each chair has a set of qualities which differentiate it from every other chair, and these individuate or particularize it. Even though the chairs in a classroom are approximately alike, the grain of the wood is different; there are scratches on one and not on another; the shapes vary slightly. If we were interested in doing so, we could give each a proper name just as, when we really are interested in individual differences, we give John and Mary proper names.

The individual differences distinguishing the members of a class are perceived, Plato argued, through our senses. They are, then, the *sensible* qualities of an object. If knowledge were limited to these qualities, it would be mere opinion. Everything the Sophists said about knowledge limited to such sensible experience is warranted—it is relative, variable, unreliable. It is impossible through the senses to *know* objects. Things are known only when we apprehend their class, generic, or universal characteristics.

The generic traits of a chair are those without which it would not be what it is. They are the characteristics by virtue of which we define "chairness," those characteristics by virtue of which we say it is a chair and not something else. They are the characteristics that are essential to it, its essence, the characteristics that go to make up the *idea* of a chair. It is by virtue of the fact that we recognize a chair as partaking of chairness, as belonging to the class, "chair," that it has meaning to us as that kind of thing. This "chairness" of which individual chairs "partake"—Plato also often thought of individuals as copies of the universal—cannot be seen or touched or smelled or in any way sensed, we should remember. No one has ever seen or touched chairness or dogness or manness or any universal or essence or idea. We can only *think* ideas; we can not sense them. This is true not only of the idea of objects, such as circles, chairs, or men, but also of relations like equality and scientific laws, and of ideals like beauty and justice and virtue. We perceive beautiful objects; but the nature of beauty —that by virtue of which we call them beautiful—can only be conceived, Plato contends. We witness particular acts of justice, but the *nature* of justice is an object of thought. How, indeed, could we know that objects were beautiful or ugly, and actions just or unjust, Plato asks, unless we had an *idea* of beauty or justice? Further details of Plato's Doctrine of Ideas or Forms will be examined shortly.

Let us return once more to the idea of circularity. The only real or "true" circle, according to Plato, is the one which is the object of thought— not the circular ring or wheel or any physical object. So, too, the only real chair or dog or man is the Idea of chairness or dogness or manness. This or that chair is a mere imperfect copy of chairness. We, you and I, are imperfect copies of manness. Since, for Plato, only *Ideas* are truly real, his viewpoint is called *Idealism*. It would more accurately be called *Idea-ism*. However, apart from euphemistic considerations, there is a sense in which the commonly used term Idealism is apt. The idea of a circle is also, let us note, the perfect circle, the *ideal* circle; it is, then, both idea and ideal. We see this easily when we are dealing with geometric figures, not so easily when dealing with chairs and dogs. (Do we see it more easily when dealing with men and women? Haven't we sometimes felt that we have an idea of what the perfect—the ideal—man or woman is like; and that, unPlatonically, we have even met one?) But Plato, under the spell of mathematics and the Pythagoreans, generalized from these examples in geometry, and was able to think easily in terms of the ideal dog or cat or chair. Obviously, it is in the context of man's pursuit of goodness, beauty, and truth that Platonic idealism becomes more meaningful. It is much easier to talk about ideals in this area than about the ideal dog or cat or chair.

Idealism as a Philosophy

Idealism is the name given to one of the most venerable and influential positions in the history of philosophy. Plato's version of it—Idea-ism, the view that only Ideas are real—is quite different from the later idealistic philosophies of Berkeley and Hegel referred to in Parts II and III. (See pp. 253, 301–302.)

Most versions of idealism, however, are agreed in describing reality in terms that are congenial to man's hopes and aspirations, and hence as permeated by purpose and charged with value. Plato implies such notions in the Idea of the Good, which he never defines for us—while setting it above all the other Ideas—but which suggests that value and purpose are categories that extend beyond the passing aims and objects of men. These idealistic philosophies are part of what has been called the genteel tradition in philosophy. William James had idealists in mind when he spoke of the "tender-minded" as contrasted to the "tough-minded" temperament. Above all, idealistic philosophies are agreed in affirming that reality is immaterial or incorporeal, and hence they define reality in terms other than those descriptive of the world of space and time. For Plato, the immateriality of the real world is found in the realm of Ideas, which, it is emphasized again, are not psychological but logical entities.

The identification of reality with logical entities, as thus described, is known as *logical realism*. No one can cope with the history of philosophy or feel at home in the history of ideas without understanding this designation. Unfortunately, the term "realism" is one of the most protean in our vocabulary. It characterizes an outlook on life, as when someone "faces realities" and sees things as they are without wishful thinking. It designates an important genre in the arts where, similarly, it refers, whether in the realm of belles-lettres or in the visual arts, to depicting objects, persons, or events as they are, without transforming or distorting them. In epistemology, realism is the view that we know or experience objects as they are. *Epistemological realism*, as this view is called, is contrasted with *epistemological dualism*, which asserts that the content of our experience is not the same as the object known; the latter is never experienced or known directly. (See pp. 216–226 for a detailed analysis.)

Metaphysical realism is the view that reality, whatever it is, and however we experience it, exists independently of our experiencing or knowing it. We are all of us naïve realists assuming, as we do, without critical reflection, that the world is not a figment of our imagination and that it does not cease to exist when we lose consciousness. As every beginning student in philosophy quickly learns, this proposition is much harder to prove—if, indeed, it can be proven at all—than, in our innocence, we hastily suppose. The opposite of realism, as thus understood, is *subjectivism*.

Now, *logical realism*, Plato's position, is a variant of metaphysical realism: that variant, namely, which asserts the independent reality of Ideas or Forms. It is easy for us to accept the proposition that physical objects or other persons are independently real, that is, exist apart from our experience of them. Are Ideas real apart from our thinking of them? Here we resist. We resist, that is, until we recur to our geometric figures. Is it necessary for us to have conceived of circularity for circularity to be whatever it is? And, whatever the nature of manness is, was it not always such, even before any man was born to exemplify it and hence before any man could have conceived of it? And is this not so, therefore, of any nature or form or essence—say the nature of mermaids, satyrs, or unicorns, not to mention lions and camels and horses? The direction of this argument suggests that forms or essences are eternal, as they are in the Platonic view. Circular objects come into being and pass away; circularity is timeless. Democracies emerge and perish. The idea of democracy is eternal. The notion that essences or forms or ideas have a being independent of our conceiving of them now seems perhaps less strange. Clearly, they possess such being as they have, even though, as with unicorns, there are no examples of them in space and time.

The opposite of the view we have been describing is *nominalism*. The polarity between nominalism and realism is one of the most important in the history of ideas. The nominalist takes the position that universals are only words or names (hence the designation "nominalism") which stand for particular things. The universal term "table," the nominalist contends, is nothing more than a name which stands for, is a symbol of, any number of particular tables. Universality accrues to the name simply in this standing-for or symbolic relation. Nothing but concrete individual things is real. As one nominalist put it, the only reality that universals have is that they are "breathings of the voice."

The debate over the reality of universals may seem an empty one to the layman, but it was anything but vacuous in the Middle Ages, for then church doctrine was at stake. The official position of the Church was realism. The Church itself, for example, was said to be a Universal Idea, which was eternal and existed, in its eternality, prior to and separate from the individual members of the Church. To attack the reality of universals, therefore, was to attack the notion of the Church eternal. To cast doubt upon the reality of universals called into question the eternality and universality of the laws of God, perhaps even God's own existence.

The medieval clergy, like medieval society itself, was, after all, a hierarchy of *classes*; the medieval church revolved about a *universal* priesthood and it emphasized the *universal* sacraments. The medieval ethic emphasized universal sin and salvation, and it recurred to the *type-woman*, Eve, and the *type-man*, Adam. Even in economic affairs—not to mention politics—transactions were not the outcome of decisions reflecting the desire of individuals to "buy for the least and sell for the most" depending on the conditions of supply and demand; transactions were governed by *over-individual* rules deriving from such doctrines as the just price, prohibitions on usury, and bans against monopolistic practices. At any rate, the theory involved these considerations, however much the ideal may have been subverted in practice.

In contrast with the realist, the nominalist is comfortable in the midst of the particularities of existence—with individual things, men, and institutions. He is like the ancient Sophists in finding man the measure of customs and morals, and he shares their skepticism of the claims of established religions. He tends to be empirically minded and is at ease in the natural sciences. He is much more at home in a modern laboratory, probing the natural world, than in the medieval cloister, contemplating the universal verities of God. The modern world belongs more to him than to the realist. In this controversy—which at first may seem to be a minor academic dispute —one finds a sign of sharply contrasting views between the Middle Ages and the modern world concerning reality, knowledge, and morality.

Ideas and Knowledge

From this digression, we may return to Plato. It seemed to him that in the doctrine of Ideas he had found an answer to the Sophists. In his *Theaetetus* Plato examines in detail some of the consequences, for knowledge, of the Protagorean doctrine that man is the measure of things. The precise statement of Protagoras, according to Plato, is as follows: "Man is the measure of all things; of existing things, that they are; and of nonexisting things that they are not."[4] With respect to knowledge, Plato interprets Protagoras' statement to mean that knowledge is perception or that knowledge is the result of what we perceive. For example, the knowledge that we have of the world and men around us—the green grass, a flowing stream, the sun, the moon, what Socrates did yesterday in the market place—is the result of what we see, hear, touch, taste, and smell: what we sense, what we perceive. Plato drives this theory into a radical skepticism. He contends that Protagoras is saying that what appears to exist to a man in his perceptions does exist for him in that way; but since no two men can perceive in the same way, they must inevitably "know" things differently and thus can have no common knowledge whatsoever. An illustration will help. Mr. A. sees a table as green, but Mr. B., who is color-blind, sees it as gray. To Mr. A. the table appears green and it is green for him. When asked what color the table is, he replies, "It is green." But Mr. B. sees the table gray and says, "It is gray." Which color is it? Does not such a doctrine make of knowledge an unverified soliloquy? The ineradicable uniqueness of sensations would seem to make knowledge impossible on this theory.

Plato rides Protagoras' thesis a good deal harder than Protagoras seems to have done or would have liked. Protagoras was fully aware of the rela-

---

[4] *Theaetetus*, 152. (Our translation.)

tivity to which this doctrine committed him, but he did not let it bother him in the form of extreme skepticism. On the color problem, he would probably have said that most men see the table green; so by convention the table is green. But if most men saw it gray, by convention it would be gray. And then he would go on about his teaching. If this seems a shabby way out, Protagoras would be anything but shabby in stressing that sense experience is inescapably individual; and if knowledge involves general or universal statements, the uniqueness of sense experience—our only access to the world around us, no matter what instruments supplement our senses —does present a problem and must be taken into account in any theory of knowledge.

If the knowledge-is-perception path leads to a dead end, what other path may be chosen? Plato points out that men compare and analyze sensations, they remember experiences, they add and subtract numbers, and they prove propositions in geometry. These are activities not of the senses but of the mind. The path to knowledge, he contends, is found in just such activities of the mind.

But, still, what is knowledge? Again and again in the dialogues, Plato uses arithmetic and geometry as examples of knowledge, as if to say, "If mathematics is not knowledge, what is?" Knowledge has the characteristics that mathematics has—it is universal, it is certain. Mathematics is concerned with Ideas and Forms which possess these characteristics. Proof is possible; and not only is possible but has been realized. There is no doubt that $2 + 2 = 4$, or that the interior angle sum of a triangle is equal to two right angles. These statements are not matters of opinion, debate, or majority vote. They are certain, and they hold anywhere at any time.

Is, then, mathematics the only knowledge that there is? Plato's answer is no. Mathematics is a model, but there can be other kinds of knowledge, perhaps more difficult to achieve. When Ideas, Forms, are grasped in other fields, knowledge will be present there also.

But what other fields? Plato asks men to attend to their discourse. Discourse is shot through and through with terms which stand for Universals. They are inescapable in most of our statements. "Socrates is a man." "A democracy is a government by the people." "Man," "democracy," "government," "people"—all are terms which stand for Ideas, Forms, Universals. To use a term like "democracy" does not mean necessarily that one knows or grasps the Universal. Men often use terms without knowing their meanings, that is, without grasping the essential characteristics of the Idea or Form. But when these characteristics are grasped, as when men can define "triangle" or "democracy," then they have knowledge.

Is knowledge, then, just a matter of definition? "Don't belittle definition," Socrates and Plato would say. At his trial, Socrates pointed out how he went about Athens asking for the meaning of "wisdom" and "justice" and other matters of that kind, and found that men were full of words and confusion and knew little of what they were talking about. In dialogue after dialogue, Socrates is portrayed as trying to help men get at the meaning of "temperance," "friendship," "courage," "virtue," "love," "piety," "justice," and "knowledge" itself. To list these terms is to list as many Platonic dialogues and more, for some have more than one dialogue devoted to them. So definition is not to be taken lightly.

But, of course, clear definition is not the whole of knowledge. If a man were a walking dictionary, he would know many things but not enough. For the Ideas are related. Knowing definitions in geometry is one thing. Knowing how to prove propositions from these definitions is quite another, and a more difficult, task. The magnificence of Euclid's *Elements* is not that he discovered a large set of novel propositions but that he was able to order the vast array of known geometrical propositions, or Ideas, as Plato would say.

Plato, too, would order Ideas or, more accurately, see the order among them. In his famous analogy of the Line in *The Republic*,[5] Plato diagrams four levels of knowing as follows:

Opinion (Concerned with Particular Things)		Knowledge (Concerned with Ideas)	
Imagining	Belief	Demonstrative Proof	Knowledge through Dialectic

The first two, imagining and belief, are actually levels of opinion, not knowledge. They are concerned with particular objects of sensible experience and not Ideas. The contrast with genuine knowledge might be illustrated by a man who had the correct belief on how to bisect a line with a compass and ruler because he had been told how to do it, but did not know how to prove the bisection as a geometer would.

The second two divisions are the realm of knowledge. The first of these is concerned with demonstrative proof as found in arithmetic and geometry, the examples Plato uses. The geometer starts with a set of hypotheses or assumptions (Plato's general term for the geometer's axioms, definitions, and postulates) and proceeds to demonstrate propositions from these assumptions. Ideas or Forms are involved in the assumptions and in every step of the proof. All demonstrative knowledge is like this, moving from a set of unproved assumptions to proved propositions. For Plato, any science worth the name would involve proof; and since all sciences begin with assumptions, they have this defective characteristic of unproved assumptions. Can this defect be remedied?

The last segment of the Line illustrates how Plato would remedy the defect. He would begin with the assumptions of the sciences, treating them not as first principles of their sciences but as propositions to be proved

---

[5] 509 ff.

after they have been simplified and carried back to the first principles of all knowledge. Plato describes this undertaking as follows (Socrates is speaking):

By the second section of the intelligible world you may understand me to mean all that unaided reasoning apprehends by the *power of dialectic*, when it treats its assumptions, not as first principles, but as *hypotheses* in the literal sense, things "laid down" like a flight of steps up which it may mount all the way to something that is not hypothetical, the first principle of all; and having grasped this, may turn back and, holding on to the consequences which depend upon it, descend at last to a conclusion, never making use of any sensible object, but only Forms, moving through Forms from one to another, and ending with Forms.[6]

An illustration may be useful. Euclid's *Elements* begins with twenty-three definitions, five postulates, and five common notions or axioms. Arithmetic, too, begins with assumptions about such matters as number and addition. Can the assumptions of these sciences be carried back to more fundamental notions in mathematics and logic? Both arithmetic and geometry use the axiom, "If equals be added to equals, the sums are equal," and other equality axioms. Can these be carried back to a fundamental notion of equality? As the assumptions in geometry, arithmetic, and other sciences are simplified and reduced, can they all be carried back to *the fundamental principle of all knowledge*, which itself is not hypothetical? If they can and this principle is grasped, then the mind can turn around and proceed to prove the very foundations of the sciences. This is Plato's claim or at least the program he outlined.

What is the meaning of this undertaking? In the first place, it is about the *unity of knowledge*. Plato insists that knowledge does not consist of an array of discrete, unrelated Ideas. The Ideas are ordered in a vast system in which there are subsystems like arithmetic, geometry, and the other sciences. The system has a fundamental unifying principle upon which the unity ultimately depends.

In the next place, it is about the *certainty of knowledge*. Demonstrative proof has a cannot-be-otherwise quality. In a subject matter like geometry, beginning with a set of definitions, postulates, and axioms, we are caught in a system in which the propositions follow of necessity from these initial assumptions. The demonstrated propositions follow, not from our likes and dislikes, but from the assumptions and in accordance with the techniques of proof. Here there is certainty, and Plato could embrace this kind of knowledge with enthusiasm. What an answer to Protagoras and the other Sophists! What a response to the men in the market place who are satisfied with their rules of thumb! Here is the refutation of all those

---

[6] *The Republic*, 511, trans. by Cornford (London: Oxford, 1941), pp. 225–226. Our italics.

laymen and philosophers who have claimed that we cannot know anything with certainty.

Yet even demonstrative proof has a flaw. The clever Sophist can puncture its claim to certainty by pointing out that a so-called solid edifice like geometry is based upon the shifting sands of assumptions. Can any structure or system be more certain than its foundation? Plato was unhappy with this last remnant of uncertainty and tried to eliminate it by carrying back the assumptions of the sciences to the first principle of knowledge which he says, is not hypothetical or an assumption. With this principle discovered, knowledge is founded as on a rock and not the sands of hypotheses. Knowledge is thus not only a vast, unified system, but also certain.

The quest for certainty, and the conviction that certainty is attainable has inspired the philosophical standpoint known as *rationalism,* a position that we shall have occasion to explore later in this volume in a number of different contexts. (See pp. 367–368.) Rationalism is only remotely, if at all, related to "rationalization"—a term employed by psychologists to designate the attempt to justify decisions already made by finding "good" reasons for them, in short, the unhappy knack of finding excuses; and employed by economists to designate such matters as scientific management and the mechanization of the production of goods. In brief, rationalism is the view that man is endowed with a faculty superior to the senses, called Reason, which enables him to know truths which observation can never provide. Pure mathematics is a case in point: it is the product of reason and reason alone. No observation could prove or refute a geometrical truth. Even propositions like "Every event has a cause," a truth about the universe, could never be asserted on the basis of sense experience alone, for not all events can be observed; yet reason enables us to make this assertion, the rationalist argues, about all past, present, and future events. Reason is the source and its own justification for such a truth. Platonism is the example, par excellence, of rationalism, and the first fully worked out and explicit formulation of the rationalist position.

Comforted with the vision of knowledge that is secure, and happy that the troublesome Sophists have been put in their place, we may be ready to lay aside our philosophic reflections and conclude that the only remaining problem of knowledge is its advancement—the discovery of those Ideas or Forms in the sciences which are truly safe and sound. But before we become too comfortable, in the spirit of Socrates another question or two should be raised.

What is this first principle which provides both the ultimate unity and certainty of knowledge? Plato in *The Republic* calls it the Good. The reader of Plato can hardly avoid puzzlement when, after much talk about mathematics, he is told that the first principle is an Idea that seems more appropriate to moral subjects or the arts than to mathematics and the sciences. One might conclude that Plato had reasons other than epistemological for the selection of this Idea, and he probably did. Even so, the question, "What is the Idea of the Good?" is perfectly legitimate; for it would seem important to know what it is since it provides the ultimate certainty to knowledge. At first most men would find the Idea of the Good far less certain than the Idea of an axiom of equality, for example. An answer to the question is crucial, but Plato never explicitly provides one, either in *The Republic* or elsewhere.

Scholars have tried to determine what Plato meant by the Idea of the Good as the first principle of knowledge. Efforts have been made to show that he was thinking of a logical principle, like the Law of Contradiction to the effect that a proposition cannot be both true and false. But the plain fact is that these efforts are only conjectures at best. If there is such a logical first principle for knowledge, Plato did not help matters by calling it the Good; for there appears no justification for the claim that an Idea which is central in moral and aesthetic considerations can alone be the basis for proving the foundation of any of the sciences. Aristotle later was to deal with this problem, asserting that each demonstrative science must make some assumptions appropriate to its subject matter, and that there is no escaping this characteristic of a demonstrative system. (See p. 117.)

There is another characteristic of Plato's first principle which bears notice: the principle itself is not hypothetical. Of course, one may ask why not. Even if the initial assumptions of the sciences were progressively reduced until only one remained, why would it not be an assumption? Why would it not be hypothetical? In this instance again, Plato's passion for certainty is seen. If this principle were not hypothetical, what would it be? It could not be a demonstrated conclusion, for it is the basis of demonstration itself. How is it then known? By *dialectic*. We shall encounter this important term in other contexts. (See pp. 301 ff.) For Plato, it is the power of the mind that is able to take the assumptions of the sciences, to reduce them ultimately to one principle, and then to grasp that principle as true and certain, simply by the power of the mind itself. The result of this last action of the mind is sometimes called *self-evident* knowledge; that is, a proposition is said to be self-evident, when, from understanding the meaning of the terms themselves, the mind certifies the proposition to be true. Thus self-evidence has often been claimed for propositions like the equality axioms of geometry; that is, if we but understand the terms, we must accept the proposition as true that when equals are added to equals the sums are equal. The trouble with self-evidence as the certification of the truth of a proposition is the plethora of propositions for which self-evidence has been claimed in the history of thought, and the disagreements among those making such claims. As indicated, some have claimed self-evidence for the axioms of geometry; however, Plato would have these axioms proved. The proposition, "God exists," has been said to be self-evident. The self-evidence of this proposition has also been denied. Self-evidence as a justification for knowledge is plagued by this kind of problem.

Ideas and Existence

When men know, they know reality, and what they know are Ideas or Forms. The perfectly real is the perfectly knowable, and the perfectly knowable is the perfectly real. Reality and the Ideas are one and the same thing. That which is and is not, the particular objects of everyday experience which come to be and pass away are not real. They are only appearances. The world of the senses is infected with unreality; the world of the mind is reality pure and undefiled. The Platonic answer to the question concerning the nature of existence—one of the oldest problems of Greek philosophy and still one of philosophy's most persistent—is embodied in statements such as these.

It would be hard to find a more succinct summary of Plato's position than that in the following quotation from *The Republic* (Socrates is contrasting the man who knows *Ideas* and hence *reality* with one who possesses belief and is thus acquainted only with *appearance*, that is, particular objects of sense experience):

So may we say that he knows, while the other has only a belief in appearances; and might we call their states of mind knowledge and belief?
Certainly.
But this person who, we say, has only belief without knowledge may be aggrieved and challenge our statement. Is there any means of soothing his resentment and converting him gently, without telling him plainly that he is not in his right mind?
We surely ought to try.
Come then, consider what we are to say to him. Or shall we ask him a question, assuring him that, far from grudging him any knowledge he may have, we shall be only too glad to find that there is something he knows? But, we shall say, tell us this: When a man knows, must there not be something that he knows? Will you answer for him, Glaucon?
My answer will be, that there must.
Something real or unreal?
Something real; how could a thing that is unreal ever be known?
Are we satisfied, then, on this point, from however many points of view we might examine it: *that the perfectly real is perfectly knowable, and the utterly unreal is entirely unknowable?*
Quite satisfied.
Good. Now if there is something so constituted that it both *is* and *is not*, will it not lie between the purely real and the utterly unreal?
It will.

Well then, as *knowledge corresponds to the real,* and *absence of knowledge necessarily to the unreal,* so, to correspond to this intermediate thing, we must look for something between igorance and knowledge, if such a thing there be.
Certainly.
Is there not a thing we call belief?
Surely.
A different power from knowledge, or the same?
Different.
Knowledge and belief, then, must have different objects, answering to their respective powers.
Yes.
And *knowledge has for its natural object the real—to know the truth about reality.*[7]

The Ideas constitute the reality of existence. They do not come into being and perish. They are, have always been, and will always be. They are the permanencies of existence. The Idea of a triangle is invariant. It was the same for Euclid, for today, and for tomorrow.

What a contrast, Plato argues, the Ideas make to the transciency of particular things—of sticks and stones or the particular triangle drawn on paper or made even of iron. Particular things, physical things, come into being and perish. Their reality is something more than nonbeing or nonexistence, but it is still a kind of unreality, for whatever perishes in any way, in that respect becomes nonbeing, nonexistent. Thus the Idea of a triangle and the drawn triangle afford for Plato as simple a contrast between the permanent and the changing, the real and what only appears to be real, as one can find. The ancient controversies in Greek philosophy over the permanent and the changing, reality and appearance, receive in Plato one of the most persuasive of solutions, not only for his day but for subsequent ages.

But the Ideas do not simply constitute the real and permanent of existence. They are an integrated order. One sees this clearly, Plato argues, in the realm of mathematics—in geometry, for example. There the Ideas are a tightly knit system, but this system is not simply characteristic of geometry as a matter of knowledge. It is also characteristic of nature. Nature itself is geometrical, a mathematical order; that is why the geometry we know applies to nature. It is not surprising, Plato would argue, that the history of science has in a sense been the history of an increasing competence in dealing with nature mathematically, for nature *is* just such a mathematical order. Thus, if there is a first principle of knowledge upon which the unity and certainty of knowledge depends, then there must be also the first principle of all existence, which performs the same function in the realm of being. But since the first principle of knowledge must also be the first principle of existence, the Idea of the Good—the

---

[7] 476–477, trans. by Cornford, *op. cit.,* pp. 184–185. Our italics.

Idea of all Ideas, one might say—is precisely this principle. The invariant principle of knowledge is the eternal foundation of existence.

Plato, the pagan philosopher, was to become a bulwark of Christian thought. Etienne Gilson, one of the most eminent students of the Middle Ages, has commented, ". . . the net result of Augustine's philosophical speculation was to achieve a platonic understanding of the Christian Revelation."[8] That Christianity should find Platonism congenial should not cause undue wonder. The Platonic contrast between the realm of Ideas, accessible only to the mind, and the world of things, the province of the senses, the true reality over against appearance, can easily be read as the realm of spirit contrasted with the perishable world of the flesh and such wordly things. If the ultimate principle of knowledge and existence is the Good, can this not be understood to be God? Not only can this be understood as God, the Christian averred, but must be; for the Ideas have their very existence in the mind of God, and God thus becomes the source of all existence and of all knowledge.

To return once more to Plato, we must now consider some of the difficulties in the Platonic view, not with a view to criticism primarily, but because they help us to see how he was endeavoring to bring science and tradition together.

There is a problem concerning the relation of the world of particular things to the realm of Ideas. If Ideas constitute the reality of existence and the objects of our sense experience are appearances, what has happened to the everyday world of shoes and ships and sealing wax? It is a sort of Alice-in-Wonderland world, a world of seeming, of make-believe, a mask, a shadow. It simply is not real. The man in the street would now be troubled. Has Plato saved knowledge and made reality secure, only to lose the world that men experience day in and day out? For most Greeks this would be a poor bargain indeed, even though the doctrine became persuasive later, in Christianity, that true reality is found in the realm of the spirit. The Sophists may have lost the certainty of knowledge and any sense of certain existence, but they at least taught a man how to get around in the world men do live in. Plato seemed to lose this world altogether. If the problem troubled the man in the street, it troubled Plato too. What *is* the relation of Ideas to things?

Plato was not of one mind for an answer. He speaks of particular things as *participating* in the Ideas and as being *imitations* of Ideas. In the first instance, Plato means that a physical triangle is a triangle insofar as it partakes of or shares in the Idea. Another way of putting this view is to say that the Idea is present or immanent in the particular thing. In the second instance, Plato means that the physical triangle is a triangle insofar

---

[8] *Reason and Revelation in the Middle Ages* (New York: Scribner, 1938), p. 23.

as it is an imitation or copy of the Idea. The Idea in this case is transcendent, totally separate from the particular instance. To illustrate further, an individual table is a table as it shares in or participates in or embodies the Idea of a Table; or it is a table because it is a copy of the Idea.

In either case Plato did not solve the problem. In the *Parmenides*[9] Plato criticizes his own metaphors. The aged Parmenides forces the young Socrates, who is defending the participation doctrine, into what is called "the third-man" argument. How, asks Parmenides, can an individual, material thing participate in a universal, immaterial thing? To have any relation, would there not have to be a third thing in which both shared? But between this third thing and the particular object, and between this third thing and the Idea there would have to be other relating factors, and so on ad infinitum. The same criticism is leveled against the "copy" thesis. The problem is unresolved.

But Plato did not become so absorbed in the Ideas that he forgot the world. In his cosmological work, *Timaeus*, he describes the development of the world as a result of God's using the eternal Ideas, especially those of mathematics, as the pattern for fashioning nature as we see it. The beautiful order of Ideas is captured in the order of nature, but how the capturing takes place remains uncertain. At best, says Plato, he can give only "a likely story"; but even if his story is only likely on this troublesome question of the relation of Ideas to things, it is clear that Plato felt that the order of nature is a logical structure accessible to man's reason. Mathematics is not simply a set of Ideas in heaven. Nature is a mathematical order "somehow," and when we know mathematics, we know the order of nature. When we know mathematics, we have truth about nature. This conviction seems to be one of the firmest in Plato.

Let us turn to a related problem. Suppose, as the reader is perusing these pages, a figure no larger than the legendary Tom Thumb were to appear before him? Or, glancing through the window he were to see a human figure one hundred feet tall standing across the field. Would these be men? Yes, it might be answered. Height does not determine what it is to be a man. Suppose a creature entered the room conversing like a man and resembling a man in every respect, except that it had two heads; would it be a man? An affirmative answer is less likely. Suppose it talked like a man, and, like Harvey, had the body of a rabbit? While all this is farfetched and preposterous, consider the following report in *The New York Times* (June 7, 1964) captioned "Early Man Stirs Science Dispute":

A sharp difference of opinion is developing over a creature that has been called the world's earliest known true man.
A British specialist doubts that the creature, named Homo habilis, should be classed as a distinct early species of man at all. He believes it should

---

[9] 131–134.

probably be classed as a subspecies of the African manapes, or near-men called the Australopithecines. . . .

Here the problem is less farfetched; indeed, scientists are engaged in a heated argument over it. At what point in the evolutionary scale should an organism be designated human, as distinguished from subhuman? Plato would say that the determination is made by reference to the nature of manness, the Idea of Man, and does not rest on our fiat. When Dr. L. S. B. Leakly argues, as he does, that Homo habilis is the earliest "true" man, he appears to be arguing like a good Platonist. Whether he is a Platonist or not depends on whether "true," as he uses it, means "consistent with accepted usage" or "conforming to some objective form or essence called man."

Many contemporary philosophers would argue against the Platonic view, and insist that the point at which the line is drawn between man and subman—while it is based, of course, on actual differences—will be determined by the purposes of the investigation at hand. For example, the division between man and subman, based upon anatomical structures may not be the same as that founded on moral considerations. For the biological man may live at a level below what we call the moral man, as when we say a man's acts are inhuman (literally not human) or amoral (outside the bounds of morality). The contemporary argument emphasizes that it is important to know in what context distinctions are made, because the context is a determining factor in the very meaning of the distinctions. For this reason, the tendency in much contemporary philosophy is to avoid a realm of fixed and clearly demarcated ideas which, the Platonists say, can be known irrespective of any context whatsoever and then can be utilized in specific situations. It is not at all clear that there is a core idea of man which will adequately serve biochemistry, anatomy, physiology, psychology, economics, politics, morals, religion, and art.

A related problem is worth exploring. Once again it will be useful to refer to our lopsided circle.　◯　There it is. May we not argue that while it is a poor example of a circle, it is an example of whatever idea or form it happens to be. Cannot any drawn figure of any shape be an example of precisely that idea or form? Why is there only one perfect Circle of which particular circles are simply good or poor approximations? Is a particular ellipse a poor copy of the idea of a circle or is it a copy of the idea of an ellipse? In fact, in Plato's language, must there not be an Idea of an Ellipse as well as the Idea of a Circle? And if an Idea of an Ellipse, where does one stop with the ideas of closed curves or any other figure? In short, is there not an unlimited number of Ideas or Forms, not only in mathematics but also in other areas of knowledge and existence? Plato did not think so. For him there is a limited number. Which are these? Well, precisely those that had been distinguished and defined by a fourth century B.C. Athenian. All of which leads us to an understanding of what Plato was really doing. He was not giving us the final truth about the nature of things. He was very much bound to the common sense and accepted wisdom of his day.

We can see, from our vantage point, that the realm of Ideas is a reflection of the everyday world experienced by a Greek citizen living in the fourth century B.C., with this important difference: it is an orderly and coherent arrangement of the common-sense world known to the Greeks, reflecting the requirements of logic and the insights of mathematics.

Ideas and Moral Ideals

If there are universal, eternal Ideas answering to such terms as "triangle," "dog," "man," and the like, are there Ideas for "justice," "wisdom," "courage," and "temperance," which are concerned with man's moral life? For if there are, they too would be universal, eternal. The Idea of Justice would not be one man's idea of justice, or the Athenians' or the Spartans'. It would be justice for all times and all places and all men. It would be not simply an idea, it would be the eternal Ideal of Justice. The Sophists and every other relativist would be answered, now and forever. The ancient wisdom had struggled to glimpse the ideal which now would be envisioned; and man could at least hope that once he had seen the Ideal, he could bring his life more nearly to conform to it. In brief compass, Plato's approach to a theory of ethics through his theory of Ideas follows this pattern. The use of the theory will be examined, first in support of the virtues as eternal ideals, and second as it is involved in the practice of virtue.

THE VIRTUES AS ETERNAL IDEALS. That there are Ideas of the virtues for which "justice," "courage," and similar terms are symbols, is a conviction of Plato's, which he expressed again and again. The Ideas of the virtues serve to make virtuous acts virtuous and form a standard for judging the conduct of man. One illustration will suffice. When Socrates asks the young Euthyphro, "What is piety?" and Euthyphro gives him examples, Socrates replies:

Do you remember that I did not ask you to give me one or two examples of piety, but to explain that very Form . . . which makes all pious things to be pious? Do you not remember that you said there was one Form [Idea] . . . which made impious acts impious, and pious acts pious? . . . Tell me, then, what is the nature of this Form [Idea] . . . so that by looking to it and using it as a pattern I may say that any act done by you or another that has such a character is pious and any act that has it not is impious.[10]

The Ideas of the virtues not only make virtuous acts virtuous, by being

---

[10] *Euthyphro* 6, trans. by Sir David Ross from his *Plato's Theory of Ideas* (Oxford at the Clarendon Press, 1951), p. 13.

present in or immanent in the act, and serve as a standard for judging acts, but they also are real in the sense that any Idea of mathematics or objects of nature is real. The passage cited previously (p. 92) about the reality of the Ideas is said to hold for the virtues and even for the Idea of Beauty. The goodness and badness of man's acts, his justice and his injustice, his courage and his cowardice, in short, man's moral life is grounded in existence as much as his knowledge or any other aspect of his life. Men cannot play fast and loose with truth, for truth is knowledge of Ideas, that is of invariant existence. Neither can men play fast and loose with moral ideals, for they are the Ideas of the virtues and are found in the realm of existence as any eternal Idea of mathematics. As the Idea of a Triangle is objective, possesses being, and is eternal, invariant, and universal; so is the Idea of Justice. There is but one Justice for all time and eternity, for all cities of men. In this way Plato would answer the relativism of the Sophists.

The Ideas of the virtues are as capable of being known as any other aspect of existence. The power of reason is as efficacious in morals as in mathematics—and as necessary, for the Ideas are known by reason and not through the senses or emotions. So close is the tie between Plato's ethics and his epistemology that he strikingly chose the Idea of the Good as the first principle of knowledge. Justice and the other virtues are said to be among the highest things to be known, but the Idea of the Good is the highest and most fundamental of all.[11] Plato places great emphasis upon the importance of reason and knowledge in man's moral conduct, an example that many an Idealist has copied since his day.

Further characteristics of the Idea of the Good should be noted. It is the most fundamental principle not only of knowledge but also of ethics. Everything that is virtuous, everything that is good and right derives from it. It is the foundation of man's moral life as well as of his knowledge. But more. The Good is the first principle of being, of existence. Even in the context of existence, the Good does not lose its moral overtones; thus, since the first principle of existence is the Good, existence itself has a moral quality to it. In the *Timaeus*, God fashioned the visible world on the model of the eternal Ideas which are good and made the world "the best of things that have become."[12] The visible world, the world of becoming, has existence and order insofar as it is patterned after the Ideas. It is also good because it is so patterned.

Plato used his theory of Ideas as a way of discriminating what he considered to be essential conditions of the moral life of man. If man is the measure of things, Plato felt that man is doomed to moral anarchy. There must be some sort of objective standard for conduct outside of man; otherwise he becomes an aimless wanderer, led now this way, now that by his

---

[11] *The Republic*, 504–505.
[12] *Timaeus*, 29, trans. by Cornford (New York: Liberal Arts, 1959), p. 17.

very human passions and desires. In the Greek tradition, there was no supreme God to hand down a Mosaic code for men to live by. Zeus was no Jehovah. What can provide the needed guide? The eternal Ideas, shining through the mist. Reason can find them. Man's rationality is his salvation. The essential conditions of the moral life are the rational conditions of conduct; and these are secure, not because they are human, but because they are grounded in existence. When reason is unfettered, it can see straight and true to the Ideas, ultimately to the Good.

IDEAS AND THE PRACTICE OF VIRTUE.   It is possible to discriminate basic conditions for the moral life without indicating how those conditions are to be achieved. Even if Plato's analysis of the conditions of virtue should be correct, the question could be raised, did he consider the manner in which these conditions can be met? It is one thing to know what virtue is; it is quite another to be virtuous. How do men become virtuous?

One of the firmest convictions which Socrates had is that men naturally seek the good. The evil that they do is the result of ignorance. That men often choose evil, no one can deny. But when men do this, Socrates argues, they choose what they *think* will bring them good; this is true of even the most tyrannical of men. One of their great flaws is mistaken logic. Another problem is that men do not know when they are ignorant. At his trial, Socrates pointed out how he endeavored to refute the oracle at Delphi, when the oracle had said that no man was wiser than Socrates himself. Socrates felt it would be a simple matter to uncover a wiser man, but he went to the great and the small, only to find that they claimed to be wise but were not. Socrates finally concluded that the oracle meant that he is wisest who, like Socrates, knows that his wisdom is worth nothing. Yes, the great trouble with men is that they do not realize how ignorant they are; hence they pursue blind folly.

Can they remedy their ignorance? Yes, but the way is hard and sometimes seems hopeless. Several of the Socratic dialogues raise questions about specific virtues, such as, "What is piety?" and "What is temperance?" After discussing the question inside and out, time and again these dialogues end inconclusively. Definitions will be proposed and rejected. A dialogue will end up in the air. The Idea has *not* been found. Again, the more general question, "What is virtue?" is proposed, and the search is made to see if virtue is a matter of knowledge; if it is, virtue can be taught, since knowledge can be taught. The question of how men become virtuous is solved if men can be taught to be virtuous. Unfortunately, the big "if" is whether virtue is a matter of knowledge. In the *Meno* Socrates cleverly shows how to teach geometry to a slave boy who knew none before; hence geometry obviously can be taught. But he finds it very puzzling that the most virtuous men of Athens, from Pericles on down, were not able to teach their rakish sons virtue. And assuredly a virtuous man would teach virtue to his own sons of all people, if he could. The dialogue ends by suggesting that virtue is a gift of the gods.

What is to be done with these dialogues? If the conditions of virtue are those described earlier—that there are eternal Ideas of the virtues which make virtuous actions possible—but if the Ideas cannot be discovered, then virtue may be a gift of the gods or a matter of chance. If the conditions of virtue cannot be realized by man, then perhaps he is back where Protagoras said he was, back on his own resources, making the best of things from day to day. The problem is not unlike that of the relation of the Ideas to objects of our experience, the Idea of the Table to the table in one's dining room. What is the relation of the Idea of Justice to the concrete dispute in the law court? From the standpoint of the dialogues referred to, at first the relation seems remote indeed.

On the other hand, the dialogues, in exhibiting Socrates in his constant enterprise of critically analyzing ideas, may point the way, if not to Ideal Justice, at least to the elimination of some degrees of ignorance. A reader cannot leave a Platonic dialogue without having cherished notions challenged and often exploded. There is merit in eliminating ignorance, in exposing to the light of reason what cannot stand examination, even if positive truth still escapes us.

But do the Ideas of the virtues always elude us? In *The Republic*, Plato comes to a decision about some. The problem is the nature of justice. After showing contradictions in, and eliminating, two commonly accepted ideas of justice—that justice is rendering each man his due, and the Thrasymachan doctrine that justice is the interest of the ruling power— Plato offers his own positive doctrine. To find justice, Socrates and his friends construct an ideal state. It is beyond the purposes of this discussion to consider the endlessly fascinating problems which come to light in *The Republic*. Only salient elements, as they are related to the Ideas and the practice of virtue, will be noted.

The ideal state is a Greek city-state consisting of three classes: the guardians or ruling class, the military, and the remainder of the citizens. After being constructed with care, the state is said to be good and to embody the virtues of wisdom, courage, temperance, and justice. Wisdom resides in the guardians, courage in the military class, and temperance— the harmonious agreement on the question of who should rule and who should be ruled—in all the classes. Justice, in the state, is then found to be that "everyone ought to perform the one function of the community for which his nature best suited him."[13] The question had also been raised as to what justice is in the individual man; that is, what is a just man? Plato finds three parts to a man's soul—his reason, emotions, and appetites—

---

[13] *The Republic*, 433, trans. by Cornford, *op. cit.*, p. 127.

corresponding to the three classes in the state. Wisdom and courage are placed in reason and the emotions respectively, and temperance pervades all parts of the soul as in the state. Justice in the individual, not surprisingly, turns out to be each part of the soul doing that for which it is best fitted. It is a kind of health and harmony of the soul. With temperance and justice present and reason ruling, a man is good.

In *The Republic*, Plato lays before his readers not only the Idea of Justice but also the Ideas of Wisdom, Courage, and Temperance. There is not the indecision and tentativeness found in other dialogues. The Ideas have been discovered which will make states and men virtuous—wise, courageous, temperate, just. But still, how can men glimpse these Ideas and realize them in their lives? The problem is one of education.

Plato and the Greeks, like twentieth-century Americans, had enormous faith in education as the means of curing their personal and social ills. Plato's emphasis, however, is upon education for virtue and not upon technical competence for making a living. For him, the end of education is the production of good men, not skilled technicians. But how? This subject is dominant in *The Republic*, and recurs again and again in other dialogues as the teachability of virtue is debated. More specifically, how can men come to glimpse the Ideas of the virtues and to agree to live in the harmony that is temperance and justice made real?

Plato begins with the traditional program of gymnastic and music and literature. He never doubts the value of a sound body to a sound mind, but the physical courage which was supreme in the ancient heroic virtue is now subordinated to wisdom. Plato censures the traditional music and literature severely. The immorality of the gods is to be purged from the myths, and the gods are to be portrayed as gods should be—the embodiment of the virtues. Music that is sensuous and passionate is also to be forbidden. Education should provide an atmosphere of the beautiful and the good. When men are reared in this kind of atmosphere, their souls come to embody beauty and goodness; and thus education ends, Plato contends, where it should, with love of beauty and the good. Men of such character are the foundation of a temperate state, and they possess that quality of temperance in their own lives which is necessary for the just and good life.

But what of the Ideas? The education just described begins at the mother's knee. The young become temperate in their climate of beauty and goodness, almost by osmosis. Where does knowledge enter? Plato reserves for his guardian class—in effect, only those of the highest intellectual capacity—a vision of the Ideas. This higher education consists, he says, of turning the eye of the soul, which is the mind, from physical things to the Ideas. The discipline is to be rigorously mathematical—using the mathematics of his day from the theoretical but not the utilitarian standpoint, theoretical astronomy, and the mathematical theory of harmony.

After ten years, the best students would be selected to study dialectic for five years. When this study is completed, they are to return to military and administrative offices of the work-a-day world for fifteen years. Finally, they lift the eye of the soul to the Good which becomes the pattern for ordering the state and their own lives. All men of the state may be temperate and just, as they go about doing that for which they are fitted. Only those of the highest intellectual capacity, however, will understand the nature of the moral principles of man's conduct.

How, then, are Plato's views on ethics and education related to the scheme of values of the folklore noted earlier? Plato, taking the traditional ideals of wisdom, courage, temperance or moderation, and justice, refashioned them, gave them certainty through the theory of Ideas, and proposed to modify the customary educational program in order to achieve them.

There is nothing novel in Plato's writing about wisdom, courage, temperance, and justice. They are as traditional Greek virtues as one can find. All these virtues are modified to some degree, however, by Plato. Wisdom still has that practical cast of being wise in the affairs of men; for the guardians where wisdom resides in the state, must administer the state after their strenuous education. But wisdom in Plato involves much more theoretical knowledge than it did before. Not only wisdom itself but the virtues in general are tied more closely to theoretical knowledge than to affairs of common sense. Wisdom demands knowledge of the sciences and not just prudence in the affairs of men.

As noted before, courage is not the supreme virtue it was in the heroic period. Wisdom has displaced it and modified it; for courage is not sheer boldness, but consists now in following reason as to what a man ought or ought not to fear. Wisdom places courage too at the service of the state.

Moderation or temperance was an ancient ideal, which changes little in Plato. In the state, he casts it as the recognition among all classes as to who should rule and who should be ruled. In the individual, there is this same "recognition" among the parts of the soul. In both cases, what is essential is the recognition that reason should rule.

Justice, in Plato's hands, received the most significant changes. The notion that justice consists of each man's doing that for which he is best fitted would have surprised many Greeks, for one of the oldest views in the Greek tradition was that justice is obedience to the law and equality before the law. A traditionalist might argue that justice is a function of law and that Plato had forgotten law altogether. Although he did not go that far, certainly Plato dismissed that sort of law which most states find necessary for their very existence—law concerning economic problems.[14] The traditionalist would be correct that Plato had substituted something else for the justice that arises out of the litigation of the law court. In fact,

---

[14] See *The Republic*, 425.

Plato dismissed another cherished notion of antiquity—that justice is rendering each man his due. Plato substituted for the more traditional view the notion that justice is a function of social organization and self-discipline. If men discipline themselves under rational control and keep to what their abilities permit, Plato insists, the usual necessities of legal justice will disappear.[15] In short, the empirical approach to justice as a function of legislative and judicial inquiry and action—an approach that both the Greeks and subsequent societies have found necessary—is considered irrelevant by Plato in the good society he envisioned. It is not necessary to repeat how Plato answered the Sophists' relativistic view of morals through the doctrine of Ideas. The traditional values are saved from disintegration, he felt, by clarifying them as indicated and grounding them in the very nature of existence.

Plato's addition to traditional education is novel and at the same time puzzling. His desired purification of the myths was not startling. The myths had been under criticism since Xenophanes. What is startling is the rigorous training in science that he requires as a prelude to administering the state. What has mathematics to do with politics? The easy answer, of course, is that science is concerned with abstract ideas, and thus if the guardians have training in the sciences, they will be at home in the realm of Ideas and will be able to find Ideas not only in mathematics but also in morals; hence the guardians will know Justice, Wisdom, and so on, even the Good. Knowing these, they will be able to translate them into the affairs of men. Certainly Plato and Platonism have been understood precisely in this manner in much of the history of philosophy.

One cannot help wondering, however, whether Plato was quite this optimistic or naïve about abstract science as a preparation for politics. Certainly history has not borne out any such optimism. But even Plato's own *Meno* is a caution against a too-ready acceptance of this interpretation. How easy it was to teach a slave boy geometry, but the noble Pericles, just and wise, could not teach his own sons virtue! There are too many dialogues running counter to *The Republic* to charge Plato either with optimism or naïveté. Could there still be merit in a statesman's studying geometry? Possibly. Not for some straight transition from the Idea of a Square to the Idea of Justice; but rather for what a man learns about objectivity, clarity, and consistency, in a system of proof like geometry. The reasoner is caught in a system; he is led by the interconnections of ideas. Propositions, like the internal angle sum of a triangle, come out certain ways whether he likes it or not. In a fundamental sense, geometry is not a subject of debate and opinion, as are war and peace, or good and evil. Geometry is a matter

---

[15] In Plato's *Laws*, which is said to be his last work, Plato writes about the second-best state, not the best state as in *The Republic*, and the more traditional view of justice as a function of law and the law court is restored.

of objective knowledge if anything is. Could it be, then, that it is profitable for the statesman to be reared first in sure and undebatable subjects before he goes on to the great debatable moral problems of life? Could it be that the habit of objectivity so cultivated can be useful in those areas where objectivity is most difficult to attain?[16] There is no surety that this will be so. But Plato does seem to feel there is hope in the attempt. What would happen if men approached matters like civil rights, socialism and capitalism, labor and management, and international relations with greater objectivity than they do?

Ideas and the Arts

What relevance does Plato's doctrine of Ideas have to the arts? If it is true that this doctrine is central to Plato's philosophy, it would seem that there should be some connection, and there is. But the nature of this relationship is confused. For Plato, the master artist of the dialogue form in philosophy, on the one hand relegates the arts to a very low order of appearance and opinion, but on the other hand he finds in the arts a way to ultimate reality and truth. Whether these apparently conflicting views can be reconciled is a problem in Platonic scholarship beyond the scope of this book.[17] But the basis of both his criticism and his praise of the arts is important for our study of Plato's concern for the traditional morality as well as his conception of knowledge. Three aspects of his treatment of the arts will be considered: art and truth, art and morality, and the Idea of Beauty.

ART AND TRUTH. Many artists and their supporters have been troubled by Plato's denigration of art in some of his works. In *The Republic*, Plato describes art as a form of representation or imitation (*mimesis*). The artist paints a representation of a physical bed, which in turn is a representation or copy of the Ideal Bed. The painting is thus a "third remove" from reality.[18] Poetry is no different from painting in this respect. The poet, in describing the just act of a man, provides at best a representation of the just act, which itself is a copy of the Idea of Justice. The poem, too, is a third remove from reality. A painting, a statue, a poem—any object of art—thus has only the appearance of reality. The work of art by its very nature cannot be true being.

Neither can painting, poetry, or the other arts be forms of knowledge, nor can they possess truth as mathematics can. The mathematician is con-

---

[16] For this interpretation, debt is owed to F. J. E. Woodbridge's *The Son of Apollo* (Boston: Houghton Mifflin, 1929), a book of great charm and wisdom.

[17] For an elaborate study see Rupert C. Lodge, *Plato's Theory of Art* (London, The Humanities Press Inc., 1953).

[18] *The Republic*, 595–602.

cerned directly with the universal Ideas, although he may draw triangles as an aid to his thinking. The painter draws an image of a particular wooden bed, itself not the true object of knowledge; hence the painter's world is the world of physical things, which leaves him only in the realm of opinion where truth cannot reside. Thus the artist spends his time with playthings of the senses instead of the hard realities and truths of the mind.

Moreover, the mathematician can prove quite clearly what he knows, while the artist cannot tell how he produced what he does. The artist creates as if in a frenzy, as if possessed by a divine madness.[19] His works in turn can lead us to frenzy; they can make us laugh or cry. The artists' world is the world of the feelings, not of the mind. We do not think with our feelings. In fact, it sometimes seems that the more we feel the less we think; the more passionate we become, the less rational we are.

Plato's indictment continues. In spite of the remoteness of their works from reality and truth, artists, he says, fraudulently claim a remarkable virtuosity of knowledge. Poets, for example, write about everything under the sun as if they know what they are writing about. But if a man needs to learn warfare, should he go to Homer or to a soldier? If a man needs to know how to construct a bed, should he go to a painter or to a carpenter? At best the artist is but a dilettante in the range of things he covers. His knowledge is poor in comparison with craftsmen who make things, and cannot compare with those who have grasped the Ideas in any field. Plato sums up his estimate of the artist by saying:

. . . the artist knows nothing worth mentioning about the subjects he represents, and . . . art is a form of play, not to be taken seriously. This description, moreover, applies above all to tragic poetry, whether in epic or dramatic form.[20]

Arguments like these occur frequently in Plato, leaving the arts low in the scale of knowledge and truth, and suspect as to their fitness for the good society. The issue that Plato raises is serious. It is the issue not only of the nature of art, but also from another approach, of the nature of knowledge, truth, and existence. If knowledge consists only of the grasp of Ideas, quite obviously a painting with all its sensuous individuality, is not an Idea, and therefore the painting cannot be knowledge. But one might retort to Plato, "Since you like mathematics so much as an example of knowledge, neither is the mathematical symbol '2' knowledge, in its sensuous particularity. Thus cannot a painting be *symbolic* of an Idea as directly as the symbol '2' of the Idea of Two? It is not at all clear why a painter's copy of the Idea of a Bed is further removed from the Idea than the carpenter's. The painter has slept on a bed and can grasp the Idea as well as the carpenter." To take a less trivial example, in the sensuous particularity of Shakespeare's *Othello* can one not be led to a closer grasp of

---

[19] *Ion*, 533–534.
[20] *The Republic*, 602, trans. by Cornford, *op. cit.*, p. 333

the Idea of Jealousy in all its evil connotations than by being jealous of one's own wife? If understanding and knowledge are the issue, it seems preferable to read Shakespeare than to be jealous. Thus, it is not obvious that the arts are a less satisfactory way of leading men to a grasp of universals than other means. In some instances, they may be the best way.

There are those who say that the objections to Plato's representational theory of art are even more serious than the criticism just made. They attack the entire range of Plato's views on knowledge, truth, and existence. The fault, they contend, is initially in Plato's theory of Ideas. How can the desiccated Ideas, stripped of the living moment and the vividness of immediate experience be reality? The immediately existent is the real. The only knowledge that possesses reality is knowledge of the moment. The function of art, therefore, is to capture this sort of authentic existence. The work of art is not symbolic of anything. It is its own moment of truth. To test art against an Idea or to make it representative of an Idea is meaningless. This kind of approach to art has numerous defenders in the contemporary world.

ART AND MORALITY. Even if Plato's views on art and truth were rebutted (no claim is made here that the rebuttal has been adequate), it would still be necessary to examine his requirement that the arts subserve the moral purposes of the community. The problem is simply this: should the artist be free to create as he sees fit, both as to the subject matter of his art and his modes of expression, or must he conform to the accepted ideals of the social order as interpreted by some controlling power or agency? In short, is it right for the community to censor art on moral grounds?

In *The Republic* Plato's answer is in the affirmative, and his answer always breeds controversy because of the severity of control that he advocates. He takes the greatest literature of Greece, from Homer to the tragic poets, and would mold it all to serve the purposes of the city-state. It must be purged of all suggestions of immorality. The gods of the traditional religion can be portrayed only as good and as living exemplary lives, the heroes only as noble and brave with never a suggestion of cowardice or other weakness. Even musical accompaniment is to be cleansed. Sensuous music is forbidden as seductive; only that which is appropriate to brave men is approved because it enhances courage. The notion that an artist might explore the development of an art form for its intrinsic quality is forbidden. The question that must remain foremost is the art form's moral effect, not merely its aesthetic effect.

Why is Plato this restrictive? His answer is very simple and clear. Art educates men, and because of this educative function, it must be watched with great care. Excellence of content, grace, and harmony of form affect character. In turn, they can be produced only by artists of good character. Not only must the artist's works be exemplary but the artist's life as well.

So, if our young men are to do their proper work in life, they must follow after these qualities wherever they may be found. And they are to be found in every sort of workmanship, such as painting, weaving, embroidery, architecture, the making of furniture; and also in the human frame and in all the works of nature: in all these grace and seemliness may be present or absent. And the absence of grace, rhythm, harmony is nearly allied to baseness of thought and expression and baseness of character; whereas their presence goes with that moral excellence and self-mastery of which they are the embodiment.[21]

Every aspect of art, therefore, must be watched, from religious poetry to household furniture; for art possesses a great power in the lives of men. Because it has this power, it is a legitimate concern of the state.

The critic might argue that Plato grossly exaggerates the power of art. Plato would welcome a continuation of that argument, leaning on his view that art is concerned with the emotions and not with the mind. The poet is a man of deep feeling, and his work sweeps us up in a flood of emotion. What man could deny this, Plato would urge, who had ever seen a great tragedy? The poetic utterance:

. . . waters the growth of the passions which should be allowed to wither away and sets them up in control, although the goodness and happiness of our lives depend on their being held in subjection. . . . We can admit into our commonwealth only the poetry which celebrates the praises of the gods and of good men. If you go further and admit the honeyed muse in epic or in lyric verse, then pleasure and pain will usurp the sovereignty of law and of the principles always recognized by common consent as the best.[22]

Here lies, Plato argues, the great problem with the arts. They loose streams of passions. It is obvious from the earlier discussion of Plato's ethics that for him one of the supreme problems of man's moral life, perhaps the supreme problem, is the ascendancy of reason over the passions and the appetites. Thus, if the arts subvert this ascendancy, they must be purified in the interest of the good life.

How is Plato to be answered? Granting Plato the power of art and its educative function, there are those who would argue that the arts help to purify men's feelings rather than to aggravate them. Aristotle suggests that tragedy, of which Plato at times was so distrustful, purges men of pity and fear rather than making them more pitiful and fearful. Plato did raise in a significant way, it is to be admitted, the problem of the psychological effects of the arts; but his analysis can be taken only as opening the problem.

A critic could also suggest that Plato unwarrantedly restricts the very educative function of art by confining its subject matter to promoting good and suppressing evil. Evil and ugliness are inescapable in life. Will not those youths who have been reared only on the good and the beautiful

---

[21] *Ibid.*, 400–401, pp. 89–90.
[22] *Ibid.*, 606–607, pp. 338–339.

be overwhelmed when they finally meet evil and ugliness? How will they be able to bear tragedy if they understand nothing about it? Reared only in the aseptic atmosphere of the good, will they not be the first to be infected with evil when they finally are confronted with it?

The problem of censorship of the arts is present in every society. The dialogue is endless. Plato made a plausible argument for control in the interest of goodness and beauty. His argument, however, as shown by his own contrasting views in other works, was in no sense conclusive, even for himself.

THE IDEA OF BEAUTY.   After one finds the poets censured in *The Republic* and the scope of their works severely limited, it comes as a surprise to read in the *Symposium*, "Who, when he thinks of Homer and Hesiod and other great poets, would not rather have their children than ordinary human ones?"[23] There is no indication in the *Symposium* that Plato wrote the dialogue primarily to recant what he said elsewhere against the arts. The dialogue is rather about love and beauty. It is about the power of love as a passion, and how it may be transformed from something worldly to something divine, from the physical to the Ideal. In this respect the *Symposium* might be quite in accord with Plato's ethical works, in that the powerful passion of love is to be controlled, through a transformation to a desire for the ideal. It may be correct to take the *Symposium* in this way, but in so doing, we should note that the arts come off much better than they do in other works of Plato, such as *The Republic*.

For now art is a way to the ultimate reality—the Idea of Beauty. But how can art be the way or Beauty be this reality, since once we learned that the ultimate reality is the Good? Remarkable things happen in the *Symposium*. Art is rehabilitated as a way to reality and truth, but, perhaps more astonishingly—or should it be—philosophy itself is said to be a form of love, as its name *philos* (love) suggests. The philosopher, too, is a lover—a lover of wisdom. He has a desire, a longing, a passion for the wisdom he does not have. No god is a philosopher, a seeker of wisdom, for a god is already wise.[24] It is only for fallible man that philosophy has any meaning. Can philosophy be passion, when passion seemed formerly to thwart philosophy? Moreover, what has mathematics, which seems so remote from passion, to do now with becoming a philosopher? Could it be that there is more than one way to become a philosopher, to pursue wisdom, to make one's pilgrimage in life to the ideal? Mathematics and the other sciences are certainly one way. Could there be other ways? The *Symposium* suggests that there are, the arts for one.

---

[23] 209, *The Dialogues of Plato*, B. Jowett trans. (New York: Random House, 1937), Vol. I, p. 333.
[24] *Symposium*, 203.

To find one's way to the Idea of Beauty—to mount Plato's Ladder of Love, as it has been called—a man should visit beautiful forms and come to love one. But these are not the Forms, the Ideas. They are very physical forms: a woman, a statue, a painting—any physical object that is called beautiful. This love should be the stimulus to fair thoughts. The lover should come to love other physical forms, and to see that the beauty of one physical form is like the beauty of another, and so on until he finds that beauty in physical objects is everywhere the same. From this rung of the ladder he sees that the beauty of the mind is preferable to that of the physical forms. The lover is now beyond the arts, to be sure, but they have helped him upward. Now he begins to see the beauty of institutions and laws. Mounting even higher, he comes to find the beauty in the sciences, and finally he mounts to the Idea of Beauty itself, which, once beheld, brings forth realities and true virtue.[25] The arts, which once seemed to thrust a man away from reality, virtue, and truth, have now impelled him toward them.

The Idea of Beauty is the first principle of existence and virtue viewed, perhaps one might say, from the perspective of the arts, but not this alone. For there is beauty even in a mathematical proof as there is in a statue. The emphasis is upon the harmonies and orders in things and ideas which, Plato would say, stir men and move them deeply. We want for words and call this characteristic the *aesthetic* aspect of things, which is simply a word of Greek origin meaning what Plato is referring to, the fitness of their existence. Some men are so moved and so perceptive that they are carried on to see this fitness, order, harmony in all things physical or of the mind. This fitness is in the most abstract knowledge as well as in concrete things. It is also, in the realm of morals, the essence of virtue. It is the ultimate nature of existence itself; for without this fitness, things could not even be. There is a unity and a harmony to existence which from one perspective is its goodness, from another its truth, from a third its beauty. The Trinity of the Good, the True, and the Beautiful—another trinity of great power and appeal in the Western tradition—receives in Plato its initial and classic expression.

Platonic Idealism, A Summary

Plato has cast a spell in every age on men of the Western tradition. His philosophy, as a statement of the ideal possibilities of existence, is the source, as noted before, of one of the main streams of philosophic reflection in the West—the philosophy of Idealism. In summary, to what have men returned to Plato's philosophy again and again for inspiration and guidance as they have reflected upon man and his place in nature?

---

[25] *Ibid.*, 210–212.

The universe is a logical order or structure. This order is the being of the universe in its most fundamental sense. Nature is a panorama of change, of particular things coming into being and passing away; but this change is dependent upon a structure which in itself is eternal and invariant. Plato describes this structure as a realm of Ideas. Whether one looks upon this realm as separate from things or immanent in them, the order discovered in nature is dependent upon the Ideas.

The logical order of the universe is accessible to man's reason. Man can know this order. In Plato's language, man can know the Ideas. The universe is no alien mystery. To be sure, man is not omniscient and very likely will never be. The order is intricate and vast. But the order is there, discoverable.

Man's knowledge is objective, real, true, and certain. The objects of knowledge are elements or aspects of the order of nature. The Ideas are not in men's minds, a view which arose to plague the empiricial philosophers in the seventeenth century and later. Knowledge is objective, not subjective. Thus there is not the problem of the reality of knowledge that confronted, say, John Locke, one of the modern empiricists. (See pp. 242 ff.). When the Ideas are grasped, this is what truth is. Knowledge is certain in the way that knowledge of mathematics is certain.

The order of the universe is a moral order. Again and again Plato finds the order of the universe to be its essential nature and capable of being known. But it is also a good order. The first principle of all existence and all knowledge is called Good.

The good life for man consists in discovering this order of nature and living a rationally ordered life in accordance with it. Reason, knowledge, rational control are primary in Plato's ethics, and they are primary in many subsequent idealistic philosophies. Plato was fully aware of the irrationalities in the lives of men. He knew the power of the passions. He would not suppress them. He was no ascetic. He would transform them. Love, for example, is a passion which can be overwhelming. It is a power in men's lives, not to be denied, but to be transformed into the love of the Ideal.

The order of nature is also a realm of beauty. There is beauty in the bloom of youth and loveliness in many physical things, and these instances of beauty come from the order and harmony in nature. But physical beauty fades. There is a higher beauty in the harmony and order of things which does not pass away. If men could ever achieve immortality, it would be in this way—to see the beauty and goodness of the Ideal that is the order and existence of all things.

Selected Readings

Demos, Raphael, *The Philosophy of Plato*, New York: Scribner, 1939.

Lodge, Rupert Clendon, *The Philosophy of Plato*, London: Routledge, 1956.

Plato, *The Dialogues of Plato*, trans. by B. Jowett, New York: Random House, 1937, 2 vols. (There are many paperback editions of individual dialogues.)

Ross, Sir David, *Plato's Theory of Ideas*, Oxford at the Clarendon Press, 1951.

Taylor, Alfred Edward, *Plato, The Man and His Work*, New York: Meridian, 1956.

Windelband, W., *History of Ancient Philosophy*, New York: Dover, 1956, pp. 174–223.

Woodbridge, Frederick James Eugene, *The Son of Apollo; Themes of Plato*, Boston: Houghton Mifflin, 1929.

CHAPTER 6

Aristotle
and
Nature

In the high tradition, philosophy is a persistent attempt to bring order into the various aspects of experience and knowledge, to resolve conflicts between science and accepted beliefs. In some cases the philosophers have been philosopher-scientists, at once extending the bounds of human knowledge and responding to the need for interpreting it—and interpreting the folklore with which it clashes in order to effect a reconciliation. Aristotle was one of those rare geniuses who both extended scientific knowledge and made this new knowledge central to his philosophy. In doing so, he corrected and modified the direction given to Greek philosophy by the Sophists and by Plato, as well as by the earlier cosmologists.

In its early period, Greek philosophers were much more absorbed with the world around man than with man himself. The Sophists redirected this focus of attention, and were, on the whole, little interested in the natural world. Socrates also busied himself with moral questions to the neglect of the physical universe. With Plato and the Platonists and their concentration on the Forms, it seems that "philosophy has become mathematics for the moderns" and "the study of nature has been abolished."

These comments about Socrates and Plato are judgments made by Aristotle in his *Metaphysics*,[1] which criticize the direction philosophy had been taking in neglecting, as he sees it, the study of nature. Aristotle's own philosophy would provide a corrective. He would not ignore mathematics, nor would he ignore man's moral and social concerns. His *Nicomachean Ethics* and his *Politics* evidence his interest in the latter concerns and are enviable contributions to ethical and political theory. But above all he would revive the attention of philosophers to the natural world.

There was something definitely wrong in what had happened in philosophy, especially in Platonism, he felt. Aristotle himself was profoundly influenced by Plato and acknowledged that influence. But, as his own thought developed, he became more and more disturbed that Plato's philosophy in effect made the sun, the moon, the stars, the mountains, the sea—the world we experience—a shadow of an Ideal world, and provided no genuine understanding of the existence of this world. What has been accomplished, he asks, if ". . . in the belief that we are accounting for their substance [visible things], we assert the existence of other substances [the Ideas]; but as to *how* the latter are the substances of the former, our explanation is worthless—for 'participation,' as we have said before, means nothing"?[2] The niceties and certainties of mathematics had bewitched philosophers into believing that its objects were the real world. The next thing men knew was that the world around them was unreal. There was something absurd about this sort of theory: to begin with the world of our experience and then, in understanding it, to lose it. Would it not be more profitable for philosophers to return to nature, to learn all that they could about it on their own and from the natural scientists, and then formulate their theories about the universe and men? Even their moral and political reflections might be more judicious if they better understood both man himself and the natural context in which his life must be lived. Aristotle would attend primarily to the world, including human concerns, and only secondarily to purely formal things—especially those dissociated from nature. Accordingly, attention would be given to logic, but it would be logic as discourse (the study of how men talk sensibly) and it would be related to rhetoric (the art of persuasion).

Logic as Sensible and Careful Talking

Aristotle was born into a philosophic tradition that, by the time of his maturity, was two and a half centuries old. The philosophic problems presented to him had been molded by the Greek folklore, the character of Greek science, and the reflections of the preceding philosophers. Aristotle

---

[1] 992a32–33.

[2] *Metaphysics*, 992a26–29, trans. by Tredennick (Cambridge: Harvard, 1936), p. 75.

was conscious of the historical background of his problems. His typical approach to a subject matter was to review and to examine critically the theories of his predecessors. Among the philosophers before him, especially since the Sophists, there had been an increasing attention to language—its nature, its place in our thinking, and its function in science. Aristotle's interest, too, was drawn to these problems. He was indebted to the work of the Sophists, to Socrates and Plato. It was he, however, who made a series of systematic studies leading to what we call "logic." In Aristotle's terms, logic is an empirical study of types of discourse, study, one might say, in sensible and careful talking. What is it that a person can assert without talking nonsense? For if what he says is self-contradictory, he does talk nonsense. Aristotle set himself to discover this, and although he began at a simple, empirical level, he soon was led to high-degree abstractions.

The empirical level had already been exhibited in the Greek folklore, in the intense concern of the Greeks with persuading, arguing, debating, discussing—in short with the varieties of verbal pursuits which were so much a part of their public life. Consequently, when Aristotle wrote his *Art of Rhetoric*, he had available to him a century of discussion and written manuals on the art of persuasion. As noted before, this art was so important to the Greeks that, by Aristotle's day, discussions of rhetoric were more a part of the folklore than technical concerns of philosophy. They had very much taken on the character of the twentieth-century how-to-win-friends manual. Aristotle's book is of this order. It is known in the history of rhetoric as one of the best and most thorough in the Greek period. Its enormous historical influence is attributable to these qualities and to his added insistence that the good speaker should have ethical and political intelligence as well as technical facility, that is, he should have something to say. Here, his *Rhetoric* is worth noting to see the level which works on persuasive discourse had reached in Aristotle's day. Studies in the art of persuasion had provided a considerable base upon which to build a more general and sophisticated analysis of the nature and function of language.

Aristotle's logical works—*Categories, On Interpretation, Prior Analytics, Posterior Analytics, Topics,* and *Sophistic Refutations* or *Fallacies*—are collectively called the Organon, the "instrument." Although the *Sophistic Refutations* is placed last among his logical works in the standard edition of Aristotle, it was one of his early studies. It is an analysis of some of the commonest types of fallacies to which men fall prey. Aristotle is the first to classify types of fallacies and to point out clearly the source of the errors. Several kinds hinge upon the ambiguity of a word. In the argument—"The end of life is the perfection of life. Death is the end of life. Therefore, death is the perfection of life." The word "end" is obviously ambiguous, meaning in the first instance "purpose or goal," in the second, "termination"; and the argument fails because of this ambiguity. Aristotle also identified other types of fallacies not dependent upon ambiguity. His survey is a classic. Although his particular classification has been improved upon, many of his distinctions are still taught to college students in beginning courses of logic. The value of the *Sophistic Refutations* is both practical and theoretical. It is, of course, useful in the ongoing arguments from day to day to avoid mistakes of one's own, and to avoid being hoodwinked by the errors of others. Its theoretical value lies in our becoming sensitive to the subtle ways in which arguments seem to prove but do not. But the detection of ambiguities, and other types of confusions in arguments, still does not provide positive canons by which a proof—or, in the more technical language of the logicians, a valid argument—can be determined. It remained for Aristotle in his other logical works to determine standards for proof itself.

In Aristotle's studies of proof, two of his major contributions will be examined: his theory of the syllogism, which is developed in the *Prior Analytics*, and his theory of the nature of a demonstrative science, which is found in the *Posterior Analytics*.

THE THEORY OF THE SYLLOGISM. Aristotle defines "syllogism" as follows:

A syllogism is discourse in which, certain things being stated, something other than what is stated follows of necessity from their being so. I mean by the last phrase that they produce the consequence, and by this, that no further term is required from without in order to make the consequence necessary.[3]

Thus, if it is stated that "All mammals are vertebrates," and "All dogs are mammals," we must conclude that "All dogs are vertebrates." From the first two statements or propositions, called the premises of the argument, the third, which is the conclusion, follows of necessity, from the first two being what they are.

The syllogism is seen to be an argument—in the technical sense of "argument" in logic, not a dispute in which individuals are angry with one another—consisting of three propositions, which contain among them three and only three terms. In this instance, the terms are "vertebrates," "mammals," and "dogs." A necessary connection between "dogs" and "vertebrates" is established through "mammals," which is called the middle term since it is common to the two premises. Of course, syllogisms may contain negative propositions, as in the case: If "No mammals are invertebrates," and "All dogs are mammals," then "No dogs are invertebrates."

After the initial discovery of the syllogism the great achievement of the *Prior Analytics* is its exploration of the possible *forms* of argument that

---

[3] *Analytica Priora* [*Prior Analytics*], 24b18–22, trans. by A. J. Jenkinson (London: Oxford, 1928).

the syllogism can take. The crucial notion is the formal structure of arguments, for instead of using terms like "dogs," "mammals," and "vertebrates," we may use merely symbols for terms with specific meanings and say: If "All B are C," and "All A are B," then "All A are C," where A, B, and C are variables in which substitutions can be made to provide specific syllogisms. The syllogism just described, using variables, is said to be one form of the syllogism. There are other forms, for example, the one using a negative proposition cited previously: If "No B are C," and "All A are B," then "No A are C." There are still other possible forms which Aristotle examined to discover which are valid, that is, those in which the conclusion follows necessarily, and those invalid, in which this is not the case. For example: If "All cats are vertebrates," and "All dogs are vertebrates," then it does not follow that "All dogs are cats." In other words, the logical form, If "All C are B," and "All A are B," then "All A are C," is an invalid or incorrect logical form or argument.

The power of this kind of analysis is that for every valid or invalid logical form, there is an indefinite number of specific arguments or substitution instances. Thus, when Aristotle proves the validity of some forms and the invalidity of others, he is, in effect, proving the validity or invalidity of countless numbers of specific arguments.

Aside from the power of symbolic analysis (which is exhibited even more dramatically in modern logic and mathematics in their greatly expanded forms), the value of Aristotle's work lay in determining the conditions of proof for certain kinds of argument—those which would fit into the syllogistic form. There are many kinds of argument which will not fit into syllogistic form, but Aristotle broke ground in showing what proof can mean and what it can be outside the realm of geometry, the only area of knowledge in which proof was systematically used and exhibited at that time. In a word, there can be careful talking, very precise talking as a matter of fact, outside mathematics.

Considering syllogisms from the standpoint of subject matter and not the formal structure of the arguments, Aristotle distinguished two kinds relevant to our discussion, dialectical and demonstrative. Dialectical syllogisms are arguments or instances of reasoning based upon opinions that are generally accepted, that is, accepted by everyone or by the majority, or by the wise.[4] An example of an opinion, accepted by all or most people would be, "The skilled man is the best at his task." Opinions of the wise (by which Aristotle seems to mean the philosophers) can also be used in dialectical syllogisms, such as, Heraclitus' "All things change." When dialectical reasoning is used correctly, the logical consequence of propositions can be obtained. This sort of exploration helps to determine the meaning of the propositions. Furthermore, it is a way of seeing whether the

---

[4] *Topics*, 100b21–22.

propositions lead to contradictory conclusions. It should be noted that, although most of Socrates' arguments were not in Aristotle's syllogistic form, the intent of Socrates' critical examination of commonly accepted opinions seems very much the same as Aristotle's intention for his dialectical syllogisms. On the other hand, the purpose of Aristotle's dialectical syllogisms is quite different from that of Plato's dialectic in *The Republic*, which would begin with the foundations of the sciences and mount to the first principle of all knowledge.

In Aristotle's discussion of dialectical syllogisms, it is clear that talking is becoming ever more precise. It is now appropriate to turn to the most precise talking of all—that found in demonstrative syllogisms that determine a demonstrative science.

THE NATURE OF A DEMONSTRATIVE SCIENCE. (The model of a demonstrative science which Aristotle had before him was geometry; and it is well to keep this model in mind as the discussion develops.) The distinction between a demonstrative science and dialectical reasoning is not in the use of the forms of the syllogism—for each may employ precisely the same logical forms—but in the nature of the premises. A demonstrative science does not begin with opinions, however well accepted, as dialectical reasoning does. It uses premises only that are *true* and *primary*, or propositions which have been derived syllogistically from true and primary premises. It is the character of the premises that makes the difference; hence the nature of these premises requires examination.

Any demonstrative science, says Aristotle, must begin with premises which are true and primary. They must also be the reasons for the conclusions; and they must be better known and prior to the conclusions. Such premises are sometimes called "first principles." The principles must be true, for the nonexistent cannot be known. Thus, that the diagonal of a square is commensurable with its side cannot be a first principle because this proposition is false. These principles are primary and cannot themselves be demonstrated. Any demonstrative science must begin with some undemonstrated propositions like the axioms of geometry; otherwise one is led into an infinite regress. In other words, demonstrative proof cannot be demanded of every proposition. The basic principles constitute the reasons for the demonstrated conclusions; they are the reasons that the conclusions cannot be other than they are. The principles are prior and better known, but prior and better known in a special sense. They are logically prior and better known, rather than being psychologically so. The first principles of Euclidean geometry were not laid down first historically with all the demonstrated propositions unfolding subsequently in proper order. The organizing principles come late; but they are logically prior, for the system depends upon them.

Some first principles are common to more than one science, for example, the equality axioms are common to geometry and arithmetic; and there are also logical first principles, like the law of contradiction, which are first principles for all demonstrative knowledge whatsoever. But every demonstrative science also has first principles applicable to it and it alone—principles concerning magnitude for geometry, and number for arithmetic—and these mark off each science from the other sciences. Thus, when Plato wished to derive by dialectic the first principles of the sciences from the Good, he asked for the impossible. (See pp. 88 ff.) At best, he could have been seeking a common axiom, as Aristotle calls it, like the law of contradiction; but from this general notion the foundations peculiar to geometry cannot be established.

How, then, are the first principles known? As noted, they cannot be demonstrated. They are immediately known, that is, not through the mediation of other propositions as in demonstration. They are known by induction, which Aristotle describes as follows:[5] Induction is a power of the mind which begins with sensation. The objects of sensation are particular things. We have memory of our sensations and their objects, and from memories of the same thing an experience results. (Experience is a kind of crude, first level universal.) Out of experiences develop the skill of the craftsman and the knowledge of the scientist, that is the universal or the principle is "seen" intellectually in the experiences, that is, in the concrete individual objects of experience and their relationships. The capacity involved is *nous*, insight, a power that men have to see the universal in things.

For example, a man may use a scale, a balance, from day to day; and in each case, when he adds equal quantities to equal quantities to find the sums in balance, he has a series of individual perceptions of equality. The memory of these perceptions constitutes an experience; and the man may come to expect the scale to balance when equal quantities are added to equal quantities, without seeing the universality and necessity of the principle involved. When he "sees" this intellectual principle, "if equals be added to equals, the sums are equal,"—sees that it holds, not just for balances with potatoes and apples but for equal quantities irrespective of kind of thing and even without reference to a balance—he has grasped or seen the universal principle. He has seen the universal exemplified, embodied, implicit in particular things.

Aristotle's view of demonstrative science looks very much like Plato's ideal of knowledge, in certain respects. Demonstrative science is true, universal, and necessary; so is Plato's knowledge. Both find *nous*, insight, a power of the mind which is essential for grasping the indubitable foundations of knowledge. Aristotle, however, rejects the Forms, not only here in

---

[5] *Posterior Analytics*, II, chap. 19.

the *Posterior Analytics*,[6] but elsewhere. This rejection implies a different view of the nature of universals, which will be discussed later with reference to his *Metaphysics*. Aristotle points out that in effect there is not Science with a capital "S," but sciences. The sciences can have unities, one might say, in common logical and mathematical notions or axioms; but, so far as we know, each science must have principles appropriate to its subject matter. For Aristotle, there is an inevitable pluralism in knowledge which Plato either forgot or wished to transcend. Like Plato, Aristotle is concerned with describing an ideal science, which is his demonstrative science. Such an ideal is the most systematic talking which man can do. How closely can it be approached? In geometry it had been achieved. How closely in the investigations of other aspects of nature, the heavens, things of the earth, living things, for example? It is interesting to note how Aristotle himself pursued his own investigations of living things in seeking an answer to these questions.

Aristotle and Living Things

Had Aristotle not written a word of philosophy, he would be remembered in the history of thought for his biological studies. He has been called the father of biology. No less a biologist than Darwin could say, "Linnaeus and Cuvier have been my two gods, though in very different ways, but they were mere schoolboys to old Aristotle."[7] Aristotle would urge philosophers to return to the study of nature, not simply in terms of what they could learn from the natural scientists, but also to conduct their own investigations. His interest in the natural world was encyclopedic, but obviously his first love was for living things, the phenomenon of life. He wrote more about living things than about any other subject, philosophic or otherwise. He was not a philosopher turned dilettante scientist. He looks more like a natural scientist turned philosopher.

What meaning, then, did his study of living things have for philosophy? Is there something about understanding the principles of life which gives a turn to a philosophy different from that provoked by the principles of mathematics? In an effort to answer these questions, certain of Aristotle's key biological concepts will be developed and then explored for their general philosophic significance.

Aristotle's *Inquiries about Animals*, his longest book, is a large collection of facts about the animal kingdom which he had made from many sources and to which he had added his own considerable and sometimes remarkable observations. It is not a theoretical book. Its purpose is to

---

[6] 77a5.

[7] From a letter to William Ogle, 1882, *The Life and Letters of Charles Darwin*, ed. by Francis Darwin (New York: Appleton, 1891), Vol. II, p. 427.

record the structural and functional characteristics of animals and to organize these data. A classification of the animal kingdom is present. Aristotle took the common-sense classification of animals which had evolved over the ages and refined it in terms of more accurate observation and discrimination. He arranged classes in the order of genus and species; and he recognized the relativity of these terms, in that a species at one level is a genus at another. He determined new classes and created terminology of his own, names that we translate as "Insects," "Crustaceans," and "Testaceans." The controlling power of the data is everywhere present. He opposed oversimplified classification schemes, which may be pretty from a logical point of view but are largely irrelevant to the complexities of animal life.[8] Perhaps no better illustration can be found of Aristotle's consciousness of the difficulties involved in the classification and study of living things than in the following passage:

> Nature proceeds little by little from things lifeless to animal life in such a way that it is impossible to determine the exact line of demarcation, nor on which side thereof an intermediate form should lie. Thus, next after lifeless things in the upward scale comes the plant, and of plants one will differ from another as to its amount of apparent vitality; and, in a word, the whole genus of plants, whilst it is devoid of life as compared with an animal, is endowed with life as compared with other corporeal entities. Indeed, as we just remarked, there is observed in plants a continuous scale of ascent toward the animal. So, in the sea, there are certain objects concerning which one would be at a loss to determine whether they be animal or vegetable. For instance, certain of these objects are fairly rooted, and in several cases perish if detached; thus the pinna is rooted to a particular spot, and the solen (or razor-shell) cannot survive withdrawal from its burrow. Indeed, broadly speaking, the entire genus of testaceans have a resemblance to vegetables, if they be contrasted with such animals as are capable of progression.[9]

The *Inquiries* is a far cry from the elevated notion of a demonstrative science found in the *Posterior Analytics*. As a man begins to dig into the complexities of the animate world, the pure, rarefied, and systematic world of logic and mathematics may seem remote indeed. As a matter of fact, in none of Aristotle's investigations of animate or inanimate things of the natural world does he produce a systematic body of knowledge answering to the criteria of the *Posterior Analytics*. Demonstrative science is an ideal of science which was exemplified in geometry, and possibly arithmetic, but nowhere else. In fact, when it comes to living things, Aristotle turns away from the *Posterior Analytics* and asks, in effect, the humbler but more

---

[8] See his vigorous criticism of the logical device of dichotomous division as a basis for classifying animals in *On the Parts of Animals*, 642b5 ff.

[9] *Historia Animalium* [*Inquiries about Animals*], 588b4–23, trans. by D'Arcy Wentworth Thompson (Oxford at the Clarendon Press, 1910).

pertinent question, "How should living things be studied?" And this question brings us to his theoretical biology, to methodological questions about the study of living things and some of his resulting views.

There are three general characteristics of living things which strike Aristotle as most fundamental to their existence as living things: their patterns of development; the unity of their structures; and the complex of their functions or, perhaps, one could simply say, their functions. Living things perpetuate themselves in kinds or species, with characteristic patterns of reproduction and growth. They have a unity of structure which has come to be called organic. If this unity is disrupted, the organisms die. Life seems pre-eminently exemplified in activity, function. In his typical, dry, matter-of-fact fashion, Aristotle comments that the difference between a dead hand and a live hand is that a dead hand cannot do the work of a live hand. It simply cannot function, and thus is a hand in name only.

How, then, should these characteristics, which are basic to the existence of living things, be studied? Or, one might ask, what are the most significant questions which, if answered, will provide knowledge of living things? Aristotle considers this problem in detail in Book I of On the Parts of Animals.

In characteristic fashion, Aristotle reviews the work of his predecessors. The early philosophers and scientists were interested in the materials of which an organ or an entire animal is composed. They asked: What is it made of? The answer to this question for an organ like the hand is found in terms of blood, flesh, sinews, and so on. Beyond this kind of answer, for want of chemistry, little could be done, except to make a speculative appeal to the role of the so-called four elements, earth, air, fire, and water, in an attempt to explain how living things are constituted. Aristotle agrees with the early investigators that the question is an imporant one for understanding an organ or a total organism. What is it made of?

A second important question is: What started the process of development? Again, this question can be asked of a specific organ or a total organism. For a total organism, this is the question of reproduction, a subject to which Aristotle devoted an entire work.

The questions thus far are important, but there are others which may provide even more significant knowledge. A dog and a cat may be composed of the same elements, but a dog is not a cat. There is the form or structure of an organism which, when known, provides knowledge that characerizes the organism better than either the materials or the process of generation. Whether one is concerned with an organ like the heart or a total organism, it seems essential to know the structure. Moreover, an organism is a structure of structures, a form composed of many forms, tightly interrelated such that if it is seriously disrupted, the organism perishes.

But gross anatomy is not enough. A dead man is a man in name only. Structures do things. They function, both the structures of individual organs and total organisms. Thus another very important question, perhaps the most important question of all, is: *What does the organ do?* What are the functions of the organism? This last question may actually be primary for understanding. To use an analogy, when we see a strange inanimate instrument lying before us, we ask, "What's it for? What does it do?" And when we learn this, we think we know in an especially important way that we did not know before. There it lies before us, the instrument, and perhaps we see much of its structure. But until we know what it does, what it is for, we do not think we know what it is. And so with the structure of any organ or organism, we think that we know, that we understand, when we know the use, the function, *the for what*, as Aristotle puts it.

These four basic questions and the answers to them are four *aitia*, as Aristotle calls them, of any living thing. They are the four factors essential to the existence of an organism: the materials of which it is composed, the agent or agency which started its development, its structure or form, and its function or functions. (The last might be called its form as function or functional form.) Aristotle's theory concerning these factors as fundamental to the existence of a living thing and to an understanding of that existence has been called his doctrine of the *four causes*: the *material cause*; the *efficient cause* (that which initiates the process of development); the *formal cause* (the structural form); and the *final cause* (the function). It should be apparent that designating Aristotle's theory as a theory of causes is a most unfortunate appellation. (Cicero can be thanked for this unhappy locution.) The difficulty lies in the meaning of "cause," which is a later designation, not Aristotle's. "Cause" has many meanings, but one of the most frequent is that of an agent or force which does something. For example, when one moving billiard ball hits a second which moves, it is said that the first is the cause of the movement of the second. Since the development of physics in the seventeenth century, this meaning especially has been given to "cause." (See pp. 159 ff. for a further account of causation.)

The problem is that only one of Aristotle's "causes" is a cause in this sense, his efficient cause. In that instance, clearly, he does mean agent or force. But in what sense do the materials cause the living organism, or does the form, or functions? The terminology of the four causes is so set historically, however, that it will be used here; but one should remember that the four causes are conditions or factors discriminated in living subject matter, a generative process. They are not four distinct ingredients put together, as one puts ingredients for a cake in a mixing bowl. The concrete individual organism is what the investigation begins with. The live animal does not result from four causes being put together.

What did Aristotle do with the doctrine of the four causes? He used it in his investigation of living things. His book, *On the Parts of Animals*, is an effort to understand structures in terms of the functions they perform. In his emphasis upon function, Aristotle felt that he went considerably beyond his predecessors, and his judgment is accurate. They had, in various ways, adumbrated the material, efficient, and formal causes, but had neglected function.

As Aristotle struggled more and more with the generative and developmental aspects of organisms, he leaned increasingly upon two additional concepts: potentiality and actuality. How do individuals of a species reproduce their kind, which then go through a characteristic pattern of development, with the process continuing on and on? Nothing, of course, was known then of chromosomes and genes; so, at best, after describing the generative organs of a number of species, Aristotle's explanation is crude. The female provides the material of development; the male is the activating agent. The material supplied by the female is potentially a new organism, that is, it must contain possible factors of development; but this potentiality must be activated by an actuality, the sperm of the male. The sperm is much more, however, than simply an activating agent. It contains within it the factors which control the pattern of development of the new organism. Again, what these factors are, Aristotle did not know. What they are, modern genetics is beginning to reveal, in one of the great revolutions in the history of biology. The actuality of the adult male thus embodies three of the causes in generation, the efficient, formal, and final causes. The process of growth is the actualizing of the potentialities of the material from the female energized by the male, with the actualizing also controlled by factors supplied by the father.

The adult structural and functional forms are not only necessary for the new organism, but also they provide the basis for understanding the patterns of development. When a man sees the tiny pulsating blood vessel in the chick embryo which becomes the heart in the adult, he has identified the organ by means of the adult form and comes to understand it in terms of the adult form.[10] Once more, Aristotle insists that with organisms the end result, that is, the "for what," or the adult functions are primary for understanding.

After all this study of living things, can one still ask, "What is life?" Aristotle would say that if this question means, "What is the essence of living things, or what is it which makes living things what they are as distinct from inanimate things?" then the question has been asked often. It has traditionally been put, he says, in the form, "What is the soul?"

This question is the subject of Aristotle's *On Soul* or *Psychology*. In his analysis of his predecessors he finds their theories to be of two kinds:

---

10 *Inquiries about Animals, op. cit.,* VI., 3.

(1) They make the soul a principle of movement in organisms, as if it were a kind of engine. The error in this theory is that they make soul and body separable. (2) They make the soul the principle of sensation and thought, influenced by such doctrines that like is known by like, with the result that the soul must be all possible combinations of known things—and thus material. Both types of theories, he rejects.

For his own answer, Aristotle suggests that in the first place the more fitting formulation of the question is "What is soul?" for the "the" in "What is the soul?" has too much the force of making soul a thing in and of itself. That soul is such a thing, Aristotle denies. The most fitting account of "soul," he says quite simply, is an account of the functions of organisms. In short, soul is what a body does. Actually, this statement oversimplifies Aristotle's theory, for he sometimes speaks of soul as both structural and functional form. The structure of the eye makes possible the actual seeing. "Soul" means both the structure and the seeing.

But, again, the most fitting account of soul is the study of the functions of organisms. Aristotle summarizes this study in terms of a hierarchy of functions: the basic biological functions—reproduction, nutrition, growth—which pervade the animate world; sensation which is narrower in scope than the basic functions, and even has its own hierarchy, with touch the most extensive and vision and hearing much narrower; locomotion; and finally, intelligence, which is present to some extent in many kinds of animals but is most highly developed in man.

As Aristotle discusses each of these levels of activity, the characteristic pattern of analysis is that the function, seeing, for example, is dependent upon an environmental actuality which activates a capacity in the organism. A color, through a medium, activates the capacity within the organism. But, for thought, how can this analysis be used? Nature, Aristotle argues, is a vast array of actual orders; nature is the order of orders, an integration of structural and functional forms, which, as described earlier in induction, act upon the mind. The order of nature is in this sense mind, actualized in nature. In a controversial and difficult passage in the *Psychology*,[11] mind in this sense is called the "active intellect." It is not a personal mind. It is the order of nature which makes it possible for personal or individual human minds to think. It is the order of nature which makes it possible for individual minds to have something to think about, and which activates their thinking. Man's knowledge is thus the discovery of orders in nature, and not personal, mental constructs in his head.

Two points need emphasis. In the first place, soul as activity is a co-operative interplay, a transaction between organism and environment. Life is this interplay. Life is not in an organism like a pea in a pod. Breathing is as much a function of air as of lungs; and if a man does not think so,

---

[11] 430a10–25.

he may try breathing without air. Vision is as much a function of color and light as of the eye. Even thought cannot be the activity of the solitary mind. It, too, is a transaction between ordered nature and individual minds.

Second, in his notion of the active intellect, is Aristotle very far from Plato's Ideas as to the order of nature? He seems at first perhaps not to be, but whether he is or not depends upon one's interpretation of the Ideas. If the Ideas are separate from the natural world, a sort of heaven of Ideas, then Aristotle's theory is clearly different; for again and again he rejects this view of the Ideas, a view which incidentally he understands Plato to mean. If the Ideas, on the other hand, are immanent, as Plato sometimes says, then an immanent order of Ideas looks very much like Aristotle's active intellect. If the immanence of Ideas is Platonism, then it seems that Aristotle did not escape the Platonism that he felt he was opposing. The issue hangs upon the transcendence of the Ideas, and since Plato seems ambivalent on precisely this point, the issue probably cannot be settled.

If one views life as a transaction of organism and environment, then certain kinds of questions have negative answers—or, in a sense, are simply out of bounds. Is there life after death? Aristotle would suggest that this question is too ambiguous even to attempt an answer. But if the question means something like, "Is Socrates immortal?" in the sense that when Socrates' body dies, his soul lives on, Aristotle's answer is in the negative. How could Socrates' soul live on? He complains against the Pythagoreans, as he might against Plato also, for flirting with transmigration of souls. The soul of Socrates, if one can speak of *the* soul, is the interaction of this organism and this environment. Destroy this organism, the body of Socrates, how can this soul persist? Rather than speculate about questions like these, which after all may be meaningless when they are analyzed carefully, men might better spend their time studying the functions of organisms—functions which extend all the way from the metabolic, essential to any living thing, to the loftiest reflections by man about the universe. Knowledge and wisdom are to be found by laboring in nature's vineyard instead of wondering what lies beyond its boundaries.

For Aristotle, the phenomenon of life is pre-eminently a matter of developmental processes, unity of structure, and activities or functions. To study life, or more accurately living things, a method appropriate to the subject matter, he contended, must be employed. This method he found in his *aitia*: What is the living thing made of? What initiated the process of its development? What is its structure, or are its structures? What are its activities or functions? Find answers to these questions and you have knowledge, he suggests, perhaps the most significant knowledge there is, about living things. They cannot be understood simply in terms of mechanical causation. Again and again, Aristotle complained about the effort of the atomists of his day to do precisely this. He argued that they, in effect, destroyed life instead of understanding it. The phenomenon of life cannot be reduced, he insists, to chance collocations of atoms. Can it or can it not? That is one of the ultimate arguments about life, and it is as active today as it was in Aristotle's time. Is life the actualizing of potentialities, as Aristotle insists, or is it simply a succession of states necessarily unfolding as a result of mechanical forces? This debate will be examined further in Part III.

From Living Things to the Good Life for Man

Can the study of living things contribute in any significant way to a theory of man's moral life? If a man is a biologist, does he tend to see questions of good or evil, right or wrong, in a light different from that of a mathematician? Sometimes it has been said that the difference between Plato's philosophy and Aristotle's is the contrast between the mathematician's and the biologist's view. The comment oversimplifies matters, but it possesses more than a kernel of truth. We may have been astonished to watch Plato convert the certainties of mathematics into a general theory of Ideas and then utilize that theory in support of eternal moral values. We may have wondered even more about his use of mathematics as a preparation for the good life. But Plato was so enamored of mathematics, he did all these things.

What might happen, then, in moral theory if, by contrast, a philosopher has spent a significant portion of his life in the study of concrete living things, instead of abstractions like numbers and geometrical figures? What if he is especially impressed with the biological rootedness of man? What if he views man as an animal—but not any old animal, rather as an animal possessing a higher level of intelligence than any of the other species— and also sees man as a social creature? What may this naturalistic view of the human condition do to and for a moral theory? In short, if man is an animal with a high degree of intelligence, and a social creature, what, one may ask, is the good life for him? This question provides the central theme of Aristotle's *Nicomachaen Ethics*[12] and his *Politics*.

The further question can be asked: If the good life for man can be found in this natural setting, and if this life should not provide a realm of eternal values after the manner of Plato (as we shall find Aristotle asserting that it will not), does it offer any answer to the extreme relativism of the Sophists? The problem can be put another way: Is there any alternative to the all-or-nothing positions into which Greek ethical theory seems to have been driven—eternal values with Plato, or no values other than the

---

[12] We shall refer to this book simply as the *Ethics*. It is said to be named after Aristotle's son, Nicomachus.

considerations of power according to Thrasymachus? Today we are often confronted with the same polarities: either, some contend, we believe in the eternal moral truths of Christianity or of some other religion, or we are condemned to complete moral relativity or anarchy. Are these the only alternatives in moral theory? Possibly there are others, and one such possibility can be found in the *Ethics* and *Politics*.

THE SOCIAL CONTEXT OF THE GOOD LIFE. Any number of important elements of Aristotle's moral theory have their roots deep in the folklore and the tradition of the city-state. The city-state as the setting for man's moral and political life; the notion of virtue as excellence (*arete*); the cluster of particular virtues, such as courage, moderation, and friendliness; the necessity of intelligence in conduct; justice and freedom as functions of law; the insistence upon the education of the young—all these and more factors essential to his ethics are found in the tradition. Does this mean that the *Ethics* and the *Politics* are merely reaffirmations of the received wisdom, a kind of last-ditch, desperate stand on Aristotle's part against the Sophists? It will be obvious that he does not desert the tradition, but it will also be perfectly clear that he does transform it and make it intellectually more secure. It remains to be seen how these modifications and reinforcements take place.

That man naturally is a social creature, a political animal (*politikon zoon*) is one of Aristotle's fundamental convictions. The firmness of this belief is illustrated in his assertion that the antisocial individual (literally, "the cityless one") is either a beast or a god but not a human being.[13] Possibly a god can live alone and maintain his divinity, but a man cannot become a man in isolation, or even retain his humanity in such a condition. For one thing, a man is born into a social unit, the family. And even the solitary family is rare. When several families unite, there is a village. From the union of several villages, the city-state naturally emerges, and can grow to the magnificence of an Athens. As the human infant can develop into a mature individual of many and varied accomplishments, so man's social organization can grow from infancy to the multiple perfection of the city-state. It is in the mature form of the city-state that man's arts and sciences flourish. The wilderness produces no Parthenon, no *Oresteia*, no geometry, no constitutional government. At last, in the city-state, the capacities of man can be brought to fruition. The good life, whatever its defining characteristics may be ultimately, is surely to be found there; for the city-state exists not simply that men may live but that they may live well. It is in this fashion that Aristotle provides the social context in which, he feels, any discussion of the good life must be carried on. A few characteristics of this basic assumption should be noted.

Aristotle retained the traditional intimacy between the individual man

---

[13] *Politics*, 1253a1 ff.

and the city-state. The love for one's city, like the love for one's family, is natural and unforced. A proud moment comes to the life of the free man when he is a citizen, participating in the deliberative and judicial functions of the state. That somehow the state, by its very nature, is oppressive —a theme characteristic of much modern political theory since the seventeenth century—would have confounded Aristotle. Of course, he knew that states can be oppressive. Any form of human association can be corrupted, even the family. But is the hallmark of the state simply force and oppression, so that men must resignedly bear the burden of the state, plaintively asserting that earth would approach heaven if there were no states at all? To say yes misses the very nature of the state, Aristotle contends. The state is a natural growth, as natural as the family and life itself. To have to justify the state, and to legitimize its authority by some fiction of the social contract—the fashion of the seventeenth and eighteenth centuries (see pp. 260 ff.)—is to ignore both how and why states come into existence at all. They exist, once more, that men may live well, to promote the good life for man. The inevitable antagonism that is often said to exist between the individual and the state finds no support whatsoever in Aristotle.

Nor does Aristotle agree with the particular version of the individual-state antagonism advanced by the Sophists, who argued that there is a natural justice of self-preservation outside society, but that law and custom within the state contrive to throttle it. The contrast between the natural and the social, which the Sophists temptingly offered as a criticism of the restraints upon man by the state, is rejected by Aristotle; for he sees the social itself as a natural development in the life of man. He goes even further: this natural development is necessary for the flowering of man's life as a human, in truth, a humane being. Yet, to live in a society is obviously not the same thing as living well or living the good life in that society; hence at least two important questions remain: (1) can the good life be described or, if one prefers, defined? and (2) if it can be defined, can it be lived?

THE GOOD LIFE AS HAPPINESS. The *Ethics* opens with the statement: "Every art and every inquiry, and likewise every practical activity and choice, seems to aim at some good; thus, it has been well said that the good is that at which all things aim."[14] The good of the art of shoemaking is the shoes the cobbler makes, the good of the musician is in playing his instrument, of the runner in the running of the race. Since every art, practical activity, and choice has a good, under this view the goods which men pursue are legion. Furthermore, "good" is so broadly conceived that it includes the goods in a drygoods store as well as an ethical good like justice. The reader may complain that in picking up a book on ethics

---

14 *Ethics*, 1094a1–3. (Our translation.)

he wants ethical matters discussed, and not shoemaking and music; that ethics is ethics, and not economics or fine arts. Aristotle would agree that he is far from making clear what the good life is for man, by saying that the good is that at which things aim. But the argument of the *Ethics* also makes it abundantly clear that if the good life for man consists in living well and doing well in the affairs of men (to anticipate one of Aristotle's conclusions), economics, fine arts, the sciences, the conduct of government—all are intertwined with that good life. Man's moral life is not lived in a vacuum which excludes the biological, economic, social, political, and psychological conditions of that life. Whatever the good life turns out to be, however good, morally good, a man becomes, the manifold conditions of life, its numerous goods, are also involved.

Although the goods which men puruse are numerous, men inevitably order their goods in terms of importance, Aristotle points out. For example, the immediate good for a family may be the construction of a house, which precludes the pursuit of other goods at the moment, the purchase of a new car or a trip to Europe. The house is more important to the family than the other possible goods. A man or a family cannot pursue all possible goods at once. In addition to this kind of limitation and selection in terms of importance, there is another. The demand for the justification of any good cannot be endless. Why does the family want the house? To improve its living conditions. Why improve its living conditions? In order that the family may be happy. Why be happy? Just to be happy. What more is there to say?

Again and again, suggests Aristotle, as men order the goods of their lives, they come to a final good, beyond which they do not seem to be able to go. If they did not come to this final end, they would be led into an infinite regress, and their desires would be futile and vain.[15] It would thus seem to be of consummate importance, for the practical conduct of life, to know what this final good is. What is it, then?

Men are generally agreed upon its name. They call the final or highest good of life, "happiness" (*eudaimonia*).[16] Moreover men, great and small alike, assert that happiness consists in living well and doing well. But here the agreement ends. What is this happiness that is living well and doing well? Some men find it in pleasure, others honor, still others wealth. Aristotle rejects each as the sole constituent of happiness, although all may be involved in happiness. After a careful analysis, he also rejects Plato's Idea of the Good as the final end.[17] His arguments are numerous and not least is the criticism that the Idea of the Good is transcendent and unattainable by man, but it is the human good which is the object of investigation.

[15] *Ibid.,* 1094a20–21.
[16] *Ibid.,* 1095a18–20.
[17] *Ibid.,* 1096a11 ff.

HAPPINESS AS A LIFE OF VIRTUE. If the good life for man is happiness, and happiness is living well and doing well, but living well does not consist of a life of pleasure, honor, or wealth, what can happiness be? Aristotle turns to an ancient Greek ideal for his approach to an answer. The good life for man, a life of happiness, is a life of virtue or excellence (*arete*).[18] If this assertion were all that Aristotle had to offer, he would be doing nothing more than returning to the past. The critical question is: What is virtue or what does Aristotle mean by "virtue"?

His definition reads as follows: "Virtue . . . is the habit of choosing the mean, the mean relative to us, determined by reason, that is, as a prudent man would determine it."[19] Much of the *Ethics* is a detailed explication and illustration of this definition. Here only certain key elements can be examined briefly, such as "the mean," "prudence," and "habit."

Aristotle's *doctrine of the mean* is probably the most famous element of his moral theory. Its renown rests in part upon its central position in the *Ethics*, and in part upon the deceptive simplicity it appears to have in providing standards for conduct. The question of standards is a critical one in moral theory. What are the standards for determining whether an act is virtuous or vicious, good or bad? And if the standards are found, what is their source and their justification? For Plato, it seems, the standard is the eternal Idea of the Good and the Ideas of Courage, Temperance, and other virtues. For Thrasymachus, the standard is what the prevailing power in society determines it to be. For the Christian, the standard is the commandments of God. For Aristotle, the standard is none of these. It is the mean. What, then, is the mean?

The virtues, says Aristotle, "are destroyed by excess and deficiency but preserved by the mean."[20] The statement has a ring of familiarity since it appears merely to reiterate the traditional doctrine of moderation. In the tradition, moderation was praised as virtuous and good, excess condemned as vicious and evil. What does Aristotle add? From the detailed discussion of the *Ethics*, it becomes apparent that Aristotle's doctrine of the mean is considerably more complicated than a simple counsel of moderation.

The mean is a midpoint between excess and deficiency. But what sort of midpoint? The number six can be said to be the midpoint between ten and two, to use Aristotle's example, since it is four from each. Is the mean in ethics this sort of "mathematical" mean? No, for this mathematical mean is constant. It would hold anywhere. The moral mean is a midpoint "relative to us." Illustrations will help.

Aristotle illustrates the mean relative to us with an example from athletics. If ten pounds of meat is too much as a diet for a wrestler, and

---

[18] *Ibid.*, 1098a15 ff. See also our previous discussion, pp. 39 ff.
[19] *Ibid.*, 1106b36–1107a2. (Our translation.)
[20] *Ibid.*, 1104a25–27. (Our translation.)

two pounds too little, is six pounds, the mathematical midpoint, the right amount? Not at all, says Aristotle. Six pounds may be too little for the great wrestler Milo, but too much for a young man beginning his training. The mean is relative to the individual.

Although the point of the illustration is that the mean is relative and not absolute, the reader may complain that the illustration is in no way apt. What does a wrestler's diet have to do with morals? It may not have much on the surface; however, Aristotle never makes a hard and fast distinction between what, in later moral theory, came to be called natural goods, such as health, and moral goods, such as courage. That health and courage can affect one another significantly would have seemed obvious to Aristotle; on the other hand, to place them in separate and distinct compartments—calling one "natural" and the other "moral"—would have struck him as very odd. For not only in athletics and matters of health but in all the arts, Aristotle argues, there is that which is appropriate, just right, the mean which is relative to the circumstances. The mean as the standard of excellence in the arts is also applicable to morals—a contention which is critical for his entire theory.

Perhaps an example from contemporary life, of considerably greater complexity than Aristotle's illustration from athletics, will be of further assistance. In a management-labor dispute over wages in a given factory, an arbitrator is called in to settle the dispute. The reader may object that the problem is "purely economic"; but Aristotle would maintain, and many contemporaries too, that questions of a just wage or justice are involved. What, then, is the just wage? Aristotle would say that there is no fixed, certain, automatic, invariant just wage. What are the circumstances in the case? The increase in labor efficiency, the present wage, the cost-of-living index in the area, the financial condition of the company, the wages in comparable industries in the community, and so on are involved. Once these factors are determined, one hopes the arbitrator has the wisdom or "prudence," as Aristotle calls it, to find the mean, the central point that achieves a balance and adjustment among these varied and often conflicting forces and conditions. The mean, determined by the prudent man, is the just wage. It is what is virtuous and good in the situation, relative to the circumstances. Obviously this mean is not the eternal Idea of the Just Wage. Neither is it a product of power or force, although powers and forces have to be taken into account. It is what is prudent and reasonable within the situation.

What is this prudence that has entered as a critical factor in the determination of the mean? It is one form of reason or intelligence. But what kind? Aristotle distinguishes prudence from the purely theoretical intelligence involved in the sciences and the intelligence utilized in those arts which are concerned with making things, as carpentry and painting.[21]

21 *Ibid.*, Bk. VI.

Prudence involves both theoretical considerations and practical action. The labor arbitrator needs to know theories of economics, and principles of law, as well as the general commitments of the society to the welfare of its citizens. But he must fashion something concrete out of the materials of the dispute at hand. He is not defining Justice in *The Republic*; he is creating justice in this dispute, in this plant, in this city, among these men. To discover the mean here and now, he needs experience, and experience is found and made in the market place, the law court, the day-to-day life among men. The prudent man can bring theoretical intelligence to bear upon the practical issues of life because of his experience in that life. So essential is experience for prudence that Aristotle insists that the young cannot be prudent. In a passage that usually affronts the young, he says:

Even though the young become geometricians and mathematicians and are skilled with respect to such matters, it seems that they are not prudent. The reason is that prudence is concerned with particular things, which come to be known from experience; but the young do not have experience. For experience is a product of years.[22]

In the doctrine of the mean, the mean determined as a prudent man would determine it, Aristotle does provide a standard for finding and judging acts to be virtuous or good. The standard is obviously a flexible one. Aristotle shies away from inflexible rules of conduct which are to be applied no matter what the circumstances. Lying generally is not to be condoned, but when a physician, knowing of his patient's fatal illness, lies to the patient about his condition because the patient cannot stand the truth, is the physician to be condemned? What would a prudent man do?

To have flexible standards for virtue is to some men, as it seems with Plato, to have no standards at all. They claim, in effect, that anything goes with Aristotle. But is this criticism justified? To say that standards of conduct cannot be invariant is not to say that there are no standards at all. The standard is prudential intelligence which does not permit anything under the sun. It is not a subjective standard, in the sense that the prudent man simply does what he likes, or satisfies his or someone else's interest. It is an objective standard in so far as it involves the critical analysis of the hard, objective conditions under which men act. It means facing up to the circumstances of the natural world, the actual institutional structure of society, and individual psychological and emotional factors. To be sure, the mean always involves human judgment, judgment which certainly is fallible. The mean selected may not turn out as reasonable as it first seemed. But the mean involves the actions of men and the conditions under which those actions take place. In fact, one might argue that this sort of standard is the most broadly based objective ethical standard of all, since it is not the result of class or individual interest, or an ideal standard removed from the

---

[22] *Ibid.*, 1142a11–16. (Our translation.)

scene of action. It is the solutions reasonable men find to the very real, specific, objective moral problems with which their social order and personal lives confront them.

Admittedly, this standard is not the eternal law of God. One hardly needs to point out, Aristotle would add, that man does not have God's omniscience, the apparent requisite for such laws. But even if the prophets can speak for God, their standards are general and are not sufficient for good and virtuous actions. "Love thy neighbor." But how? In what way? Love in general seems a vacuous love indeed. The trouble is that those who find the heart of ethics in eternal rules forget, Aristotle argues, that those rules have to be applied, that the moral situation, again, is one of action, a particular situation that always has unique elements. For this very reason Plato's Good is not the answer; it is so remote from the affairs of life that it is useless in the concrete situations that are the stuff of that life.[23] Possibly it is something for the gods to know. But after all, says Aristotle, it is the human good and human virtue that are the objects of inquiry.

Moreover, even if the standard is flexible, it is not to be confused with the suggestion of the Sophists that the good consists of power whenever and by whomsoever it may be exerted. Power can be used for good or ill, but is not itself the standard for these moral qualities. Power may overwhelm prudence, but prudence can sit in judgment of power. The hope that man has for good lies in the application of his intelligence to the problems with which he is confronted, rather than the utilization of power for class or personal interests. The critical question, Aristotle would insist, is not whether man or mankind is the measure of good and evil, as Protagoras asserted, for Aristotle would agree that mankind must determine the measure. The critical question is rather what, within the various abilities and capacities of mankind, is to determine the measure. Aristotle finds the answer in the intelligence that man can bring to bear upon the moral issues which confront him.

As estimable as Aristotle's emphasis is upon prudential intelligence, the criticism has been made that he neglects the impulsive, the spontaneous, and the passionate which, too, can make their contributions to man's moral life. The prudent man is rarely, if ever, the revolutionary, but the world is at times in need of revolutionaries and martyrs. Had Socrates been the prudent, the reasonable man, he probably would not have been convicted. But had he not died for his faith in the very intelligence Aristotle would have men cultivate, would they not cultivate it less?

In the same vein, it may be said that the prudent man tends to be the conservative man. Prudence may lead to social change, but the counsel of prudence is too often on the side of the establishment. "Don't rock the boat" is frequently urged as that which is prudent, when its real consequence is to leave a bungling captain in command.

---

[23] *Ibid.*, 1096b32.

Aristotle would agree that the middle way rarely leads to martyrdom or revolution, but it also saves individuals and societies from fanaticisms. There is nothing, he would argue, in the nature of prudential intelligence itself which stands in the way of social change. It does stand in the way of violent change. He objected to Plato's pulling up society by the roots in *The Republic,* in destroying the family and private property as these were known in most Greek states. Is this the way to the good society, or is the path by means of the effective adjustment, however slow, of the economic and social interests of competing groups? Aristotle painstakingly defends the latter in the *Politics* as well as in the *Ethics.*

LIVING THE GOOD LIFE. The standard for determining a good or virtuous act has been found, Aristotle feels. The good life for man will therefore be activity in accordance with excellent or virtuous acts,[24] and these virtuous acts are those in accordance with the mean as a prudent man would find them. Is it enough, however, to identify good or virtuous acts? The identification, if it can come off, is no insignificant accomplishment. But for Aristotle, more than this accomplishment is required. The purpose of the investigation of the *Ethics,* he says, is not simply to know what virtue is, but also to determine how we may become good; otherwise the inquiry is of no use.[25] How is it, then, that men become good?

Men become good by doing virtuous acts. By doing just acts they become just, by temperate acts temperate, by courageous acts courageous. Men are born neither virtuous nor vicious, good nor bad. They have neither taint of sin at birth nor touch of virtue. They are simply born, born the live animals that they are, with the capacity to form habits; and these habits are molded by actions from childhood to maturity. The structure of habits that a man develops is his character, we would say; and once this structure or character is formed, it, in turn, prompts men to perform virtuous or vicious acts, good or bad. We are not so much a part of all that we have met, in the words of Tennyson's Ulysses, as of all that we have done. What we do makes us what we morally are, and what we morally are affects what we do. The good man has become so by doing good and virtuous acts. He then becomes the standard for good acts, and has the disposition to continue to do them; the evil man is similarly the product of his actions, and has the propensity for actions of like kind.

But how can this be? Has not Aristotle offered us a marvelously circular argument? A man becomes good by doing good acts, and then the acts of a good man are good. But how can he do good acts in the first place until he is good?

Of course, one way out would be to have men born good or evil, either naturally or as a gift of the gods or God. But Aristotle cannot choose this

---

24 *Ibid.,* 1098a15–17.
25 *Ibid.,* 1103b27–29.

way, for he contends that men are born morally neutral. In fact, he would argue that such a solution is a poor one indeed, for look at the infants in a nursery and try to mark those at birth who will become good, those evil. Their characters seem to be known only as the infants mature and act; hence how would we know whether they are good or evil at birth?

No, we are not born knowing what the means for virtuous acts will be in the situations of life we shall face. Hitting the mean is an art, a skill that is developed, or fails to develop, as other skills develop or do not. How does one learn to play the flute? By playing it, Aristotle matter-of-factly observes; then habits are formed that enable some to play well and others poorly. So it is with developing prudence that we may learn to hit the mean. It is true, Aristotle would say, that a minimum intelligence as a natural endowment is necessary. It is difficult, in truth it would seem virtually impossible, for a fool to become a good man. Nor can a man withdraw from society and the world; for it is in the experience within that society and that world that prudence develops or does not.

A man can, however, be started on the path of virtue or vice in terms of his early education in childhood, Aristotle contends. Of course, the young are not yet prudent, but they can be taught to like excellence or virtue, and to avoid the vicious. It is not surprising, therefore, to find both the *Ethics* and the *Politics* ending on the theme of the education of the young in the way of virtue.

As a man passes from youth to maturity, and develops the habit of prudential action, he becomes a good man. He molds his own soul, his character. A man's soul is a work of art, and like a work of art in stone, it may be good or bad. When it turns out good, it is perhaps the noblest of all man's works. What greater victory wreath can a man gain than to have achieved a good life? And if he has been placed in the position where his prudential virtue has dealt with great and important matters for his city, he may finally achieve greatness of soul (*megalopsychia*).[26] Such an individual is the epitome of the virtuous man. He is proud, haughty, aristocratic. He is good and knows that he is. He has done great deeds. He is something of the ancient hero transformed into an Athenian gentleman of parts. Like the heroes of old, he is concerned with honor, but honor that comes from intelligent action of many kinds and not primarily valor on the battlefield. He is not, however, a "nice" man. He does not know what Christian humility is; and therefore he may lack the profound moral insight implicit in the Christian teaching. But he is great and accomplished in the affairs of men.

HAPPINESS AND THE LIFE OF THE MIND. Is there still something further in the good life for man? If it is man's intelligence that raises him above

---

[26] For a description of the man of greatness of soul see *Ethics,* 1123a 34 ff.

the other animals, if it is in knowing that man is peculiarly man, what would that life be like if it were devoted primarily to knowing? The *Ethics* is fundamentally concerned with doers, with men seeking prudential action in their everyday affairs. But what if a man devoted his life primarily to theoretical pursuits, the sciences, for instance? The last book of the *Ethics* raises this question.

What kind of life would the theoretical life be? It is the highest form of human happiness and goodness, since it is the function of the most distinctively human capacity. It is the most self-sufficient life, for it does not need the market place, the assembly, or the battlefield for its pursuit. Its domain is the study, the laboratory, or the starry heavens that are open for all to see. It is loved, more than any other pursuit, for its own sake. It is knowing for no other purpose than the knowing itself, although useful fruits can, of course, flow from it. If there is any divinity to man, it rests in his intelligence; hence the theoretical life is the closest that man can come to the life of the divine.

It has often been said that Aristotle finally comes to an essentially Platonic conclusion in the *Ethics*—that knowing for its own sake is the highest good and thus the happiest life for man. The comment is in part just, for Aristotle never entirely escapes the influence of Plato. But however Platonic a note the last book of the *Ethics* has, no one can deny the profound differences in the thrust of the main argument of the *Ethics* in contrast with *The Republic*—the former so immersed in the practical decisions of life, the latter controlled by the vision of ideal possibilities. And even after his apotheosis of the theoretical life, Aristotle brings the reader suddenly back to the field of action:

Now, though such considerations [concerning the theoretical life] carry some conviction, in the field of moral action truth is judged by the actual facts of life, for it is in them that the decisive element lies. So we must examine the conclusions we have reached so far by applying them to the actual facts of life: if they are in harmony with the facts we must accept them, and if they clash we must assume they are mere words.[27]

Aristotle, the naturalist, the student of living things, steered a middle course between the realm of eternal Platonic values and the extreme relativism of the Sophists. In his moral theory, he conserved the traditional Greek values and made them more secure against the conflicting winds of doctrine by placing the burden of moral decisions upon man's most distinctive characteristic, his intelligence, sharpened and chastened by practical experience in the affairs of the city-state. Plato, too, sought to conserve the tradition, but his turn to an eternal realm of values, which

---

[27] *Ethics*, 1179a17–22, Martin Oswald trans. (Indianapolis: Bobbs-Merrill, 1962), p. 294.

in their eternality need not be rooted in any time or place, made it easy for those of any age who seek the eternal to forget the Greek sources of Platonism and to use his doctrine for their own purposes. Because of Aristotle's attention to the specific moral problems of Greek life, his theory, on the surface at least, is more parochial. Yet the closer one looks at Aristotle's ethics, the more one sees that it is much more than a museum of Greek virtues. The heart of his ethics is a method for making moral decision and becoming a good man. The good life is activity in accordance with virtue; and virtue is the habit of choosing the mean, the mean relative to us, as a prudent man would determine it. "The mean relative to us." Cannot the "us" be men of the twentieth century as well as of fourth century B.C. Greece? It would seem that this naturalistic way to the good life, the application of prudential intelligence to the moral problems of life can be utilized in any age. Because of this enduring relevance to man's varied cultures, Aristotle's ethics, although rooted in the Greek experience, has become a classic model for naturalistic moral theories in the Western tradition.

What Does It Mean To Be, To Exist?

The pursuit of the theoretical life, which Aristotle eulogized, can, of course, take many directions. It can be productive of a science like geometry, apart from practical considerations of measuring the earth. It can lead to attempts to understand the movements of the heavenly bodies. It can begin in studies of language to persuade men in the assembly, and eventuate in logic as a science of systematic discourse. It can undertake to formulate the basic principles of living things, culminating in a science of biology. It can also inquire into the very nature of existence itself.

In fact, this last inquiry had been the oldest problem of Greek philosophy. When the earliest of the Greek philosophers asked, "What is nature?" they were seeking an answer to the problem of the nature of existence, although the problem itself was not yet quite clear. They thought of the problem as involving some sort of ultimate material from which all things come and into which they perish, a material that also contained within itself the source of energy, of change that was everywhere manifest in nature. To be something, to exist as something, meant to be some transformation of the basic material. It meant coming into being and perishing in terms of powers within nature that had nothing to do with the gods— if there were gods at all, something that a man might well doubt, especially if the traditional gods were the only ones there were. Thus to be something, to exist, meant, in short, to be a natural growth from the basic material.

Then mathematics appeared on the scene. Numbers and geometrical figures certainly have something to do with material things, but do they have to be tied to the things? The Pythagoreans sometimes made numbers virtually a material, but not always; and when they began to prove propositions about points, lines, and planes, material factors receded into the background. Furthermore, the same material can have different figures, forms, numbers. The same piece of string can make now a square, now a triangle; and if someone should ask about the string-as-square and the string-as-triangle, "What is it?" to answer, simply, "String," seems inadequate. Something important about the string-as-square and the string-as-triangle has been left out. The form or pattern would seem to be as significant to the existence of the figured string as the material; perhaps more so. To be sure, nature is material, but manifestly it is multiformed material. No, the nature of existence cannot be found in a material or materials alone. What is the nature of existence? What does it mean to exist as something? It means to be material with some sort of form—or formed material, if one prefers.

There is no point in repeating all that has been said in early Greek philosophy concerning this problem. It has been seen that as the problem was refined, there were those who found existence in that which is permanent, others in that which changes. What was found to be the nature of existence was called reality. What only appeared to exist, but really did not, was called appearance. Plato found existence in the Ideas. They constituted the real, real *being*. Particular things that come into being but pass away are only the appearance of real being. In Plato, the search for the nature of existence had come a long way from the first efforts of Thales or from what the man in the street would consider the true nature of existence.

All this Aristotle had before him; and he would carry on the quest. "Indeed," he says, "the question, 'What is being?' was raised long ago and is even now and will always be raised, and is always a matter of doubt. This question is 'What is substance [*ousia*]?' "[28] For Aristotle, too, the object of inquiry is to investigate the nature of being in the sense of substance.

The ancients, Aristotle suggests, in their concern with the nature of existence were asking the question, "What is being?" The question means, he continues, "What does it mean to be anything?" The question is not what it means to be a man or a horse or a table, but what it means to be anything whatsoever. What is being as being, existence as existence? What are the distinguishing characteristics of existence over against nonexistence? Aristotle continues his examination of the question itself and finds it to mean "What is substance, *ousia*?" When Thales was asking, "What is nature?" he was asking for a substance which constituted the most fundamental and pervasive natural existence, and he found it to be water. And so,

---

[28] *Metaphysics*, 1028b2–4. (Our translation.)

too, the successors of Thales sought some sort of substance or substances. What, then, is substance for Aristotle? The question is the central one of his *Metaphysics*.[29]

"Substance" for Aristotle has more than one meaning; but in its primary, most fundamental sense, "substance" means a concrete individual thing which comes into being and passes away. This man, this dog, that flower, that stone, this house—all these are substances, substances in the primary sense of "substance." Aristotle takes the world of birth and death, of coming into being and passing away, of change, of activity, as a fundamental kind of existence. What Plato saw as appearance, Aristotle sees as reality. Aristotle considers the denial of change, the exaltation of permanence over change, to be absurd. Thus, the answer to the age-old question, "What does it mean to be?" is primarily, "To be is to be a *tode ti*, a particular individual thing." But what does the "primarily" mean? Are there other senses of "substance?" And might not the question also be asked, "What more can be said of substance?"

In one sense, to be a substance is to be the primary subject of discourse. We talk about, we analyze substances more than anything else. Substances have characteristics, qualities, attributes, which we think about and discuss. "Socrates is old," "Socrates is inquisitive," "Socrates asks too many questions." Substances are the subjects of propositions, not predicates. We say, "Socrates is old," not "old is Socrates," unless we are talking for effect or trying to be cute; for the true subject is "Socrates"—not "old."

What, then can be said of substances? For one thing, any substance can be talked about; no substance is beyond the pale of discussion. But what can be said about substances? Of course many things, as of Socrates, his age, his inquisitiveness, his garrulity. All these things are interesting and may be important, but can we say what the real Socrates is? Can we get at the man, his essence? Socrates is a man. But there are many men. Socrates is white, but there are many white things. Socrates talks a lot, but so do many men. Can we say what Socrates really is? When we ask this question, when we ask for the essence of something, we want to know that which makes it what it is and not something else. We can also speak of the essence of something as substance. Thus, substance as concrete individual and substance as the essence of the individual are one and the same. Substance as essence is what can be known and stated about individual things.[30]

The statement of the essence is, of course, not the thing. Discourse is

---

29 The discussion here follows, in part, Chapter VI, "First Philosophy: The Ultimate Distinctions," of John Herman Randall, Jr.'s superb book, *Aristotle* (New York: Columbia, 1960). The core of Aristotle's discussion is found in Books, Zeta, Eta, and Theta of the *Metaphysics*.
30 *Ibid.*, 1031b6–7, 19–22.

about things; it is not the things themselves. But what things are essentially, can be put into words. Of course, not every possible thing can be known and said about the concrete individual. Many occurrences in the history of an individual remain unknown but have nothing to do with the essence of that individual, for example, how many times Socrates sat down in his lifetime. But, even though we cannot know everything about an individual thing, we can know what is essential to its existence. In the *Metaphysics*, Aristotle is quite emphatic that the careful talking he analyzed in the *Organon* is relevant to the world in which men live. Of course, this talking can go wrong; but men can, with care, put into words what things are in a fundamental sense of their being, their essence.

What else can be said of substances, besides the fact that they can be talked about and their essences put into words? To answer this question, one must go to the things themselves, go beyond the analysis of the relation of discourse to things. All primary substances are productions. They are natural—plants and animals—or artificial—tables, chairs, or houses. Each is a generative process; for example, an animal coming from parents and in turn becoming one, a table made of wood by a cabinetmaker. Any substance in the primary sense is a compound of matter and form. "Matter" is a relative term, for there is no matter without any form whatsoever. The oak is material for the table, but oak is a form of matter. Completely formless matter cannot exist. To be a substance in the primary sense, then, is to have both material and formal factors.

Also concerning any concrete individual, natural or artificial, the four *aitia* can be sought. In the *Metaphysics*, Aristotle generalizes his doctrine of the four causes to all substances, at least in the primary sense. In other words, the four factors are involved in any generative process and not simply in living processes. One can ask about any artifact as well as about a living thing: What is it made of? What began its process of development or brought it into being? What is its form? What does it do? To be a substance in the primary sense is to possess the four analyzable factors noted. Aristotle subjects the four causes to additional analysis in the *Metaphysics*. The final cause emerges as primary for understanding, as in the biological studies. The efficient, formal, and final causes at times merge into one, when Aristotle is speaking simply of the matter and form of a thing. In living things, such as a father, the structural and functional form are intimately tied together and constitute the agency for development of the offspring. The cabinetmaker is the agent, and his view of the function of the table controls the structure he gives to the oak.

The relationship of the four causes raises the question: To what extent do final causes control productions or developmental processes? The problem concerns *teleology*, the doctrine of ends or purposes. The question may be put: To what extent are occurrences in nature controlled by purposes? Is there a grand design for nature? "In the beginning God created . . ." is the way Genesis opens. God had a purpose in mind for creation and all that follows. Is God like the cabinetmaker, except that His artifact is the universe? Since Aristotle talks about ends, purposes, and *for whats*, what is his view?

Aristotle would agree that the *end-in-view* of the cabinetmaker controls what he does with his wood. The architect's plan determines how he builds. Human purposes constantly are made real in things by controlling and guiding productive processes. Is this true for nature? Aristotle's answer is in the negative. The universe is eternal. No master architect planned it and laid it out. Human purposes arise within it, but the universe answers to no purpose. Human purposes can arise in it because of the character of its productive processes. There is a natural teleology in which developmental processes eventuate in ends, structures that function; but the eventuating functions do not control the development processes that make them possible. If man is to think, he needs the apparatus that makes thinking possible. If he is to do the manifold tasks which that instrument of instruments, the hand, can do, then a structure like the hand is necessary. But nature might never have produced a thinking man or a hand. Functions require structures to function; but there is no evidence that nature set out to produce men, monkeys, and oysters. But neither are the mechanists and atomists right, Aristotle argues, in saying that the products of nature are produced by chance. He was fully aware of the sports among living things, but he found a remarkable continuity in nature. Chance collections of acorns do not produce men. You cannot get a function in any old way. But to say that God or nature foresaw that the structure of the human heart had to be what it is, is to read human purposes illegitimately into nature. Man can have purposes. Aristotle's God cannot.[31]

As Aristotle pursues his investigations of substance, he returns to one of the important distinctions in the biological studies: potentiality and actuality. All concrete individuals, natural or artificial, are actualizations of potentialities. The chicken is the actuality that developed from the potentialities of the egg. The marble was potentially the statue, and the statue became an actuality by the agency of another actuality, the sculptor. Potentialities are brought into exercise by actualities. The importance of Aristotle's potentiality is the recognition of the divergent possibilities of existence. The marble could have become a doorstep, the wood of a table might have become a chair.

But, in the *Metaphysics*, Aristotle generalizes the notion of actuality until it becomes the fundamental meaning of substance. Even in the primary sense of substance as the concrete individual, it is the individual's functions as its actuality which is the most fundamental aspect of the in-

[31] See J. H. Randall, Jr. *op. cit.*, pp. 124–125, for an excellent discussion.

dividual's existence. It is what we do, which is the most fundamental sense of what we are. As in Aristotle's biology, where functions are found primary for existence and understanding, so in his metaphysics, the generalization is made for any existence whatsoever.

The primacy of actuality as function enabled Aristotle to deal with substances that he considered eternal. In the heavenly bodies he found no coming into being and passing away, no possibilities being actualized; for they contained within themselves no potentialities. They are forever what they are, moving inexorably in their circular paths around the earth. They are pure actuality in ceaseless motion.

But why are there substances, movement, and change in the universe at all? In a reference that goes back to the theologians[32] of the folklore, such as Hesiod, Aristotle asserted that substances cannot be generated out of night. The natural philosophers failed also in trying to generate them by mixing elements together. Whatever difficulties concerning this question, in Book Lambda of the *Metaphysics*, there are—and they are numerous—it is abundantly clear that Aristotle is not asking for a theory of creation. Change is eternal; so is time. Any particular change, as one ball moving another or animals reproducing their kind, is always the result of one substance acting upon another. Of efficient causes, there is an endless chain. What is the principle that makes these changes possible and intelligible? The question, again, is not what brought change into existence, for change has always been; but rather, how would it be possible to understand that change is eternal? Must there not be an eternal condition that makes this eternal change possible? Is there not an eternal substance that is pure actuality, that would make eternal change intelligible?

What can be said of this principle? Aristotle calls this principle the *unmoved mover*. Why such a strange name? It moves the eternal heavens but is not moved, because it is the ultimate condition of movement. Anything that moves something, and itself is moved, is intermediate, like any ordinary motion we observe. The ultimate condition of motion does not itself move. Aristotle would remind us that the Law of Falling Bodies itself does not fall, nor is the Law of the Lever a lever. How can the unmoved mover move without doing anything as an efficient cause? Aristotle's analogy is that it moves as the object of desire or the object of thought moves. He struggles to describe it. It is the actuality of reason, and this is life in the ultimate sense. It is a *zoe* (initially the word for "animal"), a living thing, life, say, as thought and its object constitute life. The unmoved mover looks like the active intellect of the *Psychology*. It is the divine in nature toward which all things strive, striving to achieve the complete actuality that none can be; but it never was a first cause creating all things to serve such a purpose.

---

[32] *Metaphysics*, 1071b27.

The present book is not the place to debate whether Aristotle, the naturalist, deserted the world of becoming for the eternal and the divine. There is modern scholarship to indicate that he deserted the eternal for the temporal, that Book Lambda was written while he was still a Platonist— before turning to his investigations of nature which resulted in his analysis of substance as the concrete individual.[33] But whether or not this view is true, it is clear that later theologians, like St. Thomas Aquinas (c.1225–1274), converted the unmoved mover into God as first cause of the universe, a conversion that would have dismayed Aristotle, who was talking about a principle of intelligibility, a principle of understanding as a final cause and not a God who created in the beginning.

Aristotle's Cosmology

Aristotle's cosmology is a set of common-sense observations of heavenly and terrestrial bodies, justified as the necessarily rational and good order of nature. A curious mixture of empirical observation and a priori reasoning, it is the least successful aspect of Aristotle's philosophy as far as the development of modern knowledge is concerned; but it had enormous influence historically. The schoolmen of the Middle Ages adopted it with fervor, and in the West it remained the educated man's view of the universe until the new physics and astronomy of the seventeenth century destroyed it.

Cosmological speculations were among the first inquiries of the Greek philosophers; and as knowledge of mathematics and astronomy developed, almost every Greek philosopher had a hand in showing how the universe got to be the way it is—or at least how the universe hangs together now. Aristotle's problem was the latter, for he held the earth and the heavenly bodies to be eternally as they are.

How, then, does the universe look to Aristotle? It is a sphere, eternal, of finite size. The earth, likewise a sphere, is the center of the universe. The sun, moon, planets, and stars revolve around the earth. The heavenly bodies are composed of a special element, *aither*, which is unalterable and eternal; and they, in turn, are set in spheres composed of this material. The stars are in the outermost sphere, and their motion is the simple circular revolution of the sphere. The motion of the sun, moon, and the planets is more complex. Aristotle adapted an ingenious mathematical theory to his purposes to account for the apparent movement of the sun, moon, and planets against the background of the fixed stars. Eudoxus (408–355 B.C.) and Callippus (c.370–c.300 B.C.) had developed a purely geometrical theory of concentric spheres to explain the apparent movements by resolving them

---

[33] See Werner Jaeger, *Aristotle, Fundamentals of the History of His Development*, 2nd ed. (London: Oxford, 1948).

into combinations of circular motions. These investigators had made no assumption that there were actual physical spheres answering to their theoretical constructions.

Aristotle, with less sagacity in this area than elsewhere in his biology and philosophy, converted the mathematical into a physical theory. The spheres of Eudoxus and Callippus were now made of *aither*. They were concentric, with the earth as center, and in contact with one another. In order that the spheres of one planet should not interfere with those of another, Aristotle had to introduce additional neutralizing spheres. The entire system consisted of 55 spheres. The question of the physical causes of the apparent motions of the planets was, of course, legitimate. It is Aristotle's solution which fails. As a matter of fact, he himself was not very confident of it. "The statement of logical necessity," he says, "may be left to more competent thinkers."[34]

Except for the discussion of the 55 spheres in the *Metaphysics*, Aristotle's principal account of the heavenly bodies is found in his work, *On the Heavens*. From the composition and movements of the heavenly bodies, he turns to the composition and movements of bodies on earth. Bodies are either simple or compound. There are four simple bodies or elements: earth, water, air, and fire. Like the heavenly bodies, the terrestrial ones have appropriate, natural movements. It is natural for earth and water to fall, to move toward the center of the earth; it is natural for air and fire to rise, to move away from the center of the earth. Compound bodies, made up of these elements, tend to move in the direction in which the predominant element would move.

Other than the employment of the sophisticated mathematical theory of Eudoxus and Callippus, there is little in this cosmology, especially in the work, *On the Heavens*, that a man of common sense might not observe about the movements of heavenly and terrestrial bodies. That the heavenly bodies revolve about the earth, that fire naturally goes up, and earth, a stone, for example, naturally falls back to earth, are about as common observations as one could find. The actual mechanics of *On the Heavens* looks like common sense, pure and simple. What gives the book a distinctive power at all? Why did anyone pay attention to it? Its distinctive character is found in its theological and teleological arguments, especially that things are not simply as they are, but that they must be and that they are for the best. The theological character of the book leads Randall to call it Aristotle's natural theology, a stout attempt to reconcile science and religion.[35]

---

[34] *Metaphysics*, 1074a16–17, Hugh Tredennick trans., p. 159. For a detailed account of this entire matter from Eudoxus to Aristotle, see Sir Thomas Heath, *Aristarchus of Samos* (Oxford at the Clarendon Press, 1913), pp. 190–221.

[35] Randall, *op. cit.*, chap. VII, "The Heavens."

In this early work, even Aristotle's method of investigation is quite different from that in his biological works or that of the man who studied 158 constitutions as background for his *Politics*.

Despite the fact that he must constantly complain of our meager opportunities for observing the farther reaches of the heavens, he manages to set forth why the whole universe is as it is and why it could not be otherwise. And while wherever possible he reinforces his conclusions by appealing to observation, to what "we see," he reverses his normal order of arguing. Both in his theory of science and in his usual practice, he begins with establishing the fact that things are so, and then shows why they have to be so. Here the necessity is first shown, and then observation brought in to confirm the fact.[36]

The appeal to the religious tradition is strong. Aristotle writes:

The reasons why the primary body [the *aither*] is eternal and not subject to increase or diminution, but unaging and unalterable and unmodified, will be clear from what has been said to any one who believes in our assumptions. Our theory seems to confirm experience and to be confirmed by it. For all men have some conception of the nature of the gods, and all who believe in the existence of gods at all, whether barbarian or Greek, agree in allotting the highest place to the deity, surely because they suppose that immortal is linked with immortal and regard any other supposition as inconceivable. If then there is, as there certainly is, anything divine, what we have just said about the primary bodily substance was well said. The mere evidence of the senses is enough to convince us of this, at least with human certainty. For in the whole range of time past, so far as our inherited records reach, no change appears to have taken place either in the whole scheme of the outermost heaven or in any of its proper parts. The common name, too, which has been handed down from our distant ancestors even to our own day, seems to show that they conceived of it in the fashion which we have been expressing. The same ideas, one must believe, recur in men's minds not once or twice but again and again. And so, implying that the primary is something else beyond earth, fire, air, and water, they gave the highest place a name of its own, *aither*, derived from the fact that it "runs always" for an eternity of time. . . .

It is also clear from what has been said why the number of what we call simple bodies cannot be greater than it is. The motion of a simple body must itself be simple, and we assert that there are only these two simple motions, the circular and the straight, the latter being subdivided into motion away from and motion toward the center.[37]

Since, from the time of the ancients, no changes among the stars have been observed, the heavens are eternal. This conclusion hardly comes from the Aristotle of the *Organon*, from the biologist who knew how difficult it was to classify some animals which he had lying before him.

What, then, does *On the Heavens* offer? It offers a tight little finite

---

[36] *Ibid.*, pp. 147–148.

[37] *De Caelo* [*On the Heavens*], 270b1–31, trans. by J. L. Stocks (Oxford at the Clarendon Press, 1922).

universe in which the heavenly bodies are eternal and divine. They possess a perfection in substance and movement which are not to be found on earth. The stars are, in a sense, more divine than the planets, the sun, and the moon, for the motion of the stars is a single circular motion, that of the others, a compound of circular motions. Terrestrial bodies and motion do not have this perfection. But in their own way, they had to be what they are and are for the best. There are gradations of being and motion in nature, from that of the earth to the outermost heaven, which are gradations of perfection. In accordance with these gradations, there are proper, natural places for all the beings that there are. With each body having its appropriate place and moving in accordance with its nature, this is for the best. From all this fitting order one might conclude that this is truly the best of all possible worlds.

Conclusion

The ancient myths of Greece, as found in her great poetry, had accounted for the existence of the natural world, and also provided a pantheon which intervened in and sustained the lives of men in many ways. A man of common sense could be satisfied with the cosmological stories—they had the authority and comfort of tradition; and if he were prudent, he paid his respects to the gods and sought their aid in his daily tasks. His religion added meaning to his beliefs about nature and his own destiny. He would show his gratitude to the gods and, by the same token, add beauty to his own life by building temples in their honor and by celebrating with festivals their participation in human affairs.

As the present account has undertaken to show, this entire way of life in Greece—the conceptual framework for nature, the objects of religious worship with the consequent forms of expression of piety, the moral standards of society—was called into question and revamped by her philosophers, by means of ideas and methods of thinking that had been fostered by scientists and philosophers who were also scientists. Aristotle, the last of the Greek philosophers to be considered, had available not only the traditional Greek way of life but also a new tradition of which he was always aware, that of philosophic and scientific knowledge. Thus, when he looked at the traditional ideals, it was not through the eyes of a Xenophanes. Yet the ideals of Aristotle's *Ethics* and *Politics* are clearly recognizable Greek ideals. The ancient moral wisdom is preserved in his philosophy, but now the burden of man's conduct is placed squarely upon his own intelligence. There is little point in praising or blaming the gods, Aristotle would say, for what we are. We are good or bad in terms of what we make ourselves.

The development of science and philosophy, as Aristotle sees it, is a progressive clarification of the basic characteristics of nature. The earliest of the philosophers had raised the right question in asking, "What is nature?" meaning "What is being or existence?" or "What does it mean to be?" or, simply, "What is substance?" The Pythagoreans and Plato were correct in pointing to the formal characteristics of anything which exists. Plato erred, Aristotle feels, in making the world that lies before us a land of dreams or a shadow of something behind it all. Yes, there are forms, Aristotle agrees, and they are essential to the existence of anything, but they exist in things as the formal structures of things, not behind or apart from things. It is perfectly correct to talk about these forms, and to say that the word, "man," is a universal in standing for those formal characteristics or structures which are essential to the existence of individual men, but "man" does not stand for an ideal, eternal form, "Man."

Another difficulty arises, Aristotle insists, out of Plato's Doctrine of Forms. The concrete individual thing, which comes into being and passes away, is the nub of existence, at least on earth. It is true that the heavenly bodies are eternal, but even they are an ever-actual activity. A serious problem with the Platonists and some of their predecessors was the exaltation of permanence over change. Substances in the primary sense, as concrete individuals, are structures in exercise, potentialities being actualized. For this reason, the answer to the ancient question, "What is the nature of existence?" is "Existence is the attainment of possibilities." To be a man is to attain the possibilities of which a man is capable, to actualize his potentialities. To be is to be a process, to be active. To cease to be active, to cease to be a process, is to cease to be.

But nature is something more than a collection of processes. It is an array of ordered processes. It is a marvelous array of order. Look at living things. They reproduce their kind, their *eide*, their forms, their species. Men produce men, and not other living forms. Besides this cyclic or reproductive order, among living things there is a hierarchical order of forms from the simple to the complex, both within the plant and the animal kingdoms. In fact, as noted before (see p. 120), the orders proceed from the lifeless, through the plants, to ever more complex and higher orders in the animal kingdom. There are species that make up genera, and genera that make up higher genera. From the lifeless, the inanimate elements, to the highest terrestrial living form, man, there is order. From man, we can see higher orders among the eternal heavenly bodies. Among terrestrial things, perishable things, in the temporary existence that they have, their being consists in ever striving for the fullest realization of their possibilities. That which makes this total ordered process possible is the unmoved mover, the integrated order of all the possible orders of nature that there are. It is the order of nature which makes the tiniest, most transient terrestrial process or the eternal movement of the heavenly bodies possible; yet the unmoved mover did not create these processes. For nature is eternal.

Does not this order of nature, Aristotle suggests, truly partake of the marvelous? Is it not sufficient to excite the profoundest wonder of man? We need not keep our eyes on the stars. In the smallest insect there is the beautiful—yes, beautiful—order of nature as well as in the stars. In his own words:

Of the works of Nature there are, we hold, two kinds: those which are brought into being and perish, and those which are free from these processes throughout all ages. The latter are of the highest worth and are divine, but our opportunities for the study of them are somewhat scanty, since there is but little evidence available to our senses to enable us to consider them and all the things that we long to know about. We have better means of information, however, concerning the things that perish, that is to say, plants and animals, because we live among them; and anyone who will but take enough trouble can learn much concerning every one of their kinds. Yet each of the two groups has its attractiveness. For although our grasp of the eternal things is but slight, nevertheless the joy which it brings is, by reason of their excellence and worth, greater than that of knowing all things that are here below; just as the joy of a fleeting and partial glimpse of those whom we love is greater than that of an accurate view of other things, no matter how numerous or how great they are. But inasmuch as it is possible for us to obtain more and better information about things here on the earth, our knowledge of them has the advantage over the other; and moreover, because they are nearer to us and more akin to our Nature, they are able to make up some of their leeway as against the philosophy which contemplates the things that are divine. Of "things divine" we have already treated and have set down our views concerning them; so it now remains to speak of animals and their Nature. So far as in us lies, we will not leave out any of them, be it never so mean; for though there are animals which have no attractiveness for the senses, yet for the eye of science, for the student who is naturally of a philosophic spirit and can discern the causes of things, Nature which fashioned them provides joys which cannot be measured . . . Wherefore we must not betake ourselves to the consideration of the meaner animals with a bad grace, as though we were children; since in all natural things there is somewhat of the marvellous. . . . we ought not to hesitate nor to be abashed, but boldly to enter upon our researches concerning animals of every sort and kind, knowing that in not one of them is Nature or Beauty lacking.[38]

Here, surely, is the philosopher in what has since become his immemorial role: his eye upon both the sacred and the profane, the "divine" which mirrors our aspirations and brings us the highest joy, and "things here below" concerning which we have "better means of information." Could we be told more clearly that philosophy must encompass both?

To be sure, not all philosophers have found beauty in both. Aristotle does. We may glory more in knowledge of the heavenly bodies, which are eternal. Men always seem to treasure more that which touches the eternal. But we are fools if we do not see the divinity of nature that lies immediately

---

[38] *Parts of Animals*, 644b2–645a23, trans. by A. L. Peck (Cambridge: Harvard, 1937), pp. 97–101.

before us in all its orders. Yes, it is the order of nature that is divine. It is the actuality of reason, a life. Of course, not a life like that of a man. Xenophanes caught the sense of this order and meaning of divinity when he called it "god" but insisted it was not a person and that it "shakes all things by the thought of his mind." (See p. 60.) That last expression was still too anthropomorphic, Aristotle would say, but Xenophanes had a sense of what this sort of divinity means. Heraclitus, too, had the hang of it in his Logos. And, of course, Plato did in the Good; but you could never be sure with Plato whether the Good was the order of nature, or what we call the order of nature was just a copy of the Good.

How is it that man knows this order? Of course, by means of his mind, by *nous,* the touch of divinity that man has if he has any at all. His intelligence raises him above the other animals; it gives him a sense of what divinity is, too. Is this not the essence of true piety, to love the life of the mind and seek to understand the order of nature? Would this not be the ultimate happiness man could hope to experience? Would this not be the highest actuality of man? Is this not the natural piety for man, the knower?

Why has Aristotle excited the minds of men as much as Plato, and stirred their religious fervor, if not so much, at least deeply? Possibly there are many reasons why he has stirred men's minds, but probably the most important in arousing their religious fervor is his vision of nature, beautifully ordered from the physical elements of earth, through living things, to the eternal heavenly bodies, and finally to the unmoved mover. As with Plato, this order is not only beautiful, it is for the best.

As with Plato also, Aristotle's vision was more visionary of order than the status of knowledge warranted. Mathematics had progressed in geometry, and Aristotle took the first steps in establishing biology as a science. But speculation still outstripped what we today should consider an adequate empirical basis for a theory of nature. In fact, Aristotle's universe is much tidier in the heavens, about which he could know little, than among living things, about which he knew a great deal. He still found order and beauty in living things, but the order was many orders, not nearly so neat as the planets and the stars.

Moreover, Aristotle's analysis of discourse, productive of his theory of the syllogism based upon class relationships, and his view of a demonstrative science did not seem to deal adequately with his dynamic analyses of the processes of nature, animate and inanimate. The syllogism can formalize the class relationships among species and genera, but seems inappropriate to his dynamic analyses concerned with the functions of animals. His theory of a demonstrative science appears more appropriate to mathematics than to living things. It is not at all clear that Aristotle resolved, even to his own satisfaction, the relationship of the static and the dynamic characteristics of nature, and how these relationships can be appropriately put into discourse to constitute what we call knowledge. His works often look more like a series of studies, in which he moved from strong Platonic influences, as in On the Heavens, to his own empirical studies of biology and of man in his moral and social relations, in the Ethics and Politics.

But of this we may be sure: it was his vision of a beautifully ordered and good universe—in On the Heavens and certain passages of the Metaphysics—along with his logic of classes, that triumphed in the Middle Ages over the empirically-minded philosopher. What if the unmoved mover should be God, and the beautifully ordered and good universe created instead of eternal? What if the classes of men in society are ordained by God, as well as all things in nature? If things in nature have their appropriate place and it is best that they do, is this not also true for men in society? Each man will have his proper station and duties —the serf, the noble, and the clergyman. Truly this is God's order among men, as He has ordered all things in the universe for the best.

If Aristotle did not achieve a synthesis in his own day, there nevertheless was to be a synthesis much later, one which, however much it may have distorted Aristotle, did borrow Aristotelian concepts and did relate them, not only internally but also to the Christianity that developed in the intervening centuries. It was through the massive philosophy of St. Thomas that Aristotelianism was handed over to the modern Christian world. St. Thomas effected a synthesis of the hierarchical order suggested by Aristotle's logic and cosmology. In this system both nature and man achieved perfection, subordinated as they were to the ultimate perfection of God. The Greek Aristotle may have suffered in this transformation, but the glory of God was, through it, to be magnified and revered. In this form, Aristotelianism became the new folklore, which, in turn, was an ingredient giving rise to the need for still newer philosophies.

Why, then, did the scientists and philosophers of the seventeenth and eighteenth centuries reject Aristotle the scientist and Aristotle the philosopher? The rejection, in part, resulted from the fact that Aristotle, "the philosopher," as St. Thomas called him, became a symbol of medieval scholasticism which was the essence of barren knowledge, as the avantgarde of the new age saw it. But even Aristotle the scientist fell into disrepute. Despite his own contributions to empirical science, mainly biological, and despite his insistence on observation, and his beatification of nature, modern science superseded Aristotle because his very interest in biology that was the source of his claim to be a scientist led him to concentrate on the qualitative to the exclusion of the quantitative, and on the teleological and functional rather than the mechanical. Modern science—as Part II will show—had to abstract from the qualitative aspect of things and ignore teleology before it could move forward. (See pp. 159 ff.) Moreover, even in the area where his scientific gifts are most manifest, namely biology, Aristotle was limited by his reliance on common sense observation, albeit an uncommonly systematic and acute form of it. Given the state of knowledge of his day, this limitation was not his fault; indeed it would be captious to criticize a man who so magnificently expanded the knowledge of his time. He was also limited by his heritage from Plato, an influence that sometimes led him to emphasize formalism instead of functionalism, and hence to stress the fixity of species. Whether just or unjust to Aristotle, the investigator of nature, this was the version of his philosophy which came down to us through the Middle Ages; so that here again—as Part III will show— science, in this instance biological science, had to transcend the limitations of Aristotle's investigations before it could move forward.

Selected Readings

Aristotle, *The Works of Aristotle Translated into English*, ed. by W. D. Ross, Oxford at the Clarendon Press, 12 vols. (There are paperback editions of individual works.)

Jaeger, Werner, *Aristotle, Fundamentals of the History of His Development*, 2nd ed., New York: Oxford, 1948.

Mure, G. R. G., *Aristotle*, New York: Oxford, 1964.

Randall, John Herman, Jr., *Aristotle*, New York: Columbia, 1960.

Ross, W. D., *Aristotle*, New York: Meridian, 1959.

Windelband, W., *History of Ancient Philosophy*, New York: Dover, 1956, pp. 224–292.

Woodbridge, Frederick J. E., *Aristotle's Vision of Nature*, New York: Columbia, 1965.

PART II

IMPACT OF THE NEW PHYSICS

*If we are to draw any useful lines of demarcation
in the continuous flux of history . . . we need not scruple to say
that, in the realm of knowledge and thought, modern history
begins in the seventeenth century. Ubiquitous rebellion
against tradition, a new standard of clear and precise thought
. . . a flow of mathematical and physical discoveries so rapid
that ten years added more to the sum of knowledge
than all that had been added since the days of Archimedes,
the introduction of organized cooperation to increase knowledge
. . . a flow of mathematical and physical discoveries so rapid
that ten years added more to the sum of knowledge
than all that had been added since the days of Archimedes,
the introduction of organized cooperation to increase knowledge . . .
characterize the opening of a new era.*
J. B. Bury, *The Idea of Progress*

*A brief, and sufficiently accurate, description
of the intellectual life of the European races
during the succeeding two centuries and a quarter up to our own times
is that they have been living upon the accumulated capital of ideas
provided for them by the genius of the seventeenth century.*
A. N. Whitehead, *Science and the Modern World*

*I thus concluded that it is much more custom and example
that persuade us than any certain knowledge,
and yet in spite of this the voice of the majority does not afford a proof
of any value in truths a little difficult to discover,
because such truths are much more likely
to have been discovered by one man than by a nation.*
Descartes, *Discourse on Method*

CHAPTER 7

Introduction:
The Challenge of
Seventeenth-Century
Science to
the Older Folklore

Medievalism Become Folklore

The medieval world view, against which the new science constituted a revolt, cannot truthfully be presented as adding up to a single, agreed-upon picture. It contained many things, including science and religion, mysticism and humanism, philosophy and idolatry, and a wide panorama of its own.[1] Yet the most anguishing and complex question that the medieval philosopher had to answer was how to relate, in the light of Christian revelation, nature and man and God—nature with its many-faceted appearances, man in his triple aspect of body and mind and spirit, and God as partially revealed and yet ultimately inscrutable because of his infinite superiority to anything imaginable by man. Also, since God was universally

---

[1] Cf. G. G. Coulton, *Medieval Panorama* (Cambridge at the University Press. 1939).

believed to be the creator of the world who had left his mark on every aspect of it, nothing could finally be intelligible except as it were related to Him.

To do justice to the multiplicity of finite things and to acknowledge in a sophisticated yet humble way the unity of the infinite God—this was the task of the medieval philosopher. And the greatest of them all, St. Thomas (c. 1225-1274), did this by effecting a synthesis in the three broad areas: science, philosophy, and theology. In this synthesis, he brought together Aristotelian philosophy and Christian dogma in a way that would at the same time respect the best of natural knowledge, reason, sympathetic insight into man, and the spiritual hegemony of the Church on earth. To do this he had to search out the manifold continuities, from the lowest kind of material being to the highest of spiritual beings. In this scheme of things, man was central, in that he had to be regarded as the highest of material things and the lowest of spiritual beings. He was body and mind and spirit. Through the intermediary of the Church, he could, with faith and divine guidance, rise to greater heights, just as Beatrice could eventually lead Dante to the beatific vision of paradise. Man's spiritual pilgrimage could carry him beyond this world into eternity, and with it into the peaceful realization that was man's ultimate destiny.

Theology was one way for man to understand something of these mysteries. Another way was through the work of the anonymous architects of the gothic cathedral. The sense of structure, of wandering, and of the final oneness of things is aptly embodied in this architectural masterpiece. As one enters, for example, the cathedral of Chartres, his eye cannot but move upward from the massive columns, which line the nave, to the upper regions where they taper off to spindle-like colonnettes. And from there the eye is impelled to follow infinitely delicate tracery work, which appears much more like tensile filigree than carved stone, only for the experience to be consummated in the unearthly, mystical light of the rose window. To bring about this continuity, from the material to the half-material, half-spiritual, to the purely spiritual—this was the task of St. Thomas, even as it was the poetic revelation of Dante's *Divine Comedy* as well as the inspiriting force of the architect of the gothic cathedral.

The grandeur of the medieval synthesis provided good reason for speaking of the thirteenth century as "the greatest of all centuries." The feat of exhibiting ways of conceiving continuities, from the lowest to the highest of things, makes for a truly remarkable philosophical outlook. The question was whether men would continue to regard the universe this way. And the answer was that although the outlook persisted, it came to be challenged from a number of quarters, both from within and from without. From the inside, the synthesis was attacked in different ways by mystics and by logicians. From the outside, the scientific revolution came to be a menace to the continuance of the medieval synthesis. Although the latter chastened men's minds in the search for a new philosophical outlook, the former also cleansed away some of the impurities that would otherwise have dimmed that outlook.

St. Thomas' philosophy lent itself to reinterpretation by later Christian philosophers, because his system contained an uneasy transition between the world of matter and the world of spirit. Material things were said by him to possess "inherent forms"—that is, forms which are realized in things and which give them distinctive characteristics. These forms are embodied in matter; hence, things themselves possess real essences as a part of their nature. Aristotle had said as much when he insisted that the actualization of the potential, as when an acorn becomes an oak, is the realization of the form, which the oak is. Whether true or not, this is certainly not an absurd way of looking at material things—all of which, so far as experience goes, do become something, and hence have the form of that which they have become. But beyond material things, St. Thomas acknowledged the existence of spiritual things, like angels, cherubim, seraphim, and even higher beings, up to God. Each of these must also have a form, for all are real: one angel is like another angel in form, and so for cherubim, seraphim, and the rest. But in these cases they are not material and therefore they cannot have material form. So their forms were called "subsistent forms," forms which did not require, in fact, could not possess, matter. Because of the basic difference between material beings, which are embodied, and spiritual beings, which are disembodied, the principles of interpretation which apply to the two realms are necessarily different.

Now when philosophers—or better, philosopher-theologians—began, on the one hand, to separate completely the spiritual from the material world, and when, on the other, they began to purge the spiritual of its polytheistic connotations, then they were left with the one spiritual being, together with the awful need of imitating it, as did Thomas à Kempis (1380-1471) and Meister Eckhart (c. 1260-1327). Their objections to the Thomistic philosophy constituted the first rumblings of the Protestant revolt, in which God is sought for directly; not through the mediation of the Church. Thomas à Kempis, for example, pleads, "Let not Moses speak unto me, nor any of the prophets, but rather do thou speak, O Lord, God." Such mysticism is heresy. When this mysticism is organized, it becomes Protestantism. In medieval philosophy this mysticism has as one of its expressions "realism"—that is, a philosophy which asserts the reality of the universal. To express realism in comparative terms, we may say that the more universal a thing is the more real it is. But if reality is a function of universality, then anything less than universal is, to that extent, unreal.

Since the more universal is the more real, then the most universal is the most real. But there is only one most universal (which includes all there is), and therefore there is only one really real being, and that one really real being is God; therefore, He and He alone exists. Pushed to its logical extreme, this is where the doctrine of subsistent form comes out in the end. In the mystical Cologne school of art, it is represented by the *Madonna in the Rose Garden*, the empty, personality-less visage, with no character of its own, because its character is absorbed in God, where alone reality can reside.

Now for the doctrine of inherent form, which through a curious history was interpreted in quite opposite ways. On the one hand forms, which of course are universals, came to be interpreted as mathematical entities, and this interpretation, which became a kind of Renaissance Platonism, led the way to mathematizing nature. Natural laws, then, are best expressed as mathematical formulae, such as Kepler asserted in his third law of planetary motions in which T^2 is proportional to D^3—that is, the square of the time of the revolution of a planet is proportional to the mean distance cubed. According to this view, no knowledge is scientific knowledge unless it can be accurately and precisely expressed in mathematical characters. We shall need to explore this conception in considerable detail.

But there is another interpretation of inherent form, which, in terms of the old controversy over the interpretation of universals, turns out to be a version of nominalism instead of Platonic or mathematical realism. Nominalism, we recall, is the doctrine that universals have no independent reality. They are words; "noises" is what we usually call them today; "*flatus vocis*" the schoolmen called them—mere breaths of air. In a more sophisticated form, in the philosophy of William of Occam (died, *c.* 1349), universals have meaning, in the first instance, only as pointers. "Chair" means the class of chairs— $chair_1$, $chair_2$, $chair_3$, ... $chair_n$. Unless particular chairs exist, "chair" is meaningless. In the second instance, a pointer can point to a pointer, which in turn points to things. Thus, "furniture" can point to "chair" (as well as to "table," "bed," "hatrack," etc.). It, too, can be meaningful, provided there are chairs and tables and beds and hatracks, etc., in the world.

The importance of a pointer resides in the existence of the particulars that are pointed to. The realities then are those particulars. They constitute the referents of pointers, the things pointed to, and without them the world can be only airy nothings. Accordingly, the rock-bottom realities are sensations, for these are the ultimate particulars of experience, not reducible to anything else—this green here, this sound now, this immediate feeling of pain or cold or heat, etc. In philosophy, this view leads to sensationalism or phenomenalism—a world created sheerly out of the relations of the data of immediate experience. In the Dutch school of art, it is portrayed by Van Eyck's *Jan Arnolfini and his Wife,* where things are depicted in their utmost detail, each hair of the dog, and each little detail of the immensely complex chandelier—and then, for good measure, each detail repeated once more in the reflected image of the chandelier in the mirror!

Both the Platonic and the nominalistic interpretations of inherent form meet in their renewed interest in exploring the character of nature. Although the doctrine of subsistent form emphasizes a kind of mysticism— the inner light, which gets expressed in a variety of ways, ranging from pietism and quietism to quakerism—inherent form does not. The latter leads to an outgoing attitude. It places its faith in the virtue of curiosity and exploration, and it welcomes the novelties that result from them. The activities engendered by the interest in inherent form so interpreted lead on directly to science. Between the immediate apprehension of things in nature, that is, perceptions and the theoretical considerations of the nature of nature, that is, cosmology lies the activity which most effectively challenged the older folklore—namely, modern science.

The Challenge From Science

In science, more than in anything else, the modern world—from the Renaissance down to the twentieth century—has found an ever-present challenge to the medieval world view. Science has meant different things at different times, but in the seventeenth century it meant primarily physical science. Accordingly, scientists were bent on discovering second causes rather than the First Cause, and they increasingly dissociated their studies from final causes. Concentrating upon the study and representation of motions, Galileo (1564–1642) was probably the first of the moderns to set forth, in his law of inertial motion, a new way of conceiving of the physical world. He conceived of the physical world, not merely as having an independent existence; each body within it was thought to be capable of describing a motion independent of every other. The magnitude of the change from the older to the newer science represents a radical break in thought, profound and upsetting. The distinguished historian and philosopher of science, Alfred Koyré, asserts that the change from the older science to the Galilean science in which the law of inertial motion appears to be evident to us is so because we willingly presuppose:

(*a*) the possibility of isolating a physical body from its physical environment, (*b*) a conception of space which identifies it with the homogeneous infinite space of Euclidean geometry, and (*c*) a conception of movement—and of rest—which considers them as states and places them on the same ontological level of being.[2]

---

[2] *Philosophical Revue,* Vol. 4, No. 52 (1943), p. 337.

In this brief statement, Mr. Koyré has suggested the essence of the shift from Aristotelian science to Galilean science, and along with it, the shift from medievalism to modernism.

The humanistic world of Aristotle was made by St. Thomas into a tidy system, embodying, among other things, a geography, a human and spiritual society, and a celestial realm where man found his salvation, if he were not consigned to limbo or to the flames. Built upon an Aristotelian base, the structure contained a hierarchy of essences, each of which was qualitatively distinct from every other. Now the newly emerging system opposes this in almost every respect. Inevitably it comes out as quantitative instead of qualitative, and atomistic instead of hierarchical. The general scheme of things is mechanistic materialism as opposed to spiritualistic idealism, but the meaning of these terms will have to wait upon detailed analyses both in science and in philosophy.

In science, Galileo sought, in the words of Mr. Koyré, to isolate a physical body from its physical environment. Aristotle had had a different view; he regarded the elements of the world as moving toward their proper places, and consequently their nature could not be understood apart from those places for which they were headed and in which they would come to rest. Water and earth accordingly moved downward, which is their proper place, and the lighter elements, air and fire, moved upward toward their proper place. In fact, down and up were actually defined by the places where water and earth and where air and fire, respectively, come to rest. At least, so the theory went, they moved toward their proper places unless they were acted upon by some "unnatural" force. The world was thus regarded as stratified, and could be seen to be ordered from the more condensed to the more rarefied, topped by the most rare of all, the fifth essence (or quintessence of things). Aristotle conceived of the fifth essence as partaking of the divine, and the divine, moreover, as the ultimate goal toward which all things strive.

Today we still take nature for granted. But the nagging question is, what is it that we take for granted when we take nature for granted? Is it things in all their richness of color and scent and texture, the myriads of qualities that our senses reveal? Is it an ordered relation of things from (comparatively) simple material things to living things, to man, and possibly even to the divine? Is it material things alone in a world senseless and without colors, or, in the words of Alfred North Whitehead, "merely the hurrying of material, endlessly, meaninglessly"? Or again, is it possibly some kind of lumpiness which exists out there, we know not how, even though we are convinced that it does somehow exist? Or still again, is it possibly not material at all, but rather a realm of sprites and spirits, more like human beings than anything else? These questions philosophy desperately needs to explore and to find for them some kind of satisfactory answers. The Greeks provided a range of answers, more or less satisfactory for their times. But these times were pre-Christian. A new synthesis was required which included not only Greek philosophy but also Greek science, as well as a world in which the Christian drama of man's sin and man's salvation could be enacted. Making use of the philosophy of Aristotle and borrowing from the astronomy of Ptolemy, who regarded the sun and the planets as whirling around the earth, both St. Thomas and Dante created, as we have already mentioned, each in his own way, a magnificent synthesis, the one in the language of philosophy, the other in the language of poetry.

But turning more to the prevailing physical concepts of the medieval world view, a decisive aspect of this view consisted in the distinction between natural motion and violent motion—that is, those motions that did violence to nature. Clearly, air can be held down, as a closed container under water can be held down, and clearly, earthen things can be projected into the air. But not indefinitely. Air rises and earth falls, and it is unnatural for them to do the reverse.

The conventional wisdom did not admit of the abstraction of a body from its ambiance in the world and from its necessary relation to a place which it sought and where it ultimately belonged. Like the pieces of a puzzle, things are meaningless unless they have a place in a scheme of things. According to this view, there is no reason to pay attention to isolated things and there is no reason for them to exist. And finally, there is no proper method by which they can be known. A thing isolated from everything else is nothing of importance to anything, and can safely be ignored. For the Greeks, nature had to make sense—it had to have a pattern. And, for the schoolmen, this pattern had to be understood in relation to the Supreme Being, however imperfect it is in comparison with that Being. Things fall into kinds, and kinds are related to other kinds, so that there is a family of things that exists under a great father.

In contrast with this view, there is a complete strangeness in Galileo's conception of bodies as being either in a state of motion or rest, and of remaining in that state of motion or rest unless some meddling external force interferes with them. If Galileo is right, a moving thing does not then naturally come to rest, but it just keeps on moving forever. How absurd this must have seemed to his contemporaries, when common sense told them that things do come to rest. Heavy things, for example, do fall to the ground; they come to rest, and they require a cause to move them again. The common-sense view will have none of this moving forever—or resting forever—since this view is contradicted by all (or nearly all) that we see and know.

Bodies are like people. They have to have moving causes and they have to come to rest. And again, they are like people in that they have to be understood in terms of what they came from and in terms of what they are headed for. It seems like madness to try to understand a person who has no inheritance and who has no destiny. So also the things of the world. They, too, come from something (for nothing can come from nothing), and they too have a destiny, a place in nature (for everything has some good in it, some purpose to fulfill).

In denying all this, Galileo does require space through which things can move. But this space is, so to speak, an uninhabited space—without moving genii to keep pushing things along. Once in motion, a body continues to move endlessly; or if it does not, then and then only is an explanation required. By assuming endless space and endless motion, Galileo, by implication, totally repudiates the conventional wisdom. Accordingly, it is not motion that needs to be accounted for, but rest. And rest is not primary, something that just is; but it is, as comes out more clearly in Newton's version, a canceling of motion through the effects of equal and opposite forces. The radical shift in outlook is from one in which motion rather than rest needs to be explained to one in which rest rather than motion needs to be explained—or better, an outlook from which a change of motion needs to be explained. Aristotle, and the medieval schoolmen following him, had required four causes or principles for understanding how things change. (Cf. Part I, pp. 122 ff.) Given a body with its mass and its state of motion or rest, the new science required only one cause—the efficient cause—which would adequately explain any change in that body. Otherwise, according to the law of inertial motion, a body just continues timelessly in its state of motion or rest, quite independent of any sustaining cause, or for that matter, quite independent of anything else in the world.

For Aristotle and his medieval disciples there exists a basic distinction in kinds of motions, namely, the earthly and the heavenly. Earthly motions are, fundamentally, motions in a straight line, mostly up and down. They have a beginning, a middle, and an end, and consequently can be conceived of as the actualization of the potential, their actuality being their end. An object that is at A, but that will eventually be at B, is potentially at B, and when it arrives there it is then actually at B. Heavenly bodies move in circles. Theirs is a more perfect kind of motion, continually recurring in the same way, never coming to an end, and therefore constantly actualizing themselves; and they are divine. The received learning is thus able, sheerly in the description of the physical world, to order reality according to lower and higher in terms of the earthly and the celestial. And this order is also an order of perfection from the sheerly potential, which is formless matter, to the highest actuality, which is God.

St. Thomas formalized this view in terms of his own philosophy. Things exist in an ascending order, and inasmuch as we know them, the sciences of these things also belong in an ascending order, however different the methods of the sciences may be if they are to cope adequately with their various subject matters. So says St. Thomas:

One science may be subordinate to another in two ways. First, as a part, when its special subject is contained in a more general field: plants are included among natural bodies, and therefore botany is a species of natural science. Second, as subaltern, when the higher science provides the postulates of the lower science yet not its special subject: for instance, the human body as curable by art, not by nature, is the special interest of medical science. Thus arithmetic rules musical theory, and natural science rules medicine, chemistry, and agricultural science.

Though, in a sense, all scientific subjects are parts of general reality, which is the proper study of metaphysics, it does not follow that all the sciences are departments of metaphysics. For they employ their special methods and examine a part of being in a style quite their own and different from that of metaphysics.[3]

In contrast with St. Thomas' conception of science, the new science began to challenge this way of ordering the sciences. It did so because it began to consider nature as of a piece. Galileo made a beginning by his way of analyzing terrestrial motions. Newton (1642–1727) completed the design for the new science by accommodating both terrestrial and celestial mechanics to the same pattern. This accomplishment served to complete the revolution which was fathered by Copernicus (1473–1543) when he led men to conceive the world to be so vast, and so independent of man, that man could no longer easily think that it was created for his comfort and convenience. Implicitly, this notion led to the conception of physical nature as value free. It was no longer an anthropocentric world, that is, a world created in the image of man and especially catering to human needs.

The new science required the despiritualization of nature. It required man to reject not merely the assumption that particular physical actions are guided by a supreme spirit or a host of minor spirits, but, even more fundamentally, to reject the assumption that celestial bodies should be regarded as spiritual substances and hence as different in kind from earthly objects. The laws of nature are now universal, and apply to heavenly as well as earthly bodies. The new science could not tolerate the related notion of a hierarchy of being, in which there are degrees of reality equated with levels of value. According to the new science, all of nature is equally real; and to attribute value to any of its extra-human manifestations is meaningless and irrelevant.

Copernicus had, contrary to all common-sense experience, challenged

---

[3] Thomas Gilby, *St. Thomas Aquinas* (New York: Oxford University Press, 1960), p. 25.

the focus of the world view of the accepted learning. Man could no longer be the focus of the world, composed, as he was supposed to be, of both earthly and spiritual being; and Jerusalem could no longer be the center of the universe, below which was hell and above which was heaven. According to the new astronomy, men must regard themselves as whirling around in space at incredible speed, in spite of the fact that the senses give us no indication that this is the case. And even though the great Danish astronomer, Tycho Brahe (1546–1601), could conceive the earth as stationary, the sun as revolving about the earth, but the other planets as revolving about the sun, nevertheless his compromise could not conceal the break with the received learning. Although theoretically possible, Tycho's view was too clumsy to be very seriously entertained. Galileo's telescope had already revealed irregular motions that made Ptolemy's account of the planets suspect. New theory was now required to explain these new facts successfully.

If celestial and earthly bodies had now to be thought of as composed of the same stuff and as subject to the same laws, the conception of law itself had to be overhauled. The principle of parsimony—though actually a medieval concept—came to have new significance. This principle, that the simpler explanation is the better, begins now to be regarded as a truth of nature in a new way, namely, in the peculiarly modern sense that nature does nothing in vain. If one law will satisfy instead of two, then one law must be the reigning principle of nature, even though the heavens fall and even though the science of physics repudiates the deliverances of sense experience.

Nature may still be elegant, and the patterns of its motions may still conform to figures of exact paths. Motivated as he was by the sense of mathematical exactitude, Johannes Kepler (1571–1630) could maintain the spirit of mathematical perfectionism while still repudiating Aristotle's insistence upon circular motion as the only perfect motion. In stating his first law of planetary motion—that planets move in elliptical orbits—Kepler could maintain the perfection of their motions and at the same time take issue with the Aristotelian version. This he could do because he could conceive of the oval or ellipse as being a more adequate, because a more generalized, conception of a class of geometrical figures. In this view, the circle is just a special case of an ellipse—that in which the two foci are identical. Mathematics, then, becomes the key to the interpretation of the physical world. Thus, the second and third laws, in which Kepler asserted that planets sweep out equal areas in equal times, and that the mean distances cubed are proportional to the times squared. With this simplicity and elegance, an important part of the interpretation of nature thus became readied for a more inclusive interpretation to be given to it by Newton.

The new science was less given to the task of defining things than it was to that of analyzing nature into its parts. This emphasis becomes clearest in the new science of physics, first, because physicists had less reason for placing things in classes, and, second, because they were searching for significant predicates applicable to the whole extent of physical nature. Classification gave way to measurement, and measurement was of predicates which, by the aid of mathematical formulas, made possible an understanding of the dynamics of nature. One such predicate was that of mass. Although mass was regarded as a quality of things, there was a difference. It not merely represented the essence of a thing; it came close to being identical with the thing itself. Mass, theoretically conceived to be located at the absolute center of a body, was, in physical terms, virtually a substitute for the body itself. Color, fragrance, and sometimes even shape, were regarded as irrelevant to how a body behaves and how it acts upon others. A predicate such as mass made possible nice comparisons of bodies with one another. The laws of their relations could be stated precisely and could be employed to predict actual occurrences in nature. A formula, such as $G = \dfrac{mm'}{r^2}$, expressed with elegance and simplicity a vast range of observations and also served as a useful device, which stood the test for a century and a half. Moreover, once the various laws of physics were brought together in a system, nature could then be regarded from a sheerly mechanistic point of view. (Later we shall spell out in Chapter 12 the meaning and significance of this point of view for modern thought.)

The mechanistic approach to nature received some expression in biology too. Beginning, first of all, in anatomy, it was followed by the climactic discovery of the circulation of the blood. Andreas Vesalius (1514–1564), an outstanding anatomist, is credited with much of the pioneer work of the new biology. He dissected animals, and occasionally human corpses, and he produced the classic, *On the Construction of the Human Body*. A keen observer, a masterful draughtsman, Vesalius painstakingly and elegantly made drawings of structure and organs of the human nervous and muscular systems. His work was limited thus to a segment of nature, anatomy; but it served as a powerful influence in stimulating other work and in contributing to the mechanistic approach. This work, especially when taken in conjunction with that of Charles Estienne (1504–1564), who contributed to a knowledge of the venous and arterial systems including their valve-mechanisms, prepared the way for the remarkable discovery of the circulation of the blood by William Harvey (1578–1657).

Once these results were known, the modern world was ripe for a theory which would relate physical and biological phenomena in a total conception of the world, in short in a complete philosophy.

In addition to these fertile discoveries, there were also sterile attempts at studying nature, both in the physical and in the biological realms. These attempts were stillborn, usually because, besides being a reflection of the old intellectual folklore, they were also fused with a mysticism, neither productive in effect nor humbly religious. The work of the alchemists certainly illustrates a pseudo-scientific, abortive effort. Paracelsus (1493–1541) did toy with things like sulphur and mercury, especially in the attempt to cure disease. Believing as they did in the hidden properties of things, the alchemists thought that they could cure disease by inducing chemical substances into persons' bodies. Mercury, for example, was used as a specific to cure syphilis. Often the effects of their treatments turned out to be worse than the disease itself. Possibly the difficulty lay in the fact that alchemists such as Paracelsus paid insufficient attention to the physical aspect of medicine. He did say that "the art of medicine is rooted in the heart."[4] The alchemists actually made little contribution to the new science—much less, for instance, than the metallurgists, who actually did discover processes for the conversion of natural things into forms useful to man.

The alchemists were closer than the scientists to the tradition of the received learning, inasmuch as they thought in terms of things as having specific qualities. This way of thinking does suggest that things possess occult forms, which belong to them by nature. Moreover, it leads to easy interpretations that the explanation of anything whatsoever is to be sought in terms of these forms, as when it is said that opium makes one sleep because of its soporific (literally, "sleep making") effects. Some of the schoolmen had identified things by virtue of their specific qualities. This was true both for St. Thomas in his attempt to account for the individuation of things, and in a similar, though somewhat different, account by Duns Scotus (1265–1308), who sought to discern the individuating principle of things in a special kind of "thisness," which each thing was said to possess. Moreover, since things were regarded essentially as belonging to classes, there was set forth a doctrine of substantial forms, which had become the reigning principle of interpretation.

The Rise of Philosophy

A movement as powerful as the new science necessarily made a profound impact on men's ideas and on their way of life, and made all the more urgent a working out of a new philosophy. Philosophy was required

---

[4] Quoted by Giorgio de Santillana, *The Age of Adventure* (New York: Mentor Books, 1956), p. 192.

in order that modern man could come to terms with a world reborn in art and literature, in science and technology, in commerce and trade, and in urban centers where a whole new civilization was molding men's fate. The clash between science and the older folklore reverberated in every sphere of human life, the movement of men from the manor to the city, the inroads of reform movements on the Church, manners and morals, ideas, and virtually all the various institutions that went to structure social life. Accordingly, men needed a whole new intellectual orientation by which they could relate to the things of the world. This inevitably meant philosophy—the most inclusive intellectual interpretation which would help to make man at home in the vast, complex, new world.

The focus of seventeenth-century philosophies, quite understandably, was upon science, for science was, in its various manifestations, the area in which there were developed concepts and methods that were most contrary to the medieval folklore. The unity of nature, its lawful character, the fervor of experimentation, of empirically tracing consequences, and of the substitution of the intellect for the spirit—all of these elements of science as well as those indirectly related to it were regarded seriously by the philosophers. The methods by which men gain knowledge began to assume greater proportions. Dogma and revelation became increasingly less acceptable, and *what* the world is became insistently dependent upon *how* the world is known. This shift from being to being known, can be traced to the regard which philosophers had for science, however differently they interpreted science.

There are at least two traditions in modern philosophy that have important spokesman in the seventeenth century. Both Francis Bacon (1561-1626) and René Descartes (1596-1650) freshly approached philosophical thought and indelibly left their imprints on it. In different ways both Bacon and Descartes evolved conceptions of science and explained at length what they took to be the meaning of science. In a sense, we can say that each of them made long dialogues between philosophy and science, each in his own way attempting to show what the significance of science is. Moreover, each of these philosophers so penetrated the inner powers of science that each still has relevant words to say to us today.

Bacon had the more practical turn of mind. He was not, however, narrowly practical. Rather, he was concerned with the purposes philosophy and science could have for mankind. Of the two philosophies, Bacon's turns out to be the more brutally empirical, less given to abstractions. One historian, Benjamin Farrington, has written an essay on his philosophy with the title, *Francis Bacon: Philosopher of Industrial Science*. This characterization may be prophetic concerning the end with which philosophy may yet have to contend. At least it furnishes a point of departure for the beginning of our philosophical analysis.

The other focus is clearly the more abstract philosophy, mathematically oriented. Descartes, himself a superb mathematician, attempted to meet the upsets created by the new science by constructing a system of concepts for putting everything in its place. His appeal is much more to reason as the indispensable means to knowledge than it is to experimentation. His philosophy is more attuned to the deductive than to the inductive method. At the outset it might appear that both philosophies are necessary, because science—science in the sense of modern physics—is both mathematical and experimental. This appraisal may be essentially correct, but we cannot take much pride in it unless we know a good deal about the nature of both mathematics and experiment. We propose to begin, then, by examining the experimental method, using Bacon as our first guide.

Selected Readings

Bourke, Vernon J., *The Pocket Aquinas*, New York: Washington Square Press, 1960. (Paperback.)

Burtt, E. A., *The Metaphysical Foundations of Modern Science*, New York: Anchor Books, 1954. (Paperback.)

Galileo Galilei, *Dialogues Concerning Two New Sciences*, trans. by H. Crew and A. de Salvio, New York, Macmillan, 1914. (Also in Dover paperback.)

Hall, A. R., *The Scientific Revolution*, Boston: Beacon Press, 1954. (Paperback.)

Randall, J. H., Jr., *Making of the Modern Mind*, Boston: Houghton Mifflin, Chs. X, XI, 1926, 1940.

De Santillana, Georgio, *The Age of Adventure*, New York: Mentor Books, 1956. (Paperback.)

Whitehead, Alfred North, *Science and the Modern World*, New York: Mentor Books, 1949. (Paperback.)

Windelband, Wilhelm, *A History of Philosophy*, New York: Harper Torchbooks, 1958, Vol. I, Part 3. (Paperback.)

CHAPTER 8

Experimentation
and
Its Interpretation

The Priority of the Question of Method

In the modern mode, the knotty philosophical problem is: How to avoid the arbitrariness that results from the choice of one method rather than another? Any method is insidious, in that once we commit ourselves to its use, our commitment then dictates the kind of philosophy we are obliged to adopt. This predicament is not hopeless, since we may combine one or more methods, but always at a price.

St. Thomas, for example, showed great skill in combining science and philosophy and theology in one extraordinary system. Each division required its own peculiar method, and yet each was significantly subordinate to the next. Science, for example, required philosophical presuppositions that science itself could not provide. Or again, philosophy could prove God's existence, but it could not ascertain the fuller mysteries of His being. Because of the limitations of philosophy, St. Thomas viewed theology as the capstone of knowledge and the Church's considered, systematic interpretation of all things. Theology was the queen of the sciences and constituted the ultimate principle of intelligibility of things. The Thomistic system came to be the more or less orthodox pattern of thought;

and it increasingly attained the status of the received learning, which clearly proclaimed the primacy of the spiritual over the material world.

With the advent of the challenges to this world view, which we noted in the previous section, the need for other and new methods became increasingly urgent. The new science without doubt upset the complacent acceptance of the received learning. The question was not whether the new science could be assimilated to the philosophy of the schoolmen; clearly it could, even though the assimilation would require some major modifications of received doctrine. The real question was whether such assimilation could capture the essentials of the new science—its buoyancy, its adventuresomeness, its ecstasies in endlessly making new discoveries, and above all the new power it was giving to men in their conquest over nature. This new life could no longer adequately be regarded as a vale of tears. Men were too active, for all their reflectiveness, to be satisfied with passive meditation. The discovery of the new world, the discovery of new satellites, the new commercialism, the new bursts of energies generated by man's liberation from the manor house—all these, together with the life consonant with them, forced men to think again about how to think. New evaluations were called for. And especially the task was focused on clarifying the meaning of the new science.

Science, we must constantly remind ourselves, is a very complex undertaking. Professor A. R. Hall writes of the science of this period: "The scientific method of the seventeenth century cannot be traced to a single origin. It was not worked out logically by any one philosopher, nor was it exemplified completely in any one investigation."[1]

Whether or not any philosopher failed to work out logically the method (or should we say "methods"?) of seventeenth-century science, some of them certainly did seize upon strands of it, and certainly did succeed in disentangling them from other strands. Francis Bacon, one of the first to analyze the nature of science, deserves to have his conception of science critically, if not sympathetically, reviewed.

The Role of Science

In the *Advancement of Learning*, Francis Bacon writes:

Invention is of two kinds, very different; the one of arts and sciences, and the other of speech and arguments. The former of these I report altogether deficient, which seems to me to be such a deficience, as if in the making of an inventory touching the estate of a deceased person, it should be set down that "there is no ready money." For as money will fetch all other commodities, so by this art all the rest are obtained.[2]

---

[1] *The Scientific Revolution* (Boston: Beacon Press, 1956), p. 184.

[2] *Works of Francis Bacon*, trans. by Spedding, Ellis, and Heath (London: Spottiswood and Co., 1883), Vol. IV, pp. 407–408.

Bacon possesses a canny premonition of what the new science holds in store for men. Science is power because it is the invention of invention. Skillfully pursued, it can lead men to a control over nature and it can make human life freer.

The clue to the power of science is method. Discoveries can and have been made by chance, but they are then limited in their usefulness. Chance discoveries are limited because, apart from the systematic study of invention, they never extend to their full range of application. Prometheus did not invent fire through speculation but rather "fell upon it by accident, and, as the poets say, stole it from Zeus." Chance can be good luck; also it can be bad luck; chance is uncontrolled. To make the study of nature truly effective, man must devise a logic of invention—a consistent approach which, meticulously followed, will disclose fundamental connections between things. Superficial similarities do not help men either to understand or to control things. Men must ignore superficial similarities between things if they are to discover genuinely significant relations. A rusty nail may look like a twig, but a more authentic similarity remains hidden until the logic of invention shows, for example, the way in which the rusty nail is like a burning twig.

Logic can reveal significant similarities only as we approach nature experimentally and methodically, and utilize the skill of reasoning in connection with the manipulation of things. Experimentalism comes to have a profoundly new meaning, one which Bacon sensed more than actually developed in the course of his voluminous writings. He did not confuse experimentalism with the mere gathering of information; he clearly distinguished it from the goal of contemplation; and he unerringly avoided the pitfalls of confusing it with mystical forces, especially those employed by astrologers and alchemists, and even by such capable scientists as Gilbert, who all too facilely identified the magnet with spiritual forces, which could not be coped with on the plane of natural knowledge. The magnet was an invention by which pilots could sail their courses on the seas by day or night, bright or cloudy. It was not a course that led to the salvation of the soul or to the mystical Kingdom of Ends.

The contemporary mind more or less persistently raises the question, knowledge for what? This is often regarded as an embarrassing, if not unanswerable, question. It was for Bacon neither embarrassing nor un-unanswerable; it was a simple and straightforward question, which received a simple and straightforward answer. The purpose of science is utility, for as he says in *Novum Organum*, "Truth . . . and utility are here the very same things: and works themselves are of greater value as pledges of truth than as contributing to the comforts of life."[3] Truth is not a transcendent,

---

[3] *Op. cit.* IV, p. 110.

up-in-the-clouds essence to be contemplated, and utility is not a piggish, muddy bestiality. Both are on the same plane, for, being identical, they contribute to the well-being of man. The slogan-like answer which Bacon proposes is, "Knowledge is power."

But how is "power" to be understood? Power is often an ugly word today—just because it connotes the subjection of man to man. For Bacon it was different: it was the subjection of man to mankind, that is, to ends cooperatively realized, since it signified the full liberation of man, full because it was not a political, but rather a humanistic, liberation. It was power over nature in the interests of human society. And, equally important, it was man's power over himself, in that it was supposed to rid him of conceits and delusions and to make possible a realistic study of the workings of nature. By experimenting, the scientist changes things, and by changing them, he is able to discover how things work, because he can control the changes, instead of being at the mercy of passive observation.

Scientific method for Bacon, then, meant three things: an approach to nature, a thoroughgoing participation in the process, and above all, a formalized logic of discovery.

Like Roger Bacon (1212–1292) before him, Francis Bacon believed that man should go to nature and put his questions to her. He should turn away from authority to things, from opinions to sources, and from books to nature. This change places a serious burden on man. To probe nature he must ask the right kinds of questions; otherwise no clear answers are obtainable. Even more, he has only his own wits to rely upon in his search for knowledge. To drive home this point, Bacon invented the allegory of the New Atlantis. Situated in the Atlantic, the New Atlantis is an island where, after the hero has been shipwrecked, he establishes the foundations of the arts and the sciences. Significantly, the allegory suggests the need to start from scratch, without traditions, without any of the old folklore, and armed only with the human wit to ask his questions of nature. Above all, man needs especially to avoid confusion, since, as Bacon says, "truth will sooner come out from error than from confusion."[4] A properly designed question forces nature to reveal her secrets. It always yields knowledge.

Far from being merely passive receptiveness, the attainment of knowledge involves thoroughgoing participation. It brings the mind into play and injects a human element into nature, for in the process man converts nature from one form into another. This is the process of experimentation as opposed to mere observation. In an experiment, the scientist employs methods that bring about effects that would not otherwise occur. He

---

[4] *Ibid*, p. 149.

changes things; he manipulates them; he makes them vary in regular order, as when, for instance, he wants to discover the connection between amounts of motion and degrees of heat which the motion generates.

The intent of Bacon's remarks is clear, even though he does not always lay out the details of a program which would reveal the kind of knowledge to be sought in science. Besides, he very often relies on metaphor to carry his meaning. He applies one of his most famous metaphors to what he regards to be the authentic task of science as contrasted both with an unenlightened brute empiricism and with an empty, formalistic rationalism. Paragraph 95 of *Novum Organum* is worth quoting in full:

> Those who have handled sciences have been either men of experiment or men of dogmas. The men of experiment are like the ant; they only collect and use: the reasoners resemble spiders, who make cobwebs out of their own substance. But the bee takes a middle course; it gathers its material from the flowers of the garden and of the field, but transforms and digests it by a power of its own. Not unlike this is the true business of philosophy; for it neither relies solely or chiefly on the powers of the mind, nor does it take the matter which it gathers from natural history and mechanical experiments and lay it up in the memory whole, as it finds it; but lays it up in the understanding altered and digested. Therefore from a closer and purer league between these two faculties, the experimental and the rational, (such as has never yet been made) much may be hoped.[5]

Bacon's hard task is precisely that of finding a way to bring together the experimental and the rational to form "a closer and purer league." This task is that of a *novum organum*—a new logic to supplant the old logic of Aristotle.

The Logic of Discovery vs. the Logic of Discourse

The new logic that he envisaged was a formalized logic of discovery. Science, in other words, moves ahead by disclosing relations of things of which we were formerly unaware. If, for example, heat is recognized as a form of motion, then it is the motions of bodies that we must study. Heat, moreover, is not to be regarded as a quality of a thing, as, say, red is the quality of a rose. By regarding heat in a parallel fashion as, say, the calorific quality, we baptize the thing without coming to an understanding of it. The magic of giving a thing a name cannot yield knowledge; it is only a way of deluding ourselves by confusing words with things.

The logic of discovery is to be contrasted with the logic of discourse—just as the new organon is to be contrasted with the old—that is, Aristotle's. Aristotle's logic is the logic of discourse. Aristotle wished to provide a way of talking sensibly about things. Because things fall into classes, and because classes are related to one another in definite ways,

---

[5] *Ibid*, pp. 92–93.

logic prescribes rules for keeping things straight and for talking about them without being absurd. Elms are trees; so are oaks. Elms and oaks are thus coordinate, and an elm can never be an oak. But both are trees; and so trees are superordinate to oaks and elms. Yet trees are coordinate with shrubs, which are not trees. As long as we talk properly about these various relations we will not contradict ourselves. But if we mix them up, and say that elms are trees, and so are oaks, therefore elms are oaks, we begin to talk nonsense.

Aristotle formalized arguments so that we can tell whether a conclusion does or does not follow from the premises of an argument. This formalization he called a syllogism, namely, a form of discourse in which something being said something else follows of necessity and through what has been said. (See Chapter 6.) Since Aristotle's invention of syllogistic reasoning sounds so eminently reasonable, there is a puzzling question why Bacon should have refused to accept it. To answer this question it is necessary to elaborate Aristotle's conception of logic.

When, for example, it is said that all elms are trees, "elms" and "trees" are the terms of the proposition, and it is necessary to fix their meaning, that is, to define them. For unless terms are fixed throughout an argument, we cannot say that a conclusion follows from the premises. If trees are living things and if this elm is a tree, then this tree *must be* a living thing—"must be" *if* the terms are fixed. Is, for example, a dead elm an elm? The argument does not work unless the terms are unambiguously defined. But even more, the terms of an argument are said by Aristotle to be constituted both as "kinds of being" and also as "forms of thought." This is to say that there are general categories which tell us the kinds of things that exist, and these kinds were (usually) said to be ten in number. This limitation does make for a tidy world, or, as it has been said, it has been created by "a syllogistic gentleman with a category for every emergency." It was just this artificial tidiness to which Bacon took exception.

Nature, Bacon insists, is much too subtle to be neatly contained in the terms of a proposition, which in turn are neatly contained in categories. He says, "The syllogism consists of propositions; propositions of words; and words are the tokens and signs of notions. Now if the very notions of the mind . . . be improperly and over-hastily abstracted from facts, vague, not sufficiently definite, faulty in short in many ways, the whole edifice tumbles."[6] The "superstructure" is science, and there can be no authentic science unless the foundations are secure. What about dead and living things? What about trees and shrubs? Should we adopt a cookie-cutter view of nature and regard things of nature as having a pattern, when it is we who have actually imposed that pattern on nature? Did not Aristotle do something like this when he asserted that single bodies have each a single and

[6] *Ibid*, p. 24.

proper motion, and that if they participate in any other, then this results from an external cause? Bacon's complaint alleges that Aristotle "corrupted natural philosophy by . . . fashioning the world out of categories." A priori, in advance, he so restricted our conception of nature that his philosophy makes impossible the discovery of the true laws of nature through a well-grounded inductive method.

Although Bacon regards Aristotle as a prime object of scorn, he does not by any means regard him as the only obstacle to the development of a proper inductive method. Before considering what this new method involves, we may pause to see how, systematically, Bacon treats these various obstacles to the attainment of authentic knowledge. These obstacles to knowledge he calls the "idols"—"irrationalities," we would probably call them today. There are four of them: the idols of the tribe, the idols of the cave, the idols of the market place, and the idols of the theater.

Obstacles to Knowledge

The idols of the tribe are those errors which derive from human nature itself. They are shared generally by all men, by virtue of the fact that they confuse human nature with nature. By attributing to nature what really belongs to themselves, they make man the measure of the universe. They see nature in their own image and consequently distort and discolor things. Vividly illustrating the idols of the tribe, Bacon writes:

 . . . it was a good answer that was made by one who when they showed him hanging in a temple a picture of those who had paid their vows as having escaped shipwreck, and would have him say whether he did not now acknowledge the power of the gods,—"Aye," asked he again, "but where are they painted that were drowned after their vows?"

Remarking that this is the way of all superstition, Bacon continues, "men, having a delight in such vanities, mark the events where they are fulfilled, but where they fail, though this happen much oftener, [men] neglect and pass them by."[7]

In addition to the distortions of nature by the whole race of mankind, there are the further distortions which arise from the peculiarities of each individual man. These constitute the idols of the cave. Because of the singular character of his education, habits, and accidents of life, a man cannot easily escape his own idiosyncratic interpretation of things. He is partial to some aspects of things to the exclusion of others. He acts either with excesses or deficiencies that cloud his judgment and render his interpretation of nature inexact. Consequently, he permits subjectivities to enter into his ways of viewing things, and these make his observations useless for the advancement of science.

---

[7] *Ibid*, p. 56.

Still another idol that inhibits science is the use of words. Words come down to us as idols of the market place, for in the market much of men's time is occupied in communicating with one another. Having created words in order to communicate, people then, ironically, become dominated by their own creations. They name things that do not exist, and then they are subtly led to believe in the existence of these things just because they have invented names for them. Or again, they name things that do exist, but they define them so badly that only errors can result. As Bacon concludes, "words plainly force and overrule the understanding, and throw all into confusion, and lead men away into numberless empty controversies and idle fancies."

Finally, the idols upon which Bacon most vents his spleen: the idols of the theater. These are "the received systems" which are but "so many stage-plays, representing worlds of their own creation after an unreal and scenic fashion." The received systems are philosophies, and although Aristotelian philosophy is held up as the prime example of an idol of the theater, there are others past and present, and no doubt there will be still others to be composed. Bacon's impassioned outburst against the idols of the theater and his insistence upon annihilating them can be explained by the fact that he regards them as having usurped the rightful place of science. Superstitions, empty logical systems, barren collections of facts—these are what men employ as substitutes for science, and that make science all the harder to achieve. Theology and science do not mix; logic, that is, the logic of discourse distorts things; and although facts have to be acknowledged, the natural piety they arouse leads on to nothing useful.

Suppose then we grant the need for breaking the idols. What is the need we are granting? Is it that science requires objectivity for its advancement? or open-mindedness? or impersonality? Clearly, it requires all of these, but it requires more. Objectivity produces no knowledge, nor does open-mindedness, nor does impersonality. Only by following a method from which useful knowledge results, do we advance science. And this method must be foolproof, depending but little on the acuteness or strength of the wits. Bacon indicates by analogy how this is to be accomplished:

For as in the drawing of a straight line or a perfect circle, much depends on the steadiness and practice of the hand, if it be done by aim of hand only, but if with the aid of rule or compass, little or nothing; so is it exactly with my plan.[8]

The Inductive Method

If the idols, then, are to be regarded as the obstacles to scientific advancement, the question may then be raised, what are the objects of

[8] *Ibid.*, p. 63.

science which are knowable and which give man power? In a sense, Bacon has told us; he has said that nature is the object, because we are to put our questions to nature. But this answer will not really suffice. What is this nature that responds? Sometimes he seems to suggest that it is bodies. He did write that "in nature nothing really exists beside individual bodies. . . ." And this sounds as though nature just *is* these bodies and that our appointed task is to observe them as "performing pure individual acts." This notion will not do, and it is unlikely that Bacon thought it would, since he did not pursue the matter further. Had he done so, he would, without doubt, have discovered that the notion of bodies is itself metaphysical (as we shall later see) in a way which would prove them also to be idols of the theater.

Bacon senses that this conception of nature as being but little nuggets moving about in space is not quite appropriate to his intent, for he immediately suggests that the essence of understanding nature is understanding not nuggets but "fixed laws" and that a fixed law is a kind of rule or direction or guidance which will not deceive a person in the result and which is appropriate in the practice of deriving the result.

Although it looked at first as if Bacon were concerned with deriving a concept of nature, now we are led to believe that his real intent is not at all to provide us with a concept of nature, but rather with a method for attaining results. However odd this view may seem, it is not so if we take seriously his purpose of devising an organon of knowledge. An organon is not knowledge, but it is a set of rules which one must follow if one wants to do something—and this something, in Bacon's case, is to advance science. He seeks for rules which are the invention of invention. This end is not obtainable by tinkering with things or by getting involved in some opportunistic project. It is, instead, the involvement which is science.

Bacon explains what this involvement signifies by designating the kinds of experiments he believes are worthy of science and by singling out the ends which are their aim. Experiments, he says, are of two sorts: experiments of fruit and experiments of light. The former do not serve man well. Designed to produce quick results, they lead only to the mechanics' manipulations and fail to reveal the causal connections that make these manipulations possible. Experiments of light, on the contrary, are always decisive, for they always reveal whether or not causal connections exist. In the language of science, a "null" experiment does disclose something about nature. To know that certain things are disconnected is knowledge, just as to know that certain things are connected is knowledge. Before indicating how the experiments of light are to be conducted, however, let us consider the kind of ends they are meant to achieve.

The proximate aim of science may be said to be the formulation of laws of nature. Bacon calls them "middle axioms." By a process of careful induction, the scientist can advance from the study of particulars to lesser axioms concerning regularities in nature, and then through successive steps he may advance to the middle axioms. These axioms exist between the first stage above bare experience and the last stage of highest generality, that is, so-called first principles such as the Greeks were especially intent upon. The lesser axioms are too closely tied to sense-experience to be significant; the first principles are too general to be significant. "But the middle are the true and solid and living axioms, on which depend the affairs and fortunes of men." When understanding rises by a slow ascent, "not . . . supplied with wings, but rather hung by weights,"[9] then only does man move on to the stage of scientific knowledge.

The scientific enterprise thus turns out to be the search for causal connections, stated with such generality as enables man to understand events and to control them. Causal connections are, moreover, invariable connections in nature such that when the cause occurs the effect always occurs, and when the cause is absent the effect never occurs. Bacon's own language is not the happiest; for more in harmony with the received learning than with his spirit of protest against it, he speaks of the cause as a "form" and the effect as a "nature." He disparages Aristotle's doctrine of "efficient cause," even though he actually sets the task of science, and therefore of philosophy, which is an extension of science, as the discovery of efficient causes. This task is completed in the double interpretation whereby knowledge rises to the level of middle axioms in displaying the natures or laws of things and also the use of such axioms to deduce and devise new experiments in order to reveal even more adequately the subtleties of nature.

The processes of discovery are most effectively set forth in Bacon's interpretation of the "Tables" employed for ascertaining the forms of things. These Tables have for their content the empirical data, the various instances of natures, or the absences of them, that constitute the raw materials for the inductive process. He illustrates in detail the use of them in connection with the phenomenon of heat. By gathering from a great variety of sources instances in which heat is present, ranging from the rays of the sun, to lightning, to hot springs, to living matter, including fresh horse dung and like excrements, he means to call attention to samples which will omit no factors essential to the nature of heat. These samples or instances constitute what he calls the Table of Essence and Presence.

Realizing, however, that no scientific induction is possible without negative controls, Bacon further insists on an equally elaborate Table of Deviation or of Absence in Proximity. In each instance he wants to know in what respect there is an absence of heat. Otherwise, we confuse the proximity or nextness of things with real connections, that is, connections

---

[9] *Ibid.*, p. 97.

such that one thing cannot be present without another also being present. He recognizes that in the absence of controlled experiment, we have no basis for distinguishing between mere proximity of things and genuine connectedness. Negative instances constitute a means by which we can, often decisively, ascertain the unrelatedness of things.

There is a kind of instance which does give fairly positive proof of the real connection between things. These are instances in which there are degrees of presence or absence of a nature, connected with degrees of the form which must always be present if that nature is to occur. Heat admirably illustrates this because it possesses degrees, and although Bacon had not himself discovered a precise way of measuring degree, exact measure is nevertheless the best means we know for determining with certainty that things are related. Bacon was not opposed to mathematical measurement. In fact, he acknowledges that expressing nature in mathematical form is desirable, but he never made much effort to insist upon the formulation of experiments in mathematical terms. Actually, he was chary about the kind of broad mathematical generalizations made by Kepler and Galileo. Nevertheless, when one thing varies in proportion with another, we have a solid basis for formulating a law of nature.

The Tables as set forth by Bacon contain the instances of things, the presentations to the understanding, from which the nature of something, for example, the law of heat, can then be formulated. From the instances of heat or its absence, Bacon thus expresses the law of heat, namely, that it consists in motion. It is not, he insists, "that heat generates into motion or that motion generates heat . . . but that Heat itself, its essence and quiddity [i.e., 'whatness'], is Motion and nothing else."[10] The conclusion is enticing but nevertheless unsatisfactory. Bacon did not perform experiments, such as Joule later did when he discovered that by turning a paddle wheel in a bucket of water, heat could be generated indefinitely. Yet Bacon did suggest the formulation of a "middle axiom," which could, and eventually did, develop into a full-fledged kinetic theory of heat.

Concluding Remarks

Bacon's proposals for the advancement of knowledge lead us to ask, by way of conclusion: in what does his significance lie? First, he undercut idolatry. Second, he set forth a theory of science, including a theory of the place of science in the scheme of things, namely, philosophy. And third, he separated once and for all science and religion.

Idolatry represents the conceits of men. It is their subjectivities, magnified and projected into the world as reality. Men impose their nature,

---

[10] *Works*, IV, *op. cit.*, p. 150.

collectively and individually, on the world. They can read the book of the world only as the book of man, his exploits, his conceits, his frivolities. Language and philosophical systems, in particular, tend to prevent men from reading nature in terms of nature. The old learning is all wrong; it keeps man buried in ideas, beliefs, and feelings that can only suffocate him. He needs to be freed; and he can free himself only by the advancement of knowledge.

The advancement of knowledge requires a totally new method, the method of observation, of experiment, of culling and distilling—or, perhaps better, even of mining and smelting, for Bacon had greater respect for Agricola, who had authentic knowledge of what metals are, than for scientists who speculated more than they observed. Not reason run riot, but experimentation, planned and executed with skill—this is what he believes to be the promising road to knowledge. Reason must sift and interpret the results of experiment, but it is useless, even corruptive, when cut loose from the careful, empirical business of experimentation. Bacon believes that man should be tied neither to facts nor to reason. On the contrary, only by relating the two and discovering *laws* of nature is he freed from the life of the ant as well as from that of the spider. His rule is: by the middle axioms ye shall be freed! First there must be the gathering together of the middle axioms; in the systematization of them, knowledge in useful forms is secured to men, and through this knowledge men come to have power as they have never had before.

Is Bacon an empiricist or is he a rationalist? We can answer the question only by saying both and neither. He is an empiricist if we mean that all knowledge begins in experience, in observing particular instances of things in nature. Colors, textures, warmth, and cold—these are first got at through the senses. But the senses give us information that requires interpretation. Interpretation presupposes that we go to nature already armed with questions; otherwise, we can only stare dumbly. But interpretation also implies that we need to compare and relate and eventually to seek principles by which the information at last becomes meaningful. Reason is required if we are to ascend to that degree of generality that makes instances meaningful. Knowledge thus is applicable to things, and is not complete unless it refers to the things of experience.

Bacon is not an empiricist if we mean that the only realities are the particulars of experience, as the "here-red" or the "there-smooth" or the "now-round." To a lesser degree, John Locke (1632-1704) and to the highest degree, David Hume (1711-1776) moved to push empiricism to this extreme. But by doing this, nature became attenuated into psychological data, suggesting once more the specter of the idol of the cave. But more of this later. Bacon is not a rationalist if by a rationalist we mean one who believes that we can come by knowledge through thought and thought alone. We can prove the existence of nothing by thought. We can at best manipulate symbols that, as far as we know, stand for nothing in the world of space-time things. Reason does not tell us whether or not things exist. Rather it prescribes rules which we may follow and which, when they lead to certain kinds of results, put us into contact in the most fruitful way possible with things of the world. Mathematics can be useful in formulating rules of the connections of things—otherwise it should be shunned. Pure mathematics was no delight to Bacon and was to be regarded as one more conceit that men had better avoid.

Finally, Bacon leaves us in no doubt as to the need to refrain from confusing science and religion. Bacon was not irreligious; on the contrary, he supported religion by making it a matter of faith. Man's spiritual life ought not to be sullied by his secular doings; nor should the latter be warped by theological doctrine. They are separate and that is the end of it. Professor F. H. Anderson writes of this separation as follows:

There is no divine mind in nature or indeed a rational mind. Nature shows no divine efficiency in its movements or divine form in its structures. It possesses no divine causation, divine motivation, divine appetition, or any attributes of divinity. It is formed matter acting through varieties of local motion inherent within itself and nothing more. Bacon thus repudiates pantheism, theism, immanence, and transcendentalism.[11]

Bacon sought to interpret nature in causal terms, and he regarded all causes as strictly natural causes. Anything further is not just superfluous but also an obstacle to the correct understanding of nature.

Accordingly, Bacon is merciless in his criticism of the doctrines of final causes, which come down as doctrines from the received systems, especially, it will be recalled, from Aristotle. Final causes produce no knowledge of nature. Indeed, the inquiry into "final causes is barren, and like a virgin consecrated to God produces nothing." The study of nature is not to be obscured by anything which is not natural. There are no principles of intelligibility of nature other than those that pertain to the natural forms inherent in nature. Any other kind of interpretation is based on magic or superstitition, and would be a perversion of both science and religion.

Bacon's solution could not but produce an uneasy divorce of science and religion. Science was enhanced by him, in virtue of his devising a method for its pursuit. This was, moreover, a method with which the theologian could not very well quarrel, for to do so he would only subject himself to serious criticism. The theologian could not assume the burden of supplying man with natural knowledge. Moreover, by interfering with the secular pursuits, he would obscure the nature of the secular pursuits and also fail in his task of ministering to man's spiritual needs. Science

[11] F. H. Anderson, *The Philosophy of Francis Bacon* (Chicago: University of Chicago Press, 1948), p. 298.

and religion have, in Bacon's thought, thus been breached, and although he provided a reasonable approach to the study of nature—and to this extent a philosophy—he did not provide an approach to the study of man's spiritual nature. The dualism between nature and spirit becomes increasingly evident. By regarding nature in sheerly secular terms, and thus by forcing a renewed effort to interpret the spiritual, philosophy may yet become more appropriately grounded. In essence this is what Descartes achieved. In our analysis of Descartes' thought, we shall see an alternative mode of coping with the new science while still doing justice to the facts of human experience.

Selected Readings

Anderson, Fulton H., *The Philosophy of Francis Bacon*, Chicago: University of Chicago Press, 1948.

Bacon, Francis, *New Organon and Related Writings*, ed. by Fulton H. Anderson, New York: Liberal Arts, 1964.

Dewey, John, *Reconstruction in Philosophy*, Boston: Beacon Press, 1957, Chs. II, IV. (Paperback.)

Farrington, Benjamin, *Francis Bacon: Philosopher of Industrial Science*, New York: Collier Books, 1961. (Paperback.)

Whitehead, Alfred North, *Science and the Modern World*, New York: Mentor Books, 1949, Ch. IV, (Paperback.)

CHAPTER 9

The Light of Nature: Man and God

The Setting for Descartes' Philosophy

Man is given to action and to contemplation and without both, life is incomplete, either because it is brutish insensitivity or because it is ascetic withdrawal. There is a limitless range of philosophical interpretations for bringing these two aspects of life together. In Part I, for example, we have seen how philosophers such as Plato and Aristotle provided interpretations for understanding these elements in their various manifestations. No philosophy can legitimately ignore them, even if some philosophers try. Man does have muscles and he does have sensitivities, intellectual and emotional, and however nearly atrophied they may be, they are still part of his life.

In order to cope satisfactorily with these elements, they need to be seen in their timely as well as in their timeless phases; otherwise they will not be seen to have both structure and relevance. The Greeks, humanistic as they were, reckoned with these elements in relation to the Olympian gods *and* the drama *and* the mores *and* the city-state *and* many other insistent cultural forces. But one of the forces they did not have to cope with and that made their philosophies incomparable with those of modern western philosophers was that of the Christian Church. If for no other reason than this, Renaissance philosophy had to be different from Greek philosophy.

Moreover, modern western philosophy, we contend, has been shaped by the prevalence of another irresistible force—modern science. The compresence of Christianity and science doubly complicates the philosophical problem, for not only is there a conflict between them but also a conflict within each of them. As we have already suggested, Bacon carved out one model and, as we shall proceed to show, Descartes quite a different one. Bacon's dualism, we noted, was between knowledge and faith, and with respect to knowledge, he emphasized action rather than contemplation. Thus science meant "scientizing"—collecting, transforming, and testing, with the consequence that science meant power, and was accordingly indispensable to ethics.[1] Thus Bacon relegated contemplation primarily to the supernatural realm, the realm of faith.

Descartes' dualism is, in a sense, a more consistent one, for his temperament of mind was rather one of disinterested curiosity than of either impassioned commitment or of achieving practical results. Consequently, he read science differently and his attachments were more toward Copernicus and Kepler and Galileo than, say, toward Vesalius or Tycho Brahe or Leonardo. Descartes was searching for the "order and arrangement" of things; he believed that the world has a discernible structure. According to this view,[2] things are related in a system, so that we can move in thought from one thing to another, and then, by some curious process, arrive at a conclusion about what nature must be—or at least about what is going to happen. In this view, prediction turns out to be basically a matter of discovering the structure of the world.

Seventeenth-century science no doubt encouraged men to believe that the course of nature is predictable on the basis of natural knowledge. Accelerations of falling bodies could be predicted with greater accuracy than ever before. The motions of two pendulums striking each other could be foretold with uncanny success. The strength of materials began to be understood in usable ways. These were some of the achievements that came out of seventeenth-century physics. And these successes were added to the earlier successes of, say, astronomers who, going back to Ptolemy and before, predicted with remarkable accuracy the motions of heavenly bodies. The task of philosophy came to be, in part, that of accounting for these amazing successes, if not of adding to them, and in part that of

---

[1] The fuller consequences of this we shall observe in chap. 14, where we discuss Hobbes' conception of "the civil state."

[2] This view has already been seen in Part I as dominant in Greek philosophy, where the belief in the "cosmos" or order, contrasted with that of "chaos," is constituted as a sustained and impassioned search.

fitting the scientific advancements into a new culture. Descartes tried to show a way—a rationalistic way, we may say—of how to make the world into a balanced whole again. Although he did not quite succeed, the process he employed is of such importance that by retracing his steps we cannot fail to learn about the nagging problems of modern philosophy.

The Starting-Point of Knowledge

Modern science, we have said, is both empirical and mathematical. Bacon saw it mainly from the point of view of observation and experiment; Descartes, mainly from that of mathematics. Tycho Brahe, although he did systematize his observations of planetary motions, concentrated painstakingly on collecting data in order to arrive at inductive generalizations. Despite the fact that his science could be only incompletely experimental, it was Baconian in spirit. Galileo, even if he did make "experience the mistress of astronomy," placed his emphasis upon theory and mathematical system. Descartes could not have agreed more with Galileo that "the book of nature is written in mathematical characters." Grubby experimentation, tedious observations—these are alien to Descartes' conception of the world. A mathematician second to none, the inventor of the coordinate geometry, Descartes believed that we can achieve knowledge only by following the "light of nature," that is, by following reason. If only we can begin with some absolutely certain bit of knowledge, then we can derive from it other and still other bits of knowledge, equally certain. The crying need is to discover one indisputable truth from which others can then be deduced.

The straight path to truth, however, will not do, for it leads to dogmatism, not to truth. We know that this is the case because there are too many "truths" in the world—they conflict with one another and cancel out one another. Not only do received opinions about things clash with one another, and in such a way that they cannot all be true, but also the senses are deceiving. I see a bush for a bear; I confuse copper and glass with gold and diamonds; I build fantasies about myself and others. My disposition endlessly distorts my perception of things, so that I cannot really say that they are as they seem to be. And of crucial importance is the recognition that the things of which I seem to be most certain, the things which I now perceive about me, these things possibly do not exist where I perceive them. They may exist only in my dreams. How can I be certain of anything whatsoever? I do need some way of being unmistakably clear, at least about some things, for only then can I distinguish the true from the false, the correctly apprehended from the confusedly apprehended. The indirect path of arriving at truth forces Descartes to consider two things: first, a criterion of truth, and, second, a method for "rightly conducting the reason and seeking truth in the sciences," but sometimes he telescopes the two.

The criterion of truth resides in the clarity and distinctness of an idea. A true idea is one which is immediately recognized and accepted as being so. A true idea cannot be got from an untrue one, since untruth can breed only untruth. To make confusion the source of truth can be only confusion compounded. The true comes only from the true; therefore, somewhere we must find something that is patently true, true in its own right, something which itself bears the stamp of truth upon its own face. True ideas are clear and distinct—not as being lively or vivid to the senses, as the flowering cherry tree may be, but rather as being obvious to the intellect, as the fact that a thing once done cannot be undone. Dreams and hallucinations cannot, as sheer forms of immediate experience, be distinguished in kind from what is immediately given in perception. Shapes, sounds, fragrances—these cannot guarantee the existence of things outside of mind. Dancing snakes, even in our hallucinations, have shapes and make sounds. The pungency of eucalyptus may be no less real when we remember it or dream of it than it is when we actually smell it. Hallucinations and dreams are not only sensory; they are sensational. As sensational, the unaided senses are incapable of distinguishing their kind of reality from that of the flash of lightning or the blast of a bomb. The senses fall short of giving us knowledge, as every magician knows.

The clarity Descartes insists upon is the clarity of an axiom, the truth of which can be doubted only to prove its correctness. The part cannot be greater than the whole; things equal to the same thing cannot be unequal. These truths are self-evident, and any attempt to deny them displays only more clearly the truth that is inherent in them. To deny them is to end up with absurdity. We cannot prove them in terms of something else, for then we would have to know the truth of that something else which guaranteed their truth. Somewhere we must begin with that which is self-evidently true, which neither can be proved by anything else, nor requires proof. If there is to be any proof at all of such truths, it can be only in asserting the opposite and then observing that the opposite involves a self-contradiction.

The more taxing question, however, is whether there are any truths which attest to the existence of anything in the world. Seven stars and eight stars may always add up to fifteen stars, but this does not prove that there are any stars in the world. Descartes is not content with merely believing in the existence of the world; he wants to demonstrate, in an orderly fashion, that the world does exist and what its nature is. And he is convinced that there is an absolute starting point which is indisputable, and from which we can derive the necessary structure of the world. If only we will refrain from asserting that which we cannot know or cannot prove to be true, and if only we will adopt an appropriate method for ascertaining what our world actually is, then eminent success awaits our efforts. Method—and in this case the most abstruse method of all—provides the key to philosophical understanding.

On Method

The image of philosophy in the popular mind appears to be the deliverance of parcels of wisdom by an elderly sage who is endlessly profound in his comments upon the world. Profound reflections upon life may be set forth either as those guides to living that we call homilies, or as deep truths which give one comfort in complacent self-acknowledgement of his superiority to unlike-minded persons. If, as a matter of fact, philosophy is unable to supply some dimension of reflection and insight into things, we may well question whether it has any worth at all. Popular philosophy may have the right instincts and nevertheless be self-defeating just on this score: it fails to sustain a dimensionality of thought; its profundity fails because its alleged insights are so at odds as finally to destroy one another. Consistency may be the hobgloblin of little minds, but inconsistency can surely not be taken as the mark of greatness. Philosophy is difficult just because it must be sustained; otherwise it is worthless. Because popular philosophy fails in this regard, it is dogmatic. The contrary of its "truths" may be quite as profound as its own assertions. Hence, something more is needed if it is authentically to satisfy the philosophical impulse. Only method can supply the deficiency of popular philosophy; and in the beginnings of modern philosophy we have already seen that philosophers are painfully self-conscious about how they will go about philosophizing. In fact, it is this self-consciousness about method which more than anything else places the stamp of modernity on modern philosophy.

Descartes believes that philosophic method is needed because there is nothing to take its place in providing the foundations of knowledge. There are various kinds of imposters who speak of that of which they are ignorant. Alchemists, astrologers, magicians boast of a knowledge they do not have. Seeking for a more secure science, Descartes resolves to study "that which could be found in myself, or at least in the great book of the world." Theology, logic, and mathematics—each of these fails in some way to satisfy the demands for his new science of self and nature.

Respectful of the teachings of the Church fathers (who had taught him in the college of La Flèche), and humble before revealed truth— to which he could not himself hope to aspire—he confessed that he could not follow the way of theology. He said that in order to pursue this subject he would need "assistance from above and to be more than a mere man." Sometimes he sounds ironical in what he says about theology and the teachings of the Church. After all, Bruno was burned at the stake in 1600 and Galileo did recant his subversive teachings. But at other times, he sounds genuinely humble before the power and majesty of Church teachings. In any event, he cannot accept contradictory doctrines, and, above all, the method of philosophy is rational, and he has no choice but to follow reason wherever it may lead.

Why not then follow the lead of logic and mathematics in order to arrive at the truth? Logic will not do. Like Bacon before him, Descartes regards logic—the syllogism—as incapable of being employed for the discovery of new things. What we already know can be put into logical form, and can effectively be conveyed to others, but the syllogism is not adapted to the procurement of anything new. The premises must be given, and the conclusion is contained in the premises; were this not so, there would be no way of drawing it out as a consequence of the premises.

Descartes is no less critical of mathematics—algebra in particular— than he is of logic. It, too, is a formal subject based upon rules and formulas that end in "the construction of an art which is confused and obscure and which embarrasses the mind." Mathematics is too abstract; being so very abstract, it has no actual use, and, he adds somewhat ingenuously, it "fatigues" the imagination. This latter is of all criticisms the most odd. If the attainment of knowledge should prove to be difficult and tiring, does this mean that it is not worth the effort or that we should refuse to pursue this method, even if it were the proper one? Even more odd is that this criticism comes from one who contributed so greatly to the advance of the subject. In truth, Descartes almost immediately retracts this perplexing criticism in his proposals of the method he advocates for philosophy.

Turning to these proposals, he states them as follows:

The first of these was to accept nothing as true which I did not clearly recognize to be so: that is to say, carefully to avoid precipitation and prejudice in judgments, and to accept in them nothing more than what was presented to my mind so clearly and distinctly that I could have no occasion to doubt it.

The second was to divide up each of the difficulties which I examined into as many parts as possible, and as seemed requisite in order that it might be resolved in the best manner possible.

The third was to carry on my reflections in due order, commencing with objects that were the most simple and easy to understand, in order to rise little by little, or by degrees, to knowledge of the most complex, assuming an order, even if a fictitious one, among those which do not follow a natural sequence relatively to one another.

The last was in all cases to make enumerations so complete and reviews so general that I should be certain of having omitted nothing.[3]

[3] *Philosophical Works of Descartes*, trans. by E. S. Haldane and G. R. T. Ross (Cambridge at the University Press, 1931) p. 92.

There we have the rules of method for rightly conducting the reason and for seeking the truth in the sciences. A few comments about each may better prepare us to see the pattern that is intended to make a go of philosophy. First of all, we are advised to put aside everything that is not clearly and distinctly known. Is there anything actually that is so clear and distinct that we cannot doubt it? Although we shall soon see that Descartes does believe there is one idea about existence that measures up to this standard, the initial suggestion is a sweeping skepticism that sets everything aside. In his *Meditations*, this is exactly what he proposes. We must break with the past, if we are ever to acquire firm knowledge. We must take an inventory of everything anew. Unless we are willing to doubt the reality of all things, we are not sufficiently bold and incisive to be philosophers at all. We must eliminate everything eliminable in order to prepare ourselves with the kind of philosophical humility required for philosophical development. As men of the world, we may need to hold to a code of morals, but as philosophers we must radically suspend judgment on everything suspendible. Only out of radical skepticisim does knowledge come.

Once we have surveyed the resulting problems, we can proceed by dividing our difficulties into their elements. Knowledge of "the thing as a whole" is, when one knows nothing of the parts, no knowledge at all. He who knows the right conclusions, but does not know how to establish them, knows nothing. In fact, he is a menace, an imposter, an obfuscator of true knowledge. A picture which is said to be clear, but in which none of the parts is clearly grasped, is like the smile of a Lewis Carroll cat without a face. Knowledge can only be precise, and the only way it can be precise is for its elements to be known clearly and distinctly.

If the elements are known, then one can proceed to know the complex in terms of the simple. In the physical world, resultant forces are vectors which are added together. The parallelogram of forces is intelligible because the vectors, having both direction and quantity, can be combined in a precise way. Taking two vectors at a time, the resultant force can be calculated. Then it, considered as a single vector, can be added to another, and so on, until the total force is computed. This is the kind of knowledge Descartes is after, and he clearly sees that it is obtainable by dealing not with gross things, but only with simple things, leading on to the complex.

Since our calculations can be in error, it is important finally to check them in the interests of accuracy. Mistakes easily creep into reasoning, and we can eliminate them only as we use the utmost care in reviewing the course of the argument. Step by step, then, we arrive at conclusions that give us confidence that we have a true grasp on things.

As Descartes evolves his rules of method, it becomes increasingly apparent that they are the method of geometry. Immediately after stating them, he tells us that, being impressed by "the long chains of reasoning

. . . of which geometricians make use," he came to believe that all knowledge is to be regarded as falling into this pattern. Mathematics is a formal science, capable of yielding certainty; but it is also applicable to nature, which is to be conceived according to a mathematical structure. By understanding the only things which are truly understandable in nature —the "relationships or proportions present in objects"—we discover that the mathematical method is the only one which provides true knowledge of nature. There must then be a kind of universal mathematics, which constitutes the ultimate science, the final kind of knowledge to which we may aspire.

Looking back once more to the rules of method, we can now see them in a new light. Rule One, concerning the acceptance of nothing which is not clearly and distinctly apprehended, is the sort of thing best illustrated by the axioms and postulates of Euclidean geometry. The first rule, then, is to begin with truths, such as Euclidean geometry could be conceived of as embodying—at least before the advent of non-Euclidean geometry. Once we begin with self-evident truth, then, according to Rule Two, we can prove various theorems, each one of which is also true because it follows from the axioms, postulates, and definitions, or from other theorems proved by their use. Rule Three proposes the adoption of an order of theorems from the simple to the complex. For example, the Pythagorean theorem will not precede the proof of the theorem concerning the sum of the interior angles of a triangle being equal to two right angles, etc. Rule Four contains the obvious suggestion that we review our demonstrations to be certain we have made no errors. The application of algebra to geometry appeared to Descartes the perfect way to insure confidence in the proof of conclusions, inasmuch as geometry could be used to correct algebra and algebra to correct geometry. When the results of both agreed, our confidence could be unbounded.

From Method to Existence: Number One, the Self

In the Cartesian view, method is indispensable to the pursuit of philosophy; nevertheless method is not to be confused with philosophy. In addition to the employment of method, we need to know about the *existence* of things. The question is: how can we employ the mathematical or philosophical method in order to obtain the knowledge which can be found in the self and in the great book of the world? The first rule of method, we have seen, is to seek for indubitable truth; its other face is to reject everything dubitable. Descartes combines the two in order to arrive at indubitable knowledge of the self. Because skepticism is self-defeating, we can, by pursuing it ruthlessly, arrive at certain and indubitable truth.

Cogito ergo sum—"I think, therefore I am"—is his familiar argument.

Be as skeptical as we like, doubt the existence of everything in the world, consider, if we like, that life is one long dream; however thoroughgoing our doubts, one thing we cannot doubt is that we are doubting. Thinking is a form of conscious activity. Doubting is a form of thinking. We cannot think, and, even more, we cannot doubt, without being aware that we are doing so. Thus, Descartes concludes, whenever I think, I know that I am. To doubt this conclusion is once more to prove that it is true. Skepticism thus proves itself false. To doubt, to deny, is a conscious activity which does not allow us to deny consciousness without at the same time exhibiting it to ourselves. The denial affirms the existence of that which we attempt to deny.

This argument was not new in the history of thought. Early in the fifth century, St. Augustine had used it, but with a radically different intent. He used it in order to probe the psyche. He had recognized in it a way of exploring the inner depths of man, and eventually of discovering the spiritual being of man, which could come only from God himself. Descartes, on the contrary, was more of a surface psychologist. For him, awareness or consciousness appears in any activity of the self, whether it is seeing, dreaming, believing, willing, or whatever. Descartes did not hesitate to regard these activities as just strung along, all of which together are said to be thought, the attribute that belongs to the self. He thereby shifted the whole focus of the analysis of the self so that he could speak of it indifferently as soul or mind or consciousness or, formally, as "a thing which thinks." The form of the argument was medieval, but its content suggested a whole new approach to the "science [of] that which could be found in myself." The agonizing introspectiveness of St. Augustine was now lost in the analytic cataloguing of the functions of mind. The bothersome question became: What is this self which has the attribute of thought or consciousness? Two answers are given, one intuitive, the other formal.

Descartes appears to have most confidence in the intuitive answer. By doubting, I cannot but perceive that I exist. Proof, in other words, must begin with something; and that something can come only from the intuitively clear, which is given immediately to the mind. In Objections II of the *Meditations*, Descartes was challenged on this very point, and he there gave an unambiguous answer, worth quoting.

. . . when we become aware that we are thinking beings, this is a primitive act of knowledge derived from no syllogistic reasoning. He who says, "*I think, hence I am, or exist,*" does not deduce existence from thought by a syllogism, but, by a simple act of mental vision, recognizes it as if it were a thing that is known *per se*.[4]

---

[4] *Ibid.*, Vol. II, p. 38. Third Reply to Objections II.

According to this statement, existence is not found by some kind of linguistic prestidigitation, but by the prior knowledge of existence, through experience. The formal answer differs from the intuitive, in that it casts knowledge derived from the mental vision into a verbal form.

The formal answer is as simple as it is unconvincing. Qualities appear, but they can exist only as qualities of something. Red does not exist in itself. A rose is red, or an apple is red, or a flag is red; red as a quality must inhere in something else. The world has no "floating qualities"; they are always attached to something, and cannot exist apart. Some qualities, like color or shape, are material qualities, that is, qualities of material things. But there are other kinds of qualities, such as thinking or doubting or asserting. These qualities are spiritual or mental; hence they must belong to spiritual or thinking things.

In short, they are *minds* which think. " . . . when we perceive any attribute," writes Descartes, "we therefore conclude that some existing thing or substance to which it may be attributed, is *necessarily* present."[5] The formal answer then runs as follows: When I doubt the existence of myself, I am aware of doubting. Doubting is a quality, but since a quality must be attributed to a substance, there must exist a substance which doubts. Since doubting is a thinking or spiritual quality, the substance to which it is attributed must be a thinking or spiritual substance. Therefore, I exist as a spiritual substance, and to doubt it is only once more to assert the existence of myself as such a being.

The form of the argument is worth considering. It is an argument which presupposes the existence of something in the denial of it. The question is whether this argument, which is intended to prove the existence of the thinker, is one which, say, is the kind of statement which appears to be self-defeating, as when one declares for example, "You can't prove anything by a generalization." If it is of this form, it quite clearly violates the logic of types.[6] If, however, it is not a statement which is meant to apply to itself, but rather an activity which is involved whenever one thinks (doubting being a form of thinking); then the presence of that activity is in truth indubitable. The further question, and this is the crux of the matter, is whether that activity proves the existence of an agent or actor—namely, a substance who thinks.

The formal answer does not settle this question; it begs it. It assumes what is supposed to be proved. It assumes that qualities involve substances. The verbal syntax does, of course, lead us to this conclusion, for qualities are considered to be qualities *of*. But then the question turns out to be whether we should call them qualities. If we do not, we may assume that thinking goes on without our having to assume that it goes on in a thinker.

---

[5] *Principles of Philosophy*, LII. (Our italics.)
[6] Cf. Part IV, pp. 475 ff.

This may sound odd, but it is not absurd or self-contradictory. The formal answer settles the question, as Descartes himself pointed out, only if there is truth, and not just formal validity, in the answer.

The formal answer is open to criticism in that it doesn't really prove anything. Because the formal answer is defective, however, we are not therefore entitled to say that the thinker or mind does not exist. Descartes' trump card is to say that it is "a simple act of mental vision" that reveals the existence of mind. In this case we are confronted not with an argument but rather with a disclosure of what he alleges to be a reality. He believes the existence of this reality is grasped in a clear and distinct idea. From this point of view, each person has to settle this question for himself, for the awareness of consciousness is an individual act, open only to the introspective illumination of the person himself. Actually, the more interesting question is to ask what Descartes does with this analysis. Does it have any genuine significance in helping us to understand ourselves and the book of nature?

His further analysis proceeds by his distinction between "what I am" and "that I am." The fact "that I am" is established by each act of consciousness. We know immediately and directly our own existence, not that of the world. As an impressive example, Descartes asks us to consider a piece of wax newly taken from a beehive. It possesses a distinctive yellow color; it is cool, hard, and has a definite shape; it is sweet and still retains a fragrance from the fields from which it has been removed. As the wax is brought near the fire, it begins to lose all its former qualities—its flavor, odor, shape, color, texture. All are different. What do these changes prove? Do we know what the wax is? However clearly we perceive the wax, and this clarity of perception is open to doubt, "it certainly follows much more clearly that I am or that I exist myself from the fact that I see it."[7] It may even be that the wax does not really exist, but I cannot doubt that I exist.

Granting then that nothing is more certain than my own existence, the further question requires an answer: *What* am I? In reply to this question, he answers straightforwardly: I am a thing that thinks—i.e., a thing that doubts, understands, affirms, denies, wills, refuses, and also imagines and feels. We might say these are the faculties of the mind by which we conduct our mental activities, in accordance with our abilities. As we shall see, they are not perfect faculties; but so long as we do not misuse them, they do serve our purposes. In fact, Descartes believes that because they are not perfect, we can establish the existence of a being who is perfect. Moreover, by means of the existence of this perfect being, he thinks we can further establish some important truths about the world. We need therefore to follow carefully the course of his argument.

---

[7] See *op. cit.*, pp. 154 ff.

The Arguments for God's Existence

There are two strains in Descartes' attitude toward God. One is that of a rationalist intent upon rigorously proving propositions, as a mathematician would prove a theorem. Sentiment, reverence, awe—in short, the feelings—have no place in this activity, for proof is made of sterner stuff and is not to be compromised by any kind of sentimentality. The other does involve a sense of humility, a pious acknowledgment of forces, not just beyond our control, but even beyond our understanding. It is, existential-like, a confrontation of the finite by the infinite, where we as finite beings are at a loss to cope with the infinite, or to recognize anything much but our dependence upon it. This latter strain is not really developed by Descartes, but he does base an argument on it insofar as God is the sustaining cause of that which cannot sustain itself—namely, finite beings like us. Although we need not become deeply involved in examining this strain, we do on occasion need to acknowledge it.

The rationalist strain, on the other hand, goes to the core of Descartes' philosophy. Although the minute details of the argument can be better got from the text itself, we need to observe its major steps. We need this, not so much to see whether Descartes actually proved God's existence—for clearly he did not—but rather to discover the attributes he gave to God and therefore to the kind of intelligibility that he thought belonged to the world, and how he reconciled the existence of God with modern science. We may accordingly abbreviate the argument and proceed expeditiously to its significance.

Man is finite and he knows it. He knows that he is not all-powerful or all-knowing or all-loving or all-merciful, etc. Descartes takes this recognition as an obvious fact, which we, living among men, had better not dispute. Being finite and knowing it, we also know the infinite (in-finite). The finite is the limited or imperfect. Knowledge of the imperfect implies knowledge of the perfect, as the limited implies the unlimited—or so Descartes believes. Having the idea of the perfect, there must be a cause of the idea of the perfect in me; I cannot be the cause of the idea of perfection, for then the greater would come from the lesser and then something would come from nothing. (Shades of Aristotle and St. Thomas.) The cause, moreover, must be an adequate cause, for if not, there would be more reality in the effect than in the cause, which Descartes thinks would be absurd. The only cause adequate to the effect is God Himself. Therefore God exists.

One may object: Something else could be the cause of the idea besides God. Descartes anticipates this objection and asserts that instead of disproving God's existence, it merely pushes the argument back a step. Suppose that our parents or teachers have implanted the idea of God in us, then the question is: Where did they come by it? Our objection is to no purpose; it merely forces the argument to retreat in order to re-assert itself once again. Then, instead of accounting for the idea in us, we need to account for it in them and in us. And again he argues, the only adequate cause of the idea, first in them, and second in us, is God. Hence God exists. We have added some steps to the proof, but nothing fundamental is changed.

His argument combines two elements of a rather different order. First it relies upon the formal nature of God, and second upon his causal connection with a part of the world, or, more specifically, with an idea in me. The formal is constituted as the so-called ontological argument of God's existence; the causal as the cosmological argument for his existence, although each is altered in important ways in Descartes' treatment of them.

The ontological argument stems from the medieval realists and St. Anselm, who believed that the most real thing is the most universal of all things, not the particulars of experience. The argument is simple: it asserts that God is a perfect being and that perfection involves existence. God has all the superlative qualities. He is "that [of] which no greater can be conceived." Were this to exist only in my thought and not in reality, I could conceive of a greater who existed in reality as well as in thought. Therefore, that of which no greater can be conceived must exist in reality too. Putting it a little differently, suppose God had all the superlative qualities, save one, namely existence. Then we could say he is omniscient, omnipotent, all-loving, etc. But we could not say he exists. This, however, is absurd, because lacking this quality he would be imperfect. Since God's nature is to be perfect, he must possess the quality of existence as well as the others. Therefore, He exists.[8]

Actually, Descartes telescopes the ontological argument with the cosmological argument, insisting, as he does, that the finite is incomplete and requires the infinite to account for and sustain it. In the peculiar causal argument he employs, the cause is the cause of one idea only—the idea of God in me. Having a character of perfection, the effect can be caused only by a perfect being. In this case, Descartes argues from effect to cause , and since the effect is undeniable, the cause too is undeniable. In the deeper strain mentioned above, he argues more generally from the fact that he is a limited and imperfect being, incapable of sustaining himself; he can be sustained only by the perfect being, God, who there-fore exists. Usually, the cosmological argument proceeds from the need for a sustaining cause of the world. But since Descartes has not yet arrived at the point where he can say that he has a clear and distinct idea of the existence of the world, he cannot use the world as a starting-point

[8] For an incisive criticism of the ontological argument, see Paul Henle, *Philosophical Review*, Vol. LXX (Jan., 1961), pp. 102–109.

for proving God's existence. Instead, he uses the imperfect nature of his being as a thinking thing to arrive at the adequate cause which alone can sustain such a being. The scientists, such as Newton, could use the argument from the cause of the existence of the world, but this was because there was a yawning gap between the theory of inertial states and the fact that there should be anything at all which is at rest or in motion. The cosmos requires a sustainer and that is God. For Descartes, man needs a sustainer, and that is God.

"That God exists" is questioned in only a formal way—really only in order to prove that He exists. This procedure accorded very well with the received learning, and the renewal of this learning kept the world as a cozy place to live in. As for the cosmological part of the argument, Descartes added nothing important, and it was actually disfunctional to the main stream of his argument. The cosmological argument, save possibly for the insistence upon a first cause, a creator of the world, explained nothing important about the texture of the world, or how we are to go about knowing it. God's omnipotence seems to have been of less interest to Descartes than God's omniscience. And even then his philosophical interest in omniscience was of a very special sort. As a philosopher, Descartes wanted God to be omniscient, not in the sense that He knew Adam and Eve had sinned, even though they were hiding, but in the sense that He knew analytic geometry. For in this sense He could be the guarantor of the validity of clear and distinct ideas. God may not be interested in the garden of Versailles, or in the clandestine things that might have taken place there, but He could not but be interested in the geometry of which it was an expression. God's existence turns out to have only a limited value for interpreting nature, namely, the purely formal aspects of nature. Descartes observes in Meditation IV that because God is "immense, incomprehensible, and infinite," this convinces him that final causes have "no useful employment in physical [or natural] things; for it does not appear to me that I can without temerity seek to investigate the [inscrutable] ends of God." But, in the attempt to answer to "what God is," one cannot but reflect that which one takes to be of first importance—whether it is love, or knowledge, or power, or whatever. Descartes makes it out as knowledge, and as knowledge which is contained in clear and distinct ideas. Hence, he insists that anything which we know clearly and distinctly is vouchsafed by God. It is God-like; it is our approach to the divine. But if it is divine, it is also the way to the knowledge of what God has created—namely, the world. The Cartesian world is, as we shall see, a reflection of the divine, and because it is, we can have knowledge of it. The ontological argument is important because it is an expression of knowledge that is perfected. It establishes, not the existence of mysteries, which cannot be established, but the existence of intelligibility, which can be established—in the sense in which we can say we have knowledge of the world. The task of philosophy thus turns out to be one of exhibiting the nature of knowledge, and of suggesting how man may go about constantly learning more of what there is to know. This part of Descartes' argument is the briefest of all, but it turns out to be the most consequential.

Selected Readings

The Philosophical Works of Descartes, trans. by E. S. Haldane and G. R. T. Ross, Cambridge at The University Press, 1931, and New York: Dover, 1955, Vol. I, *Meditations,* I-III, Discourse on Method. (Paperback.)

CHAPTER 10

The Light of Nature: Nature

The Arguments for the Existence of the World

The question, Does the world exist? appears to be idle and absurd. Why not dismiss the question at once and go on to serious work? For two reasons, modern philosophy could not afford summarily to dismiss it. First, there was a clearly felt need to provide a bridge between the received learning and the new science; and second, to make sure that the new way of conceiving of the self would be certain to have a spatial counterpart as an indisputable reality.

The emphasis on the received learning required the exploration of "inner experience," whereas the emphasis on the emerging science required the exploration of "outer experience." This shift could not be satisfied by the Book of Genesis, which describes a world much too richly endowed to be properly understood by science. The world, including the heavens above and the earth beneath with all they contained, had to be simplified into abstract bodies moving about in abstract Euclidean space. But, however abstract was the nature of the bodies, and however abstract was the space within which they moved, both the bodies and the space had to be unquestionably real. Otherwise science could not be distinguished from fantasy. The reality of the world therefore had to be proved, and in such a way that it declared the Glory of God and the Rightness of Euclid. Reason therefore must be supreme in satisfactorily relating the Christian God and the Galilean science. Nothing short of a proof of the existence of the world, conforming to these specifications, would do. This could be accomplished by a simple argument.

But second, and much more complexly, the world had to be proved to exist in conformity with the new way of thinking of the self. According to the conventional wisdom, the self was chiefly an immortal soul whose destiny was realized after a transient passage through temporal affairs. But according to the new learning, the self was chiefly a mind, a consciousness, with ideas excited by forces impinging upon the human body from the outside. This new view made it urgent that the inside be able to demonstrate that there is an outside, and also to demonstrate what that outside consists of. This demonstration, bound to be complex, was desperately needed to provide a bridge across another kind of dualism —that across mind and nature. This bridge was required, not so much because of the conflict between science and religion as because of the conflict between science and common sense.

Descartes provides a convenient starting point for the analysis of both these problems, inasmuch as he provides us with two kinds of arguments to prove the existence of the world, the one simple and the other complex. They are very different; and eventually they come to mark the difference between a mathematical and a psychological interpretation of the world. The simple argument reflects the spirit of mathematics, and he puts it forth with great confidence; not so the complex argument.

The Simple Argument for the Existence of the World

The simple argument for the existence of the world is that anything which I perceive clearly and distinctly must exist, for otherwise God would be a deceiver. He cannot be a deceiver because then he would be imperfect. Since he cannot be both perfect and imperfect, he cannot deceive us about anything clearly and distinctly perceived. There are pitfalls here if we do not take care to understand what is meant by that which is clearly and distinctly perceived. In fact, Descartes' interpretation of this turns out to be the most fruitful part of his philosophy. But before examining it, we may pause to see what this argument for the existence of the world comes to.

God cannot be a deceiver, because if he were a mendacious being, we could not be sure of knowing anything at all. He guarantees the truth of our ideas, that is, of our clear and distinct ones. Descartes is really not justified in saying this. He has said, first, that anything which is clearly and distinctly apprehended, that is, which is indubitable, is true. "I exist"—I know this indubitably, and I know "God exists" indubitably. Thus, when he further argues that God is the guarantor of the truth of clear and distinct ideas, he argues in a circle, and it is illegitimate for him to have it both coming and going. He may say that God exists *because* we have a clear and distinct idea of him, or he may say that *because* God exists and cannot be a deceiver, anything clearly and distinctly perceived is true. But he cannot simultaneously prove the second proposition by the first and the first by the second, any more than one can prove that because a girl is good she is a virgin and that because she is a virgin she is good.[1] What then does the argument about God's not being a deceiver prove?

Actually it proves nothing, and when we remember that the ways of God are inscrutable, the argument is preposterous. But as an expression of faith, it is an attempt to make the world safe for mathematics. Since the mathematical method is the method of using clear and distinct ideas for discovering the order which the world exhibits, the world must contain an order which makes such knowledge possible. If God were a deceiver, not merely would the world exhibit no order, but reason itself would suffer defeat. If deception *at this level* is possible, then the true would be the false and the false true, and no statement would be contradictable, and nothing could be intelligible. Descartes' argument then is not so much an argument as a limitless faith in the capacity of reason to reveal the nature of nature. Having assumed this, his genius appears in the specific way in which he makes reason the instrument for forcing nature to reveal the order it possesses.

By insisting that nature fits the dictates of reason, Descartes' theory of nature not only harmonizes with the Galilean mode of thought but it also becomes oriented in a total philosophy. Galileo embodies mathematics in his view of nature; Descartes embodies mathematics in his whole philosophy—nature, God, and man. With respect to the first, Descartes anticipates the world of nature as a machine, subject to unchanging law, and best expressed in mathematical formulas. Order and proportion are of the essence of nature, and the things which are ordered are capable of being measured and weighed and timed, and therefore reckoned with in quantitative terms. Because of this, the intellect can apprehend things clearly and distinctly.

[1] There is a subtle distinction to be drawn between a clear and distinct *idea*, which is the content of experience, and the *judgment* that the idea clearly and distinctly apprehended is *true*. Even though Descartes does not always speak strictly, he says, strictly speaking, only the judgment has truth. However, he does make God the author of truth itself when he writes in Part IV of the *Discourse*, "But if we did not know that all that is in us of reality and truth proceeds from a perfect and infinite Being, however clear and distinct were our ideas, we should not have any reason to assure ourselves that they had the perfection of being true." The further assurance can only be circular, groundless, and factitious.

The process by which this occurs involves the reduction of the multitudinous richness of experience to the simplicities inherent in nature, unencumbered by subjective feelings. The essence of nature is to be extended. To be extended is to be a body, to occupy space, to possess a definite figure and weight, and to be in motion. At one point, Descartes believed that nature consisted of simple things, "so clear and so distinct that they cannot be analyzed by the mind into others more distinctly known."[2] To conceive of nature in such terms is to be able to apprehend things as they are purely distilled in nature.

The organ by which the things of nature are apprehended is the intellect, that superb faculty which in this world is the distinctive property of man. Man possesses mind and can therefore come to know what nature is in itself, for through mind he is suited to understand the essence of nature. One can hear echoing in this Cartesian doctrine that which Kepler so confidently stated when he said, "As the eye for colors, as the ear for sounds, so the mind is made for understanding not qualities but quantities."[3] By regarding nature in quantitative terms, one can rely on the power of the intellect to put things in perspective and so avoid the confusions and obscurities to which man is subjected when he relies upon the senses. Whatever insult this attitude does to common sense, it is the lifeblood of the new physical science.

Physics is to be dissociated from poetry. Yellow and black and pale and hectic red may do for poetry; they will not do for physics. Colors, sounds, tastes, odors are "subjective" qualities that, under certain circumstances, exist in us, not in things. Hence, Descartes seems to resolve the old riddle about whether a tree makes a sound when it falls in the forest if no mind is present to hear it; for him it does not. In more technical language, as Democritus had already suggested in Greek times, primary qualities belong to things in themselves; secondary qualities do not. Primary qualities are extension, figure, motion, and mass. Secondary qualities are colors, sounds, odors, and tastes. The latter depend upon sense organs and consciousness; they belong to man insofar as he has feelings. Primary qualities do not depend on man, but he is capable of apprehending them through his intellect. The intellect is therefore the faculty of mind which penetrates the essence of nature. The order of things in nature is the very same order which universal mathematics possesses. This is not a coincidence but is inherent in the very intelligiblity which things have and which mind knows. True knowledge is thus mathematical, and the mechanical system of nature is the exemplification

---

[2] Cf. *Rules for the Direction of the Mind, Philosophical Works of Descartes*, trans. by Haldane and Ross (Cambridge at The University Press, 1931), pp. 40 ff.

[3] Cf. Giorgio de Santillana, *Age of Adventure* (New York: Mentor Books), especially pp. 200 ff.

of mathematics insofar as it pertains to extended things. It is consequently the meeting of the divine and the mechanical.

Nature exists that way and God must have planned it that way—otherwise he would be a deceiver, and nothing would be knowable. Newton was absolutely right when he wrote the *Mathematical Principles of Natural Philosophy* (that is, physics) because that is the only way an intelligible account of nature can be written. It is systematic; it is mathematical; it is the account which alone tells what nature is in itself. Thus, mathematics provides a bridge between mind—especially the infinite all-comprehensive mind—and nature; and it constitutes the basis of the ontological argument.

The ontological argument for the existence of nature is, in the final analysis, an assertion that nature is understandable only in mathematical terms. To perfect our understanding of nature we must, therefore, perfect our knowledge of mathematics. God has this perfection insofar as he is intellect. At one point Descartes actually says, in a parenthesis about God, that it is in Him that "all the treasures of science and wisdom are contained," and he thereby underscores the importance of God's intellect. To imitate God in perfecting this faculty of ours is the task of the natural philosopher. This task then is to become mathematicians of nature, that is to say, to discern in nature its mathematical structure and to express it in mathematical formulas. But then nature must have a certain kind of structure, if mathematics is to be applied to it: it must be structured according to primary qualities, and, indeed, these qualities constitute the basis for the mechanistic interpretation of nature. In his treatise on *The World; or Essay on Light*, Descartes tells us something of what this interpretation signifies. In Chapter VII he writes:

Know, then, in the first place, that by nature I do not here understand any goddess or any other sort of imaginary power, but I make use of this word to signify matter itself, in so far as I consider it with all the qualities I have attributed to it, taken as a whole, and under this condition, that God continues to preserve it in the same way that he has created it; for, from the simple fact that he continues thus to preserve it, it necessarily follows that there must be many changes in its parts, which not being, as it seems to me, properly attributed to the Divine activity—because that does not change—I attribute them to nature; and the rules in accordance with which these changes occur I call the laws of nature.[4]

It is worth observing that although Descartes introduces God in his description of nature, he virtually nullifies God's powers. The "Divine activity . . . does not change" and may consequently be neglected in the interests of examining those changes in nature which are lawful-like and which may be formulated as the "laws of nature." The variousness of nature is not attributed to God, but to the regularities that can be

---

[4] See *Descartes: Selections*, ed. by R. M. Eaton (New York: Scribner's, 1927), p. 322.

precisely expressed without appealing to any special interventions by God. The resultant laws of mechanics entitle us to speak of the whole body of them taken together as the mechanistic interpretation of nature. Descartes prided himself on applying mechanistic theory so that every day he could make at least some new discovery. Before indicating what some of these were, we may first note his treatment of biological things, and how they too might be understood as an integral part of mechanics.

Earlier (pp. 165f.) we have had occasion to refer to some of the remarkable developments of Renaissance biology: Vesalius' studies of anatomy; Estienne's work on the arterial and venous systems, including their valve mechanisms; and especially, Harvey's discovery of the circulation of the blood. Seizing upon the results of these biological investigations, Descartes incorporated them in his own conception of nature and thus accommodated biology to the mechanistic interpretation of nature. The importance he attributed to this task is apparent in the fact that he devotes the whole of Part V of the *Discourse on Method* to a discussion of the circulatory system.

Although his treatment of the subject is inferior to that of Harvey, nevertheless he achieved a notable result in accommodating biology to physics. Using the theory of the circulation of the blood as an example of how biological phenomena can be interpreted mechanically, he engages in a detailed explanation of the expansions and contractions of the heart, the propelling of the blood first through the arteries and then through the veins, from which, of course, it returns again to the heart. The constant repetition of the processes, rhythmically working, can then be understood in mechanical terms. The underlying principles are like those of any pumping system, not at all different, say, from the way in which seepage is pumped from a mine. Once understood, the circulation of the blood could be interpreted as merely a complicated pumping of fluid through tubes. Thus the principle could be incorporated into those of the mechanics of fluids—that is, made a part of the science of hydraulics. If such a complex affair as the circulatory system in animals could be adequately interpreted in mechanistic terms, then there was reason to believe that all phases of animal life could be similarly interpreted —at least of animals other than man. So Descartes believed.

His own original investigations into nature were mostly into the order of physical events. He made elaborate investigations, for example, into the principles of the refraction of light. This led him to the study of lenses, and especially into questions of the magnification of objects by the use of lenses. By employing a great variety of mathematical models, he calculated the refractions of various kinds of lenses. Throughout these studies, his ability to apply mathematics to the investigation of nature is everywhere evident. Extending this work, he launched into a detailed study of the rainbow. He inquired in this study, not only into the refraction of light, but into the very nature of light itself, involving as it did a theory of the order of the various colors when sunlight is broken up into its parts. And, even more ingeniously, he worked out a theory of why the rainbow always appears at an angle between 42 and 52 degrees. Although most of his theories were proved wrong and superseded by Newton's, they nevertheless mark him as a scientist of uncommon genius. By virtue of the philosophical theory which underlay these investigations and the effect they had on others, he, more than any other, is responsible for setting a new pattern of thought in opposition to the medieval pattern, while simultaneously employing the medieval vocabulary and invoking principles basic to the medieval mode of thought.

The fact, however, that Descartes' own theories about nature had eventually to be abandoned raises a disquieting question about his method in particular and his theory of knowledge in general. Could it be that clear and distinct ideas can be false? For all the confidence that he and his fellow Cartesians placed in them, we still have soberly to reply that such ideas can be false. To see this more clearly it will be well to observe, first, the analysis he himself gave to the question of error in his simple argument for the existence of the world, and then to observe his own uneasiness in the complex argument for asserting its existence.

The simple answer has been stated to be that clear and distinct ideas are true; otherwise God is a deceiver. But that God should be a deceiver is absurd and impossible. Should we not inquire, then, why are not *all* ideas true, for would not God be a deceiver if any of them were false? He is our maker. Therefore he is responsible for what we are. In terms reminiscent of St. Augustine, Descartes replies that God has given us the faculties by which we can come to know the world; they are perfectly suited to their functions. It is up to us to use them correctly. Just as St. Augustine said man is free to sin or not to sin, so Descartes says man is free to assert or to refrain from asserting the truth of ideas. Assertion and denial are acts of the will and are infinite—that is, we can assert or deny anything we like, and most people do. But we are also capable of refraining from asserting or denying—although most people do not. The understanding is limited; no mortal understands all things. Yet we are capable of understanding some things—those of which we have clear and distinct ideas. If we refrain from asserting the truth of all ideas except the clear and distinct ones, we will not fall into error. Error comes from:

the sole fact that since the will is much wider in its range and compass than the understanding, I do not restrain it within the same bounds, but extend it also to things which I do not understand: and as the will is of itself indifferent to these, it easily falls into error and sin, and chooses the evil for the good, or the false for the true.[5]

---

[5] *Philosophical Works, op. cit., Meditation* IV, pp. 175–176.

God is the guarantor of the truth of clear and distinct ideas. Or, to put it in more secular terms, coordinate geometry is the guarantor of clear and distinct ideas, because algebra is a check on geometry and geometry is a check on algebra.

The argument is, we repeat, a circular one, and will not do. At least it will not do unless we can prove that there is only one geometry and only one algebra, and that they mutually confirm each other. Unfortunately, modern mathematics has demonstrated that there are more than one of each, and that their results may conflict with one another. Therefore, the secular form of the argument breaks down, and with it the non-secular form too, for even God cannot make the sum of the interior angles of a triangle both equal and unequal to two right angles. Perhaps there is, however, a *universal mathematics* from which all others are derived and perhaps this alone is the "true" mathematics? If there is such a mathematics, it has not been discovered. And even if there were such a mathematics, a modern Cartesian could not but be embarrassed by the fact that the mathematics which had been regarded as composed of clear and distinct ideas should, after some two hundred years, be discovered after all not to be so composed. However fruitful the simple argument proved to be, we can no longer rely upon it. Does this then mean that false ideas may be useful? We had better not try to answer this question until we are clearer on the meaning of truth and falsity. Regardless of the question of utility, one can no longer reasonably conclude the existence of anything from the having of a clear and distinct idea. Is there, perhaps, then some other way by which we can conclude the existence of things in nature? To consider this question we turn now to the more complex argument.

The Complex Argument for the Existence of the World

This argument revolves about the question: What can feeling and the secondary qualities inform me about the existence of material things? Descartes remains unwavering in his assertion that we do have indubitable knowledge of material things, insofar as they are considered as the objects of pure mathematics. These are clear and distinct ideas, and even the Almighty would not deceive us about them. But what of the things that we perceive only confusedly and obscurely, that is, of the things which come to us through the senses and which, like taste or scent or color or sound, are not capable, in their direct sensuousness, of being grasped as objects of pure mathematics? This question has far-reaching implications and is, as one can see in *Meditation VI*, the most tortuous philosophical question that Descartes raises.

Ideas, he has told us, are of of three sorts. They are either innate or adventitious or fictitious. Innate ideas are clear and distinct ideas, and they possess this character either because they are directly grasped as true, as, for example, when we are supposed to see that something cannot come from nothing, or because they are grasped as implications of directly grasped ideas, as when from human imperfection the existence of God is demonstrated. Calling them innate may be somewhat misleading (it did mislead John Locke), but clearly Descartes means to show them to be basically like mathematical statements, either as self-evident axioms or as deductions from such axioms. In any case, they are said to be evident to reason, not to the senses.

At the other extreme are fictitious ideas. These are ideas which the human mind has itself formed and it knows that it has formed them. These are the fantasies of life, the invention of such ideas as centaurs and mermaids that people a realm of fiction in which we may take delight. Since there is no serious thought that these are realities other than as fictions of the mind, they appear to cause no formidable problems about truth and error. As fantasies and as recognized to be fantasies, they are never confused with clear and distinct ideas; and they are no more a challenge to truth than poetry is to mathematics. They are different.

But, as for adventitious ideas, we are confronted with nagging questions about their truth or falsity. In the Cartesian scheme, their challenge is not in whether they are taken for innate ideas, but in whether they have any power of revealing to us anything about material things. Difficulties arise from the fact that they are created neither by the mind nor the object alone, but apparently by both together. Things act upon the mind; they "excite" the senses and out of these excitations there come to consciousness sensations, which may or may not resemble qualities that exist in nature.

Basically the problem may be put this way. Sensations are immediately present in the mind. About this there is no doubt. We do experience colors and sounds and tastes. But are the colors and sounds and tastes in the objects too, or are they just in us, or possibly are they just *are*? However we answer the question, the outstanding difficulty resides in the fact that the source of our knowledge is the datum, that is, the sensation itself. How can the sensation reveal knowledge beyond itself, when all we can be sure of is the sensation itself? Of course, we can just take an easy way out and say that sensations are always sensations *of*. Thus, it is the sensation *of* the red apple or *of* its tartness or *of* its squishiness. But this way out is, in a sense, too easy. It does, of course, follow the lead of language, and that may be in its favor, but does it also conform to the deliverances of experience? I say the apple is tart; you say it is sweet. Can we say then that it is both tart and sweet, when tart (meaning sour) and sweet are not just names but opposite qualities? From Plato and before to Bishop Berkeley and after, philosophers have had a great time pointing to the absurdities of saying that things can have mutually exclusive properties. No wonder then that Descartes can readily speak of adventitious ideas as being confused and obscure. But, at the same time, he cannot, as I suppose we cannot, just dismiss secondary qualities, saying that they provide no basis for judging things about the world.

Descartes does vacillate about whether and what adventitious ideas tell us about material objects. On the one hand, the new science regards reality as structural rather than sensuous, but on the other, common sense tells us that things are somewhat as they seem to be. No doubt we can share his discomfort, to the extent that we apply ourselves to puzzling out the kind of disclosures that secondary qualities may make. To deny them any validity for knowledge of external things closets us with our feelings in a suffocating kind of existence. If secondary qualities belong only to the inner recesses of the mind, we are limited to subjective enjoyment quite unrelated to outer reality. Basil Willey elaborates this theme in relation to poetry and quotes what Dryden wrote in his *Apology for Heroic Poetry* that we were to be "pleased with the image, without being cozened by the fiction."[6] If sensations are of this kind, we would be more accurate if we said that we suffer our sensations. They are more in the nature of a shock than of a disclosure of anything that exists. And surely shock is not the best way for a man to come to know the world.

What are we to say about what seems so obviously real to us? We seem obviously to exist, and it seems equally obvious that we have head and hands and feet. Moreover, it seems that other things of the world also must exist, not just this body of mine that appears so inseparable from my existence. These other things appear, whether or not I will them to. My consent or its absence—except when I shut my eyes—makes no difference. I open my eyes and there stands the eucalyptus. It is a stubborn and recalcitrant reality, not to be thought out of existence. Descartes is well aware of all these considerations, as well as of those pertaining to illusions and sleep, such that I can never be sure that things are as I see them. That distant square tower looks round, a person whose leg has been cut off appears to feel pain in a part that has been amputated; things appear vivid in sleep, only to vanish as one awakens. Despite all the possibilities of error, there nevertheless seem to be good reasons for believing that the things I perceive exist, even if not in quite the way I perceive them. Although we may doubt some things that the senses seem to reveal, Descartes observes, "I do not think that I should doubt them all universally."

The argument gets complicated because, in making his case, he combines his faith in God's not being a deceiver with an analysis of adventitious ideas, which, as we have amply observed, are not clear and distinct.

---

6 *The Seventeenth-Century Background* (London: Chatto & Windus, 1949), p. 87.

First, a word about God's not being a deceiver. We saw in the simple argument that the assertion that God is not a deceiver amounts to a faith in the intelligibility of the mathematical view of the universe. This faith can never be proved, even though it led to remarkable discoveries in the physical world. The assertion about God's not being a deceiver produced no such results when coupled with the arguments for proving by means of adventitious ideas that material things exist. In the complex argument, the faith is necessarily weak because the conclusion is itself weak and tentative. The best Descartes can do is to suggest that sensations point to the existence of material things, but they do not prove that such things exist. He writes:

I conjecture with *probability* that body does exist; but this is only with *probability*, and although I examine all things with care, I nevertheless do **not** find that from this distinct idea of corporeal nature, which I have in my imagination, I can derive any argument from which there will necessarily be deduced the existence of body.[7]

The question is: Is it proper to appeal to God in order to establish the *probability* that bodies exist?

God may be a being in whom we have faith and in whom we trust. If God is good, then one might assume that on judgment day one will be judged with justice, if not with compassion. But a faith which leaves us in doubt as to whether God is good is then no faith at all. It is not merely self-defeating, it makes God an object of suspicion. Similarly with the Cartesian argument. I may believe that God guarantees the truth of what I cannot doubt. But to believe that God is the guarantor of what cannot be guaranteed, and to know that it cannot be guaranteed is— we will not say hypocrisy, but it is to take the name of the Lord in vain. This appeal is one which makes God functionless in the argument, and which therefore neither adds to nor detracts from what is otherwise its strength. Then what is otherwise its strength?

The total strength of the argument from adventitious ideas to the existence of material things derives from the analysis of *experience*. Rejecting strict empiricism, Descartes relies upon two arguments, neither of which is quite convincing, and he knows it. The first is an argument from the faculties of the mind; the second, an argument from the nature of perception.

Man has two faculties that, although related to the intellect, are different from it: imagination, and feeling or sensation. By the intellect one can prove theorems about a triangle. In these proofs, the intellect may be assisted by the imagination—the way in which one apprehends the "three lines as present by the power and inward vision" of the mind. But, in a

[7] *Sixth Meditation*, from *The Philosophical Works of Descartes, op. cit.*, p. 187. (Our italics.)

proof concerning a figure of a hundred or a thousand sides, the imagination cannot in the same way support the intellect. Among contemporary philosophers, Bertrand Russell has been especially concerned with drawing a similar distinction between the intellect and the imagination. His symbolic logic has taught us that we are easily misled when we rely upon a model or figure in trying to prove a theorem. A completely abstract formulation, such as is contained in symbolic logic, is required if we are not to go astray. The distinction between the intellect and the imagination has become a commonplace in contemporary mathematics. This faculty of the imagination is employed for picture thinking, as when we say, "Imagine a right-angled triangle lying on its hypotenuse." These words exemplify not pure thought but a kind of picturization of thought. Recognizing this distinction, Descartes frees the imagination from the intellect and links it to feeling, that is, sensation.

Both imagination and sensation are closely related to bodies, and the mind regards these faculties as containing forms of consciousness to which there is some conforming thing outside the mind—that is, some conforming body. Therefore, we think some such bodies exist. Although imagination and feeling are not of the essence of mind, in the sense in which the intellect is of its essence, they do nevertheless act as intermediaries between thought and body, and constitute an argument for the existence of bodies. Imagination and feeling "must be attached to some corporeal or extended substance, and not to an intelligent substance, since in the clear and distinct conception of these there is some sort of extension found to be present, but no intellection at all."[8] The conclusion does, of course, contain a kind of vagueness of which his writing is usually free, but it is nevertheless understandable in view of the subject matter with which he is dealing.

The second argument is more straightforwardly naturalistic. The things of sense experience come to me from another source. I have ideas of sense, passively received, and which cannot come from me, since the faculty from which they come does not presuppose thought. Moreover, these ideas of sense "are often produced in me without my contributing in any way to the same, and often even against my will."[9] Because they contain no thought and are independent of my will, I must attribute them to a source beyond me. Surely they must come from bodies themselves, even though, since they are obscure and confused, they are not likely to be quite the same in the objects as they are in our feelings. The marked difference, however, between sensation and intellect serves as the guide for believing that the one comes from a source outside, whereas the other comes from thought itself.

---

[8] *Ibid.*, p. 190.
[9] *Ibid.*, p. 191.

Of course, one might say that the external source is not a body but rather another mind. This suggestion, ironically, turns out to be trivial. For, if this other mind is God, as Bishop Berkeley (1685-1753) later insisted, the difference is terminological rather than fundamental. "God" becomes in this case another word for "nature." Interestingly enough, Descartes is led to suggest the very same thing. In this same muddy Meditation he writes, "for by nature, considered in general, I now understand no other thing than either God Himself or else the order and disposition which God has established in created things; and by my nature in particular I understand no other thing than the complexus of all the things which God has given me."[10] The language is theological, but the argument naturalistic and its intent empirical. How do I discover nature? By discovering the order of created things. "God is manifest in his works" becomes "God is his works." He is nature and we discover Him by discovering the order present in things. The position suggested by these words is elaborately, if not definitively, worked out in the *Ethics* of Spinoza (1632-1677).

We are now ready for Descartes' conclusion to the *Meditations*, a conclusion inevitable and yet so contrary to the opening that we are forced to reconsider the whole course of his argument. But first the conclusion. His startling acknowledgment is that "I ought to set aside all the doubts of these past days as hyperbolical and ridiculous, particularly that very common uncertainty respecting sleep." The suggestion is disconcerting; possibly the inquiry need not have been entered into at all. Life cannot be one long dream, or if it is, there is no sense in calling it a dream: it is life itself. As a matter of fact, there is dream life and there is waking life, and the difference is apparent. The images in sleep are phantoms. They come and go without reason, coming from no known source and disappearing quite as mysteriously. Things in dreams are unconnected and therefore not quite intelligible. True perceptions are different. "I know distinctly both the place from which [things] proceed, and that in which they are, and the time at which they appeared to me; and when, without any interruption, I can connect *the perceptions which I have of them with the whole course of my life,* I am perfectly assured that these perceptions occur while I am waking and not during sleep."[11] The notion of truth suggested here is totally different from that contained in the doctrine of clear and distinct ideas. This notion is bound to engender error and we must consequently "acknowledge the infirmity of our nature." On the other hand, truth derived from innate, or clear and distinct ideas is indubitably true. Can we reconcile these divergent points of view? The reply to this question turns upon the fundamental issues

10 *Ibid.*, p. 192.
11 *Ibid.*, p. 199. (Our italics.)

of modern science: what kind of knowledge can we gain from mathematics and what kind from empirical observation? We need to know how to cope with them both.

The Cartesian Theory of Knowledge Reconsidered

Truth as contained in innate ideas is rationality raised to its highest pitch, while truth as contained in adventitious ideas is inescapably empirical. The former relies upon clear and distinct ideas and has mathematical truth as its ideal. In the end, this means a universal mathematics which explains all of nature. ("The book of nature is written in mathematical characters.") From the *Principia Mathematica* of Newton to the method of extensive abstraction of Alfred North Whitehead, this ideal has moved men to regard nature as the expression of elemental notions that are primarily affairs of the intellect. The other theory, that truth resides in adventitious ideas, has a range of forms which we need to point to, in order to suggest the ambiguities which lurk in it. Better to begin with the latter theory, in order to perceive its bearing upon the ideal of rational and indisputable knowledge.

Theories of knowledge based upon adventitious ideas have two extreme forms, as well as a number of intermediate forms. The extreme forms may be designated as atomism and coherence. The atomistic theory of empirical knowledge attempts to arrive at true statements about the world on the basis of simple ideas, not further analyzable; and because these ideas are simple and unanalyzable, they may be regarded as a kind of atom. Heat, for example, may be regarded as a simple idea. In approaching the stove, I may at first feel heat. The sensation of heat is an adventitious idea. It is excited by the stove, and I may say, "The stove is hot." The hotness of the stove is thought to be the counterpart of the heat which I feel. It is not clear, however, whether the heat of the stove is the same quality as the heat which I feel. If, for example, I touch the stove, I am burned and feel pain. We do not say that the pain is in the stove. Are we then really entitled to say that the heat is there either? The trouble, in saying that the quality which I feel also resides in the object, consists in the fact that all I know is what I feel; and from the simple fact of feeling, I have no right to attribute the same quality to the thing itself. The atomistic theory is not very promising for reaching judgments about things in nature independently of what I feel. Nevertheless, this theory is thoroughly explored by the empiricists, Locke, Berkeley, and Hume. We shall analyze (in Chapter 13) the argument in some detail.

The coherence theory attempts to surmount the basic difficulty of the atomistic sensation by considering adventitious ideas to come in an order, which makes truth depend, not just on the correspondence of an idea with a quality of a thing, but rather on the assumption that an idea is true only when it fits in with a total pattern. Reality itself is assumed to be coherent, in that things do not just bluntly exist, but they exist in such a way that anything involves everything else. Things do not exist as specters or phantoms, appearing and disappearing as a snapshot; rather, they are connected as the continuous scenes of a good movie are connected, each reinforcing the others. Or to repeat the Cartesian language, I can connect the perceptions with the whole course of my life. The connections thus confirm the fact that I am in contact with reality instead of a dream world where things are incoherent and spasmodic.

Of course, we are forced to admit that our experience is not very coherent, and that it is more often a "blooming buzzing confusion" than a harmoniously rounded picture. This objection to the coherence theory is by no means fatal. In fact, the incoherences, the jarrings or difficulties we encounter, can be and have been interpreted by philosophers as a stimulus to search for a greater harmony, because the mind cannot regard contradictions as characteristics of reality. Both Hegel and Marx, to mention only two, regarded contradictions as the lifeblood of the dialectical process for pushing thought on to conclusions which would overcome contradictions. In forcing the theory to the extreme, Hegel so far from being satisfied with connecting ideas with "the whole course of [man's] life," insisted that final coherence could be attained only for absolute mind, that is, the mind of God.

But we must not forget that it is we—finite beings and fallible—who are searching for truth. Does the coherence theory help to explain man's search for truth? The advocates of the coherence theory can answer yes. In doing so, however, they need to introduce a new element in the theory of knowledge—the element of probability. Some things we know only very unsatisfactorily; some things more satisfactorily. Hence there may well be what we call degrees of knowledge. Or, as applied to the coherence theory, degrees of coherence, since things may be knit together more closely or less closely. Some things affect other things only minimally or trivially, as say the attraction of the Empire State Building to the moon. Other attractions may be significant as, for example, the attraction of the ocean to the moon. Some connections are loose and tenuous; some are tight and intimate. To ignore the former may lead to error, but not serious error. With respect to the latter, however, the error may be serious. According to the coherence theory, the absence of all error depends on our knowing all reality. Since this we cannot do, knowledge is at best probable and always affected with some error. The degree of probable error thus becomes an inescapable part of all knowledge, a factor of which the scientist is painfully aware and carefully introduces into the results of his investigations.

The atomistic theory of adventitious ideas gives us no basis for asserting the truth or falsity of an idea. The coherence theory makes absolute truth a vain search, but it does provide a way of regarding ideas as more or less true. Between the atomistic and the coherence theories there are others, such as various forms of conventionalism and operationism, too complex to discuss at this time. In all these theories, it appears that we are unable to reach infallible empirical knowledge. The best we can hope for is a degree of knowledge, more or less imprecise. We may now observe the consequences of this conclusion for both the complex and the simple argument that Descartes employs to prove the existence of material things.

The consequences for the complex argument are easy to observe. Adventitious ideas can never be indubitably true. We cannot say that the color we see in the orange or the heat we feel from the stove is in either the orange or the stove. In fact, we cannot even legitimately say that the ideas resemble the qualities in the objects, because the basis of our judgment would require a knowledge of both the idea and the quality as well as of their similarity. But, if we knew the quality, the idea would be superfluous and we could make a true statement, not on the basis of the adventitious idea, but on the basis of direct knowledge. Accordingly, about secondary qualities, we may say with Descartes that "there is something in it," that is, in the object, but we are at a loss to say just what it is that is in it. We may nevertheless be "taught somewhat by nature," and our knowledge may be more or less adequate, even though we are sometimes deceived or confused. Ideas may serve as "signs" of things to come, and they may be supported by past experience, but never infallibly. To add, in this connection, that God is not a deceiver is to express an irrelevant sentiment.

What then about the simple argument that we have a clear and distinct idea of the existence of material things, and that God cannot deceive us in this? The controversial question is whether we actually do have a clear and distinct idea about such things. Let us grant that we do have clear and distinct ideas in connection with mathematics in general and co-ordinate geometry in particular. Are these also clear and distinct ideas of material things? The answer is unequivocally no. Neither formal algebra nor geometry nor a combination of the two entitles us to say what things exist or how they exist. We may be reminded here of Bertrand Russell's famous observation that mathematics is a science in which we never know what we are talking about or whether what we say is true. What and how, then, do we know of the existence of material things? Let us assume with Descartes—and with Kepler and Galileo—that we know the primary qualities of figure, extension, motion. Let us assume, moreover, that we can measure things—weigh them, time them, calibrate them in many ways—that is, that we can employ mathematics in our treatment of them.

Even assuming these points, we are still forced to admit that our results are never infallible. There is always a probable degree of error in measuring anything. Or, to reckon more broadly with error, why are we not just as much subject to illusions with respect to primary qualities as with respect to secondary? The stick in water appears bent, the railroad tracks appear to converge, figures drawn on paper appear to move, etc.

The only way to avoid error in relation to what material things exist and how, is to legislate for them in advance of experience. Indeed, this seems to be what Descartes does, even as both Galileo and Newton also did in their approach to the study of nature. The law of inertial motion is not proved or provable. It contains assumptions which, by their very nature, are not ultimately testable. Similarly, laws are assumed which hold only for freely falling bodies, or for perfectly elastic bodies. In such matters, the best we can do is to observe empirically that there is something approximating these ideal conditions. Hence, our ideas pertain to concepts or laws directly and to the existence of material things only indirectly and inadequately. Although we may have clear and distinct ideas about a theoretical world, they are not such as will prove the existence of material things—even as theoretical models may be useful, yet false to reality. Men are fallible with respect to knowledge of primary qualities, just as they are with respect to secondary qualities, and therefore even the appeal to God cannot guarantee the truth of ideas which do in fact contain illusion and error.

When we consider the simple argument in the light of the complex one, we observe that the results of the latter upon the former are devastating. I cannot refrain from judgments about primary qualities any more than I can about secondary. And in neither case do I possess clear and distinct ideas. Therefore, it is inept of Descartes to suggest that with respect to primary qualities we can refrain from error if only we restrain our will—that is, if we refuse to assert that an idea is either true or false unless it is clear and distinct. There are clear and distinct ideas in mathematics, but not in physics. Consequently, even God cannot guarantee us true ideas of the physical world—at least not in terms of natural knowledge. However benevolent God may be, men cannot but suffer the infirmities which are inherent in their empirical undertakings. There are always hazards in this kind of undertaking, and although scientific methods can minimize them, they cannot eliminate them.

Reluctantly, we are forced to conclude that the theoretical pinnings of Descartes' theory of knowledge are faulty. Are we also to conclude that his basic insights are faulty? In order to pursue this question, we need now to consider, first, the Cartesian dualism, and, second, the mechanistic interpretation of nature.

Selected Readings

The Philosophical Works of Descartes, trans. by E. S. Haldane and G. R. T. Ross, Cambridge at The University Press, 1931; and Dover, 1955, Vol. I, *Meditations,* IV-VI. (Paperback.)

Descartes: Selections, ed. by R. M. Eaton, New York, Scribners, 1927, pp. 312-349, and pp. 361-403. (Also in paperback.)

CHAPTER 11

Dualism

Cartesian Dualism

As we look back over Descartes' arguments, imperfect as they may formally be, we are nevertheless confronted with two, if not three, formidable ideas—all pertaining to existence. His concern is with the existence of finite thinking things, finite material things, and the infinite thinking thing. We need to consider these, not just separately, but also in their relations to one another, their likenesses, their differences, and the ways in which they affect one another. By considering them in this order, we can gain an insight into seventeenth-century philosophy, and observe how it so remarkably mediated between the conventional wisdom and the new mechanistic science.

The Thinking Thing

However faulty Descartes' argument about the existence of the self, whether in the intuitive form or in the analytic (see pp. 191ff), can we seriously deny that man is a thinking thing? A hasty answer to this question is not called for, because the question itself needs to be cleaned up before we are entitled to respond to it. There is an obvious sense in which man is an unthinking being. He often acts irrationally—or possibly just nonrationally—as subject to impulses, and especially to habits, such that he might be regarded as a kind of machine, rather than as a thinking being. We need not belittle these various considerations, which come down to us from such different quarters as Freudianism, behaviorism, and, more recently, cybernetics. They are largely, but not entirely, irrelevant to the kind of question Descartes meant to pose. He was, in the first instance, concerned with the undeniable fact that man is a conscious being, and that the more serious we are in denying it, the more we discover consciousness as inescapably belonging to man's nature. Descartes' illustration, of the piece of wax apparently changing its qualities as it is placed near the fire, is designed to prove not the existence of the wax but the existence of consciousness.

"Man is a thinking thing." Each of the terms of this statement contains overwhelming connotations—"man," "thinking," "thing." Let us, for strategic reasons, consider the middle one first. What is "thinking"? Is it an activity, or the result of an activity, or a special kind of one or the other, or none of these? These questions suggest that Descartes may be somewhat ambiguous in the way he employs the term. No doubt he is, but in context the term is usually fairly definite, especially when we distinguish between a generic use of the term and a more specific one.

In the generic sense, thinking appears to be any form of conscious activity. The forms can be listed as perceiving, willing, asserting, denying, remembering, doubting, imagining, and so on indefinitely. Man, then, as a thinking thing is a conscious being who possesses the distinctive attitude of being aware. Mind is mind*ing*; it is being alert to items, being able to discriminate between one item and another. Minds can single out things and distinguish them from one another. All this seems obvious enough, and our first reaction is likely to acknowledge it and say, "So what?" And there really is no good answer to the "so what?" unless we can move to the formulation of some underlying question to which the acknowledgment of these characteristics of mind supply an answer. The clue to the answer is the specific sense in which Descartes uses the term.

Specifically, "thinking" is the kind of activity in which the mathematician engages, for the essence of mathematical thinking is that its ideas are clear and distinct and they pertain not to perceiving, willing, remembering, imagining, and the like, but to the intellect and the intellect alone. Why single out this one activity from the countless conscious activities in which men can engage? The answer, which becomes abundantly apparent in the Cartesian analysis, is that only through this activity can man come to have knowledge. Clear and distinct ideas, the meats on which the intellect feeds, give us a grasp of reality. The rest may soothe us or irritate us or depress us or excite us, but they cannot supply us with what Descartes most intensely wants—knowledge. Why all this intensity for knowledge?

The Middle Ages gave man God—solace, comfort, a degree of security, and a reasonable hope for eternal salvation. It did not give him knowledge of the vast world in which he lived. Copernicus made a good start; so did Vesalius and Harvey. But the astronomers and the physicists did most to enlighten men about the world. Descartes himself wanted answers to questions about lenses and rainbows that Aristotle and the new Aristotelianism of St. Thomas and the later scholastics did not provide. These answers were to be had only through mathematics, and this was primarily an affair of the intellect, rather than of seeing and remembering and becoming ecstatic about such things as rainbows. Of all forms of consciousness, the intellect seems to be farthest removed from space-time things, and is not likely to be confused with them. The intellect is expressed as ideas, which are true or false; things are bodies, which either do or do not exist, but as such are neither true nor false.

Being farthest removed from things, ideas need to be characterized in a way which will mark their extreme diversity from things. Things are extended. As extended they are corporeal, that is, they are body-like; they are divisible, have figure and motion, but are insensitive. Ideas are not material, and therefore that of which they are expressions—minds— are also not material. Mind is nonextended and indivisible. Literally, minds have no weight nor solidity, nor any of the other properties that material things have. In fact, they are in every way opposed to such things—*non*extended, *in*corporeal, *in*divisible, etc. The intellect, specifically, is to be so characterized; so are all the generic activities of mind— perceiving, remembering, imagining, willing, and the rest. Since they are nonmaterial, these activities belong to a being which is also nonmaterial. This being is mind or spirit or soul, or in the language of the schoolmen, a substance—nonmaterial, of course. It exists, therefore it is a thing; for whatever exists is a thing or substance. To be is to be a substance.

There is concealed in this language a difficulty, however. The formal definition of substance is that which we conceive of as "an existent thing which requires nothing but itself in order to exist." As Descartes himself points out, "nothing but God answers to this description as being that which is absolutely self-sustaining, for we perceive that there is no other created thing which can exist without being sustained by his power."[1] Spinoza took over this definition of substance and used it quite literally, so that only one substance, God or Nature, exists. But Descartes preferred

---

[1] *Principles of Philosophy*, LI. See also LII for further explanation. *Descartes: Selections*, ed. by R. M. Eaton (New York, Scribner's, 1927), pp. 275–276.

to use the concept in a somewhat inexact sense, and was satisfied with asserting the existence of a substance wherever an attribute can be found. Since there is thinking, there must be thinking substances. The adoption of this formal way of speaking leads to grave philosophical difficulties, and actually obscures some of the most important things Descartes had to say. For the present, we may point to one difficulty only, and this leads us to consider the third term above—"man."

Man is a thinking being, but man is also body, an extended being. Supposedly, we have clear and distinct ideas of both thinking and extended things. Man, moreover, is unique among all beings, in that he is the only one who both thinks and has a body. Animals do not think, not even in the generic sense of being conscious. They are automatons, completely and adequately understandable as a kind of machine. Not so, man. He thinks and he also moves about, causing other things to move and being moved by other things. Therefore, in the case of man, we need to consider what is the relation of mind and body.

There is a limited number of alternatives for conceiving of man in these terms. Either he is just mind or just body or both. The idealist says just mind; the materialist, just body. Others say both. If both, body may be the controlling factor, with consciousness a kind of effect of body, but itself having no genuine power. In this case, we can say that mind is an "epiphenomenon"—an appearance, but not a causal agency. Or, similarly, mind could be said to be the controlling factor, and then body would be regarded as an "epiphenomenon," without any real effect upon man's life. Again, both could be said to be equally real, but not affecting one another, as for example, when Spinoza regards both thought and extension as attributes of some underlying substance which manifests itself in both ways. According to this view, bodies never effect ideas or ideas bodies. Or, as we sometimes say, you can fight ideas only with ideas.

Finally, we might say that both bodies and minds are real, and that they interact upon each other. If we are not queasy, we might ask the man on the street, "Do you have a body?" Assuming that he did not react violently, that he was accustomed to being polled, and that he was willing to answer the question, he probably would reply, "Yes." "Do you have a mind?" Again making those doubtful assumptions, he would probably repeat, "Yes." "Do they react upon each other?" "Of course." Surely we do have ideas and our ideas do lead to actions. Thoughts guide the body, within limits, to do our will. Again, things happen to the body, and they affect our thoughts. Hatred, revenge, love, and a multitude of reactions in response to how the world has affected us, imply that bodily actions do affect our minds. This seems so obvious—we might almost say, so clear and distinct—that we cannot deny it. So, in essence, Descartes thought.

The Mind-Body Problem

The mind-body problem is inevitable in the Cartesian philosophy. Honestly, deliberately, and with reason, Descartes has been forced into it. The grounds for asserting that man is a conscious being are overwhelmingly strong and undeniable. Coupled with his adoption of the medieval mode of substantial forms, mind cannot but be said to be an immaterial substance. Now we have entered upon a dangerous path. Mind is now something in and of itself. Had Descartes taken the path of idealism, such as Malebranche (1638-1715) did, he would, in one sense, have had an easy course to follow, for then he could have avoided any serious mind-body problem. But he was unwilling to take that easy way. Why? Because, it seems, he would then have lost out on the exciting, scientific adventure of exploring the world.

To avoid making the mind narcissistically capable of appreciating only itself, he seized upon the specially prized aspect of the mind, the intellect, which by its clear and distinct ideas enabled man to advance knowledge of the world. Descartes was playing for high stakes and the game was costly. By making the intellect the arbiter of truth, he could regard as true only that which is clear and distinct. We have had ample occasion to observe that the consequence was the mechanistic interpretation of nature, and that only the primary qualities of things could be clearly and distinctly apprehended; consequently, he took them to constitute the essence of nature. This bold move made is possible to relate to the work of the new science, and to use mathematics as the open-sesame to the secrets of nature.

One may say that both the virtues and the vices of Descartes' philosophy come from his coupling the old with the new—the reconciliation of the new science with the old folklore. The old folklore, in this case, is specifically the doctrine of substantial forms. This doctrine belonged appropriately to the older hierarchical conception and with it to a metaphysics that could only be at odds with a competing metaphysics, which was atomistic. Descartes insisted that bodies are substantial forms; they are substances which are extended. Their properties are extension in length, breadth, and depth—qualities that are inherent in bodies. Although he did believe that there are more subtle and rarefied extended things, not quite observable, nevertheless the essence of their qualities was likewise to be regarded as occupying space.

By combining the old and the new metaphysics, he proved himself sensitive to the conventional wisdom as well as to the challenge of the new science. The two could live together only if a harmonizing principle could join them in a union which would at the same time liberate each. He believed that there is just such a principle—the natural light of reason, that is, so far as the study of nature is concerned, universal mathematics. Universal mathematics is the intellect perfected to the highest degree. It is the essence of knowledge, for it contains the ideas by which things can be related to one another. Moreover, things are themselves related in just these ways. So we are entitled to say, as Spinoza did say more explicitly than Descartes, "the order and connection of ideas is the order and connection of things." This notion is, as we have seen, the very essence of the ontological argument. Ideas and things are inseparably related. They must be that way, because we must think that way. Such a relationship exists, of course, only when ideas are clear and distinct. God's ideas are of that sort; and the natural light of reason is of that sort, because it is the divine in us.

But the marriage of ideas and things holds only for the intellect, that is, for thought in the specific sense. What about thought in the generic sense which, in including all forms of consciousness, contains secondary qualities, emotions and feelings of varieties from the most obscure and confused to those only less so? Here the agony begins. We know what mind is, and we know what body is, but how can one possibly act upon the other? Mind is nonextended, incorporeal, indivisible. Body is extended, corporeal, divisible. Their natures are opposites, and it can only be a miracle that one could affect the other. Thoughts are not physical. How then can they produce physical results? Mechanical events pertain only to the movements of bodies. How can they determine thoughts in the mind? The mystery is deeper even than action at a distance, for mind being nonextended cannot really be said to be close or far, in touch or not in touch, moving or motionless. Being incomparable, they can no more be related than can smokiness and tartness be related. They are unmitigatedly different. The truth of the matter is that in this view minds cannot consistently be located anywhere without involving a fundamental category mistake.[2]

The details of Descartes' elaborate theory of how mind and body are supposed to interact are not worth discussing. Suffice it to say that he believed that each acts upon the other through rarefied animal spirits, and that the point of interaction is in the pineal gland, lodged at the base of the brain, and therefore strategically related to the various, symmetrical parts of the brain. In this gland, thoughts affect the spirits, which in turn stimulate the nerves to activate bodily motions or, in reverse, the nerves to carry "messages" to the gland, which are then translated as thoughts of which we are said to be conscious. The theoretical foundations of this doctrine are shaky and the physiology impossible. Nevertheless, its influence

---

[2] This notion, together with what the distinguished contemporary philosopher, Gilbert Ryle, has called "the dogma of the ghost in the machine," is discussed in Part III, pp. 347 ff.

on modern thought has had an importance difficult to exaggerate, for the dualism it engendered has left a heritage almost inescapable.

Dualism Reconsidered

The mind-body relation is only one aspect of Descartes' dualism; and, if inevitable, nevertheless the least satisfactory aspect of his dualism. He was forced to adopt the interaction theory, not because of its intrinsic virtues, but because of his deeper-lying conception of man and the world. That Descartes was not happy with his "solution" of the mind-body problem is seen from his desperate attempts to bring together body and soul into a real union; and this he does, in spite of the fact that he has endlessly insisted on the radical difference between material and immaterial things. For example, he writes in *Meditation VI*:

Nature also teaches me by these sensations of pain, hunger, thirst, etc., that I am not only lodged in my body as a pilot in a vessel, but that I am very closely united to it, and so to speak so intermingled with it that I seem to compose with it one whole. . . . For all these sensations of hunger, thirst, pain, etc. are in truth none other than certain confused modes of thought which are produced by the union and apparent intermingling of mind and body.[3]

The theory of the interaction of mind and body is certainly awkward to defend. Is it also awkward to defend the separation between man as thinking being and nature as extended being?

Bacon's dualism was an easy one—the dualism between natural knowledge and the supernatural. The one pertains to experimentation, action, and power; the other to religious faith. They are different and need not be confused. Like the theory of separation of Church and State, this separation permits us to do Caesar's work, that is, science, without mixing it up with God's work, that is religion. But then, Bacon did not worry about analyzing the difference between consciousness and matter. He was apparently more concerned with experimental testing and the use of knowledge than he was with trying to separate man's soul from his body, the effect of which would reduce rather than contribute to man's power.

Even apart from the theological questions, into which we shall presently inquire more carefully, Descartes' problems were different. As a mathematician and metaphysician, he wanted to prove things; he wanted to attain indubitable knowledge by demonstration; not just laboriously to experiment and by means of an inductive leap to seize upon generalizations about nature. The mechanistic interpretation, which provided clear and distinct ideas of how nature works, was a godsend for him. The laws of nature were mathematical, and coherently related to one another. Deductions were possible in a neat and tidy world, in which all motions were predetermined

---

3 In *Philosophical Works of Descartes, op. cit.*, p. 192.

by physical forces. Copernicus, Kepler, and Galileo had prepared the ground for this interpretation, and their scientific successes overwhelmingly proved the reliability of their methods.

Descartes believed that the intellect could demonstrate what the world is. He did show how scientific intellect and the mechanism which is nature were different, yet complements of each other. Design becomes increasingly apparent in nature, and design is intelligible only to the intellect—because, in the final analysis, design can be created only by the intellect. Since intellect forces its pattern on nature, intellect can, of course, rediscover that pattern which it has forced on nature. Therefore the dualism of mind and nature provides a remarkable solution of understanding both—that is, mind as intellect and nature as machine. Moreover, the machine concept applies not just to the so-called inorganic world. It applies to animals too, which are automata. It applies to everything except to the intellect and to the passions of the soul—to all those things "which [are] in us and which we cannot in any way conceive as possibly pertaining to a body."[4] The weakness of his dualism appears when he attempts to unravel the relation of the passions of the soul to the actions of the body. At this point, he is forced to deal with adventitious ideas and feelings, unclear and indistinct. And, refusing to employ the mechanistic theory to explain them, he leaves us with a most unsatisfactory account.

In this account, the Cartesian heritage is one which combines extreme objectivism in the analysis of the physical world and extreme subjectivism in that of consciousness. The first may be conveniently spoken of as physical nature regarded as a world-machine. Later, Newton delineated its principles with a care and precision that remained virtually unchallenged until the late nineteenth century. The second comes down to us mainly in the form of associational psychology, and its method was largely introspective. It, too, lasted on as structural psychology. And although it has now been thoroughly superseded, it has nevertheless been hallowed as the stream of consciousness in the novels of Proust and the poetry of Gertrude Stein.

The question still remains as to how we should interpret the significance of the infinite spiritual substance. We have noted above an ambiguity in Descartes' ontological argument for the existence of God. Man is finite and limited in two ways: in his knowledge and in his power.[5] He is neither

---

[4] *The Passions of the Soul*, Part I, Article III. In *Descartes: Selections*, ed. by R. M. Eaton (New York: Scribners, 1927), p. 362.

[5] Actually, Descartes should have recognized a third way in which man is limited—namely, in his feelings. Even though Descartes acknowledges man's limitations in regard to mercy—God being all-merciful—he characteristically fails to recognize the importance of this feeling-aspect of man's nature. Although he does analyze the passions of the soul in his psychology, he fails completey to take serious account of the capacity of the feelings to open up a whole new dimension of life, the aesthetic dimension. This omission means that there is no proper analysis of beauty as a facet of either human existence or of divine being.

omniscient nor omnipotent. Since the limited implies the unlimited, we must have at least the idea of the unlimited or perfect being. Then, we recall, that by means of the necessity for a cause for the idea, Descartes thinks he proves the existence of God. But the important question remains: What is God?

GOD IS THE INFINITE SPIRITUAL BEING. Now, however, we need also to recall how the term "spirit" has been redefined in this philosophy. To be a spiritual being is to be a thinking being, and the faculty by which thought is carried on is the intellect. Hence the essence of God's nature is to know; He has the most perfect intellect conceivable. We have already analyzed what this means in connection with Descartes' philosophy—how, in other words, the intellect is most perfectly expressed in universal mathematical knowledge. But two other considerations press in on us. What of God's power? And what of his role in traditional Christianity?

GOD'S POWER. Immediately we are confronted with a vexing question. How can a spiritual thinking being exercise power? The simple answer is that it cannot. It has no power other than that of thought. In fact, were it to have power and to manifest it, it would be continually meddling in the world; and then the mechanistic interpretation would be rendered disserviceable. Its power would produce all kinds of miracles; and then the law-like descriptions, expressed in mathematics, would be false to what goes on in the world. Sensitive to the problem, Descartes ironically attempts in Chapter VI of *The World* to describe a new world, one which he supposes not really to exist, but which is nevertheless of the essence of a mechanistic world. He begins, then, to develop the principles by which this "purely imaginary" world can be understood, without any appeal to supernatural agencies. When the supernatural intervenes, then is thought stymied.

If there is to be anything miraculous, perhaps there should be just one big miracle, and we may call this the First Cause of the world. This creation appears to be the work of an all-powerful being, especially if, as Christian theology has it, God created the world out of nothing. Sheerly out of his command, the world came into being. Although the First Cause cannot be investigated in the way the scientist investigates second causes in nature, one can assume that the First Cause makes possible the discovery of second causes. The Great Watchmaker not only makes the watch but also stipulates the laws in accordance with which the watch runs. Hence, by studying the workings, we can also come to know the laws of their operation. Descartes and the scientists inevitably came to some such notion of the omnipotence of God insofar as He made manifest His power in the natural world. The extension from a substance's being spiritual to its being omnipotent is illegitimate, but this extension derived understandably from the difference between thinking and a corporeal being.

One final aspect of this dualism, expressed in the gulf between God and nature, is important to note. How well does Cartesian philosophy comport with traditional Christianity? Technically and strictly interpreted, this philosophy does not harmonize well with the Christian tradition. By placing its emphasis upon the intellect and upon the world as intellectually knowable, it suggests, in essence, more of a secular point of view than a religious one, especially once the implications of mind as a natural phenomenon are traced out. Nevertheless, two considerations made the philosophy more palatable to the believer—its inherent ambiguities, and its reinterpretation by other Cartesians.

The ambiguities are, at times, dodges by which Descartes attempted to avoid censure from the Church. He was aware of the heresies which caused Bruno's being burned and of Galileo's retractions. He was not anxious to run afoul of the clergy. Besides, he did have a very real respect for the clergy, even an affection for many of them—Father Mersenne, in particular. Aside, however, from some obvious attempts to dodge conflicts with the Church, he was not a naturalist, and his dualism of spiritual and material things was most certainly an honest disavowal of naturalism —at least in the form of a consistent materialism. It would be an easy extension from the assertion of the existence of a perfect thinker to other qualities traditionally lumped together as part of God's perfection. By a combination of wits and witlessness, believers could accept this masterful attempt to meet the challenge of science and to effect a working arrangement between it and the folklore with which it seemed to clash.

Besides, there were excellent minds who, instead of merely swallowing whole Descartes' philosophy, prepared, according to their own recipes, variations of the Cartesian metaphysics. Among them were Malebranche, Geulincx, and, above all, Blaise Pascal (1623-1662). Pascal is, in many ways, the most interesting of these Cartesians. Like Descartes, he was a superb mathematician. He wrote a skillfull treatise on conic sections at the age of sixteen, and he also did a significant piece on probability. In science, he made fresh discoveries, as well as inventing the calculating machine. He knew the nature of the "geometric mind," and he contrasted it with the "acute mind," capable of penetrating things of sense and feeling, which the geometric mind could not. Sensitive to what real geometry is, Pascal clearly recognized the ridiculousness of trying to use definitions and principles on acute matters, where the methods of reasoning do not belong.

In his now famous words, "the heart has its reasons, which the reason knows nothing about: a thousand things testify to it. . . . This is what faith is: God known by the heart, not by reason." The dualism could not be made plainer. Reason can prove things about the natural world; it is powerless to prove anything about man's relation to God. In the one case man confronts the finite, and can cope with it. But "Unity joined to the infinite augments it in nothing any more than a foot added to an infinite measure. The finite is annihilated in the presence of the infinite, and becomes a pure nothing. Thus our mind before God; thus our justice before the divine justice."[6] Arguments for the existence of God are of no real help. Even if we succeed in proving it, we fail to have conviction in the proofs. We can prove, moreover, that God exists without knowing what he is, just as we can prove that infinite numbers exist without knowing whether they are odd or even.

Possibly we should not call Pascal a Cartesian. His faith in reason is severely limited. His *Thoughts* contrast the knowable with the unknowable. Pascal is aware of sin, Descartes only of error. Pascal believes in eternal life, Descartes in timeless knowledge. Pascal is a mystic, Descartes a believer in the natural light of reason. Pascal is a Christian, Descartes is more of a Deist. Being absorbed by the Christian mysteries, Pascal makes his mark by his sheer mathematical and scientific brilliance. The modern philosophical tradition, however, comes down through Descartes rather than through Pascal. It regarded seriously the need for interpreting things naturalistically. In the broad sense, this came to mean interpreting things mechanistically. We turn now to an analysis of what this means.

Selected Readings

Blaise Pascal, *Pensées*, trans. by J. M. Cohen, Harmondsworth: Penguin, 1961, Parts I, II. (Paperback.)
Randall, J. H., Jr., *The Career of Philosophy*, New York: Columbia, 1962, Bk. III, Chaps. II-IV.
Ryle, Gilbert, *Concept of Mind*, New York: Barnes and Noble, 1949, Ch. 1. (Paperback.)

[6] *Thoughts*, trans. by O. W. Wight (Boston: Houghton Mifflin, 1887), p. 251.

CHAPTER 12

Mechanism

The Mechanistic Interpretation

Mechanism is a form of naturalism. Although naturalism is not easy to define, naturalists, and therefore mechanists, do rally together in repudiating the existence of a final cause or end which determines the course of nature. They insist that nature, including human beings, is all there is, and that the laws of nature are the most adequate explanations we can find for things. Destiny is nothing more than a sequence of causes by which, of necessity, one thing happens after another. But there is no cause of causes which predetermines a final end to which all things must conspire. There is no will of God or other reality independent of nature which employs nature to serve its purpose. The "will of God" is nothing more than a human fiction which men invent to satisfy their sentiments. Neither in reason nor nature nor experience is there anything which compels us to believe in the existence of any causes controlling nature other than nature itself.

The naturalistic point of view, if not radical today, was certainly regarded that way in the seventeenth century. In fact, it was so radical that scarcely anyone in the seventeenth century dared to propose it seriously. Descartes in *The World* did so very tentatively; Hobbes did so somewhat more boldly; and Spinoza did so under the guise of a pantheism, where nature and God being identified, one could take his choice in regarding this philosophy as either naturalistic or not. Novalis believed Spinoza's philosophy to be nonnaturalistic and said that it was written by "a God-intoxicated" man. Clearly, however, a new spirit pervades the work of these philosophers, and marks a contrast between their outlook and that of the medieval schoolmen. When these philosophers speak of God—and they all do—it is in a different sense from that in which St. Thomas or St. Bonaventure speaks of God.

Spinoza, especially, can speak, one might almost say sonorously, of "God or Nature," and assert that "all things flow from God" in a way that is diametrically opposed to "Praise God, from whom all blessings flow." For Spinoza, things flow from God "as it flows from the nature of a triangle that the sum of its interior angles is equal to two right angles." God's nature is nature, and in nature whatever happens is caused by its antecedents. Or, more accurately speaking, it is caused by a necessity better expressed as ground and consequent. By analogy we might say, given the solar system, the motions of the planets are also given, for they are deducible from the character of the system itself. There is nothing miraculous that enters into the system; it is explicable only in terms of itself. Just as the axioms, postulates, and definitions of Euclidean geometry involve the totality of theorems which are demonstrable within that system, so from the existence of nature, the totality of events is similarly demonstrable. Mathematics, not piety, is the clue to the understanding of nature. To know the world according to the method of geometry has nothing to do with the mysteries of creation or the will of God or of men's prayers for divine grace to save their souls. Knowledge of nature, not the search for final causes, is the only hope for salvation. The search for final causes, the reliance upon the will of God, is regarded in this philosophy, according to Spinoza, as "the refuge for ignorance."

The contrast between the medieval point of view and the modern comes out most sharply in the attitude toward God and some final end or meaning or purpose of nature that transcends nature. For the medievalist, nature without God is meaningless. Man's hope and man's destiny are capable of realization only as he can resurrect the spirit, dissociate it from the earth, and unite it beatifically with God. Prayer, practice, and the intervention of the Church in performing the sacraments for men is, when divinely illuminated, the path to salvation. What is causally efficacious in respect to the spirit requires techniques and considerations totally alien to the causal efficacies in nature. Faith, supernatural knowledge, and the offices of the Church have no clear relevance to worldly adventure, experimental knowledge, and the use of physical implements for the satisfaction of wants or the enhancement of power. Profits, men may seek on earth; salvation only in the heavens. No wonder the medievalist distinguished terrestrial mechanics from the celestial, and applied different principles to each. When scientists applied the same kind of mechanics to each, the philosopher was inevitably led to call into question final causes, and eventually to assert that only efficient causes can provide adequate knowledge of the world.

Empiricist and rationalist alike become increasingly alienated from the older pattern. Bacon's insistence upon the need for a new logic of discovery and his translation of it in tables for experimentation underscore his repugnance to the medieval mode of interpretation. Moreover, a shift to new human ends becomes inescapable—from salvation to power, from blessedness to freedom, from meditation to instrumentation. Bacon was an incomplete naturalist, as were the other seventeenth-century philosophers. But the direction to naturalism was pointed out, and further refinements in philosophy could not but lead the main stream of eighteenth-century philosophy into the cool lakes of naturalism. The rationalists had the profounder influence upon this development. In Part III we shall see how naturalism was modified under the influence of biology; but in the seventeenth century only the science of physical objects and their movements had definitely achieved its own maturity, and naturalism therefore took the form of a mechanistic materialism. Nature consists of extended bodies in motion and, once the laws of moving bodies are formulated, mechanistic theory becomes irresistible.

The general theory of materialism is contained in three fundamental principles, none of which is absent in the classic version of this theory. Materialism is: (1) atomistic, (2) reductionistic, and (3) constituted as a closed system capable of perpetuating itself without end. These principles were first spelled out in the ancient Greek atomism of Democritus. Modern materialism differs in tone, rather than in substance. It runs into opposition to Christianity rather than to polytheism and anthropomorphism, as the older atomism did. It does, of course, make use of more sophisticated forms of mathematics, such as coordinate geometry and the theory of fluxions or modern calculus. And above all, it is supported by a science far more experimental and systematic than anything the Greek materialists could possibly have known. The modern theory of mechanistic materialism surely could not have caught on had it not been for the massive experimental and systematized work of the many scientists whose results were finally organized in Newton's *Principia*. The resultant theory may properly be called either mechanism or materialism or mechanistic materialism, depending on whether emphasis is placed upon its dynamics or upon its elements or upon both equally.

Because this modern mechanistic materialism ran into opposition to Christian piety and Christian ideals, it was looked upon with suspicion. The material world was contrasted with the spiritual, and a materialistic person was regarded as one concerned more with the gratifications and adornments of the body than with the humility and devotion appropriate to Christian ends. Ethical materialism is related to mechanistic materialism, but they are by no means identical. It is ordinarily castigated by Christian pietists because of its sensual rather than its material character. So interpreted, materialism is a function of things which cater to sensual delight, not to the delight itself, which is nonmaterial. Although the lifeblood of materialism is natural knowledge, this is not so easily criticizable. Mathematics and physical science, which make materialism possible, do, after all, depend upon the cultivation of the intellect, and are far removed from the life of sensuality. Nevertheless, because they serve ends which concern life here, rather than an after-life, they subvert the old folklore. The new science could not but set loose powerful forces for reorganizing society in accordance with ideals more appropriate to a naturalistic and secular outlook. Presently we shall wish to inquire into this movement in detail. But before we do so, we should understand mechanistic materialism.

MATERIALISM IS ATOMISTIC. In its classic form, materialism requires the existence of bodies or bits of stuff, and space or that in which bodies exist and through which they move. The bits of stuff are primordial. They cannot be accounted for. They are; they always have been; and they always will be. These assertions taken together constitute the principle of the conservation of matter. Matter, it is said, is neither created nor destructible. Why should it exist? The question is impertinent and incompetent. It is a wrong question, and from the materialistic point of view it can be given only a wrong answer, for it is born out of ignorance or sentimentality. The answer can therefore be only misleading or a bit of poetry or both. But surely there is a mystery of why the realm of bodies should exist? If there is a mystery, it is an ultimate one, and the only reasonable attitude toward it is that of acknowledgment or, as Santayana calls it, "natural piety." Those who adopt this attitude accept the world. To attempt to account for the beginning of things is only to incur, to no effect, one mystery after another —the material coming from the nonmaterial, time coming from the timeless, space from the spaceless, together with a host of questions of why a spiritual being, especially if he were a perfect one, would ever want to create a plaything out of his own being. Could it possibly signify anything but his own imperfection?

The alternative question, meaningful in this scheme of things, is an inquiry into the nature of bodies which exist and their relations to one another. In the Greek version, bodies exist as atoms, uncuttable pieces of matter. In the seventeenth-century version, the indivisibility of bodies is less important, because, for example, gravity is regarded as concentrated at the center of a body, whether or not it is divisible. Except for the question of whether bodies are composed of tiny nuggets no longer divisible, the other properties attributed to bodies agree very well, even if the later version introduces refinements. A body is, first of all, something that occupies space—it is extended. Second, the space it occupies also defines its figure, which is inherent in the body itself. And then, finally, there is the weight of the body, also an inherent property. For Newton, the major refinement is to substitute mass for weight, since the former is regarded as a constant, the latter varying with atmospheric conditions. There is, of course, the further topic of motion, but to understand this, one must assume the existence of space through which objects can move.

Space is an ultimate. It is the great receptacle of the world, but one without sides or top or bottom, since space is in every direction infinite. Consequently, the world is no longer picturable, and since the infinite was not yet satisfactorily analyzed, the concept of space remained fuzzy—even for Newton. Nevertheless, the notion of spaces seemed to cause no insuperable difficulties for the understanding, at least until about the time of Einstein and relativity theory. Until these modern innovations, the motion of a body from one place to another appeared capable of reasonably clear analysis. Hence, with space or spaces and bodies given, precise analysis could be undertaken.

The triumph of mechanistic materialism came with the ability to predict motions. Parallel to the assumption of the law of conservation of matter (mass) was the law of the conservation of motion (force). Greek atomism was again crude in this respect, whereas Newton achieved the most remarkable results. The law of the parallelogram of forces may be taken as constituting the essence of mechanistic determinism. By the geometrical device of representing two vectors of forces at one time as lines having a common origin in which both direction and length count, and by completing the parallelogram, the diagonal then represents the resultant force. Hence, the vector, which includes force and its direction, is predictable. Whether it be a terrestrial or a celestial body, its position and motion are, theoretically, determinable at any moment. This determinism, which results from the mechanistic world view, constitutes its very core. It represents the ideal knowledge of all that happens in nature, describable sheerly in terms of bodies in motion. Nothing is left indeterminate, even though our ignorance may make it appear otherwise. If we only knew the masses and motions of every body at any moment—really we would have to know them at any two moments—we could then predict their positions for any other moment. The amount of knowledge required would be staggering, and hence it proves convenient, in order to bring it off, to call upon an omniscient being. But the kind of knowledge such a being needs is not different from that which is required for the adding of two vectors together, since the assumption is that it is necessary to add together only two vectors at a time.[1]

MATERIALISM IS REDUCTIVE. Since all things are, according to this conception, determined by the motions of bodies, materialism is reductive. It is reductive in two ways: secondary qualities are reduced to primary, and the higher categories are reduced to the lower. Since we have dealt with the first kind of reduction at length in connection with the Cartesian conception of the material world, we need here only recapitulate. The qualities which belong to matter are the primary qualities—those which can be measured or counted and thus expressed in mathematical terms. Most important are mass and motion and these can be determined by the balance scale, the measuring rod and the clock. As long as we are dealing with matter in a solid state, these, plus perhaps the telescope, are the most important instruments. Gases, waves, magnetism, and electricity make for many complications. But much of the genius of the materialistic interpretation consisted in making various phenomena intelligible in terms of bodies in motion, such, for example, as the kinetic theory of gases. The secondary qualities, then, may be regarded as adventitious ideas, caused by bodies' stimulating the sense organs. The secondary may also be used as indicators of the presence of primary qualities; nevertheless, grounded knowledge consists in the statement of precise relations among primary qualities. In employing such

formulas as $F = ma$ or $G = \dfrac{m\,m'}{r^2}$, knowledge can be approximated for

practical purposes and the formulas can be assumed to hold for ideal connections.

Mechanistic materialism means, first, the science of mechanics, and, by extension, the science of physics. In its simpler form, the mechanistic world view signifies that conception of the world which makes physics the paramount science, in that all things can ultimately be understood as motions of bodies. Whatever comes to be comes from such motions, and whatever passes away passes away into just such motions. This conception does raise a serious problem: How are we to understand the manifest richness of the world? Since experience is infinitely rich, we cannot expect to cope with it, save as we can order the world through some classificatory means.

One of the simplest classifications—much too simple, but useful for a beginning—is that which divides all things into matter, life, and mind. These divisions appear fairly obvious. We are certainly accustomed to

---

[1] Of course, if there were an infinite number of bodies in motion, the ideal of complete knowledge could never be realized. In this case, we would not be capable of conceiving the kind of knowledge an infinite mind might have.

distinguishing between living and non-living things. Although this distinction appears to be basic, the drawing of a line between the two is of no great importance for the mechanist, and his reason is not difficult to see. He believes there is no authentic difference between the two. Biological things differ only in complexity, not in kind, from other physical things. They are of the same nature—they are automata or machines completely understandable in terms of the delicate motions of their minute parts in relation to one another. The so-called distinctive processes in biological phenomena are our gross perceptions of their various responses. Properly analyzed and thoroughly understood, these phenomena are reducible, without remainder, to physical processes. From this point of view, the science of biology is truly scientific only as it becomes one with physics. Otherwise, living processes are incompletely known. Once they are completely known, they are incorporated into the one truly basic science—physics.

The relation between the biological and the physical turns out to be one of identity. The true and completely adequate analysis of biological processes discloses them to be physical. In the seventeenth century, this reduction was effected rather crudely. Hobbes was most insistent upon this kind of reduction. Descartes insisted upon it for animals but not for man. Even here, he compromised the two, sometimes with almost ludicrous results. Compare, for example, his descriptions of love and laughter in *The Passions of the Soul*:

Now in considering the various alterations which experience causes us to observe in our body while our soul is agitated by various passions, I notice in love that when it occurs alone, that is, when it is unaccompanied by any strong joy, desire, or sadness, the beating of the pulse is equal and much fuller and stronger than is usually the case, that we feel a gentle heat in the breast, and that the digestion of food is accomplished very quickly in the stomach. In this way this passion is useful to health.

Or again,

Laughter consists in the fact that the blood, which proceeds from the right orifice in the heart by the arterial vein, inflating the lungs suddenly and repeatedly, causes the air which they contain to be constrained to pass out from them with an impetus by the windpipe, where it forms an inarticulate and explosive utterance; and the lungs in expanding equally with the air as it rushes out, set in motion all the muscles of the diaphragm from the chest to the neck, by which means they cause motion in the facial muscles, which have a certain connection with them. And it is just this action of the face with this inarticulate and explosive voice that we call laughter.[2]

The reductive point of view is, in the twentieth century, carried out with care and sophistication, and often with astonishing results. In the con-

---

[2] In *Descartes: Selections*, ed. by R. M. Eaton (New York: Scribners, 1927), pp. 385, 388.

temporary mode, the reduction is usually attempted by reducing the biological to biochemical and chemical processes. For instance, the study of the complex molecular formula of DNA's in the genetic processes has revolutionized our whole notion of reproduction. A staggering list of illustrations could easily be compiled. Although these illustrations do not prove the correctness of the mechanistic point of view, they do provide us with mounting evidence that deserves a respectful hearing.

When we move up to the level of mind, materialism requires another kind of reduction—namely, that of the mental to the biological. The question is then whether there is scientific evidence for the correctness of reducing the mental to the biological. Although there are many difficulties in an affirmative answer, there are also astonishing results produced by regarding psychological processes in terms of biological, especially physiological, processes. One aspect of the question has been raised in connection with the learning process. In the now classic experiment, Pavlov presented dogs with food and induced them to salivate. At the same time the food was presented, a bell was struck. After some repetitions of the process, the dogs salivated at the sound of the bell alone. This transfer of response has come to be known as the conditioned reflex, and this kind of learned response, which is to be discussed in some detail later, has been the mainstay of behavioristic psychology. A complete mechanistic explanation of psychological phenomena would then require double reduction, from the psychological to the biological, and then from the latter to the physical.

Categorial Materialism

There is another way of regarding materialism, not so much opposed to that of reducing the higher categories to the lower, as it is a way of emphasizing a unique kind of explanation within each category itself. This is the method of categorial atomism. It is worth exploring.

The atomistic theory of the ancient Greeks was a full-fledged materialism. According to Democritus, the universe itself is to be regarded as constituted of indivisible atoms, neither created nor capable of being destroyed. The explanation of all things physical is to be expressed sheerly in terms of the motions of these atoms, the way they come together in aggregates and the way aggregates dissolve into lesser aggregates, or even into the separate atoms. In analogous fashion we can say that the materialistic interpretation of things in any category is one which analyzes them into their least parts and explains the complex in terms of these parts, which are not further analyzable *upon that level*. Hence, they may be regarded as atoms only with respect to the particular category under consideration.

In the biological sciences, the atom is the single cell. This assumes that the cell possesses the characteristics of a living thing—at least insofar as it is sensitive and capable of being regenerated. In some instances, it is even capable of reproducing itself. Although the cell may be regarded as the atom of the organism, the analogy to the physical atom is not otherwise very close. The properties of the cell may be studied separately, just as, theoretically, the properties of the atom may be studied separately. But, because we can add weights of atoms or motions of the separate parts of an inorganic thing, it does not follow that we can similarly add the properties of cells in order to derive the nature of the organism. The peculiar biological relations of cells to one another depend on biological things themselves, and cannot be derived from knowledge of the constitution of physical things like, say, a granite rock.

On the level of mind, categorial atomism calls for the analysis of the complex mental processes into sensations. Sensations are the simplest mental processes, in the sense that they are the simplest forms of consciousness and cannot be further reduced without destroying their unique character of being mental. To reduce them to nerve stimulations or to physical vibrations is to destroy this character, and thus to reduce them to a lower category. But if we regard sensations of color, tone, simple taste, and the like, as the elements of mind, then we may attempt to account for the higher mental processes in terms of these elements. Thus, we attempt to account for the complex processes of memory, imagination, and reasoning as so many different ways of relating sensations to one another, whether through some process of reinstating them, recombining them ("imagination is decayed sense"), or adding and subtracting them, arithmetically or algebraically, in accounting for the complex processes of reasoning. Wundt (1832-1920), Titchener (1867-1927), and the whole school of "structural psychology," who followed in the footsteps of the British empiricists and the French sensationalists, devoted themselves to just this approach to the study of mind.

Finally, society, too, may be said to have its atoms—in this case, individuals. Individuals are capable of coming together in a variety of ways, in the markets and thoroughfares, in legislative assemblies and the courts of law, as well as in numberless other places, public and private. Here they carry on their sundry negotiations and pleadings, in order to make things conform more to the desires of their hearts. From this point of view, the essential reality is the individual, and the institutions which are erected are considered valuable only as they cater to the satisfactions of individuals. The business of government is accordingly conceived to be legitimate only as a public means to private ends. It itself is without intrinsic worth, for it can be at best only a necessary evil, and the less the better—"that government governs best which governs least." The atomization of society has traditionally been identified, in the Anglo-American world, with democracy, but it is often precariously confused with anarchy.

Only the policeman or "night watchman" is allowed to intervene, and this in order to prevent the atoms from destroying one another.

Categorial atomism is rarely applied to spiritual things. Devoted essentially to mystical ends, spiritual beings are more concerned with union with the godhead than in their separate identities. To be absorbed in a greater reality, to lose one's trivial identity—"one must lose oneself in order to find oneself"—this is in keeping with the tradition of great religious teachings. Some, like Immanuel Kant (1724-1804), may propose the spiritual life as a "Kingdom of Ends," but this proposal may be more an indication of Kant's being infected with the mechanistic point of view than his being humbled by the spirit of pietism. Even though categorical mechanism is not absent from Protestant Christianity, by and large it is foreign to the major teachings of religion—and it is positively anathema to Catholicism. To take it seriously is to undermine the religious tradition and to convert it eventually into secularism, as modern history convincingly teaches.

MATERIALISM, A CLOSED SYSTEM. Being atomistic and reductive, mechanistic materialism is also characterized as a self-contained system, in which everything in the universe happens as a consequence of motions predetermined by mechanical necessity. This necessity is expressed in causal laws. Bodies move, not haphazardly, but predictably in accordance with a pattern. The causal forces in the world are motions of bodies which predetermine the motions of other bodies, just as one billiard ball striking another causes it to move with a certain motion in a certain direction. Motion is conserved, if not in the obvious movements of bodies, then in the form of heat or some other form of energy. But heat, too, is a form of motion, at least according to the kinetic theory, which applied to gases proved to be a dramatic confirmation of the mechanistic hypothesis. Thus, in the kinetic theory of gases, the higher the temperature of a gas, the more forceful the bombardment of the molecules against the sides of its container, and consequently the greater the pressure that the gas exerts. If, moreover, light, electricity, and magnetism can be similarly interpreted as forms of energy convertible into motion, the mechanistic theory becomes virtually complete.

The reason the mechanist regards the universe as a closed system is that, otherwise, forces other than physical may be determinants. In this case, physical motions or their equivalents cannot constitute the complete explanatory principle of things, and recourse must be had to other principles—such as the mysterious workings of genii or of gods or of something else essentially capricious and incomprehensible. The beauty of the mechanistic hypothesis is its simplicity and its all-inclusiveness. If a multitude of principles must be appealed to, or if explanations are only partial, the value of science is curtailed, and men would have to rely upon guess-work or prayer or incantations in order to reckon with the future.

Mechanistic materialism requires the extrusion of the observer from the material world. If, in the attempt to gain knowledge of the world, the experimenter intrudes himself into that world, he cannot know the world as just physical but, if at all, only as human-physical. Those who insist that men can "see the world only through their own eyes" and that what they see is colored by the seeing-process are forced to conclude that we never can know things as they exist in their own right. Such persons are idealists, not materialists. They make mind central, not just to knowing, but also to that which is known. The mechanist repudiates idealism. He insists on the capacity of man to know things as they are in themselves, and without projecting himself into nature. Idealism is anthropomorphic, in that it structures nature in the image of man. The materialist divorces man and the world. Knowledge is like a searchlight, which reveals nature but does not alter it in the process. (The analogy should not be taken too literally.) Man as a physical being is part of the physical world, affected by and affecting other things. But man as a knower can, in prin-ciple, know the world and therefore can predict the future.

Since the world is a closed system, and since it works like a machine, it can be considered to be the only perpetual motion machine. It never runs down, because energy cannot escape from it. There is no place outside for energy to go, because there is no outside. Therefore energy cannot be lost or destroyed. There is a problem here in connection with the second law of thermodynamics, the law of entropy. This law states that energy becomes reduced to a form in which it is no longer available to produce work. Through friction and the loss of heat in mechanical processes, energy escapes, and cannot be recaptured. The inferior form means that eventually all bodies will have the same temperature. Then since no more energy will be available for work, the world will be dead. In this final state, the works will exist but not the workings.

Conclusion

By way of conclusion to this discussion of the mechanistic interpreta-tion of nature, we may ask once more whether Descartes was not in essence right when he expressed his philosophy in dualistic—or possibly, trialistic—terms. Nature is a machine; matter and motion are its principles; granted this, every future state of the world is in theory predictable. But predictable by what? by man? by God? by the intellect? by the mathemati-cal method? In a sense, by all of these. But especially by man, insofar as he perfects his intellect and makes use of the mathematical method. This perfected intellect is God; it is the ideal of knowledge, that is, omniscience. Man then is god-like, and the more advanced his knowledge, the more god-like he is.

The intellect is the superior faculty. It secures the world to man, for man can be secure and realize his ends only as he comes to know. This is the Cartesian interpretation of Aristotle's opening sentence of the *Metaphysics*, "All men desire to know." The further question is. To know what? Descartes' answer is again clear: "To know myself and the book of the world." The book of the world is the science of physics. It is the mechanistic interpretation of nature, completely worked out and adequately expressed in mathematical language. This knowledge was made virtually real in Newton's *Principia*. The Cartesian design of knowledge of the world is realized in a form so clear and so complete that it was not seriously undermined until the twentieth century. A philosophy which gave such adequate expression to this mechanistic conception of nature, for this reason alone could not but be the regnant philosophy in a world of newly-emerging science.

Adequate as this expression may have been in relation to physical science, was it also adequate in relation to the study of man? Enthroning reason as he did, Descartes saw clearly that the intellect is the only tool by which man could find certainty. Tenaciously holding to this ideal, and thus, by implication, repudiating the conventional wisdom of Christianity, Descartes subordinated everything to the structure and proportions which could be discovered in nature. The tool for understanding was the intellect; everything else was an obstacle: the senses, the emotions, the will, and the practical necessities of life. This austerity, this asceticism, could only cause him to depreciate anything not essential to mathematical knowledge of nature. The passions of the soul, too, he explains as far as he can in terms, not of the human issues of life, but their biologico-medical underpinnings. Love and laughter, for example, have no intrinsic virtues—because they are not forms of knowledge. They are more intelligible in their bodily manifestations than in their soul-blasting eruptions.

If man can be judged only in relation to the world machine, God too can only so be judged. As knower, he too knows the world as we do—only better. As creator, he can erect only a world that conforms to a mathematical pattern, because it is the only kind of knowable world. He must have created it that way and only that way. The pattern of the world is a machine. A machine is an artifact and, as such, it can be regarded as embodying a purpose—all of men's machines do. God's purpose can be only the creation of the most perfect machine—a perpetual motion machine. The earth then declares the glory of God; it is an adumbration of his intellect. Inevitably the kind of theology this conception entails is Deism. God is the creator of the world, but his handiwork is so perfect it does not further require his intervention in the world. This closed system, the world, is completely understandable in terms of itself alone.

Mechanism depends on our having clear and distinct ideas. But to conceive of minds in these terms alone is clearly inadequate. Descartes was embarrassed by the presence of obscure and confused ideas, that is, adventitious ideas. He nevertheless had to acknowledge them, even though he could not satisfactorily cope with them. He could not cope with what Aristotle recognized in the second sentence of the *Metaphysics*, "An indication of this [that all men by nature desire to know] is the delight we take in our senses; for even apart from their usefulness they are loved for themselves; and above all others the sense of sight." Other philosophers did attempt to cope with these "obscure and confused ideas," while still retaining the mechanistic interpretation of nature. By developing the categorial mechanistic theory of mind, John Locke substituted the introspective method for the mathematical method. He was thus enabled to supply content, which the mathematical method could only fraudulently introduce into its account of the world. In other words, the world could not be explained by the Cartesian "natural light of reason" dissociated from Baconian experimentalism. The marriage of the two, however, involves a major reconstruction.

Selected Readings

The Philosophical Works of Descartes, trans. by E. S. Haldane and G. R. T. Ross, New York: Dover, 1955, Vol. I. (Paperback.)

Randall, J. H., Jr., *The Career of Philosophy*, New York: Columbia, 1962, Book III, Chaps. II–IV.

Scott, Joseph F., *The Scientific Work of Descartes*, London: Taylor and Francis, 1952.

Smith, Norman Kemp, *New Studies in the Philosophy of Descartes*, London: Macmillan, 1952.

Spinoza: Selections, ed. by J. Wild, New York: Scribners, 1930, *Ethics*, Bk I, especially Appendix. (Paperback.)

Willey, Basil, *The Seventeenth-Century Background*, London: Chatto & Windus, 1949.

CHAPTER 13

The Mechanics
of Mind

From Matter to Mind

Cartesian dualism made the world safe for physics. It facilitated the mechanistic interpretation of nature, and it declared the existence of extended bodies that are moved about in determinate ways. It asserted that the cause of the motion of a body is the motion of another body. Moreover, it assumed that the world is constituted as a closed mechanical system, which neither requires nor involves any final purpose to make it understandable. Possibly the world has been created, but once this occurred it moved on endlessly by its own power. The intellect is capable of understanding its essence by employing mathematics as its tool. The tool is employable because nature is inherently mathematical. Quantity and proportion are the essence of nature; they constitute its structure.

Does Cartesian dualism similarly make the world safe for an understanding of mind? If mind is to be regarded as belonging to a different category, and therefore not reducible to matter, it too must have not only structure but also a method by which it can be analyzed. Descartes did not himself provide any satisfactory means of analysis. He suggested that mind could be divided into ideas—fictitious, adventitious, and innate. But the only analysis he offered was of innate ideas, and even these he analyzed only partially. He assumed the priority of the intellect, and he suggested the axiomatic character of basic ideas from which others could be formally derived. Beyond this, he provided a home for ideas but no notion of the kinds of intimacies that take place in it. Without some means of exploring the actions of the mind, knowledge of it is grossly insufficient. It remained for others to complete the dualistic philosophy by developing a method appropriate to the study of mind.

The question is: What kind of mechanics provides a method appropriate to this subject matter? The success of the mechanistic point of view applied to physical nature could only stir the seventeenth-century genius to a like success for investigating the mind. Some, like Hobbes, did apply the reductive method, and considered the mind to be nothing but the bodily responses. This overambitious method dissipated not just the spiritual life, but the mental as well. According to the critics of the so-called "Hobbist Creed," God then becomes "Almighty matter," angels are "not incorporeal substances, (those words implying a contradiction) but preternatural impressions on the brain of man"; and finally the soul of man "is the temperament of his body."[1] A materialism so complete infuriated the divines, and left the conventional wisdom completely unreconciled. Moreover, it affronted common sense, because it left unsatisfied the claims of conscious activity to be regarded as different from motions of the body. Consciousness might be closely associated with the senses, but surely it could not be denied its own peculiar kind of existence—the kind that belongs to mind rather than to body. Maybe, as Professor Gilbert Ryle now insists, there are not two kinds of existence. But this insistence would not do for the seventeenth century. With the advent of Newtonian science, one could neither deny the existence of material things, like water or rocks or planets, nor identify minds with existences such as these. A new answer had to be sought, and that answer had to be a kind of parallel to that which had proved to be so satisfactory for physics. Mind is a mechanism too, but mental. What kind of atoms, they asked, are mental atoms? The answer forthcoming was that mental atoms are sensations; therefore mind must be understood in terms of sensations. The resultant theory is a form of categoreal mechanism, not reductive mechanism. John Locke gave the theory its initial impetus, but a theory so radical was not easily elaborated and purified. Other philosophers besides Locke were required to complete the task he had begun.

---

[1] The Huntington Library contains a volume from which these excerpts are taken: *The Creed of Mr. Hobbes Examined in a feigned Conference between Him and a Student of Divinity*, The Second Edition, much corrected, London, 1671, by Thomis Tenison.

The Starting-Point of the Analysis of Mind

Thinking things are not the same as extended things. Descartes had asserted this, and to most philosophers, it appeared undeniable. Similar to the analysis of nature, the task is, as we have said, to ascertain the elements of mind. Right off, there is a sticky question. How can mind or consciousness have elements? If we look inward—introspect—we find no consciousness at all. This is so, even though we may *be* conscious. Where is consciousness located? What is its nature? What are its elements? We may spend sleepless nights, in anguished consciousness, and still not discover that illusive being we call consciousness. We see things or we hear things, but we do not see "seeing" or hear "hearing," or have any direct awareness of them. The colors we see and the sounds we hear are not conscious. We do not say that; we say we are conscious *of* the colors and sounds, and the preposition makes a difference. Just as we may have an idea of patriotism without being patriotic, so the color seen is a seen color, but is not therefore conscious. How can we make it into something of the nature of mind, rather than just a quality of an extended thing?

There seems to be one way out of the fix. Suppose that instead of calling it a color, we call it a sensation. Sensations are not things, like apples or chairs or moons, or even like the qualities of them. They are feelings, or something like that. Feelings are not solid or hard or extended—like billiard balls; they are painful or pleasant or wholesome or dreaded or bright or dull, etc. Sensations may qualify as candidates for the elements of what we call mind. And, to make sure that they remain elements of mind, we may use the language of the seventeenth-century philosophers and call them "ideas," utterly different as the term here used is from the use which Plato made of it. Ideas seem to stay put—in mind. They cannot exist anywhere else. Granting, however, that they are the elements, why all the bother? Does the discovery of elements make any difference to anything we might conceivably be interested in? The answer, for seventeenth-century philosophers, is yes. It makes a difference to our understanding of what knowledge is, including the kinds of things we can know and the extent to which we can gain knowledge.

Locke raised this question as a result of his own distressing experience. Meeting with his gentlemen's discussion club, he was disturbed by the fact that the men did not agree. He believed that the failure of men of intelligence and good will to come to agreement on fundamental questions required an explanation. Like Newton, he believed that something should have occurred that did not and therefore an explanation was necessary. Just as it requires an explanation of why the moon does not fall to the ground as apples fall to the ground, so it requires an explanation why men who are supposedly endowed with the natural light of reason do not agree. If gravity is the basic principle which relates bodies, surely there should be some principle which relates ideas. This latter principle should serve to explain both the agreements and the disagreements of men, and thus give us some notion of what we can expect of ourselves and of others. Accordingly, in his *Essay Concerning the Human Understanding* (1690), Locke sets out to find an answer to that most abstruse question of all. What is knowledge? He first insists that we seek the origin of knowledge. Only after discovering the origin, he believes, are we in a position to discover the certainty and extent of human knowledge. This method of analyzing knowledge calls for some warnings and explanations.

It seems as if to have knowledge is enough, and that inquiring into its origins is useless and pedantic. $6 + 7 = 13$. What is the original? Does it have any? If we do not know that this equation is true, or at least if we do not know some simpler version, like $1 + 1 = 2$, then we could not know anything at all. Because Descartes believed in the truth of such equations, he thought it unnecessary to inquire into origins, and said simply that their truth depends on our having clear and distinct ideas of them. In other words, knowledge is immediate, and it is madness to try to derive it from something else, which is not knowledge. That is why he said clear and distinct ideas are innate. He did not mean that infants arrive in the world, screaming, at birth, "$6 + 7 = 13!$" or even "$1 + 1 = 2!$" Rather he meant that when 6 and 7 are added the sum must be 13. Or, to take a different example, that a bell once rung cannot be un-rung. These truths he regarded as so, whether or not newborn infants knew them, and that there is no necessity for tracing the lives of infants to observe when they become mathematicians, or wise about bells. For if we did not have this kind of knowledge to begin with, we would not gain it by observing how infants become knowing beings. Locke disagrees.

Locke believes that there are no innate ideas and that knowledge comes from experience. At birth mind is a "blank paper"—this is Locke's borrowed metaphor. Hence there is no knowledge at birth, and therefore no innate ideas. There are no ideas which all people have at all times, and there are no "unconscious ideas." The first is easily acknowledged. The second is so because an unconscious idea is a contradiction in terms. He defines an idea as "whatsoever is the *object* of the understanding when a man thinks."[2] We may grant all this, and still ask wherein do Descartes and Locke actually disagree?

The disagreement is so fundamental that it is scarcely possible to compare the two. They are not talking about the same thing at all. Clearly,

---

[2] See *An Essay Concerning Human Understanding*, Vol. I, p. 134. References are to *The Philosophical Works of John Locke*, ed. by J. A. St. John (London: George Bell and Sons, Bohn's Standard Library, 1905), 2 volumes.

Locke does not mean to deny that 6 and 7 really are 13, and he does not mean to say that maybe they are really equal to 12 or that sometimes they may be 12. This would be arrant nonsense for an English gentleman as well as for a logical Frenchman. But the gentleman does sometimes get confused or carried away and thinks that he can prove such things by counting 6's and 7's, and finding that the sum holds true of apples and cookies and pigs, and therefore this *must* hold true of all other things too. But then again, the logical Frenchman can also get carried away in another direction, and insist that we know indubitably that the rainbow must appear between an angle of 42 and 52 degrees. Descartes seeks ways to compel agreement to propositions by means of proof or demonstration. Locke seeks ways to explain how reasonable persons can disagree.

The difference in outlook between the two philosophers is no less than that between mathematics and medicine. Descartes is a mathematician and can be satisfied with nothing less than a demonstration. Since mathematics is of the essence of demonstration, it is therefore the perfect science, and since physics approximates mathematics, it is nearly perfect. Locke, an admirer of Sydenham, is a physician and is satisfied with a cure, even though the way in which a drug works may never be known. Medicine is a practical art and as such is concerned with the health of man. Because of his realistic interests, not just in biomedical things, but also in social affairs, Locke could scarcely have been anything but an empiricist. His reflections on the purpose of government led him to consider the relation of social conditions to the goals of life. He wrote about these things in that now classic piece which he entitled *An Essay Concerning the True Original, Extent and End of Civil Government.* The method of Descartes is the mathematical method; that of Locke, "the historical, plain method."[3]

They may use the same words, but they use them in a different sense. Locke explicitly acknowledges this when he writes in the Epistle to the Reader of his *Essay Concerning Human Understanding,* "Clear and distinct ideas are terms which, though familiar and frequent in men's mouths, I have reason to think everyone who uses does not perfectly understand." He suggests that he prefers to replace them by the terms "determinate" or "determined." And he explains, "By *determinate,* when applied to a simple idea, I mean that simple appearance which the mind has in its view, or perceives in itself, when that idea is said to be in it; by *determined,* when applied to a complex idea, I mean such a one as consists of a determinate number of certain simple or less complex ideas . . ." This is a beginning; we can expect now that he will employ the empirical method to reveal the character of complex ideas by disclosing how they come from

---

[3] The above distinctions may be overdrawn. They are rejected by an impressive Locke scholar, James Gibson. See his *Locke's Theory of Knowledge and Its Historical Relations* (London: Cambridge at The University Press, 1917).

simple ideas. His authentic concern is to analyze in this fashion what Descartes called adventitious ideas, rather than the clear and distinct ones.

We begin to see what Locke is aiming at in his inquiry into "the original, certainty, and extent of human knowledge, together with the grounds and degrees of belief, opinion and assent." Less confident that there is indubitable knowledge of nature, we may have to settle for something less, namely, for *"degrees of belief"* or what he later calls "probable knowledge." We may have determinate ideas, but in themselves they do not constitute knowledge. For instance, we may have an idea of red. But the idea of red does not count for knowledge unless we relate it to something else, as when we say that the tulip is red. As a case of knowledge, this is of course very limited. We may say of this tulip that it is red. Possibly, every tulip we have ever seen was red. Still there is no inherent necessity why tulips *must be* red. And once we see a purple or a white one, we can make no case at all for tulips being necessarily red. Locke's point is that we cannot know tulips at all unless we have determinate ideas of red and purple and white, and of smooth and waxy feels, etc.

If we are to come to know things in the world, we have to begin with something, not clear and distinct, but determinate. Qualities are thought to be determinate. They are the stuff of knowledge. The genetic method, that is, "the historical, plain method," traces knowledge from this source. So the infant comes into the world with a mind which is as a blank paper upon which impressions are made. Locke may be wrong about infants; maybe they do arrive in a "blooming buzzing confusion." But even if this were their mode of entrance into the world, it could not be used to account for knowledge. Confusion and buzzings sound more like un-mind than like mind, or more like the psychopathic disorders than like a source of knowledge. But whether or not order comes out of disorder, strategy may dictate the wisdom of assuming the existence of determinate ideas as the foundation of knowledge.

All knowledge should, according to Locke's strategy, be traced back to simple ideas. These are basic in that we have no capacity to create them. They are the creatures of sense-experience. The congenitally blind will never know what color is; the congenitally deaf, sound. If the blind man says that "red" is "a loud blast of the trumpet," he deserves our admiration in creating a skillful metaphor; but he has not described red. Simple ideas are original—just because they are simple. Locke is not interested in reducing them further to bodily or physiological movements, because then they would not be ideas. Simple ideas are in a sense ultimates. If we have ever sensed them, we know what they are; if we never have, we never will know.

Now it may be that our ideas come not as simple, but as complex perception. Instead of a simple sensation of color, we may see a whole panorama, as in a football stadium, dotted with colors and forms here and there, filled with roars and bands, and all the other confusions and complexities. Yet, from this we can nevertheless pick out the simple ideas; for example, the "plump" which is the sound of the fullback kicking the football, is just such a determinate idea. It can be revealed only by the ear; it can never be manufactured or in any way summoned up by one who has never himself heard it. It is simple and original, and is to be acknowledged as such. So, also, with the other simples—the red of the jersey, the smell of chrysanthemum, the taste of the hot dog, etc. For analytic purposes, it makes no difference whether the ideas come singly or in packets. Each idea has its unique nature, which experience alone can disclose to us. How they enter into complex experience, however, is a question of a different sort from that which is directed at the origin of knowledge.

Simple ideas come first of all from the senses, whether from one sense or a number of senses—as, for example, motions or figures. But second, simple ideas come from the operations of the mind itself. The activities of the mind in perceiving, remembering, imagining, discerning—in short, all those "ing" activities of the mind—these leave their traces on the mind and are open to the mind as it observes itself. Through introspection we are able to apprehend their imprint on the mind. The metaphor of "the blank tablet" becomes now less appropriate, since blank tablets do not do anything. The confusion would probably not be great if these were the only activities in which the mind engaged. Unfortunately, Locke makes it responsible for much more, in that it also "combines, unites, and repeats" ideas in an infinite variety of ways. But, before bothering about what this does to his analysis, we should pause to note certain complications with respect to simple ideas.

Some Resultant Clashes and Ambiguities

Even more than Descartes, Locke is committed to the new science. He accepts the physics of "the incomparable Mr. Newton," and he accepts the distinction between the primary and the secondary qualities. There are those qualities, the "bulk, figure, number, situation, and motion or rest,"[4] which belong to bodies in their own right whether or not we perceive them. Then there are the secondary qualities, such as color, sound, taste, fragrance, which come into being by virtue of the "power" of the primary qualities acting upon the senses. Accordingly the "original" simple ideas appear in an entirely new light. Instead of the relatively easy analysis of showing how complex ideas arise from simple ideas, Locke has subscribed to an ontology and a causal theory of perception. The ontology is under-

---

4 *Works, op. cit.,* p. 250.

standable: it is the Galilean-Cartesian-Newtonian version of nature. In other words, he has gratuitously subscribed to the mechanistic interpretation of nature. However correct this interpretation may be, he has not prepared us for it by way of any argument at all. He has committed himself to it, but he has not come around to it by virtue of anything which in his philosophical assumptions compels him to do so. Ideas—those objects of the understanding when a man thinks—yes, these he is committed to, whether simple or complex. But, these do not also commit him to the view that some are objects apart from the understanding and exist whether or not a man thinks. Ideas do not come to us, some tagged as being independent of mind and others as mind-dependent. This distinction raises many thorny questions, as well as painful doubts.

The causal theory of perception is a further manifestation of this doubtful distinction. It is put forth because Locke has confused his analysis of mind with his commitment to Newtonian science. Instead of holding to his design in his "Introduction" that he will not "meddle with the physical consideration of mind . . . and whether . . . ideas do, in their formation, any or all of them, depend on matter or not," Locke betrays his original resolve and thereby creates endless problems. His analysis of mind is now compromised by both an ontology and an epistemology. The ontology, or mechanistic theory of nature, is warranted by neither the simple nor complex ideas, for they are *ideas* and *not qualities* of things. This being so, his epistemology, that is, his theory of knowledge, cannot stand. He wants to say that the ideas of primary qualities are true ideas because they resemble things in nature, whereas the ideas of secondary qualities do not, and therefore are not true.

However much we sympathize with Locke's objective, we nevertheless cannot be cozened into a conclusion which his presuppositions do not allow. All knowledge comes from experience—"in all that our knowledge is founded, and from that it ultimately derives." We have then ideas of objects or sensations, as well as ideas of reflection on the operation of the mind. The former we may assume, without too much incredulity, come through the inlets of the senses. But does the knowledge that some of these ideas, the primary qualities, are also in the object, and some of them, the secondary qualities, are not in the object—does this knowledge, too, come through the inlets of the senses? The answer can only be, certainly not! He cannot establish the resemblance of ideas to objects by means of ideas; his only alternative is to fall back upon an argument. But in doing so, he has turned rationalist and has forsaken empiricism. The causal theory of perception, too, is rationalistic philosophy. For, unless the existence of objects can be established by argument rather than by sense-experience, they would be constituted, not as objects in themselves, but as objects of consciousness, that is, percepts, and would therefore be mind-dependent.

Since the causal theory cannot suffer this conclusion, it must seek to rest its case on an *argument* which can establish the independent existence of the physical object. Weak or strong, the argument is of the form, "There must be an independent object, otherwise . . ."

Locke was aware of his predicament. In his attempt to establish the existence of material substances, he does rely upon an argument, even though he is forced to concede its weakness. The argument is, like Descartes', that qualities cannot exist alone, they are qualities *of*, or dependent *upon*, something. Secondary qualities depend upon primary qualities, which in turn are qualities of substance. Therefore, substances exist. However convincing the argument may be—and as we have seen it, it is not very convincing—it dethrones experience in favor of reason, and marks the failure of the empirical philosophy. Nevertheless, Locke is wise enough to leave us in some doubt. He falls back upon a parable to explain the kind of support qualities require. An Indian was asked what supports the world? He replied, "A great tortoise." What supports the tortoise? "A great elephant." What supports the elephant? "That which I know not what." Substance is then a "that-which-I-know-not-what." But the question is how we are to understand this conclusion.

Locke is unquestionably of two minds in his conclusion about substance. It both is and it is not. As a common-sense Englishman, he knows that he cannot relinquish the concept of substance without calling into question the existence of the world itself. Clearly it is absurd to deny the existence of the world—especially the kind of world that Newton speaks about. Masses clearly exist, but not in themselves. Bodies have mass. Mass is a property of a body. Since masses exist—they can after all be measured—the bodies of which they are properties must also exist. Yet the conclusion runs into conflict with his most cherished principle: knowledge comes through the inlet of the senses. By what sense then do we know bodies?

By the sense of sight? No. Sight reveals colors, light and dark, figure, and motion. But these are not bodies; they are qualities, not substances, Perhaps we know bodies by means of touch? A solid body, like a brick, does not yield to the pressure of my fingers. Consequently there must be something there which resists pressure. But what is it the fingers "know"? The suggestion is insuppressible that they "know" only the smoothness of the brick as a tactile sensation or the resistance of the brick as a muscular sensation. They are ideas, and ideas do not literally touch anything. They occur.

Now this analysis may be all wrong. Modern Englishmen, like G. E. Moore, insist that it is. There is a perfectly good sense in which we know not ideas but objects, like bricks and fingers, etc. Moore may be right about this, but Locke cannot be right. Locke's novel pitch is that knowledge consists in having ideas, and that this involves analyzing the contents of the mind. He is not being a physicist, and his job is not to reinforce the mechanical interpretation of nature. But he has got himself into a predicament, by virtue of having accepted Descartes' dualism and of illegitimately supporting this dualism when his distinctive task was to create a philosophy by analyzing the contents of mind. He has set himself the problem of showing that complex ideas result from simple ideas. His unique virtue is to be found, first, in his approach to simple ideas, and second, in his historical, plain method by which he is to account for complex ideas.

It is not difficult to discover the source of his confusion. He has confused the analysis of mind with the analysis of knowledge. With respect to the first, he has made a profoundly important beginning. With respect to the second, he pays honor to Descartes and Newton, but at the cost of restricting his own originality. His revolutionary approach has been partly annulled by acquiescing to a counterrevolutionary doctrine. The historical, genetic method has been conned by the analytical mathematical method— and just as Locke was on the verge of a brilliant break-through in philosophical analysis. The power of Newtonian science and the strength of common sense were obstacles too great to permit his insight to come to fulfillment. Yet, in the pages of the *Essay*, enough comes through to make us realize how radical an approach is portended.

One example of this portentous method is seen in his approach to the analysis of spiritual substance. He gets off to a slow start. With real insight he probes the question of what constitutes the identity of a person, but he begins with a dull discussion, first, of how the parts of an organism hang together, and second, of what constitutes the unity of the soul. The latter, he lamely concludes, consists in the fact that the soul is immortal. But after these preliminaries, he raises the more exciting question: How is it that I can say I am the same person now as ten minutes ago, or a year ago, or ten years ago? Clearly, he does not mean by this question that I am the same dull unchanging being now as before. On the contrary, he is concerned precisely with the question of how, even though changing, I can assert my identity. The question then is actually one of accounting for the continuity of human life in the course of change.

His answer is both simple and convincing. Identity is a function of consciousness and memory. Consciousness directly reveals sensations and perceptions, without which there would be no experience of anything whatsoever. And memory relates past and present, and thus provides whatever continuity there may be in our conscious existence. The conviction and elegance by which Locke expresses these ideas make it worthwhile to quote his own words:

When we see, hear, smell, taste, feel, meditate, or will anything, we know that we do so. Thus it is always as to our present sensations and perceptions:

and by this everyone is to himself that which he calls *self*; it not being considered, in this case, whether the same self be continued in the same or diverse substances. For, since consciousness always accompanies thinking, and it is that which makes everyone to be what he calls self, and thereby distinguishes himself from all other thinking things: in this alone consists personal identity, i.e., the sameness of a rational being; and as far as this consciousness can be extended backwards to any past action or thought, so far reaches the identity of that person; it is the same self now it was then; and it is by the same self with this present one that now reflects on it, that that action was done.[5]

And again, in order to emphasize the importance of memory, this passage is noteworthy:

For as far as any intelligent being can repeat the idea of any past action with the same consciousness it had of it at first, and with the same consciousness it has of any present action; so far it is the same personal self. For it is by the consciousness it has of its present thoughts and actions, that it is self to itself now, and so will be the same self, as far as the same consciousness can extend to actions past or to come; and would be by distance of time, or change of substance, no more two persons, than a man be two men by wearing other clothes today than he did yesterday, with a long or short sleep between: the same consciousness uniting those distant actions into the same person, whatever substances contributed to their production.[6]

Peter and Paul never confuse their identities with each other, because their experiences are not the same. If they, in fact, had the same experiences, Locke would not hesitate to call them the same person. Clearly, he now recognizes that rationalistic notions of substance are irrelevant. He insists that "being the same consciousness . . . makes a man be himself to himself." And he adds pungently, "Personal identity depends on that only, whether it be annexed solely to one individual substance, or can be continued in a succession of several substances."

By giving to the concept of "that which thinks" a content, the empirical point of view is beginning to show results. Instead of being a buried nugget incapable of being observed, it is becoming an adult and meaningful experience, having a past, and, very likely, a future. The "that which thinks" does not individuate; but the power of past experience brought into the present does individuate. David Hume accepted the doctrine; and although he sometimes misrepresented the self by speaking of it as "a bundle of impressions," he more generally recognized its importance when he regarded the identity of a person as being constituted by the "ease of transition" from one experience to another. The transition, the fluidity of experience, deserves metaphors more appropriate than those of "blank paper" or "bundles." William James caught the spirit of the requirement when he made it into "the stream of thought." Experience flows, and it flows

---

[5] *Ibid.*, pp. 466–467.
[6] *Ibid.* p. 468.

cumulatively. The stream of thought catches up the past, which is never quite lost and which adds more or less to the content of individuality. The stream is a continuum, but never repetitious; it is always new and at the same time it is always old. Or to change the metaphor, as he did, experience may be of "flights and perches," but the perches are ways of realizing the full impact of the flights. We never experience thunder simply; it is thunder-preceded-by-and-followed-by silence. Even silence is full and meaningful in human experience. From this point of view nothing is empty, save unconsciousness.

"The historical, plain method" cannot but come into conflict with "the mathematical method." Immanuel Kant recognized the conflict, but Locke could not recognize it, or did not want to. Wedded as he was to the Newtonian position, he could not divorce it, even though his originality in philosophy was incompatible with it. Personal identity had nothing to do with substances. What about the identity of objects? And what about the certainty of the laws of nature? Could they remain secure in the presence of the onslaught of this radical, subversive, empirical approach to the study of things, of *all* things? Curiously enough, it was an Irish theologian, Bishop Berkeley, who took the next decisive step for the advancement of the empirical philosophy.

The Inroad of Empiricism: The Laws of Association

The conflict between seventeenth-century science and folklore requires for its resolution the adoption of a new method of thought. And that method had to prove itself by its results. The mathematical method proved itself in Newtonian science, and it caught on. No merely theoretical arguments about the superiority of some other method could weaken the seventeenth-century attachment to mathematics. If another method were to gain headway, it, too, would have to show results. Although Locke had titillated the imagination in recommending courses of analysis in getting at the originals of experience, he did not make good use of these originals for deriving new knowledge. The final book, Book IV, of his *Essay* is a disappointing, dilute form of Cartesian philosophy, somewhat confused, even if somewhat suggestive, but certainly not decisive. As a nominalist, he focused upon the importance of particulars rather than universals. His analysis of knowledge of coexistence pointed in the direction of empirical analysis, but it was hedged in by other forms of knowledge, not empirical but rationalistic.

Bishop Berkeley took the decisive step by narrowing down to size a small problem which expressed the heart of Lockean empiricism. If ideas are really not innate, then some appropriate technique should be devised for showing how ideas that are complex do derive from simples. The good

Bishop thought he could show this by analyzing our perception of objects at a distance. His incisive question was: How do we judge the distance of objects? The question, it should be noted, is distinctively a psychological question—not one of physiology and not one of metaphysics. In his *Essay Towards a New Theory of Vision*, he is inquiring into the way in which a certain kind of perception comes into being.

In accordance with Lockean empiricism, we may assume that some ideas are given as simple, original ideas, and therefore need not be accounted for. The perception of color patterns in a two-dimensional plane might be regarded as original or underived ideas. The question that then is framed is: How do we come to perceive objects in the third dimension? On the assumption that things appear to the eye as two dimensional, how can we judge that some are closer, some farther away, on condition, of course, that one does not partially obscure the vision of another? Or to put it slightly differently, why should a larger unobscured object farther away appear like a smaller object nearer? Clearly, judgment is called for, that is, something more than is given to direct perception as simple ideas. Berkeley convincingly shows that the problem cannot be solved in terms of visual ideas alone.

Distance is judged not just by the eye, but by the muscles as well. To judge distance we reach for things which we see, or we step off distances, and our judgments improve in the course of experience. No doubt, the process begins in the nursery. The movements of a newborn infant are wild, random movements, uncoordinated. With continued practice, it reaches for the breast or the bottle with increasing success. Gradually it coordinates eyes and muscles. Or, more accurately, it coordinates visual and kinesthetic appearances, for these are the ideas which are relevant to the explanation of the problem. By combining ideas from different sensory departments, it begins to perceive something different from either—namely, the perception of things at a distance. This radically new idea is explained as a complex idea based upon two different kinds of sense experience.

What is so astonishing about this explanation is that incomparables become the basis for new complex ideas. This paradox is driven home by one of the favorite eighteenth-century puzzles: Would a person born blind and who later gained sight know by vision alone forms of things which he previously knew only by touch? The point is that a form recognized by vision is not the same form as that recognized by touch. The seen thing and the touched thing are no more alike than smoky is like Middle C, or blue is like tart. Yet experience yields acceptable combinations—tones are silvery, or colors are soft or warm, or tastes are brown, etc. These things are so, not because objects are so, but because experience is so. Disparate qualities, that is, ideas, exist together in the mind, and therefore become *associated* with one another. Complex ideas then come about as associations of ideas. Because ideas are experienced as contiguous in space or in time or both, they produce something new, namely, complex ideas.

Berkeley's experiment on perceiving things at a distance turned out to be momentous. If a problem of this magnitude can be solved, is not the underlying principle one that holds the key to the interpretation of all the problems of adult experience? The historical, plain method has now really proved itself, and its radical implications can now be drawn without fear of discrediting the method. Only metaphysical problems are discredited, for they can all be reduced to psychological problems. Berkeley himself was unwilling to go all the way; he cherished spiritual substances, but otherwise he ruthlessly ruled out material things and any connections among things of nature except as they were sustained by the will of God. But his theological designs were inevitably undermined by his method, which could support naturalism but which was incompatible with supernaturalism. The consistent application of this method could not but reveal the necessity for rejecting the hard dogmatisms of Cartesian dualism, as well as the necessity for making man and the world the subject matter of endlessly fresh inquiries.

The End of Dogma

The belief in material substances is the belief in a dogma. Such substances are never revealed in experience and are not revealable—because they do not exist. We never do or can, see, touch, taste, smell, hear, or in any other way perceive substances. Whatever exists is a color or a form or a fragrance or a sound, etc., or some kind of pleasure or pain or intellectual activity or emotional upset—in Locke's language, they are ideas of sensation or of reflection. But even more importantly, there is no use to appeal to material substances. They explain nothing whatsoever; they are fictions, which neither titillate the imagination nor serve any purpose of explaining anything that a man could possibly care to know. They cannot be useful to science, for there is no way of measuring them, testing them, or employing them to make knowledge secure. They are worse than gremlins, for they are emotionally flat, and they are not even as plausible as the so-called ether, because they are intellectually vacuous. So Berkeley concluded, and so Hume agreed, and so have agreed all philosophers who have studied Berkeley and Hume.

The final *coup de grâce* was executed by the scientists. Empirically minded, they came increasingly to realize that although they were free to invent all kinds of fictions about the world, that unless these fictions were checked out empirically, they could achieve no status worthier than theories. They could not be laws, which are theories that test out, or which are general statements derived from theories that test out. Laws may in time prove to be untrue, but as long as they remain as laws, there is a preponderance of evidence for believing that they are true, regardless of what future judgments may be. Thus, instead of insisting upon the "nugget theory" of the universe, scientists became increasingly concerned with such questions as the existence of waves, electromagnetics, and their cognate phenomena, which do not easily assimilate to the substance-theory of reality. In this view, theory is not ignored; rather it is at the same time freed and tied in with scientific investigations. It is freed, in the sense that mathematics is not regarded as prescribing what nature must be. It is tied, in the sense that by crossing mathematics with explicit inquiries, both mathematics and experiments become pricelessly more significant. In other words, the progress of science revealed the necessity for harmonizing the Baconian and the Cartesian methods. The British empiricists indirectly forced philosophical thought into just such a mold.

But to return to Berkeley and Hume, we can see in them the exorcising of the rest of the dogmas that confused the analyses of natural knowledge, especially as knowledge was advancing through scientific inquiry. When it came to the analysis of natural events, Berkeley's thought moved masterfully in eliminating obstacles to the recognition and acknowledgment of repeated patterns in nature. He readily acknowledged that unsupported bodies fall to the ground. But he was also keen in pointing out that "gravity" is no explanation of falling bodies. The term represents nothing but a pattern of motion in which the variables are the masses and the distance. There is no extra "force" to be seen or touched or felt in any way. "Gravity" is a name for the relation of variables according to a unique formula; it is not a thing. If, in the future, unsupported bodies move in some regular fashion upward rather than downward, we would similarly describe the motions by a law of "levity." But, again, there would be no force of levity in nature—unless, we wish to call "the will of God" a force in nature.

Berkeley's analysis of nature is thoroughly functional. Whatever we observe must exist, for to exist is to be observed. Whatever can not be observed or perceived in any way is nothing of which we need to take account. Or more simply, it is nothing. Scientists get along just because they acknowledge what is confirmable, for that which in no way manifests itself is that which they can safely ignore. This is precisely the way they got rid of the ether. If there is an ether, they agreed, there must be an ether drag. They found no ether drag, therefore they concluded there is no ether. One might say that nevertheless the ether could exist and still not be detected. Like the scientist's answer, Berkeley's answer to this kind of statement is to call it meaningless. It is like saying, "Scientific laws affect falling bodies." Anything that is not observable does not exist. Abstract things are neither observable nor existent.

Once more, then, we are led to analyze nature into particulars, or, in

Berkeley's language, into ideas. All "the choir of heaven and furniture of the earth" exist only as ideas. Ideas, however, are inert and causally inefficacious; they exist, but they can not produce anything. Taking his clue from his analysis of perceiving things at a distance, Berkeley concludes that an idea can be a "sign" for another. A sound, "the bark," can be the sign of "the furry thing standing at the screen door." The bark does not cause the dog to be at the door. But I can associate the one with the other, and if I go to the door, chances are I will see and smell the dog there. Things are conjoined in our minds only because we have had opportunity to observe them on a sufficient number of occasions to expect the second occurrence to follow the first. Sounds do not cause sights and smells, but one can stand for another.

David Hume elaborated this theme. Things regarded as causally related contain no necessary connections; they are only constantly conjoined. The event, which is said to be the cause, always precedes that which is said to be the effect, and the second never to our knowledge occurs without the first. Nevertheless, reason does not disclose any basis for asserting that a cause is always necessary. Any a priori argument that we employ to establish this proposition is circular, and therefore begs the question. He examines those arguments that he can find in the literature, and they all prove to be insufficient. Moreover, experience does not disclose any necessary connections. An honest appraisal of experience reveals nothing more than that patterns of events recur. We interpret them as involving necessary connections.

Fire causes water to boil, but we see, hear, taste, etc., no causes—only colors, sounds, flavors, etc. Prior to experience of the sequence of events, we would have no way of knowing what would happen when heat was applied to water. There is nothing in fire itself which could tell us, and there is nothing observable in the relation that could tell us. All that we observe is one thing preceding the other, their proximity. This constant conjunction in experience, thus, leads us to expect the second to follow upon the first. Hume's classic analysis deserves a careful reading of the orginal by every student of philosophy. It is one more of the fruits of the historical, plain method.

Finally, Hume subjects the alleged existence of spiritual substances to the rigors of analysis. He destroys any possible remaining illusion that we can, according to this empirical method, discover any spiritual substance. In a celebrated passage on personal identity from the *Treatise* Hume writes:

If any impression gives rise to the idea of self, that impression must continue invariably the same, thro' the whole course of our lives; since self is suppos'd to exist after that manner. But there is no impression constant and invariable.[7]

---

[7] David Hume, A *Treatise of Human Nature*, ed. by L. A. Selly-Bigge (Oxford at the Clarendon Press, 1888, reprinted, 1946), p. 251.

Insisting that there are only impressions such as "pain and pleasure, grief and joy, passions and sentiments, [which] succeed each other, and never all exist at the same time," he clinches the analysis:

For my part, when I enter most intimately into what I call *myself*, I always stumble on some particular perception or other, of heat or cold, light or shade, love or hatred, pain or pleasure. I never can catch *myself* at any time without a perception, and never can observe anything but the perception. When my perceptions are remov'd for any time, as by sound sleep; so long am I insensible of myself, and may truly be said not to exist. And were all my perceptions remov'd by death, and cou'd I neither think, nor feel, nor see, nor love, nor hate after the dissolution of my body, I shou'd be entirely annihilated, nor do I conceive what is farther requisite to make me a perfect nonentity.[8]

The last remaining vestiges of the argument for support of ideas in a mind or spiritual substance are snatched from us. We are left with phenomenalism complete—a rigorous, positivistic, empirical analysis.

Conclusion

"The perception of ideas is to the soul what motion is to the body." In insisting upon a method for the analysis of mind, Locke pointed the way for a revolution counter to the Copernican. Although it was Immanuel Kant who thought he concluded the counterrevolution, the British empiricists actually made mind primary in philosophical analysis, in the sense in which they concentrated attention upon the facts of perception. This makes the starting point of all analysis the contents of human experience. Perceptions, not the world, are given to man. The world is secondary; it is an achievement which comes about as perceptions come to be ordered in the course of adult experience. Things are three dimensional, because various sense organs work together to provide three-dimensional pictures. The complex data of experience framed in an orderly pattern signify all we can know about the world, as well as about ourselves.

Read in the light of British empiricism, Descartes' philosophy requires a new interpretation. Now it appears that he was right in beginning where he did—namely, with thinking, perceiving, judging, and the like. These activities, taken with their contents, are the stubborn, irreducible facts of experience. But—and here is where Descartes misled us—he appealed to a logical home for experience, a substance in which it was made to rest, instead of allowing it to find its own fulfillment in the course of time. Multitudinous facts come together in some order—or else men are deluged by chaos. This is the way of empiricism. Descartes, however, insisted upon beginning with a map of all reality, before sending out an expeditionary force to learn what the terrain was actually like. Consequently, his various

---

[8] *Ibid.*, p. 252.

ontological arguments could end only in dualism because that is where he began. Substances are all that exist; they are either extended or thinking; therefore, where there is thought there are minds, or where there is extension, there are bodies. The Copernican revolution had made the latter necessary; common sense, the former. Man and the world were both safeguarded—by the benevolence of God. Therefore, science, common sense, and the folklore of theology were brought together in a Cartesian happy harmony.

The upshot of empirical analysis was to transform Cartesian dualism into a dualism of two kinds of propositions: synthetic and analytic. Only in this way could dogmatism be avoided and mathematics saved. As for matters of fact, epistemological etiquette requires humility in the face of them. We cannot summon up facts, in the way we can numbers or polygons. If lemons are yellow or maples are deciduous, this is not because predicates are contained in subjects, as squareness is contained in cubedness. There is no "because"; they just are. They are *synthetic* propositions: their predicates assert something that reason itself cannot evolve out of the subject terms. The truth or falsity of the statements rests upon the empirical test. "Yellow" or "deciduous" is not manifestation of a substance, such that it could not be otherwise. Observation does permit us to make generalizations about things, which moreover, we can expect to hold true in the future—even if the future should disappoint us.

But though many things can be learned from observation and experiment, some things cannot, such as, $a^2 + b^2 = r^2$, or that "all generals are officers." Locke, for example, tried to overdo it. He thought that numbers, even infinity could be learned empirically; and Berkeley got so enthusiastic about particulars as opposed to universals that he had to go through bizarre cerebral summersaults to save geometry. Hume alone saw clearly that mathematical propositions are analytic and a priori. They do not depend on experience; they are understandable as ideas of reason; they are not matters of fact. In the modern idiom, they are tautologies, and they do not require empirical tests. Their "truth" is postulated, or they are arrived at by definition or as purely formal consequences of postulates, or definitions. Hence they legislate nothing, and they are secure from being overthrown by discoveries in nature, since they are independent of nature.

In terms of the new dualism of synthetic or empirical statements and analytic or formal statements, science, even Newtonian science, became better established than could be expected through Cartesian philosophy. If Newtonian science were to become inadequate, Descartes' philosophy could not make it adequate. All his ontological arguments could not guarantee the correctness of the mechanistic interpretation. They could reasonably do no more than to show how mathematics could be employed to make clearer ideas which could not be made so clear without mathematics. But this service was very different from that which could be rendered by establishing beyond the shadow of a doubt the truth of the mechanistic interpretation of nature.

Dogmatism has no place in science. But mathematics does; so does experimentation. British empiricism fostered an empirical point of view, though possibly one which relied more on observational techniques than upon experimentation. It had gained in clarity over, say, the Baconian view, but it had also lost something of the fervor and radicalness of the Baconian method. Science would get along, of course, with or without Descartes or Bacon or the later British philosophers. But science would not be so well understood without them, and it would not be reconciled with other things important to man—especially the relation of men to men. This whole dimension of experience the social, was scarcely touched upon by Descartes; and although it was of concern to Locke and to Hume, we can more profitably look at it in the seventeenth-century context, especially as it was related to the dominant mechanistic interpretation of the time. For if the mechanistic interpretation were the correct interpretation of reality, it should be able to reveal truth in every cranny of reality, the mental as well as physical, the social as well as the theological.

Selected Readings

Ayer, A. J., *Language, Truth and Logic*, New York: Dover. (Paperback.)

Berkeley, George, *Essay Toward a New Theory of Vision*, New York: Dutton Everyman Paperback.

Berkeley, George, *Three Dialogues between Hylas and Philonous*, La Salle, Ill.: Open Court, 1947. (Paperback.)

Hume, David, *Treatise of Human Nature*, New York: Dolphin Books. (Paperback.)

Locke, John, *Essay Concerning the Human Understanding*, La Salle, Ill., Open Court, 1927. (Paperback.)

CHAPTER 14

Civil Society

The Folklore in Flux

The change from serf to citizen marks so radical a step that it represents a shift from a medieval to a modern point of view. Not only does it represent a shift in emphasis from security to freedom, but also from the hierarchical medieval folklore to the new atomistic science of nature and of man. Sir Henry Maine phrased it well when he spoke of it as a change "from status to contract." Status was a characteristic of the old society. A man was born a serf or a nobleman and, no matter what he did, he could not move from one class to the other. In this sense, social relations were fixed, just as if they were exemplars or eternal plans in the mind of God. Each member had his work to do; his duties and his rights were set in the social system of which he was a part. As serf, he had menial tasks to perform, but he could expect the protection of the lord he served—in fact, the lord had a sacred obligation to protect him from the vicissitudes of life.

A system of obligations so completely defined as those that prevailed under the feudal system almost cried out for a Thomistic theology as its counterpart in heaven. The fixedness of social relations under the guardianship of the manorial baron was a secular counterpart of the fixedness of of the relations of spiritual beings above. A system in which relations are so clearly defined and which are grounded in first principles can be, and indeed was, expressed in law. And since these relations are said to "share in right reason," they derive from "the eternal law." Applied to the conditions of social life, they are positive law, which according to St. Thomas:

. . . is a dictate of the practical reason, whose processes are similar to those of theoretical reason. Both proceed from principles to conclusions. In the theoretical reason the conclusions of the different sciences, which are not naturally self-evident but discovered by effort, are based on first principles. Similarly the practical reason proceeds to make concrete the precepts of the natural law, which are like general and indemonstrable principles. These decisions are called human laws, so long as they fulfill the . . . conditions essential to law.[1]

The feudal order, dependent as it was upon serfs to do the menial work and upon a system of vassalage, that is, obedience of vassal to lord, could maintain itself as long as agriculture remained the staple of life. It tied serfs to the soil; it made obedience of vassals to lords reasonable, and the good faith of lords to vassals indispensable; and finally, it constituted an order that appeared to be lasting, worthy of being consecrated by the Church itself. Once, however, trade and production began to entice men from the manorial estates, a new wealth, a sense of independence, and the lure of adventure began to upset the old order. From the sheer fact that men were able to move about in the world, they achieved a liberation that presaged a whole new order. We have seen what this liberation meant to the intellectual life, embodied as it was in the new science, and elaborated in the new philosophies, especially the Cartesian. The physical world came to be understood, with a scope and a precision of method, as it never had before. The human mind was explored systematically and in a detail such as had not happened since the time of Aristotle. The new science had not as yet been embarrassed by the study of theology. But something radical was portended in the social movements which made the political state a contender for first power, even as against the Church. England did break with Rome, and the rise of Christian sects destroyed the tidiness of things contained in the Church Universal.

Above all, this political development signified the need for a new authority, as well as a sanction for it. The authority required was one which could cope with the new secular activities. Small scale production and trade—these activities were stimulated by the growth of cities. Capitalistic enterprise began to reach new heights, and in some instances were promoted by nations themselves, as in seventeenth-century mercantilism. Barriers to trade, such as customs inspections and tariffs, hampered the development of capitalism, whereas the nation-state fostered capitalism. Little wonder, then, that the newly-emerging class of traders and capitalists favored the development of a strong secular state, which could support

---

[1] *Summa Theologica of St. Thomas Aquinas,* ed. and trans, by Thomas Gilby (New York: Oxford, Galaxy, 1960), pp. 359–360.

them in their own productive activities. Utilizing the fortuitous system of vassalage, kings consolidated their powers implicit in feudalism and employed them in furthering new mercantile enterprise. This consolidation marked the establishment of the nation-state as the most powerful of all institutions in the modern world.

Developments of the magnitude of the nation-state require not just power but sanctions, too—a way of making that power rationally legitimate. The state has a function to serve, and it needs power in order to realize its function. But, also, it needs a theory by which its function can be understood. The task of relating political realities as well as physical and psychological realities in a coherent scheme of things falls to philosophy. Descartes did this in respect to the last two; but, other than a limited statement of a code of morals, including obedience to the laws and customs of his country, he ignored in his philosophy anything even remotely connected with the reality of the state. The urgent question became: How is the sanction of the power of the state to be conceived?

The fact of having power is no justification of it. Tyrants have power, but are supposed not to have it. If governments do exercise power legitimately, there should be some way of justifying it, whether they hold it because God has so willed, or because they serve some useful purpose, or possibly some combination of good reasons. One of the philosophically interesting justifications came from England in the writings of King James I, who insisted that the rightful power of the king derives from God. God alone has the authority to appoint a king to rule, and the king, in turn, is responsible only to Him. The theory does not entail the consequence that the king can do no wrong. He may or may not do wrong, but under no circumstances is he to be taken to task by his subjects, since he is accountable only to God.

The genius of the theory resides in the appeal to God as the source of legitimacy of power, coupled with application to political matters. The seventeenth-century ear was attuned to this supernatural source of power: the Church had employed it to substantiate its own legitimacy. If the pope were to be regarded as the vicar of God for things spiritual, so the king could be regarded as His vicar for things temporal. The belief in the benevolence of God could induce subjects to unquestioning acceptance of the king as their ruler, and at the same time make it possible for him to use his office for promoting the well-being of his "flock." The theory had the effect of reducing the shock of the shift from a society oriented primarily toward religious concerns to one increasingly oriented toward political concerns. The political problem was forcing itself inevitably upon the seventeenth century, especially in England where the break with the Church had already occurred. This break began to force the issue of where the power within the state should lie, as well as how the state could be responsive to the needs of the growing middle class.

The Church was increasingly incompetent to cope with the new problems, in part, because they concerned a new kind of temporal affairs, in part, because with the rise of Protestant sects, the Church was no longer universal in fact. The religious wars, such as flourished in England, provided no solution, just because Roman Catholics, Anglicans, and the Puritan sects were all fighting for Rightness and the glory of God. Christian brotherhood could not be an effective appeal for the resolutions of conflict when Christian sects, each dedicated to its own interpretation of Christianity, were fighting one another. Their belief in God increased, instead of lessened, the intensity of their struggles. Under these circumstances another kind of authority was desperately needed. Kingship looked as if it could provide a way, above the religious battle, to enable men to get on together. But the House of Stuart provided no such way, since that required a religious neutrality that no Stuart king could assume; and when, after the Protectorate, some seeming overtures for closer ties with Rome became public, the consequences were disastrous. They led to the demise of James II, and to the Glorious Revolution of 1688.

The New Political Philosophy

During the turmoil, philosophy in England was not quiescent. The most remarkable and shocking of political philosophies was that of Thomas Hobbes—remarkable because it reflected a mathematical clarity in idea such as Descartes had urged in his method, and shocking because it appealed not to religious motives but to motives almost purely utilitarian. Hobbes' philosophy was radical, in that it was founded on a full-fledged materialism, devoid of sectarian religion, and aimed at the utilities of man. So extreme was this point of view that on October 17, 1666, there was ordered a select Committee of Parliament which "should be empowered to receive information touching such books as tend to atheism, blasphemy, and profaneness, or against the essence and absence of God and in particular a book published in the name of one White and the book of Mr. Hobbes called the *Leviathan*, and to report the matter with their opinion to the House of Commons."[2]

Although the Hobbesian philosophy was rejected in all quarters, it nevertheless set a style which has influenced the writing of political philosophy to this day. Because of its mechanistic interpretation of politics, it is peculiarly relevant to the development of seventeenth-century thought. It begins with individual men in a state of nature and, through a social contract, evolves a civil society in which men come to have obligations.

---

[2] Quoted by George Croom Robertson, "Hobbes," *Encyclopaedia Britannica*, 9th ed., 1881.

The State of Nature

The argument begins with the unhappy state of men living in a world alien to their aspirations, and incapable of satisfying their longings. Hobbes traces this condition back to the state of nature, in which men are moved only by desire and aversion. Desire is expressed as a positive response which leads men to act to gain the objects they seek; aversion is expressed as a negative response by which men attempt to avoid objects which are distasteful to them. To the extent to which they are able to gain the one and avoid the other, the responses are satisfactory and pleasure accrues to their actions. The opposite, of course, brings them displeasure or pain. In a state of nature, men are consequently under the domination of pleasure and pain, attempting to maximize the one and minimize the other. The corresponding ethic is called hedonism, that ethic in which only pleasure and pain are and ought to be responsible for swaying the actions of men. There is no good, except as pleasure comes about in human actions, and there is no bad, except as pain comes about. Hence, right and wrong can be defined only as a course of action leads to a preponderance of pleasure or of pain, respectively. This maxim is then expressed as "might makes right"—the power to achieve what one desires or to avoid successfully what one has an aversion to—and constitutes the only standard of right and wrong.

This doctrine of the maximization of pleasure and minimization of pain is usually called utilitarianism. Hobbes speaks of it as the principle of felicity, and defines felicity as the *"Continuall successe* in obtaining those things which a man from time to time desireth, that is to say, continuall prospering." Or again as he puts it, "Felicity is a continuall progresse of the desire, from one object to another; the attaining of the former, being still but the way to the latter." And he adds, "The cause whereof is, That the object of mans desire, is not to enjoy once only, and for one instant of time; but to assure for ever, the way of his future desire."[3] The simplicity and naïve freshness of this doctrine makes it attractive. Men employ their power to gain their ends, which in turn are defined by their appetites and aversions, that is, their tastes and distastes. Each can judge these for himself, knowing what it is that he wants to have or wants to be free from.

Attractive as this simple doctrine is, felicity or the contented life is not for man. Men's desires are not only not easily satisfied, but they are incapable of being satisfied. Men come into conflict with one another. Desiring the

---

[3] Thomas Hobbes, *Leviathan* (Oxford at the Clarendon Press, 1947, reprinted from the edition of 1651), pp. 48, 75.

same things, or to assert themselves over one another, or to demonstrate their various superiorities, they cannot but compete and clash, and thus engage in "a war of all against all." This state of warfare cannot but defeat the very possibility of the contented life. The defeat is not just incidental; it is inherent in the state of nature and is unavoidable. The reason is not far to seek. In the state of nature, men are equal, not in any moral sense, but in the sense of exercising power over another. This does not mean that some are not physically stronger than others, for clearly they are. And some are faster, or better coordinated, or brighter, or more wily, or have any of innumerable other advantages. But no one person possesses all these advantages together, or any of them to such an extent that he can indefinitely hold another down—a temporary advantage, yes, but a permanent one, no.[4] The consequence is that no person is really safe, or indefinitely secure in maintaining his position, or even in surviving. His lot is, of necessity, an unhappy one, described by Hobbes in his famous adjectives, "solitary, poore, nasty, brutish, and short."

This universal warfare makes impossible the attainment of anything man holds dear in life. When he has no security other than that which he gains by his own strength, his life is so poverty-stricken as to make it not worth living, even if one somehow could survive. Hobbes' inventory of what such a life lacks is the clue to his authentic contribution to political thought. It should be quoted in full:

In such condition [that is, of universal war, where every man is enemy of every man], there is no place for Industry; because the fruit thereof is uncertain: and consequently no Culture of the Earth; no Navigation, nor use of the commodities that may be imported by Sea; no commodious Building; no Instruments of moving, and removing such things as require much force; no Knowledge of the face of the Earth; no account of Time; no Arts; no Letters; no Society.[5]

The quest for felicity in the state of nature is doomed to fail. By asserting himself, man causes his own destruction. If he is to prosper he must, in conjunction with others, seek another way, and thereby quit the state of nature, which is the worst of all possible worlds.

The Commonweath

Man's only out is to give up his natural rights, which are not rights at all, but only directionless power, on condition that others too give up their rights, or power. By relinquishing their natural power, they are enabled to come together and to create that which never can come about in the state of nature—namely, society or the commonwealth. Men create this

---

[4] *Ibid.*, chap. 13.
[5] *Ibid.*, pp. 96–97.

new life by covenanting with one another, that is, consenting to live together in society. Thereby they create "a reall Unitie of them all, in one and the same Person, made by Covenant of every man with every man." In such manner, "the Multitude so united in one Person, is called a COMMON-WEALTH . . . this is the Generation of that great LEVIA-THAN, or rather (to speak more reverently) of that *Mortall God* to which wee owe under the *Immortall God,* our peace and defence."[6] Only by leaving the state of nature and so joining together can man acquire a measure of peace and security. He thus brings about a total transformation of life, from the brutish to that which, if not the best of all possible worlds, is at least one which has authority and reasonableness.

The state of nature is neither moral nor immoral. In it, men do what they are able, and that is not much. In exercising their powers there is no justice and no injustice; they just do what they can. Force and fraud are neither right nor wrong, but they are the elements at work in a state of warfare. Hobbes thinks we are committed to this position because in a state of nature there is no law, and no law because there is no common power. Moreover, where there is no law there is no right or wrong, justice or injustice. "These qualities," he insists, "relate to men in Society, not in Solitude." They are not faculties of the mind, nor of the body, and they belong not to individuals but only to society. Property depends upon "propriety," for there is nothing proper or improper except as authority confers them upon persons in society. In the state of nature there exists things, and men may of course appropriate them—if they have the power to do so. Such power, however, does not carry right with it. To say that "might is right" is in this sense a tautology; it means merely "might equals might."

By reason of the covenant of all with all, that is, the social contract, something new has come into being, namely, society. Society, moreover, is not just an aggregate of individuals. It is a commonwealth, literally, the wealth which is common to the members of a society—which in the absence of society is nonexistent. There is nothing strange about this. Hobbes is insisting that the commonwealth exists by virtue of the fact that law, not just the strength of individuals, prevails. The ascription of rights and duties is possible under law; it is not possible in the absence of law, such as would be the case in times of universal warfare. Rights and duties are not inherent in persons, even if Locke tried to make them out to be so. Hobbes certainly has the upper hand in this argument. Warfare has no niceties, any more than one could sanely suggest that animals should be nice to one another and not eat one another. The point is that human beings are animals in a state of nature, for there they can act only on their appetites.

---

6 *Ibid.,* p. 132.

Law may be said to be responsible for the change from the state of nature to the civil state. Law involves two things: (1) the ascription of rights and duties to persons, and (2) an authority not just responsible for ascribing them but also capable of defending the rights and enforcing the duties so ascribed.

(1) Rights and duties do involve a society of some stability, for unless there are some patterns, some regularizations of actions, law could be only an *ad hoc* intrusion—a new law for each act. Unless there were categories for actions, like buyers, sellers, renters, bailees, employers, trustees, fathers, wives, children, guardians, etc., there would be no way of knowing what rights or obligations persons have. Law is a kind of second-order system of social arrangements, a system which protects and reinforces certain kinds of activities and prohibits others. It declares, ordinarily in advance, which are to be protected and which are to be prohibited, and thus informs persons what they can expect by way of protection or penalty if they engage in lawful or lawbreaking practices. Laws therefore are promulgated —they are publicly made known or published in order that persons may know what is and what is not lawful.

(2) Laws pertain not just to publication but to habits created in people —to the acknowledgment or expression of laws in their actions. A "law" nullified or safely ignored is no law. It must be enforced, or at least enforceable. Authority entails power and not just moral suasion, or, in the words of Hobbes, "Covenants, without the Sword, are but Words, and of no strength to secure a man at all." A man must be in awe of something and tied to some power greater than himself, if he is to be bound in the civil state and not relapse into a state of nature, where, of course, there is no law, just the law of the jungle. The civil state therefore requires not just a covenant whereby all become associated with all, but, in addition, a power which can promulgate and enforce law for the purpose of securing the ends of the civil state. There may have to be some arbitrariness here as to what the laws are, but then there is always some arbitrariness in law, otherwise law could never get under way.[7] Law may be made by a single individual, and responsibility for enforcing it may rest in him, or the making and enforcement of law may be done by a body of individuals. The form of government differs in the two cases, but not the character of law. For various reasons, Hobbes preferred the monarchial form, but this proposal is incidental and for historic reasons; it is not essential to the argument itself.

Hobbes did struggle to make the ruler or sovereign free from criticism

---

[7] Equity is a recognition of the arbitrariness of law, which, because it speaks in general terms, may create excessive hardships. Equity is then an attempt to make law more fair. But in making law more equitable, equity itself cannot but introduce new arbitrariness, which itself may have to be made more equitable, etc.

by his subjects, and, at the same time, to prevent law from being wholly arbitrary and capricious. He believed that if the sovereign were subject to criticism, his authority would be undermined and the state made ineffectual. Therefore, he insisted that in whatever he did, the sovereign could be guilty of no injustice, but at most an inequity. Not very convincingly, he argued in support of the conclusion that since the authority of the sovereign comes from his subjects through the covenant, he is, in whatever he does, expressing their will. Hobbes does not suggest, however, that law can be an expression of just any arbitrary whim of the sovereign. He disavows laws which are not for the safety of the people, and by safety he includes not merely the people's "bare Preservation, but also all other Contentments of life."[8] And he makes certain that the interest of the sovereign is not at variance with that of the people. "A Law may be conceived to be Good, when it is for the benefit of the sovereign; though it be not Necessary for the People; but it is not so. For the good of the Sovereign and People cannot be separated."[9] In this identification he reasserts the purpose of the civil society and he suggests the conditions in accordance with which the laws of society should be made.

Hobbes is no mere formalist. In fact, he is attempting to cope with the two most troublesome problems of social philosophy: How to establish a workable authority in society? and; How to determine the ends for which that authority shall work? The first question was forced upon him because England was confronted with internecine warfare and was without guidelines to show the way to stable government. The second question was forced upon him because authority for the sake of authority makes no sense. Governments do derive their just power from the governed, and therefore a covenant is necessary to invest a governor with legitimate power. Yet, legitimate power must be legitimated—that is, employed to serve those ends for which it was invested—the good or safety of the people. Now we can detect what that good is, namely, peace and security.

Peace and security are not vague abstractions in Hobbes' conception of civil society. They are the peaceful arts: the making of things commodious and useful; growing things to eat; moving things, heavy things, about; being moved about, through navigation; and along with these the fine arts, including belles lettres; and the sciences. The cultivation of these arts alone shows what it is to be free from the universal warfare, the universal degradation of man, in the state of nature. There is no reason to hesitate in choosing the one rather than the other, and this choice is to be made even though it binds man by "Artificiall Chains, called *Civill Laws*."[10] For as Hobbes declares, it is an easy thing for men to be deceived "by the

---

[8] *Ibid.*, p. 258.
[9] *Ibid.*, p. 268.
[10] See *Ibid.*, ch. 21, and especially p. 162.

specious name of Libertie." They fail to distinguish between their private inheritance and their public bounty, and thus they fail to recognize the existence of liberty in relation to the bonds which secure life—namely, civil law. Law cannot create the utilities which support civil life; but, in the absence of law, the utilities bog down because men are too busy destroying one another to engage in the peaceful arts.

Hobbes' Significance

Hobbes' theory of the civil state is, first, functional—it copes both with the utilities that make human life possible and with the authority that regulates their interrelationships. Second, it couches morality in social terms and provides a meaningful concept of liberty. Finally, it gears into seventeenth-century thought by extending the mechanistic mode into the analysis of political life, and thus advances the philosophical task in meeting the challenge to the old folklore by the new science.

HIS FUNCTIONALISM. Life can be purposive and enhancing, or it can be aimless and degrading. The former is concerned with utilities or usefulness in life, where necessities, comforts, and the making of things of art are realized through the full employment of men's faculties. From the time of the discovery of the hoe, the axe, fire, and the wheel, man immediately elevated himself above the other animals and began moving toward the civil society. In contrast to the contemporary development of technologies, man's first discoveries were long in coming, and primitive. The more he discovered, the more he was able to discover; for he increasingly discovered how to discover. Something like this happened when Greek science was born; and for several centuries men made great strides in the advancement of science, especially in the realms of physics, astronomy, and medicine. Any attempt to describe the quality of life which omits these developments is like describing a clock with no works. Yet philosophers have often tried to do just this.

Technology is the peculiar goal of a society. This fact is recognized in the names which we commonly give to certain kinds of society, such as nomadic, herding, agricultural, industrial, militaristic, as well as their various subdivisions. Each of these technologies has its own peculiar virtues, but it is not our purpose to attempt to evaluate them, if that were possible.[11] Yet it is worth observing that a society is severely limited both in its arts and sciences by the kind of technology it possesses. Historians have even found it possible to write their stories in terms of the basic technologies of a society.

But it should not be forgotten that technologies are capable of advancing, and it may not be too extravagant to suggest that an advancing society

---

[11] See this volume, Part IV, p. 502 ff., for a discussion of this problem.

is precisely one with advancing technologies. A knotty problem remains with respect to militarism, since we are not always quick to say that advancement in techniques of destruction is the mark of an advancing society. For this reason, it seems appropriate to limit advancement, as Hobbes did, to the peaceful arts, including among these the techniques for a society to protect itself from marauders.

Once we consider society in terms of its actual activities, together with the continuities among them, we have a strategy for understanding it realistically. We can better understand the potentials of persons by virtue of the tools or machines they have at their disposal, and by how these instruments influence the most productive relations these persons can bear to one another. By means of this approach we do avoid the naïveté of regarding men's conduct as if it proceeded only from drives and appetites centered within themselves. Hobbes never made this kind of mistake; in fact, he used the state of nature, not as an historical account of human life, but as a device for showing how preposterous the state of nature is, and how absurd a philosophy it presupposes. It was employed as a crude device for contrasting animal (*lupus* or wolf) and man (rational and living in civil society). Animal life is, in these terms, the life of desire and aversion, which never leads to contentment or felicity, but only to a solitariness, both brutish and short. Desires and aversions are concerned with single objects that are wants or antipathies, as for example a ripe banana or a mosquito bite. The ideal of contentment in passing from one satisfaction to another is hopeless, because, even if it could come about, it is not the stuff of contentment. A passage from one satisfaction to another lacks any cumulative continuity. In spite of the somewhat activistic connotation of desire and aversion, the end which is prized is more one for a listless consumer than for an active participant in human life. Life is impoverished to the extent that it fails to appreciate the rational and the creative capacities of man, together with their results—science and the arts.

Sometimes Hobbes speaks as if all that is necessary for man to pass from the state of nature to the civil state is to add reason to desire—then the social contract, then the commonwealth, then the sovereign, then the peaceful arts. But the whole argument is really inverted. Reason gets under way only with the practice of the arts, which, when regulated and coordinated by the sovereign, produce the commonwealth, which in turn brings about a new solidarity, and this is the truth of the social contract. The social contract is a reconciliation, a renewal of fellowship, begun when men first cooperate in the practice of the arts, and it is consummated when, through formalization of the state, they become critically and discriminatingly reconciled. This process is one in which people, in the language of the preamble to the constitution, "form a more perfect union." The contract is consummated, not by some verbal or written solemnization, but by habits and social procedures through which a people carry on their business. What makes this functional is the advancements of the arts through which the business of life is carried on. In *The Citizen*, Hobbes describes this clearly with respect to three things "expedient for the enriching of subjects":

For the first, those laws will be useful which countenance the arts that improve the increase of the earth and water, such as are husbandry and fishing. For the second, all laws against idleness, and such as quicken industry, are profitable; the art of navigation . . . and the mechanics . . . and the mathematical sciences, the fountains of navigatory and mechanic employments, are held in due esteem and honour. For the third, those laws are useful, whereby all inordinate expense, as well in meats as in clothes, and universally in all things which are consumed with usage, is forbidden. Now because such laws are beneficial to the ends above specified, it belongs also to the office of supreme magistrates to establish them.[12]

These words unmistakably place this political philosophy in the vanguard of those concerned with the realities of political life, rather than the rituals of vacuous pieties.

MORALITY IS SOCIAL. Hobbes has already been quoted as saying that justice and injustice concern men in society, not in solitude. Ethics, we may say, is the study of the right relations among men. But this study is the essence of the civil state—to be civil is to treat other human beings as if they count, and count as human beings, not just as things. This quality of civility becomes more evident when we compare the civil state with the state of nature. In the state of nature, men are self-centered; they are after things, and other men are regarded as things. Might or power is the only "law" man knows in the state of nature, for it is a war of all against all. There is nothing proper or improper, right or wrong, moral or immoral. The state of nature is that amoral state in which one survives as best as he can.

In civil society all this is changed. Man now has obligations to perform. In order to pursue the objectives of peace and safety, he is obliged to accommodate himself to other men, not to gain an advantage over them, but to gain advantages in common. The distinctive mark of the civil state is the existence of common objectives or values, and that is why it is called the commonwealth. The security of the individual man then is bound up with the security of the commonwealth, and anything which threatens the latter also threatens the former. For this reason man is obligated not just to join in the commonwealth but also to devote the energy necessary to preserve it. Since a man's own good is inextricably combined with the good of civil society, to act contrary to that society

---

[12] *De Cive or the Citizen*, ed. by Sterling P. Lamprecht (New York: Appleton-Century-Crofts, 1949), p. 151.

is to undermine his own good. In this basic sense, then, men consent to live together in the commonwealth.

There is another sense, however, in which consent is not empty. The commonwealth is an on-going process, constantly being defined by the utilities, old and new, which embody the values that make living possible —or more important, living better. In order to regulate men's relations in the pursuit of their activities, laws have to be enforced. And when old laws are inadequate or inappropriate, new laws need to be enacted and enforced. In the commonwealth, men are bound not just by the old laws, but also by the new ones. These laws define, in specified situations, the relations that men are to bear to one another. They are indispensable conditions by which men can achieve utilities in life under peaceful and safe circumstances. And Hobbes would add that this is still the case, even if men obey the laws through fear of the consequences if they did not obey, for commonwealths are not possible without laws and therefore without lawmakers and law enforcers—or, in his language, without sovereigns.

Right relations are initially sanctioned by the social contract, and thereafter by the sovereign, who makes laws in the light of the utilities which men have or might have. Men can do wrong in the civil state—they can be declared guilty of inflicting injury on another. This kind of wrong —injurious action—is a wrong precisely because it is contrary to public policy, which in turn exists because there also exist utilities affected with the public interest. These interests, Hobbes was for the most part content to describe simply as the peace and safety of the community. The implication is clear that peace and safety can prevail only as a public good, not as a private one, except that private persons can of course enjoy public benefit. Yet the nature of the good is essentially civil, and therefore belongs to society primarily and to private persons secondarily.

That this is the correct priority of the nature of the good is seen in the further implications for the topic of liberty. These priorities apply to liberty in the civil state rather than to that in the state of nature. The latter is an unenviable kind of liberty which Hobbes calls "unfruitful liberty." This is the liberty man has in the state of nature and which profits him nothing. It is that form of liberty which we speak of in saying a man is free whenever he is not restrained from doing anything he likes. It is the freedom of being led by one's desires and aversions, and its consequences are catastrophic for all; it can end only in destruction. So we are confronted with the paradoxical question: Is man free only when he is bound? The question sounds absurd; yet in all soberness it has to be faced, and having been faced it has, by many including Hobbes, been answered in the affirmative. In *The Citizen*, Hobbes elaborates his answer by contrasting civil liberty with the unfruitful liberty in nature as follows.

. . . he who by reason of his own liberty acts all at his own will, must also by reason of the same liberty in others suffer all at another's will. But in a constituted city [that is, in a civil society], every subject retains to himself as much freedom as suffices him to live well and quietly, and there is so much taken away from others, as may make them not to be feared. Out of this [civil] state, every man hath such a right to all, as yet he can enjoy nothing; in it, each one securely enjoys his limited right. Out of it, any man may rightly spoil or kill another; in it, none but one. . . . Out of it, no man is sure of the fruit of his labours; in it, all men are. Lastly, out of it, there is a dominion of passions, war, fear, poverty, slovenliness, solitude, barbarism, ignorance, cruelty; in it, the dominion of reason, peace, security, riches, decency, society, elegancy, sciences, and benevolence.[13]

Man's liberty in nature is powerless and unfruitful; in society it is productive and worth having. Hobbes wants to solve the paradox in that by limiting one's freedom he gains all. Unlimited freedom is frightful and self-destructive. Limited freedom is the only freedom man can know, and the limitations are to be determined by the sovereign without any control by the subjects.

Is tyranny then the price to be paid for freedom? Posed in this fashion, the question appears absurd. Hobbes would not have admitted the question, or at least would formally have replied to it by insisting that the sovereign's acts can only be lawful, and that "every Subject is Author of every act the Sovereign doth."[14] The formal answer relinquishes too much because it is based upon empty consent—a blank check offered to the sovereign. But underlying the formal answer is an insight Hobbes did not, and could not yet, sufficiently delineate—that is, the spelling out of peace and security as the peaceful arts constituting the utilities of man. Yet these arts flourish only as the expression of human rationality, for they depend on science and technology and the sensitivities that characterize human life. They do not grow out of tyranny; they grow out of the liberation of man both from the dead dogma and from exhausting warfare. Hobbes was the first to see how man could avoid both, and by combining the utilities of man with a mechanistic outlook, he saw how man could at the same time be freed of the conventional wisdom and from the horrors of warfare. His genius was precisely that of translating seventeenth-century mechanism into a social outlook, free from the dead hand of the past and the internecine wars fanned by religious sects. Peace, if it were at all possible, would have to be effected through secular values, protected and advanced by secular, political powers. Hobbes' political philosophy was in advance of his time, but it was an integral part of the mechanistic point of view, which was an inexorable consequence of Galilean science.

---

[13] Ibid., p. 114.
[14] Leviathan, p. 163.

Hobbes' Mechanism

Hobbes' metaphysical predilections are clearly mechanistic. Since metaphysics is the study of reality, and since Hobbes unambiguously asserts that the realities of the world are bodies, he has only to tell us what kind of bodies there are and how they are related to one another. Bodies are material and they are in motion or at rest. Organic bodies are likewise material, in that they are complex arrangements of physical things. There are no new kinds of elements that enter into them, for there are no elements which are not material. Living things are only complexes of nonliving things. Finally, bodies are natural or artificial. The latter, made by man, are either inorganic, that is, machines, or organic, that is, states, such as the Leviathan. Hobbes' analysis pretty well fits the classical scheme of mechanistic philosophy in every way except one—his analysis of the civil state. Our question is whether this is basically mechanistic in outlook.

This question arises from the fact that his analysis of the civil state involves principles at variance with those of the state of nature. The former entails morality, the latter does not. In the former, man can act on the basis of reason; in the latter, only desire and aversion. In the former he is man, in the latter he is animal. In the one, he prizes peaceful pursuits; in the other, he is doomed to ceaseless warfare. The one is altruistic; the other egoistic. The oppositions may well arouse our suspicions, since it is inconceivable that the state of nature could contain the potentialities of social life which are characteristic of the civil state. By its very nature, then, the social contract could not have been an historical event, for it would have required an obligation to enter into an obligation, which in turn would have required a preceding obligation, and thus would engender an infinite regress. Putting it differently, we can say that if men are motivated only by desires and aversions, there is no basis for them to enter into a contract. Desires and aversions are for specific things like a drink of water or avoiding the blistering sun. The contract, however, is not for satisfying a specific desire or for avoiding some present pain. It is designed to make for a different kind of life; its intent is not to satisfy or avoid some desire or aversion, but to establish the conditions for peace, that is, for a peaceful existence. Like happiness, it specifies no object. Rather it is, at best, a stipulation for conditions under which life may be led. Or like "law and order," the concern is for an arrangement by which men can jointly pursue their common ends, and be free to do other things, jointly or individually, which do not jeopardize these conditions that make common ends possible.[15] Civil life cannot be adequately

---

[15] Professor C. B. MacPherson gives an alternative reading of Hobbes' individualism, linking it more closely to bourgeois capitalism, rather than to the peaceful arts as cooperative undertakings. See *The Political Theory of Possessive Individualism* (Oxford at the Clarendon Press, 1962).

described in terms of desires and aversions. It is much too significant for that kind of description, and must not be confused with wants and aversions, which if not immoral, are nonmoral. Hence, the question whether Hobbes has, in his social view of morality, proffered a mechanistic concept of civil society.

The reductive atomistic view of mechanism is much too individualistic in outlook to satisfy Hobbes' highly sophisticated conception of society. It appears that the mechanistic point of view more appropriately entails a notion of government as a necessary evil, and that the social contract is entered into only because it is a way of maintaining as much independence of one another as possible. Carlyle succinctly stated this point of view as "anarchy plus the constable." According to this view, government and joint activity have no intrinsic worth. They are justifiable only as means for preserving the greatest possible independence among individuals, whose satisfactions alone constitute value. There is nothing of the fraternal idea in this. Government and nations and other men are looked upon with distrust. The social contract has only made the hot war into a cold one. And it is an uneasy state capable of erupting at any moment.

Hobbes' framework is entirely different. His is a commonwealth where, even when men are aloof, they have an obligation not to disturb others' safety. And if they are not obligated to initiate peaceful pursuits with others, at least they are obligated to respond to the laws of the sovereign which aim at the promotion of peaceful pursuits for the common good. Because Hobbes assumed that initiative would come from men—after all, they are animals with desires and aversions—he placed the emphasis on the circumstances which would control initiative in order that men could live together as human beings. Whatever initiative need not be inhibited was permitted—that is, left to individuals to do or fail to do with it as they pleased. This political philosophy as so conceived is the forerunner of that of Rousseau, in which fraternity or the common good is held to be primary, and liberty and equality are derivative from fraternity. In both Hobbes and Rousseau, freedom thus means the free society in which men can participate, not free individuals such as make society impossible. Since the quality of civil society could not, except by a factitious social contract, be created by individuals totally lacking in that quality of civility, the mechanistic interpretation of society appears not adequate to Hobbes' philosophical outlook.

Yet, in a modified form, his philosophy bears the mechanistic stamp. In this form the elements are not the individuals but their arts or utilities. Thus society is analyzable into its arts as constituting its elements, and men into their roles in these arts. Farming requires farmers; navigation, seamen; building, carpenters; fishing, fishermen; belles lettres, belle lettrists; and science, scientists, etc. Peace and security or the contented life, which is the end of government, is the totality of the arts, including that of governing, whereby civil society flourishes, for civil society is nothing other than these arts added together. The practical arts, science, and the fine arts do possess in their practice the qualities which Hobbes prizes in the civil state. They are the utilities of society, and Hobbes was the first of the utilitarians in modern philosophic thought. Moreover, the utilities are undergirded by the motions of bodies, where any motion is regarded as causally determined by prior motions. Utilitarianism, or a kind of categoreal mechanism in the social arena, is the logical consequence of mechanism in nature. Hobbes saw this in the seventeenth century; Diderot and the Encyclopedists reaffirmed it less ambiguously in the eighteenth century. In this sophisticated form of mechanism, Hobbes left his indelible imprint on the writing of political theory.

Selected Readings

Ayres, Clarence, *Towards a Reasonable Society*, Austin: University of Texas Press, 1961.

Barker, Ernest, *The Social Contract* (Introduction and Essays by Locke, Hume, and Rousseau), London: Oxford University Press, 1947.

Collingwood, R. G., *The New Leviathan*, Oxford at the Clarendon Press, 1942.

Hobbes, Thomas, *Leviathan*, ed. by Herbert W. Schneider, New York: Liberal Arts, 1958, Parts I, II, and Introduction. (Paperback.)

Hobbes, Thomas, *De Cive or The Citizen*, ed. by S. P. Lamprecht, New York, Appleton-Century-Crofts 1949.

For important and variant interpretations of Hobbes, see:

MacPherson, C. B., *The Poliitcal Theory of Possessive Individualism: Hobbes to Locke*, Oxford at the Clarendon Press, 1962. (Also paperback.)

Warrender, Howard, *The Political Philosophy of Hobbes: His Theory of Obligation*, Oxford at the Clarendon Press, 1961.

CHAPTER 15

Secularism Is Enough

The New Quest for Religion

The Cartesian philosophy attempted to confine the mechanistic interpretation to the natural world; spiritual beings were regarded as of another order, even though Descartes was compelled to admit some relations between the two. Although the two orders were supposed to make nature safe for science and man safe for religion, their conciliation was, as we have seen, an uneasy one. This uneasiness was less a matter of Descartes' ingenuity than it was a basic restlessness in the search for God. While this intense desire to seek new forms of religious expression was abroad, science was, as a matter of fact, making inroads upon traditional religious leliefs. The constant collision between science and the conventional religious folkways could not long permit a compartmentalization of religion and science. One or both must give, even if science were ultimately proven to be the stronger force.

The phalanx of Catholicism had been broken by the spirit of Protestantism. The intensity of the drive for new religious experience caused men to seek for a more immediate relation between man and God, bypassing the Church and sometimes creating new churches or conventicles which would permit more intimate forms of fellowship in pursuit of religion. Formalities, such as the sacraments, were regarded as of less significance than the immediacies of religious experience. Simplicity was sought not just in the conduct of life but also in the forms of worship and in the plainness of the houses of worship, sometimes not even called "houses" but rather "meetings."

Pietism, quietism, quakerism—these were some of the forms the new religious spirit took. They combined the inner spirit with a society devoted to its cultivation, producing novel forms of religious exercise. Described by the late F. L. Nussbaum, the new mysticism differed from that of the thirteenth century in the form of its institutionalization. He writes:

In general . . . mysticism in this period was democratized in the form of societies and institutions rather than illustrated by the extraordinary experiences of individuals. The experience of God became a matter of *collegia pietatis*, of conventicles, of meetings, rather than of withdrawal into solitude and silence.[1]

Although these seventeenth-century religious expressions required social support, they were nevertheless dominated by the search for the inner light, the religious counterpart of Descartes' "natural light of reason." By making the strong separation between the inner and outer man, Descartes, as we have seen, did contribute to the philosophic orientation that supported both religion and mechanistic science. Nevertheless, the power of mechanistic science could not be limited to the analysis of material bodies in motion. Locke and his fellow Britishers soon applied it to the mind itself, and Hobbes applied it to the analysis of society. If, now, the same application could be made to religion, then the delicately balanced dualism of Descartes would have to give way to new and other philosophic modes.

Even in the seventeenth century there were premonitions that Cartesian dualism occupied a precarious position. Descartes' own attitude was certainly not one inspired with religious fervor, and there were those who, like Lord Herbert of Cherbury (1583-1648) and Hugo Grotius (1583-1645), were more deistic than theistic in outlook. The mysteries of religion more and more were coming under attack. Revealed knowledge was becoming increasingly suspect. And in its place was the desire to make religion rational. Perhaps the existence of God could be demonstrated, for it was commonly believed that the world had to be created, even if, once created, reason could discover its laws. Then, also, there was no doubt that virtuous living was required of man, for morals are themselves a part of the rational order of things. And finally, since there is an incompatibility between virtuous living and unhappiness, or between vice and happiness, there must be a system of rewards and punishments apportioned out in accordance with virtue and vice, respectively.

These principles of deism were later spelled out by John Toland (1670-

---

[1] *The Triumph of Science and Reason, 1660–1685* (New York: Harper Torchbooks, 1962) p. 189.

1721) in his *Christianity, Not Mysterious* and by John Locke in his *Reasonableness of Christianity*. Each of these writers was trying desperately to find reason in the world, and thus was imbued with the Cartesian—and scientific—spirit of the age, of which the ontological arguments were supreme examples. For them, the knotty problems were moral rather than theological. They could not countenance disorder, confusion, and wickedness here, any more than they could be countenanced in the system of planetary motions. Locke wrestles with the problem of the moral order in these terms:

. . . "Why did God give so bad a law to mankind . . . ?"

Answer.   It was such a law as the purity of God's nature required, and must be the law of such a creature as man; unless God would have made him a rational creature, and not required him to have lived by the law of reason; but would have countenanced in him irregularity and disobedience to that light which he had, and that rule which was suitable to his nature; which would have been to have authorised disorder, confusion, and wickedness in his creatures: for that this law was the law of reason, or, as it is called, of nature; we shall see by and by: and if rational creatures will not live up to the rule of their reason, who shall excuse them? If you will admit them to forsake reason in one point, why not in another? Where will you stop? To disobey God in any part of his commands, (and 'tis he that commands what reason does,) is direct rebellion; which, if dispensed with in any point, government and order are at an end; and there can be no bounds set to the lawless exorbitancy of unconfined man. The law therefore was, as St. Paul tells us, Rom. vii. 12, "holy, just, and good," and such as it ought, and could not otherwise be.[2]

Then there is also the question of rewards and of the coming of Christ and their relation, which must also fit the dictates of reason if Christianity is to be the truly reasonable religion. Locke is worth quoting again on these points. In explication of them, he observes:

Neither, indeed, could it be otherwise; for life, eternal life, being the reward of justice or righteousness only, appointed by the righteous God (who is of purer eyes than to behold iniquity) to those who only had no taint or infection of sin upon them, it is impossible that he should justify those who had no regard to justice at all whatever they believed. This would have been to encourage iniquity, contrary to the purity of his nature; and to have condemned that eternal law of right, which is holy, just, and good; of which no one precept or rule is abrogated or repealed; nor indeed can be, whilst God is an holy, just, and righteous God, and man a rational creature. The duties of that law, arising from the constitution of his very nature, are of eternal obligation; nor can it be taken away or dispensed with, without changing the nature of things, overturning the measures of right and wrong, and thereby introducing and authorising irregularity, confusion, and disorder in the world. Christ's coming into the world was not for such an end as that; but, on the contrary, to reform the corrupt state of degenerate man; and out of those who would mend their lives, and bring forth fruit meet for repentance, erect a new kingdom.[3]

[2] *Reasonableness of Christianity*, 11th ed. (London: 1812), p. 11.
[3] *Ibid.*, pp. 111–112.

To make religion rational is a difficult task, and it is doubly difficult to make sectarian religion rational. In the case of deism, all men are required to adopt not only the religion of an all-powerful, righteous being, but also the being of Christ too. Locke's task is thus the formidable one of reconciling with the basic principle of deism the reasonableness of Christian mysteries. Accordingly, the Bible is to be believed, not because it is the revealed word, but because it is Logos in the sense of the rational word, capable of being demonstrated by anyone who will properly employ his natural faculties.

Deism is not so much a religion satisfying the deepest impulses of man, as it is a desire for tidying up the bookkeeping of the world. It acknowledges and welcomes a kempt appearance of things. Just as mathematics can express the order in physical nature, so can arithmetic add up virtues and vices and strike a balance according to which men achieve their just deserts in after-life. Nevertheless, despite all the ingenuity of the deists, they cannot conceal the yawning gap between the physical and the spiritual, and the need to bridge that gap. Rationality of disembodied spirits does not well comport with rationality of minds that are originally "blank papers." Life eternal, being so greatly removed from biological, or psychological, or even social life, its principles cannot appropriately apply to the natural world.

The Ascendency of Moral Questions

Although the dualism expressed in these terms cannot be bridged, there is a possibility of bridging the natural and the moral. Realistically speaking, this bridge is more than hinted at by Locke. He does want a moral order; he is concerned with justice; he castigates rebellion and "the lawless exorbitancy of unconfined man"; he is an advocate of natural law in nature and the laws of nature (morality) in society. And in all this, he is pre-eminently concerned with government and with "political power," which he takes to be "a right of making laws with penalties of death, and consequently all less penalties, for the regulating and preserving of property, and of employing the force of the community in the execution of such laws, and in the defence of the commonwealth from foreign injury, and all this only for the public good."[4] Order can be projected in the realm of eternal life, or it can be aimed at in social life so that every man may come to terms in pursuing the goals of life. In justifying the Glorious Revolution, which justification, after all, was the explicit intent of his *Second Treatise*, Locke meant by order something vastly different from what one could mean by it in the conception of life eternal.

By concentrating attention upon the social as the bridge between

---

[4] *Second Treatise on Civil Government*, Ch. 1.

nature and man, we can better appreciate the inevitable criticism of deism by atheists. Baron d'Holbach (1723–1789) developed his atheism, following a lead by La Mettrie, precisely because he insisted that reforms in society could come about only as men give up their religious superstitions. He writes:

When we shall be disposed usefully to occupy ourselves with the happiness of men, it is with the Gods in heaven that the reform must commence; it is by abstracting these imaginary beings, destined to affright people who are ignorant and in a state of infancy, that we shall be able to promise ourselves to conduct man to a state of maturity. . . . No wise government can found itself upon a despotic God, he will always make tyrants of his representatives. No laws will be good without consulting the nature and the end of society. No jurisprudence can be advantageous for nations, if it is regulated upon the caprice and passions of deified tyrants. No education will be rational, unless it be founded upon reason, and not upon chimeras and prejudices. In short there is no virtue, no probity, no talents, under corrupt masters, and under the conduct of those priests who render men the enemies of themselves and of others, and who seek to stifle in them the germs of reason, science, and courage. . . .[5]

Holbach belongs to the group of Encyclopedists during the eighteenth-century Enlightenment. A naturalist and materialist, he comes to see that deism must give way to atheism. Men have to be responsible for their own destiny. Religion stands in the way of men's coming to terms with their authentic goods and in this sense, as was later insisted, it is the opiate of the people. Men must prepare themselves to take an active part in directing the course of their lives, collectively as well as individually. They cannot lead the good life if they supinely remain subjects of a monarch. The climax of atheism, and the Enlightenment of which it was a part, could only be the French Revolution, in which men must shout and battle for liberty, equality, and fraternity, even if the revolutionary movement could not stop short of excesses. In the Reign of Terror under Robespierre, the religion of reason did come to be expressed as the love of beauty in women. This last step occurred when prostitutes were worshipped in the Cathedral of Notre Dame.

During the Enlightenment, the effects of science began to be acknowledged in the popular mind, and the eighteenth-century *philosophes* consciously made use of science to proclaim the need for, if not the inevitability of, a new social order. The French Revolution was a direct consequence of political, economic, and intellectual unrest; and with the destruction of the old regime, feudalism tottered. Religion could henceforth hold a place second only to politics. Science had finally turned the course of man to an intense concern for things secular—popular government, new codes

---

[5] *System of Nature*, trans. by H. D. Robinson (Boston: J. P. Mendum, 1889), pp. 323–324.

of laws, public education, scientific societies, technological innovations, increased production and trade, and, especially, a sense of national loyalty that consolidated these interests in a viable social scheme.

There is the world before and the world after the French Revolution. The events which occurred were crucial; and so a whole new vocabulary is needed to understand these worlds before and after. Harold Laski vividly portrays the difference between them, when he writes:

Before 1789 there was not, in the modern sense, any social problem. Men asked how the poor were to be relieved, not, as afterwards, what part they were to play in the State. . . . Before 1789 socialist ideas were simply moral theories which lived in a vacuum and had no chance of effective realization. After 1789 . . . men had seen the deliberate introduction of proposals the purpose of which was to legislate for equality. . . . Before 1789 society was divided into privileged and unprivileged; since 1789 it has been divided into rich and poor.[6]

The philosophical question remains, can dualism still provide an intellectual accommodation to interpert a satisfactory range of human experience? In one sense, we must admit that it did. In the eighteenth and nineeenth centuries, few people were atheists, and whether or not the religious spirit was strong, Christian churches were an inseparable part of social life. Nor does it appear that by virtue of this there was outspoken antagonism to science—until, of course, the publication of the *Origin of Species*. May we not conclude, then, that Cartesian dualism did prevail? In a sense, we are forced to say that such is the case. The popular view certainly included the mechanistic science of nature, but it equally accepted a subjective view of happiness as the great and chief end of man. Nature's laws were taught in the schools, however much they were regarded as a beneficent expression of God; and the happiness principle became an ever-more-absorbing theme.

Not merely was happiness regarded as the end of man, but it became, at least in the Anglo-Saxon world, the slogan-like doctrine of both politics and economics. Pursuit of happiness gave meaning to life and liberty. And the very fact that it was interpreted as "pursuit" meant that it was up to each person to give it content relevant to his unique life. Descartes' individualism becomes incisive, just as his subjectivism also becomes incisive. Happiness rests on consciousness, and is known by each individual in his own way. To preserve its privacy, Jefferson, following Locke, made it into a natural and inalienable right. Similarly, the happiness principle is used in order to provide the motive for economic behavior. Man's natural disposition is to pursue his own interests in the exchange of goods in the market. His prudence, subject to no will but his own, employs intelligence

---

[6] *Socialist Tradition in the French Revolution* (London: G. Allen and Unwin, 1930), pp. 34–35.

as a means of maximizing his utilities—that is, to exercise that choice which brings him the greatest possible pleasure.

If the spirit of politics interpreted as natural rights and the spirit of economics interpreted as capitalistic enterprise are concrete, institutionalized embodiments of the happiness principle, its most general formulation is morality interpreted as the Protestant ideal which ought to govern human life. Enterprise, initiative, and self-reliance are the subjective sources which lead to individual happiness, and, miracle of miracles, to the sublimely good public state. Natural law so prevails that by submitting to the Protestant ethic, man also acts as testimony to the glory of God. The dualism actually expands into a trialism, where the spirit of the Cartesian philosophy becomes transformed into accepted practice.

Practice so constituted then becomes conventional wisdom. The eighteenth and nineteenth centuries provide abundant evidence for the correctness of this interpretation. The rigor of the mathematical method becomes the rigor of the Protestant ethic. Whatever shortcomings Descartes' philosophy as philosophy may have, it is fairly congruent with the puritan spirit of the new ethic. Mathematical exactness parallels the exactness required in human conduct, and the whole structure is arched by natural law which testifies to the beneficence of God. Couched in these terms, Cartesianism displays its virtues and its defects. Its virtues have been sufficiently elaborated; we need to turn now to its defects.

Cartesian Inadequacies

The received learning, arising as it did out of a Baroque spirit, is transformed into a Victorian prudery. The mathematical ideal is abstract. It whittles experience down to a formula, which covers a vast, possibly infinite, range of occurrences. In arithmetic, we are told that we cannot add together chickens and eggs and marbles and cabbages, but that we can add things of a common denominator. The same is true in physics. Before general laws can be formulated, the physicist must somehow decide upon the kinds of things he is to study, whether like mass, or heat or particles or what-not. In classical mechanics, physicists made the decision to study the so-called primary qualities of things and to formulate laws accordingly. The decision was momentous, both for the advancement of science and for the depreciation of art. Rich as the early Baroque period of art was, with its Holbeins and Rembrandts and Berninis, its Miltons and Corneilles and Racines, it becomes dilute in its later manifestations of Molières and Voltaires, Swifts and Fieldings, Bouchers and Fragonards, together with the sophistications of society, more interested in wit and satire than in probing the depths of human consciousness. The same restless spirit that produced great art and great science and great philosophy in the seventeenth century had lost its fervor in the sophistications of the eighteenth century, such as were displayed in the drawing rooms of Paris. Clearly, there was something missing, which neither Cartesian dualism nor Hobbes' monism could supply.

The missing element was the emotional life expressed in forms significant not just for inner feeling but also for outer manifestations in the dialogue and works of man. Feeling may be regarded as inner, the ghost within the machine. Although, in our own time, Professor Gilbert Ryle questions whether there is an inner, Cartesian philosophy certainly did provide a framework for an inner and an outer, such that artistic expressions were regarded as belonging to the one and scientific to the other. Actually, this had the effect of reducing the significance of both art and science. The point needs to be spelled out.

The usual contrast is something like this: Science is universal, art is unique; science depends on the intellect, art on the feelings; science is impersonal, art is personal; science is concerned with things, art with human beings, etc.[7] The scientific spirit and the artistic spirit are contrasted as far as possible, just because science deals with the "real" world, the world of things, and art with the inner life, especially with suffering and joy, desperation and elation, a whole range of intense experience, vivid, and ego-centered. In this romanticized version of art, its significance gets lost rather than advanced by being totally opposed to the scientific spirit. This version ends by separating irreparably fact and value, making science into a caricature of cold, emotionless, dispassionate study and art as warm, creative, emotional, expressive. This is the dualism, traceable to Descartes and most fully expressed in Immanuel Kant, which has plagued contemporary philosophy. (This is explained at length in Part IV, chap. 30.)

German romanticism, in the magisterial poetry of Goethe and the equally magisterial philosophies of Hegel (1770–1831) and Schopenhauer (1788–1860), attempted to cope with the human, made superhuman, in making the spiritual life a step above the power men gain through science. Faust has power, but it is self-destructive. To avoid the pitfalls, man must not sell out to science. Hegel places science on a lower level of dialectic, but in doing so he fails to give science its due and makes the dialectic appear ludicrous. However clever their intellectual schemata, and however productive their philosophical talents, philosophers cannot prove by any dialectic how many planets must exist. Nothing discredited Hegel's philosophic method more than his failure to acknowledge facts and to refrain

---

[7] Joseph Wood Krutch glibly depreciates scientific analysis in *The Modern Temper*, especially in Chap. 3, "The Disillusion with the Laboratory." Max Eastman acknowledges the distinction as between "water" as "H₂O" and as "wet" in *The Enjoyment of Poetry*, Chap. 2, "Names Practical and Poetic." And Alfred North Whitehead attempts to combat the separation of the scientific and artistic spirit in his *Science and the Modern World*, chap. 13.

from inventing necessities of what nature must be as a consequence of some allegedly philosophic insight. One can sympathize with Schopenhauer's more radical flight to the mysterious, which instead of encompassing all reality becomes, in its contemplative purity, a realism where the will is rendered powerless and where the infinite is totally absorbing. But none of these attempts, noble as they are in intent, can satisfy the demands of coping with both science and art in their objective and demanding expressions.

Science and art need not be regarded as opposites so much as they need be regarded as complementaries. Their methods are different and so are their results. It would be foolish to try to make science into art or art into science, but it is blindness to fail to see the artistic in science or the scientific in art. The motives, the creative impulses, in science require for their expression not just an elegance of formulation into simple laws, but also an intuition of how those laws get expressed in the particularities of nature and thereby make nature more human.[8] This, in essence, is the artistic impulse, similar to the spirit of the ontological argument, which sought to bring thought and nature together in a way which makes them genuine complementaries instead of casual coincidences. The old ontological arguments were no doubt defective in their alleged proofs. But their emotional commitments stand as affirmations of the need to relate intimately man and nature. In their enthusiasms for working with the complexities of nature, or perhaps even in their unenthusiastic drilled habits, scientists may overlook the potentialities of their activities to re-establish contact with nature. This contact, nevertheless, may be regarded as a clue to how the artistic spirit becomes fused with the scientific.

Or from the other side, art, too, can become more adequately expressed when it takes science seriously. Instead of being cloyingly obsessed with particularity or uniqueness, it can find genuine liberation in searching for the universal in the particular. Sheer particularity is sheer sensation, which in turn is sheer shock, as meaningless as anything could be. Art must, of course, always be shocking; otherwise it is not art. This property makes both its mystery and its spice. By virtue of it, art avoids the humdrum. Art endlessly searches for something new. But it must be more than just "unusual," which is sometimes popularly taken to be the essence of art, though it may equally well be a way of dismissing a work as, after all, not really worth the bother. Some works are no doubt abortive art, stopping short of significant expression. This contrast can be brought out by comparing the art of the day with the classics. In the former we are struck by novelty; in the latter we are absorbed by its insight. "To be struck." "To be absorbed." These again represent extreme aspects of art, both of which

---

[8] See the illuminating study by J. Bronowski, *Science and Human Values* (New York: Harper Torchbook, 1956).

are to be comprised in art if it is to have both vitality and significance. Novelty can come only from sheer talent, but absorption depends on structure, on relatedness of things, and if anything is comprised in science, surely it is relatedness. Art ignores science only to its own detriment. The Cartesian philosophy is totally inadequate to cope with the problem in those terms. One need only read Descartes' philosophy to be convinced of the truth of this harsh judgment. In translating the most commonplace feeling into its bodily concomitants, Descartes did no service either to enlightening men about their sensitivities or in providing more than commonplaces about their physical capacities.

Concluding Remarks on Man's Social Nature

Finally, we may observe the failure of the seventeenth century to come to terms adequately with man's social nature. Two powerful forces were at work to confuse the authentic issues, even though shafts of light sometimes brilliantly illuminated the human condition. Hobbes' social thought contained genius, but even this was aborted by his concern for the peculiarities of revolutionary England. From another angle, Locke, with this insistence upon individual requisites, was also diverted from producing a philosophy of sufficient generality to be quite acceptable. Rousseau stands alone as one who reached a level of abstraction which could make social philosophy into a monumental analysis, constantly stimulative to thought and suggestive in its implications.

From the beginnings of the Renaissance, when the collision between science and folklore was most intense, European thought—and practice—had to cope with two movements, sometimes divergent, sometimes dovetailing, but each with its own demanding necessities. These were, of course, nascent nationalism and nascent individualism. Each had a logic of its own, even though its urgency depended upon the particular crises which had to be met from time to time. Sometimes the consolidation of centralized power seemed to be the most pressing of demands, sometimes the liberating of individual energies and the new talents which the expanding world made relevant and important. Monarchs and sovereignty were indispensable to the one, the advance of trade and invention, science and technology to the other. The more enlightened monarchs perceived the necessities for encouraging the expression of the many talents of persons which would, at the same time, enlarge the power and prestige of the state, thereby bringing about what Hegel later called "the well-constituted state." The march of events progressively showed that the problems in both areas, national and personal, were fundamentally secular, and that naturalism was an ally of both. The scientific revolution made its impact upon the need for new social orientations, just as it had upon the need for new orientations in thought.

The only institution which could rival the Church for giving expression to human longings of great numbers of persons and which could become an object of intense devotion was the nation-state. Despite the need for reconciling the old folklore, especially in its religious manifestations, with the new secularism, the temporal power in organized life was increasing at the expense of the spiritual power. Hobbes saw this with crystal clearness. Without any attempt to conceal the need for making civil power supreme, he insisted upon there being a "sovereign," who could alone bring order out of social chaos. The function of the sovereign was to embody that power which was required for men to carry on their business with one another, and thereby to advance the common good. No wonder that the popular term for expressing this function was "the commonwealth." By regarding it as a common possession, wealth could be wholeheartedly espoused by men pursuing their secular interests and at the same time creating a new folklore which could enlarge their view of a common destiny and hallow their activities in what they regarded as the business of life.

In the narrow sense, wealth may pertain to making money, but for our forefathers it clearly connoted something far more important. It connoted "weal" or "well-being" or "prosperity" in the sense, not just of amassing goods, but in the sense of the development of the self in a society in which all could develop themselves. Private property could consequently be considered important, not because one was justified in hoarding things, but because one was using, making, or creating things that helped others as well as himself. When Locke made private property into "the great and chief end" of the state, he did it, as his Introduction to *Civil Government* clearly states, for the purpose of serving "the public good." In his political writings, he wishes to justify men's actions which better themselves, and he does this by insisting upon the privacy of property rights—the rights of "life, liberty, and estate." These are not to be interfered with—because, and this is the principal point of theoretical interest, by leaving these matters to individual decisions, the greatest good for the commonwealth is achieved. In other words, Locke writes the political version of what he regarded as men's overriding needs, just as Adam Smith writes the economic version. In this connection, we cannot overemphasize the im-importance of the harmony which was supposed to exist between the individual's actions and the general welfare. The very title of his great work makes Smith's intent quite unambiguous. His concern is for the *Wealth of Nations*, and that wealth is possible only as individuals by their own works produce wealth.

This newly-emerging folklore may better be expressed in terms of "the law of nature," which, of course, is nonnatural. The law of nature is God's law—the moral law imposed upon man by God. By respecting natural law, men can live in harmony with themselves. Their motives may be private interest, but the ends which they achieve are public—namely, the public good. In this sense, "private vices are public virtues." And although "every man is to be his own priest," the new mechanistic pattern still serves the ends of society and therefore is God's will. This theme Carl Becker has elegantly drawn out in his *Heavenly City of the Eighteenth-Century Philosophers*.[9] Becker believes that this spirit of natural law is the eighteenth-century reading of nature, which bears a closer resemblance to the spirit of medievalism than it does to modern naturalism.

We are left finally with a question rather than a dogmatic conclusion. The question is: Is secularism enough? The eighteenth-century is not quite clear on the subject. The persisting question is whether we are clear on the subject. Eighteenth-century philosophy is highly suggestive; it is, of course, not conclusive. The question still remains for us to resolve in the very best way we can, using the very best of our resources. But however we resolve it, we need to be faithful to the insights of the whole range of human experience, and we need to reckon with the power that science has justly had in shaping our mentalities. The philosophical task remains important, because science is important and because it continues to collide with our hallowed beliefs and with our common-sense experience. The extension of the mechanistic interpretation clearly demonstrates this mentality in the seventeenth and eighteenth centuries, and the extension of evolutionary naturalism further demonstrates it in the nineteenth and twentieth centuries. The shift is from an emphasis in which physics constitutes the goading power to one in which biology serves such a purpose. Philosophy can afford to ignore neither of these sources of knowledge nor the imposing structures built upon them.

Selected Readings

Becker, Carl, *The Heavenly City of the Eighteenth-Century Philosophers*, New Haven: Yale University Press, 1959. (Paperback.)

Bronowski, J., *Science and Human Values*, New York: Harper Torchbooks, 1956. (Paperback.)

Laski, H. J., *The Rise of Liberalism*, New York: Harper & Row, 1936.

Locke, John, *On The Reasonableness of Christianity*, Chicago: Gateway, 1965. (Paperback.)

Martin, Kingsley, *French Liberal Thought in the Eighteenth Century*, New York: Harper Torchbooks, 1963. (Paperback.)

Nussbaum, F. L., *The Triumph of Science and Reason, 1660–1685*, New York: Harper Torchbooks, 1962. (Paperback.)

Weber, Max, *The Protestant Ethic and the Spirit of Capitalism*, London: 1930 (trans. by Talcott Parsons). (Also in Scribner paperback.)

---

[9] New Haven: Yale, paperback, 1959.

PART **III**

PHILOSOPHICAL RESPONSES
TO DARWINISM

The thing that hath been, it is that which will be; and that which is done, is that which shall be done; and there is no new thing under the sun.

ECCLESIASTES 1:9

. . . we are not here concerned with hopes or fears, only with the truth as far as our reason permits us to discover it; and I have given the evidence to the best of my ability.

CHARLES DARWIN, *The Descent of Man*

Doubtless the greatest dissolvent in contemporary thought of old questions, the greatest precipitant of new methods, new intentions, new problems, is the one effected by the scientific revolution that found its climax in the "Origin of Species."

JOHN DEWEY, *The Influence of Darwin on Philosophy*

CHAPTER 16

Before Darwin

The Mechanistic World View—Recapitulation

Despite the difficulties to which it gave rise, the world view associated with the names of Galileo, Descartes, and Newton provided such a satisfying answer to the questions troubling thoughtful Europeans that it nearly dominated the outlook of the eighteenth century. These three towering geniuses supplied the basic ideas in terms of which modern man, once he broke with the medieval tradition, understood the "nature of things." This understanding was not merely the property of a handful of gifted men; it became during the period of the "Enlightenment" the possession of the educated classes of Europe.

It may be well at this point to recapitulate the basic assumptions with which, under the influence of Descartes and Newton, the modern era opened. To begin with, these assumptions included a *mechanistic* description of the physical universe and a *dualistic* treatment of the knower as a detached onlooker. In this dualistic view man, in his distinguishing aspect of mind, was not included in the system of nature, and neither, therefore, were the institutions by which he lives: man was something special and apart, and for most the study of man and society belonged, not to science, but to the province of metaphysics and theology. It should be emphasized at this point that mechanism had certain profound implications concerning which it is important to be completely explicit. Mechanism committed the followers of Descartes and Newton to the idea of a *closed* or what William James has called a *block* universe: it is finished and complete, proceeding endlessly through the same revolutions like an elaborately-fashioned watch. Hence the mechanistic interpretation of nature involving, as it does, the notions of uniformity, constancy, repetitiousness, led to a belief in the possibility of achieving *complete and finished knowledge*: one has only to learn the laws by which the machine is governed to know with certainty what the machine will be doing in the indefinite future. This is the *rationalistic ideal of knowledge* which, arrived at by a different route, modern science at its inception shared with the scholastic tradition that preceded it. Even today, while conceding that the world mechanism is much more complex than the Age of Reason imagined it to be, many thoughtful people tend to regard the conquests of science as bringing us closer and closer to a fixed body of static truths to which, in the judgment of the more optimistic, we shall one day attain.

All of the machines that we have known are artificial. When we say this we mean that they have not assembled themselves and they are not found, so to speak, in a "state of nature." They are artifacts—the products, in every case, of contrivance. They have been wrought, fashioned, designed, brought into being at a given instant in time. Every machine, in other words, suggests an *act of creation* to which *time is incidental*. If the universe is a machine, it too has been created, and hence owes its origin not to processes involving vast spans of time, but to a special act.

The architects of the world view under examination were far from disavowing the theistic implications of such a creationist view of the origins of the universe. On the contrary, as we have seen, they emphatically affirmed the presence of an all-powerful deity who not only created the universe but keeps it moving in its appointed course. To be sure, they shrewdly appealed to the idea of God's greatness to argue that it is impertinent of mere mortals to search out his motives, so that the search for final causes had better be abandoned for theological as well as scientific reasons. And they argued from the notion of his perfection to one of the basic requirements of their science, namely the idea of the regularity of the laws of nature: God being perfect would have no occasion to change his mind, and Nature can therefore go on forever in its inexorable and immutable way, as Galileo said, "never passing the bounds of the laws assigned her." Nevertheless, as the preceding pages have shown, if they used the idea of God in a way that served the requirements of science they also believed in God with sincere devotion. What is more pertinent to the later developments inspired by Darwin is the ease with which their creationist views permitted and even encouraged the Newtonians to regard the world as having come into being only a relatively short while ago. They had torn apart the narrow spatial boundaries of the medieval universe; the temporal boundaries remained intact. On this score, there was no real quarrel with the biblical account of creation and this agreement extended to the biblical account of the origin of living species.

Living species were regarded as having the same form as when they had issued complete and full-grown from the hands of the Creator: the *immutability of species* was generally taken for granted. Those same fixed forms, which had been expunged from the physical world and had given way to the Galilean principle of change, remained securely lodged in the realm of living things to which, indeed, they seemed especially apt. In the strictly orthodox view, it was assumed that all living species had been created simultaneously, and hence that the myriad species are genetically unrelated and separate: one species is not descended from another, nor does one species imperceptibly merge with another; the species are discrete, that is—with troublesome exceptions—they are clearly and distinctly demarcated. To be sure, careful observers like Linnaeus (1707–1778) belatedly reckoned with the appearance of new species; these he explained as an effect of hybridizing.[1] Others, like Cuvier (1769–1832), accepted fossil remains as evidence of extinct species, even if he postulated general cataclysms or catastrophes to explain them. But these were only minor amendments to the orthodox doctrine as this was expounded, for example, by the Catholic Suarez (1548–1617), and movingly described in Milton's *Paradise Lost*. As late as the middle of the nineteenth century, one could encounter the view that fossil remains were not of animal or vegetable origin, but had been deposited in the earth by God—or Satan—to test the faith of man.

Traditional assumptions of this kind coincided nicely with the deliverances of common sense which readily testified to the fixity of living forms. Surely one can find no more striking example of constancy in nature than the sameness with which the species reproduce themselves. Within the memory of man all new generations of living things have been born with the traits of their ancestors. Occasionally sports and monstrosities remind us that nature may depart wildly from her accustomed course, but these, even if they survive, do not repeat themselves. Here and there, common sense stumbles upon the remains of some no longer extant type of organism, but these it explains more readily, as did Cuvier, by postulating great natural catastrophes that wiped out whole populations—an easy enough assumption for those familiar with nature's destructive vagaries—than by regarding strange fossils as progenitors of the species we know today.

---

[1] It was not until 1766, thirty-one years after his celebrated *Systema Naturae* first appeared, that Linnaeus abandoned his famous dictum: *nullae species novae*. "We reckon as many species as issued in pairs from the hands of the Creator," he had said. However, a few—Diderot, for example—did not accept the immutability of species.

Such, in large outline, was the prevalent view of the world at the close of the eighteenth century: an initial act of creation, a closed, timeless universe operating according to necessary law, the separateness and autonomy of man, the fixity of species. This view was contested by brilliant philosophers, as when Berkeley and Hume challenged its basic assumptions, but most thoughtful people found it satisfactory—until a series of developments in the nineteenth century rendered it untenable. The most significant of these by far was the advent of scientific evolutionism. The details of this great revolution in biology must be fully reviewed if some of the most important changes through which philosophy has passed in the last one hundred years are to be even partly understood.

However, it is a common error to suppose that the history of pure science is self-contained, so that great innovations are thought to follow from earlier scientific developments without reference to other tendencies in the history of ideas. This may be so for minor scientific discoveries, but major scientific reorientations of the kind associated with the name of Darwin are likely to be connected with other trends in the culture. Two of these—the cult of progress and the romantic movement—deserve special attention.

The Idea of Progress

An analysis of the idea of progress belongs properly to the philosophy of history for it is primarily a theory concerning the nature of historical change. The eighteenth century, stirred by great improvements in technology and rapid advances in the natural sciences, committed itself wholeheartedly and uncritically to the belief that society, if not indeed the cosmos, is steadily improving and moving inevitably toward a state of perfection. This was a new dogma, quite alien to the Greeks who regarded their golden age as in the past. The Greeks tended to think of change in terms of world cycles endlessly repeating themselves. Similarly the medieval period, dominated by the idea of Providence and Predestination and man's fall from a state of original grace, was hardly receptive to the idea of progress.

Indeed, the Cartesian-Newtonian outlook, which regarded the natural world as analagous to a great machine, hardly provided metaphysical assumptions consistent with a concept which implies qualitative transformations. The idea of progress does, of course, imply such transformations—in a direction involving improvement—but it would be hard to understand what was meant by a machine that underwent such development. As we have seen, machines by definition are characterized by regularity of movement, sameness, periodicity. However, since the system of nature was not yet conceived as encompassing man and society, there was no great theoretical obstacle to viewing human history in terms of the idea of progress. The idea was directly—and perhaps inseparably—related to the new sense of mastery over nature and control over his own future with which western man became imbued after the seventeenth century. A typical expression may be found in the words of Priestley:

. . . men will make their situation in this world abundantly more easy and comfortable; they will probably prolong their existence in it, and will grow daily more happy . . . Thus whatever was the beginning of this world, the end will be glorious and paradisiacal, beyond what our imaginations can now conceive.[2]

Later, Herbert Spencer wrote:

. . . the ultimate development of the ideal man is logically certain—as certain as any conclusion in which we place the most implicit faith; for instance that all men will die. . . . Progress, therefore, is not an accident, but a necessity.[3]

Exponents of the idea of progress begged the question of value, failing to understand that at the very least "improvement" and "perfectibility" require some agreement on standards of value to be meaningful. They were guilty of the most extravagant optimism, and often fell into the vulgar error of confusing progress with mere increase in size or speed—a common enough confusion in America today. Even worse was a disposition to identify progress with the prosperity of merchants and manufacturers—they became indeed the most zealous propagandists for the idea—and to ignore the welfare of the rest of society. Some even argued, as did Spencer, that, since progress is a law of nature, social legislation is nothing but tinkering and meddling; nature should be left to take its course.

Today, after two wars separated by a prolonged depression, with the shadow of the atomic bomb hovering over us, we are not as optimistic as our forefathers of the eighteenth and nineteenth centuries, and probably a good deal more self-critical. Pessimists among us are prone to dismiss the idea of progress as an obsolete myth if not a transparent hoax. However, there is much in the idea of progress that is enduring, and to dismiss it as the dross of a class overanxious to vindicate itself, or an age intoxicated with its own achievements is to neglect some fundamental insights. Quite apart from the important fact that it is inspired by and reflects the conviction that man can be master of his own fate, the idea of progress involves a recognition of the proposition that the world will not be the same as it was or is, and hence an acceptance of the idea of novelty. Consequently, what has yet to come takes on new significance, so that the idea of progress is associated with an orientation toward the future rather than the past. All this is typically and even uniquely modern in spirit. More relevantly, the

[2] *Selections*, ed. by Iva Brown (University Park: Pennsylvania State University Press, 1962), pp. 152–153.
[3] *Social Statics* (London: John Chapman, 1851), pp. 64–65.

evolutionary principle could not make sense except in a climate of opinion at least partly conditioned to accept the idea that change may involve more than mere shift of location in space, and more than the kind of cyclical transformations through which organisms pass; change may also manifest itself in the completely new. Neither the age of Plato nor the "century of genius" to which Descartes and Newton belonged was hospitable to such an idea, much as people may take it for granted today. The new climate was at least partly prepared by the idea of progress.

Romanticism

The complex and conflicting attitudes and tendencies known as the romantic movement came into prominence in the first half of the nineteenth century. Romanticism was primarily a protest against the mechanism, the intellectualism, and what it called the crass utilitarianism and narrow egoism of the eighteenth century Enlightenment. It saw the French Revolution—which enthroned Science and Reason—as an example of the evil excesses to which Reason can go when unanchored by feeling, sentiment, love of tradition, and a sense of the continuity of history.[4] The cold impersonal terms in which the mechanist describes reality were dismissed by the romanticists as a distortion of nature. Nature in its fullness and variety cannot be reduced to a set of mathematical equations. Even physics, declared Goethe, "must describe itself as something distinct from mathematics." The romanticists condemned what they called the "dissection of Nature" by the Newtonians and Cartesians whose analytical method breaks living wholes into lifeless fragments and whose uniformities and generalizations efface the individuality and variety of the experienced world. Wordsworth's lines are famous:

> Our meddling intellect
> Mis-shapes the beauteous forms of things:
> —We murder to dissect.

And Keats wrote disconsolately of the regnant mechanistic philosophy:

> . . . Do not all charms fly
> At the mere touch of cold philosophy?
> There was an awful rainbow once in heaven:
> We know her woof, her texture; she is given
> In the dull catalogue of common things.
> Philosophy will clip an angel's wings,
> Conquer all mysteries by rule and line,
> Empty the haunted air; and gnomed mine . . .

---

[4] Among the many "conflicting tendencies" referred to above is the archromantic, Rousseau, serving (though not by choice) as patron saint of the French Revolution; and Spinoza, who worshipped mathematics, evoking the admiration of the romantics, who despised it.

Herder, German prophet of romanticism, wrote books prompting Goethe to exult that nature is a "compost heap teeming with life." It was in "concrete" organic rather than abstract mechanistic terms that romanticists insisted the real world be viewed. And if this was true of reality in general, so, too, was it true of society; neither can society be regarded as a mere aggregate of atomic individuals: "those who are living, those who are dead, and those who are to be born"—to use the words of Burke— comprise with their traditions and institutions an organic unity, a whole that is more than the mere sum of its parts.

Such a living whole, whether it be DeMaistre's royalist and Catholic France, or Wordsworth's Nature must be grasped through our feelings and sensibilities rather than through Reason; for Reason deals in pale and lifeless abstractions and expresses itself, in practical affairs, in a meticulous computation of interests. And it is, indeed, the emotional and irrational side of man that romanticism stresses, scorning the rational, calculating creatures glorified by the French *philosophes* and the English classical economists. Man is ruled—and better ruled—by his heart than by his head. For a deeper insight into the nature of man we must reckon with his passions and sentiments, not his intellect. Descartes' *Je pense, donc je suis* becomes for the romanticist *Je sens, donc je suis.* Moreover, man's moral, religious, and aesthetic experiences provide a better insight, not merely into the nature of man—this might readily be conceded—but into the nature of *reality*, than is obtained from the experience embraced by what we call science.

One is tempted to raise questions. Had the Age of Reason made a cult of science, had science degenerated into scient*ism* and, if so, was the romantic movement no more than a healthy corrective tendency? Was it a way, peculiar to the nineteenth century, of responding to the limitations of a too mechanistic science? Or is romanticism better described as the perennial recourse of an embattled folklore summoning its best minds to resist the inroads of science, by challenging the very assumptions on which science is based? Is the romantic spirit essentially hostile to science or is it an attitude which contributes, for all its defects, to a more enlightened folklore and an amplified science? Or, are we perhaps dealing with another kind of competition, that between the scientific and the aesthetic ideal; even more, with the alternation of the human spirit between its love of order—the orderliness of Greek classic art (against which romanticism is also a protest) or of a mathematical system—and the spirit's own spontaneity, waywardness, even madness?

These are provocative issues the exploration of which must be left to others. Here it is more appropriate to turn briefly to German Idealism in which the ideas and tendencies associated with romanticism received their most elaborate formulation.

Absolute Idealism

German Idealism dominated the philosophy of the first half of the nineteenth century not only on the continent, but in Britain and America. The opaque prose and cloudy obscurities so dear to the German philosophers of that day are difficult to summarize, but a brief account is important to an understanding of the period immediately preceding the advent of Darwin. Such an account requires us to go back at least as far as Immanuel Kant, one of the towering figures in the whole history of philosophy.

No philosopher ever strove more perseveringly to establish a basis for both science and the faith of his fathers than did Kant in his monumental works, *The Critique of Pure Reason*, *The Critique of Practical Reason*, and *The Critique of Judgment*. If, as we have assumed, the reconciliation of science and accepted belief has been historically the main task of philosophers, Kant performed this role in a profound and original way. Kant had read the works of David Hume who has appropriately been called the prince of skeptics. He agreed with much of the brilliant Scot's negative analysis, commenting in a famous phrase that Hume had "roused him from his dogmatic slumber." Hume had argued, it will be recalled (see Part II, p. 255), that experience fails to disclose those necessary connections in nature on which the principle of causality and all natural law are commonly thought to depend. Neither does experience substantiate the claims, extravagant or modest, of metaphysics and theology. If experience fails us, so too must reason, if we mean by reason some special faculty for apprehending truth above and beyond experience.[5] There is no such alternative source of truth. Reason does indeed yield necessary truths, as in logic and mathematics, but these express the relations of ideas and hence cannot tell us anything, such as that events have causes, that God exists, etc. Truths are necessary only if their opposite is inconceivable and, while it is inconceivable that circles should be square or that uncles not have nieces or nephews, it is quite conceivable that a billiard ball will when dropped hit the ceiling, as it is conceivable that the sun should stand still, and as it is—the "ontological" argument notwithstanding—that God does not exist.[6]

If, then, we are unable to find through experience or apprehend through reason those necessary connections in nature on which causal relationships and the rule of law—not to mention much of metaphysics and theology—appear to depend, it seemed to Kant that the whole basis for relying on science as a source of truth about nature has been destroyed. If falling ob-

---

[5] Cf. 367–368.
[6] Cf. 194–197.

jects are under no compulsion to obey the law of gravity, how may we make predictions about them? If there is no necessary connection between heat and the boiling of water how can we count on water boiling the next time a pot is put on the fire? In a brilliant, but ponderously elaborate and difficult, argument Kant sought to restore the basis of science. His argument is too complex to detain us here. It is more pertinent to note that, having established, as he thought, the competence of science to give us certain knowledge of the natural world, Kant then went on to argue that when, as in traditional theology and metaphysics, reason attempts to go beyond what man can experience, that is, beyond what science can confirm, it reaches a dead end. This is evidenced by reason's involvement in what he called *antinomies* in which mutually contradictory propositions can be demonstrated as valid. Thus, it is possible, Kant contended, to prove both (the *thesis*), that the world must have a beginning in time and a limit in space and (the *antithesis*) that the world can have no beginning in time nor limit in space; or, another instance, that there must be a first cause (the *thesis*), and that a first cause is inconceivable (the *antithesis*). Hence Kant called these *dialectical* assertions: "because the thesis, as well as the antithesis, can be shown by equally clear, evident, and irresistible proofs."[7] Such assertions are not gratuitous; Kant gave reasons for contending that the nature of the understanding is such that it must make such assertions even though the outcome is inevitably bafflement and frustration. Clearly, Reason lives in the shadow of Sisyphus. Kant calls it the "transcendental illusion."

At this point a decisive qualification must be noted, which lies at the heart of Kant's philosophy. While, for Kant, *theoretical* reason may not indulge in theological or metaphysical speculation that carries it beyond the bounds of experience without becoming involved in contradictions, certain metaphysical or theological assumptions are essential if our moral experience is to make sense. We do have such moral experience. Therefore the nature of reality must be such as to make this experience possible, even though our "theoretical" reason cannot tell us what this nature is. We must make certain *assumptions* about man and God and reality. We cannot test these assumptions as we do propositions—such as that bodies expand when heated—nor can we demonstrate them—as we do the proposition that the sum of the angles of a triangle is equal to two right angles. But, unless we postulate them, the moral imperatives by which we guide or ought to guide our conduct become meaningless. Our "practical" reason thus leads us to them, even though they may not be known to our "theoretical" reason. Such are the propositions that man is capable of exercising free will, that he is a member of a spiritual order, that he is

---

[7] *The Prolegomena to Any Future Metaphysics* (New York: Liberal Arts Press, 1951), p. 87.

immortal, and that there is a God who is able to guarantee his immortality.

The complex argument by means of which Kant reaches this conclusion is not important for our present purpose. What is important is his contention that man must seek through his moral—others were to stress the religious and aesthetic—experience, and not through the kind of knowledge on which logic and mathematics and science are based, for the most important of all truths. For Kant, it must be remembered, these truths cannot be demonstrated. They can only be postulated; they are articles of *faith*. One of the most famous phrases in philosophical literature is his declaration that "I have . . . found it necessary to deny *knowledge* [of God, freedom, and immortality], in order to make room for *faith*."[8] Here, in stressing the limitations of reason and affirming an indispensable role for faith, Kant provided the philosophical taproot that nourished much of the romantic movement. In this he shares responsibility with Rousseau whose emphasis on immediate faith and feeling had avowedly influenced Kant as well as the romanticists who followed him. Kant would have been the last to reject reason—as stressed above, he sought only to confine it to its proper sphere—and hence he would have shunned the sheer irrationalism to which much of the romantic movement succumbed. But he gave the rejection of reason a decisive impetus, the kind of impetus that made it possible for a Schopenhauer, who thought of himself as a true Kantian, to substitute for reason the endless desiring and striving of blind will as the key to a true understanding of reality.

Two points must be noted. First, although Kant limited the theoretical understanding (science) to a knowledge of *phenomena*, that is, to a knowledge of that which presents itself or appears, he was not a *phenomenalist*. This is a term that may properly be associated with Hume, who said, as we have seen, that there is nothing and no evidence for anything except that which presents itself to the senses, which appears. Kant believed, whether convincingly or unconvincingly, that there is more than phenomena, that there is a reality lying beyond, of which phenomena are only an appearance, even though we cannot know what that reality is—only that it is. To this extent Kant was a *realist*—in the fourth sense of realism outlined in Part I.[9] He believed that there is a reality independent of what we experience, even though we are not able to say what that reality is like—not even that it is spatial or temporal or a substance or involved in causal relationships. These are attributes of *phenomena* (the objects of scientific knowledge) and as such are "forms" imposed by us as knowers on the content of experience. But, although they are therefore creations of the mind (or sensibility) in organizing (synthesizing) the content of experi-

---

[8] *Critique of Pure Reason*, trans. by Norman Kemp Smith (London: Macmillan and Co., 1929), p. 29.

[9] Cf. p. 84.

ence and are in this respect mental or "ideal,"[10] Kant is insistent that the *noumenal*, the thing-in-itself, is not mind-created or ideal or anything else that we can imagine or surmise.

Second, it must be remembered that, for Kant, all attempts at describing the reality beyond experience, which he called the thing-in-itself, must perish in a dialectical cul-de-sac where opposite statements are equally demonstrable.

The Idealists, better called Absolute Idealists, who followed him— Fichte, Schelling, Hegel—ignored both of these Kantian teachings. Kant's insistence on the active creative role of mind in synthesizing or organizing the raw manifold or brute content of experience[11] was exaggerated into the claim that *all* reality is a creation of or manifestation of or objectification of mind or ego in one or other of its characteristic activities—moral, aesthetic, or rational. And, especially in the case of Hegel, that same dialectical conflict, which for Kant warned that thought had exceeded its bounds and come to a halt, became the very basis of the rational process. The dialectical process is nothing less than the progressive development of what Hegel called the Absolute Spirit or Ego manifesting itself in successive stages from the particular and least inclusive to the universal and most inclusive. Insofar, it is also a progress from the abstract to the concrete, since those same independent, unitary, homogeneous existences or atoms or "least parts" which the mechanist treats as ultimate reality and the building blocks of everything else are mere abstractions; only complex wholes are concrete—and therefore real. Since, for Hegel, the order of ideas is the same as the order of things, this progress is both a logical and ontological one, and it is dialectical in a curiously creative way: each earlier, lower level, because it is partial and limited and fragmentary, that is to say, an only imperfect expression of a later, higher, more inclusive idea or reality, develops contradictions. Every *thesis* thus generates its *antithesis*. But this does not paralyze thought or balk development or halt history; on the contrary, it drives thought or transforms existence or moves human history—these for Hegel are all manifestations of the same process—in the direction of finding a *synthesis* in which the contradictions are as it were taken up, contained, and reconciled. But since this synthesis, although more inclusive, is still only partial and limited, contradiction in the form

---

[10] They are both subjective and objective: the former in that they are imposed by the knower on the content of experience, expressing, as Kant said, "the conditions under which alone we are able to apprehend or understand the object"; the latter, in that the object of experience can be had by us in no other way since they are conditions governing all knowing subjects and hence are hardly discretionary.

[11] Kant's view here is in contrast to that of the eighteenth-century sensationalists who tended to regard mind as passive (like a sealing wax) in receiving sense impressions. His stress on an active, creative role for mind is one of his more enduring insights.

of a new thesis and antithesis breaks out, only to be reconciled at a still more inclusive level in a new synthesis, and so on and on until the all-inclusive, the concrete universal, the Absolute, is attained. "In this way," Hegel tells us, Reason or the "World-Spirit" unfolds itself, which is to say, becomes conscious of itself, in a development or progression that proceeds by triads, often described as a great waltz-like movement, from thesis to antithesis to synthesis. This, to repeat, is as true of the existent as of the conceptual, since in the Hegelian system they are indentical: "The real is the rational and the rational is the real."

It follows that nothing has meaning or reality save as a contribution to or part of the whole or, since the whole is in process, as a "moment" in the development of the whole, a totality which, since it contains all these passing moments can be known only in terms of its past, that is, under the form of history. "History is mind clothing itself with the form of events . . ."[12] The *history* of the Real is its *nature*; time, to borrow a phrase from Woodbridge, enters into its substance. That is why "Philosophy concerns itself only with the glory of the Idea mirroring itself in the History of the World." And "that which interests it [Philosophy] is the recognition of the process of development which the Idea has passed through in realizing itself. . . ."[13]

Here, greatly abbreviated, are the major premises of romanticism: the rejection of a mechanistic order for an interpretation of reality in personal or "spiritual" terms, the stress on interrelatedness so that everything is what it is by virtue of its relationship to the whole of which it is a part, the view of reality as involved in progressive self-development, the assertion that reality is inexplicable except in terms of its past because its past is in a definitive sense contained in it. While Hegel was critical of romanticism, his whole grandiose system was rooted in it.

The hostility of romanticism, not merely to mechanistic science, but to science in general, was noted earlier. Romanticism, it was suggested, could be the shining shield with which tradition parries the deadly thrusts of science. If this is so, the paradox is that nineteenth-century romanticism paved the way for a new and great scientific triumph.

Just as the seventeenth-century view of reality as a Machine suggests an act of creation and hence an instantaneous origin, so, as has been seen, the romantic view of reality as an Organism or as an objectification of a Self or Spirit or *"Geist"* suggests growth and development. The past of a machine, unless there have been "outside influences," is the same as its present, and hence to know its present is to know it fully; nothing is added to our

---

[12] *Philosophy of Right*, trans. by T. M. Knox (London: Oxford, 1942), p. 217.

[13] G. W. F. Hegel, *The Philosophy of History*, trans. by J. Sibree (New York: Dover, 1956), p. 457.

knowledge of it by examining its history. (In the strict sense it has no history.) Not so an organism. What it was does differ from what it has become, so that much may be learned about what it now is by turning to its past. More than this. The past of organisms—through conditioning, memory, etc.—enters into and is constitutive of them in a sense that does not seem to be true of a machine. To understand an organism fully, therefore, we need to see it in another dimension—in *time* as well as in space. The *organic* point of view may thus be seen to involve an *historical* orientation.

However, the romanticist arrives at such an orientation by more than one route. If we are to discard what Burke called the "fallible and feeble contrivances of our reason," our recourse in the realm of social policy must be to the "wisdom of the ages." The *rational* approach to laws and institutions is by reference to whether they are working badly or well, that is to say, in terms of their consequences in weal or woe. Reason is in this sense utilitarian (if not "crassly" so), for the rational man is one who tries to realize his purpose in the most efficient way, and he may well ask, therefore, if institutions promote or subvert the ends they are intended to serve. But if rational tests are to be ignored or slighted, the basic justification of institutions is that they have always been, they have a long history, they are the work of our revered ancestors who have handed them down from the past. It is no accident that so many of the romanticists idealized the Middle Ages; most of them venerated tradition. Historicism, as it has been called, and romanticism go hand in hand. Here—whatever else we may have—is the emphasis on time, on origins, on slow development, that the evolutionists needed.

The sequence of ideas is well described by Ernst Cassirer:

How was it possible for evolutionary history to attain to such value and significance in the biological thinking of the nineteenth century that all else disappeared beside it—all other interests and problems being swallowed up, as it were. Was it merely the weight of the empirical proofs advanced by Darwin that caused the scale to turn? It is known how incomplete his material was at first, and how disappointing the findings of paleontology still are . . . That such lacunae should have been readily and cheerfully overlooked, however, is explained by a deep-seated characteristic of general intellectual history in the nineteenth century.

This century presents the first encounter and first reckoning between the two great ideals of knowledge. The ideal of the mathematical sciences, which had engrossed and dominated the seventeenth century, was paramount no longer. Since the time of Herder and romanticism another mentality and spiritual force had been opposing it with increasing vigor and conviction. Here, for the first time, the *primacy of history* was proclaimed by both philosophy and science.[14]

---

[14] *Problem of Knowledge* (New Haven: Yale, 1950), p. 170.

Time is a passage from the past through the present to the future. The idea of progress gave man a new sense of the future. The romantic movement imbued him with a sense of the past. The outcome was a new consciousness of the category of time—not clock-time, which is a convention, but time as a dimension of reality, as an essential aspect of the experienced world. Without such a concept of time Darwin and his precursors could not have thought—at any rate, could not have thought clearly—in terms of the evolutionary principle.

Scientific Precursors of Darwin

If these were the tendencies in general intellectual history that nourished evolutionary theory and encouraged the reception of Darwinism, there were developments within the history of science that were also noteworthy. Before turning to these more obvious influences it must be emphasized that Darwin did not invent the *idea* of evolution. Also, it should be noted that there is a great difference between evolution as a speculative idea and as a scientific generalization. Speculation, while it may be characterized by shrewd insights and result in lucky guesses, is content with meager and insufficient evidence, and hence is merely surmise and conjecture; in science, truth is not enough, it must have been found by proper methods and procedures.

Dim premonitions of evolutionary change may be found in the cosmogonies of preliterate societies. Speculation about evolution goes back at least as far as the Greeks who had a word for this, as, proverbially, they had for everything else. The Roman poet-philosopher, Lucretius, shrewdly commented that:

> Nature she changeth all, compelleth all
> To transformation . . .
> The nature of the whole wide world, and earth
> Taketh one status after other. And what
> She bore of old, she now can bear no longer,
> And what she never bore, she can today.[15]

But, as with his atomic theory, Lucretius' basis is still speculative. In 1749, over one hundred years before the publication of *Origin of Species,* the great naturalist, Buffon, wrote that nature "is not a fixed thing, a static being." He even dared suggest that, if it were not for the contrary authority of the Bible, one might suppose a common origin for man and monkey—a suggestion which, having no stomach for martyrdom, he later withdrew. The concluding words of the recantation forced on him by the theological

---

[15] *Of the Nature of Things,* trans. by W. E. Leonard (Everyman edition), Book V, pp. 221–222. Cf. H. F. Osborn, *From the Greek to Darwin* (New York: Scribner's, 1929) for an historical account of evolutionary theory.

faculty of the Sorbonne are interesting: "I abandon everything in my book respecting the formation of the earth, and generally all which may be contrary to the narrative of Moses." Notwithstanding, by the end of the eighteenth century the "transmutation" or "development" theory, as it was then known, was advocated independently by Charles Darwin's grandfather, Erasmus Darwin, by Geoffrey St. Hilaire, and by that many-sided German genius, Goethe. With them, Hooke (1635-1703), Ray (1627-1705), and Maupertuis (1698-1759) deserve honorable mention.

Herbert Spencer, in a famous article written in 1852, came as close as anyone of prominence to anticipating the ideas of Darwin, even originating the expression "survival of the fittest," although he limited his speculation to human populations. Indeed, the classical political economy for which he became the most doctrinaire spokesman, while it never attained to an evolutionary view in its treatment of social institutions, was in a sense Darwinian before Darwin. The stress of Adam Smith and Ricardo on competition and the emphasis in the economic tradition in general on scarcity surely justifies Lord Keynes' remark that the principle of the survival of the fittest was "a vast generalization of Ricardian economics."

However, it was the French naturalist Lamarck (1744–1829) who, despite his inadequacies, may be fairly said to have initiated the scientific discussion of evolution. In Lamarck's *Philosophie Zoologique* (1809) the genetic approach to living species begins to acquire a solid foundation in fact. Discredited as his reliance on the inheritance of acquired traits may be, his search for a systematic explanation of how variability in species comes about must be regarded as a bold, pioneering effort. But the great impetus to evolutionary theory was to come from the physical rather than the life sciences.

Evolutionary theory was already asserting itself in the physical sciences as early as the publication of Laplace's celebrated *Système du Monde* in 1796, in which creationism was rejected for the view that the solar system has evolved from a rotating mass of incandescent gas. Kant had suggested a similar idea in 1775, although Laplace does not appear to have been aware of it. It is reported that Laplace, reproached by Napoleon for having no mention of the Creator in a book purporting to deal with the origins of the universe, responded: "I have no need for that hypothesis."

It was inevitable that the theories of Laplace should direct attention to the origins of the earth, whose characteristic features continued to be explained by reference to cataclysms suggested in the biblical cosmogonies. James Hutton, the "father" of modern geology, in his *Theory of the Earth,* (1785) and Sir Charles Lyell in his famous *Principles of Geology* (1830–1832) asserted the contrary. Hutton, though he never fully freed himself from the older cataclysmic theories, declared that he could find "no traces of a beginning nor signs of an end." Both Hutton and Lyell contended that, not special acts, but natural processes still taking place, such as erosion and sedimentation, account for the formation of the earth's surface. This contention, formulated by Hutton as the principle of *uniformitarianism*, was simply, in his words, that "The past history of our globe must be explained by what can be seen happening now."

Now the forces presently shaping the surface of the earth operate very slowly, so that the principle of uniformitarianism suggests an antiquity for the earth beyond anything even remotely imagined by the creationists. ". . . confined notions in regard to the quantity of past time, have tended, more than any other prepossessions, to retard the progress of sound theoretical views in geology. . . ," declared Lyell, "and until we habituate ourselves to contemplate the possibility of an indefinite lapse of ages . . . we shall be in danger of forming most erroneous and partial views in geology."[17] It was precisely such a vast span of time that Darwin needed before the evolutionary hypothesis could make sense in biology. Hutton came a generation before his time, but Lyell profoundly influenced Darwin, and Lyell's work may be said to have finally embarked science on the genetic study of nature.

Selected Readings

Bury, J. B., *The Idea of Progress*, New York: Macmillan, 1932. (Also Dover paperback.)

Eiseley, Loren, *Darwin's Century*, New York: Doubleday, 1958. (Also Anchor Books paperback.)

Hegel, G. W. F., *The Philosophy of History*, "Introduction," trans. by J. Sibree, New York: Dover Press, 1956. (Paperback.)

Mead, G. H., *Movements of Thought in the Nineteenth Century*, ed. by M. H. Moore, Chicago: University of Chicago Press, 1936, pp. 51–153.

Randall, J. H., Jr., *The Making of the Modern Mind*, Boston: Houghton Mifflin, 1940, chaps. XVI–XVIII.

Scoon, Robert, "The Rise and Impact of Evolutionary Ideas" in *Evolutionary Thought in America*, ed. by Stow Persons, New Haven: Yale University Press, 1950.

---

[17] *Principles of Geology* (London: John Murray, 1833), Vol. III, p. 97.

CHAPTER 17

The Darwinian Heresy

The Reception of Darwin

The appearance of Darwin's *Origin of Species* in 1859 marks a major reorientation in the intellectual history of western man. For science it was a breakthrough comparable in significance to the appearance of Newton's *Principia*. Some books have been more widely read; few, if any, have had such impact. Henceforth, men saw themselves and the world in which they lived in terms of their agreement or disagreement with Darwin. For those who disagreed, Darwinism posed a threat to which they often responded with disproportionate fury; for those who agreed, Darwin's great work seemed to banish confusion, dispel doubt, and raise the mind to a new level of understanding.

It is difficult for the contemporary student to grasp the magnitude of Darwin's departure from established belief. After all, opinion had been prepared by the activities of Lamarck and the then anonymous author of the widely read and debated *Vestiges of the Natural History of Creation* —even if Darwin disparaged them—as by Lyell, Spencer, and others. Indeed, evolution was so much "in the air"[1] that Darwin was nearly pre-

---

[1] However, Darwin's own testimony is striking: "It has sometimes been said that the success of the 'Origin' proved 'that the subject was in the air,' or 'that men's minds were prepared for it.' I do not think that this is strictly true, for I occasionally sounded not a few naturalists, and never happened to come across a single one who seemed to doubt about the permanence of species." [*Life and Letters of Charles Darwin*, ed. by Francis Darwin (London: John Murray, 1888), Vol. I, p. 87.]

empted by Alfred Russell Wallace who, laboring quite independently (in the remote Celebes) formulated the very principles for which Darwin has become celebrated. We receive a hint of the enormity of Darwin's heresy when we find him adding, after confiding in 1844 to his friend Joseph Hooker that he was "almost" convinced that species are not immutable, "it is like confessing a murder."

This was no farfetched comparison. The outcry of protest and the volume of savage abuse which *Origin of Species* evoked from scientists as well as prelates was torrential. Dr. Whewell, Master of Trinity and a historian of science, refused to permit a copy in the Trinity College library. Darwin's professor of geology, the Reverend Adam Sedgwick, declared that his former student had betrayed a "demoralized understanding" and suggested that Darwin was "deep in the mire of folly." Wilberforce, Bishop of Oxford, wrote in the *Quarterly Review* (July, 1860) of Darwin's "jungle of fanciful assumption," his "flimsy speculation," and his "utterly rotten fabric of guess and speculation."[2] In America, Louis Agassiz, Harvard's great naturalist, more charitably believed that Darwin would outlive his "mania."

Everything seemed threatened: the authority of the Bible, the purposefulness of the universe, the autonomy of man, the efficacy of God. "... years had to pass away," wrote T. H. Huxley, "before misrepresentation, ridicule, and denunciation, ceased to be the most notable constituents of the majority of multitudinous criticisms of his work which poured from the press."[3] True, there were also formidable men to champion Darwin: Huxley himself and Lyell and Hooker and Spencer in England, Asa Gray and John Fiske in America, Haeckel in Germany. Thanks to them the battle was successfully joined. The smoke has only recently cleared.

The centennial of the publication of *Origin of Species* was celebrated less than a decade ago. By this time generations of students have had ample time to explore its implications and to understand that they required a new philosophy of man and of the universe. Such an understanding did not come easily, but today all philosophers would agree with William James that to revert to pre-Darwinian thinking is to be guilty of an "absolute anachronism."

An historian recently observed that there are events in the life of nations, such as the American Civil War and the French Revolution, cutting their history in two so that nothing is ever the same again. Such events are as close as history comes to presenting us with a clean break between the past and the present: the past is irretrievably gone in a way that would not have seemed possible a short interval before and everything associated with it is suddenly antiquated; the present, with everything in it that earlier

---

[2] *Ibid.*, Vol. II, p. 325.
[3] *Ibid.*, pp. 182–183.

had seemed extravagant and forbidding, is clamorously upon us, exacting recognition even from the most reluctant. If this is true of the history of nations, it is also true of the history of ideas where the appearance of *Origin of Species* was precisely such an event. Thereafter, as the following pages are intended to suggest, nothing was the same.

The Main Tenets

The main tenet of the evolutionary principle as it applies to biology is that species have a common origin and are thereby changing and related. The immutability of species is denied and so, too, is the idea that they were separately created. Over vast stretches of time complex organisms have derived from simpler organisms and ultimately from the simplest microscopic organisms. Thus species change in form: new species come into being; existing species become extinct. This is the minimal claim.

In this limited formulation, the evolutionary principle embraces no view concerning the origin of the simplest forms of life, that is to say, of life itself; neither does it decree concerning the origin of man. These are much more controversial issues, consideration of which may be deferred. Indeed, as thus formulated, the evolutionary principle, after surmounting the first wave of indignation, might have affronted none except fundamentalists, who correctly find it incompatible with a literal interpretation of the Book of Genesis and a threat to the authority of the Bible. As for a theistic point of view as such, it is a matter of indifference whether the forms of life are changing or fixed; Deity might express itself as appropriately by initiating an evolutionary process as by producing separate, distinct, and immutable species.

Whether it considers evolution in this restricted sense or in the more general sense yet to be discussed, science, as distinguished from speculation, must deal with two questions: (1) How do species vary; what accounts for the appearance and disappearance of species, that is to say, for speciation or the process of variation by which species become differentiated? (2) What is the evidence that species vary?

An answer to the second question requires the gathering of facts: that whales have buried hind limbs; that, in spite of markedly different superficial appearance, the bone structure of the walking limb of a dog, the flying limb of a bird, and the swimming limb of a seal are similar enough to suggest a close relationship; that extinct trilobites are built much like lobsters, and dinosaurs like lizards; that gill slits occur in the fetus of the mammal; and so on and on. To be sure, the procedure involves more than mere fact finding; most of the facts cited in *Origin of Species* would not have been noted or—if noted—their relationship to one another, including their common import and bearing, would not have been appreciated without a guiding hypothesis—in this case the theory of common origin. When Darwin declares: "I worked on true Baconian principles, and without any theory collected facts on a wholesale scale . . ."[4] we may fairly suspect him of oversimplifying his own procedure. Isolated and detached facts are of little interest to science; of itself, for example, the fact that man has a rudimentary tail is hardly worth noting; viewed in the light of the theory of common descent it takes on great significance.

The procedure by which science has established *that* evolution takes place is called *empirical*. Now, in this narrow sense of the term, knowledge that is called empirical is of a rather low order. Thus, in medicine we often refer to empirical or *merely* empirical remedies such as cortisone in the treatment of arthritis. In the absence of more knowledge it is, to be sure, a great advance to discover *that* cortisone relieves arthritis. But until we know *how* cortisone produces this effect our knowledge is greatly handicapped. To know the causal relationship involved is to be able to alter the conditions so that, for example, a crude remedy may be purified of unnecessary, and even harmful, ingredients. A knowledge of causal relationships enormously increases our efficiency because we are in a position to predict more accurately and to control. It is to such a higher level of knowledge that science always aspires. Such knowledge is also empirical in the broader sense that it is based on experience—so that the use of the term empirical for one type of knowledge and not another is unfortunate and confusing; yet the distinction between the two levels of knowledge is needed. This brings one to the first of the two questions posed for science, for the knowledge *that* evolution occurs is bound to be superficial and precarious, that is, *merely* empirical in the narrow sense, until we have learned *how* it occurs.

Charles Darwin towers above his contemporaries and is reckoned one of the great geniuses in the history of science because of the way in which he addressed himself to both questions, the question of fact and the question of cause. Few men have been more avid for facts, and the painstaking way in which he marshaled them to prove his point—from geology, from paleontology, from comparative anatomy, from embryology, from accumulated knowledge about plant and animal breeding—is a model of scientific scruple. So, too, was the meticulous way in which he reckoned with seemingly contrary evidence. But the facts, however multitudinous,

---

[4] *Ibid.*, Vol. I, p. 83. Earlier in the same autobiographical account he says, ". . . I worked to the utmost during the voyage from the mere pleasure of investigation, and from my strong desire to add a few facts to the great mass of facts in Natural Science." (p. 65.) Just the same, Darwin had the first volume of Lyell's *Principles* with him on the *Beagle*. He studiously addressed himself to it and, we may assume, to the interpretative principles it set forth, even though "sagacious" Henslow, the geologist who called the volume to his attention, warned him "on no account to accept the views therein advocated." (Vol. I, pp. 72–73.)

were mute until Darwin made them eloquent with an explanation of the mechanism of evolution which he called natural selection. It is to this explanation of how evolution takes place that, strictly speaking, the name Darwinism is applied. In the form that Darwin gave it, the explanation is simple enough—so much so that, after reading *Origin of Species*, Huxley exclaimed, "How extremely stupid not to have thought of that!" Moreover, Darwin came upon the idea of natural selection quite fortuitously (as, by a striking coincidence, did Wallace) by reading "for amusement" [sic] Malthus' *Essay on Population*.

Reduced to its essentials Malthus' *Essay* notes the overwhelming disparity between man's capacity to reproduce and the capacity of the environment to sustain his increased population. According to Malthus, man —in whom he was exclusively interested—can double his population every generation in a geometric progression whereas the resources on which he depends for sustenance can be increased only in arithmetic progression, that is, by increments of constant value. What Darwin thought of the melancholy and controversial social and economic conclusions derived by Malthus from this disparity is unimportant; what is of enormous significance is his realization that the disparity which Malthus had noted applied to *all* living things. The capacity of animal organisms and plants to increase their number is enormous. Nevertheless, over a period of time their number remains constant—limited by the availability of subsistence (and space). Clearly, a struggle for survival must ensue which will be won by those most favorably endowed. There is, in other words, a natural selection.

"In October 1838 . . . I happened to read . . . 'Malthus on Population'" writes Darwin, "and being well prepared to appreciate the struggle for existence which everywhere goes on from long-continued observation of the habits of animals and plants, it at once struck me that under these circumstances favourable variations would tend to be preserved, and unfavourable ones to be destroyed. The result of this would be the formation of new species. Here then I had at last got a theory by which to work."[5]

As Darwin developed the theory, he began by postulating "chance" variations, later known as mutations, of a type which the parent transmits to its offspring. They must be distinguished in kind from changes which, since they are not heritable, affect the individual organism only and have no place in an explanation of the origin of species. Darwin noted that, in the nature of the case, some of these variations would give the organism an advantage in the struggle for survival (or in the competition for a mate), others—indeed most—would handicap it. An organism inheriting or undergoing a variation having survival value would live to mate and transmit this character to its offspring and the variation would thereby be preserved. The accumulation of such variations—Darwin has been

[5] *Ibid.*, Vol. I, p. 83.

vindicated in thinking of them as small rather than large variations—accounts for the differences that distinguish species. It is in this way that the myriad species are explained as products of natural selection.

Now Darwin's theory of natural selection is an oversimplification which has only recently been adequately supplemented. The science of genetics was unknown to Darwin and his contemporaries. Darwin knew nothing of the distinction between germ cells and body cells and hence nothing of the role of germ cells in the transmission of hereditary traits. Although the great pioneering work of Mendel was published in 1865—in time to be known to Darwin—Mendel was an obscure Austrian monk and the provincial journal in which Mendel's discoveries were first reported understandably escaped the attention of many learned men. It has been argued that, in any case, the prevailing interests in science were not such as to encourage the exploitation of Mendel's experiments. Consequently, Darwin was ignorant of the particular nature of hereditary traits: that they are unitary and indivisible (like atoms) and do not blend with each other (like paints); and that the gene for any given character will persist in the hereditary makeup of a group of organisms even though the character itself (phenotype) is not manifest.[6] On the assumption accepted by Darwin that hereditary traits blend with each other, it is difficult if not impossible to see why the small variations postulated by him are not "swamped," much as a dab of red paint would lose its identity in a bucket of black. Darwin was also ignorant of the cause of mutations, and such efforts as he made to provide an explanation went far astray. Moreover, while much more is known today about the causes of heritable variation or mutation, the science of genetics is still far short of filling the gap. In sum, the explanation of evolution has turned out to be much more complex than T. H. Huxley, in the remark cited earlier, imagined it to be.

Despite these gaps and errors, the fundamental principles expounded by Darwin have—after an interlude of comparative desuetude—been fully confirmed by recent research. Today the evolutionary principle rests on a more solid foundation than that provided by Darwin; but the work has been done on the site that he surveyed. An account of developments in evolutionary theory since Darwin is of interest to the student of science rather than the historian of ideas or the student of philosophical problems and need not be explored here. What remains to be done is to examine the evolutionary principle in its broader and more controversial applications. These concern the origin of life and the origin of man, which is to say, the origin of the very simplest and—to our best knowledge—the most complex forms of life.

---

[6] For a caution against a crudely particulate view, see, Julian Huxley, *Evolution: The Modern Synthesis* (New York: Harper & Row, 1943), p. 19.

The Origin of Man and of Life

Except for a deliberately perfunctory observation in the concluding passages, the problem of man's relationship to other organisms receives no direct attention in *Origin of Species.* "Much light," Darwin promises, "will be thrown on the origin of man and his history."[7] It was not until 1871, twelve years after the appearance of his magnum opus, that Darwin's *Descent of Man* was published. In asserting that man, too, is related by descent to simpler organisms and is a product of natural selection, Darwin was, of course, challenging the most sacred of all dogmas. No conviction is more tenaciously held than the belief in the separateness and uniqueness of Man. Seventeenth-century dualistic philosophy, instead of tampering with this belief, established it more firmly. Hence, one of the great Victorians could well ask: "What is the question now placed before society with a glib assurance the most astounding? The question is this—Is man an ape or an angel? My Lord, I am on the side of the angels." So declared Disraeli in a speech at Oxford in 1864, and his view reflected the received learning.[8] And, even if the descent of man be conceded, Darwin's theory of how such descent occurred was bound to encounter especially vigorous opposition. Thus, even A. R. Wallace, Darwin's brilliant rival whose essay on evolution anticipated all the basic arguments of the *Origin* including the theory of natural selection, recoiled from explaining the origin of man in terms of natural selection. Warmly as he embraced the inclusion of man under the notion of common origin, something more than natural selection is needed to explain how man is produced, he contended.

The proposition that man has evolved through natural selection has profound philosophical implications that will shortly be examined in detail. Here it need be noted only that science since the time of Darwin has amassed such conclusive evidence for extending the theory of common origin and, in its recently amended form, the principle of natural selection to man that hardly any reputable scientist would dissent.

Evolutionary theory—enlisting the resources of new sciences such as biochemistry and cytology—has also dealt with the other end of the "chain of being." Science has made great progress toward finding intermediate stages between the organic and inorganic, and it is increasingly challenging the traditional and common-sense emphasis on a complete and clear-cut break between living and nonliving substance. Darwin's indirect contribution to this development will be noted later (pp. 329–330). The great

---

[7] (New York: Random House, Modern Library edition, 1936), p. 373.

[8] Quoted in William Irvine's *Apes, Angels and Victorians* (New York: McGraw-Hill, 1955). Darwin's *Descent* did not evoke as much indignation as his *Origin*, no doubt because his views about man had already been anticipated.

majority of scientists now believe that self-producing particles or "proto-organisms" evolved by natural processes out of inorganic materials. They have simulated such processes more and more closely, and their view is that only the complexity of the problem in relationship to the present level of their science keeps them from synthesizing the simplest forms of life in the laboratory. G. G. Simpson probably expresses a consensus among scientists when he writes that ". . . studies show that there is no theoretical difficulty, under the conditions that may well have existed early in the history of the earth, in the chance organization of a complex carbon-containing molecule capable of influencing or directing the synthesis of other units like itself. Such a unit would be, in barest essentials, alive."[9]

Selected Readings

Darwin, Charles, *The Origin of Species*, New York: Random House, Modern Library edition, 1936. (Also paperbacks by Collier, Dolphin, Mentor.)

Darwin, Charles, *The Descent of Man*, New York: Random House, Modern Library edition, 1936.

Darwin, Charles, *Life and Letters*, ed. by Francis Darwin, 3 vols. London: John Murray, 1888; also 2 vols., ed by Francis Darwin, New York: Basic Books, 1959. (Also paperbacks by Collier, Dover.)

Dobzhansky, T., *Mankind Evolving*, New Haven: Yale, 1962. (Paperback.)

Huxley, Julian, *Evolution: The Modern Synthesis*, New York: Harper & Row, 1943. (Also Sci. Ed. paperback.)

Simpson, George G., *The Meaning of Evolution*, New Haven: Yale, 1950. (Paperback.)

---

[9] *The Meaning of Evolution* (New Haven: Yale, 1950), pp. 14–15.

CHAPTER 18

Darwinism
and
the Category of Change

I t now becomes meaningful to examine or—where they have already been touched upon—to elaborate the profound philosophical implications of the evolutionary principle in its Darwinian and post-Darwinian formulations.

Of Description and Classification

To begin with, the use of the evolutionary principle in the study of biological species represented a long stride toward establishing *change* as a universal or "categorial" aspect of reality. The first step had been taken by Galileo, when he sought to understand the physical universe in terms of the laws of occurrence and change. As noted earlier, the fixed forms which Galileo and those who worked in the Galilean tradition had expelled from the physical universe remained intact in the world of biology—to which, indeed, they seemed especially apt—with the result that the biological sciences continued to be mainly occupied with mere description and classification.

Here again the status of classes or universals comes to the forefront, as in Parts I and II, and it may be well to examine the issue in this new context. Disproportionate emphasis on classification is characteristic of every science in its beginnings. This may be called the taxonomic phase. At the end of the eighteenth century biology was still in its infancy. The great biological works of the period were the *Systema naturae* (1735) and *Philosophica botanica* (1751) of Linnaeus—triumphs of taxonomy in which the whole of animate nature was arranged with an order and precision heretofore unachieved. Such classification is, of course, important, and, in fact, Darwin himself was greatly helped by the tireless labors of Linnaeus. But, as the discussion in Part II has indicated, the shortcomings and limitations of a science that is confined to classification are manifold.

Discontinuity is as much a feature of the organic world as continuity and a good classification will be based upon groupings or "clusters" that do in fact occur in nature. Moreover, a good classification helps us to see genetic relationships that might otherwise not be evident (as when whales are classified as mammals rather than fish), but it is primarily a way of organizing the knowledge we already have, rather than a way of discovering new knowledge. Also, we are prone to forget the extent to which the classifications we employ are a reflection of our own interests or even of the structure of our language, that is to say, constructs of which we are the authors, rather than disclosures or reflections of real groupings and distinctions in nature. This, as the earlier discussion has shown, was the central error of Platonism, as of much scholastic science, and, as late as the eighteenth century, it was the error of renowned natural scientists like Cuvier and the botanist Candolle.[1] Moreover, classes or types are fixed and static and the lines of demarcation stress their separateness. If it should prove to be the case that the reality of which they purport to be a representation is, on the contrary, fluid and continuous, or that we can operate with reality more successfully by viewing it as fluid and continuous —analogous, to use the figure of Heraclitus, to a flowing stream—then the result of classification will be to distort and falsify and to inhibit progress.

As indicated in the earlier discussion of scholasticism, the emphasis in classification is on what an object is, that is, on its aspect as being rather than becoming. Hence we tend to accept the object as it presents itself. We

---

[1] "To Cuvier or Candolle 'type' was an expression of definite and basic constant relationships in the structure of living things that are fixed and unalterable and upon which all knowledge of them depends." E. Cassirer, *Problem of Knowledge*, p. 138. In Chapter VI entitled "The Problem of Classifying and Systematizing Natural Forms" Cassirer provides a useful discussion of the topic as does T. Dobzhansky in an essay "Species after Darwin" in *A Century of Darwin*, ed. by S. A. Barnett (Cambridge: Harvard University Press, 1958). Cf. also Darwin's discussion of species in *Origin*, p. 371, Modern Library Edition and above, Part I, pp. 95–97.

tend not to look beneath the surface to find the forces that brought the object into being or make it pass away. Moreover, our attitude as observers is essentially a passive one: if we are oblivious to the forces in nature that give it this dynamic aspect, it will not occur *to us* to manipulate these forces in such a way as to alter the conditions under which the observed object comes into being and passes away. This is to say that our attitude is contemplative, in the sense of merely beholding or noting the object, rather than experimental. Important as this contemplative attitude may be in other contexts, it fails to advance greatly the goal of science, which is to predict and control. To repeat what has been said before: only when we raise the question "How?" is this goal substantially advanced, and this question will not be raised until we stress the dynamic aspect of reality and view objects as in a state of flux. Such a view is shunned by the taxonomist whose tendency may well be—as it was with Plato and the medieval thinkers who were influenced by him—to avoid and disparage change just because it upsets the applecart: we no sooner have a classification worked out than things alter and our well-ordered arrangements no longer apply.

If all this was more or less accepted by the physical scientists who followed Galileo and Newton, it was only dimly or sporadically perceived by biologists until Darwin's confirmation of the evolutionary principle concentrated attention on the mutability of species. At that point, many of the life sciences burgeoned: natural history became experimental and thus developed into the science of ecology, genetics received a decisive (if delayed) impetus, the study of embryology was provided with new and important insights and thereby greatly stimulated, and, in general, new vistas opened up. But the consequences were even broader.

Ever since men have thought seriously about the world—and possibly before—they have alternated between stressing those aspects of reality that are fixed and permanent and those features that are changing. More than they have known they have been influenced by their moods and by the kind of world in which they lived. Those who have stressed the stability of nature and have been drawn to that which abides are possibly the less venturesome and the more insecure. Those who prefer to brave the flux belong to the ranks of the "tough-minded," to use the term made famous by James in his lectures on pragmatism. As we have seen, the lines were first clearly drawn in ancient Greece by Parmenides and Heraclitus: Parmenides who found that change is an illusion and that true being is static; Heraclitus who found the world like an eternal Fire "with measures kindling and measures going out." On the whole the Greeks followed Parmenides, as did the Middle Ages. But in modern times it is the spirit of Heraclitus that has prevailed and Darwin did a great deal to tip the scales in his favor.

Novelty and Contingency

So much for change in general. There is, however, much more that can be said about change, provided we complete the account of evolutionary change, as such change pertains to biology. Evolution, it must be clearly understood, applies only to groups of organisms, that is to say, to populations. Biologically speaking, an individual does not evolve. Individuals do, indeed, vary from other individuals, including their parents, and this too is change. But it is not evolution. This will be better understood when it is noted that individuals may vary in any one of three ways which must be carefully distinguished.

They vary in the first place because each individual represents a different combination of genes and, since the number of possible combinations is astronomically great, each individual is overwhelmingly likely to differ from every other. However, variation of this kind does not yield new species. It goes on within fixed limits: human beings may vary in height but no human being will be 20 feet tall, their hair may vary in color but no one has green hair, etc. If the genes and chromosomes in their totality are likened to a great deck of cards, we can say that while each shuffle of the deck will, in all probability, produce a new combination of cards, no amount of shuffling can yield a combination containing cards not in the deck.

A second kind of change is produced by environmental influences where this is understood to include the effects of use and disuse and the effects of internal as well as external influences. Obvious examples are the bulging muscles of a wrestler, the increased height of second-generation Japanese-Americans, the tanned skin of a beachcomber. It is sometimes difficult to determine whether given variations are mainly a result of heredity or have been brought about primarily by environmental influences, but the difference between the two is basic. The effects of environment, while they may indeed influence the expression of genes, are not themselves inherited, although a whole school of thought—the Lamarckian and neo-Lamarckian —was based on the assumption that they are.[2] Since they are not inherited, such changes affect only single organisms and hence are not a basic factor in evolution.

A third kind of variation has already been noted. It is especially relevant to the evolutionary process for two reasons: (1) because, unlike environ-

---

[2] Darwin believed that the effects of use and disuse are inherited and, while disparaging Lamarck's work as "a wretched book," relied in part on Lamarckian theory. Neo-Lamarckianism is in virtually total eclipse—except in the Soviet Union where new rulers, after having withdrawn the political seal of approval it enjoyed under Stalin, appear to be reviving it.

mentally influenced change, this third kind of variation is heritable and hence affects populations and not just individuals, and (2) because, unlike variations that are the product of new combinations of the same genes, it is a result of the appearance of genes and chromosomes (or groups of genes and chromosomes) that are entirely new. Such variations have come to be known as *mutations*. To recur to the analogy between the genes and a great deck of cards, it can now be said that the deck contains "wild" cards, indeed very wild cards, since they can stand for anything!

Now the recognition of mutations has a significance far beyond the role they play in biology. Mutations force us to reckon with the *novel* and *contingent*. It is of the essence of novelty that it cannot be mathematically demonstrated, which is to say, it cannot be deduced from the antecedent events of which it is an effect and is in this sense contingent. The difference represented by novelty is a *sensible* phenomenon (i.e., a sensed difference) and hence susceptible of descriptive generalization only; it is more than a mere quantitative variation expressible in mathematical equations.

When Aristotle reckoned with contingency he regarded it as a mark of corporeality and therefore as devoid of—or inferior in—reality. In general, he and those who followed him found contingency only in the realm of the physical: in vagaries of the weather, in shifting sands, in frothing waves, in eddying waters, in flickering fire; but not in the orderly movements of the heavenly bodies—heavenly bodies were not, let us recall, regarded as corporeal—nor in the growth cycles of living organisms. Quite differently with the mechanistic point of view, born of seventeenth-century physical science; there change is seen exclusively in terms of the movement of an invariant unit in space (or space-time). The principle of orderliness and with it the promise of completely certain knowledge are found among those very physical processes which had seemed so refractory to the Greek and medieval mind. However, the possibility of novelty is rejected; contingency has no place in the vocabulary of strict mechanism. Indeed, in the Newtonian scheme, God—once he has created the universe—is assigned the heavy responsibility of guarding against contingency. Hence, everything in nature proceeds with complete regularity according to inexorable law which, once discovered, permits one to read the future with all the certitude of a mathematical calculation. This was, let us remember, the ideal of knowledge that dominated the thinking of the seventeenth and eighteenth centuries.[3]

---

[3] Actually, as the discussion in Part II has shown, there were two tendencies—one experimental and empirical as represented by Bacon, Gilbert, Harvey, Boyle, and Tycho Brahe; the other mathematical and deductive as represented by Copernicus, Kepler, Galileo and Descartes. Both tendencies were manifest in Newton. See E. A. Burtt's *Metaphysical Foundations of Modern Physical Science* (New York: Doubleday Anchor Books, 1954.) See also above, Part II, p. 185. Nevertheless, there is no place in the Newtonian world for novelty. Once God has brought order out of the primal chaos

Since the nineteenth century we have come to see that among the rhythms and repetitions of nature there is an element of contingency; the constancies upon which seventeenth-century science built the reign of universal and necessary law are still there, but they are infected with the irregular and unpredictable; uniformity in nature is now qualified by difference, unity by diversity, the certain by the precarious; we are always to some degree at the mercy of the adventitious and fortuitous. "We live," as John Dewey says, "in a world which is an impressive and irresistible mixture of sufficiencies, tight completeness, order, recurrences which make possible prediction and control, and singularities, ambiguities, uncertain possibilities, processes going on to consequences as yet indeterminate."[4]

Thus, what had seemed in the older view to be finished and complete must be recognized as always "in the making."[5] Nature is not a closed system; the future is open. One cannot deal with nature in terms of finalities; nature is forever unfinished, replete with novelty, and to this extent indeterminate. From this it must follow that the rational ideal of knowledge as a body of fixed and final truths is, necessarily, illusory; the evidence can never *all* be in. With Professor Broad we must say that "Whatever is has become, and the sum total of the existent is continually augmented by becoming."[6]

Nature may be regarded as a complex of histories some of which have ended, some of which still go on, and some of which have yet to begin. Whether we emphasize such histories, or stress the constancies, repetitions, and regularities in nature depends on whether our interests are primarily aesthetic or practical. As Henri Bergson has written:

> In so far as we are geometricians . . . we regret the unforeseeable. We might accept it, assuredly, in so far as we are artists, for art lives on creation and implies a latent belief in the spontaneity of nature. But disinterested art is a luxury, like pure speculation. Long before being artists, we are artisans; and all fabrication, however rudimentary, lives on likeness and repetition, like the natural geometry which serves as its fulcrum. Fabrication works on models which it sets out to reproduce; and even when it invents it proceeds, or imagines itself to proceed, by a new arrangement of elements already known.[7]

he becomes, in Professor Burtt's words, the "cosmic conservative." "His aim is to maintain the *status quo*. The day of novelty is all in the past; there is no further advance in time. Periodic reformation when necessary . . . but no new creative activity—to this routine of temporal housekeeping is the Deity at present confined." (*Ibid.*, p. 294.)

4 *Experience and Nature* (New York: Norton, 1925), p. 47. For a discussion on contingency in the physical world, see Morris Raphael Cohen's *Reason and Nature* (Glencoe: Free Press, 1953), pp. 222 ff. and below, pp. 352–359.

5 The phrase is William James'. *Pragmatism* (New York: Longmans, 1907), p. 257.

6 *Scientific Thought* (London: Routledge, 1949), p. 69.

7 H. Bergson, *Creative Evolution*, Mitchell trans. (New York: Holt, Rinehart, and Winston, 1911), p. 45.

Our interest in the novel or repetitious varies also with how large a segment of time we consider. If the Newtonians could have reckoned with longer spans of time in connection with their observations of the movements of heavenly bodies they would not have exclusively stressed the recurrent and periodic. Without our vast temporal perspective they could not know that even their favorite model of regularity, the solar system, was not always as it is now, that it too has a history.[8] In short, there is a great deal that *is* new under the sun—including the sun itself.

The realization of all this must surely kindle a sense of adventure, which could hardly be inspired by a vista of the future as simply an endless and monotonous repetition of what has gone before. This is surely an important factor in helping us to understand why, unlike their predecessors and neighbors, the western peoples are futuristically oriented. If the future is wide open, we can make it—we need not resign ourselves to it. Surely this helps explain why westerners, fortified by a dynamic technology, became imbued with the Promethean spirit. To be sure, it may well be that we of the west have become so preoccupied with improving the future that we neglect the art of living in the present and that some balance between the fatalism and resignation of the Orient and the restless optimism and driving energy of the West would be preferable. We may be in danger of becoming the fool whom Shaw's Devil describes as pursuing the better before he has secured the good. But this is an issue to be explored elsewhere.

Now, it would be too much to impute the shift in emphasis just described entirely to the recognition of biological mutations and the appearance of new species. All kinds of developments, from the positivism of David Hume to recent trends in physics, have contributed to the same result.[9] Also, as observed before, society itself in the nineteenth century —at any rate the society of Western Europe—presented a spectacle of social change in radical contrast to the comparatively static culture of earlier periods. We are so habituated to having our world kaleidescopically transformed from one decade to another that we are prone to take such change for granted. We need to remind ourselves that there was a time when the society of Europe was comparatively static, when social change was so slight and slow as to be imperceptible and when, in any case, men were too lacking in historical perspective to feel the cumulative impact of such change as had occurred. In such circumstances, they could hardly have been expected to be as cognizant of novelty and spontaneity in nature as they have since become. But, when all this has been said, the new

---

[8] The age of the earth is now estimated to be at least three billion years.

[9] For the contribution of twentieth-century trends in physics, see Albert Einstein and Leopold Infield, *The Evolution of Physics* (New York: Simon and Schuster, 1951) pp. 295–313.

biological point of view, to which the recognition of mutations and the appearance of new species made so decisive a contribution, enormously facilitated the shift in emphasis, as the older mathematical orientation of the seventeenth century could not.

One can find no more eloquent reminder of such a shift in thinking than in the pages of seminal thinkers like Charles S. Peirce and Henri Bergson. For Pierce, ". . . conformity to law exists only within a limited range of events and even there is not perfect, for an element of pure spontaneity or lawless originality mingles . . . with law everywhere."[10] "Chance," "irregularity," "variety," "spontaneity," these are clarion words in Peirce's increasingly influential writings and, although he was primarily a mathematical philosopher, his vocabulary was inspired by his reading of Darwin. Bergson writes of the "absolute originality and unforeseeability of forms," of a "situation that is unique of its kind, that has never yet occurred and will never occur again,"[11] of the "continual elaboration of the absolutely new."[12] While Bergson was no true Darwinian, the notion of "creative evolution" could hardly have played so decisive a role in his philosophy without the work of Darwin.

Guided and Unguided Change

If the evolutionary principle calls attention to the ubiquity of change—in particular that kind of qualitative change which manifests itself as novelty—it must now also be noted that, in the Darwinian formulation of the principle, the change involved is *undirected*. The "received" or established view might, indeed, have accommodated itself to the idea of evolution, were it not that the Darwinian explanation of evolution dispenses with a guiding agency. It is, of course, just because Darwin did not rely on a teleological explanation of evolutionary change that the Darwinian principle may be regarded as a scientific hypothesis, for, as the scientists of the seventeenth century discerned and the earlier discussion of Bacon reminds us, recourse to final causes is an *"asylum ignorantiae."* When we are at loss for the explanation of a phenomenon, we often have recourse to purposes or ends; men who are ignorant of the causes tend to attribute earthquakes to the wrath of the gods.

This is not to deny that human beings have conscious purposes; nor to exclude the teleological type of explanation in the areas of biology and sociology, when understood in a carefully restricted sense as involving reference to the function of a vital process or organ or the function of a social process or institution. Clearly, we have not fully explained an organ like the heart until its role in maintaining the characteristic activities of

---

[10] *Collected Papers* (Cambridge: Harvard, 1931), Vol. I, p. 223.
[11] *Creative Evolution, Op. cit.*, pp. 28–29.
[12] *Ibid.*, p. 11.

the organism as a whole has been described. Similarly, we do not adequately understand the institution of marriage if we limit ourselves to mere description and neglect a functional explanation of the part played by marriage, in one or other of its forms, in relation to the total culture of which it is a part. Such functional explanations are often called "teleological" by scientists since, in a sense, an "end" is served. But the end is part of no design, and no purposeful agent or agency defined it as a goal in the sense in which persons set up goals for themselves and seek to realize them.

However, if science accepts the dictum of Spinoza that "nature has no fixed aim in view, and that all final causes are merely fabrications of men,"[13] common sense does not concur, and neither for that matter have many scientists (who, when they depart from their professional role, are, to be sure, usually no more than spokesmen for common sense). ". . . whence arises all that order and beauty which we see in the world?" asked Isaac Newton. "How came the bodies of animals to be contrived with so much art, and for what ends were their several parts? Was the eye contrived without skill in optics, or the ear without knowledge of sounds?"[14] Even the greatest scientists, it may be observed, are not merely or not always scientists; they are also lovers, gourmets, art devotees—and humble believers. Newton answered the questions cited above by invoking divine agency.

At the level of common sense, it is tempting to pass from the adaptive nature of many of the characteristics of an organism to the conclusion that such adaptations are evidence of the operation of a purposeful agency. The lizard appears to be provided with a coloration that blends it with its background *in order to* protect it from its enemies; the giraffe, with a long neck *in order that* it may reach the higher foliage; man—to compensate for an unarmored, nearly unarmed, and relatively slow-moving body—with intelligence. One recalls the story of the elderly lady who said, upon seeing a tiny kangaroo peer out of the "pocket" with which mother kangaroos are provided: "Good heavens, what will they think of next?"

Darwin himself notes the situation with more than usual eloquence:

How have all those exquisite adaptations of one part of the organization to another part, and to the conditions of life, and of one organic being to another being, been perfected? We see these beautiful co-adaptations most plainly in the woodpecker and mistletoe; and only a little less plainly in the humblest parasite which clings to the hairs of a quadruped or feathers of a bird; in the structure of the beetle which dives through the water; in the plumed seed which

---

[13] The famous Appendix to Part One of Spinoza's *Ethics* from which these words are taken is a *locus classicus*. *Works*, Vol. II, Elwes trans. (New York, Dover, 1951), p. 74 ff.

[14] *Opticks* (London: W. & J. Innys, 1721), 3rd ed., pp. 344 ff.

is wafted by the gentlest breeze; in short, we see beautiful adaptations everywhere and in every part of the organic world.[15]

But Darwin was writing almost two centuries after Newton and, unlike Newton, he did not "explain" these marvels by appealing to the idea of purposeful intervention. In the Darwinian scheme heritable variations occur at *random;* they are blind and purposeless and do not happen *in order to* further the survival of the organism. The overwhelming majority of variations are, in fact, harmful or lethal to the organism, thereby reducing its chances for survival. Sir Julian Huxley notes that "since the gene-complex is an elaborately co-ordinated system, any changes in it are much more likely to act as defects rather than improvements. Further, the larger the change the less likely is it to be an improvement . . ."[16] The distinguished geneticist, R. A. Fisher, speaks of "a storm of adverse mutations." The fossil record testifies eloquently to the innumerable failures. Darwin erroneously ascribed heritable variations to the effects of use and disuse and the influences of the environment, but he also, and increasingly, referred to them as "chance" variations, by which he meant, not that they are without a cause, but that we are ignorant of the cause,[17] and he thought of them as "accidental as far as purpose is concerned."

It is upon such variations that *natural* selection works. Natural selection provides an explanation of evolutionary change and of an orienting factor in evolutionary change without postulating a teleological principle; there is no need for a "vital force" (*élan vital*) or "inherent tendency" or "inner perfecting principle" or "entelechy" or any other of the inscrutable agencies which substitute mere words for genuine explanation.[18] The orienting factor—by which one means not a supernatural force or agency, or predetermined goal that guides change but a factor that permits us to discern a direction in change—is *adaptation;* organisms have changed in the direction of becoming more and more adapted to their environment.[19] There

---

15 *Origin* (New York: Random House, Modern Library Edition, 1936), p. 51.

16 *Evolution: The Modern Synthesis* (New York: Harper & Row, 1943), p. 115.

17 *Origin, op. cit.,* pp. 101–102.

18 We have here a classical example of the potency of mere names, and our tendency to suppose that in christening something we thereby disclose its nature. The pedantic doctor in *Le Bourgeois Gentilhomme* who "explains" the sleep-producing properties of opium by referring to its "dormitive powers" is a universal character. Aborigines and children ascribe explanatory value to names, and science, too, in its infancy, is prone to regard names as revelatory.

19 Julian Huxley writes: "It has been for some years the fashion among certain schools of biological thought to decry the study or even to deny the fact of adaptation. Its alleged teleological flavor is supposed to debar it from orthdox scientific consideration, and its study is assumed to prevent the biologist from paying attention to his proper business of mechanistic analysis. Both these strictures are unjustified. It was one of the great merits of Darwin himself to show that the purposiveness of organic structure and function was apparent only. The teleology of adaptation is a pseudo-teleology, capable of being accounted for on good mechanistic principles, without the intervention of purpose, conscious or subconscious, either on the part of the organism or of any outside power." *Op. cit.,* p. 412.

is nothing inevitable about this tendency, as Darwin was well aware, although his words sometimes lend themselves to a contrary interpretation.[20] "Degeneration," declares J. B. S. Haldane, "is a far commoner phenomenon than progress. . . . If we consider any given evolutionary level we generally find one or two lines leading up to it, and dozens leading down."[21]

Darwin is by no means completely free of teleological influence, and he himself confessed, when dealing with his difficulties in explaining traits lacking in survival value, that "I was not . . . able to annul the influence of my former belief, then almost universal, that each species has been purposely created."[22] But in principle Darwin's explanation of the origin of species dispenses with appeals to laws of purposeful development of the kind so dear to the romanticist philosophers who preceded him, as it dispenses with creative acts, and relies entirely on the operation of natural forces. When he wrote in the *Origin* that "species are produced and exterminated by slowly acting and still existing causes,"[23] Hutton's principle of uniformitarianism was at last extended to the world of living organisms.

The naturalistic framework, in terms of which Descartes had sought to understand the organic world, thus finds impressive scientific vindication. It should be remembered, of course, that the work of Vesalius (1514–1564) in anatomy, and of Harvey (1578–1657) and Malpighi (1628–1694) and Borelli (1608–1679) in physiology, had already initiated a naturalistic approach to the study of organisms. Until Harvey discovered the mechanical principles governing circulation of the blood, and Borelli (*c.* 1670) the mechanics of muscular motion, the functioning of organisms had been explained since the time of Galen and the Greeks almost entirely by reference to an assortment of "animal spirits" which were thought to inhabit living bodies. The great chemist, Laviosier, and his followers, in applying the theory of combustion to the processes of respiration, nutrition, and the generation of animal heat carried this work forward. Darwin, by

---

[20] For example: "Man selects only for his own good: Nature only for that of the being which she tends." (*Origin*, Modern Library Edition, p. 65) "Can we wonder that Nature's productions should be far 'truer' in character than man's productions; that they should be infinitely better adapted to the most complex conditions of life, and should plainly bear the stamp of far higher workmanship?" (p. 66) ". . . as natural selection works solely by and for the good of each being, all corporeal and mental endowments will tend to progress towards perfection." (p. 373)

However, misinterpretation is possible only if sentences like the former are taken out of context. When Darwin writes that "natural selection is daily and hourly scrutinizing . . . the slightest variations; rejecting those that are bad, preserving and adding up all that are good; silently and insensibly working, *whenever and wherever opportunity offers*, at the improvement of each organic being in relation to its organic and inorganic conditions of life," (p. 66) he emphasizes that he is speaking metaphorically.

[21] *Causes of Evolution* (New York: Harper & Row, 1932), pp. 152–153.

[22] *Descent of Man* (New York: Modern Library Edition, 1936), p. 442.

[23] P. 372. For other expressions of his views on providential design see *Life and Letters of Charles Darwin*, ed. by F. Darwin (London, John Murray, 1888), Vol. I, pp. 313–315.

extending naturalistic principles to an understanding of individual variation and the origin of species, brings this work to a culmination.

But what of the origin of life itself, of that "simple" beginning from
which all living species have richly proliferated? Until this question and
the question of the origin of man are settled, naturalism recoils before
a compound mystery. Before returning to these crucial questions it will be
well again to indicate in a general way what the term naturalism means
to philosophers. This will require us to review and expand upon what has
been said in earlier discussions.[24]

Selected Readings

Braithwaite, R. B., *Scientific Explanation*, Cambridge at the University Press,
    1953, "Teleological Explanation," pp. 322–336. Reprinted in *Con-
    temporary Philosophical Problems*, ed. by Y. H. Krikorian and A. Edel,
    New York: Macmillan, 1959, pp. 367–379. (Also Harper Torchbooks
    paperback.)
Dewey, John, *The Influence of Darwin on Philosophy*, Gloucester, Mass.:
    Peter Smith, 1951, pp. 1–20. Reprinted from *Popular Science Monthly*,
    July, 1909. (Also paperback by Indiana University Press.)
Nagel, Ernest, *The Structure of Science*, New York: Harcourt, Brace & World,
    1961. See selected readings after next chapter.
Randall, J. H., Jr., "The Changing Impact of Darwin on Philosophy," *Journal
    of the History of Ideas*, Vol. XXII, No. 4 (Oct.-Dec., 1961), pp. 435–462.

----

[24] See pp. 227 ff.

CHAPTER 19

The Nature
and
Origin of Life

The Meanings of Naturalism

Naturalism is a key word in the philosophical vocabulary. It is the view that the system of nature is all-inclusive. As such it involves the denial of a supernatural (or extranatural) realm or agency. But none of this can have much meaning until we know what is signified by "nature" and the "natural." Unfortunately, these terms have nearly as many meanings as there are schools of philosophy. The following more common uses may be distinguished:

(1) Natural and normal are often used interchangeably. One would say that it is not natural for saucer-like objects without ascertainable owners to be flying about at great rates of speed, for lightning to strike twice—or perhaps thrice—in the same place, for a child to have green hair. Natural in this sense is the opposite of unusual or abnormal.

(2) Natural may refer to the essential or real or fundamental character of anything as distinguished from its accidental or apparent, or distorted, character. Thus naturalism in art and literature refers to literal transcriptions of "reality," that is, to dealing with things as they are. So, too, Lucretius

writes "On the Nature of Things" (*De Rerum Natura*). We speak of "human nature" and we advise each other—although in many contexts such advice may be taken as suspect—that "you can't go contrary to human nature," meaning, to man as he is. Implied in this use is a distinction of things as they are, from things as they appear to be, and hence the ancient Greek dichotomy between appearance and reality; or, the distinction made familiar by Aristotle between the essential or inherent or definitive character of something and what is accidental or extrinsic or incidental to it.

(3) Natural is used to mean not made by man and hence existing in a state of nature. A natural object is here distinguished from an artifact. This distinction is also implicit in the ancient Sophist contrast between nature and law or "convention." Natural in this sense is the opposite of artificial. This broadens into the wider use in which anything, or any event, which is the consequence of plan or contrivance or design is excluded so that (with certain qualifications) a naturalistic explanation would be the opposite of a teleological explanation.

(4) The natural may be contrasted to the human in yet another sense, as when nature is understood as comprising the physical world and (usually) all living organisms other than man, and man is regarded as something special and apart. This is the notion of nature associated with the Galilean-Cartesian-Newtonian view discussed earlier. It is a notion that continues to be congenial to prevailing common sense and it is reflected in the archaic nomenclature by which we still differentiate between the "natural" sciences and the "social," i.e., the human sciences—as though the social sciences dealt with phenomena falling outside the realm of the natural. Man is excluded from and opposed to nature not by virtue of his bodily processes which, as will be noted in some detail later, are generally regarded as "natural," but by virtue of his spiritual or mental side. Hence the use of the term natural broadens into more than a polarization of man and the "external" world; it differentiates a world of the spirit, or of spirits—which historically includes much more than man's spirit—and the material, corporeal, physical world of space and time.

(5) Finally, at least as far as this enumeration is concerned, any object or event is natural if it can be observed and described by more than one person—though not necessarily in the same way[1]—and is related to other things and events, in such a way that the relationship can be expressed in terms of a causal or probability law such that the occurrence of later events or combination of events can theoretically be predicted from or traced back to the occurrence of an earlier event or combination of events. Today, when the term is used philosophically, this is the sense that is usually intended. To be natural is to be part of the system of such re-

---

[1] A dentist's experience of his patient's toothache is different from his patient's, or else there would be no dentists! Cf. pp. 361–362.

lationships. Nature is simply the totality of objects and events involved in such relationships. By definition, therefore, naturalism involves the rejection of miracles, so-called, as it involves the rejection of a first cause —the attribute traditionally assigned to deity—or of events that are traced back to a first cause. It follows that for naturalism everything is amenable to scientific investigation and description, since, in Adolf Grünbaum's words, "it is the essence of a scientific explanation in any field outside of pure mathematics to 'explain' a past phenomenon or predict a future event by showing that these are instances of a certain law (or laws) and that their occurrence is attributable to the fact that the conditions for the applicability of the relevant law(s) were satisfied."[2] Nevertheless, naturalism need not affirm that the scientific is the only way of apprehending nature.[3] Moreover, as will be seen later, naturalism as such is not committed to understanding nature in physical or biological or any other particular set or sets of terms.[4]

It is especially important to distinguish naturalism from materialism, with which it is often confused. Materialism is, as we have seen, one of the variants of naturalism. Materialism or—as it would better be called— physicalism describes all of nature exclusively in terms of the laws and generalizations of the physical sciences. All materialists are naturalists, but the converse is not the case, and, as the later discussion will indicate, the difference between materialists and many naturalists is of crucial importance.

Finally, it may be observed that naturalism—at any rate, as understood here—is committed to the continuity or "connectedness" of nature. This is not always noted or emphasized but it follows from what has been said. Continuity refers to the fact that every event is antecedent to and preceded by other events to some of which it is causally related.[5] It must follow that the naturalist abhors and rejects metaphysical positions that deal in radical discontinuities. Metaphysical dualism, as espoused by Descartes for example, is anathema to the naturalist. The reasons for this will become evident as the discussion proceeds.

Darwin's Views

These considerations may now be applied to the two questions raised earlier. What, in the first place, of the origin of life? Can the origin of life be understood in naturalistic terms, and how did Darwin's views

---

[2] *American Scientist*, 40, 1952. Reprinted in *Readings in the Philosophy of Science*, ed. by Feigl and Brodbeck (New York: Appleton-Century-Crofts, 1953), p. 767.

[3] Cf. pp. 361, 364.

[4] Cf. pp. 362 ff.

[5] Cf. pp. 351–352.

influence such an understanding? The noble concluding passage of the *Origin of Species* reads: "There is grandeur in this view of life, with its several powers, *having been originally breathed by the Creator into a few forms or into one;* and that, whilst this planet has gone cycling on according to the fixed law of gravity, from so simple a beginning endless forms most beautiful and most wonderful have been, and are being evolved." But there is no reason to believe that Darwin meant the italicized words— not similarly emphasized in the text—to be taken literally. On the contrary, on this issue Darwin confronted the limitations of his science in the second half of the nineteenth century, and, in 1863, in a letter to J. D. Hooker, said: "It is mere rubbish, thinking at present of the origin of life; one might as well think of the origin of matter." He adds in the same letter that "I have long regretted that I truckled to public opinion, and used the Pentateuchal term of creation, by which I really meant 'appeared' by some wholly unknown process." However, elsewhere he allowed himself to reflect: ". . . if (and oh! what a big if!) we could conceive in some warm little pond, with all sorts of ammonia and phosphoric salts, light, heat, electricity, etc., present, that a proteine compound was chemically formed ready to undergo still more complex changes, at the present day such matter would be instantly devoured or absorbed, which would not have been the case before living creatures were formed."[6]

What Darwin said on this specific issue—where the shortcomings of his science necessarily limited him to speculation—is not so important as the enormous impetus that his general theory gave to the quest for a naturalistic explanation of the origin of life. Men were bound to seek here for the same natural causes which Darwin had found for them in explaining the origin of species. Moreover, the evolutionary approach had accustomed them to finding continuities and relationships in the organic world where discontinuities had heretofore been taken for granted. The same habit of thought that finds living species related and erases the sharp line of demarcation which had traditionally divided them will, in good time, seek for continuity and relatedness between the living and nonliving.

Mechanism

Three points of view concerning the origin of life and its relationship to the physical world are broadly distinguishable. Inevitably they involve us—as they well should—in considerations relating to the nature of life.

The first of these may be called Mechanism. It will be useful to restate what has been said about mechanism in Part II (pp. 227–239) with special

---

[6] *Life and Letters*, ed. F. Darwin (London: John Murray, 1888), Vol. III, p. 18. The parenthetical remark is Darwin's. He is not referring specifically to his use of the term "creation" in the final passage of *Origin*, but the point is the same nonetheless.

emphasis here on mechanism as a biological standpoint. As concerning the nature and origin of life, mechanism asserts, in Professor Broad's words, "that a living body is composed only of constituents which do or might occur in nonliving bodies, and that its characteristic behavior is wholly deducible from its structure and components and from the chemical, physical and dynamical laws which these materials would obey if they were isolated or were in nonliving combinations."[7] The laws governing the functioning and origin of organisms are, in other words, completely deducible from the laws of the physical sciences. Descartes, as noted earlier (Part II, pp. 233), was a strict mechanist in this limited sense. In our century, a distinguished scientist, Jacques Loeb, adopted a mechanistic position when he wrote that living organisms are "chemical machines consisting chiefly of collodial material and possessing the peculiarity of preserving and reproducing themselves."[8]

While the significance of this point may not become evident until all the views under examination have been detailed, it is especially important to note that the mechanist goes beyond saying that the characteristic qualities of life are caused by or *determined* by its chemical and ultimately its physical constituents combining under determinate physical conditions; he asserts that its qualities are deducible from them in quite the same way that the properties of a physical aggregate—say a collection of billiard balls—are deducible from the laws governing its component parts. Water is a product of, and is insofar determined by, hydrogen and oxygen molecules appropriately combined. The question is: Could the qualities or properties of water be deduced from a knowledge of the properties of hydrogen and oxygen molecules taken in separation? The mechanist would answer in the affirmative. Similarly, the mechanist would contend, the properties of a living organism can be deduced solely from a knowledge of its chemical constituents. In point of fact, we do not have the knowledge, but such a deduction is possible, in principle, according to the mechanist. "The essence of mechanical explanation . . . is to regard the future and the past as calculable functions of the present, and thus to claim that *all is given*. On this hypothesis, past, present and future would be open at a glance to a superhuman intellect capable of making the calculation."[9]

---

[7] *Mind and Its Place in Nature* (New York: Harcourt, Brace, 1929), p. 46.

[8] *The Organism as a Whole* (New York and London: G. P. Putnam's Sons, 1916), p. 128.

[9] H. Bergson, *Creative Evolution*, Mitchell trans. (New York: Holt, Rinehart and Winston, 1911), p. 37. Bertrand Russell states the mechanist position as assuming that "There are such invariable relations between different events at the same or different times that, given the state of the whole universe throughout any finite time, however short, every previous or subsequent event can theoretically be determined as a function of the given events during that time." *Our Knowledge of the External World* (Chicago: Open Court, 1914, p. 221).

In short, mechanism, as a biological standpoint, involves two basic contentions: (1) that vital phenomena are causally derivative from nonvital phenomena, and (2) that vital phenomena, in point of fact, do not differ in kind from, and are no more than, nonvital phenomena. Both contentions are involved in the assertion that vital phenomena are completely explicable in physiochemical terms. This is what is called the "reducibility of biological laws."

In defending his case, the mechanist points out that his position accords with science in banishing final causes. He notes that an approach which unifies the organic and inorganic coincides with the unifying tendencies in science whereby the most diverse phenomena from light to electricity to magnetism have been subsumed under the same laws. He cites the enormous progress that science has made in explaining vital phenomena in physicochemical terms. It was supposed, for example, that so-called organic compounds could not be made by artificial means, that is, without the cooperation of some "vital force" which chemists could not command, until Liebig and Wöhler, in 1828, synthesized urea. "The most marked feature of early twentieth-century physiology was the extension of the methods of physics and chemistry to physiological problems," declares a distinguished historian of science. He adds: "Indeed, it can almost be said that physiology was resolved into biophysics and biochemistry."[10]

The mechanist argues that all the evidence we have suggests that the material world antedated living organisms and that the vital must therefore be regarded as having derived from the nonvital; such an assumption, at any rate, most nearly accords with our knowledge concerning the conditions necessary for sustaining life, which could hardly have survived travel through interstellar space or the temperatures of the earth when it was still a molten mass. He is unembarrassed by the failure of biochemists to make the simplest forms of life in their laboratories; he points out that, on the contrary, they have approximated vital processes more and more closely, and their knowledge of substances apparently intermediate between the organic and inorganic—for example, viruses which are crystals and yet have some of the properties of living organisms—is increasing rapidly.

Undoubtedly mechanism received enormous encouragement from Darwinism. However, its greatest impetus comes from recent work in biophysics and biochemistry. Molecular biologists, so-called, are at this very time brilliantly probing the complex chemical control system by which heredity is governed, and are finding in the incredibly complex self-duplicating, protein-making DNA molecule, weighing two ten-trillionths of an ounce, the control chemicals by means of which the nature of all living organisms is determined. Meanwhile, we find the boldest expression

[10] Sir Wm. C. Dampier, *A History of Science* (Cambridge at the University Press; New York: Macmillan, both 1949), p. 332.

of mechanism in the literature of cybernetics, where we learn that in a mathematical laboratory of the University of Cambridge there is a machine than can "profit by experience," that electronic computers have "memory" in the sense that they can store up information for future use, and that it is possible to make machines (*horrible dictu*) which can reproduce themselves![11]

Vitalism

A second point of view concerning the nature and origin of life is called Vitalism. Vitalism—neovitalism, as it might better be called—came into prominence at the turn of the century before evolutionary theory had absorbed the results of recent genetical studies. The contributions of brilliant biologists like J. B. S. Haldane, Sewall Wright, R. A. Fisher, and T. Dobzhansky were not yet available to solve a number of problems with which classical Darwinian theory had been unable to cope. For a brief period Darwinism was in semi-eclipse.

Vitalism asserts that life is original—primordial. Life is irreducible and underived. It cannot be understood in terms of, or resolved into, simpler chemical components. Neither was it at some remote time in the past, under whatever favorable circumstances, the product, result or effect of some complex configuration of physical forces. If material substance was not causally prior, neither, presumably, was it temporally antecedent to living substance; living substance has always existed. Either that, or it has been brought into being by some supernatural agency.

It must follow that a living cell will never be made in a scientist's laboratory any more than in nature's laboratory. The inability of scientists to make even the simplest forms of life is not the result of a temporary shortcoming, to be overcome with the progress of learning; it is inherent

---

[11] "Edsac is a merciful abbreviation of 'electronic delay storage automatic calculator,' The machine can be trained like a dog to respond to external stimuli, meaning that it has reflexes that can be conditioned. The newest Cambridge version of Edsac either responds to any number between zero and seven or else throws back an 'x' to indicate that it cannot make up its mind . . .

"Similar machines have been constructed in this country. In one a mechanical mouse blunders about in a complicated maze until by a process of trial and error it finds its way to a piece of 'cheese' in the corner. Placed in the maze a second time the mouse runs directly to the 'cheese.' The performance is much better than that of a live mouse in the same situation.

"But the machine that commands . . . admiration is one proposed by Dr. John Von Neumann—a machine that reproduces itself . . . Von Neumann has shown mathematically that reproduction is possible. . . . one of these hypothetical but possible machines will collect parts from its environment and assemble them to produce a duplicate which then starts collecting parts to construct a triplicate and so on ad infinitum . . ." (Waldemar Kaempffert in "Science in Review," *The New York Times*, May 3, 1953.) The geneticist, L. S. Penrose, has recently devised models of machines which approximate Von Neumann's proposal.

in the nature of life: the phenomenon of life imposes upon science an absolute and indefeasible limitation. Thus Immanuel Kant wrote: "It is indeed quite certain that we cannot adequately cognize, much less explain, organized beings and their internal possibility, according to mere mechanical principles of nature; and we can say boldly it is alike certain that it is absurd for men to make any such attempt or to hope that another *Newton* will arise in the future, who shall make comprehensible by us the production of a blade of grass according to natural laws which no design has ordered. We must absolutely deny this insight to men."[12] Not *ignoramus*—we do not know, but *ignorabimus*—we never shall know; such is the vitalist's verdict.

The vitalist tends to reify life, to regard it as something substantive, to speak of a life-stuff—much as Descartes regarded mind. Hans Driesch first called it a "something" without spatial character, then a psychoid and finally an "entelechy." In general, the vitalist is, like Descartes, a metaphysical dualist, except that the vitalist bifurcates reality at a different point: the dividing line is not between the psychological and the physical but between the vital and the physical.[13] Descartes was a mechanist with respect to living things, asserting that all biological phenomena can be understood in terms of mechanical processes; the vitalist, on the other hand, proclaims the absolute "autonomy"—the term is Kant's—of biology. But both agree that there is an ultimate and irreducible difference between the two kinds of reality.

In the passage from Kant cited above, a teleological orientation is suggested which is characteristic of vitalistic theories. The vitalist dwells upon the fantastic odds that prevail against a merely chance combination of the factors necessary to produce the simplest forms of life, not to mention its more complex manifestations. Gustav Wolff argued that the theory of natural selection with its reliance on mere chance could never explain how an organ as complicated as the human eye could arise or how it could restore itself after an injury. E. Bleuler calculated that the probability of a chance occurrence of the location of cornea, lens, vitreous humor, and retina would be about $1:10^{42}$ and that for the origin of the whole organ the probability would be astronomically more remote. Bergson, while he rejected the idea of a plan "given in advance," cited the resemblance between the eye of a mollusk and the eye of a vertebrate, that is to say, the presence of identical organs in very different organisms, and from

---

[12] *Critique of Judgment*, trans. by J. H. Bernard, 2nd ed., rev. (London: Macmillan, 1914), pp. 312–313.
[13] Often, life is regarded as an elementary form of mind. *Cf.* M. R. Cohen, *Reason and Nature* (Glencoe: Free Press, 1953), pp. 250–254. Also, vitalism may take the form of hylozoism—the view espoused by the early Milesians, that life is a property of all matter. More recently Haeckel (1834–1919) took this position when he declared that "every atom is endowed with sensations and motion."

this reasoned: "Suppose . . . that the mechanistic explanation is the true one: evolution must then have occurred through a series of accidents added to one another, each new accident being preserved by selection if it is advantageous to that sum of former advantageous accidents which the present form of the living being represents. What likelihood is there that, by two entirely different series of accidents being added together, two entirely different evolutions will arrive at similar results? The more two lines of evolution diverge, the less probability is there that accidental outer influences or accidental inner variations bring about the construction of the same apparatus. . . , especially if there was no trace of this apparatus at the moment of divergence." If we do not assume an *"original impetus,"* according to Bergson, an impetus "passing from one generation of germs to the following generation of germs through the developed organisms which bridge the interval between the generations," such phenomena are unintelligible.[14] To be sure, this is not as serious a charge as it might seem since, as Bergson himself agrees, the original life impetus or vital force is also unintelligible—known only to intuition. Julian Huxley comments: "To say that an adaptive trend towards a particular specialization or towards all-around biological efficiency is explained by an *élan vital* is like saying that the movement of a railway train is 'explained' by an *élan locomotif* of the engine."[15]

The vitalist not only recoils from what he regards as the inadequacies of the physical sciences, so far as an explanation of life is concerned, and he not only affirms the irreducible difference of the vital and the nonvital; he removes life from the purview of science altogether. If vital phenomena, like the *res cogitans* of Descartes, are excluded from the system of nature, they presumably obey a higher law. Unfortunately, men have always disagreed concerning what that higher law is and have found no way of resolving their differences.

It must be evident that vitalism and mechanism appeal to different types of attitude and disposition. Vitalism is in accord with the traditional, accepted point of view and is on the whole more congenial to the great majority of people for whom the "miracle of life" is more than a manner of speaking. This is evidenced by the enthusiastic reception enjoyed by a book like Lecomte du Noüy's *Human Destiny* in which the argument from

---

[14] *Op. cit.*, p. 54. *Cf.* pp. 87ff.

[15] *Op. cit.*, p. 458. For the same author's comments on the argument from improbability, see p. 474. For a scientist's answer to the point made by Bergson, see Simpson's *The Meaning of Evolution* (New Haven: Yale University Press, 1950), pp. 168–175. Simpson points out, for example, that the eyes of a mollusc and vertebrate arose as adaptive responses to similar environments by radically different evolutionary pathways. Hence the environment is the selecting agent and not any mystical force of the kind postulated by Bergson. In truth, as Simpson points out, the eyes of a mollusc and vertebrate are by no means as alike as they seemed to Bergson.

improbability is used with plausibility and persuasiveness against the theory of natural selection. Such people regard mechanism as the only alternative to vitalism and they view mechanism as a cold, impersonal philosophy that deprives life of all meaning. For obvious reasons, those who are theistically oriented have generally preferred the vitalistic point of view.

Mechanism, on the other hand, speaks in the name of science and bases its claim on what science has done and may be expected to do in the future. In the eighteenth and nineteenth centuries great scientists like Xavier Bechat (1771-1802), one of the founders of the modern science of biology, and Claude Bernard (1813-1878) could be classified as vitalists. As recently as a few decades ago some scientists could be found flirting with, and in a few cases embracing, vitalism; hardly any may be counted as vitalists now, and in scientific circles a book like du Noüy's is likely to be branded a pious imposture.

But must the choice be limited to reductive mechanism which ignores the distinctive qualities of life and an obscurantist vitalism which preserves these differences by excluding life from the system of nature? Granted that a naturalistic and not a vitalistic interpretation of life is a proper inference from the teachings of Darwinism and the recent achievements of biochemistry and biophysics, must such an interpretation imply a mechanistic philosophy?

Some of the most significant philosophy of the twentieth century has given a negative answer to the foregoing questions and, in providing a third view of the nature and origin of life, has received its inspiration from the work of Darwin. This third view has been variously called evolutionary naturalism (Sellars), emergent vitalism (Broad), emergent evolution (Morgan, Wheeler), critical naturalism (Randall). But critical naturalism—as it will be called here—is far more than a philosophy concerning the nature and origin of life; it refers to possible transformations that may have taken place in the physical universe and—more relevantly to the problem at hand—to the status of man and his works. Before turning to an account of critical naturalism it would be well, therefore, to explore the second and more crucial of the two questions raised earlier: What light does Darwin throw on the origin and nature of man?

Selected Readings

Cohen, Morris Raphael, *Reason and Nature*, 2nd ed., Glencoe, Ill.: Free Press, 1953, Bk. II, chap. 3, "Law and Purpose in Biology." (Also rev. ed. paperback.)

Dewey, John, *Experience and Nature*, New York: Norton, 1925, chap. VII, "Nature, Life and Body-Mind." (Also paperbacks by Dover, Open Court.)

Nagel, Ernest, *The Structure of Science*, New York, Harcourt, Brace & World, 1961, chap. 11, "The Reduction of Theories"; chap. 12, "Mechanistic Explanation and Organismic Biology."

Schlick, Moritz, "Philosophy of Organic Life," (reprinted from "Naturphilosophie") in *Readings in the Philosophy of Science*, ed. by H. Feigl and M. Brodbeck, New York: Appleton-Century-Crofts, 1953, pp. 523–536.

CHAPTER 20

The Nature
and
Origin of Man

Darwin's Views

Darwinism had revolutionary implications for the status of man as for the status of life and, if these implications encountered greater resistance, they were also more firmly grounded in Darwinian principles. For it must be remembered that the derivation of the vital from the non-vital is primarily a complex chemical problem on which the evidence for a common origin of species and the principle of natural selection throws no direct light. On the other hand, Darwin was able to employ the same *kind* of evidence and the same explanatory principles in relating man to the primates as in relating the primates to other species. In brief, the impetus that Darwin gave to naturalism is more direct in the case of the origin of man than in the case of the origin of life. And, in the *Descent of Man* he did not hesitate to derive a naturalistic conclusion.

"We have now seen," he declares, "that man is variable in body and mind; and that the variations are induced, either directly or indirectly, *by the same general laws* as with the lower animals."[1] and, in the memorable final passage of the *Descent of Man,* he concludes: "We must . . . acknowledge, as it seems to me, that man with all his noble qualities, with sympathy which feels for the most debased, with benevolence which extends not only to other men but to the humblest living creature, with his god-like intellect which has penetrated into the movements and constitution of the solar system—with all these exalted powers—Man still bears in his bodily frame the indelible stamp of his lowly origin." Another passage is worth citing in full:

The main conclusion arrived at in this work, namely that man is descended from some lowly organized form, will, I regret to think, be highly distasteful to many. But there can hardly be a doubt that we are descended from barbarians. The astonishment which I felt on first seeing a party of Fuegians on a wild and broken shore will never be forgotten by me, for the reflection at once rushed into my mind—such were our ancestors. These men were absolutely naked and bedaubed with paint, their long hair was tangled, their mouths frothed with excitement, and their expression was wild, startled, and distrustful. They possessed hardly any arts and like wild animals lived on what they could catch; they had no government and were merciless to everyone not of their own small tribe. . . . For my own part I would as soon be descended from that heroic little monkey, who braved his dreaded enemy in order to save the life of his keeper, or from that old baboon, who descending from the mountains, carried away in triumph his young comrade from a crowd of astonished dogs—as from a savage who delights to torture his enemies, offers up bloody sacrifices, practices infanticide without remorse, treats his wives like slaves, knows no decency, and is haunted by the grossest superstitions.[2]

Darwin is severe with aborigines. Had he lived in the twentieth century he might have discussed a possibly more mortifying biological kinship with Hitler and Stalin. At any rate, it is here, in his treatment of man as a phenomenon of nature, that Darwin most directly affected the course of subsequent thinking and it is here that he broke most spectacularly with the past. In the seventeenth century Descartes had made the system of nature almost all-inclusive—embracing celestial objects as well as terrestrial, the organic as well as the inorganic, human organisms as well as subhuman organisms. The inclusion of living organisms in the system of nature was therefore no Darwinian innovation. On this score, Darwin simply amplified and reinforced what Descartes and others had already affirmed. But, as we have seen earlier, Descartes had scrupulously

---

[1] Modern Library Edition, pp. 430–431. Italics added. "I am aware," he declares, "that the conclusions arrived at in this work will be denounced by some as highly irreligious; but he who denounces them is bound to shew why it is more irreligious to explain the origin of man as a distinct species by descent from some lower form, through the laws of variation and natural selection, than to explain the birth of the individual through the laws of ordinary reproduction." *Ibid.*, pp. 914–915.

[2] *Ibid.*, pp. 919–920.

withheld the mind and soul of man. Between man in his distinctive aspect and the natural world a great chasm yawned. Darwin bridged this gap.

This is not to say that the inclusion of man within the system of nature is limited to post-Darwinian philosophy. Reference has already been made to Hobbes and Spinoza. Long before them there were Democritus and Lucretius. As noted in Part I, there is much in the writings of Aristotle to inspire the contemporary naturalist. But post-Darwinian philosophy has been able to invoke the authority of science for including man in the system of nature and has thereby proceeded with a new kind of conviction. Moreover, post-Darwinian philosophy can speak with the assurance that this phase of its teaching will be heard by more than a handful of avant-garde contemporaries.

Traditionally and by general consent the distinctive attributes of man are those which mark him off as a thinking being and a morally responsible agent. His role as a cognitive, reflective being is associated with his *mind* and, traditionally, his role as a moral agent is associated with his *soul*. Western thought tends strongly either to treat mind as one aspect of the soul, or to identify mind and soul—as when Socrates described the soul as "whatever it is in us that has knowledge or ignorance, goodness or badness." In the popular view, the soul of man is his link with the supernatural, and since it partakes of the supernatural, it is also accorded immortality.

When the status of man is under discussion it is usually the status of his mind or soul that is at issue and here, as with the nature and origin of life, the disputants have engaged in prolonged polemics—only more fiercely and implacably. The issue has changed but—if we can omit those systems of thought that treat mind as a cosmic principle or identify it with all reality—the contestants continue to fall into three camps.

Metaphysical Behaviorism

One group consists of the *behaviorists* whose position regarding the status of mind corresponds to the mechanist's treatment of life and who marshal much the same arguments. It is important, however, to distinguish between *methodological* and *metaphysical* behaviorism. Methodological behaviorism was a response to the discontent of most psychologists with the status of their science at a time when it relied largely on introspective report for its data. Now, introspection may be extremely important to the individual who engages in it, it no doubt serves useful purposes in clinical psychology, the verbal responses in which it is reported are themselves significant data for study, and it most assuredly has had important literary manifestations as in the writings of Marcel Proust. But the data of introspection are incorrigibly private: whatever it is I find when I "look into" myself only I can see. It is the nature of introspective reports, therefore, to be *subjective*. The psychologist aspiring to *objectivity*—as all scientists must—has sought data whicih are public, i.e., amenable to observation by more than one person. Hence he has insisted that scientific as contrasted to literary psychology concern itself with the study of overt behavior and of neurophysiological processes. This is generally accepted as a sound methodological postulate and, in this sense, probably all professional psychologists are behavioristic,[3] although needless to say, behavioristic psychologists may differ greatly over what aspect of behavior they emphasize, the vocabularies they use, the hypothetical constructs they employ, and so on.

Metaphysical behaviorism identifies mental states with the neurophysiological conditions determining them. It passes from the methodological precept that psychology achieves scientific status by concerning itself with the study of overt behavior, to the ontological statement that such behavior exhausts the nature of the human organism, that, in other words, there is nothing but overt behavior of varying degrees of complexity. Ontology, often identified with metaphysics, is a venerable part of philosophy dealing with the nature of being. Behaviorism, at this point, is ontological in that behaviorists are not merely commenting on good and bad procedure in the science of psychology; they are making statements about what *is*, i.e., about the nature of being: if by consciousness or mind or soul is meant something other than, or more than, certain bodily states, then consciousness or mind or soul does not exist, is without being. However, at this point psychologists are something more than scientists; they are philosophers—good or bad.

But professional psychologists have not wanted for encouragement from

---

[3] To the extent that they rely on the verbal reports of their subjects the situation is complicated by the fact that, however objectively recorded and checked and crosschecked these reports may be, they are nevertheless the products of introspection. Denying that this involves a concession or capitulation to introspectionism Kenneth Spence writes:

> The introspectionist . . . assumed a strict one-to-one relationship between the verbal responses of his subjects and the inner mental processes. Accordingly, he accepted these introspective reports as *facts* or *data* about the inner mental events which they represented. The behavior scientist takes a very different position. He accepts verbal response as just one more form of behavior and he proposes to use this type of data in exactly the same manner as he does other types of behavior variables. . . . In contrast, then, to the introspectionist's conception of these verbal reports as mirroring directly inner mental events, *i.e.*, facts, the behaviorist uses them either as data in their own right to be related to other data, or as a base from which to infer theoretical constructs which presumably represent internal or covert activities of their subjects.

"The Postulates and Methods of 'Behaviorism,'" rep. from the *Psychological Review*, 55, 1948, in *Readings in the Philosophy of Science*, ed. by Feigl and Brodbeck (New York: Appleton-Century-Crofts, 1953), p. 574.

philosophers as evidenced by a revival of the spirit of Democritus and Hobbes in the latter half of the nineteenth century. The Roman philosopher-poet, Lucretius, who wrote that "mind and soul are formed of bodily nature" which is "made of tiny particles"[4] found new adherents well before Watson and his followers came on the scene to express their dissatisfaction with introspectionism. The German philosopher, Ludwig Feuerbach (1804-1872), while he disassociated himself from reductive materialists, summed up their position in a famous pun: *"Der Mensch ist was er isst"* (Man is what he eats). He was echoed by Nietzsche's (1844-1900) Zarathustra who declares: ". . . body am I entirely, and nothing else; and soul is only a word for something about the body."[5]

In France, Auguste Comte (1798-1857), father of the nineteenth-century positivist tradition, outlawed introspective psychology, describing it as mere illusion and as a last phase of theology. The mind, Comte says, "may observe all phenomena but its own." Hence, "there can be nothing like scientific observation of the passions, except from without. . . ." This is equally true of the "intellectual observation of intellectual processes." He concludes: "After two thousand years of psychological pursuit, no one proposition is established to the satisfaction of its followers. . . . This interior observation gives birth to almost as many theories as there are observers."[6] Positivists reject all statements not capable of verification by the methods of empirical science. Since a consistent positivist finds the assumptions of materialism as unverifiable as other metaphysical assumptions (including those of idealism), Comte eschewed materialism. Nevertheless, in regarding the generalizations of physiology as completely adequate to an understanding of the data of psychology, he inevitably encouraged metaphysical behaviorism.

In our time Logical Positivism or, as it has come to be known, "logical empiricism" or "scientific empiricism," has been the most influential movement in denying the reality—in the vocabulary that positivists prefer, the "meaningfulness"—of such terms as mind and soul, if these are intended to designate nonphysical phenomena. Since logical positivism will be discussed in some detail later (pp. 410–417) only a brief comment is needed here. While claiming descent from Hume, Comte, Mach, and others, it represents a complete break with the great philosophical tradition. In the view of logical positivists, statements are without meaning unless they are subject to experimental confirmation and, since, as they contend, statements embraced by the traditional philosophical sys-

---

[4] *On the Nature of Things*, trans. by Bailey (Oxford at the Clarendon Press, 1910), Bk. III, 173–204.

[5] *Thus Spoke Zarathustra* in the *Portable Nietzsche*, ed. and trans. by Walter Kaufmann (New York: Viking, 1954), p. 146.

[6] *The Positive Philosophy of August Comte*, trans. by Harriet Martineau (London: Trubner and Co., 1853), Vol. I, chap. 1, pp. 9–10.

tems cannot be verified, i.e., can be neither proved nor disproved, they are meaningless. This holds for all generalizations in metaphysics and ontology. Their status is noncognitive. The meaningful statements that philosophers do make are statements about matter of fact falling outside their field of competence which would be much better made by appropriately trained and specialized scientists. The philosophers' purported explanations of reality are, therefore "pseudoexplanations."

Logical positivists, while thus disavowing interest in ontological problems, subscribe in their own way to behaviorism, preferring to call their position "logical behaviorism." Rejecting materialism as "meaningless" because it is a metaphysical position which purports to describe the ultimate nature of reality, they nevertheless do not shun the designation "physicalism," which they interpret as asserting that the language of psychological theories and constructs is "translatable" into the language of physics.[7] Their approach to the status of mind, while it has undergone some change since the movement was initiated several decades ago, is exemplified by the late Hans Reichenbach. He asks us to assume that scientists have constructed a perfect robot that in every way behaves like a human being. "The machine would talk, answer questions, do what it is ordered to do, and give all kinds of information wanted. . . . It would be a perfect machine but without a mind." Reichenbach asks: "How do you know it has no mind?" Reichenbach answers that the question is "meaningless" because "there is no verifiable difference between the two states of the person and if we assume he has a mind in one state, we have also to admit the mind for the other state. The mind is inseparable from a certain state of bodily organization. *It follows that mind and bodily organization are the same thing.*"[8]

Thus, both from the point of view of a logical analysis of meaning and a psychological description of behavior, the familiar quip is apt for at least some students of psychology that they first lost their soul, they then lost their mind, and they finally lost consciousness!

---

[7] Thus, Herbert Feigl, while deploring the "confusion of physicalism with 'mechanistic materialism,'" nevertheless interprets the physicalist thesis as implying that "The set of physical laws which enables us to deduce the facts of chemistry will also be sufficient for biology and psychology." "Unity of Science and Unitary Science" in *Readings in the Philosophy of Science*, p. 384. For a fuller statement see his "The Mind-Body Problem in the Development of Logical Empiricism" in the same volume.

On the other hand, the "strict" physicalist thesis that the laws of psychology or biology can be reduced to or derived from the laws of physics, i.e., the mechanistic position, can be rejected in sympathetic accounts of logical positivism, as by Gustav Bergmann in his discussion of methodological problems in psychology in the same volume. ("On Some Methodological Problems of Psychology." Rep. from *Philosophy of Science*, 7, 1940), pp. 627–636.

[8] *Rise of Scientific Philosophy* (Berkeley: University of California Press, 1957), pp. 271–272. Italics added.

Psychophysical Dualism

The second of the three positions referred to earlier may be called *psychophysical dualism*. In modern form, this view is best exemplified by Cartesianism. As we have seen, the Cartesian treatment of mind corresponds to the vitalist treatment of life. Indeed, vitalism may be called biophysical dualism.

Cartesianism, we may recall from the discussion in Part II (pp. 216–225) asserts the absolute duality of mind and matter. Emphasis on the difference of mind takes the extreme form of asserting its complete disparateness. Mind is neither derived from matter nor reducible to it. Mind is an ultimate principle or "stuff," equally real and having nothing in common with matter. Minds are "spiritual" entities and, although they are completely devoid of spatial attributes, they somehow inhabit human bodies where they engage in perceiving, thinking, willing, etc. Above all, they are possessed of a reflexive faculty which enables them to be aware of themselves in what we generally call self-consciousness.

Dualists may differ over whether this immaterial substance is one or many, whether it is capable of existing independently or is irrevocably chained to a body, whether it interacts with the body or pursues a course which somehow parallels the bodily processes, but they are alike in disjoining mind from physical or physiological processes and thereby detaching it from nature.[9] Mind obeys laws that are exclusively its own; psychology is a completely autonomous discipline.

Psychophysical dualism as thus described is so completely in accord with the traditional point of view and so appealing to common sense that Professor Gilbert Ryle calls it the "official doctrine."[10] As Bertrand Russell points out, "Few things are more firmly established in popular philosophy than the distinction between mind and matter. Those who are not professional metaphysicians are willing to confess that they do not know what mind actually is, or how matter is constituted; but they remain convinced that there is an impassible gulf between the two, and that both belong to what actually exists in the world."[11]

Mind-body dualism accords with man's view of himself as an exalted being, the "lord of nature," in Kant's words, "the *ultimate purpose* of

---

[9] Not all of this is always conceded and some will speak of a "natural science of the inner sense" and of psychology as the "science" of inner experience. Cf. Windelband, *History of Philosophy* (New York: Macmillan, 1901), p. 304. Also W. E. Hocking's "Mind and Near Mind," *Proceedings of the Sixth International Congress of Philosophy*, 1926, p. 209.

[10] *The Concept of Mind* (London: Hutchinson, 1949), p. 11.

[11] *Analysis of Mind* (London: G. Allen, 1921), p. 10.

nature here on earth."[12] Either man is a special creature endowed with a mind which by a miraculous feat of transcendence illumines and discloses the far-flung recesses of an ulterior reality, or he is no more than a dumb beast in the field. Either he is a unique being capable of exercising free will and of distinguishing between good and evil who is therefore morally responsible for his conduct, or he is a mere automaton at the mercy of blind, mechanical forces which completely determine his action and leave no room for moral agency. These are the alternatives as the psychophysical dualist sees them. He supports the first alternative. Darwinism, in affirming man's derivation from simpler organisms, appears to him to support the second alternative. Therefore, however ready he may be to accept the evolutionary principle on the biological level, along with a naturalistic account of the origin of life, the psychophysical dualist rejects the Darwinian explanation of the origin of man as, of course, he must reject much that is taught by modern science.

Selected Readings

Anderson, A. R., ed. *Minds and Machines,* Englewood Cliffs, N. J.: Prentice-Hall, 1964.

Blanshard, Brand, "The Nature of Mind" in *American Philosophers at Work,* New York: Criterion Books, 1956, pp. 183–193.

Broad, C. D., *The Mind and Its Place in Nature,* New York: Harcourt, Brace & World, 1929, especially chap. II "Mechanism and Its Alternatives."

Dewey, John, *Experience and Nature,* New York: Norton, 1925, chaps. 6, 7. (Also paperbacks by Dover, Open Court.)

Hook, Sidney, ed., *Dimensions of Mind,* New York: Collier Books, 1960.

Mead, G. H., *Mind, Self and Society,* Chicago: University of Chicago Press, 1934.

Morris, C. W., *Six Theories of Mind,* Chicago: University of Chicago Press, 1932.

Russell, Bertrand, *Analysis of Mind,* London: G. Allen and Unwin, 1921.

Ryle, Gilbert, *The Concept of Mind,* London: Hutchinson, 1949. (Also Barnes and Noble paperback.)

Spence, K. W., "The Postulates and Methods of 'Behaviorism,'" *Psychological Review,* 55, 1948. Reprinted in *Readings in the Philosophy of Science,* ed. by H. Feigl and M. Brodbeck, New York: Appleton-Century-Crofts, 1953, pp. 571–583.

Wisdom, John, *Problems of Mind and Matter,* Cambridge at the University Press, 1963.

---

[12] *Critique of Judgment,* trans. by J. H. Bernard, 2nd ed., rev. (London: Macmillan, 1914), p. 352.

CHAPTER 21

Critical Naturalism

As with the differences between the mechanists and dualists over the nature and origin of life, one must ask if the alternatives discussed in the last chapter are the only ones. Metaphysical behaviorism, in reducing the psychological to the biological appears to ignore the qualities that distinguish psychological phenomena. Psychophysical dualism does indeed recognize significant differences, but at the price of removing mind from the system of nature. Mind and body are, indeed, so polarized that their actual relationships become inexplicable. Let us recall some of the problems posed in Part II: How, for example, can the mind, which Descartes described as nonspatial, be "located" in a physical object like an organism? And how can this same nonphysical object act upon and be acted upon by physical objects, as when one wills to move his arm, or as when one's mind is affected by a drug? As we know from our earlier exploration of these questions, Cartesianism ultimately foundered on these difficulties. Accordingly, much contemporary philosophy has rejected both alternatives in favor of a third, represented by the standpoint of *critical naturalism.*

In America, the main outlines of critical naturalism were worked out during the first several decades of this century by a number of brilliant philosophers differing greatly in their emphases and interests but concurring on fundamentals, notably John Dewey, William James, George Santayana (with qualifications), Frederick Woodbridge, and Morris Raphael Cohen. It would be surprising indeed if there were complete agreement among their successors, and, of course, there is not. Any description of the naturalist position is bound to invite dissent at some point or other, from one or another "naturalist." Certainly no one can claim to speak for all. Nevertheless, there is an impressive consensus among critical naturalists and the account of their criticism of dualism and monism which follows should evoke general agreement.

Naturalism and Dualism

Critical naturalists, along with nearly all contemporary scientists and philosophers, are at war against the dualistic conception of man as a kind of robot inhabited by a ghostly pilot operating a complicated set of mechanical controls—Gilbert Ryle calls it the "dogma of the Ghost in the Machine"—as they are against the vitalist notion of life as an imponderable breath animating otherwise inanimate lumps of clay. They are undeterred by the fact that the man in the street clings to these occult entities with a tenacity born of long conviction and inveterate verbal habits.

Professor Ryle's illustration of the verbal habit is worth citing. Anyone who has visited England and traveled to Oxford University has found Balliol, University College, Magdalen, the Ashmolean Museum, Christ Church, the Bodleian Library, and much else, but no Oxford University! Where, the visitor is prone to ask, is Oxford University? When the foregoing items are again enumerated he is likely to be perplexed. What is Oxford University? he may well plead. Oxford University has become the name of an entity on its own and he is not easily reconciled to the assertion that it is nothing but a collection of "related" colleges, churches, etc. He may remain adamant even after we have told him how they are related, for it is Oxford University that he always believed that students were attending, and after all, Professor Ryle is himself an Oxonian. Professor Ryle calls this and the "dogma of the Ghost in the Machine" by the name of "category-mistake." Such a mistake "represents the facts of mental life as if they belonged to one type or category . . . when they actually belong to another." Category mistakes are made by people who, while competent to apply concepts in situations with which they are familiar, are liable, in certain cases, in their abstract thinking "to allocate those concepts to logical types to which they do not belong."[1]

We must see that "Oxford University" is a convenient shorthand for numerous entities and groups of entities involved in a complex set of relationships. When this is forgotten and Oxford University itself comes

[1] *Concept of Mind* (London: Hutchinson, 1949), pp. 16–17.

to be regarded as an entity, we are on the road to confusion. Similarly with the terms "Life" and "Mind." It would make for clarity if, as nouns,— especially capitalized nouns—they were banished from the vocabulary and we spoke instead, adjectivally, of living things and minded organisms. So long as they are nouns, we shall be tempted to look for the entities they designate. For example, in distinguishing between man and other organisms it is common to say: "Man possesses a mind which enables him to look ahead." Much confusion would be avoided if we were to say: "Man's looking ahead (among other activities) *is* his mind." The former manner of speaking suggests a separate agency possessing an identity of its own that does the looking ahead. It is one of those cases in which, to use the famous words of a contemporary philosopher, "our language has gone on a vacation." The second and more accurate manner of speaking identifies the agent, i.e., the mind, with the looking ahead —along with such other activities as may be called mental.

Observation fails to disclose substantial entities of the kind which loose linguistic habits and ancient preconceptions have led us to expect, according to the critical naturalist. Beyond this, the assumption that such entities exist has created the insoluble problems noted earlier, those same problems that eventually rendered Cartesianism untenable. Finally, dualism is a surrender to ignorance. Excluding life or mind or any other property or manifestation of being from the system of nature forecloses the possibility of finding out anything about them, at any rate, by the scientific methods that have demonstrated their enormous potency here as elsewhere. These are the methods which, over the centuries, have been extended steadily to forbidden areas, in every case increasing our understanding and our power to predict and control. The issue can be stated another way. Science—the quest for intelligibility and control—is a quest for relationships. We find out about something by discovering its relationships to other things. Dualists, in stressing the separateness of mind, abdicate this quest.

In the seventeenth century, as the discussion in Part II has disclosed, dualism made it possible for science and theology to live together, and thus served a profoundly important historic purpose. It was the inevitable outcome of a view that regarded nature in exclusively mechanistic terms, and hence was lacking in a vocabulary with which to deal with the phenomena of mind. In general, dualists deserve great credit for refusing to ignore important differences. But, when they erect these differences into radical disjunctures, they cut off inquiry at the point where it is most needed. To be sure, an adequate philosophy must explain why Professor Ryle's "ghost in the machine" continues to haunt us after it has been banished so often. It must somehow reckon with everyday, common-sense convictions, especially those to which common sense clings stubbornly.

Dualism has done this. But for philosophy, as for science, the assumptions of common sense must be the starting point of analysis and inquiry, not the conclusion.

Naturalism and Materialism

Critical naturalism also rejects *monism:* not merely the now virtually defunct idealistic monisms that identified reality with Mind or Spirit, but materialism, which identifies all of reality with its physical manifestations. This is the materialism to which mechanism in biology and behaviorism in psychology are allied. To be sure, materialism as understood today must not be confused with the crude materialism of Democritus and Lucretius: inert lumps of matter and solid pellets have been replaced in the vocabulary of the materialist by energy configurations and electric charges and such other refinements as modern physics may suggest. Not even the mechanist is prepared to say that—to borrow a phrase from Ortega y Gasset—we are launched into existence like a shot from a gun, with its trajectory absolutely determined. But the language and categories of materialism are the language and categories of physics: physics is the basic science and the laws or descriptive generalizations of physics are all-sufficing.

Now critical naturalism and materialism have much in common. As noted earlier, each standpoint dispenses with supernatural agencies or purposes and hence excludes the kind of teleological approach which postulates preconceived goals or ends-in-view in explaining natural events. They agree in regarding the system of nature as all-inclusive. They each regard physical phenomena as temporally prior and causally antecedent to biological, psychological and sociological phenomena.[2] Each respects the competence of science and scientific method, although at this point agreement starts breaking down. Many critical naturalists are not so disposed to emphasize the *omni*competence of science; and their orientation, as some of the ensuing comments will indicate, is on the whole more influenced by the biological than by the physical sciences.

The basic difference between these two varieties of naturalism stems (1) from the materialist assumption that "derived from" means "identical with" (for all significant purposes), and (2) from the materialist conversion of methodological postulates (which are in their way cognitive processes or ways of knowing) into ontological predicates. The details of the indictment are not as formidably technical as the foregoing language may suggest. The charges will be considered in reverse order and hence-

---

[2] The critical naturalist is not committed, however, to the ultimacy of matter which may itself be derived from something more primitive; although, admittedly, such considerations are purely speculative.

forth, in the interest of simplicity, the term "naturalist" will be reserved for the critical naturalist, that is, the naturalist who is also a critic of materialism.

One of the most prolific sources of confusion in the history of philosophy is the tendency to misuse the various procedures of science, once these procedures have come to be explicitly defined and consciously employed and have proven themselves impressively successful. Ways of dealing with the objects of experience get confused with the objects themselves. This was the case with the Platonic doctrine of Ideas which, as indicated in Part I, mistook logical abstractions for self-subsistent entities, treating a way of knowing as though it were a mode of being. In the argot of philosophers this is called *hypostatization*. Similarly with materialism: our knowledge of things is enormously advanced if we ignore, that is, abstract from, their qualitative differences (thereby carrying abstraction a step further than does the traditional logic of kinds or classes) and view them in quantitative terms as homogeneous particles in motion or configurations of energy in space-time. But materialists are guilty of forgetting that this is a way of dealing with the objects of experience and is not to be identified with the object themselves. Once again, a way of thinking gets converted into a mode of being. Behaviorism affords still another example, on the psychological level, of what Dewey has called the "substantialization of the function of being a tool"[3] when it converts a canon of method—that psychologists must study publicly observable behavior—into a dogma of metaphysics—that there are no covert (subjective) mental states corresponding to overt (objective) behavioral processes. To deny the existence of consciousness simply because psychology finds it more useful to limit itself to "accessible" data is, in the words of C. I. Lewis, "as if one should deny the existence of colors because, for purposes of exact investigation, the colors must be defined as frequencies of vibratory motion."[4] One is reminded of Santayana's reference to those *esprits forts* who, having led a life of vice, think that the universe must be composed of nothing but dice and billiard balls.

The other criticism of materialism is also basic. Materialism, it should be recalled, asserts that all phenomena are conditioned or determined by physical events and physical relationships. To this, the naturalist assents, but with a decisive reservation: the circumstance that all psychological and biological phenomena vary with variations in physical conditions, and the fact that the origin of all such phenomena, if traced back far enough, must be sought in a physical matrix, does not preclude their being different from the physical—so different, indeed, that their full understanding requires generalizations not applicable to physical objects and events. The occurrence of a mental event does indeed depend upon, i.e., is con-

---

[3] *Quest for Certainty* (New York: Minton, 1929), p. 248.
[4] *Mind and the World Order* (New York: Scribner, 1929), p. 5.

ditioned by neurophysiological processes, which are in turn determined by biochemical and biophysical changes. From the point of view of controlling or manipulating mental processes, it would be well, therefore, to learn the physicochemical changes which produce the neurophysiological which in turn bring about the mental changes. But this is not enough. We would need also to learn about the supervening properties on each new level and how *these* affect the result. It is these properties which the materialist, given his mechanistic predilections, either ignores or treats as *epiphenomenal*, that is, as having no effect on the course of events so that whatever happens can be deduced without reference to them.

To be sure, the materialist's "mechanistic" orientation no longer commits him to explanation in terms of the fundamental concepts of the science of mechanics. He is not so oblivious to recent developments in physics as to continue regarding classical mechanics as the universal science of nature. But he continues to be dominated by the subject-matter and methods of the physical sciences, however the data and procedures of these sciences are presently conceived, and this leads him to stress the homogeneity of data and the constancy of relationships to the exclusion of difference and novelty. That is to say, it commits him, in the interest of a mistaken ideal of simplicity, to a "homogenized" universe. This is what naturalists mean when they charge materialists with "reductionism."

Pluralism

Critical naturalists are not dualists. They are not monists. They are pluralists. They believe, that is, that nature manifests itself in many ways of which the physical is only one and the mental another. But they are pluralists in a sense quite different from the sense in which dualists, as thus far described, are dualistic: they do not exclude anything from nature nor do they disjoin the several aspects or levels of nature that are discriminated, however much they may insist that these are irreducibly different. The several levels into which nature is distinguished are, it must be remembered, causally related; the continuity of nature is unbroken.

The idea of continuity requires brief comment. It has been involved in seemingly unnecessary differences of opinion among those who might be expected to agree. Professor Ernest Nagel speaks almost unkindly of "professed" naturalists "who make a fetish of continuity" and he suspects "that the cardinal importance philosophers assign to the alleged universality of such continuity is a lingering survival of that ancient conception, according to which things are intelligible only when seen as teleological systems producing definite ends. . . ."[5]

---

[5] "Naturalism Reconsidered," *Proceedings and Addresses of the American Philosophical Association,* 1954–1955, pp. 10–11; cf. also, Thelma Lavine's "Naturalism and the Sociological Analysis of Knowledge," in *Naturalism and the Human Spirit* (New York: Columbia, 1944), pp. 183–186.

Others will find it difficult to see why Professor Nagel finds so innocent a concept as suspect as the foregoing comment suggests. Naturalists who emphasize continuity do so because they fear that their insistence on recognizing irreducible differences will otherwise be construed dualistically. It is because they do not want differences confused with *dis*continuity that they emphasize continuity, by which is meant nothing more mysterious than causal relatedness. Dewey, with whom Nagel is usually to be found in broad agreement, in referring to the "continuity of the lower (less complex) and the higher (more complex) activities and forms," adds: "The idea of continuity is not self-explanatory. But its meaning excludes complete rupture on one side and mere repetition of identities on the other; it precludes reduction of the 'higher' to the 'lower' just as it precludes complete breaks and gaps." He continues: "What *is* excluded by the postulate of continuity is the appearance upon the scene of a totally new outside force as a cause of changes that occur. Perhaps from mutations that are due to some form of radio-activity a strikingly new form emerges. But radio-activity is not invented *ad hoc* and introduced from without in order to account for such transformation. It is first known to exist in nature, and then, if this particular theory of the origin of mutations is confirmed, is found actually to occur in biological phenomena and to be operative among them in observable and describable fashion."[6]

How, more specifically, do naturalists reach and formulate this conclusion? At this point the discussion may return to Darwin and Darwinism, from which it may seem to have strayed, for "critical" naturalism begins with that aspect of change upon which Darwin's work focuses attention, that aspect, namely, which manifests itself as novelty.

Mutations and the new species to which beneficial mutations may give rise are, it has already been noted, genuine novelties; they mark the appearance in nature of properties not heretofore manifest. By virtue of them, nature—in this instance organic nature—is different from what it was before. In short, those same Darwinian principles, which were construed as reducing man to the status of a brute because his ancestry was found in subhuman organisms, actually pointed the way to an escape from reductionism by forcing thinkers to reject the ancient maxim that the effect may never "exceed" (that is, be of a different nature from) the cause—lest something come from nothing. As Whitehead points out, "A thoroughgoing evolutionary philosophy is inconsistent with materialism."[7] Perhaps for the first time it was necessary to reckon seriously with the proposition that there can be more in the consequent than there was in the antecedent.

---

[6] *Logic* (New York: Holt, Rinehart & Winston, 1938), pp. 23–24. Ironically, this work is one in which Dewey generously declares that "I have availed myself freely of the superior knowledge and competency of Dr. Ernest Nagel."

[7] *Science and the Modern World* (New York: Macmillan, 1962), p. 157.

Ex nihilo nihil fit. This ancient dogma that "there cannot be more in the effect than in the cause" was regarded as axiomatic by Greek materialists as by medieval schoolmen and seventeenth-century mechanists, until insights suggested by the principle of evolution compelled its re-examination.[8]

These insights have been epitomized in a concept which, although its usefulness has recently come into question among many naturalists, has played a key role in the thinking of scientists and philosophers since the early part of this century. This is the concept of *emergence.* The view of nature as a series of emergent levels rather than a succession of rearrangements of the same elements is not the least of the philosophical consequences partly inspired by the work of Darwin. It is, of course, as old as Aristotle and what he called "the coming-to-be of what is not."[9]

Before turning to an examination of the concept of emergence we must understand that, however naturalists finally deal with this concept, they are unanimously committed to a stress on the multiplicity, the variety, the richness of nature: ". . . how marvelous the swarming atoms, in their unintentional, perpetual fertility!"[10] All naturalists would echo these words of Santayana.

The Concept of Emergence

An emergent property—as the idea of emergence was first formulated—is to be distinguished from a *resultant.* G. H. Lewes—who suggested the terminology—described a resultant as additive and subtractive only, and as predictable. An emergent, on the other hand, is new and initially unpredictable, although both resultants and emergents "fall under the rubric of uniform causation."[11] Simple examples are cited on the chemical level although not with quite the same confidence as on the biological and psychological levels. Thus, when molecules of hydrogen combine with molecules of oxygen they form water. But many of the qualities and properties of water bear no resemblance to the qualities and properties of hydrogen or oxygen. Neither hydrogen nor oxygen is a liquid, translucent substance, nor can either one quench thirst or nourish plants. The molecular weight of water at ordinary temperatures is the sum of the molecular weights of its components—this is an additive *resultant* that could have

---

[8] Cf. A. O. Lovejoy's "The Meaning of 'Emergence' and its Modes" for a fuller discussion. *Proceedings of the Sixth International Congress of Philosophy,* Harvard University, Sept., 1926, rep. in *Readings in The Philosophy of Science,* ed. by P. P. Wiener (New York: Scribner, 1953), pp. 585–596.

[9] *De Generatione* II, 10:336a. Cf. also J. H. Randall, Jr's, *Aristotle* (New York: Columbia, 1960), especially chap. X.

[10] G. Santayana, *Three Philosophical Poets* (Cambridge: Harvard, 1927), p. 37.

[11] Lloyd Morgan, *Emergent Evolution* (New York: Holt, Rinehart, & Winston, 1931), p. 3.

been predicted in advance of the formation of the compound called water. But, it has been argued, no amount of knowledge of the properties of hydrogen and oxygen in isolation and no amount of knowledge of the other compounds into which they enter would enable one to predict the distinguishing properties and qualities of water in advance of our having experienced these qualities. These, then, are *emergent* qualities. Needless to say, once one has observed the sequence of events represented in the forming of water by hydrogen and oxygen one may then predict that a substance possessing the qualities and properties of water will be produced again under like circumstances.

What is said of chemical compounds is also claimed *a fortiori* for living things. Thus, in Professor Broad's words, "The only way to find out the characteristic behavior of living bodies may be to study living bodies as such. And no amount of knowledge about how the constituents of a living body behave in isolation or in other and nonliving wholes might suffice to enable us to predict the characteristic behavior of a living organism." Professor Broad adds that "this possibility is perfectly compatible with the view that the characteristic behavior of a living body is completely determined by the nature and arrangement of the chemical compounds which compose it . . ."[12]

Among the phenomena usually cited as emergent on the biological level are growth, regeneration, reproduction, and heredity for which laws are formulable (for example, Mendel's laws of inheritance) without reference to merely physical or chemical processes. Often the "goal-directed" behavior of living things, by virtue of which they may be described in a qualified sense as teleological systems, is cited:

> The interactions of the various constituent parts of a plant take place in such ways as to tend to continue a characteristically organized activity; they tend to utilize conserved consequences of past activities so as to adapt subsequent changes to the needs of the integral system to which they belong. . . . Iron as such exhibits characteristics of bias or selective reactions, but it shows no bias in favor of remaining simple iron; it had just as soon, so to speak, become iron-oxide. It shows no tendency in its interaction with water to modify the interaction so that consequences will perpetuate the characteristics of pure iron. If if did, it would have the marks of a living body, and would be called an organism.[13]

Stated otherwise, biological organisms do react sensitively in a great variety of ways. Capable of primitive tropistic responses, they turn toward or away from such stimuli as food, water, sun and various chemicals. The response is not, for example, quite like the reaction of a photographic plate to light. It is a response to a stimulus by the whole organism, which, never-

---

[12] C. D. Broad, *Mind and Its Place in Nature* (New York: Harcourt, Brace and World, 1929), p. 67.
[13] John Dewey, *Experience and Nature* (New York: Norton, 1925), p. 254.

theless, maintains its identity and capacity to adjust and to react again and again, but not just like a bouncing ball, to a variety of stimuli. It maintains this capacity unless, of course, the stimulus is strong enough to destroy the organism or permanently to impair its capacity to respond, as may be the case under conditions of excessive heat.

Finally, it is argued that organisms are not mere collections or aggregates of parts; the cells of an organism, unlike grains of sand or billiard balls, derive their character from their relationship to each other and to the whole of which they are a part. The relationship of the parts of an organism is internal rather than external; that is, a part cannot be separated from the whole without losing its identity, nor can it be fully described or understood apart from its relationship to the whole. Unlike a machine, an organism cannot be broken down into elementary components from which it can then be reconstructed. Organisms are wholes which cannot be analyzed into their constituent parts without remainder, that is to say, such organized wholes possess properties not possessed by or discernible in their constituent parts—emergent properties not describable in physicochemical terms. This is the view of so-called "organismic" biology which notes the relatively small role that physicochemical terms have played in explaining biological phenomena and asserts that the mechanistic type of explanation is inherently inapplicable to some of the major problems of biology.

A similar position has been defended in psychology. Thus, the distinguished psychologist, Edward Tolman—who called himself a "Purposive Behaviorist"—subscribed to an emergent view of psychological phenomena when he declared that "Behavior *qua* molar possesses characteristic *molar* properties which a mere detailed, *molecular* . . . description of its underlying physics and physiology completely leaves out." By "molar" phenomena he refers to such organic activities as are the result of past learning or capable of future learning.[14] More specifically, "molar" properties characterize behavior when "if a given behavior-act in a given environment proves relatively unsuccessful, i.e., does not get to the demanded type of goal-object at all or gets there only by a relatively long distance . . . , it will on subsequent occasions, tend to give way to an act or acts which *will* tend to get the organism to this demanded type of goal-object and will tend to get him to it by a relatively short route."[15] By "molecular" behavior Tolman means a conception of behavior which stresses its physical and physiological character. While "Purposive Behaviorism," as he called it, agrees with strict behaviorism in asserting that "organisms, their behavior and the environmental and organic conditions which induce the latter, are all that there is to be studied," it differs in asserting that "behavior *qua* molar has characteristic descriptive properties all its own." According to Tolman, "be-

---

[14] *Purposive Behavior in Animals and Men* (New York: Century, 1932), p. 438.
[15] *Ibid.*, pp. 442–443.

havior has *emergent* patterns and meanings which are *other than* the patterns and meaning of the gland secretions and muscle contractions which underlie it, though no doubt they are completely dependent on the latter."[16]

In the emergent view, while one will avoid speaking in dualistic fashion of organisms with minds—except in a Pickwickian sense—"mindedness" will be regarded as distinctive and irreducible, designating the totality of those activities in which "minded" organisms engage when they are abstracting, generalizing, recalling, projecting. Such processes are peculiarly mental, obeying their own laws and having their own different consequences. Sub-human organisms are incapable of engaging in such activities, except in a rudimentary way, and hence may not be described as "minded." There is no reason to suppose, for example, that any organism—other than man—can perform the feat of histrionics which Professor G. H. Mead called "taking the role of the other" and brilliantly analyzed as providing the basis for communication and thought.[17] There is nothing mysterious about the fact that, uniquely among organisms, man is capable of such activities. Their general biological basis has long been familiar, however elusive the details may be. But they are called emergent because they do not occur, except in the most rudimentary form, on the prehuman level.

Emergent qualities are not, of course, limited to the domains of chemistry, biology, and psychology. Matter itself may be an emergent deriving, it has been suggested, from some primal mist; and, at the other end of the scale of complexity, social phenomena, as we shall soon see, may be said to exhibit emergent qualities requiring us to employ concepts and evolve generalizations peculiar to the study of society. And, if one accepts the view that ethical deliberation is something more than the direction of conduct by reference to established rules or accepted goals—if one agrees, that is, that ethical deliberation is an achievement of which human organisms are capable only after their social relationships have reached a highly complex and peculiarly ordered level, then the exercise of ethical choice and decision may well be characterized as an emergent. Similarly with those of man's activities in which he is moved by beauty and worships God—where the concept of God is something other than childlike or primitive father-imagery. Finally, nature may manifest itself in ways that our meager imagination cannot even remotely envisage.

It must be emphasized that, in the view under consideration, an emergent property, in the nature of the case, can be ascertained only *after* the experience of its occurrence. This is because it is something novel, something more than, or—since the difference cannot be fully stated in quantita-

16 *Ibid.*, pp. 417–418. Italics added. Cf. also, pp. 7–8.
17 *Mind, Self, and Society*, ed. by C. W. Morris (Chicago: University of Chicago Press, 1934), p. 73.

tive terms—other than a regrouping or rearrangement of pre-existent events or entities. If new relations "supervene," relations of such a nature that their presence makes an "effective" difference in what takes place in the world,[18] then the statements we make about them cannot be a priori. As Broad points out, such statements must come after observation and experiment. Thus, the emergent approach, as so far described, would appear to reduce the scope of deductive procedures in science—which is large, to the extent that one encounters sameness and regularity in nature—and to increase the scope of observation and experiment—which is large, to the extent that one encounters difference and contingency.

The point is well made by the biologist, H. S. Jennings, who writes:

> For mechanical evolution (i.e., mechanism) the ideal scientific method is mainly rationalistic, to but a minimal extent empirical. From the examination of any small part of the universe, at any time, it is possible to discover the laws of action, of grouping, for all its parts and for all periods. Only a few preliminary observations should be required—of the particles, their arrangements and motions. The rest is a matter of computing, of reasoning. . . . From a sample of the universe we ought to be able to reason out the rest. . . .
>
> For the doctrine of emergent evolution, on the other hand, observation and experiment are the primary and the final methods of science. . . . On the basis of what they bring forth, reasoning, computation, may indeed act, so long as these stay within the restricted circle that shows nothing new, nothing emergent. . . . The new things, the new modes of action, that come in evolution, cannot be discovered by reasoning, but only by observation and experiment.[19]

The concept of emergence has lately been rejected by many naturalists because it is often used in ways repugnant to naturalism: emergents have been cited as proof of an external creative activity,[20] emergent qualities have been converted into substances—as by the vitalists and psychophysical dualists; and the concept of emergent levels has been used as a loom on which to weave such highly speculative metaphysical systems as those elaborated by S. Alexander (*Space, Time and Deity*, 1920) and Lloyd Morgan (*Life, Mind and Spirit*, 1926). But many will insist that these are misuses of the emergent principle and not reasons for discarding it. More challenging is the argument that, in calling an effect an emergent we give up the attempt to understand it, and substitute a word for an explanation, which is to say, provide a pseudo-explanation. Thus Hempel and Oppenheim conclude that the "emergence of a characteristic is not an ontological trait inherent in some phenomena; rather it is indicative of the scope of our knowledge at a given time. . . . What is emergent with respect

---

[18] L. Morgan, *op. cit.*, p. 9.

[19] *The Biological Basis of Human Nature* (New York: Norton, 1930), pp. 371–372.

[20] Joseph Needham in the *Encyclopedia of the Social Sciences* (1st ed.), improperly describes *all* emergent theories as evoking an "external creative force" and stressing the "discontinuity view." Vol. V, p. 649b.

to the theories available today may lose its emergent status tomorrow."[21] Professor Ernest Nagel, although he believes that "the manifest plurality and variety of things . . . are an irreducible feature of the cosmos,"[22] has argued similarly and with impressive scientific erudition. The distinction between a whole that is the sum and a whole that is not the sum of its parts is not an absolute one, but is always relative to some body of theory, he contends in criticism of so-called "organismic" biology and its stress on the principle of emergence. Accordingly:

. . . though a given whole may not be the sum of its parts relative to one theory, it may indeed be such a sum relative to another. Thus, though the thermal behavior of solids is not the sum of the behavior of its parts relative to the classic kinetic theory of matter, it is such a sum relative to modern quantum mechanics. To say, therefore, that the behavior of an organism is not the sum of the behavior of its parts, and that its total behavior cannot be understood adequately in physicochemical terms even though the behavior of each of its parts is explicable mechanistically, can only mean that no body of general theory is now available from which statements about the total behavior of the organism are derivable.[23]

The issue is sufficiently important to warrant citing at some length the divergent opinion of Professor Arthur Lovejoy.

To characterize an effect as "emergent," it is urged, is to give up the attempt to "explain" it; and since science cannot give up this attempt, the characterization can have, at best, no more than a provisional validity, as a way of admitting that certain things have not as yet been completely "explained." Now, what sort of explanation is it that these critics desiderate in theories of emergence? "Causal explanation" in the empirical sense—the assumption that every event follows upon some other *nach einer Regel*, the "determinism of the experimentalist" is . . . entirely compatible with the belief in emergence. The sort of explanation which . . . emergent evolution, would exclude, is . . . the conception of an event as *neither* (*a*) manifesting any law, or mode of uniform behavior, *nor* (*b*) containing any existent, not found in the antecedent

21 "The Logic of Explanation," rep. from *Philosophy of Science*, 15, 1948 in *Readings in the Philosophy of Science*, ed. by Feigl and Brodbeck (New York: Appleton-Century-Crofts, 1953), pp. 335–336. Cf. also, W. P. Montague's "A Materialistic Theory of Emergent Evolution," in *Essays in Honor of John Dewey* (New York: Holt, 1929), especially pp. 264–265.

22 "Naturalism Reconsidered," *Proceedings and Addresses of the American Philosophical Association* Vol. XXVIII (Oct., 1955), p. 9.

23 "Mechanistic Explanation and Organismic Biology," *Philosophy and Phenomenological Research*, Vol. II, (1951), p. 335. Reprinted in *American Philosophers at Work*, ed. by S. Hook, pp. 106–120. Cf. also his "The Meaning of Reduction in the Natural Sciences," in *Science and Civilization*, ed. by Robert Stauffer (Madison: University of Wisconsin Press, 1949). Here also Professor Nagel writes that when controversies over the scope of physics "overlook the fact that the reduction of one science to another involves a tacit reference to a date, they assume the character of typically irresoluble debates over what are alleged to be metaphysical ultimates; and differences and similarities between departments of inquiry that may possess only a temporary autonomy with respect to one another come to be cited as evidence for some immutably final account of the inherent nature of things" (p. 129).

phase of the sequence to which it belongs. To maintain then, that everything is "explicable," in the sense incongruous with emergence . . . is to imply, for example, that, barring mere summations or rearrangements, there is to be found in the present phase of terrestrial history no existence whatever—no quality, type of entity, or kind of process—which could not already have been discerned by a scientific angel observing the cold-gaseous-nebula stage of the development of our solar system. This proposition cannot be said to have a high degree of *prima facie* plausibility; and its truth cannot be assumed *a priori* merely because it is one of the two conceivable ways of satisfying the demand for a special type of so-called "explanation" which is not practically indispensable to science.[24]

Clearly, the issue is one on which naturalists are not in accord. With Professor Nagel, many will find the assertion that "certain properties of compounds are inherently novel relative to the properties of the elements" one of the "dogmas of a footless ontology."[25] Others will continue to accept the presence of emergent properties in nature with natural humility if not "natural piety," contending that no metaphysical mystery is implied—only the recognition of an indefeasible limitation on the predictive powers of science. They will say that the advent in nature of genuine, i.e., irreducible novelty, to which every *critical* naturalist must assent, precludes the prediction of such novelty on the basis of generalizations formulated before its appearance. This should disappoint only those who fail to realize that science no more than philosophy can be the spectator of all time and all existence.

The Scope of Science

The conclusion just reached prompts a somewhat closer examination of the position of the naturalist concerning the scope of science in general and the physical sciences in particular. Earlier, in contrasting critical naturalism with materialism, it was observed that, while both stress the competence of science and scientific method, the former is less likely to stress the omnicompetence of science and is more likely to be oriented toward the biological than toward the physical sciences. To the extent that naturalists have stressed the advent of novelty and relied on the emergent principle, their biological bias is clear although, as Professor Nagel's asseverations attest, there is by no means complete agreement. In general, the position of the critical naturalist with respect to the scope of scientific method is not without its ambiguities, and he often seems to be affirming

---

[24] "The Meaning of 'Emergence' and Its Modes," *Proceedings of the Sixth International Congress of Philosophy, op. cit.*; reprinted in *Contemporary Philosophic Problems*, ed. by Y. H. Krokorian and A. Edel (New York: Macmillan, 1959) and *Readings in Philosophy of Science*, ed. by P. P. *Wiener* (New York: Scribner, 1953), pp. 585–596.

[25] *Ibid.*, "The Meaning of Reduction in the Natural Sciences," p. 134.

a point of view very close indeed to that of the materialist. This is especially true when scientific method is construed so as to imply a denial of the reality of mental states. But at this point it would be well to permit critical naturalists to speak for themselves.

A collection of essays published in 1944 entitled *Naturalism and the Human Spirit* comes as close as anything we have to providing a testament for the naturalist point of view. In one of the essays Professor William R. Dennes sets forth the idea which, more than any other, unites the able contributors to this volume, when he writes:

> . . . there is for naturalism no knowledge except that of the type ordinarily called 'scientific'. But such knowledge cannot be said to be restricted by its method to any limited field of subject matter—to the exclusion, let us say, of the processes called 'history' and the 'fine arts'. For whether a question is about forces 'within the atom,' or about the distribution of galaxies, or about the qualities and pattern of sound called Beethoven's Second Rasumowski Quartette and the joy some men have found in them—in any case there is no serious way to approach controlled hypothesis as to what the answers should be except by inspection of the relevant evidence and by inductive inference from it.[26]

The kind of dedication to scientific method to which Professor Dennes calls attention has provoked criticism both from within and without the ranks of naturalists. Among the former is Thelma Levine,[27] who charges that in their preoccuption with scientific method many naturalists are forfeiting their status as constructive philosophers. Naturalism, as they formulate it, would convert philosophy into a mere methodological principle conceived of in terms of experiment or empirical verifiability and "sweeping the nonexperimental under the rug." Can philosophy have escaped the role assigned to it in the Middle Ages, of handmaiden to theology, only to become the handyman of science? Even those who may be guilty would repudiate the suggestion that naturalism implies such a role for philosophy.[28] Meanwhile, other criticism has come, as might be expected, from nonnaturalists, such as W. H. Sheldon, who charged that naturalists are, in fact, surreptitious materialists. "Their naturalism is just materialism over again under a softer name," he asserts. The naturalist's "adoration" of scientific method limits him exclusively to affirmations about the physical world, Sheldon contends, citing by way of illustration another contributor to the volume referred to above: ". . . perhaps the sole

---

27 "Note to Naturalists on the Human Spirit," *The Journal of Philosophy* (Vol. L, No. 5 (Feb. 26, 1953), pp. 145–154, rep. in *Philosophy of the Social Sciences*, ed. by M. Natanson (New York: *Random House*, 1963) pp. 250–261.
28 Cf. Ernest Nagel's "On the Method of *Verstehen* as the Sole Method of Philosophy," *The Journal of Philosophy*, Vol. L, No. 5 (February 26, 1953), pp. 154–157, rep. in *Philosophy of the Social Sciences*, ed. by M. Natanson, pp. 262–265.

bond uniting all varieties of naturalists is that temper of mind which seeks to understand the flux of events in terms of the *behavior of indentifiable bodies.*"[29]

When naturalists speak of method, argues Sheldon, it is the procedures of the purely physical sciences they have in mind as evidenced by their treatment of the critical issue of mind and consciousness in exclusively behavioristic terms. Since there is no knowledge except scientific knowledge, since scientific knowledge has to do only with what is accessible to public observation, and since mental states are not amenable to such observation, the naturalist's acceptance of such mental states is mere lip service. This is the argument by which Professor Sheldon arrives at the conclusion that the difference between naturalism and materialism is merely verbal.

Professors Dewey, Hook, and Nagel in a joint response to Sheldon's critique, while reaffirming their conviction that scientific method is the "most reliable" method for achieving knowledge, point out that men have other experiences besides those involved in knowing: they suffer pain and enjoy pleasure, they appreciate beauty, they have mystic experiences, and so on. All these are mental "states," but they are not ways of knowing, although, to be sure, they can become objects of knowledge. "Accordingly, while he [the naturalist] insists that the world may be encountered in other ways than through knowledge and admits that scientific method possesses no valid claim to be the sole avenue for such encounters, he also insists that not every encounter with the world is a case of knowledge. Indeed, for many naturalists, the experience of scientific method is instrumental to the enrichment of other modes of experience."[30]

Moreover, mental states may be publicly verifiable even though they are not directly observed by others, just as propositions about subatomic phenomena are verifiable although the phenomena are not directly observed. Hence such mental states are proper objects of knowledge and, far from ignoring or denying them, the naturalist says that propositions may be meaningfully asserted about them. More than this, to assert that propositions about mental states are publicly verifiable by indirect means, such as by the use of psychogalvanometers, "lie detectors," etc., is not to exclude their being verified directly:

> . . . the naturalist will recognize that the proposition that A is experiencing a pain is verifiable in two ways: directly by A, in virtue of the privileged position in which A's body occurs; and indirectly by everyone (including A) who is in a position to observe processes causally connected with the felt pain.
> However . . . the fact that A can directly verify the proposition that he is in

---

[29] *Ibid.*, p. 211. Italics added.
[30] *Journal of Philosophy*, Vol. XLII, No. 19 (Sept. 13, 1945), p. 523. Use of "most reliable" in characterizing scientific method suggests an avoidance of "only." Clearly, the naturalists cited above are not as explicit as they could have been—at any rate in this particular expression of their credo.

pain, without having to consult a surgeon or dentist, does not make the proposition any the less *publicly verifiable*. For the surgeon or dentist can also verify it, not, to be sure, by sharing A's qualitative experience, but in other ways: by asking A, for example, or by noting the condition of A's body. In brief, therefore, to maintain that propositions about the occurrence of pains and other mental states are publicly veri*fiable*, does not mean that they must always be veri*fied* indirectly; and, conversely, to acknowledge that propositions about mental states have been indirectly veri*fied* is not incompatible with the thesis that they are publicly veri*fiable*.[31]

Finally, naturalists have pointed out that "scientific method," while many of its essentials are common to all subject matters, varies in important respects with the kind of data under examination and the character of our interest. Professor Nagel has distinguished four types of explanation: deductive, probabilistic, functional or teleological, genetic.[32] The deductive method obviously lends itself to data exhibiting relative constancy and uniformity; the probabilistic is appropriate for those areas where we must content ourselves (as in statements about subatomic phenomena) with statistical regularities; the functional where, as with organisms and societies, we are dealing with the contribution of a part in maintaining the character of the whole of which it is a member, or of an action in contributing to an end or goal; the genetic where we are dealing with development or evolution. Thus, when we explain the behavior of living things we must deal not only with the spatial relations of their mass and velocity to other moving objects (deductive and probabilistic), but also with their temporal relations to their own past (genetic) and future (teleological). W. P. Montague was only pointing out what many others have noted when he observed that, since the reactions of a living being to its environment "are controlled primarily by its actual past history and secondarily by its potential future history," time replaces space "as the primary *milieu* of all that lives." Animal life is distinguished from vegetative life in that in the former the organism controls "its reactions to the present environment, not merely by an *inherited* past, but by an *individually acquired* past." In other words, the animal organism (as every animal trainer knows) uses two histories and not, as in the case of plants, only one.[33]

The validity requirements are different for each kind of subject matter, even though we often obscure these differences by saying that in every case "evidence" must be required. The difference is clearest and greatest when the subject matter is not physical objects or organisms, but *human* organisms, that is to say organisms which are *motivated* in their action and which, given their capacity to communicate and use symbols, find *meaning*

[31] *Ibid.*, p. 525.

[32] *Structure of Science* (New York: Harcourt, Brace & World, 1961), pp. 21–26.

[33] "A Materialist Theory of Emergent Evolution" in *Essays in Honor of John Dewey* (New York: Holt, Rinehart, & Winston, 1929), pp. 257–259.

in what they do. Such motivations and meanings also play a part, when we are dealing with human behavior, in influencing the sequence of events. From the standpoint of causation, there is a difference, Professor R. M. MacIver has reminded us, between a piece of paper blown before a wind and a man running from a pursuing mob, and this difference is missed by those who, taking what they call an "objective" position, insist that science is limited to the observation of behavior only. "The paper knows no fear and the wind no hate, but without fear and hate the man would not fly nor the crowd pursue."[34]

A method, sometimes called Verstehen—the method of "understanding," sometimes the *phenomenological* method—has been proposed as a necessary supplement to the methods used when we are dealing with subhuman phenomena. This method, first hinted at by Comte, and later explicitly formulated by Max Weber and Wilhelm Dilthey (as well as the American sociologist, H. E. Cooley) reflects the claim that to understand social phenomena we must reckon with the intentions of the participants, we must by an act of empathy (or the like)—at any rate by a method that can hardly be called "experimental"—understand the *meaning* which an act has for the individual engaging in it.

This is obviously not the place to explore the highly controversial issues raised by the method of Verstehen, which, Professor Thelma Lavine, for example, has ably defended as a necessary concern of naturalistis.[35] It is merely intended to show that, once one reaches the level of social behavior, understanding may well require methods other than the kind of experimentation and canons of evidence characteristic of the biological and physical sciences.

It is arguable that this is nowhere truer than in the realm of ethics. Can we appreciate or understand the nature of moral deliberation if we limit ourselves to taking the standpoint of the external observer? Must we not follow Professor C. A. Campbell's advice and "place ourselves imaginatively at the standpoint of the agent engaged in the typical moral situation"[36] if we are to have any sense of what goes on when individuals find themselves involved in moral dilemmas, find themselves confronted, that is to say, by alternatives involving competing values? Must we not, as Kant insisted and as the law recognizes, know how an act is willed before we can appraise it morally? Is not a new dimension involved here just as, earlier, we had to reckon with a new dimension—time—in understanding organic phe-

---

[34] *Society: An Introductory Analysis*, new ed. with C. H. Page (New York: Rinehart, 1949), p. 628.

[35] Cf. "Note to Naturalists on the Human Spirit," *Journal of Philosophy*, Vol. L, No. 5 (Feb. 26, 1953), pp. 145–154.

[36] "Is 'Free Will' a Pseudo-Problem?" *Mind*, Vol. LX (1951), pp. 441–465, reprinted in *Freedom and Responsibility*, ed. by Herbert Morris (Stanford, Calif.: Stanford University Press, 1961), p. 485.

nomena? As Santayana pointed out, God is not to be found by exploring the heavens with a telescope any more than we shall find the human mind if we search the human brain with a microscope.[37] Indeed, naturalists have gone so far as to say that the procedures involved in the scientific method are not the only way of knowing—although here, to be sure, they have not been entirely consistent. The following statement by John Dewey deserves extensive quotation.

The formulation of ideas of experienced objects in terms of measured quantities . . . does not say that this is the way they *must* be thought, the *only* valid way of thinking of them. . . . For purposes except that of general and extensive translation of one conception into another, it does not follow that the "scientific" way is the best way of thinking of an affair. The nearer we come to an action that is to have an individualized unique object of experience for its conclusion the less do we think the things in question in these exclusively metric terms. The physician will not think in terms as general and abstract as those of the physiologist in the laboratory, nor the engineer in the field in those as free from special application as will the physicist in his workshop. There are many ways of thinking things in relation to one another. . . .

There is something both ridiculous and disconcerting in the way in which men have let themselves be imposed upon, so as to infer that scientific ways of thinking of objects give the inner reality of things, and that they put a mark of spuriousness upon all other ways of thinking of them, and of perceiving and enjoying them. It is ludicrous because these scientific conceptions, like other instruments are hand-made by man in pursuit of realization of a certain interest—that of maximum convertibility of every object of thought into any and every other. It is a wonderful ideal; the ingenuity which man has shown in devising means of realizing the interest is even more marvelous. But these ways of thinking are no more rivals of or substitutes for objects as directly perceived and enjoyed than the power-loom . . . is a substitute and rival for cloth.[38]

To compare this statement with the words of Professor Dennes cited initially, not to mention some of John Dewey's other statements, is to discover that naturalists are not of one mind on this important issue. Here all that can be done is to state the issue and perhaps suggest that its complete resolution still belongs for naturalists to the category of "unfinished business."

At any rate, the realization that nature is broad enough to embrace, and the scientific tools for understanding it flexible enough to comprehend, all the phenomena that are in fact disclosed in experience, accounts in large part for the decline of the once regnant philosophies of dualism and idealism. These were responses to a philosophy of nature dominated by

---

[37] *The Life of Reason, Works* (New York: Scribner, Triton Edition, 1936), Vol. III, p. 101.

[38] *Quest for Certainty*, pp. 135–136. Again, "If experience actually presents aesthetic and moral traits, then these traits may also be supposed to reach down into nature, and to testify to something that belongs to nature as truly as does the mechanical structure aattributed to it in physical science." (*Experience and Nature*, p. 2.)

the methods and concepts of the science of mechanics and hence too narrow to explain the phenomena of man's rich mental and spiritual life, not to mention the complex world of living organisms in general. In the newer view, then, the inclusion of man in the system of nature does not degrade him; rather it testifies to the opulence of nature. Professor John Herman Randall, Jr. has said it with characteristic felicity when he reminds us that:

A world with man in it contains the richness of human experience. It holds terror and love and thinking and imagination, good and evil and the wrestling with them, knowledge and ignorance and the search for truth, failure, frustration, defeat, beauty and vision and tragedy and comedy, the abyss of despair and the love of God. It has the reflective commentary of the spirit of man on all these wonders, the imaginative expression of what man has felt and suffered and thought and judged, the concentration of it all in words, and paint and stone and sound. It has the pursuit of the ideal and the vision of the divine.[39]

Clearly, naturalism as thus described serves both the interests of science and that common wisdom which contains what Whitehead has called "the more concrete intuitions of the universe."[40]

Selected Readings

Krikorian, Y. H., et al, *Naturalism and the Human Spirit*, New York: Columbia, 1944.

Lovejoy, Arthur O., "The Meaning of 'Emergence' and Its Modes," *Proceedings of the Sixth International Congress of Philosophy*, 1926. Reprinted in *Contemporary Philosophic Problems*, ed. by Y. H. Krikorian and A. Edel, New York: Macmillan, 1959, pp. 380–392.

Montague, W. P., "A Materialistic Theory of Emergent Evolution," in *Essays in Honor of John Dewey*, New York: Holt, Rhinehart, and Winston, 1929, pp. 257–273.

Nagel, Ernest, "Naturalism Reconsidered," *Proceedings and Addresses of the American Philosophical Association*, Vol. 28. Reprinted in *Contemporary Philosophical Problems*, New York: Harcourt, Brace & World, 1961, pp. 337–349.

[39] "The Changing Impact of Darwin on Philosophy," *Journal of the History of Ideas*, Vol. XXII, No. 4 (Oct.–Dec., 1961), p. 454.

[40] *Science and the Modern World* (New York: Macmillan, 1962), p. 88.

CHAPTER 22

The Nature
and Limits
of Knowledge

The work of Darwin brought about a new conception of nature and man's place in nature. Darwin's work not only generated the need for a philosophy that would embody such new conceptions; it inspired the insights that made such a philosophy possible. But the catalogue of philosophical developments suggested by Darwin's ideas is not complete. The extension of Darwinian principles to explain the origin of man has suggested a re-examination of the nature of knowledge, and has resulted in a major effort at recasting the traditional conceptions of knowing and the nature of truth. The effort found its chief expression in the United States, in the work of a number of brilliant philosophers, notably Charles Peirce, William James, George Mead, and John Dewey. Of these John Dewey, in part because of his long life and voluminous publications, is the most pre-eminent, so that an account of pragmatism or instrumentalism, as the new view has come to be known, is to a considerable extent an account of Dewey's philosophy.

Rationalism Reviewed

Of the two major traditions in western philosophy, the historically more influential has regarded knowing as an affair of making inferences from self-evident premises. Reason is treated as a power or faculty above and beyond experience, to which the principles from which all knowledge is derived are somehow manifest. Known as *rationalism*, this view has already been examined in Parts I and II. As noted there, rationalism is the view that Mind (appropriately capitalized) intuitively apprehends principles or truths which are absolute, timeless and universal—principles or truths from which it is possible by deductive reasoning to achieve complete and certan knowledge about the "ultimate" nature of things. In the technical parlance of philosophers such truths are called "a priori": they are prior to, which is to say, independent of, observation or experience. Rationalists differ over the role they assign to experience, but they are agreed in relegating it to an inferior position. The senses may yield information of a sort—they may prompt and suggest and remind—but the senses are notoriously misleading and fallible: certainty is supplied by reason alone. In the history of philosophy most great thinkers from Plato to Descartes to Hegel have shared a sublime confidence in the capacity of such a rational faculty to yield certain knowledge and, by and large, the western theological tradition with its commitment to a body of universal and absolute truths has concurred. To be sure, western religion exhibits a strong mystical tendency which eschews reason and relies on "feeling" and revelation as a source of truth. But, happily, our religious tradition did not, as in the East, divorce itself from reason and succumb to mysticism—a circumstance which may help explain why science was able to grow and flourish in the West and not in the East.

As noted earlier, Descartes is the modern rationalist par excellence. The third rule of his *Rules for the Direction of the Mind* is one of the clearest expositions of the rationalist position. There he proposes to "take note of all those mental operations by which we are able, wholly without fear of illusion, to arrive at the knowledge of things." Of these he admits only two, namely, intuition and deduction.

By *intuition* I understand, not the fluctuating testimony of the senses . . . but the conception which an unclouded and attentive mind gives us so readily and distinctly that we are wholly freed from doubt about that which we understand . . . *intuition* springs from the light of reason alone. . . . Thus each individual can mentally have intuition of the fact that he exists, and that he thinks; that the triangle is bounded by three lines only . . . and so on.

. . . by *deduction* we understand all necessary inference from other facts that are known with certainty. . . . many things are known with certainty, though not by themselves evident, but only deduced from true and known principles by the continuous and uninterrupted action of a mind that has a clear vision of each step in the process.[1]

Empiricism Re-examined

Rationalism, as thus understood, is not the only influential standpoint in the western philosophical tradition. The earlier account of Baconianism reminded us of another persistent tendency, *empiricism*, today in the ascendant, which views knowledge as originating in experience. This is not the place to explore the different meanings of experience, which is a notoriously ambiguous term. However, no matter how much they may differ over their interpretation of experience, all empiricists are agreed in rejecting the claim that a priori reasoning and the criterion of self-evidence can give us significant knowledge. If mathematics once supplied the model to which rationalists appealed because it appeared to afford an ideal example of reasoning from axioms or self-evident principles, empiricists point out that this is no longer true. As the discussion in Part II indicated (pp. 189–205), Descartes' quest for a universal mathematics turns out to have been illusory. In mathematics, so-called axioms are no longer regarded as true or false in themselves; they are treated as postulates or assumptions, either to be kept or discarded, depending on their usefulness, or as providing the logical basis for purely theoretical systems that have no relevance to "real" objects.

A priori reasoning, the empiricists contend, can yield only tautologies as when, in mathematics, we elaborate or develop the implications contained in our definitions. As Hume pointed out (Part II, p. 257), it cannot give us *factual* knowledge. Such knowledge can come only through experience; and since, necessarily, experience is always limited, empiricists also reject the rationalist ideal of *certain* knowledge, which they regard as chimerical. They point out that the so-called self-evident propositions from which the rationalist makes his inferences have failed to evoke that universal assent which we are entitled to expect the "self-evident" to command. Such propositions turn out, upon examination, to be unconscious borrowings from common sense. When they do win general assent, this is because they are true by definition: it is self-evident that all points on the periphery of a circle are equidistant from a point called the center, as it is that all bodies are extended and all men mortal, for the good reason that we have so defined these notions that they already contain the predicates attributed to them. Such propositions make no addition to our knowledge, indispensable as they may be in making our ideas explicit and internally consistent. To add to our knowledge we must have recourse to observation. Clearly, empiricism, as thus far described, is in harmony with the spirit and

---

[1] *Selections,* ed. by R. M. Eaton (New York: Scribner, 1927), pp. 46–47.

method of science where the only basis for the acceptance of a theory consists of its agreement with the evidence derived from observation or experiment.

Up to this point, pragmatists or instrumentalists regard themselves as belonging to the empirical tradition. It is when they come to describe the nature of the agreement between our ideas or theories, on the one hand, and the realities with which our ideas deal, on the other, that pragmatists part company with traditional empiricism. The nature of this agreement between our ideas and the reality to which they refer has, indeed, raised profound problems. Some of these have been explored earlier, in the discussion of what Descartes called adventitious ideas. For the most part traditional empiricism—and to this common sense assents—has viewed knowing as an affair in which an experiencing subject somehow "lays hold of," grasps, apprehends, ulterior objects.[2] The proposition that reality antedates, and is independent of, the sentient beings in whom and to whom it now—perhaps only intermittently and transiently—manifests itself is converted into the conclusion that the *object of knowledge* is something apart from, and prior to, the operations of inquiry and the consequences to which these operations may lead. When an object is truly known there is said to be a *correspondence* between it and our ideas of it. It is suggested that there is a kind of doubleness in experience such that, when our experiences are veridical, an inner order of ideas corresponds to an outer order of events. This correspondence may be variously regarded, sometimes as analogous to the relationship between objects and their images in a mirror, sometimes to the relationship between a terrain and its delineation on a map. Often mind is implicitly if not explicitly conceived as if it were a kind of mirror held up to an ulterior reality and passively reflecting it. Or, man in his role as knower may be regarded as a spectator viewing finished pictures—and scientists as more avid and indefatigable viewers. The knower —even though nature and mind are included, as by Bertrand Russell, in "one single system"—is nevertheless regarded as apart from the objects known; he is indeed "detached." Objects somehow get depicted, revealed, disclosed, as we observe or experience them through our senses, so that sensations may be regarded as revelatory, as cognitive, as constituting in themselves items of knowledge about the real.

Now by any odds the cognitive relationship is as complex as it is marvelous. The trouble, according to pragmatists, is that, as traditionally understood, whether by empiricists or rationalists, it is also inexplicable, and

---

[2] Empiricism may take either a "realist" or "phenomenalist" form. For the purpose of this discussion, phenomenalism, although an important philosophical standpoint, will be ignored. (Cf. above p. 300.) "Realism," as the discussion in Part I has shown, is without doubt the most protean word in the philosophical vocabulary. As here used, realism means that the objects of knowledge exist independently of their being perceived or known.

that attempts to explain it have bred a formidable pseudo-science, *episte-mology*. Modern philosophy has been mired in epistemology to its baffle-ment and frustration because it wrestles with a problem which is rendered insoluble by the nature of the terms in which it is posed. What is the nature of knowing? How is knowledge possible?—this is the epistemological ques-tion, the so-called problem of knowledge. But, once the knower and the known are polarized and set over against each other as subject and object— where the subject is somehow the locus of an "inner" reflection of an "external" referent—and once the cognitive relationship is treated as "different" *in the sense of being quite unrelated to any other process in nature*, is not knowing rendered utterly mysterious?

To treat knowing as the activity of a "rational faculty" and to speak of the "natural light of reason," as does the rationalist, is to invoke an occult agency if not to play with words. But the empiricist, who assumes that knowledge is a process through which we get outside ourselves and are thus able to duplicate or otherwise apprehend independent objects, is equally guilty of rendering knowing incomprehensible. There is, indeed, as Augustine observed, "a certain wonderful power" in the mind by which it can contain "*tanta coeli, terrae marisque spatia.*" But by what feat of transcendence is the mind able to get outside itself to reflect the wide world? Does the mind glow like a magic ray as it brings "illumination"? If so, it is an evanescence for which there is no analogue in nature and, moreover, in the conventional view, it appears to glow quite gratuitously: the fact that its activities serve the purposes of the organism is a happy one but presumably quite incidental to the knowing process itself. The very words reflect, grasp, view, see, apprehend (Latin: *prehendere*, to seize), which we use to express the cognitive relationship are surely not meant to be taken literally. Does the mind really reflect like a mirror, or grasp like a hand, or see like an eye or illuminate like a light? If, on second thought, all these terms are found to be used in a metaphorical sense, in what sense is the "given" in experience given to us?

In short, it is all very well to insist, with the naturalist, that reflective processes are as much natural processes as other processes in nature, and that the mental is not extraneous but that manifestation of nature through which nature becomes "aware" of itself. But what is this awareness? Spirit, Santayana has written with his usual elegance, is nature's comment on herself. But the comment is one we have yet to decipher. The naturalist's account would appear to be still incomplete.

One more question: How in the conventional view can we ever know that we know? If we grant that the test of knowing is the congruence of our ideas with what is external to them, and if, as we must be, we are confined to the circle of our ideas, how can we ascertain that there is such a congruence? This is the dilemma, thought by many to be fatal, of the so-called "correspondence" theory of truth.

Pragmatism and the Biological Approach

How do we determine the truth of our ideas? The answer of the pragmatist is influenced negatively by the difficulties cited above, and positively by the Darwinian teaching that man is an organism and as such is part of the biological order. It is to biology that the pragmatist therefore first directs us: "Suppose we take seriously the contribution made to our idea of experience by biology," Dewey proposes, in the introductory essay to a now-classic collection of essays entitled *Creative Intelligence*. If we do, the basic relationship in terms of which to understand man must be the "intercourse of a living being with its physical and social environment."[3] To understand experience we must see it as an aspect of living, which is to say, an aspect of the process through which an organism responds to an environment in such a way as to further survival. The theme of this early essay (1917) is repeated again and again. In *Reconstruction in Philosophy* he writes, ". . . the interaction of organism and environment, resulting in some adaptation which secures utilization of the latter, is the primary fact, the basic category. . . . *Knowledge is not something separate and self-sufficient, but involved in the process by which life is sustained and evolved.*"[4] Elsewhere we are cautioned against taking intellectual experience and its material as primary. To do this, we are told, is to cut the cord that binds experience and nature.

That the physiological organism . . . whether . . . in man or the lower animals, is concerned with making adaptations and uses of material in the interest of maintenance of the life-process, cannot be denied. The brain and nervous system are primarily organs of action-undergoing; biologically, it can be asserted without contravention that primary experience is of a corresponding type. Hence, *unless there is a breach of historic and natural continuity, cognitive experience must originate within that of a non-cognitive sort.* And unless we start from knowing as a factor in action and undergoing we are inevitably committed to the intrusion of an extra-natural, if not a supernatural, agency or principle.[5]

In short, if we are to understand knowing we must not treat it as "detached"; we must address ourselves to the situation in which knowing takes place and we must establish its continuity with other processes in nature. Again in his *Logic* (1938) Dewey writes: "If one denies the super-

---

[3] "The Need for a Reovery in Philosophy" in *Creative Intelligence* (New York: Holt, Rinehart, & Winston, 1917), pp. 7–8.

[4] (New York: Holt, Rinehart, & Winston, 1920), p. 87. Italics added.

[5] *Experience and Nature* (New York: Norton, 1925), p. 23. Italics added. Elsewhere he writes: ". . . it [instrumentalism] holds that thinking does not mean any transcendent states or acts suddenly introduced into a previously natural scene, but that the operations of knowing are (or are artfully derived from) natural responses of the organism . . ." *Essays in Experimental Logic* (New York: Dover, 1953), p. 332.

natural, then one has the intellectual responsibility of indicating how the logical may be connected with the biological in a process of continuous development." By the biological is meant those processes that involve dynamic interaction of the organism and its environment.

When the balance within a given activity is disturbed . . . then there is exhibited need, search and fulfilment (or satisfaction) in the objective meaning of those terms. The greater the differentiation of structures and their corresponding activities becomes, the more difficult it is to keep the balance. Indeed, living may be regarded as a continual rhythm of disequilibrations and recoveries of equilibrium. The "higher" the organism, the more serious become the disturbances and the more energetic . . . are the efforts necessary for its reestablishment. The state of disturbed equilibrium constitutes *need*. The movement towards its restoration is search and exploration. The recovery is fulfillment or satisfaction.[6]

Every accommodation, we are reminded, is an unstable one, every equilibrium precarious. Moreover, accommodation implies no passive submission to the environment; the "higher" the organism the more it is engaged in actively manipulating its environment.[7] But, in any case, if it is accommodation that the organism seeks then "success and failure are the primary 'categories' of life."[8]

What, then, is knowing? It is, says Dewey, intelligently conducted doing. It is not merely contemplative, but practical. Thinking does not originate in a vacuum—or an ivory tower; it is produced by our needs, needs which, moreover, are by no means always simple creature needs, but as multiple and various as man's complex and shifting interests have decreed that they shall be. Thinking originates in confusion, uncertainty, trouble. It is a mode of "directed overt action" and ideas are "anticipatory plans"[9] designed to resolve a difficulty or solve a problem. Ideas are hypotheses to be tested by reference to their success in removing the difficulty which generated them. Since they are essentially tools, instruments—hence "instrumentalism"— their value is determined by reference to whether or not they work.

If ideas, meanings, conceptions, notions, theories, systems are instrumental to an active reorganization of the given environment, to a removal of some specific trouble or perplexity, then the test of their validity and value lies in accomplishing this work . . . Now an idea or conception is a claim . . . or plan to *act* in a certain way as the way to arrive at the clearing up of a specific situation. When the claim or pretension or plan is acted upon *it guides us truly or*

---

[6] (New York: Holt, Rinehart & Winston), pp. 25–27.

[7] Cf. *Reconstruction in Philosophy* (New York: Holt, Rinehart, & Winston, 1920), pp. 84–85. The point is unusually important to an understanding of Dewey's social philosophy and of its major difference from the use of biological accommodation to argue against social reform; Dewey stressed the active role of the organism in achieving accommodation, thereby advancing his deep interest in social reconstruction.

[8] *Creative Intelligence*, p. 13.

[9] *Quest for Certainty*, (New York: Minton, 1929), pp. 166–167.

falsely; it leads to our end or away from it. Its active, dynamic function is the all-important thing about it, and in the quality of activity induced by it lies all its truth and falsity. The hypothesis that works is the *true* one.[10]

The procedures of modern experimental science are cited as confirming this interpretation of knowing and doing as inseparable. Science, we are told, is a "mode of directed practical doing."[11] Contrary to the assumptions of the seventeenth-century natural philosophers, the scientific manner of thinking does not disclose the inner reality of things any more than does any other way of thinking. The scientific is rather a way, albeit a very versatile way, of *dealing* with things. If the function of thought "is not to conform to or reproduce the characters already possessed by objects but to judge them as potentialities of what they become through an indicated operation," then "to think of the world in terms of mathematical formulae of space, time and motion is not to have a picture of the independent and fixed essence of the universe." It is, says Dewey, "to describe experiencable objects as material upon which certain operations are performed."[12]

Often we say that *pure* science is removed from purposes, and in a profoundly important sense this is the case. These are practical purposes that have to do with immediate or proximate serviceability or utility—which is left to applied science or technology. In this way pure science is left free to generate new purposes. But, however this may be, in a different sense pure science is dependent on ends or purposes at every point, observes Dewey. The difference is that pure science "generates them within its own procedures and tests them by its own operations."[13]

The foregoing is an attenuated account of a position that involves many complications. There has been much criticism, some of it invited by the oversimplified and even misleading formulation of the pragmatic viewpoint in the writings of William James, who was much more effective as a critic of traditional views than as a constructive philosopher.[14] This is not

---

[10] *Reconstruction in Philosophy,* p. 156.

[11] *Quest for Certainty,* p. 24.

[12] *Ibid.,* p. 137.

[13] *Ibid.,* p. 138.

[14] Criticism of Dewey has centered about his contention that the processes of knowing, i.e., the operations involved in resolving a problematic situation, generate the object of knowledge. His critics freely concede that Dewey reckons with antecedently existing objects of experience. But Dewey denies that such felt or perceived objects have cognitive status—his chief criticism of eighteenth-century empiricists is that they accord cognitive status to sense data—and he distinguishes between these, as the "subject matter *for* knowledge" (*Journal of Philosophy,* Vol. XXVII, p. 273), and those which are the outcome of the act of inquiry.

To many naturalists, especially those who, like Professor Sterling Lamprecht, have been influenced by Woodbridge, when "our inquiry is not *how* to do something, but what something *is* or *was*," then "the act of investigating the problem could not possibly constitute the object said to be known . . ." ("Empiricism and Natural Knowledge," in *University of California Publications in Philosophy,* Vol. 16, p. 85. Italics added.) To

the place to deal with the way in which later pragmatists have met criticisms of their position, nor with the often subtle and brilliant analysis by which Mead and Dewey explore the processes by which in man, thanks to his capacity to use tools and employ symbols, the cognitive has emerged from the noncognitive. The main intent has been to show how, in the climate of opinion generated by the Darwinian treatment of man as part of the biological order, a new conception of the nature of knowledge and truth has become possible.

Selected Readings

Ayer, A. J., *The Problem of Knowledge*, London, Macmillan, 1956, chaps. 1, 2. (Also Penguin paperback.)
Cohen, Morris Raphael, *Reason and Nature*, 2nd ed., New York: Harcourt, Brace, & World, 1931. (Also Free Press paperback.)
Dewey, John, *Reconstruction in Philosophy*, New York: Holt, Rinehart, & Winston, 1920, Ch. IV. (Also Beacon paperback.)
Lewis, Clarence I., *Mind and the World Order*, New York: Scribner, 1929.

---

assume that it does, entails "the breaking down of the distinction between theoretical and practical objectives, that is, between theoretical efforts to know what has been and is, and practical efforts to guide choices wisely . . ." (*Ibid.*, p. 87.)

For a similar criticism see A. E. Murphy's "Dewey's Epistemology and Metaphysics," in *The Philosophy of John Dewey*, ed. by P. A. Schilpp (Evanston: Northwestern University, 1939), espec. pp. 201 *ff*. Dewey's rejoinder will be found in the same volume, pp. 565 *ff*.

CHAPTER 23

The Nature
of
the Social

Language and the Social

In the foregoing account of knowing, when attention has been concentrated on the interaction of organism and environment, on adaptation and equilibria and disequilibria, it is the categories of biology that have been in the foreground. When reference is made to sensory perception or to "directed overt action" (Tolman's "molar" behavior-acts), we have moved into the area of psychology. However, once attention is directed, as of course it must be in any account of thinking or knowing, to ideas, meanings, conceptions, theories, a new dimension is added; we are now dealing with man as a *social* organism. For there could be no ideas or meanings, and therefore no thinking or knowing, in the absence of communication, in the absence, that is to say, of a *culture* embracing the use of *symbols* in what we call language. Thus, for us the sound for "stone" is not merely a stimulus exciting a chain of responses, either conditioned or inherited, as would be true with subhuman organisms. It is not merely a signal; it is a symbol or surrogate standing for, or meaning, something to throw at an attacker or an object with which to build a house or to chip into a tool.

Language, to be sure, has its base in such anatomical conditions as the voice box and certain peculiarities of brain structure, and it has its psychological conditions in the stream of brute experience—visual, auditory, tactual, olfactory, etc.—which comprise the stuff about which language is a report. Obviously, too, language has its origins in the signal systems of simpler organisms. And, if this were all, the generalizations of psychology and biology would suffice for a full understanding of communication. But, as we have been constantly reminded in recent decades, it is not all. If the signals by means of which subhuman organisms influence each other's behavior can be explained in terms of the purely psychological mechanism of stimulus and response, communication by means of *symbols*, which is what language is, presupposes a *social* relationship. We are unable to explore here the social processes by means of which a sound or signal becomes a symbol and enters into discourse. But the following seminal comments of G. H. Mead will indicate the area in which these processes must be sought:

We say the animal does not think. He does not put himself in a position for which he is responsible; he does not put himself in the place of the other person and say, in effect, "He will act in such a way and I will act in this way." If the individual can act in this way, and the attitude which he calls out in himself can become a stimulus to him for another act, we have meaningful conduct. Where the response of the other person is called out and becomes a stimulus to control his action, then he has the meaning of the other person's act in his own experience. That is the general mechanism of what we term "thought," for in order that thought may exist there must be symbols, vocal gestures generally, which arouse in the individual himself the response which he is calling out in the other, and such that from the point of view of that response he is able to direct his later conduct. It involves not only communication in the sense in which birds and animals communicate with each other, but also an arousal within the individual himself of the response which he is calling out in the other individual, a taking of the role of the other, a tendency to act as the other person acts.[1]

The dependence of thinking, and the meanings and ideas that are involved in thinking, on communication as thus described is a modern insight. It reverses the traditional view that language is a mere physical vehicle consisting of visible characters or gestures or spoken sounds which are either necessarily connected with or get "associated" with pre-existent meanings or ideas—meanings or ideas which individuals command simply and solely by virtue of their possession of "minds" and hence without essential reference to social relationships. The act of role-taking, described by Mead in the passage above, could not occur except in a socially structured group. And, while some would not go so far as Mead went in

[1] *Mind, Self, and Society*, ed. by C. W. Morris (Chicago: University of Chicago Press, 1934), p. 73.

affirming that what we call mind is a social derivative, there is much to be said for his thesis that self-consciousness and the higher thought processes are a product of our intercourse with other selves.[2] Such intercourse would not occur in those primal hordes once postulated by armchair anthropologists as the condition of early man, any more than among animal groups; it presupposes institutionalized group life, a culture, in brief, a society in the true sense of that word.

We are thus brought in the concluding chapter of this part to a consideration of the status of culture and of social institutions, where once again it is useful to raise the question explored in considering the status of life and mind. May human culture, in all of its institutional manifestations, be said to possess qualities other than those belonging to the individuals who partake of that culture? Or, can all social phenomena be described, without remainder, in terms of the generalizations of biology and psychology? The status of social phenomena, like the status of vital and mental phenomena, has been in much dispute between those who may be called mechanistic reductionists, and those whose exaggeration of differences which defy reduction has led them to a position corresponding to dualism. This is an important issue which has been a primary concern of what has come to be known as social philosophy. It is appropriate, before turning, in the concluding portion of this volume, to the impact of the social sciences on accepted belief, that we see how the issues raised by Darwinism and the way they have been resolved have affected the answers to these questions.

Social Reductionism

The mechanist has been as undaunted by the cultural or institutional life of man as by its physiological or psychological manifestations. For him, as indicated in Part II (pp. 285–287), society is no more than an aggregate of individuals corresponding to the homogeneous particles in physical compounds. All social phenomena may be explained by reference to the laws governing individual human nature. In J. S. Mill's well-known words, "Men . . . in a state of society are still men; their actions and passions are obedient to the laws of individual human nature. Men are not, when brought together, converted into another kind of substance, with different properties: as hydrogen and oxygen are different from water. . . . Human beings in society have no properties but those which are derived from, and may be resolved into, the laws of the nature of individual

---

[2] Even soliloquy and introspection become, in this view, a kind of internalized discourse in which we pluralize our self into several selves and hold a "conversation" among them. Thus, reflection or deliberation is not the prior condition of communication but a concomitant of it.

man."[3] Classical political economy from the time of Adam Smith until well after the turn of the twentieth century took this assumption for granted. The behavior of the individual qua individual was regarded, not merely as a necessary, but as a sufficient, condition for understanding social phenomena and the institutions through which social relationships are structured.

Differences did indeed arise concerning the nature of the individual and the drives which move him. Hobbes, well before the time of Adam Smith, described the individual as seeking his self-preservation, and he explained the origins of the state by reference to the rational decisions of such individuals to further their self-interest by ending the "warre of every man against every man" and placing themselves irrevocably under the authority of an absolute sovereign. Bentham described man as moved exclusively by a desire for pleasure and an aversion to pain. The great majority of nineteenth-century economists, accordingly, sought to understand all economic phenomena in terms of the efforts of such men, under the conditions prevailing in a market economy based upon a division of labor and exchange, to maximize gains and minimize costs, where gains and costs were either explicitly or implicity understood as magnitudes of pleasures and pains, or, in the later terminology, satisfactions and dissatisfactions. What men find serviceable or unserviceable to the self, pleasurable or painful, satisfying or dissatisfying, is, to a significant extent, conditioned by the kind of social institutions prevalent at any given time or place; but this fact was largely ignored. Cultural influences were treated as incidental. Human nature was thought to be a constant, expressing itself always and everywhere in an aversion to work, in a desire for gain, and in meticulous calculations of profits and losses. It has become clear to a more sophisticated generation of psychologists and economists that these were not eternal manifestations of human nature, but ways in which human nature expressed itself under the special and transient conditions prevailing in early capitalist England and America. But this was not clear during a long period which emphasized the priority and self-sufficiency of the individual, and therefore reduced the science of society to the study of individual human nature, that is, to psychology.

Such reductionism, exquisitely fashioned, if not intentionally designed, to serve the interests of the middle class, achieved a crude extreme in the popular doctrine known as "social Darwinism." Darwin's assumption, that among living species there is a competition for survival in which the fittest survive, was first oversimplified and then applied without modification to human relationships. That "nature red in tooth and claw" was the lurid language of Tennyson's *In Memoriam* and not Darwin's did not deter the social Darwinists. Men were said to be engaged in such a struggle, vary-

---

[3] *A System of Logic* (London: Longmans, 1941), p. 573.

ing in its savagery with the ratio of population to available resources. Those who prospered were those who were most fit, and all efforts to mitigate the rigors of competition by helping the destitute at the expense of the rich, that is, all efforts at social reform, were deplored as interfering with the law of nature which, among men as among beasts, beneficently weeds out the weak and rewards the strong.

Chief exponents of this view, which Darwin himself never espoused in this crude form,[4] were William Graham Sumner in the United States and Herbert Spencer in England. Many economists, Sumner complained, are frightened by competition because it "bears harshly on the weak."

They do not perceive that here "the strong" and "the weak" are terms which admit of no definition unless they are made equivalent to the industrious and the idle, the frugal and the extravagant. They do not perceive, furthermore, that if we do not like the survival of the fittest, we have only one possible alternative, and that is the survival of the unfittest.[5]

As noted earlier, even before the publication of *Origin of Species* Spencer had written of the "survival of the fittest," and in *Social Statics* he found that "the poverty of the incapable, the distresses that come upon the imprudent, the starvation of the idle, and those shoulderings aside of the weak by the strong, which leave so many 'in shallows and in miseries,' are the decrees of a large, far-seeing benevolence."[6] The law of survival applies indifferently to men or beasts; institutions make no substantive difference. Nor is it significant to social Darwinists that "fitness," which has an objective and specific meaning in biology—where it refers at the very least to success in having offspring sufficient to maintain the population level of the species—reflects value judgments, when used in a social context, which have nothing to do with the only modest record of tycoons in fathering children.[7] Biologism, as it may be called, was not to be hindered by such discrepancies. It may be noted in passing that social Darwinists varied in attributing "fitness" to individuals, classes, nations, and races and, especially on the Continent, natural selection was used to justify colonialism, war and, finally, as the pseudological blended with the pathological, genocide.

Discredited observations, such as those of the social Darwinists, are cited here not for the purpose of criticism, but to suggest the extent to which reductionism was carried, even among those who, like Sumner and Spencer, were associated with the birth of anthropology and sociology. But reductionism, it must now be added, is by no means limited to classical or

---

[4] See *The Descent of Man* (London: 1874), pp. 151–152 for evidence of his own proto social Darwinism.

[5] *Essays*, II, 56. Cited by Richard Hofstadter in *Social Darwinism in American Thought* (Philadelphia: University of Pennsylvania Press, 1945), p. 43.

[6] (London: John Chapman, 1851), Chap. XXV, Sec. 6.

[7] For an account of the radical difference between natural and social selection, see R. M. MacIver and C. H. Page, *Society* (New York: Rinehart, 1959), chap. 24.

neoclassical economists and social Darwinists, unconsciously providing an apology for the more predatory manifestations of colonialism, racism, nationalism or early modern capitalism. It is notorious that Freud and orthodox Freudians find their explanation for conduct, both individual and collective, in the biography of the individual, his infantile experiences and instinctual drives, and in mechanisms of repression which assertedly are common to and function in the same way for all men. While it would be unfair to ignore Freud's occasional concessions to the influence of culture,[8] the fact is that these concessions are generally obscured by his overwhelming psychological bias and his assumption that the role of culture is restrictive rather than directive and creative. In this respect he would have benefited greatly had he been familiar with the social psychology of G. H. Mead.

Freud's great contribution to our understanding of the role of the irrational in conduct and other cognate subjects need not concern us. At issue here is the reductionism implicit in the Freudian position. This is best illustrated by his assumptions concerning the Oedipus complex, that is, the sexual attraction which all children are said to feel to the parent of the opposite sex and the resultant jealousy directed at the other parent.[9] The Oedipus complex is not culturally conditioned and therefore not stronger or weaker, present or absent in different social environments; it is part of our biological legacy. This legacy includes, for Freud, the inheritance of acquired traits, and the recall of prenatal events such as the "memory" of an act of primal parricide when, as members of a presocial "horde," jealous sons rebelled against a father who monopolized all the women in the horde, and slew and ate him![10]

---

[8] Typical of the views of many Freudians are those expressed by Géza Róheim. Culture, he says, "is but the extension of delayed infancy in which the memory images or symbols of past generations are united with parent and child. Therefore, when we talk of phenomena explained in terms of culture what we are really talking about is psychology." *Psychoanalysis and Anthropology* (New York: International Universities Press, 1950), p. 439. Since psychology as understood by Freud is biologically oriented, it was easy for him to treat psychology as a branch of physiology, thereby carrying the reduction a step further.

The better known works in which Freud concerned himself with culture are *Totem and Taboo* (1912), *Civilization and its Discontents* (1930), *Moses and Monotheism* (1939). For an excellent discussion of this whole issue as it pertains to Freud, cf. the discussions by Abram Kardiner, Ernest van den Haag and Alex Inkeles in *Psychoanalysis, Scientific Method and Philosophy*, ed. by S. Hook (New York: New York University Press, 1959), pp. 81–128.

[9] When counter evidence is cited such as healthy adults in whom no traces of an Oedipus complex can be found, the response is likely to be that the complex was there but successfully repressed. When counter evidence in the form of a close tie between parent and child of the same sex was cited, Freud amended his theory to include a homosexual or "inverted" Oedipus complex as well as a heterosexual or "normal" one.

[10] See his *Totem and Taboo* in the *Complete Psychological Works of Sigmund Freud* (London: Hogarth, 1955), pp. 140–143.

Similarly, when Freud found, as he did, that women (presumably Viennese) are more jealous than men, he assumed that the phenomenon was constant and universal—a dubious thesis—and promptly attributed it to the female's sense of lack in not possessing male genitalia, her consequent wish for the next best, namely, sexual intercourse, and her envy of other women who have been gratified. Here the reduction of the sociological to the psychological and the psychological to the biological is almost complete. However, Freud, not to mention his women patients, was a product of his time and, as Karen Horney points out, in the nineteenth century when Freud formulated his basic ideas "there was little knowledge regarding cultural differences, and the prevailing trend was to ascribe peculiarities of one's own culture to human nature in general." Horney continues: "In accordance with these views Freud believes that the human being he sees, the picture which he observes and tries to interpret, has a general validity the world over. . . . he is inclined to regard cultural phenomena as the result of essentially biological instinctual structures." In appropriately describing this as "mechanistic" thinking she consistently concludes that for Freud, "present manifestations are not only conditioned by the past; nothing really new is created in the process of development; what we see today is only the old in a changed form."[11]

For a useful summary of the mechanistic interpretation of society we may conclude with the comments of J. S. N. Watkins:

> . . . the ultimate constituents of the social world are individual people who act more or less appropriately in the light of their dispositions and understanding of their situation. Every complex social situation, institution or event is the result of a particular configuration of individuals, their dispositions, situations, beliefs, and physical resources and environment. There may be unfinished or half-way explanations of large-scale social phenomena (say, full employment); but we shall not have arrived at rock-bottom explanations of such large-scale phenomena until we have deduced an account of them from statements about the dispositions, beliefs, resources and inter-relations of individuals.[12]

The Culturalistic Fallacy

Opposed to reductionism as thus defined are those who would insist on what has been called the "autonomy of sociology." The extreme version

---

[11] *The New Ways of Psychoanalysis* (New York: Norton, 1939), pp. 40–42.

[12] "Ideal Types and Historical Explanation," *British Journal for the Philosophy of Science*, Vol. 3 (1952), p. 29. Cited by Nagel in the *Structure of Science*, p. 541. This is the ideal of what has recently come to be known as *micro-economics* which, as expounded by Frederick Hayek and Ludwig von Mises, would attempt to derive all generalizations about large-scale economic phenomena (e.g., unemployment, inflation, over-saving, etc.) from the preferences and propensities of individuals as they engage in economic transactions. Cf. F. A. Hayek, *The Counter Revolution of Science* (New York: The Free Press of Glencoe, 1952), pp. 25–35, esp. pp. 31 ff., and pp. 38 ff.

of this view is analagous to the dualistic treatment of life and mind. Complex systems of social relationships are reified, and cultures are regarded as independent realities having a life of their own. Such metaphysical supra-organic or supra-individual entities, viewed as independent of the individuals composing or partaking of them, and obeying laws of their own, are exemplified by Rousseau's "General Will" (*volonté générale*) by Hegel's nation-state, and, in the realm of psychoanalysis, by Jung's "collective unconscious."

Hegel's comments concerning the state, if extreme and turgid, are eloquently illustrative. He tells us in a celebrated pronouncement that, "The state is the Divine Idea as it exists on Earth." It is "the Idea of Spirit in the external manifestation of human Will and its Freedom." He goes on to speak of "that concrete reality which is the State" and tells us that it is "the shape assumed by [Spirit] in its complete realization in phenomenal existence."[13] Elsewhere we are told that "The nation-state is mind in its substantive rationality and immediate actuality and is therefore the absolute power on earth." In it "self-consciousness finds in an organic development the actuality of its substantive knowing and willing. . . ."[14]

Rarely has a collectivity—in this instance the Prussian state of Frederick III, which Hegel really had in mind—undergone such a bland apotheosis and blunt hypostasis. As noted earlier, Hegel's was only one of many attempts to find in social development, if not in the cosmos itself, the gradual self-revelation of a pre-existent Ego or Spirit. Such efforts, often relying on garbled versions of Darwin, were quite common until well into the twentieth century.

Quite apart from Hegel's metaphysical and political biases, some modern sociologists and anthropologists, in their zeal to preserve the autonomy of sociology and anthropology, have likewise been guilty of treating systems of relationships as though they were self-subsistent entities. Thus, one of the great pioneers of modern anthropology, A. L. Kroeber, declared that mental activity (and therefore the science of psychology that describes it) "proves nothing whatever as to social events. Mentality relates to the individual. The social or cultural, on the other hand, is in its very essence nonindividual. Civilization as such begins only where the individual ends. . . ."[15] Elsewhere, Kroeber referred to civilization as "an entity in itself," adding, "The entity civilization has intrinsically nothing to do with individual men nor with the aggregates of men on whom it rests. It springs

---

[13] *The Philosophy of History*, trans. by J. Sibree (New York: Dover, 1956), pp. 39, 47, 50, 54.
[14] *Philosophy of Right*, trans. by T. M. Knox (Oxford at the Clarendon Press, 1942), paragraphs 331, 360.
[15] "The Superorganic," *American Anthropologist*, Vol. XIX (1917), pp. 192–193.

from the organic but is independent of it."[16] In a commendable effort to recognize the distinctiveness of social and cultural data, Kroeber appears, in the use of terms like "susbtance" and "entity" and in stressing the independence of what he called the "superorganic," to have erected a dangerous dualism suggestive of the dualism associated with Descartes and later vitalists, and inviting many of the same difficulties.

Similarly, R. H. Lowie has described culture as a "closed system" declaring that "Culture is a thing *sui generis* which can be explained only in terms of itself."[17] Even so, Kroeber's and Lowie's position was not nearly as extreme as that of the distinguished sociologist, Talcott Parsons, who, in his earlier writings, postulated a primordially creative element, independent of the natural world of heredity and environment, as indispensible to our understanding of the social data represented by valuation and the choice of goals.[18]

This has aptly been called the "culturalistic fallacy." This fallacy occurs, as David Bidney points out, "when one defines culture as an ideational abstraction and then proceeds to convert or reify this *ens rationis* into an independent ontological entity subject to its own laws of development and conceived through it alone." Bidney adds:

The culturalistic fallacy is committed . . . when this logical abstraction comes to be regarded as if it actually were a reality *sui generis*, a superpsychic, supersocial entity independent of man, individually and collectively. The . . . fallacy is the result of "elevating" a pure form or abstraction to the level of a substantial natural force which is self-explanatory and ontologically self-sufficient—a procedure which is reminiscent of the Platonic doctrine of transcendental Forms. . . .[19]

Evolutionary Naturalism and Society

Clearly, sociologists and anthropologists cannot adequately deal with social phenomena unless they reckon with actual human individuals, that is to say, with organisms characterized by certain biological and psychological traits living in a given physical environment. Even if natural selection, however indispensable to an understanding of biological evolution, is irrelevant to social evolution, where the use of this concept has

---

[16] "Eighteen Professions," *American Anthropologist*, Vol. XVII (1915), pp. 283–288. Cited by David Bidney, *Theoretical Anthropology* (New York: Columbia, 1953), p. 38.

[17] *Culture and Ethnology* (New York: Douglas C. McMurtrie, 1917), p. 66. Elsewhere Lowie takes a less extreme position.

[18] "The place of Ultimate Values in Sociological Theory," *International Journal of Ethics*, Vol. 45 (1934–35), pp. 282–316. In later statements (e.g., "Values, Motives, and Systems of Action," in *Toward a General Theory of Action*, pp. 247–275.) Parsons drastically changes his course in the direction of a naturalistic position. (*Cf.* "The Changing Foundations of the Parsonian Action Scheme," John Finley Scott, *American Sociological Review*, Oct. 1963, pp. 716–735.)

[19] *Theoretical Anthropology* (New York: Columbia, 1953), p. 51.

bred only mischief and confusion, the student of society must reckon with such biological data as sex and hunger drives, the long period of dependency of the human infant, the fact that mating is not seasonal among humans, etc.

On the other hand, it is obvious that cultures have varied widely while man as an animal organism, within the same span of time, has remained the same and some of his fundamental psychological characteristics have remained constant; and, also, that cultures have undergone great changes within the same physical environment. Clearly, then, one must look to processes within the culture, processes operative at the social level, if one is to understand cultural or institutional variation and change. One must see that, in addition to such influences as are described in the generalizations of physiology and ecology and psychology, the social represents a qualitatively different manifestation of nature which cannot be adequately understood without generalizations peculiar to that level. If the concept of emergence be taken seriously, such *macro-laws*, as they may be called, cannot be deduced from generalizations describing (or laws governing) the behavior of individuals, any more than the psychological generalizations describing the behavior of individuals could be deduced from a knowledge of the underlying facts of physics and physiology.[20] Many would say that this limitation is *ontological* and not merely *methodological*, that is to say, it stems from the nature of the data and not from the state of our knowledge of the data at any given time.[21]

Thus, once again the theory of evolutionary naturalism suggests, in the concept of emergence, a way of avoiding dualism and its hypostatizations,

[20] Cf. pp. 355–357.

[21] Not all naturalists would support this statement for there is among them a disagreement between those who, in the tradition of the Greeks and Aristotle, prefer the language of being for expressing these differences, and the "terminists" who prefer to deal with such differences, not as levels or aspects of Being, but as differences in statement or method or mode of analysis dictated by the level of our knowledge at a given time. The latter, of whom, as we have seen, Professor Nagel is an outstanding example, are therefore much more concerned with the language of science, i.e., with formal logic and mathematics, and hence more in accord with the antimetaphysical bias of most recent philosophy which has led it to concentrate on language analysis.

The question of ontology nevertheless persistently intrudes itself: by virtue of what traits in the structure of reality are such different theories or theoretical constructs necessary? And, if our different languages or methods are *merely* and *solely* a reflection of the progress of our knowledge in any given area, and not a reflection of the character of the real, as Professor Nagel often seems to say, is not the case conceded to those very reductionists whom naturalists initially set out to revise and correct? The issue is a technical one beyond the scope of this treatment. The reader who wishes to explore further may consult Nagel's *The Structure of Science* (New York: Harcourt, Brace & World, 1961), chap. 11, and *Naturalism and the Human Spirit*, ed. by Y. H. Krikorian (New York: Columbia, 1944), starting perhaps with those pages (379–380) in which Professor Randall summarizes the problem, and then turning to Nagel's "Logic Without Ontology" (pp. 210–244).

on the one hand, and reductionism, on the other. That concept, interpreted in the spirit of critical or evolutionary naturalism, at once implies continuity and difference. It leads us to see that economic phenomena, for example, not only require reference to psychological principles for their full understanding, but also require reference to cultural factors. Capitalism would be incomprehensible without reckoning with such psychological data as man's capacity for thrift and enterprise—or avarice and greed, depending, as R. H. Tawney has reminded us, on one's point of view. On the other hand, it would be equally incomprehensible if one failed to seek in English history, that is, in the cultural setting of eighteenth- and nineteenth-century England, for those social factors which, for the first time, emphasized and encouraged the expression of these personality traits and gave them the peculiar institutional manifestation we call industrial capitalism. A contingent and isolated event, such as Arkwright's invention of the "water frame" in 1769, would not explain the rise of modern capitalism. Neither would such geographic factors as England's coal deposits, her temperate climate or her insular situation—although all this would be helpful. Similar events have occurred and like conditions have prevailed elsewhere without producing capitalism and the putative sovereignty of the free market. Required in addition, and decisively important, are such *social* phenomena as the emergence in England of parliamentary government, the appearance of a powerful middle class, the disestablishment of a church rooted in the feudal agrarian society of the Middle Ages, the enclosure acts and, perhaps—as stressed by the great sociologist Max Weber—the influence of the Protestant ethic.

How, to take other examples, is the spread of Protestantism to be explained, if we rely exclusively on biological or psychological principles? Why did the great rebirth of science in Arabia in the eleventh and twelfth centuries prove abortive? Why did the Orient fail to develop a tradition of pure science despite an early technological advantage? Why are the Kikuyu of Kenya largely herbiferous, despite the fact that in consequence their men are no stronger than the women of the neighboring omniverous tribe and disease is more prevalent among them? Why is the suicide rate greater among Scandinavians than among other comparable peoples?

Reference to suicide should remind us that Émile Durkheim's famous study of suicide rates is generally regarded as the first example of scientific sociological research. Durkheim explicitly renounced psychological explanations affirming that "for sociology to be possible, it must above all have an object all its own. It must take cognizance of a reality which is not in the domain of other sciences." And, "if no reality exists outside of individual consciousness, it [sociology] wholly lacks any material of its own. In that case, the only possible subject of observation is the mental states of the individual, since nothing else exists. That, however, is the field of psychology."[22] In this pioneering effort to carry out Comte's injunction and establish a place for sociology, Durkheim understandably carried his anti-psychologism to an extreme. Most sociologists know now that psychology cannot be dismissed in this way. If they are able to exploit the resources of psychology and ecology and physiology and still preserve the autonomy of the science of society, this may well be, in great part, because a theoretical framework has been provided by the insights of evolutionary naturalism in which such opposites as continuity and discontinuity, sameness and novelty, regularity and contingency no longer appear as incompatible.

The Marxist View

Most of the insights thus achieved were anticipated by Karl Marx, whose views had a decisive influence in this as in other areas of social philosophy and therefore deserve special attention. Marx's A *Contribution to the Critique of Political Economy*, which contains perhaps the best statement of his philosophy of history, appeared in the same year (1859) as *Origin of Species*. His rejection of reductionism antedates his reading of Darwin. Nevertheless, Marx was so much impressed by the *Origin* that he offered to dedicate his *magnum opus, Capital*, to Darwin (who politely refused). He thought of himself as accomplishing for the social sciences what Darwin had accomplished for our understanding of living species. He believed that, just as Darwin had found the dynamic principle that made the evolution of species intelligible, he, Marx, had found and formulated the law that explains the change, transformation and development of social institutions. It is no accident that his friend and collaborator, Friedrich Engels, in a graveside eulogy, compared him with Darwin.

Marx's position is epitomized in his famous dictum: "It is not the consciousness of men that determines their existence, but, on the contrary, their social existence determines their consciousness."[23] While this cryptic comment was directed against Hegel's idealism, and not against psychologism as such, it nevertheless expresses Marx's conviction that psychological generalizations are inadequate to an understanding of human behavior, and that to comprehend man one must consider his social environment. Human nature, which is to say, man's interests, motives, aspirations, ideals, cannot be understood unless we reckon with the social institutions which condition—Marx would say *determine*—their expression. Moral aspirations, aesthetic ideals, religious commitments, above all, eco-

---

[22] *Suicide*, trans. by J. A. Spaulding and George Simpson (Glencoe: The Free Press, 1951), p. 38.
[23] *Critique of Political Economy* (Chicago: Charles H. Kerr and Co., 1918), pp. 11–12.

nomic motives—these are, of course, all psychological phenomena. But they express themselves in multifarious ways and the form they take depends on the kind of social institutions that prevail at any given time. To say this is to suggest that social institutions change, and it is to Marx's abiding credit that he recognized not only the role of social institutions in molding human nature, but their evolving character.

This is, of course, only one part of the story. Marx, in stressing the role of social institutions, emphasizes—some would say, places almost exclusive emphasis on—economic institutions. Economic forces determine the course of history and the character of any given culture. The word "determine" is used advisedly, for Marx's theory (more accurately the theory of Marx and Engels) is called *economic determinism*. What Marxism affirms is that economic factors, that is to say, the "forces of production" (physical and human resources, level of technology) and the "relations of production" (the system of class relationships, for example, slavery, feudalism, capitalism) which prevail at any given time determine the direction of social change and with this the form and content of all our other institutions—familial, political, religious, educational—not to mention our aesthetic and moral ideals and even our science. As a historic force, the individual does not count, even though it must be individuals who ultimately feel and reflect the forces at work. Only classes and their interests, as these reflect the "forces" and "relations" of production, are historically significant. That is why Khrushchev's denunciation of the "cult of personality" in his now celebrated denigration of Stalin was strictly canonical for listeners steeped in the teachings of Marx.

By class relationships Marx meant *economic* classes, which he defined by reference to the relationship of the individual to private property (the means of production), whether as master or slave, lord or serf, employer or worker. Individuals may, of course, be classified in other ways—by nationality, race, age, and so on—and these may be important. But Marx taught that the economic class to which they belong enlists their primary loyalty (even though they are not always conscious of this); all other loyalties are subordinate to class loyalty, and all other interests and aspirations fundamentally *determined* by it. "The history of all hitherto existing society," declares the *Communist Manifesto*, "is the history of class struggles." Elsewhere, Engels wrote that "all political struggles are class struggles, and all class struggles for emancipation, despite their necessarily political form . . . turn ultimately on the question of *economic* emancipation."[24]

The dynamic factor in history is, then, as a latter-day socialist has said, "the attempt of successive social classes, themselves set in motion by

[24] *Ludwig Feuerbach and the End of Classical German Philosophy* in *Marx and Engels Selected Works* (Moscow: Foreign Languages Publishing House, 1962), p. 394.

technical and economic changes, to remould society to suit themselves."[25]

As understood by Marxists, a determining condition is not merely one without which an event cannot occur; it is a sufficient condition: no matter what changes occur in other conditions its presence suffices to bring the event about; it is the *decisive* even if not the *sole* factor.[26] Two famous passages, one from the writings of Engels, the other from Marx, summarize the position thus far described. In *Anti-Dühring* Engels writes:

The materialist conception of history starts from the principle that production, and with production the exchange of its products, is the basis of every social order; that in every society which has appeared in history the distribution of the products, and with it the division of society into classes . . . is determined by what is produced and how it is produced, and how the product is exchanged. According to this conception, the ultimate causes of all social changes and political revolutions are to be sought, not in the minds of men, in their increasing insight into eternal truth and justice, but in changes in the mode of production and exchange; they are to be sought not in the *philosophy* but in the *economics* of the epoch concerned.[27]

Earlier, Marx had written in the *Critique of Political Economy*:

In the social production which men carry on they enter into definite relations that are indispensable and independent of their will; these relations of production correspond to a definite stage of development of their material powers of production. The sum total of these relations of production constitutes the economic structure of society—the real foundation, on which rise legal and political superstructures and to which correspond definite forms of social consciousness. The mode of production in material life determines the general character of the social, political, and spiritual processes of life.[28]

---

[25] John Strachey, *The Theory and Practice of Socialism* (New York: Random House, 1936), pp. 382–383. Long before his death, Strachey, a leading theoretician of the British Labour Party, abandoned the orthodox socialism he advocated in this volume.

[26] Marx and Engels are often interpreted as if they said that economic conditions are the *only* dynamic factor in history, an interpretation to which they often lend themselves. However, Engels wrote:

According to the materialist conception of history the determining element in history is *ultimately* the production and reproduction in real life. More than this neither Marx nor I have ever asserted. If therefore someone twists this into the statement that the economic element is the *only* determining one, he transforms it into a meaningless, abstract and absurd phrase. The economic situation is the basis, but the various elements of the superstructure—political forms of the class struggle and its consequences, constitutions established by the victorious class after a successful battle, etc.—forms of law—and then even the reflexes of all these actual struggles in the brains of the combatants: political, legal, philosophical theories, religious ideas . . . also exercise their influence upon the course of the historical struggles and in many cases preponderate in determining their *form*. There is an interaction of all these elements, in which . . . the economic movement finally asserts itself as necessary.

Marx-Engels Correspondence (New York: International Publishers, 1942), p. 475.

[27] (London: Martin Lawrence Ltd., 1935), p. 300.

[28] *Op. cit.*, p. 11.

It is a fair verdict to conclude that Marx and Engels deserve great credit for calling attention to the role of economic institutions in shaping history, at a time when economic forces were generally ignored in favor of an exaggeration of the role of individuals in history or an exclusive emphasis on political reform as the decisive factor in bringing about social change. Thanks in large part to Marx, this is no longer true, even among those who reject his other teaching. Marx also deserves credit for emphasizing class exploitation and its attendant friction and conflict, at a time when attention was too much occupied with spurious harmony theories. The reference here is not merely to Adam Smith's "natural harmony of interests" but to idealistic philosophies where society is treated as analogous to an organism in which all the parts harmoniously perform their alloted roles.

But it must also be noted, even if the proof cannot be given here, that Marx and Engels exaggerated the part played by economic forces, important though the role of such forces surely is, that class loyalties have been far from playing the central role assigned to them by Marx and Marxists, and that class struggle is by no means inseparably associated with private ownership of the means of production when the power attendant on such ownership is judiciously limited and responsibly exercised. Indeed, as far as his views concerning the class struggle are concerned, Marx was guilty of the same misuse of Darwin as those who invoked Darwin to place the stamp of science on the inhumanities of the profit system. "Darwin's book is very important," he wrote to the socialist, Ferdinand La Salle, "and serves me as a basis in natural science for the class struggle in history."[29] It may be said, however, that, despite these and other shortcomings, Marx's recognition of the institutional, and therefore the social, basis of behavior was one of the most important insights of a century hovering between the psychologism of Mill and Bentham and the trans-empirical pseudo-entities postulated by Fichte or Hegel.

Although they were mainly concerned with preserving the autonomy of political economy, Marx and Engels were quite clear in rejecting mechanistic science in general. Engels was especially explicit and remarkably acute on this issue. He credits mechanistic science with great accomplishments: "The analysis of nature into its individual parts, the grouping of the different natural processes and objects in different classes, the study of the internal anatomy of organic bodies in their manifold forms—these were the fundamental conditions of the gigantic strides in our knowledge of Nature that have been made during the last four hundred years." However, the next passage, if it had been in iambic pentameter, could as well have been written by Wadsworth as by Engels. The mechanistic method, he observes, "has also left us as a legacy the habit of observing natural objects and natural

[29] Cited by Sidney Hook in *Towards the Understanding of Karl Marx* (New York: John Day, 1933), p. 96. The same point is made in a letter to Engels.

processes in their isolation, detached from the whole vast interconnection of things; and therefore not in their motion, but in their repose; not as essentially changing, but as fixed constants; not in their life, but in their death."[30]

For a mechanistic materialism Marx and Engels substituted a philosophy which Marxists call *dialectical materialism*—a kind of illicit union of Hegelian methodology (see pp. 301–302) with the materialism they learned from the German philosopher, Ludwig Feuerbach.[31] Dialectical materialism is variously described by its adherents as a theory which "regards every historically developed social form as in fluid movement, and therefore takes into account its transient nature not less than its momentary existence," that is, which involves "recognition of the existing state of things, [and] at the same time . . . the recognition of the negation of that state"[32] (Marx), or, more inclusively, as "the science of the general laws of motion, both of the external world and of human thought . . ."[33] (Engels). Thanks to the dialectical method—(it is at once a method and a theory about the structure of reality—events are no longer seen as *externally related*, that is, as possessing their essential identity independently of their relations to other events and to the totality of events. On the contrary, events are disclosed as *internally related*, as "interconnected," each having a necessary role to play in the development of nature (including man and society) as a whole. Here, as with Hegel, development proceeds through a series of contradictions. The difference is that, for Marxists, the conflict is not between ideas, but between material forces reflecting themselves at the social level in contending class (economic) interests; and the contradiction is not associated with an incomplete manifestation of Hegel's Absolute Spirit, but with incompletely developed economic systems which, so long as they are based on private ownership of the means of production, must generate disparities between the actual conditions and the potentialities of the prevailing productive system.

The aim here is not to examine dialectical materialism, which has few adherents nowadays west of Moscow, but to indicate that it was primarily German philosophy—including German romantic idealism—rather than Darwin's work that initially suggested or provided the theoretical frame-

---

[30] F. Engels, *Anti-Dühring*, pp. 27–28.

[31] "The mystification which dialectic suffers in Hegel's hands, by no means prevents him from being the first to present its general form of working in a comprehensive and conscious manner. With him it is standing on its head. It must be turned right side up again, if you would discover the rational kernel within the mystical shell." *Capital*, Vol. I, Preface to the 2nd ed., p. 25, trans. by E. Moore and A. Aveling (Chicago: Charles H. Kerr & Co., 1932).

[32] *Ibid.*, p. 26.

[33] Engels, *Ludwig Feuerbach* . . . , p. 387. It was Engels rather than Marx who applied the theory beyond human society, but he credits Marx with formulating the "leading, basic principles."

work for such contentions as that "Nature . . . does not move in the eternal oneness of a perpetually recurring circle, but goes through a real historical evolution." Clearly, however, such notions concerning transformation and development, on which an autonomous science of society must be based, derived welcome nourishment from the pages of *Origin of Species*. To this Engels attested when, after the above statement, he added: "In this connection Darwin must be named before all others. He dealt the metaphysical [i.e., mechanistic] conception of Nature the heaviest blow. . . ."[34]

Conclusion

The science of society, whether as sociology or anthropology or any one of the more restricted social sciences, rests upon the assumption that man is part of the system of nature. Without this assumption, although we might have social "studies," we would not have social science. As already noted, Marx and others derived their materialist and naturalist assumptions largely from other sources, but, to the extent that Darwinism was responsible for this great change in our view of man, it may also be regarded as having contributed greatly to the birth of a true science of society. But more than this. If an adequate science of society requires us to view social phenomena as genuinely novel and therefore as calling for generalizations peculiar to them, the Darwinian outlook, with its implied rejection of reductionism, again helped to point the way.

To be sure, Darwinian principles, as recorded above, were often thoroughly misapplied. This was true not only with what we have already referred to as social Darwinism; for decades, in anthropology, in sociology, in political economy, social scientists, misinterpreting Darwin, uncritically assumed that all social institutions undergo a unilinear change, in the course of which they must pass through predetermined stages of development. With a great deal of wasted erudition these stages were carefully defined and described, as, for example, by Lewis Henry Morgan in his influential *Ancient Society* (1877). The famous law of the "three stages" of Auguste Comte,[35] who coined the term "sociology," provided a prototype for this

---

[34] *Socialism: Utopian and Scientific*, Vol. II, pp. 131–132. Cf. also, Engels, *Ludwig Feuerbach*, p. 389. Engels uses the term "metaphysical" in the Hegelian sense as meaning "mechanistic."

[35] "From the study of the development of human intelligence, in all directions, and through all times, the discovery arises of a great fundamental law, to which it is necessarily subject, and which has a solid foundation of proof, both in the facts of our organization and in our historical experience. The law is this:—that each of our leading conceptions,—each branch of our knowledge,—passes successively through three different theoretical conditions: the Theological, or fictitious; the Metaphysical, or abstract; and the Scientific, or positive. In other words, the human mind, by its nature, employs in its progress three methods of philosophizing, the character of which is essentially different, and even radically opposed: viz., the theological method, the metaphysical, and the positive." *The Positive Philosophy of Auguste Comte*, trans. by Harriet Martineau (London: Kegan Paul, 1893), Vol. 1, pp. 1–2.

kind of often highly suggestive surmise. Similarly, Marxists are cardinal sinners, as when Engels wrote that "all successive historical systems are only transitory stages in the endless course of development of human society from the lower to the higher," adding that "each stage is necessary. . . ."[36] For Marxists, development proceeds after the manner of a spiral rather than a straight line, but it is nonetheless regarded as prescribed in its pattern and inevitable. Evolution*ism* is now in eclipse, although even here we have a legacy of enduring insight, namely, that social institutions are not fixed and static, as prescientific students of society too often supposed, but dynamic and changing—therefore subject to deliberate reconstruction.

At any rate, the study of society in all of its institutional and cultural manifestations is no longer the exclusive province of metaphysics and theology. The church sanctifies marriage and the family; the state is still sometimes said to be ordained of God; property rights—if not royal rights— are genuinely regarded by many as though they were divine or "natural"; history, in some quarters, is still thought to be the march of an Hegelian or Marxist-Hegelian Absolute. But the family, the state, the church, property and everything else that pertains to societies and their histories—including man's aesthetic, moral and spiritual life—have now become proper subjects of scientific inquiry. The result has been a new kind of conflict and a new ambivalence. Today, not so much the formal sciences or the physical sciences or the life sciences, but the social sciences collide with the folklore, challenging our preconceptions and straining traditional modes of thought. It is with the tensions produced by this conflict and the manner of their resolution that the next section is therefore largely occupied.

Selected Readings

Bidney, David, *Theoretical Anthropology*, New York: Columbia University Press, 1953, chaps. 2, 4, 5.

Bukharin, N. I., et al. *Marxism and Modern Thought*, trans. by Ralph Fox, London: Routledge, 1935, "Marx's Teaching and Its Historical Importance," pp. 29–46. Reprinted in *Contemporary Historical Problems*, ed. by Y. H. Krikorian and A. Edel, New York: Macmillan, 1959, pp. 435–449.

Cassirer, Ernst, *An Essay on Man*, New York: Doubleday, 1959. (Anchor paperback.)

Dewey, John, *Experience and Nature*, New York: Norton, 1925, chap. V, "Nature, Communication and Meaning."

Durkheim, Émile, *The Rules of Sociological Method*, Glencoe: Free Press, 1938. (Paperback.)

---

[36] Engels, *Ludwig Feuerbach* . . . p. 362.

Engels, Friedrich, *Ludwig Feuerbach and the End of Classical German Philosophy*, in Marx and Engels, *Selected Works*, Moscow: Foreign Languages Publishing House, 1962.

Hook, Sidney, "Dialectic in Society and History," in *Reason, Social Myths and Democracy*, New York: Humanities Press, 1951, chap. 11.

Hook, Sidney, "A Pragmatic Critique of the Historico-Genetic Method," in *Essays in Honor of John Dewey*, New York: Holt, Rinehart & Winston, 1929, pp. 156–174.

Hook, Sidney, editor, *Psychoanalysis, Scientific Method and Philosophy*, New York: New York University Press, 1959, Pt. III, "Psychoanalysis and Society." (Also Grove Press paperback.)

Lundberg, George A., *Foundations of Sociology*, New York: Macmillan, 1939, pp. 5–44.

Popper, Karl R., *The Open Society and Its Enemies*, Princeton: Princeton University Press, 1950, chap. 14, "The Autonomy of Sociology." (Also Harper Torchbooks paperback, in two vols.)

P A R T IV

THE CONTEMPORARY SCENE

Clarity is not enough.

H. H. PRICE

I'm tired of nihilism.

ALBERT CAMUS

. . . it is silly
To refuse the tasks of time
And, overlooking our lives,
Cry—'Miserable wretched me,
How interesting I am!'

W. H. AUDEN, *Age of Anxiety*

The impact of the behavioral sciences on our society is far greater
than most people realize. At one level they are providing technical
solutions for important human problems. But at a deeper level
they are changing the conception of human nature—our fundamental
ideas about human desires and human possibilities. When such
conceptions change, society changes.

From the Report of the Behavioral
Sciences Subpanel of the President's
Science Advisory Committee, 1962

CHAPTER **24**

New Problems

Philosophy has a history in that it is both a response to tensions created in society and an intellectual development created by the momentum of ideas. Sometimes philosophy is most responsive to the clash between the new and the old in society, as when tradition or folklore and science are in opposition. At other times, when philosophical ideas are already embodied in a culture, they undergo at the hands of philosophers a process of refinement, a kind of internal criticism or development, often called "the dialectic of ideas." Actually, the discussions in the preceding chapters illustrate both kinds of history, but, for the most part, the emphasis has been on the role of philosophy as interpreting and overcoming the tensions between the traditional beliefs and the ideas that arise from the new science of an epoch. This phase of philosophy is the most dramatic, and culturally is no doubt the most important. The other phase of philosophy becomes proportionately more technical, and its spokesmen may be said to be philosophers for philosophers, rather than for the wider public. Nevertheless, the difference is more one of degree than of kind, since cultural philosophy requires analysis to sustain it, and analytic philosophy cannot last very long unless it refers to the larger social context from which it evolves and to which it must again relate. Although the preceding chapters are not intended to be histories of philosophy, they have taken

397

their materials from historical epochs in order to show what philosophy is and why it does have a history.

Part I was concerned with the beginnings of western philosophy as rising out of the need for reconciling the old myths and the old morality, about which Homer and Hesiod had written, with the new attitudes that were expressed in the cosmologies of Thales and his followers. The Pythagoreans, in this first phase of philosophy, were especially intent on reconciling religious and moral attitudes with a formulation in which the new science, defined in terms of numbers, was taken as the clue to the understanding of the essences of all things. There is an internal development of ideas from Thales and the Milesians, to Pythagoras and Parmenides, and finally to the pluralists who were attempting to account for the phenomena of nature—and for man, too—as an integral aspect of nature. This led them to distinguish between illusion and reality, the one and the many, the ideal and the actual, and the like. Such dualisms were engendered in most of Greek philosophy, and became especially prominent and sharply defined in the philosophy of Plato. These dualisms, pagan in origin, were later carried over into Christian thought, only to become, sometimes in Platonic, sometimes in Aristotelian form, the philosophical underpinnings of a later folklore.

The conclusions of Part II, it will be remembered, underlined several critical dualisms found in the work of Descartes and his followers. The most central dualistic split was seen to be that of thinking beings and extended beings, a split which was to be found first in man, as between soul and body, and second in nature at large, as between spiritual and material things. Following upon the Cartesian dualism, there were seen to be related splits clustering around (and depreciating) the emotional and imaginative life of man, such as to forecast the "two culture" division between art and science that we talk about today. A corollary and further related split was seen in the failure of philosophers adequately to come to terms with man's social nature. Mostly, the difficulty was seen to be a result of the infatuation of seventeenth- and eighteenth-century philosophers with the mechanistic interpretation of nature. The price of the new science came high, and a philosophy so enamored of physics could not accommodate itself to the realities of experience and to the importance of creative talent. No merely dialectical development of ideas could overcome the inadequacies of these philosophies. The inadequacies were not clearly disclosed until such philosophies and the folklore in which they were embedded received a profound shock, which was delivered primarily by the advent of the work of Darwin.

Part III depicted the intellectual accommodations that followed upon the trauma produced by evolutionary doctrine. A new form of naturalism, supplementing, and in some cases revolutionizing, seventeenth-century naturalism, inevitably followed. Some of the older dualisms had to be overcome, or at least softened. This was accomplished largely through a new philosophy which was in opposition to the mechanistic practice of attempting to reduce higher things to lower things. Accordingly, man becomes reinterpreted as being a more integral part of nature without losing anything of his unique character. In order to clarify and support this interpretation, man had to be seen as one with nature and yet as possessing distinctive qualities which set him apart from other forms of life. Man shares his nature with plant and animal; but insofar as he possesses a developed consciousness and self-consciousness, these mark him off as a separate species. The truth of both "mechanism" and "vitalism," it was seen, must be acknowledged and reconciled in any adequate theory about the truth of man.

Evolutionary naturalism cries out for the new accommodation, not just for regarding man as a genuine part of nature, but also for delineating more adequately his human and social qualities in the widest range of their cultural expression—including art and religion, economics and politics, manners, sports, the family, war and peace; in short, including the whole range of activities and aspirations and frustrations which are peculiar to contemporary man.

Twentieth-century philosophy must cope with a whole new set of problems. We may look to the past for some guidance, but there is in this procedure the danger of ignoring, or of grossly misrepresenting, the questions that are uniquely contemporary. In this sense, the past is easier to understand (or so it is usually made out) than the present. If the study of the past is of any help, it is by suggesting a strategy for coping with the present. In the broad sense, there is a strategy suggested by the preceding analyses—that of explicitly acknowledging the major task of philosophy as that of accommodating the old to the new. This is the overwhelming task of philosophy. A likely approach is to consider a number of the persisting questions of today as being constituted by the need for reconciling the folklore of modern attitudes engendered in the philosophy of the Enlightenment and of the recent past with the challenge from the new studies and insights of the social sciences. This approach does not attempt to include the whole range of philosophical questions, but it does have the advantage of focus, and it holds a promise of providing a better understanding of "the predicament of modern man."

In any field of experience, the results of new theories and new data will present a challenge to the conventional wisdom, but especially is this so when the new knowledge probes some of the most vulnerable and sensitive areas of our beliefs. For nowhere are human interests more vested than here, in the very nature of man and his relation to his fellows. In a double fashion, then—because of their relative youth and because of their subject matter—the social-behavioral studies present a special challenge today.

By concentrating on this challenge, we are not unmindful of natural science, now or in the past. That impact, as it manifested itself in earlier centuries, has already been discussed. And it is an impact that has deepened and widened its pressure as the twentieth-century revolutions in the physical and life sciences have set unforeseeable forces in motion. The overt manifestations of the ever-continuing scientific revolution are so familiar from our newspapers that even a bare inventory should prove superfluous. It is unlikely that many of our readers have failed to respond one way or another to the dramas—often tragic, occasionally comic, always exciting—of the release of nuclear energy, automation and computers, space travel and communication, or even to such frontier sciences as psychopharmacology with its undreamed-of possibilities.

It is somewhat less likely that such readers have responded as sensitively to the equally dramatic impact of scientific *theory*, despite the fact that for more than half a century the "new physics" has been in a state of ferment. Yet, even here, there has been popularization, often vulgarization, of concepts deriving from relativity, quantum mechanics, discontinuity and causal indeterminism, cybernetics, psychosomatics, and many more. These very terms themselves seem to suggest a shattering collision with common sense and received opinion; and it is unquestionable that vast and rapid developments in the natural sciences have engendered whole new philosophic concerns and techniques.

Nevertheless, although it would be too strong to say that the folklore has made its peace with the natural sciences, an uneasy truce does seem to prevail. For example, any controversies which may remain about the biblical account of creation or of the origin of man carry with them an archaic ring. Few thoughtful people are touched by them, and those who are will be unlikely to influence the course of events or the history of ideas.

This uneasy truce also depends, in part, on the fact that many modern scientists do not regard their work as a disclosure of the nature of reality, as did the great seventeenth-century thinkers like Galileo and Newton. Science is thus supposed to be concerned only with *phenomena*, that is, with *that which appears* and not with a reality supposed to exist behind appearances.[1] Such scientists also believe that their work must avoid value judgments. This position is known as *positivism*. It suggests another reason why physicists and biologists no longer step so heavily on people's toes. A

---

[1] This position has noticeably weakened in recent years, at least in the controversies surrounding the interpretation of the behavior of single physical particles. (See pp. 499–502.)

modern counterpart of Galileo would hardly be called upon to recant his views—not in the nontotalitarian western world as we now know it.

There are, to be sure, awesome disparities between our common sense view of things and the strange world of astro- and atomic physics. But such disparities do not appear to challenge any cherished beliefs. No one has a vital commitment to the corpuscular, as over against the wave, theory of light, in the sense that men once had a stake in the perfect sphericity of the moon or the geocentric system of Ptolemy. Moreover, its sheer technicality tends to remove much of natural science from areas of controversy that might seriously engage the layman. Beyond this, if the physicist of today must have recourse to non-Euclidean geometries and the intricate mathematics of relativity and quantum mechanics when he explores interstellar space and the interior of the atom, both he and the common man continue to be well served by Euclidean geometry and Newtonian mechanics in the world of middle-size objects where both physicist and common man reside. In all but the most specialized of experiences the common-sense notions of space, time, and motion rely on theories that are not in frontal collision with the more scientifically sophisticated ones, and so they can jog along together in comfort.

It must also be noted that the folklore does change, and new accommodations do arise. Just as the "prejudices of the vulgar" could not stand forever against Newton, so, in this Age of the Astronauts, we are beginning to adjust, at least vicariously, to the most uncommon sense experiences— weightlessness, curved space, speeds approaching the limits of speed, variable time, disorientation from the earth, if not from the solar system— and it would be no rash prophet who would foretell that possibly in a century the common wisdom will be what the advanced textbooks now teach, scientific fiction already having become prosaic.

Is there a comparable elasticity to be expected in the received beliefs about society and social institutions? In some areas, clearly, there has been a conspicuous and occasionally over-hasty readjustment of prevailing ideas. The rapid spread of psychoanalysis—at least what passes for psychoanalysis—in certain sectors of the public, the revolution in the care and training of very young children, the quick acceptance of the techniques of estimating public opinion, even the sometimes grudging acquiescence to social security and other concepts of the welfare state—these would provide some indication that the social folklore is by no means entirely resistant to new ideas.

At the same time, it is undeniable that a main source of tension today stems from the social-behavioral sciences and the strains they impose on traditional beliefs about man and society. In the areas dealt with by these sciences, we have strong and even passionate commitments. Despite the facile acceptance of psychoanalysis, it is outrageous to be told that every display of affection by a child toward its parents is an incestuous fantasy, even if the proposition were as demonstrable as some Freudians think. It is intolerable, if one believes in the inferiority of the black race, to learn that northern Negroes score higher on intelligence tests than do some southern whites. And when most prominent economists tell us that the fear of an unbalanced budget is an irrational fear based on mistaken analogies and assumptions, for many members of the business community, and of Congress, this is still a strange and subversive notion.

It would seem, then, that there is an ambivalent reception given to the findings of the sciences of man. We are not, of course, considering here the prevalent debiting of science with unwelcome things like "the Bomb." Such reactions involve entirely different matters from those being handled at this point. Perhaps it is chiefly the youth of social science that is responsible for this, rather than the material in question (although there is danger—as the saying goes—that its youth may become its oldest tradition). After all, it would still be premature to speak of a full-grown Scientific Revolution in the social field, although the evidence is clear that a revolution is well under way: it may even have reached the stage of Kepler or possibly Galileo, although not yet that of Newton.

In any case, these are some of the reasons why particular attention will be given, later in Part IV, to some of the problems arising in the areas covered by social-behavioral science.

It is not easy to observe contemporary folklore in its continual adjustment to new knowledge. Too often our observations of what is going on under our very eyes tend to become clichés, or to verge on the pontifical. It is merely facile to keep repeating the slogans about "living in a revolution."

This is evident as we turn to the dominating interests of present-day philosophy and find that much of contemporary academic philosophy seems easily to escape from the formula—from the attempt to accommodate scientific information, particularly in the field of the social sciences, to the conventional wisdom. But has there been such a successful escape? An investigation of some of the leading concerns of contemporary philosophy may indicate that, no more than in earlier days, can philosophy think to cut all ties with its cultural setting.

CHAPTER 25

The Contemporary Scene:
Logical Analysis

W hat is to be included within the range of "contemporary philosophy"? If "contemporary" is to be understood, as students seem to
understand it, as that which is not much older than they are or possibly
than their parents, the answer is reasonably clear. At least so far as Western
academic philosophy is concerned, two patterns of thought, poles apart
in aim and technique, tend to dominate the scene: logical—or, more
accurately, linguistic—analysis, and existentialism. However, neither name
is entirely satisfactory.

The first is connected with more than half a century of British thought
whose antecedents trace back to Locke, Berkeley, and Hume, and it has
varied in its ideas as much as in its names: "analysis," "logical atomism,"
"logical positivism," "logical empiricism," "logical analysis," "linguistic
analysis," and "linguistic phenomenology"—the last representing the approach of J. L. Austin. Certainly, some form of "analysis" (but not
"psycho-") is the appropriate label for what has been called, perhaps in
overstatement, a veritable revolution in philosophy. Nor can "existentialism"
be looked upon as representing a single movement; indeed, the name
itself has been successively rejected by nearly all of its supposed practition-

ers. But, in this brief discussion, we will use the terms, "linguistic analysis" (or just "linguistic philosophy") and "existentialism" as the two contrasting philosophies since approximately the time of the Second World War.

Philosophy is ordinarily given to the long view—it must be remembered that "modern" philosophy begins in the seventeenth century—and so the year 1900 has frequently been used as a marker for contemporary philosophy, not simply because we like round numbers (actually, the nineteenth century may be appropriately said to have come to an end in 1914, when World War I began), but because the opening years of the twentieth century saw a sharp reaction set in against the prevailing theories of German Absolute Idealism. (See pp. 298–302.) In England, this was represented by the early work of G. E. Moore and Bertrand Russell, which signaled a revolt against obscurantism and imprecision, and emphasized common sense, clarity, and analysis (with Moore) and epistemological realism and mathematics (with Russell). In the United States, at the same time, there was a corresponding break with German metaphysics in the pragmatic philosophies of Charles Peirce, William James, and John Dewey. Even the quite different ideas of Henri Bergson in France represented a self-conscious attempt at a fresh point of view; so that the transition from the nineteenth century to the twentieth century did usher in what may at one time have seemed like a consistent mood of "contemporary philosophy."

The trouble with the long view of contemporary philosophy is that it is either not long enough, or it is too long. Perhaps the year 2000 may disclose the pattern of twentieth-century thought; although at this point only a prophet could foretell whether it will be called an Age of Analysis or of Ontology or of Scientific Philosophy, or of something quite unforeseen. In any case, the "Age," whatever it be, would picture no more accurately what went on during these hundred years than the "Age of Romanticism" described the nineteenth, or the "Age of Reason" the seventeenth and eighteenth centuries. If we cannot wait until 2000, neither can we look back to 1900 to help us with "contemporary philosophy." For in the roughly two generations of active thinking since then, many movements have come forward and then receded, perhaps to remain in the background or to advance again in a new guise. (It will be understood that we are not discussing here "nonacademic" philosophies such as Marxism or Freudianism.)

Take the various forms of American pragmatism that have been noted in Part III (pp. 371–374). This philosophy never transported easily and made little impression outside North America (except for the work of the Oxford philosopher, F. C. S. Schiller, which he called "humanism"). Even in the United States pragmatism reached its peak of influence in the 1920's and early 1930's, just before the collapse of the League of Nations, the onset of the Depression, and the spiraling rise of movements like Fascism, Nazism, and Communism—all of them seeming to be fatal rejoinders to the confident, "progressive," democratic and pro-scientific ideas that were associated with pragmatism. At that time pragmatism was, at least in the United States, truly "contemporary"—whether for praise or blame—but now, despite the fact that a number of distinguished living American philosophers still accept the name, it has largely been passed over as old-fashioned. Yet there are some indications of resurgent interest among younger philosophers, especially along the lines of adapting some of the pragmatic themes to the present climate of opinion. Also, in certain significant ways, pragmatism has already achieved its purpose in providing a working, if possibly unrecognized, basis for prevailing methods in the law, education, art, and social science.

"Contemporary philosophy"—roughly that since World War II—has developed for the most part in different directions. One of these has firmly guided Anglo-American philosophy for almost a generation and only very recently has it shown signs of relaxing its grip. This, as mentioned before, is the philosophy best nominated by terms like "linguistic" or "conceptual analysis," or even more generally as "analytical philosophy."

The Analytical Movement

"Analysis" is a designation as antique as it is up-to-date. In some fundamental ways the entire philosophic enterprise has been analytical in that, at least since Socrates, it has been seriously engaged in trying to clarify the meaning of men's beliefs and ideas. From Plato's *Euthyphro* to the most recent examination of the nuances of ordinary language, a major theme in the history of ideas has been to define concepts and to explicate their uses. Certain periods have been more given to such investigation than others; the present age in philosophy, as in literary criticism, is, or just has been, one with an unusually strong interest in such inquiry.

But what exactly does "analysis" mean? It is a highly approved word, yet it does not stand for any single method or technique, any more than it indicates just what is to be analyzed. The basic meaning of "analysis" is to reduce something to its parts, its elements, its common denominators. It is contrasted with "synthesis"—the putting-together of parts; so that it would be easier to "analyze" than to "synthesize" a clock. Science has ordinarily been regarded as "analytic," since characteristicly it has sought for irreducible elements (for example, true "atoms"— now, the numerous "particles" making up a physical atom) on the basis of which to construct a reliable system of "compounds." Whether the life sciences and social sciences can be so construed provides one of the interesting items in contemporary discussions of scientific method. But what are the irreducible elements or "atoms" for which philosophical analysis strives? What are the basic common denominators of language, concepts, ideas, and definition? This is not an easy question to answer. Even G. E. Moore, rightly regarded as one of the fathers of contemporary analytical philosophy, expressed his perplexity.[2]

According to the method of analytical philosophy, the way to analyze a statement (the *analysand*) is to supply another statement (the *analysans*) which supposedly replaces it with elements that are unambiguous and verbally clear. An almost classic paradigm of verbal analysis is: "*x* is a sister" reduces to "*x* is a female sibling." Now, what is the value or point of such a translation? On the positive side, an arbitrary and conventional word, "sister," is replaced by empirical, biological terms, which may be said to explain the former word. We all undoubtedly learned the meaning of "sister" by rote, by an ostensive "pointing," as it were. But what is necessary to be a "sister" is now clearly spelled out, in the longer but more explicit *analysans*. This is a very simple case. Suppose we take the word "gold." Its definition, like many definitions, is clearly analytical, breaking down the familiar, yet necessarily vague, idea to "a precious yellow metal, highly malleable and ductile, free from tendency to rust, with an atomic weight of 197.2 and a specific gravity of 19.3." In one sense, this extended translation is much less "simple" than the original term, since some of the defining properties, like atomic weight, may be unfamiliar. In another sense, it is more "simple," for it connects "gold" with a set of common denominators, all of them more "elemental" and more far-reaching than "gold" itself, thereby making it possible to fit the word to significant statements applying to many other things.

But the question can still be raised: Why paraphrase? If the analysis results in a synonym, however technical it may be ("sibling"), then it is trivial; but if the paraphrase is not synonymous, then it is false to the original *analysand*. This is known as "the paradox of analysis." Analysis is puzzling, but it is no more perplexing than some of the similar problems of definition. Should we happen, for example, to look up the word "bee" in the dictionary, we discover that, among other things, it stands for an "hymenopterous insect," as though this phrase were more familiar than the word to be defined. That which is to be defined (the *definiendum*) is replaced by something else to be defined, and, logically, the process could be open-ended. But definition does come to a close when, in an admittedly arbitrary fashion, sufficient information is given to account for the usage of the particular term. Similarly, analysis, again in an arbitrary fashion,

---

[2] See *The Philosophy of G. E. Moore*, ed. by Paul Schilpp (Library of Living Philosophers, Evanston: Northwestern University Press, 1942) pp. 660–667, espec. 665–667.

comes to a close when a proposition is made clear and explicit, not necessarily in terms of new information, but by having the original statement translated, if possible, into one that is unique and unambiguous. In this respect, analysis is close to the explicative function of deduction. For instance, to aver that a whale suckles its young since it is a mammal, and all mammals do that, is not to produce any new knowledge about whales, for all of it is implicit in the acceptance that whales are mammals. But the explicit conclusion may make some of us take another look at whales, if only by rereading *Moby Dick*.

There are many problems involved in the general analytic process. For example, can all statements be analyzed? Are not some statements genuinely atomic and reducible no further, for example, "x is yellow" or "x is good"? (See pp. 459, 461.) Other questions ask in just what way analysis is applicable to all statements; how far it can be carried; what are its relations to synthesis—to that synoptic vision celebrated by Plato—and whether it is self-justifying or needs to be appraised by its undoubted relevance in solving significant problems. Responses to questions like these have provided almost a resumé of much of contemporary philosophy.

Common Sense Defended

There can be no attempt here to detail the history of twentieth-century analytic philosophy, but the several major phases will be given a brief mention. Even such a necessarily inadequate account may suggest that the interests of contemporary analysis are not free of the tensions generated by the criticism and defense of common sense.

Actually, for more than two generations, one of the central purposes of analytical philosophy has been to defend the ordinary notions of common sense, as well as the language in which they are customarily expressed. It was pointed out that early in the twentieth century a pronounced reaction set in against Hegelian idealism with its downgrading of empirical science and the senses in favor of logic and dialectic. Moore, the leading English figure in that reaction, introduced into recent philosophy the novel and refreshing idea that what philosophers were often saying simply made no sense. At least not to Moore. For example, take the proposition: "The material world is unreal." From the ancient Greeks to modern times, in the Orient as in the Occident, this has been a familiar, and often commended, contention, Moore professed a total incomprehension of what the proposition could be supposed to mean. During one now-famous lecture, he extended his two hands in front of his face, and then insisted that certainly here were two real things! Therefore, it was just false to say that "the material world is unreal." Upon other occasions, Moore went beyond his hands, and proceeded to draw up an inventory of ordinary beliefs that could in no way be doubted.[3]

It is not easy to capture, at second hand, Moore's method, much less the wide-eyed innocence of his puzzlement over statements like "The Absolute does not exist in time," or even something seemingly less obscure such as William James's "The true is what is useful." Moore's method was to search for the possible meaning of what appeared to him outrageously false statements ("Time is unreal" or "The good is what produces happiness"), and he was persuaded that he was not deceived by appearances—for, indeed, they were outrageously false statements. But, first, they had to be made clear. This was his task, and that of philosophy as he understood it. Philosophy was to be neither rhetorical nor hortatory, but analytical.

As he admitted, Moore was concerned not with the world but with statements made about the world. He wrote: "I do not think that the world or the sciences would ever have suggested to me any philosophical problems. What has suggested philosophical problems to me is things which other philosophers have said about the world or the sciences."[4] To put this in more recent terminology, the philosopher devotes himself to "second-order" statements rather than to "first-order" ones. The latter would be such as: "Love is good, and cruelty bad,"; "The world is, after all, a beautiful place"; "Brahma is the only reality, but we see it through illusion, the veil of Maya." A second-order approach would, first of all, seek for clarification of meaning: "Whether or not love is good, just what do you intend by 'good' or 'goodness'?" "What are the criteria of what you call 'beauty' or 'beautiful'?" "If ordinary 'reality' is somehow illusory, what does it take to be 'really real'?" Relevant answers to questions like these would also be of the second order, since they would be dealing with words, propositions, concepts rather than with their applicability to things. Before predicating something of the world we have to be sure that the predicate is meaningful, can stand the test of analysis. Tools must be sharpened before they can be used, and philosophy is—or should be—the sharpener and the analyzer. Better never to use a tool than to hack away with a poor one.

Moore was an expert sharpener. He had a very high boiling point, to shift the metaphor, so far as metaphysical curiosity was concerned, but an unusually low one where language was involved. Some later English philosophers have understood him to be defending the ordinary language of common sense, but he himself thought he was doing much more than that; he was concerned, he said, with the truth of concepts and not simply with

---

[3] See "A Defense of Common Sense," in *Contemporary British Philosophy*, 2nd Series, 1925 (London: G. Allen, reissued, 1953) pp. 193ff., and "Proof of an External World" Hertz Lecture. (London: Humphrey Milford, 1939).

[4] Schilpp, *op. cit.*, p. 14.

the appropriateness of the words used to express them.[5] What makes G. E. Moore the very model of a modern English philosopher and (along with Ludwig Wittgenstein) the most important influence upon recent British thought, is his unconcern with theory and his concentration on practicing—or, as it has become known since, "doing"—philosophy. Einstein once reminded us not to pay attention to what scientists say but to what they do. And to "do" philosophy is, for much of the profession to-day, to analyze what philosophers—"other" philosophers, that is—say. More than that, it is to take literally what other philosophers say and show it to be, if it is, unclear, or incomplete, or downright false when not simply nonsense. The criteria for these strictures? Moore was quite clear on this point. The common-sense world was the most appropriate standard. Clearly-stated beliefs about the world which are widely entertained have the best claim to be true. That the world exists very much as it appears to us, that time is real, that man's will is free, that we just "know" when something is right or wrong: to stop there—these have the strongest claim upon us. In any case, the burden of proof rests definitely and heavily upon those who would question such items of common sense. The questioners would be constrained to show that the enduring and eminently workable ideas that men have fashioned about themselves and their surroundings are somehow in error—and this, Moore felt, would be very hard to do. Although Moore was very critical of at least one aspect of pragmatism— William James' theory of truth—his own defense of common sense would appear to rest firmly on a pragmatic test, that of durable success.

When common sense is challenged, it by no means yields. As has been seen earlier, conventional wisdom may be assimilated to new knowledge or it may resist. Moore is defending common sense not so much against science as against philosophy itself, at least against a supposedly unclear and unanalyzed philosophy. He is defending it strongly, and on very simple grounds, so simple as to be startling. When Moore raised his two hands before him and asserted that they were real, this was a notable event in English philosophy; yet when Dr. Johnson kicked a stone to refute Bishop Berkeley, he was patronized as not comprehending what was involved. For Berkeley never contended that a foot would go through a stone. No more, it may be suspected, did Hegel or F. H. Bradley (the English Hegelian, a dominating figure during Moore's most productive years) question that a man actually has two hands. Their concern was other things, such as the relation of organs like hands to everything else. Moore was unpuzzled about these "other things." He had no metaphysical system to defend. What did puzzle him was the way philosophers talked, and in this he strikingly anticipated the kind of thinker Ludwig Wittgenstein was to celebrate if not exemplify.

[5] *Ibid.*, p. 675.

Moore's great hold upon all subsequent Anglo-American philosophy was his passion for clarity, his reliance upon analytical techniques—even though he confessed some doubts about them—his honest attempt to respond to the long tradition of philosophic lore as if he were hearing it for the first time. More than that, for a half century he practiced not what he preached, for he did not preach, but what he believed to be the purpose and discipline of philosophy. If there is anything revolutionary about contemporary philosophy, the quiet and donnish Moore was a veritable revolutionist. If, however, the all-out defense of common sense and the accompanying unconcern with the grand visions and ideals of Western thought are counterrevolutionary, then he was a leader here, too.

Logical Positivism

Although contemporary philosophy (with the exception of existentialism) has been largely professional and intramural, one phase of it has penetrated beyond the academy; this is the movement known as "logical positivism," although other names have been applied to the same ideas. That "metaphysics is nonsense"; that ethics and aesthetics, if not exactly nonsense, are constituted by emotive statements with no claim to truth; that empirical verification (such as is found in science) and logical consistency (such as operates in mathematics) are the only allowable cognitive methods —pronouncements with such a "positivistic" flavor have spilled over, not simply into science, but into the lay world as well, achieving a notoriety and a dramatic impact rare for philosophic statements. Despite this flair, the movement itself has been relatively short-lived, although its influence will undoubtedly be permanent. In this it resembles early (Watsonian) behaviorism and, possibly, even pragmatism. The verb "has been" is not inadvised. Both A. J. Ayer, whose *Language, Truth, and Logic* was regarded as almost the scripture of logical positivism, and Rudolph Carnap, a leader in the Vienna Circle and later in the United States have testified[6] that there is no longer a recognizable philosophy to be identified as "logical positivism," although neither would wish to underplay, even if he could, the lasting significance of positivisitic ideas.

But this is going too fast. What about "analysis," which is the theme of

---

[6] See Ayer's edited work *Logical Positivism* (Glencoe, Ill.: Free Press, 1959), Intro., espec. pp. 3–10; and *The Philosophy of Rudolf Carnap*, P. A. Schilpp, ed. (La Salle, Ill.: Open Court, 1963), chiefly Carnap's introductory remarks, pp. 3–84, espec. pp. 81–84; and pp. 1009–1013 of his concluding remarks. Also, in this connection, a summary by Professor Herbert Feigl, one of the early leaders of logical positivism, is very revealing. Cf. his prefatory remarks to his Presidential Address before the American Philosophical Association (Western Division), "The Power of Positivistic Thinking," *Proceedings and Addresses of the American Philosophical Association* (Yellow Springs, Ohio: Antioch Press, 1963), pp. 21–23.

this section? How does it function vis-à-vis logical positivism? To answer this, a brief historical note must be included about "logical atomism," the theory connected with the names of Bertrand Russell and Ludwig Wittgenstein (at least in the first phase of his thought).[7] As we saw, G. E. Moore analyzed the statements made by philosophers to discover if they jibed with common sense. But Russell wanted to analyze "facts" into their elements. These elements, in the tradition of Locke and Hume, were to be "sense data" or "sensa," which, like the "simple ideas" of Locke, were irreducible and automatically valid deliverances of the senses, such as "This is red," or, more exactly, "here-now red." Not "This is a stop sign" or "That is a Communist emblem," for those are inferences and therefore debatable. But that I am experiencing a sense datum is not debatable; it can be denied only if I am a deliberate and elaborate deceiver. It is what Russell called "knowledge by acquaintance." All other knowledge is compounded out of this primary type, and is "knowledge by description," resting for its authenticity upon the hard or primitive data. To say "I see a dog" is always subject to error, since I may be dreaming, or mistake one kind of animal for another, or be put off by an ingenious toy. But to say—allowing for Russell's sense of mischief—"I see a canoid-shaped patch of color" is indubitable. Even if I dream I see something. Like Descartes, Russell was looking for what cannot be doubted, and he thought he had found it by analyzing both facts and the knowledge of facts into the most simple and basic atoms, such as patches of color, sound, touch, and the like.

There is no need to go into the rise and fall of sense-datum theory, except to record that few philosophers today subscribe to it in an unmodified form. Even Moore admitted he had never encountered a truly atomic proposition, and in recent years perhaps the *coup de grâce* was given to the theory by J. L. Austin.[8] Furthermore, psychologists have just about demonstrated that the whole idea is part of the mythology of perception. It may well be that analysis can break down objects into perceptions, and perceptions into bare sensory elements, and, for some purposes, such analysis is soundly conceived and fruitful. But, to read back the *products* of analysis (for example, "this-that") as what we initially do perceive is to commit what has been termed "*the* philosophic fallacy." Russell has said that "the point of philosophy is to start with something so simple as not to seem worth stating [I see a cat] and to end with something so paradoxical that no one will believe it [I see nothing but a feline-shaped patch of color]," which may prove to be a notable epitaph for logical atomism.

Another important aspect of this theory needs to be mentioned. If "facts"

---

[7] Cf. J. O. Urmson, *Philosophical Analysis* (Oxford at the Clarendon Press, 1956), Sections 4–6, Part I.

[8] In his *Sense and Sensibilia* (Oxford at the Clarendon Press, 1961).

are to be analyzed into "sense data," then the propositions which refer to facts must themselves be reducible to truly atomic elements, perhaps such as "this-that." Propositions, at least the fundamental ones, were somehow to picture not facts but the skeletons of facts. There was to be a one-to-one relation between language and the world, a relation like a photograph or a (realistic) picture or a mirror image to an object, like a phonograph record to a musical theme. These analogies come from a famous work by Wittgenstein, the *Tractatus Logico-Philosophicus*, one of the seminal books of twentieth-century thought. The same idea is also found in a number of Russell's writings, chiefly his lectures, *Logical Atomism*; he also wrote the Introduction to the *Tractatus*, underscoring the same point, although not to Wittgenstein's liking. Moreover, the prodigious three-volume *Principia Mathematica*, which Russell wrote in collaboration with Alfred North Whitehead (a notable landmark in the history of symbolic logic), is an attempt to construct a perfect language—rather, the syntax of a perfect language—based on the assumption that the atoms of language can be indeed identified and rationalized.[9] Further discussion of these matters would become too technical and also would be of historical interest only, because both Russell and Wittgenstein long ago rejected, or at least abandoned, the picture theory of language. In the brilliant little book by Geoffrey Warnock, *English Philosophy Since 1900*, it is maintained that philosophies are rarely refuted; they simply fade away. "They are citadels much shot at perhaps but never taken by storm, which are discovered one day to be no longer inhabited"[10]. Logical atomism is only one of many systems to which this applies. Later Warnock specifies logical atomism, when, referring to a cryptic passage in Wittgenstein's *Tractatus*, he notes that Wittgenstein had, as it were, placed a time bomb in the basement of the philosophy but "when it went off [at the time of Wittgenstein's *Investigations*], the early proponents had already vacated the premises."[11]

---

[9] For students who have had some logic: the concept of "truth functions" is one which plays a deciding part in Wittgenstein's *Tractatus* as well as in Russell's work in this area. In a capsule, the "truth" of a compound statement depends entirely on the "truth" of its components, even if the results are sometimes paradoxical. If the propositions p and q are true, and we follow correctly the rules for putting them together, then the resulting combinations must hold. Of course, as has been pointed out, it is not always as simple as this. For instance, the truth of "all men are mortal" depends on the truth of "x is mortal," "y is mortal," . . . "n is mortal," but upon something else, too, i.e., "and that's all the men there are." As Russell himself recognized, this suggests that the truth-function calculus (as in the familiar "truth tables") is not self-sufficient. It should be added that "all men are mortal" also means "*if* x is a man, *then* x is mortal," which interpretation does not depend upon a complete enumeration.

[10] (London: Oxford, 1958), p. 11.

[11] *Ibid.*, p. 42.

Cognitive Language

There is a direct connection between logical atomism and the more formidable logical positivism, for the sense datum theory is a significant aspect of the positivistic understanding of knowledge. Any piece of reliable information can be reduced to basic propositions (*Protokollsätze*), which are of the "here-now-blue" type. Furthermore, the reduction of all cognitive propositions to two exclusive types is also a by-product of atomic analysis, although this goes back at least to Hume and Kant. These two types, it will be recalled, are the empirical (also known as a posteriori, or synthetic, that dealing with matters of fact) and the analytical (also, a priori, that dealing with relations of ideas). All statements making a claim to truth or validity must be fitted into one of these categories. To illustrate: "Some men are blondes" is an empirical statement, depending for its truth or falsity upon simple sensory evidence. But "Either some men are blondes or no men are," depends for its validity not on the content of the argument, for that is irrelevant, but on its form. This is an example of one form of logical contradiction, of the relation between a universal negative (E) proposition and a particular affirmative (I). If one of these is true, the other must be false, and if one is false the other must be true. This is a formal, syntactical matter, so that this kind of proposition offers no problem except the technical ones found in logic and mathematics. Other examples of analytical statements would be tautologies such as "A is A," or "A red apple is an apple," or "If x is south of y, then y is north of x."

What about empirical statements? Here we meet the famous "verification principle," a major plank in the positivistic platform. It is disarmingly simple. Any meaningful (empirical) statement must be capable of being verified or disverified, and, although there are real problems about strong and weak verification and direct and indirect, it can be said that a statement is verified when a sense-datum sentence (a protocol—or original—sentence) is present to vouch for it. The phrase "verification principle" may be new, but the idea is ancient, reaching back at least to the Greek empiricists, and found throughout the entire philosophic tradition, becoming particularly prominent in the work of the British philosophers of the seventeenth and eighteenth centuries and in American pragmatism. What was new about modern positivism was its belligerent rejection of any claim which could not meet the verification test. The leading candidates for rejection, of course, were the metaphysical and theological claims. A statement such as that of F. H. Bradley, "The Absolute is itself incapable of evolution or progress," would be almost a model of meaninglessness, or, less politely, of non-sense. It certainly is not an analytic statement, since its contradictory does not create a logical or linguistic absurdity, as if we were to say that a green apple was not an apple, or that y is not north of x, although x is indeed south of y. And it certainly is not verifiable or disverifiable by any known criterion. Indeed, no one intended it that way. It is really poetry.

Disenchantment with the ponderous pronouncements of metaphysics and theology is, to be sure, a long-time disenchantment. What gives logical positivism its new version of an old complaint is its focus on language, an emphasis which ties together nearly all aspects of contemporary philosophy. It is the systematic misuse of propositions so as to give them the appearance but not the substance of meaningfulness ("Time is unreal"; "God is both immanent and transcendent") which has upset the logical positivist. He has reacted in two different ways. One reaction was to turn to the possibility of a purified, artificial language of which the syntax and referents would be impeccable. This has been the interest of the group of which Carnap has been the leader. He has attempted to construct various calculi, not simply for the purpose of supplanting ordinary language by an unimpeachable set of symbols, but in order also to talk constructively about language from an "outside" perspective, by means of a deliberate "metalanguage," to talk about language, that is, "formally" and not merely "materially." However, the issues amenable to this astringent approach have turned out to be few. The second reaction began at Cambridge and developed further niceties at Oxford and in this country It explored meticulously the nuances of ordinary language, in the course of which the positivistic suspicion of everyday language was almost totally reversed.

The positivistic attempt to rectify language, as with Carnap, provides an intimate liaison between philosophy and the sciences. (The early continental logical positivists, especially those of the so-called Vienna Circle, which flourished from the end of World War I to the *Anschluss* of Austria with Germany under Hitler, were expert scientists as well as philosophers.) Being firmly persuaded that philosophy could no longer deal with the world, as traditional metaphysics held, and that science could and did, and believing therefore that philosophy was in no sense a rival of science and endowed with an extra-special, superfine method of knowing, the logical positivist regarded his function as a philosopher to be that of supplementing the sciences, and possibly unifying them. The supplement, as might be suspected, was linguistic. Philosophy was to clarify and sharpen the symbols used by the sciences. This task turned out to be a double one. One phase was that of "semantics," that is, concern with the referents of symbols, the objects and events for which symbols acted as surrogates; the other was "syntactics," the internal structure or grammar of symbols as they were used in concert.

The positivist was scandalized, first by the fact that terms such as "consciousness," "causality," "will," "time," "energy," and scores of others were current coin in both science and everyday speech. He was further shocked by the recognition that—as C. D. Broad has pointed out—we do not know the grammar of our own language; we are insensitive, for instance, to the many different kinds of English sentence, usually lumping together quite distinct shades of meaning into a single gross category, such as the declarative or the subjunctive. Without going into details, it can be said that the function of philosophy vis-à-vis science (or vis-à-vis anything else, for that matter) was to clear up the meaning of terms and to make more precise their relations. Science had other things to do, such as gathering of data, formulating problems, creating and testing hypotheses; it could not also be expected, at least so it was argued, to scrutinize the language it used. But philosophy had nothing else to do. Indeed, it was exhausted by its contribution to the meaning of meaning. And for many philosophers since, even those who have rejected positivism, this is still the sole function of philosophy.

It is clear, then, that, unlike Moore, the positivist was no celebrator of common sense, for too frequently it was fuzzy and opaque. Moreover, its techniques for verification could not meet the rigid requirements of science. For the positivist, only certain kinds of experience could be counted as verificatory; unreconstructed common sense was not likely to be included. Thus, philosophy was to be limited in its scope and common sense in its significance. Science was limited too, and not simply by the need to have its symbols renovated and unified. It was limited because it could have no dealings with values.

Emotive Language

The nub of the positivistic approach to value is found in the "emotive theory." This theory is stated most succinctly and dramatically in A. J. Ayer's *Language, Truth, and Logic*. However, it has been so modified by Ayer himself and by many others, principally the American, C. L. Stevenson, that it is doubtful whether any philosopher today subscribes exactly to the program as outlined in the first edition of *Language, Truth, and Logic*. Nevertheless, the book has had enormous influence and the starkness of Ayer's presentation allows the theory to stand out in all its strength and weakness.

It begins with the now-familiar analysis of cognitive statements into the empirical and the a priori. Ethical propositions are evidently neither one nor the other, and so can represent only a kind of pseudo-proposition, one giving the appearance but not the substance of an allowable statement. For example, "monogamy is the official marriage practice of the Western world" and "monogamy is good" are propositions which resemble each other, but only structurally. The former is an empirical claim capable of verification, the latter proffers no way of being tested: it is a different kind of statement. Is it analytical or a priori? Even if "good" could be defined, which most positivists would not admit, the proposition is totally different from a tautology, or an explication, or one whose contradiction presents an absurdity. What, then, is "monogamy is good"? Mere nonsense? Ayer and the emotivists would not go so far. A sentence like this does have meaning, but not cognitive meaning. "Monogamy is good" or "promiscuity is bad" report simply my approval of the first and my disapproval of the second. Through them I evince my likings and dislikings, my emotions, but I have obviously made no claim which could be judged true or false—except the trivial one that I actually did or did not make such statements. I have not talked about facts or my belief in them but only about my attitudes. Ayer puts it this way:

> The presence of an ethical symbol in a proposition adds nothing to its factual content. . . . If I say to someone "you acted wrongly in stealing that money," I am not stating anything more than if I had simply said "you stole that money." In adding that this action is wrong I am simply evincing my moral disapproval of it. It is as if I had said, "You stole that money," in a peculiar tone of horror, or written it with the addition of some special exclamation marks. The tone, or the exclamation marks, adds nothing to the literal meaning of the sentence. It merely serves to show that the expression of it is attended by certain feelings of the speaker.[12]

Value propositions (for what applies to ethics applies also to aesthetics and the "poetic" parts of metaphysics) belong to a different realm of language from that of the cognitive: it is the "emotive"or "affective" realm (these terms going back to I. A. Richards). This is the language of commitment and interest, but not of prediction or description. If someone tells me to go to the devil, I do not expect to be provided with a map. It is also the language of persuasion. One of the modifications of the emotive theory, that of Stevenson, suggests that far from being "merely" emotive, the function of affective language is to exhort, to persuade others to change their attitudes. To say "*x* is good" is not merely to say "I approve of *x*," but also "Would that you approve of *x* too." Where such persuasion is impossible, we can but scream at each other. No appeal to facts can help.

The English analyst, Mary Warnock, has said that "the extreme simplicity of Ayer's remarks about ethics (which he himself called attention to in the preface to the 1947 edition of the book), as well as their brevity, made them peculiarly suitable as dogma, and this is what emotivism, in one form or another, became."[13] But philosophies have a way of becoming dogmatic. What is more perplexing about the positivist approach to value is this: Just what enterprise, if any, is to concern itself with human values? Who can traverse the frightening no man's land between fact and value?

---

[12] *Language, Truth and Logic,* 2nd ed. (London: Gollancz, 1946), p. 107.
[13] *Ethics Since 1900* (London: Oxford, 1960), p. 85.

Science must deal solely with facts, and philosophy with clarifying the language of science and (possibly) of common sense; classic philosophy, that is, metaphysics, theology, ethics, politics, is innocent of meaning, and common sense of no particular concern. Apparently, then, the ordinary citizen must muddle through with his own untutored emotions. The logical positivist, as philosopher, can furnish him no help in facing his frightening and ever-increasing moral problems. Are the problems so frightening that professional philosophy, in all honesty, has had to abdicate? Have the almost insupportable tensions engendered by the collision between what we know and what we want, between science and the mores, brought about a frankly neuter philosophy? Or, risking a pun, should not the questions be put more "positively"?—Do not our terms, certainly our value-terms, need to be made clear before anything else can be essayed or accomplished? Without such clarification, are we not courting disaster as well as confusion, as when "peace-loving nations" may well have to be translated into "warlike nations"? These last, of course, are rhetorical questions, since the answers are clear. But it is still not clear what is meant by the "clarification" of language. Can it be renovated or must we take it as it is?

Linguistic Analysis

It may not be easy to persuade the beginner in philosophy that for nearly a generation the almost exclusive concern of the leading figures in English philosophy has been to study the subtleties of the English language and to conclude that it is doing very well. A great many American philosophers, somewhat handicapped by the American language, have characteristically followed suit. It might be even more difficult to persuade the beginner that much of mid-twentieth-century philosophy—to quote Professor Abraham Kaplan—"takes no notice of war, revolution, nationalism, nuclear energy, the exploration of space"—not to mention the ethics of racial discrimination, overpopulation, or even juvenile delinquency. But this is starting off on the wrong foot. Perhaps a brief account of the way contemporary linguistic philosophy developed might prove to be helpful if not persuasive.

Professor Urmson has said that English philosophy after World War II was conspicuously different from that before the war, even though these new movements were foreshadowed in the 1930's. In 1931, for example, Gilbert Ryle suggested that "philosophical analysis might be the sole and whole function of philosophy," and that such a function would involve detecting "the sources in linguistic idioms of recurrent misconceptions and absurd theories."[14] The war, then, cannot be held responsible for the new emphases except perhaps, as in France with existentialism, that the disloca-

---

[14] In "Systematically Misleading Statements," printed in *Proceedings of the Aristotelian Society*, 1931–1932; reprinted in *Logic and Language*, 1st Series, Antony Flew, ed. (Oxford: Blackwell, 1955), p. 36.

tions and disillusionments brought about by war provided a climate congenial to drastic innovation of any kind. Even the place of philosophy shifted slightly, from Cambridge to Oxford. It must be made clear, however, that no "school" of philosophy was to emerge at Oxford in the 1940's. But there was a distinct pattern of new interests, into which was woven the influence of the ideas of Ludwig Wittgenstein—or at least what his ideas were believed to be. Wittgenstein was an enigmatic figure whose impact on subsequent thought, at least professional thought, in England and America, had been astonishingly determinative, his name being quoted in certain circles with the reverence given, in other circles, to Marx and Freud. He has been met before, in the discussion of logical atomism, for his *Tractatus* was a source of the picture-theory of language. It was, among other things, his shift from this theory of a unique role for language to the denial, in Wittgenstein's *Investigations* (1953), of any such role that helped to set the new pattern.

But it was a pattern of *analysis* and therefore not entirely new; moreover, it was analysis of *language*, and this, too, was familiar in England all throughout the first half of the twentieth century. What proved, however, to be novel and exciting about this kind of linguistic analysis was its idol-breaking, seemingly more disarming but actually more destructive than the iconoclasm of the logical positivists. For philosophical problems were now to be regarded simply as those which arise when "our language has gone on vacation." Consequently, philosophy itself should be "nothing other than a battle against the bewitchment of our intelligence by language." Quotations like these from Wittgenstein have become so familiar that they no longer need any identification for sophisticated readers; not only are they as well-known as many scriptural passages are to the layman, but they are often treated with the same respect—an outcome Wittgenstein himself would have been the first to decry. Despite this, his provocative and epigrammatic statements are still the aptest way of presenting the challenge of linguistic philosophy.

That challenge is to insist that philosophy is a method, and not something with a special content or subject matter. To be sure, such a challenge could be accommodated to much of the tradition, since philosophy has largely thought of itself as a critic and explainer. But when Wittgenstein goes on to say that philosophy is "not a body of propositions but to make propositions clear," he is breaking with the tradition, for "clear" and "philosophical" have not always been synonymous. Indeed, lack of clarity has more often than not been associated with a putative profundity. Not for the linguistic analysts. "Whatever can be said at all, can be said clearly." But not all things can be said. Perhaps the best-known line of Wittgenstein is that which closes the *Tractatus*: "Whereof one cannot speak, thereof one must be silent." This, coupled with the preceding dictum, would have enforced silence upon an astounding number of the world's thinkers. It also anticipates an unmistakable and characteristic note of mysticism in Wittgenstein.

The general demand for philosophic clarity did not constitute the real impact of his work: it was something more intricate; although almost any general statement about the man and his ideas would be challenged by one or another of his commentators. "What Wittgenstein really meant" has become something of a quite unfrivolous game. This something more intricate has to do with the very form of philosophical problems. They are not due to ignorance. Difficulties due to ignorance can be repaired by knowledge. At least we know the *kind* of answer that would prove satisfactory. If I am puzzled about life in interstellar space, I am aware of what it is that I want to find out, as I am of what would suffice as information. But what of questions where this does not hold, where we are unsure what kind of answer would match the question we pose? If, according to the Wittgensteinian, we raise typically philosophic problems like: "Is time real?" "Does the world have a beginning?" "Does the world conserve values?" "Is everything determined?" "Is beauty of a higher order than goodness?" "Is the world one or many?"—we would not be able to recognize or accept *any* answer, since the very form of the question demonstrates that I don't know my way about. Consider, for example, when we ask whether time is real, the enormous complexity of the word "real." What do all "real" objects and events have in common? "We apply the word 'real,'" says G. J. Warnock, "to many things, to things of all kinds—we speak of a real (as opposed to an illusory) advantage, of a real (as opposed to a false) beard, of a real (as opposed to a toy) pistol, of real (as opposed to hallucinatory) pink rats . . ."[15] There just is no property which all "real" things have in common.

Take even words like "picture" and "language" itself. Here is where the Wittgenstein of the *Investigations* challenges the Wittgenstein of the *Tractatus*. "A picture held us captive," he says, referring to the picture- or copy-theory of language, basic to logical atomism. "We" were held captive because, apparently, we thought that the word "picture" was simple and could be equated with mirror images or phonograph records or other kinds of "copies." We were betwitched by a single meaning of "picture," but there are many meanings.[16] What had to be done was to recover from our "superstitious" errors, to see things a new way. "We must turn the whole examination around," avoiding any preconceived view, even of language

---

15 *English Philosophy Since 1900* (London: Oxford, 1958), p. 82.

16 Nonetheless, the one-to-one interpretation of the relation of "picture" to object is a very significant one, and is the basis for a good bit of what we now know as "information theory." Also, there are some authorities, like Professor Paul Wienpahl, who feel that there is no serious discrepancy between the *Tractatus* and the *Investigations*.

itself. For "language" refers to no single entity, any more than "game" does. Many things can be called "games"—baseball and chess, poker and polo—which have little in common. At most there is only a family resemblance. The same with "language" itself. It is essentially inexhaustible and nothing decisive can be said about the resemblances, say, between mathematics and gestures, both of them "languages." No wonder we have been bewitched, like the author of the *Tractatus* himself.

But newcomers to philosophy will still wonder why all this seems so important. To put it in schematic form, Wittgenstein and the philosophers who followed him seemed to assume that *every* philosophic problem was a linguistic one; at least that such problems *originated* in language even if they were not necessarily *about* language. Remember the dictum that philosophy can be "nothing other than a battle against the bewitchment of our intelligence by language." Now, no one can deny that some philosophic problems, perhaps a great many, arise from linguistic imprecision and its evident fascinations. But the unreconstructed linguistic philosophers went further than this, and might thus be said to illustrate an occupational hazard few philosophers have managed to avoid—to push a good idea too far. In sum, old-fashioned philosophy was somehow a language disease, up-to-date philosophy was to be its cure. In what way?

Here again, as Urmson notes, we meet what have come to be slogans, such as "Don't ask for the meaning, ask for the use." Don't think about language, just look at it. (Had Wittgenstein been an American, his maxim might well have come to be regarded as vulgarly pragmatic.) We need, therefore, to gather examples of words and see how they are actually used. It is becoming evident why the post-Wittgenstein philosophy, at least at Oxford, is called "ordinary language" philosophy. Everyday usage plus a good dictionary (such as the Oxford) will provide most of what we need to know about the English language, including its therapeutic values for philosophy.

Although we are still in the general realm of "analysis"—since the function of philosophers is to inquire minutely into the enormous variety of word usages and sentence structures—it is no longer reductive analysis, as in logical positivism. For example, the "emotive" and "cognitive" categories of language are much too constricting. We cannot set up in advance a few kinds of language, and let it go at that; language is multifariously subtle. For instance, to illustrate from the late J. L. Austin—possibly the most acute of the linguistic philosophers—language does an enormous number of things such as promising, making claims, congratulating, commanding, giving decisions or verdicts, retailing anecdotes, offering hypotheses—to go no further; to think that all of these activities can be grouped under classes like "descriptive" or "prescriptive" is to do serious injustice to what actually happens when language is used.

But how will recognitions like this—that ordinary language is much richer and more trustworthy than hitherto believed—help to cure men of yielding to philosophy as it used to be? How will a painstaking study of the subtleties of everyday speech provide a prophylaxis against future philosophic infection? The answer is relatively simple, although it has proved to be one of Wittgenstein's most controversial utterances: "Philosophy may in no way interfere with the actual use of language; it can in the end only describe it. For it cannot give it any foundation either. It leaves everything as it is."[17] The last sentence, of course, is the crucial one. For if "everything" is to be interpreted literally, then the treatment for (old-style) philosophy would seem to be incuriousness, very much like Moore's incuriousness about the world. The world is what is; the comments about it are alone puzzling. The trouble is that if language is also part of the "everything"—as it certainly seems to be—and if it, too, is to be left as it is, then there really is not much point in investigating it, unless, of course, the only point of (new-style) philosophy is therapy. While Wittgenstein's cryptic remark that philosophy "leaves everything as it is" has been interpreted in many different ways, at least this seems to be clear: if we do see what puzzles or "cramps" language has got us into, then the assumption is that we shall be free of the cramps. The connection with psychoanalysis appears to be a close one.

Ordinary Language

To show how the Wittgensteinian therapy developed, it is necessary to say something about the situation after his death. As Warnock puts it, "new questions" arose which were less "deep" than those troubling Wittgenstein; the "cramps" were less severe. These new questions had to do with the intricacies of word usage, with the enormous range of shades of linguistic meaning, and they were pursued with immense energy and professional skill. Perhaps the best way to illustrate might be to cite some examples from J. L. Austin.

"Voluntarily" and "involuntarily" . . . are not opposed in the obvious sort of way that they are made to be in philosophy or jurisprudence. The "opposite," or rather "opposites," of "voluntarily" might be "under constraint" of some sort, duress or obligation or influence: (footnote: But remember, when I sign a checque in the normal way, I do *not* do so *either* "voluntarily" *or* "under constraint") the opposite of "involuntarily" might be "deliberately" or "on purpose" or the like. Such divergences in opposites indicate that "voluntarily" and "involuntarily," in spite of their apparent connexion, are fish from very different kettles. In general, it will pay us to take nothing for granted or as obvious about negations and opposites. It does not pay to assume that a word must have an opposite, or one opposite, whether it is a "positive" word like

17 *Philosophical Investigations* (New York: The Macmillan Co.), p. 49e.

"wilfully" or a "negative" word like "inadvertently." Rather, we should be asking ourselves such questions as why there is no use for the adverb "advertently."[18]

It is the use of the expressions "I know" and "I promise" (first person singular, present indicative tense) alone that is being considered. "If I knew, I can't have been wrong" or "If she knows she can't be wrong" are not worrying in the way that "If I ('you') know I ('you') can't be wrong" is worrying. Or again, "I promise" is quite different from "he promises": if I say "I promise," I don't say I *say* I promise, I *promise*, just as if he says he promises, he doesn't say he says he promises, he promises: whereas if I say "he promises," I do (only) say he *says* he promises—in the other "sense" of "promise," the "sense" in which *I* say I promise only *he* can say he promises. I *describe* his promising, but I *do* my own promising and he must do his own.[19]

This latter selection must be understood against the background of an issue considered important by many contemporary English philosophers, that of the difference between "performative" sentences (illustrated by "I promise") and nonperformative sentences. The recognition of that difference should help to clarify, it is held, a number of ethical questions. Many other passages could be presented from different sources to give the flavor of these new techniques, passages dealing with the significance of quotation marks ("inverted commas" in English English), with the distinction between "namely" and "i.e.," and with the insight that sentences do not "refer" since only "uses" do—but instead we include one which demonstrates a welcome and not infrequent Austinian mood, that of a relieving humor giving the bare hint that all this may be less grim than it sometimes appears.

You have a donkey, so have I, and they graze in the same field. The day comes when I conceive a dislike for mine. I go to shoot it, draw a bead on it, fire; the brute falls in its tracks. I inspect the victim, and find to my horror that it is *your* donkey. I appear on your doorstep with the remains and say—what? "I say, old sport, I'm awfully sorry, etc., I've shot your donkey *by accident?*" Or "*by mistake*"? Then again, I go to shoot my donkey as before, draw a bead on it, fire—but as I do so, the beasts move, and to my horror yours falls. Again the scene on the doorstep—what do I say? "By mistake"? Or "by accident"?[20]

Perhaps these quotations need more of a context. What, after all, are these philosophers proposing to do, and why? Again, it may be best to let them speak for themselves.

Nothing excessive is here being claimed for our ordinary language. There undoubtedly exist some areas or topics of discussion in which our everyday idioms would be of very little interest indeed . . . But where the topic at issue really is one that does constantly concern most people in some practical way—as for example perception, the ascription of responsibility, or the assessment of

---

[18] J. L. Austin, *Philosophical Papers*, ed. by Urmson and Warnock (Oxford at the Clarendon Press, 1961), pp. 139–140.

[19] *Ibid.*, pp. 66–67, fn.

[20] *Ibid.*, p. 133, fn.

human character and conduct—then it is certain that everyday language is as it is for some extremely good reasons; its verbal variety is certain to provide clues to important distinctions; and it is *almost* certain to be more illuminating, to work much better, than any artificial, technical vocabulary would do. In such areas language is, as it were, a store-house of long-garnered principles and distinctions, enshrined there because they have been found important enough to merit specific linguistic recognition. If so, then on the one hand we override these distinctions at our peril; and on the other, if we wish to learn just what distinctions there are, it is to language that we can most hopefully turn for an answer.[21]

The following is Austin's summary of the significance of the study of ordinary language. It is important, because in addition to underlining his almost complete reliance upon words for the purposes of analysis, it also points out clearly the distinction between words and things. In doing this, Austin is delineating a separate world of things, even if his own philosophic interests are turned elsewhere.

First, words are our tools, and, as a minimum, we should use clean tools; we should know what we mean and what we do not, and we must forearm ourselves against the traps that language set us. Secondly, words are not (except in their own little corner) facts or things: we need therefore to prise them off the world, to hold them apart from and against it, so that we can realize their inadequacies and arbitrariness, and can relook at the world without blinkers. Thirdly, and more hopefully, our common stock of words embodies all the distinctions men have found worth making, in the lifetimes of many generations; these surely are likely to be more numerous, more sound, since they have stood up to the long test of the survival of the fittest, and more subtle, at least in all ordinary and reasonably practical matters, than any that you or I are likely to think up in our arm-chairs of an afternoon—the most favoured alternative method.[22]

Concluding Remarks

The above quotations present some of the reasons why what has come to be known as "Oxford" or "linguistic" philosophy is regarded as extraordinarily pertinent, so much so that it has almost pre-empted recent philosophic discussion in the United States and in Great Britain. Yet it is almost impossible to appraise this "philosophy" because, for one thing, there is no single point of view which would be accepted as definitive by any of the practitioners. As was noticed earlier, there is allegedly no "school," there is only a pattern of similar interests; even so, those interests have a spread so wide as to forestall any blanket judgment. At one extreme, there is simply the contention that *some* philosophic issues have sprung from verbal disorder, added to which is the disarming admission that one enjoys looking into such disorders to the end of achieving verbal precision. So far as this

21 Warnock, *English Philosophy Since 1900*, pp. 150–151.
22 *Philosophical Papers, ibid.*, pp. 129–130.

goes it is an unexceptionable position, although there would be some question as to how far it goes. At the other extreme, it seems to be argued—if any post-Wittgensteinian could be found to argue it today—that there just are no problems which can be called "philosophical"; all we have to do with is the way language is used or abused. Unlike the other extreme, this is exciting, although exciting in the way euthanasia is. It also has the effect of making some people, Bertrand Russell, for instance, extraordinarily angry. In the middle, of course, there are a number of subpositions, perhaps the most characteristic being that found in some of Warnock's statements, in which he acknowledges that certain problems can correctly be called "philosophical" but goes on to insist that such problems can be fully understood only by turning to the way language is used or misused.

Despite this range, there is enough similarity in practice among linguistic philosophers to suggest at least one preliminary observation. Let us recur to the locution, "x is necessary but not sufficient for y." That philosophy must seek to achieve clarity of thought and expression can in no way be challenged; nor have many philosophers overtly challenged it. That philosophy should do nothing else but clarify thought and language is an idea that resided only in English and American university philosophy departments for some fifteen or twenty years after World War II.[23] It is in no way a description of what, in *ordinary language*, has been known as "philosophy," and, as a suggested programmatic reform, it has not yet spread much beyond a small circle of academic philosophers. To be sure, whether linguistic analysis is accepted as a sufficient condition for the practice of philosophy will depend on how one reacts to what philosophy has come to mean historically. The "traditional" philosopher, in addition to seeking for clarity of meaning, sought also for vision, for new ways of seeing the world and man in it; he attempted to synthesize knowledge as well as to analyze it, even though many of his attempts proved to be opaque; and, consciously or unconsciously, he seemed to address himself to the problems of his culture and, as a result of such concern, to recommend to men a set of values.

It is here, then, that the break between the old and the new philosophy

---

[23] The past tense, once more, is not out of place. One by one the leading English philosophers have turned to somewhat different interests; and they have been quite conscious of this. See, for example, their reports in the interesting if popular interviews given to Ved Mehta of the *New Yorker* magazine, later published as *Fly and the Fly-Bottle* (Boston: Little, Brown, 1963). See also some of their more recent statements in *Clarity is not Enough*, ed by H. D. Lewis (New York: Humanities Press, 1963) and also A. J. Ayer's Oxford inaugural address in 1960, "Philosophy and Language," published as the opening chapter in his *The Concept of a Person and Other Essays* (New York: St. Martin's Press, 1963). As evidence of the turning to new interests by language philosophers, two titles may be noted: P. F. Strawson's *Individuals* (London: Methuen, 1959), and S. N. Hampshire's *Thought and Action* (New York: Viking, 1960), both showing signs of a return, in part to traditional philosophic concerns.

(the Anglo-American new) is sharpest, and if indeed there has been a revolution in philosophy it is to be found not so much in the fascinations of analysis and language as in the deliberate and successful attempt to limit the scope of philosophy and to make it "professional." What does this involve? As Gilbert Ryle pointed out, it means, first of all, that (British and American) philosophers now write for other philosophers, not for the educated public. It is not only the style and content of the writing but the places where it appears. Nineteenth-century thinkers like John Stuart Mill, Herbert Spencer, William James, and even Charles Peirce wrote for the most part in the general literary periodicals; in the twentieth century philosophers write for the professional journals which only their colleagues read. "Professional" means much more than this, however. It also implies that philosophers now are engaged with techniques not with beliefs. "It is at any rate certain," Warnock writes, "that questions of 'belief'—questions of a religious, moral, political, or generally 'cosmic' variety—are seldom if at all directly dealt with in contemporary philosophy." Why should the philosopher qua philosopher have any more to do with establishing or influencing belief than the philologist, or mathematician, or botanist? No one asks the mathematician in his capacity as a mathematician about happiness, the United Nations, or racial discrimination. He is engaged in other things. As a man and a citizen he will entertain beliefs, but not as a professional. The case is no different with the professional philosopher. In any case, adds Warnock, the politician, the novelist, the theologian will handle "beliefs."

One wonders if this is meant seriously. Even if it is, the problem is the same as that which confronted logical positivism—just *who* will competently handle questions of values? Who will mediate between the old and the new in our changing world? Who will adjust new scientific insights to ancient wisdom, or disturbing fact to precious myth? Warnock seems to suggest "the other fellow" will do it. But, in all candor, will the contemporary English philosopher be in any way impressed by such a fellow or recommend his ideas to anyone? Will not the language and the ideas of politicians, scientists, theologians, and professed moralists be, at best, unclear and their perspectives unprofessional? The old question remains: *Who* can talk intelligently about beliefs?

For all this, there is much strength in the case for professionalism. No one, concludes Warnock, should fear what has happened to much of present-day philosophy except those who do not welcome a "clear intellectual air and a low temperature of argument." This is cool and clean (even if it inevitably recalls Whitehead's epigrammatic retort that "man cannot live by antiseptics alone"), and the attempt to restrict philosophy to manageable limits and to conduct discussion in an undogmatic manner is novel enough to evoke a surprised and positive reaction. Moreover, the competency and meticulousness resulting from concentration on a single and readily available subject matter has produced a spate of technical papers that have kept philosophers busy and the journals full, items required by any academic profession.

Yet it would be leaning over backward not to mention that the "professional" approach to philosophy has provoked strong negative reactions and from some of the most distinguished of English thinkers. This comment is from C. D. Broad:

> An influential contemporary school . . . would reduce philosophy to the modest task of attempting to cure the occupational diseases of philosophers . . . [I will not speculate] how long an impoverished community, such as contemporary England, will continue to pay the salaries of individuals whose only function, on their showing, is to treat a disease which they catch from each other and impart to their pupils.[24]

And this from Bertrand Russell in his Introduction to Ernest Gellner's *Words and Things*:

> When I was a boy, I had a clock with a pendulum which could be lifted off. I found that the clock went very much faster without the pendulum. If the main purpose of a clock is to go, the clock was the better for losing its pendulum. True, it could no longer tell the time, but that did not matter if one could teach oneself to be indifferent to the passage of time. The linguistic philosophy, which cares only about language, and not about the world, is like the boy who preferred the clock without the pendulum because, although it no longer told the time, it went more easily than before and at a more exhilarating pace.[25]

The most angry and sustained attack against "professionalism" is found in Gellner's book. It is an unusually complete and detailed critique of language philosophy, although it lacks appeal because it is so polemical and therefore overstated and repetitious.

A major criticism of the Oxford philosophic venture rests on the assumption that human thought does not appear in a social vacuum. "Sociology of knowledge," in its broadest sense, would appear especially applicable to contemporary philosophy since a good part of contemporary philosophy has deliberately cut itself off from "the world" and deals with, in Wittgenstein's language, its own particular "game." Even if the rules of this particular game can be determined internally, the choice of the game, the selection and rejection of its problems, and the ways of solving them, as well as the conviction, by some, that a revolution has taken place—all this cannot easily be divorced from the prevailing climate of opinion. To try and understand why contemporary philosophy is dominated at one end by linguistic

---

[24] *Inquiry* (Oslo: Oslo University Press, Summer 1958), p. 102. Reprinted in *Clarity is Not Enough*, H. D. Lewis, ed. (New York: Humanities Press, 1964), p. 45.
[25] (Boston: Beacon Press, 1959), p. 15.

analysis, and at the other by existentialism, without in some way tying up these "revolutionary" or "counterrevolutionary" movements with contemporary social and political dislocations would be to forfeit understanding.

The social argument can, of course, be pushed too far. For example, Gellner feels that linguistic analysis simply provides something for intelligent and educated gentlemen to do in a world collapsing about their ears. Parkinson's Law operates here as elsewhere: (unnecessary) work will be found so as to keep (unnecessary) personnel occupied. Veblen's ideas might also be called upon to disclose present-day English philosophy as an illustration of "conspicuous waste" and systematic triviality; and Marx can be invoked to show that the defense of the English language may be imperialism's last ditch, since nothing else of the British Empire is left to defend.

This all may be taken in good fun. As a matter of fact, the ploy here has been to admit much of the allegation and simply to point out that no particular harm is being done by a small body of admittedly ineffectual professors who happen to enjoy this particular game. Like logicians and mathematicians, philosophers are members of a restricted profession and, in their capacity as members, have no concern with the "larger" issues. Why get angry about it? It is difficult sometimes to sift out the quotations in order to discover whether we are indeed in the realm of gamesmanship. Especially is this true in the last few years when, as John Wisdom puts it, everyone seems now to have changed his mind, and it would not be easy to say at this point just which individual would be a target for the critic's shafts. But one must not exaggerate the differences. It is undeniable that there is, or just has been, a prevailing mood in Anglo-American philosophy, whatever its correct designation. It is also undeniable that in this mood the philosophy concerned has deliberately and systematically turned away from questions of value, and of the nature of the world and man, and from the tensions in which man finds himself. Finally, it would be suggestive to point out that such an abdication by philosophy can not be regarded as an historical accident.

This account of linguistic philosophy appropriately ends with what has become a well-known and even notorious example from Antony Flew, one of the leading linguistic analysts: "The clue to the whole business now seems to lie in mastering what has recently been usefully named, The Argument of the Paradigm Case . . . Since the meaning of 'of his own free will' can be taught by reference to such paradigm cases as that in which a man, under no social pressure, marries the girl he wants to marry (how else *could* it be taught?): it cannot be right, on any grounds whatsoever, to say that no one *ever* acts of his own freewill."[26] This is a frank and not untypical

26 From *Essays in Conceptual Analysis*, ed. by Flew; the passage is from the opening chapter, "Philosophy and Language," written by Flew (London: Macmillan, 1956), p.

disclosure of one way to handle the classic problems. It is very economical: great issues can be disposed of quickly and cheaply. A single smiling bridegroom can overcome the whole deterministic clan. Also, it provides a secure defense not only for common language but for common sense as well. Instead of being revolutionary, such a way of addressing problems might rather be regarded as conformist or even conservative. In addition, this particular way to do philosophy makes philosophy formal rather than substantive, and so ultimately would tend to ally it with logic and mathematics, a goal very much in the forefront of present-day thinking, although not so far in front as to have escaped serious criticism from many mathematicians and philosophers. Finally, it goes without saying that the way of the Paradigm Case needs to have no traffic with values.

Here, then, is a complex of ideas which seems itself to provide a paradigm or model of what philosophy *ought* to be like today. For even analysis has value implications. The model is designed to limit rational discourse by excluding substantive and scientific matters. Yet, like many other contemporary models, it seems to contain a built-in obsolescence. Already it has proved difficult to keep certain interests out-of-bounds. Not many have followed Mr. Flew in thinking that the free-will issue has now been dissolved by one happily married young man; but even those who do are finding themselves confronted with the ideas of Freud, Marx, Spinoza, Kant, all of which the model was constructed to keep off limits.

This present model of philosophy, to conclude, does not necessarily testify against the suggestion that philosophy arises as a result of cultural conflict. What it does testify to is that philosophy may respond by deliberately ignoring, or at least sidestepping, such conflict, and that the attempt may prove to be, for a time, a professionally successful one.

Selected Readings

Austin, J. L., *Philosophical Papers,* London: Oxford, 1961.

Ayer, A. J., ed., *Logical Positivism,* Glencoe, Ill.: Free Press, 1959.

Ayer, A. J., ed., *Language, Truth, and Logic,* London: Gollancz, 1946. (Also Dover paperback.)

Caton, C. E., *Philosophy and Ordinary Language,* Urbana: University of Illinois Press, 1963.(Paperback.)

Lewis, H. D., ed., *Clarity is Not Enough,* New York: Humanities Press, 1964.

Passmore, J., *A Hundred Years of Philosophy,* New York: Macmillan, 1957.

Pitcher, George, *The Philosophy of Wittgenstein,* New York: Prentice-Hall, 1964.

---

19. It should be added that few analysts would now be willing to regard the paradigm approach as central or decisive.

Ryle, G. et al., *The Revolution in Philosophy*, New York: St Martin's, 1956.
Schilpp, P. A., ed. *The Philosophy of G. E. Moore*, Evanston, Ill.: Northwestern University Press, 1942.
Schilpp, P. A., ed., *The Philosophy of Bertrand Russell*, Evanston, Ill.: Northwestern University Press, 1944.
Schilpp, P. A., ed., *The Philosophy of Rudolph Carnap*, LaSalle, Ill.: Open Court, 1963.
Urmson, J. O., *Philosophical Analysis*, Oxford at the Clarendon Press, 1956.
Warnock, Geoffrey, *English Philosophy since 1900*, London: Oxford, 1958.
White, A. R., *G. E. Moore: A Critical Exposition* Oxford: Blackwell, 1958.

CHAPTER 26

The Contemporary Scene: Existentialism

The Setting

Just as analysis has pre-empted academic philosophy in this country, so existentialism has come to signify philosophy for many laymen, and especially for the young. Unfortunately for existentialism, the interest of many of the young people has been in the "beat" variety. The following exposition is "square." The popularity of this philosophy, however, has not precluded a strong academic interest in existentialism; this has been the case for decades on the Continent and there is now a great deal of interest showing from the English and American universities. Unlike analysis, existentialism is clearly a nonprofessional, even an antiprofessional, movement, seeking to recover for philosophy its historical concern with a way of life, however bizarre or irrational that way may be. Furthermore, the indebtedness of existentialism to the contemporary chaos is evident, recognizable, and even celebrated, so that there is little problem in relating at least this particular philosophy to historical and cultural upheaval. In all these ways, not to mention the gulf between the austere and aseptic clarity of analytical argument and the emotional ardency of existentialist metaphor, the two reigning philosophies are light-years apart. Nevertheless, they do have certain common features and these will be noted later.

The complex of ideas now known as existentialism goes back, in most of its major points, to the work of the unorthodox Protestant theologian, Sören Kierkegaard, more than a century ago. Yet it is only since the end of World War II that these ideas have come into their own, and with explosive power. Every writer on the subject—there are now many of them— has easily found the cause of the detonation, each one finding it in his own particular catalogue of horrors. The most familiar, of course, is The Bomb. That the world is about to blow up and that the resulting unbearable tension has prepared the ground for an offbeat, nonconformist, and rebellious irrationalism, often miscalled "existentialism," has become almost a journalistic slogan. Yet slogans may well report what is the case, and certainly only an incorrigible and nearsighted optimist could fail these days to be anxious. It must be remembered, however, that "The Wasteland" goes back to 1922 and Auden's "Age of Anxiety" to 1947; that art has been "irrational" since the time of the post-impressionists and that "decadent" literature was part of nineteenth-century romanticism; that protoexistentialists like Dostoevski, Nietzsche, and Rilke thought that they, too, saw collapse and failure of nerve all about them; and that even William James has now been rehabilitated because, unlike other American thinkers, he reckoned with the despair and loneliness of "the sick soul" in an empty world. Existentialism may well have been detonated by the atomic flash of postwar disillusionment but the powder train stretched a long way back.

A detailed and sympathetic picture of the century-old malaise that is now reaching its fevered climax is found in the second chapter of William Barrett's *Irrational Man*, one of the most dramatic accounts of existentialism.[1] The chapter is entitled "The Encounter with Nothingness." It provides an excellent sketch of the historical and social background of existentialism. The problem, in brief, is this: Man himself has been too long forgotten by a massive world of science, industry, and "rationality" (more on this provocative term presently), a world which ignored "the human situation" and tragically failed to realize man's limitations. America was the paradigm case for such a world: a young, pioneering, buoyant, middle-class, and refreshingly "materialistic" culture for which any *Weltschmerz* was simply Old World despair and defeatism. The American thought of the human being as having no foreseeable limits and he thought of Nothingness— if he ever thought of it—as simply nothing. But, according to the indictment, he was seriously deluding himself.

The "encounter with nothingness" is more than a figure of speech. "Nothingness" serves as a reminder of the ordering and rationalizing of life, in which individual man has simply been lost to sight and his "condition" fused with the general social order. His life, it is alleged, has lost its

[1] (New York: Doubleday, 1958.) See also his more recent *What is Existentialism?* (New York: Grove Press, 1964).

unique and interior preciousness and has been forced outward into the "lonely crowd," where novelties abound and artificial wants fester, where men all eat the same thing, dress alike, and dwell in indistinguishable houses in unidentifiable suburbs. Depersonalization has taken over. At this point, the literate reader will have dozens of familar sources to draw upon.[2] The inventory of bourgeois conformist miseries is a rich one. It is an inventory of the ways in which men are unmade. Yet all this is not really new. It may be argued that the onset of World War I in August, 1914 showed that the "materialistic" and "rationalized" culture of Europe, dominant since about 1870, rested on a void, and that it had for long been slowly dissolving. The signs of that dissolution were supposedly evident in the "irrational" nature of the painting, literature, and music that were already well-installed long before 1914. It is, however, the contemporary period which has so fused all this as to make existentialism "the philosophy of the Atomic Age," which is also the Age of Irrationality.

What is the meaning, then, of "rational" and how is it different from "reasonable"? As has already been suggested, "rational" tends to mean "organized," "ordered," "regulated." The trouble is that these in-themselves respectable conditions have been deflected to the service of a leviathan culture in which the individual man has come to be looked upon as a nonentity, a cipher, a part of a mass-mind manipulated by the advertising impresario and the controller of communications. Our lives are being made *for* us and not *by* us. This is what must be rebelled against. Thus, to be "irrational" is not necessarily to be "unreasonable," just as a war can be waged "rationally," although the whole enterprise be psychotic, not merely "unreasonable." In this particular usage, "rational" is not to be contrasted with "emotional" or "impulsive." The contrast, instead, is between "already organized" and "creative," between "imposition" and "spontaneity," between the "social" and the "individual." For more than a century, "rationalism's" greatest mistake, it is held, has been to deny, perhaps unconsciously, the creative, the spontaneous, and the individual—in other words, to have denied men. This is why the Furies have now been unloosed.

Still another assault on the rational emerges from the discovery that science has itself come up against the unordered, the uncertain, the paradoxical. It is not simply that the sciences of man, like anthropology and depth psychology, have uncovered the deep irrational roots of the human animal, but physics, too, has stubbed its toe. And even mathematics. In

[2] These would include such familiar books as those of David Riesman (along with R. Denny and N. Glazer), *The Lonely Crowd* (New Haven: Yale, 1950); W. H. Whyte, *The Organization Man* (New York: Simon and Schuster, 1956); Colin Wilson, *The Outsider* (Boston: Houghton Mifflin, 1956); Vance Packard, *The Status Seekers* (New York: McKay, 1959); Joseph Wood Krutch, *The Meaure of Man* (Indianapolis: Bobbs-Merrill, 1954); A. C. Spectorsky, *The Exurbanites* (Philadelphia: Lippincott, 1955); and many more.

every area human finitude is disclosed and "the pathos of knowledge" broods over all. Barrett, for example, makes much of the Heisenberg Uncertainty Principle, of Bohr's Principle of Complementarity (the electron can be regarded as both a particle and a wave), and of Gödel's Proof (all mathematical systems contain an unresolvable contradiction); and he uses effectively two important quotations: "I can choose to observe one experimental set-up, A, and ruin B, or choose to observe B and ruin A; I cannot choose not to ruin one of them." (Von Pauli, the eminent German physicist.) And, "We have tried to storm Heaven and have succeeded only in piling up the Tower of Babel." (The distinguished mathematician, Hermann Weyl.) The most rationalized sciences have now encountered Nothingness.

Into such a Nothingness has, of course, fallen the "rational man" of the eighteenth and nineteenth centuries—at least so it has been insisted. This had been the man motivated by self-interest alone, one who weighed the consequences before acting, who looked before he leaped, and who guided his conduct consistently by the attempt to maximize pleasure and minimize pain. He was the "economic man" who always sold in the highest and bought in the lowest market, who satisfied his desires with the least exertion, and whose private interests inevitably led to public gains. The picture of such a man, especially as he operated in the business world, has been one of the cherished portraits in the gallery of our folklore.

Suspicion of such a regularized self-seeker did not wait until the age of irrational man. Have we not already seen that the first part of the nineteenth century (in one of our constant attempts to oversimplify history) was called the "Age of Romanticism"—a turning away, as in Faust, from gray wisdom to the greenness of life? From the romantic protestations of English, French, and German poets early in the nineteenth century to the latest pronouncements of a beat generation, there has been a consistent strand of antirationalistic revulsion, revulsion against the greengrocer ethic (as Nietzsche put it) of the calculating man figuring out his own interests, and an equal revulsion against the increasing sweep of science. Some of this may be regarded as no more than a kind of dialectical swing from one extreme of the pendulum to the other. But much of it can be attributed to the devastating examinations by Marx and Freud of the alleged "rationality" of our actions—one regarding it as a function of class interest, the other as a false front erected to justify the thrust of deep compelling drives; and much of the criticism of "rational man" is also the result of the increasing sophistication of the behavioral sciences.

Indeed, that man is irrational has itself become an established item of present conventional wisdom. As early as 1939 the American writer, Max Lerner, could declare that "the discovery of the irrational marks the genius of our age . . . The intellectual revolution of the twentieth century is likely to prove the charting of the *terra incognita* of the irrational and the extraction of its implications for every area of human thought." This is, he tells us, "nothing short of a Copernican revolution in ideas," since "the rational right-thinking man has as surely ceased to be the center of our intellectual system as the earth has ceased to be the center of our planetary system."[3]

So much then for the background, for this picture of a world we never made, against which there are now rebels with a cause. Many writers have been saying more or less the same thing. Whether what these apologists have been saying is itself "reasonable" is something to be examined further on. But without this lurid background, existentialism loses much of its illumination. After all, the incandescence of existentialism is Atomic.

The Meaning of "Existence"

At the outset, it must be noted that there can be no attempt to present *the* philosophy of existentialism. There is, in fact, no single body of doctrine to be so labeled, although there is certainly a set of preoccupations that make some people existentialists and others not. Yet a "school" of existentialism would tend to forfeit a characteristic connotation of the philosophy, that of incorrigible individualism. The philosophy is fundamentally one of revolt and the very opposite of anything like "togetherness." Actually, with the possible exception of Jean-Paul Sartre, nearly every reputed "existentialist" has renounced the label. Nonetheless there is a recognizable attitude, as well as a consensus applying to the names of those who, since Kierkegaard—if not before—may be regarded as in the existentialist spirit. The approach to existence, as might be expected, is a cardinal element in such a spirit, and it is found in both atheistic and religious existentialism. The present discussion is based largely on the ideas of Sartre and, with some reservations, of Heidegger, and not on the religious expression of the philosophy, such as Kierkegaard's. However, it is almost impossible to keep the two aspects clearly separated.

There is a familiar short sentence which has become almost a slogan—"Existence precedes Essence." The flat statement is Sartre's, although the idea is general, and even if there is a simplistic tinge to the pronouncement, it nevertheless is vital for understanding at least the use of the term "existentialism."

In this context the "essence" of anything is its definition, or the law or principle which sets it off from anything else, its Platonic "form," the universal of which it is a transient shadow, or, in at least one of its several uses, an Aristotelian "substance" (see pp. 138–140). To illustrate: The essence of a circle is its definition—a locus of points all equidistant from a single point. As noted earlier, in the Platonic view such a definition or

---

[3] Quoted by Arthur O. Lovejoy in *Reflections on Human Nature* (Baltimore: The John Hopkins Press, 1961), p. 22.

concept applies only to The Circle, a universal form not existing in ordinary space and time, and it is to *this* circle alone that the "laws" of the circle refer, such as $A = \pi r^2$. Such laws can refer only imperfectly and approximately to actually existing circles of wood or glass or chalk marks and pencil lines, for these empirical circles can never completely fulfill the requirements of the concept. No such precise locus could ever be realized in the physical world. Consider that even Euclid's definition of point gives it no extension—it does not occupy space—so how could we ever experience existentially a collection of extensionless points? And lines are made of points—or, which amounts to the same thing, lines have but one dimension. Even if we put aside the Platonic realm (which has never failed to fascinate the mathematician), and talk a purely conventional or notational language, making circles *merely* definitions with no metaphysical grounding, we have the same result. For an arbitrary definition (essence) is still different from the application of that definition (existence), the pure is separable from the applied. In arithmetic, for example, we do not add *objects*, we add *numbers*, which is why one plus one *must* equal two. The definition of integers and of their operating rules makes such a result necessary and certain, despite the fact it does not help with two drops of water or of mercury, or with a lion and a lamb, or even with two rabbits. This is why Bertrand Russell can, in his pixie way, describe mathematics as the science in which "we do not know what we're talking about or whether what we say is true," and Descartes can be sure about triangularity, but not about the existence of any individual triangle.

Although mathematics and the theoretical formulations of science provide the most apt examples of "essence," traditional philosophy sought to apply the idea everywhere. All existing things were dependent upon antecedent and determining concepts. "Man," for instance, was defined in many ways, the most familiar being the Aristotelian dictum that he was a rational or thinking animal. Rationality was a built-in capacity or goal which, if not realized, meant that man was not complete, not a real man. "Essence" and "existence," then, were separate, although they could intersect. For rationalists like Spinoza, no essence could guarantee existence except all-encompassing Substance or Nature or God. Moreover, logically if not chronologically, essence preceded existence: to be an existent implied that an essence had already exercised its constitutive powers. This idea was developed more consistently and exaggeratedly in the philosophy of Hegel, against which Kierkegaard proved to be only one of many protesters.

This dependence of existence upon essence is totally reversed by existentialism. To put it simply: We can define anything—satyrs, mermaids, golden mountains—anything except flat contradictions, like a square circle. But it does not follow from the definition of anything that it exists. Existence may indeed be dependent on essence in the sense that *we* usually have to have an idea of something before we can make it. And if all existing things are thought of as having been created analogously to the way in which we create things, then it might appear that their creator must have had antecedent "ideas" of them. But, at least for atheistic existentialism, there is no such creator or definer. Things—man, above all—must stand on their own and define, even create, themselves.

Unlike the rationalistic thinkers who took great pains to describe essence but seemed to take existence for granted, the existentialist has an almost pathological concern with trying to tell of existence. First, this interest in existence is a caveat against any form of logical reductionism. For existence cannot be explained away or discounted in the facile manner employed perennially by rationalists—or "essence-ialists." Take the "frontier situations" of danger, death, or nothingness in which men must choose and in choosing establish their existence. This situation—that is, the human condition—is one for which Pascal seems to have provided the classic description. "When I consider the short duration of my life, swallowed up in the eternity before and after, the little space which I fill, and even can see, engulfed in the infinite immensity of spaces of which I am ignorant, and which know me not, I am frightened, and am astonished at being here rather than there; for there is no reason why here rather than there, why now rather than then."[4] Sartre recalls Pascal in his recognition of a world where everything is given but nothing ever explained. But this is existence. Existence is not something far-off and logically disinfected. Existence is where it is found, in the "little homely things," as Kierkegaard put it. The one thing I can be sure of is my immediate experience, my "phenomenological" deliverances. I can always be sure that I am experiencing, but cannot be sure *what* I am experiencing. Brute experience is existence, explanation essence. For it is always *this* world that must be reckoned with not another one of laws and universals and remote essences. And this world is inescapably one of individual experience.

The Quality of Existence

Now the problem is, what is the character of these individual experiences? Theoretically and empirically, they could be—and undoubtedly are for many persons—serene, quiet, untroubled, if not always interesting. But the existentialist discovers in *his* experiences a whole new world of anxiety and forlornness, of loneliness, separateness, and homelessness. He proceeds to insist that this is the experience of all of us, unless we have fallen under the narcosis of the busy, ordered, and rational life so distinctive of mass-men. Immediate experience, untampered with by the social order, sounds inevitably the overtones of dereliction and melancholy. This is not

---

[4] *Pensées*, 205 (New York: Modern Library edition, 1941), p. 74.

simply a psychological aberration. The encounter with nothingness, with human finitude as exemplified by sickness, bad luck, sin, and death, is a metaphysical confrontation, a clue to the "essential" meaninglessness of the universe. Man's anguish, so it is averred, is cosmic, not neurotic. Indeed, it is the rest of men outside the existentialist fraternity who are neurotic, since the lives they lead are no more than desperate devices used to cover up the unacknowledged but ineradicable glimpses of emptiness which leave them shivering. They become teachers, fathers and mothers, lawyers, presidents, scientists, they lead the "serious life" replete with its bourgeois virtues, all to no effect. The absurdity of their condition induces a nausea that cannot be overcome, whereas the truly existing man honestly and openly accepts the alienation, the absurdity. Like Sartre, he understands that to exist is simply to be here, to turn up; that there is no reason for it, it cannot be deduced or inferred from anything else; existence is an absolute datum, an irreducible surd. Perhaps a few quotations from the literary expressions of the pangs of genuine existence may help to make all this more real and moving.

Existence, liberated, detached, floods over me. I exist . . . I jump up; it would be much better if I could only stop thinking. Thoughts are the dullest things. Duller than flesh . . . They leave a funny taste in the mouth . . . I exist. How serpentine is this feeling of existence—I unwind it slowly . . . If I exist, it is because I am horrified at existing. *I am the one* who pulls myself from the nothingness to which I aspire; the hatred, the disgust of existing . . .

People. You must love people. Men are admirable. I want to vomit—and suddenly there it is: the Nausea . . . Now I know: I exist—the world exists—and I know that the world exists. That's all. It makes no difference to me. It's strange that everything makes so little difference to me: it frightens me . . . I am in the midst of things, nameless things. Alone, without words, defenseless, they surround me, are beneath me, behind me, above me. They demand nothing, they don't impose themselves; they are there . . . I would so like to let myself go, forget myself, sleep. But I can't. I'm suffocating: existence penetrates me everywhere, through the eyes, the nose, the mouth . . . And suddenly the veil is torn away, I have understood. I have *seen*.[5]

O, Caesonia, I knew that men felt anguish, but I didn't know what the word, anguish, meant. Like everyone else I fancied it was a sickness of the mind—no more. But no, it's my body that's in pain. Pain everywhere, in my chest, in my legs and arms. Even my skin is raw, my head is buzzing, I feel like vomiting. But worst of all is this queer taste in my mouth. Not blood, or death, or fever, but a mixture of all three. I've only to stir my tongue, and the world goes black, and everyone looks . . . horrible. How hard, how cruel, it is, this process of becoming a man![6]

It must be remembered that despite these agonizings over existence, it is a positive and creative state that man rescues from the night of nothing-

---

[5] From some of Antoine's many soliloquies in Sartre's *Nausea,* Alexander tr. (Norfolk, Conn.: New Directions, 1959.)

[6] Albert Camus, *Caligula,* Gilbert tr. (London: Hamish Hamilton, 1947.)

ness and that can slip back into nothingness once the tension is relaxed. At least this is the case with *authentic* existence, existence-for-itself, which man alone can enjoy. Special terms are used to symbolize this authentic condition, such as *Dasein* (Heidegger) and *"être-pour-soi* as opposed to mere *être-en-soi* (Sartre). If "enjoy" seems ambiguous, it needs to be kept in mind that the whole philosophy is deliberately and systematically ambiguous, for such actually is the nature of things. When men are not anguished and forlorn, when the sense of straining rebellion and of fevered self-concern abates, when, in short, the "serious soul," the bourgeois mind, takes over—then inauthentic existence, existence simply in-itself—that of stones and animals—reclaims its own, and man loses his precious moment of creative triumph. Thus, the nausea and the pride in it, the loneliness and the cherishing of it, the woes of being an outsider and the utter rejection of joining—all must be kept suspended togther in an almost unbearable tension. This is why it is so hard to become a man.

What to do about all this? Where is the recipe for a life? First of all, one must clearly recognize genuine existence for the ambivalent thing it is. One must realize he is an alien in the world, a stranger. *The Stranger* is the title of one of Camus' most memorable novels; and the hero of a Kafka novel, such as "K" in *The Trial* or in *The Castle*, is an almost model existentialist, at least in the symptomatic stage, as is the unfortunate man-turned-into-bug of the gruesome absurdity, *Metamorphosis*. One must come to grips with his own isolation, he must remain free of illusion, he must not kid himself, for "there ain't any Santa Claus." Even the religious existentialist insists upon this. Such pride in not being fooled is close to that of Bertrand Russell's "free man,"[7] who girds up his loins in an action of heroic despair and proceeds then to thumb his nose at the alien "accidental collocation of atoms" which makes up the universe. This, then, is the first step of redemption: not to compromise with absurdity.

A second follows easily: Be self-consciously absurd, go along with the game. This perhaps is said too quickly for, as noted before, it is impossible to generalize about existentialists and the best solution is to present a kind of composite picture. For instance, a most moving expression of self-conscious absurdity is found in Camus' *The Stranger*, especially the closing sections, also in his "Myth of Sisyphus" and in many of the novels and plays of Sartre. But Camus proceeded to reject existentialism, and his later novels like *The Plague* and *The Fall* turn in quite a different direction, while Sartre also has turned more "serious" and more political. Yet Sisyphus, as Camus portrays him, stands as a kind of tragic hero. The stone he rolls up the hill will never get there, it is fated to roll back. Now, were Sisyphus a vulgar serious fellow, he would continue to spit on his hands

---

[7] Cf. his "A Free Man's Worship," found most conveniently in *Mysticism and Logic*, (London: Geo. Allen & Unwin, 1917; also an Anchor paperback.)

and say "Next time, damn it!" This would betray that one does not understand what it's all about, would be a relapse into brute, uncomprehending naturalism. But the existentialist Sisyphus will laugh uproariously, not so much when he pushes the stone up as when he sees it go rolling back. "There it goes again!" he howls in glee. He contemplates his own torments and makes them a joke. Thus only can he be free of the stone.

Given this special situation of Greek frustration, the disarming reaction of Sisyphus may seem laudable and appealing. There are not many ways to laugh at a stone, but there are many ways to be self-consciously absurd. Assuming that the myth does reveal an eternal verity about the world, the refusal to take the world seriously can take a number of forms, some of them quite desperate and bizarre. For example, at one period of his thinking, Camus considered that "the only significant philosophical problem" was that of suicide, not why men killed themselves but why they did not. This reminds us again that there is a wide range of views to be found under the general label of "existentialism," even if the extreme at either end would undoubtedly be denied its rightful use. Yet even what looks like a "middle" position on absurdity will seem to many as no more than a familiar romantic attempt "to shock the middle class" (*épater la bourgeoisie*).

In the existentialist novels and plays, for instance, the way to reject the serious life seems to be largely a matter of "fooling around" through sex, violence, and general mischief. The description of the ordinary life of the citizen is nothing short of scatological, and although many of the "heroes" are dedicated revolutionaries or counterrevolutionaries, or at least solitary outsiders, others represent with insight and sympathy the young rebel without a cause so familiar now in the international cinema. With the latter, it is always difficult to know where to draw the line, where, that is, the beatnik or the delinquent takes over, or where the sophisticated "gratuitous act" of an André Gide turns into the sadistic and deliberate terror of the city streets. In the same way, it is not always easy to distinguish the existential memorializing of the absurd from the art of the absurd or, rather, the so-called "anti-art" of recent years.

No attempt is being made here to hold a respectable and formidable philosophy liable for what one does not like about contemporary youth or contemporary art. (After all, there are those who debit "progressive" education with juvenile delinquency.) Nor are these remarks a sign of obtuseness about the desperate conditions which young and old alike must face and react to one way or the other every day. The point, to repeat, is to try to understand how wide is the range of the antirational protest which can be attributed to the philosophy of existentialism. It is evident that this philosophy is in the long tradition of the romantic revolt against reason, and that such a tradition is now an honored section of the history of ideas.

Recall that at one time even the young heroes of Goethe's writings were looked upon as sentimental posturers. But the question still persists: What is the degree of absurdity required to reject the "serious spirit" and to overcome the false suasion of reason? Kierkegaard's flaming statement that "the conclusions of passion are the only reliable ones" and many others like it make an excellent conversation piece, but if they are more than gestures, then, with Bertrand Russell, one must wonder what further enormities face us once man—should it be possible—"becomes entirely unloosed from reason," or even from the "rational."

Less dramatically, one must also note that the preoccupation with failure, dread, death, and disaster, the rejection of the serene and the cheerful and even of a sense of humor, the elevation of subjective experience over all—these, for a long time, have been the marks of the romantic "hero." This makes them neither right nor wrong, but it may introduce a sense of proportion. Preoccupation with the self, like the moral holiday, is a perennial response of the human animal when things get tough. It is unquestionably a healthy and even a therapeutic response. That it also lays down the determining elements of "the human condition" and traces the very anatomy of existence is an altogether different matter.

Existentialism and Freedom

Contrary to Descartes, the existentialist says, "I am—not because I think—but because I choose." This should be clear from the very nature and quality of existence, since I lose my very being when I do not exercise choice or when I do not exercise it authentically. A mechanical or habitual choice is no choice at all. We have seen that existentialism is focused on man; it is—in a favorable sense—anthropocentric; it imputes whatever value and meaning there may be in the world to man's indomitable ability to assert himself, to define himself, "to turn up" and demand being taken into account. That existence precedes essence testifies to this electric push, for man has no prior essential being, but only the specific existence he hammers out for himself. Man alone can and does bring some measure or order out of chaos and makes a world out of nothing. But how? By asserting his freedom, his power to choose.

Adam was, of course, innocent before he had to choose, Kierkegaard reminds us, but his innocence was metaphysical as much as moral. He really did not exist as a genuine being until the great decision was forced upon him. He had been no more than a cipher. But the freedom which came with the power and necessity to choose provided Adam with "the very being of existence" (to use Jaspers' terminology). It also provided him with anxiety. This is a key existentialist concept, and the seeming paradox which joins the agony of choice with the certification of existence is deliberate and not inadvertent. The perversity of the situation was already apparent in God's prohibition, for Adam was instilled with the inevitable desire to use his freedom even if disastrously. Again, in Kierkegaard's words, "choose —if only to choose despair." Unless we choose we would be as infinite as God Himself or as nonentic as an oyster. As it is, "There is an Either/Or which makes man greater than the angels," for man's limitation, his finitude, is disclosed to him—more accurately, created by him—in his ability to choose. Perhaps Kierkegaard's most important book is *Either/Or*, the title of which captures the fight for freedom, for the future. But it must be insisted that both the freedom and the agony are much more than psychological; for the existentialist these are unimpeachable clues to the nature of things. Freedom is a creative and constituting force which literally brings into existence one whole area of being, that of man; so that freedom is no mere attachment, no adjective for "will"—man *is* freedom, freedom *is* man.

It is a "dreadful freedom." The dread and the "nausea" are not the neurotic's compulsive fear of some specific event or thing, but rather a pervasive and completely general anxiety, hovering over the abyss of "nothingness." For if our very existence is "determined" by our free act, it can also "go out" because of our "bad faith," our shirking from choice. We can annihilate (*néantir*) or "nothing" (*nichten*) existence by acting unfreely, like a machine, or living like a vegetable. The responsibility is indeed overpowering. Like an Atlas, the free man holds the very world on his shoulders and well may he tremble!

There is still another source of anxiety. It is, as Kierkegaard puts it, "the next day." Man lives projectively, into the future; he anticipates, makes plans, attempts to foresee. But the future, like "being" itself, simply does not yet exist: it is nothing. So that man, above all a creature of time, is necessarily living in nothingness, in the what-yet-has-not-come-to-be. Even the past is no secure foundation, since in each act of free decision, man negates his past; and the present moment is surely a "specious" one, since it is "the way the future becomes the past." Thus, the precariousness of man's existence, resting as it does on a choice that anticipates a nonexisting and highly contingent future.

One is tempted to ask: What about those persons who do not feel nauseated, who have no general anxiety, who do not dread the next day since they are quite content with this one, thank you, who are in nowise disgusted by what Sartre calls the "sticky" or "slimy" or "viscous" feel of emptiness, and who choose or fail to choose without tears? Is the phenomenology of their experience of any worth? The existentialist undoubtedly would answer: These disgustingly healthy individuals are simply deceiving themselves. They live systematically in bad faith and cover their inescapable dread with the plaster of so-called "serious affairs." They are

pedestrian souls and do not truly "exist." In other words, for the existentialist negative evidence is as good as positive.

The awful responsibility of freedom should by now be apparent. No
wonder that men have striven to "escape from freedom," as well as to save
it. Yet, paradoxically, man cannot really escape. As Sartre puts it, he is
fated, condemned, to be free. There is no contradiction here, according to
Sartre, because since man makes himself—at least whatever is characteristically human about himself—the very conditions of selfhood are also made
as an act of free choice. "Determinism" in a bad sense would be possible
only if man were created by some other maker (God, say), but not when
he deliberately creates himself. Having brought himself into existence, man
is irretrievably bound to the nature of that existence.

If this is not entirely persuasive, it must be remembered that "paradox"
is not a negative term for existentialism, and that if "Man is condemned
to be free" seems ambiguous, it is no more so than the whole human situation itself. We must choose, choice produces anxiety, yet the nausea of
anxiety is not to be prevented by something like Dramamine. This would
be "inauthentic" therapy. The burning sense of paradox dramatizes the true
dilemma of our lives, the dilemma of choice. When an officer orders men
into battle, he is condemning some men to die; but had he chosen otherwise, or had he not exercised any decision at all, he would have condemned
other men to die. "You can't win" is the gloomy conclusion—if by "winning" one naïvely means secure, unambiguous, and unanxious deliverance
from choice.

"We were never more free," says Sartre, "than during the German occupation." But the paradox here is surely an intelligible and approved one.
"For every one of our gestures had the weight of a solemn commitment."
We are most alive when we are in a "frontier" situation, say, at the point
of meeting violent death, as a matador in front of a bull, or a fighter in the
resistance movement at any hour, not simply at "five in the afternoon."
Being in these "limit-situations" is, once more, a free decision, but even
for the more sedentary of us, we have chosen our true existence and with it
the necessary concomitant of ultimate nonexistence, of nothingness. Freedom, then, means that a man can say "No!" which is his final dignity. To
be sure, he can say "Yes," too, but freedom seems here in existentialism
to carry a sense of denial. Freedom is thus the origin of all value, as it is
of existence. The moral imperative is to choose. And should this prove to
be, as William Barrett phrases it, a "demoniacal freedom," this is only
testimony to the alien position of man launched by his own creative futility
into an obdurate glass-cold emptiness. The Age of Anxiety or of Paradox is
not merely a fashionable posture to be described by poets and social psychologists; it is a faithful reflection of the way things really are.

The paradox stretches into the field of politics. Most readers will know,
if only from the newspapers, that Jean-Paul Sartre is an "authentic" revolu-

tionary and far over to the left. In his practical political activity he has generally, although not always, followed the prevailing line of the Communist Party. However, he has rejected the Marxist ideology and so has proven to be a strange, yet very effective, adversary of the Communist theoreticians. The reason is clear—this matter of freedom. For according to the Communist ideology, man is allegedly trapped by economic and historical forces beyond his control. More than that, by cosmic forces, since the dialectical process of thesis-antithesis-synthesis is not limited to this planet: the way the universe itself rolls on is through-and-through an illustration of the dialectical pattern. The history of the world is the law of the world and the "rightness" of it, too. Change comes by way of impersonal giant forces, and the individual man is but an agent and carrier of such forces—although one might ask, to be sure, whether the *man* Lenin had anything to do with the course and development of the Russian Revolution.

Sartre has been unimpressed by this part of the Marxist argument. Man's revolutionary activity, just as any other, is based not on some objective historical movement but on his free, truly free, choice. Sartre has also been unimpressed by the Utopian dream of the inevitable classless society, the last synthesis where economic and political conflict will have ended.[8] As already noted, man is alone, cosmically alone; he is an alien and his existence is fundamentally absurd since there is no *reason* for his being here at all. This forlornness cannot be assuaged by making him a part, however noble, of some grand impersonal process, historical or otherwise. Sartre is a total atheist and will have man created by no "god," not even one who moves dialectically. Man is free, solitary, and inescapably an outsider, and would remain so in any society.

In concluding a discussion of existentialism and freedom, it might be suggested that existentialism—at least this phase of it—is an effort to make sense out of freedom against a background of thinking, much or most of it scientifically oriented, which seems not to provide a place for freedom. The existentialist seems to be saying, "Let's put aside argument and the parade of logic. I *feel* free and I affirm its importance and that is sufficient." He seems, in a sophisticated, sometimes obscure, and often poetic, way to be reaffirming the intuitions of common sense.

Existentialism and Humanism

Sartre's most popular book is the report of a lecture, which carries the French title, *L'existentialisme est un humanisme*. In England it appears as *Existentialism and Humanism*, but in this country simply as *Existentialism*.

---

[8] However, Sartre has recently been endeavoring to bring existentialism and Marxism together. See W. Desan's *The Marxism of Jean-Paul Sartre* (New York: Doubleday, 1965), and *Marxism and Existentialism* by W. Odajnyk (New York: Doubleday, 1965), both of which are expositions and interpretations of Sartre's still untranslated 1961 book, *Critique de la raison dialectique*.

Putting aside for the moment the general meaning of "humanism," the specific claims made by Sartre as a humanist are as follows: Man cannot be defined by an anterior essence but only by his own free actions. He makes himself as he exercises choice, as he repudiates tradition and the customary. No God is responsible for him, and no metaphysical force. He alone is to be credited or debited for the quality of his existence—and this is the core of "humanism." More than that: as he chooses freedom, he is also helping to achieve the freedom of others. Freedom, the top value for existentialism, would be self-stultifying and even without meaning were it only partial. It has to be universalized, as with Kant, and so in opting to be free I am at the same time helping to secure your freedom. There is a moral solidarity, as there should be a political, and this constitutes still another "humanistic" element of this philosophy.

That existentialism is admittedly an ambiguous philosophy has already been noted. Therefore it may be pointless to suggest that this laudable social ideal of mutual freedom seems to be, if not actually a political improvisation, at least seriously at odds with the basic theory of human relationship worked out chiefly in Sartre's *Being and Nothingness* and dramatically illustrated in his novels and plays. The relationships between men are those of conflict, not Marxian conflict, but a possibly more deadly one, fought out on a personal man-to-man—more frequently, a man-to-woman—level. Take the matter of freedom. A "social" interpretation of existentialist freedom has just been given, but such freedom is a most ambivalent idea. For it appears that the human condition is, among other things, a battleground of opposed freedoms, since my neighbor's freedom may well mean my doom. In this connection the perfervid subjectivism and individuality of the existentialist must be recalled. I am indeed a subject to myself but an object to others. And as an object I can be literally "nothinged." Consider these expressions:

They see me—no, not even that: *it* sees me. He was *the object* of looking. A look that . . . was not his own look; an impenetrable look . . . condemning him to be himself . . . Himself, quivering beneath that look and defying it. That look! I am *seen* . . . But by whom? "I am not alone," said Daniel aloud.[9]

What I apprehend immediately when I hear the branches crackling behind me is not that there is someone there; it is that I am vulnerable, that I have a body which can be hurt, that I occupy a place, and that I cannot in any case escape from the space in which I am without defense—in short that I am seen.[10]

These are not simply expressions of a morbid sensitivity, any more than

---

[9] Jean-Paul Sartre, *The Reprieve*, Sutton tr. (New York: Knopf, 1947).
[10] Jean-Paul Sartre, *Being and Nothingness*, Barnes tr. (New York: Philosophical Library, 1956), p. 259.

is the distaste for stickiness, mentioned earlier. The violation of privacy has ontological implications—not merely psychological ones—and, as might be expected, these implications are two-edged. In one sense, I must never be an object for another, since such "objectification" tends to unmake me, to reduce me to passivity; it implies that, like any inanimate "thing," I can be regarded by another with impunity. When so regarded, my position is subtly changed from one of project to one of posture, as if I were caught in the act of eavesdropping. Yet in another sense, I need the look of the other to provide limits for my existence. I should not know shame or guilt or even pride were it not for the existence of the other who sees me as an object. And this is Hell—"Hell is the other fellow," which is the theme of Sartre's well-known play *Huis Clos (No Exit)*.[11] In sex this whole ambiguity becomes exasperatingly smug, smug to the point of cruelty, for love can mean only "the wish to be loved." I need love to "exist" me, but I do not need to give love. And sex is as important as it is for literary existentialism because it is an incarnation of the one who is loved. Consider the two snakes, each having the other's tail in its mouth, that proceed mutually to swallow one another. The battle of the sexes is more deadly than James Thurber ever imagined.

Were it not for the paradoxical character of existentialism, one would be tempted to reject out of hand the notion that this kind of tension and stress in the relations among men could be considered "humanistic." Sartre's observations of men are extraordinarily shrewd and penetrating, and they may well be correct, but they have an acid quality which is almost dehumanizing, if one can also indulge in ambiguity. In any case, "humanism" seems too "sentimental" to be appropriate for what he describes. Yet, at times, Sartre does come upon the social and cooperative character of men—certainly an aspect any genuine "humanism" must emphasize—as when he speaks of the unity of Frenchmen under a situation such as the German occupation. Just as men were freest then, so were they most brotherly. But (unfortunately?) such frontier situations end, and men relapse into conflict again, a conflict that makes and unmakes them, inevitable as it is dreadful. "How hard it is, this process of becoming a man!"

Concluding Remarks

We have discussed some of the relatively familiar themes of existentialism, but have left untouched a number of its central doctrines. These would include the confrontation of Being and Nothingness, the special ways of knowing demanded by such metaphysical categories, and, what has become of great interest in recent years, the existentialist approach to a

---

[11] Sartre's major discussion of this matter is found in the section on "The Look" in Part 3 of his *Being and Nothingness*, espec. p. 252ff.

non-Freudian psychoanalysis. Perhaps the interested student may wish to explore for himself some of these more technical matters. But before we leave existentialism, a few words on the relations between the two reigning philosophies of the present may be suggested.

The contrasts between existentialism and logical analysis are clear. Putting it oversimply, one philosophy is concerned rigorously with what some would hold to be trivial and even frivolous affairs, whereas the other deals unclearly and equivocally with the most important matters. One prizes the logical cleanliness of the academy, the other forces philosophy into the streets where it well may become muddy. A great fissure seems to open between these two philosophic approaches. Yet in some ways the gulf is not so wide as it seems; there may be some improvised bridges crossing it.

For one thing, both analysis and existentialism seem to lie intentionally outside the area covered by science. It is, of course, true that the positivistic phase of analysis made philosophy almost the handmaiden of science. Its function was to clarify the language of science. The linguistic philosophers have been more concerned with ordinary language than with scientific. Yet by both of these it is assumed that philosophy can profit very little from what science has to offer, and any attempt to blur the boundaries between them is most ill-advised. The existentialist would tend to go along with them. As the German philosopher, Karl Jaspers, puts it, "The scientist builds a castle and lives next door in a shanty." Science can provide no help with the lives men lead, nor with the important questions men raise. (An exception might be made in the case of existential psychiatry.) Nor can it provide any help with other strange and puzzling questions, the kind raised by Wittgenstein as well as by Kierkegaard. True, Wittgenstein hoped that such questions might disappear when probed, while Kierkegaard felt that plunging into them would reveal new insights into human existence; but it was the unusual and unscientific nature of the questions which set the philosophic tone for both.

Another area of agreement between these two generally opposed philosophies is their tendency to underplay the social factor in the development of the person. Each one is "individualistic" in its own fashion, the one relying upon the solitary feelings of the truly-existing subject, the other upon the acuity of the trained analyst. Neither is concerned with the social origins of language or of the self; indeed, such an interest is regarded as fallacious or, at best, irrelevant. The genesis of x may be of interest to the scientist but not to the philosopher, since the latter, it is maintained, is concerned not with history but with the analysis of immediate experience, be it "phenomenological" or linguistic.

In the matter of value, both philosophies would be inclined to reject the possibility of knowledge of good and evil. Unlike Adam, they will not risk being driven from the Garden. Existentialism holds value to be entirely subjective and thus impervious to intellectual or scientific inquiry, but this imperviousness is something to be cherished and nurtured. Philosophy must indeed deal with values, but in the peculiar ways recommended by a romantic preoccupation with self. The analytical tradition has varied on this issue. The logical positivist, such as the early A. J. Ayer, found values to be "subjective" and therefore not amenable to logical or true-false treatment; they were mere emotional ejaculations. The linguistic analysts have not been subjectivistic in this same sense, since their concern has been with the objective meaning of value terms; nevertheless that concern has not gone beyond a certain way of using language. Anyone interested in ethics and human problems, Professor John Wisdom has announced, should steer clear of present-day English philosophy.

This whole discussion of the contemporary scene has deliberately concentrated on two influential and contrasting—although related—philosophic movements. Naturally, there has been no attempt to present a complete inventory of current thought, which, as might be expected, extends in many directions beyond the limits of existentialism and linguistic analysis. Mathematical logic, philosophy of science, history of ideas, new insights into metaphysics and epistemology, interest in legal philosophy and in philosophy of art—these and many other ventures have been among the current concerns of philosophers. Nevertheless, the two movements described here have played a particularly dominant part in contemporary thought, and have, in their diverse ways, represented a characteristic mood of yesterday and today—one of disenchantment with the substantive efforts of human reason to solve human problems. At least, this has been a characteristic mood in professional philosophy.

The mood may be only temporary. In fact, it does seem to be changing, although in what direction is far from clear. Disenchantment has been a natural and periodic reaction to the crises that scarify man at recurring intervals; and if philosophy is a reaction, if only in part, to cultural conflict, then what Socrates called "misology"—hatred or contempt of reason —would seem to be one of the expected possible reactions. Read "science" or "technology" for "reason" in this connection, and one discovers a quick entry into certain distinguished areas of contemporary thought. The paradox, if not the tragedy, of the situation is that as intelligent inquiry, in the form of scientific method, reaches its high point in solving certain problems, it is judged incompetent to handle other problems, such as those dealing with values. The split between the two worlds of things and ideals is thereby widened and an Age of Frustration seems nominated to succeed an Age of Paradox. But contemporary philosophy is in so fluid a state that it may presently become disenchanted itself with frustration.

Selected Readings

Barrett, William, *Irrational Man*, New York: Doubleday, 1958. (Paperback.)
Blackham, H., *Six Existentialist Thinkers*, New York: Harper & Row, 1951.
    (Paperback.)
Collins, J., *The Existentialists*, Chicago: Regnery, 1962. (Paperback.)
Grene, M., *Dreadful Freedom*, Chicago: University of Chicago, 1948.
Kaufmann, W., *Existentialism from Dostoevsky to Sartre*, New York: Meridian
    Books, Inc., 1956. (Paperback.)
Murdoch, Iris, *Sartre*, London: Hillary, 1959. Also Yale paperback.
Schrag, C. O., *Existentialism and Freedom*, Evanston: Northwestern University
    Press, 1961.
Wahl, Jean, *A Short History of Existentialism*, New York: Philosophical
    Library, 1949. (Paperback.)
Wild, John, *The Challenge of Existentialism*, Bloomington: Indiana University Press, 1955. (Paperback.)

CHAPTER 27

Fact and Value

The split between the two worlds of things and ideals, mentioned at the close of the last chapter, is not simply a characteristic of contemporary thought. A dominating and perennial feature of at least Western culture has been the presence of a whole series of opposed pairs, such as value-fact, ends-means, mind-body, reality-appearance, individual-social, even humanities-sciences—a split for which C. P. Snow has coined the popular new phrase, the "two cultures." Polarizations like these, and there are many more, have helped to illustrate, or even to establish, a pervasive climate of dualism, so familiar as to pass almost unnoticed.

To some, these signs of dualism, built so strongly into our culture and our language, are clear evidence of deep insights into the way things really are, or at least the way human things are. To others, the classic polarities may reveal, instead, equally clear evidence of historical origins, and their hold upon us may be attributed to the power of cultural institutions. Yet, in either case, the dualities are part of our continuing experience.

The current guise of this ancient split is found in the familiar statement that "Science can deal only with facts and not with values." This can be rephrased in many ways. One statement, by no means confined to journalism or the pulpit, is that science can give only knowledge, whereas something else (not always identified) must provide wisdom. Another version is that science deals with means only, not with ends.

The undoubted strength of propositions like these will be attested to by almost any reader, and he would not have to rely upon "mere" common sense or folklore, since he would be fully supported by the overwhelming majority of present-day scientists, including social scientists, and of philosophers as well. Indeed, folklore and science would come together on this issue.

The same support would be given to a similar observation, that is, that in some way science is in collision with other aspects of contemporary culture; and to deny this observation, whatever it may be called, would be irresponsible to the point of frivolousness. Not that the problem of the "two cultures" is itself contemporary; earlier sections of this book have traced it back at least to early Greece. But the paradox presented by a world literally thrusting its technological control to the stars, coexisting uneasily with another world which sometimes seems to be populated by naughty and ill-witted children, is a spectacle no literate or sensitive observer can fail to note. Whatever form it may take, the tragic juxtaposition of knowledge and ignorance, of control and drift, of technical competence and moral helplessness is almost the key signature of our times.

Fact and Value

Of all the dualisms met in our discussions perhaps none is so pervasive as this between fact and value. Certainly none of them is now so widely celebrated or so highly certified. The complex of statements elaborating it has become so familiar as to be almost banal. That "You cannot derive a conclusion containing an 'ought' from premises containing only an 'is' "; that "The normative can never be reduced to the descriptive, just as the descriptive can never generate the prescriptive"; that "Science can make no moral judgments"—these and countless other similar propositions have become clichés. Now, there is nothing necessarily wrong about a cliché; a truism, even if trivial, is at least true. And some commonplaces, although not all, are truisms. The problem is to distinguish between the commonplaces that can stand up to analysis and those that reflect no more than stubborn adherence to unreasoned commitments.

First of all, we must acknowledge the strength of the "is-ought" dualism and its long tradition. The cleavage has appeared many times in a variety of period costumes, but the centuries since the Scientific Revolution have seen it take on a prominence not manifest before, and in the Nuclear Revolution it has been illuminated to the point of incandescence. David Hume's familiar words may stand as a convenient model of uncounted testimonies, this despite the fact that, casually if not systematically, he proceeded to ignore his own caveat:

In every system of morality which I have hitherto met with, I have always remarked that the author proceeds for some time in the ordinary way of reasoning, and establishes the being of a God, or makes observations concerning human affairs; when of a sudden I am surprised to find, that instead of the usual copulations of propositions, *is* and *is not*, I meet with no proposition that is not connected with an *ought* or an *ought not*. This change is imperceptible; but is, however, of the last consequence. For as this *ought*, or *ought not*, expresses some new relation or affirmation, it is necessary that it should be observed and explained; and at the same time that a reason should be given for what seems altogether inconceivable, how this new relation can be a deduction from others, which are entirely different from it. But as authors do not commonly use this precaution, I shall presume to recommend it to the readers; and am persuaded, that this small attention would subvert all the vulgar systems of morality . . .[1]

The sense of this is very clear. What men do is no criterion for what they should do. What men should do is not a reflection of what they do indeed do. The spirit is willing but the flesh is weak. And to call these commonplaces is only to describe them. Statistics, to continue, can provide no basis for moral judgment: should a new Dr. Kinsey discover that nearly all men and women were unfaithful to their marriage vows, would this be in any way relevant to judging the moral worth of monogamy? After all, Saint Augustine would have found nothing surprising in such a discrepancy between conduct and ideal, for were not men fallen creatures indelibly programmed to sin?

There is another formulation of the impasse, connected with the name of G. E. Moore, who coined the phrase, "the naturalistic fallacy." This we commit when we try to talk about values such as "good," in factual terms such as "happiness" or "survival." To be more precise:

It may be true that all things which are good are also something else, just as it is true that all things which are yellowish produce a certain kind of vibration in the light. And it is a fact that Ethics aims at discovering what are those other properties belonging to all things which are good. But far too many philosophers have thought that when they named those other properties they were actually defining good; that these properties, in fact, were simply not "other," but absolutely and entirely the same with goodness. This view I propose to call the "naturalistic fallacy . . ."[2]

Thus, "everything is what it is, and not another thing," a dictum from Bishop Butler that Moore uses as the motto for his book. If, for instance, one is talking about pleasure, Moore goes on to say, one is talking about psychology and not about ethics. It will be seen that an approach like this is concerned with definition; it has even been suggested that if any fallacy is involved here it should be called the "definistic fallacy," since it

---

[1] *The Treatise of Human Nature*, Book III, Part I, last paragraph of section 1.
[2] *Principia Ethica* (Cambridge at the University Press, 1903), p. 10.

has supposedly to do with the confusion of two different properties one with the other and it really makes no difference whether the properties are "natural" or "nonnatural." But Moore was at least calling our attention to the meaning and clarification of terms like "good," an enterprise than which nothing is more congenial to contemporary philosophers, although he himself averred that he was doing much more than this. In short, the error—if it be an error—is to talk about value judgments without including the factor of commendation and obligation.

Value as Indefinable and Nonnatural

This, then, is what "the problem of value" seems to signify for much of recent thought. The "the" in the phrase may appear simplistic, since, for one thing, there are many problems of value; moreover, what is problematic in the field of human conduct and decision did not wait to be uncovered by modern thinkers. Nevertheless, there is some warrant for the locution. For value theory has become something of a specialized industry in modern Anglo-American philosophy, with feeder-lines tapping science, theology, journalism, and the arts; and a newly-exploited natural (in G. E. Moore's language, "nonnatural") resource seems to have provided much of the raw material for it. (Where the material is lacking, plastic substitutes have been provided.) This resource, natural or synthetic, turns out to be an unanalyzable sense of obligation or fittingness: an intuitive, immediate, indefinable grasp of what is intrinsically worthwhile. To illustrate:

One of the most dramatic of many dramatic episodes in Dostoevsky's *The Brothers Karamazov* is that in which Ivan is prepared, as he says, "to turn in his ticket." To use a modern vulgarism, he wants out. Why? He tells the story of a young blameless peasant girl who has been cruelly and obscenely persecuted by her ignorant, sadistic parents. Her innocent tears and undeserved anguish elicit no response, not from her bestial parents to be sure, but none either from a world which callously rolls along, seeming to include her inarticulate and piteous suffering as part of its whole scheme. If this is indeed the case, if the universe necessitates—in a logical or dialectical way—the unrequited and totally unjust misery of one single child, Ivan wants no part of it. He *feels* the child's baffled horror and *knows* it to be wrong, whatever else may be true.

Let us make the case even stronger. Suppose the torture of this one innocent girl were to bring about as its result the greatest good for the greatest number, an end to war, to injustice, to hate. Suppose the end clearly justified this particular means, one small horror and death to be compensated by the savings of millions of lives and all the promises of the most imaginative Utopia. Who would torture this girl to death—or consent to the torture—to bring about all these laudable results? Rather let us say if, in an allegedly realistic manner, one would so consent (since in so doing he would hope to be effecting a surplus of good), would he not regret the nature of the choice? Would he not regard the act as perhaps necessary, but if so, as a necessary *evil*? Why? Why are not the empirical consequences of the act sufficient to determine its moral worth? One answer is assertedly that we simply *know* it is wrong to inflict underserved suffering. We *know* it is wrong to repay love with hate and cruelty. In fact, we *know* that love is better than hate. Even if the child herself consented to be sacrificed for the greater glory of man, although we should marvel and rejoice at her martyrdom, we would still know it was somehow a bad thing, that it would be better if she were not sacrificed. Not to know this would be regarded as moral blindness.

Let us put the case in reverse. A pilot in a jet trainer develops serious engine trouble. He is flying over a village and rather than eject himself from the falling plane he chooses to remain with it to attempt to guide the machine away from the houses. He manages finally to zoom over a crowded school at the very edge of the village and crash into a field—where he falls upon a picnicking family. Where is the moral onus, if any, to be located? After all, the hero inadvertently caused the death of a family of five. Is he responsible? Do the consequences alone determine the moral worth of an act? Would anyone but a morally blind person blame the pilot for what he did? Was his moral obligation to try and save lives any the less demanding because of the circumstances that followed? This is not intended to be an exercise in casuistry. If any technical term is involved, it would be "deontology," i.e., that branch of ethics concerned alone with the sense of "rightness," of duty and obligation, with what we "ought" or "ought not" to do.

There has always been a tradition in philosophy, it will be recalled, which has underlined the intention rather than the result, will rather than consequence. The Hebrew ethic of righteousness, the Stoic reverence for duty, both of them committed to the majesty of law and obedience to it, would be illustrative. So would the Kantian approach, which contended that the moral value of an action does not reside in the effect which is expected from it, but only in the sense of duty to an inner moral law. Even English common sense has gone along. In the late seventeenth and eighteenth centuries there was, first, the "intuitive" or "rationalist" school of ethics—led by Richard Price. Here moral truth was seen to be as impeccable as mathematical truth. "Things equal to the same thing are equal to each other," was no more certain than that justice (the equating of good with good and bad with bad) was right and injustice wrong. Plato's doctrine of Truth applied to both kinds of propositions. The moral sense philosophers (Hutcheson, Shaftesbury and, in a special sense, Hume) were in a somewhat different category, the empirical rather than the rationalist, yet the idea that moral vision is like color vision was still congenial. There are moral-blind individuals just as there are color-blind individuals.

But twentieth-century philosophy, especially of the British variety, has developed the intuitive approach to heights of sophistication it had not been able to reach before.[3] And it has tended thereby to reinforce the dualism between value and fact. Above all, the "nonnaturalistic" element has been thrown into unprecedented prominence. Now, a "naturalistic" approach to ethics is one that considers the realm of values to be significantly related to other aspects of human experience, and that goes on to regard all experience as at least potentially and theoretically amenable to description and analysis deriving from historical and scientific method. This does not imply, as the argument in Part III has abundantly shown, "reducing" values to something else, nor that human experience is all of a piece; but it does suggest that neither value nor experience is an immaculate and inexplicable deliverance forever opaque to intelligent inquiry.

"Nonnaturalism" would consider this last comment invidious. For its approach to value is one which claims to be genuinely empirical, since it professes to report what is actually the case. And this is that what men fundamentally prize and hold to be good can be analyzed no further: ordinary experience and language seem to dictate this—at least, so it is argued—just as does the analytical process itself. When men try desperately to discover what is truly and unimpeachably good they are inescapably forced into the realm of indefinables: happiness, pleasure, duty, self-realization, sacrifice—whatever may coerce them with its obligatory power. It is the simple imperative force of "ought" and not the content which determines the moral realm. Moral content seems often a later rationalization of what is immediately and compellingly experienced, and often an unsatisfactory rationalization at that.

To turn to logic, analysis must at some point reach bedrock. If there are compounds, there must be elements, and what is elemental is just that: not reducible further. For example, the primitive constitutents of mathematics are definitions, undefined elements, postulates, and operations, and although these are all subject to amendment and substitution, they cannot themselves be reduced further. This is what an element means. Euclid's first axiom may or may not be a suitable one, but it is not subject to proof or disproof, since proof or disproof would demand something more simple

---

[3] The chief names here, although these philosophers differ in many ways among themselves, would be Moore, Ross, Ewing, Broad, and Pritchard. See books such as G. E. Moore's *Principia Ethica* (*op. cit.*); W. D. Ross, *The Right and the Good* (Oxford at the Clarendon Press, 1930), and *The Foundations of Ethics* (Oxford at the Clarendon Press, 1939); A. C. Ewing, *The Definition of Good* (New York: Macmillan, 1947); C. D. Broad, *Five Types of Ethical Theory* (London: Routledge, 1930); and *Ethics and the History of Philosophy* (London: Routledge, 1952); and H. A. Pritchard, *Moral Obligation* (Oxford at the Clarendon Press, 1949).

than the axiom, on which the demonstration or lack of it could be based; in that case the first Euclidean axiom (things equal to the same thing are equal to each other) would no longer be an axiom. Mathematics has a clear advantage here, in that it is dealing largely with tautologies, so that if a primitive element is further analyzable it would thereby not be primitive.

Is an ethical intuition a tautology? Is it something like "A is A"? Few contemporary moralists would go quite so far as to make such a claim. Instead, it is urged that the *quality* of moral feeling is what is elemental and irreducible and hence not subject to ordinary empirical examination. Such a contention is the heart of ethical "nonnaturalism." This particular use of "naturalism" and anti- or non-"naturalism" is different from the metaphysical use of these terms, a use which has been discussed earlier in this book in quite different connections. The present use, in the field of ethics, stems as we have seen from the work of G. E. Moore and others. (Also "nonnaturalism" should not be equated with "supernaturalism.")

A conscientious objector, for instance, may or may not be able to convince others that nonviolent resistance would bring peace to a world organized as ours is at present—which, of course, is the only world with which we can now deal. He may even be troubled a little, unless he approach fanaticism, by such things as resistance to Hitlerism, the Hungarian uprising of 1956, the Indian reaction to Chinese invasion, and he may wish to propose a pragmatic argument on challenges like these. But his fundamental beliefs are not dependent upon such argument or evidence, for he *knows* it is absolutely wrong to kill, to bear arms, to use violence of any sort. His "conscience"—another term for intuition or a sense of "oughtness"—is sanction enough. After all, to what could his "feeling" be reduced? To be sure, there are other forms of pacifism that do not involve "conscience," and other manifestations of "conscience" that do not involve pacifism.

Perhaps the point has been made. Since it is not the point of the present approach, its strength should be made clear and in no way underestimated. Nonnaturalism is a persuasive position and, according to its own logic, is not disprovable (nor is it provable, either, since intuitions do not lend themselves to proof). But what are some of the other possible approaches to the field of value?

The Language of Fact and of Value

The problem of definition is everywhere a sticky one, nowhere more so than here, for the questions are nothing less than these: Can men ever talk a common language about things of importance? Are there indeed two languages, those of "fact" and of "value"? If there are, should they be pushed further apart, or, if possible, drawn closer together?

There is also the question of the value of definition itself and whether it should come at the beginning or the end of a discussion. On one side it may be argued that some sort of definition or classification, even if unsatisfactory, is better than none, since we have to be able to delimit what we are talking about and then give it a name; indeed, we can not very well talk about something unless or until it does have a name. There must be something identifiable, however imperfectly, before discussion can begin. On the other side, it may be pointed out that to begin with a definition, particularly in such a debatable area as this, is simply to beg the question at the very beginning, since a "value" would then simply be what we or others have said it is. Therefore, it may be maintained, a definition should be allowed to emerge as a result of a long look at the whole area of what can be called preferential behavior. Between these extremes, of an advance definition or none at all, there are many degrees, and the present approach will hit somewhere within the extremes.

One simple item of definition may be disposed of forthwith. "Value" is a term which is found in many fields besides ethics, as in economics and aesthetics. But there is a clear difference between the moral and the nonmoral use. In economics, "value" may depend upon demand or upon "utility" or upon cost of production, or some meeting point of all of them; in aesthetics, it may derive from a choice among a number of even more controversial criteria. But in neither case is there the clear-cut presence of the distinction between "desired" and "desirable," which may be said to pinpoint the difference between the moral and the nonmoral. However we approach the uniqueness of moral judgment, naturalistically or the reverse, it cannot be denied that the conflict between what men actually do and what they "should" do is its very signature. Men do desire, say, power; this is a purely descriptive matter, one to be handled perhaps by social psychology or history. Is it desirable that men seek power? Ought they seek power? These questions, by their very language, introduce another dimension.

Does such a recognition hand the issue over to those who are persuaded that the sense of "oughtness" or "obligation" is an unanalyzable and unique experience? Or is it, in more up-to-date phrasing, that the crucial difference between fact and value, between "is" and "ought," lies in the special status of what may be called the "-able" words: desirable, lovable, laudable, culpable, judgeable, and so on? (Not that all "-able" words fit into this category.) The function of such words, as of all truly ethical terms, is not to report some nonnatural quality or sense of fitness, but rather to exhort, to exercise some measure of control. This is a dominating theme in recent Anglo-American ethical theory, fascinated as its exponents are by language. They point out that ethical terms do many things—express emotion, persuade, order, commend and command, prescribe and ascribe, indicate performance, even that they "goad" and "guide."

The discourse of ethics, thus, is a practical one. Indeed, this is what "ought" means: at most to urge others to act, at least to testify how one feels.[4] In either case no "facts" are involved, beyond the obvious one that people actually do express their emotions and try to get others to share and to act in accordance with them, so there is nothing that can be judged true or false or that can be approached rationally. To attempt to go from "is" to "ought" would be to violate linguistic usage and literally to talk nonsense. This is clearly a last line of defense and unquestionably a sophisticated one. It is therefore necessary to take a more extended look at this whole issue of fact-and-value and, while acknowledging the cogency of the arguments directed to severing totally the realm of value from that of fact and even accepting them in part, to suggest another approach.

Take this crucial item of the invulnerability of "ought"—invulnerable logically, empirically, and linguistically.[5] "Ought" simply cannot be reached, so it is customarily held, from an "is"; facts can never generate values. Many would say there is less there than meets the eye. To be sure, there is a difference between fact and value. But it certainly is not an obvious difference. For one thing, whatever we decide "values" to be, they are certainly part of the inventory of "facts," although this is so broad an observation that no conclusion can follow from it. And what are facts? Certainly nothing obvious. For facts are highly selective, *capta*, or *things taken*, rather than *data*, or *things given*; and perhaps all we can say, if inelegantly, is that they are simply what you have to take into account. If this is so, then "value," it will be argued, has a clear claim to factual status. Human preferences and judgments present a record which must be acknowledged. No matter how values come to be defined, they cannot be excluded from what one has to take into account. This is perhaps a trivial point, even if it is enshrined in ordinary language.

Less trivial is the observation that "fact" words are not easily or entirely separated from "value" words. The vocabulary of social science, for example, contains terms which are to a degree normative, "culture," for one. Such a term, it may be said, does not simply denote what has to be taken into account; it also connotes a living and an intelligible social order. The word is more than merely descriptive. So is the word "state," not to mention the "welfare state"; and so are others like "supply and demand," "a balanced budget," "deficit financing," "security," "freedom," as well as the many obviously loaded slogans of politics and economics. But, it will be retorted, these words are really value-words, covertly if not overtly.

---

[4] Among the names associated with this approach to ethical language would be those of A. J. Ayer, C. L. Stevenson, R. M. Hare, and H. L. A. Hart.

[5] There is some recent evidence that this particular linguistic impasse is, to a measure, being cut through; see, for instance, a paper by Professor Max Black, "The Gap Between 'Is' and 'Ought,'" in the *Philosophical Review* Vol. 73, No. 2 (April, 1964), pp. 165–181.

This double function is precisely what is being noted here, that it is not easy to separate clearly prescriptive from descriptive language. A "parent" is a biological and social term, yet it has an aura which certainly includes "responsibility," "love," "obedience," and many other "value" or "value-like" words. These illustrations may be somewhat slanted, and there is no intention to deny that there are innumerable statements which seem innocent of anything but a straight matter-of-fact interpretation. "This is Monday, June 28, 1965," might be such a case, except, of course, for those who celebrate or mourn the day as an anniversay. Such signpost language constitutes but one of the limits of a range of meaning that merges imperceptibly into language of evaluation. "This is a banana" changes quickly in its interpretation into "This is an overripe (that is, bad) banana." "The traffic light has just turned red," is a factual assertion, but it gets its significance from a whole complex of social directives and imperatives. "Hitler was a paranoic," is more than a label in psychopathology. It suggests that we do not look favorably upon paranoics or that they require treatment of a sort.

There is nothing strange in this overlapping of language, nor do these illustrations "prove" anything. The overlapping is not strange because all human experience has this double aspect of fact and value: Janus-like, it points two ways. And language represents this ambivalence in a more or less accurate fashion. Words about facts and words about value blend into each other. But an argument based on linguistic usage can count on an equivocal reception, today more than ever. The reason, as we have already seen, is that from one end of the philosophic spectrum (the violet?) ordinary language is regarded as the repository of the common wisdom and can be tampered with only at our peril, while from the other end (the red?), it is looked upon as almost an institutionalizing of error and confusion and needs drastic renovation. Therefore, it is difficult to know how much weight to give to the evident overlapping of descriptive (cognitive) and normative (evaluative) language.

Even the logic of the distinction between "is" and "ought" is not as clear as David Hume seemed to think. It will be recalled that he—and nearly everyone since—deplored the misguided effort to go from a premise containing only descriptive terms to a conclusion in which, lo! a normative term suddenly and surreptitiously appears. Yet this really has little to do with any special problem of "is-and-ought." A logical fallacy is committed whenever *any* term is found in the conclusion of an argument without the term having already appeared in one of the premises. I cannot talk about "angels" at the end when I have talked only about "men" and "animals" in the beginning—and this has nothing to do with the fact that "angels" are not natural in the way that "men" and "animals" are. To go from "is" language to "ought" language may indeed be fallacious but it is not a "naturalistic" fallacy, just a good, old-fashioned mistake in logic. Only, this kind of mistake is rarely made! For as Professor Abraham Edel has shown, when a term, or even a whole proposition, turns up for the first time at the conclusion of an argument, certain missing terms or premises are implied. Few arguments are found in complete canonical form, whether syllogistic or not; indeed a major task of logic is to discover the suppressed parts and to recover the approved form of an argument.

This search for connectives is in order even when a *quality* is found suddenly in the conclusion when it had not been detected earlier. Take this abbreviated claim: "*x* is an object that reflects light waves of the length of about 6500 ängstrom units; therefore it is red." This is a kind of "naturalistic fallacy" since the word for an irreducible (phenomenological) experience is found in the conclusion, whereas only analytical and reducible terms, those dealing with light waves, had been used up to that point. But no one will be disturbed by this. The argument is simply an enthymeme, that is, there is a missing proposition, in this case, the major premise: "All objects having etc., etc." Ordinarily, when one argues from "is" to "ought," he is—rightly or wrongly—counting upon an assumed but missing link, and it would be a poor reasoner who could not find a justifying "ought" somewhere along the line. But, of course, this is not the real issue, which is whether at *any* point we can proceed from "is" to "ought." After all, it will be said, both light waves and colors are still within the same factual dimension; it would be only if I said, "I hate the color red," or "I order you not to wear red," or "You ought not to wear red," that a totally different kind of statement would present itself. Can this kind of statement remain invulnerable to factual penetration at any level, linguistic, logical, or empirical?

The Naturalistic Fallacy

A further consideration of the naturalistic fallacy will reveal that it is a major obstacle to overcoming the dualism of fact and value. Its special hindrance is that it obscures the way in which science can provide means for relating facts with values. G. E. Moore's statement of the fallacy has already been given (pp. 451–452); it can be amplified. Suppose I say that what I mean by "good" is "the greatest happiness, or the greatest pleasure, for the greatest number." Then I should be able to substitute the *definiens* ("the greatest happiness . . .") for the *definiendum* ("the good"). So that if I then asked, "Is the greatest happiness . . . good?" I should be able to make the question nonsense by rephrasing it, "Is the 'good' good?" But it is quite clear that the original question is far from nonsense. Indeed, if you defined the good in any way whatever, call it *x*,

I could still continue to make sense by asking, "But is x really good?"

Compare the definition of "good" with that of "cousin," as "the son or daughter of my aunt or uncle." Now if I asked, despite the definition, "But is my cousin really the son or daughter of my aunt or uncle?" I should certainly be talking nonsense, or, more politely, I should be violating customary linguistic usage, since I should only be asking, "But is my cousin really my cousin?" This uniqueness of "good" and of other ethical terms indicated to Moore (and to many others) that such words cannot be defined in the usual way, that they are essentially indefinable, that they are *sui generis* and understandable only through something like intuition.

There is a whole literature on this particular issue, in the course of which Moore himself modified his original position;[6] and there are ethical theorists (like John Dewey) who have not even acknowledged the existence of "The Fallacy." In any case, if values are ever to be handled as other things are handled—waiving the alleged impossibility of such a suggestion —the so-called naturalistic fallacy has either to be run around or run over.

This alleged fallacy can be appraised from several different vantage points. One of them, already noted, is that of definition, or rather of its impossibility. Here Moore has called our attention to what is undeniable, that there are indefinable, not to say ineffable elements at the root of moral experience—of all experience, for that matter. It needs to be added that in itself this is in no way obstructive of further inquiry. Any universe of discourse has its undefined elements, and in certain logical and mathematical universes these elements constitute perhaps the most interesting part of the systems. Moore himself demonstrated that indefinability is no block to discussion by proceeding in the *Principia Ethica* and elsewhere to write enough material on the "good" to fill two books and more. If the fallacy did nothing but underline the limits of definition, it could be regarded as unexceptionable if not exactly exciting. But it goes quite beyond this.

For one thing, many of the exploiters of the fallacy use indefinability not merely as a note of caution but as a warrant for regarding "good" and other ethical words as referring *positively* to some simple nonnatural or irreducible quality. This does not follow. For the indefinability of "good" stands up only so far and so long as the term is kept abstract, out of any context, so long as it is supposed to refer to a *single* and unchanging quality. But as shown by Professor Paul Edwards in *The Logic of Moral Discourse*, the meaning of "good" varies with different contexts, just as "nice" does. A "nice" day for one person may be hot and steamy, for another

---

[6] A good summary of this discussion will be found in *The Philosophy of G. E. Moore*, ed. by Paul Schilpp (Evanston, Ill.: Northwestern University Press, 1942), chaps. I-IV, and espec. pp. 535–611.

crisp and tangy. "Good" in one situation (to quote Edwards) may mean "truthful, loving, gentle, and free from envy or malice"; but elsewhere (these are not his exact words) it might refer to something like "God-fearing, pure, always truthful, intolerant of sinlike conduct," or possibly "strong, loyal to the Party, intolerant of hesitation or doubt, zealous and fearless." Edwards proposes the word "polyguous" for this multiple-referring character of "good," and of many other terms; there is a necessary vagueness and open-endedness in their use. "But though this implies," he writes, "that *in a sense* 'good' is indefinable, it does not imply any more than a similar fact implies this in the case of 'bald' or 'rich' that 'good' has no referent or that it has a non-natural referent." The nonnaturalist, like Moore, seems to beg the whole question, not only by assuming at once that "good" stands for a single indefinable quality, but also that such a quality is therefore beyond analysis.

There is still another *petitio principii* (question-begging) to be discovered in the exploitation of the naturalistic fallacy. Take the maxim referred to earlier that "Everything is what it is, and not another thing." This revered pronouncement of Bishop Butler, one of the most perceptive ethical thinkers of the eighteenth century, may well hold within a restricted setting, but it becomes an exercise in pure obscurantism when it is generalized, as it usually is, so as to hold secure from any further analysis or inquiry some particular area of human experience such as the ethical. Consider the color yellow, which Moore uses to show the similarity between two ineffable experiences. Just as a blind or a colorblind man could not be talked into seeing yellow, he argues, so no one could be talked into understanding the meaning of "good"; he would have to come upon it directly and immediately. Neither the color nor the moral quality can be reduced to anything simpler. Now, that there are such "phenomenological" experiences can scarcely be challenged, and that they constitute a prized possession of man is equally unquestionable. The realms of the arts, of play, of the many sensuous joys, indeed all those consummations of experience that poets and philosophers have had before them when they have tried to describe what man's life might be—each of these could serve as illustration for the precious and the inexpressible.[7]

But there is a rhythm to experience. Among the rhythms, for there are a number of them, is the oscillation between what we are and what we want to be, between enjoyment and the engineering of enjoyment, between the direct and the indirect, the "having" and the "knowing." Water

---

[7] Some pages of the material used in this chapter and also in the following chapters have already appeared in a slightly different form in George R. Geiger's, *John Dewey in Perspective*, and are used here with the kind permission of Oxford University Press, holders of the original 1958 copyright. The book also appeared in a 1964 paperback edition, published by McGraw-Hill. The specific pages referred to are 458, 461–463, 467–469, 486–487, 513–517, 528–531, 523–524.

as that which satisfies thirst and water as the object of search or of chemical analysis presents two different kinds of things. So does a fire when we poke it simply to enjoy the sparks or when we are trying to get the wood to burn by removing the ash. Or again, there is after-dinner conversation between friends, in which the words become as autonomous and satisfying as the cigars and brandy, and then there is talk to explain something or to make a political conversion. Although different, these are not, of course, separate gears of experience between which we have to shift with some effort and noise. They can replace each other subtly and quickly, and sometimes, as when we poke the fire, it might be difficult to determine in precisely which gear we are moving. "Knowing," when it is not a chore or dull routine, is to some degree consummatory and final: the words we use to describe may themselves become enjoyed for their own sake. Contrariwise, "havings" and enjoyments are not necessarily final in the sense of being irresponsible and unforeseeing. Culminations are also beginnings. Authentic experience carries on; it is instrumental as well as final, fruitful in that it leads to other genuine experiences. But no single aspect of experience is exhaustive, since experience is not all of a piece; it is not all of a piece because, as has been intimated by these examples, problems arise and situations become indeterminate and confused. Directly enjoyed experiences are interrupted, or they begin to pall; breaks of one kind or another appear and something needs to be done.

To return to the matter of color. What the antinaturalist approach overlooks is that the immediate experience of color does not in itself present a problem; it is not a matter of "knowing" or "meaning" but of the sheer relish of quality. It cannot be talked about, perhaps, any more than can the "good." But this intrinsic simplicity of a quality like color or good (if it be such) does not exhaust the experience of which it is one focus. To limit the entire meaning of the color phenomenon to what is directly grasped is, perversely, to put one's self in the position of being unable to answer some very significant questions about color: why some people can see it and others not, how it changes and how it can be controlled, what is the larger context of which this particular phenomenon is a part; in other words, how color can be understood, as in aesthetics and optics.

Judgments about color are not made in terms of color. To say, therefore, that "Everything is what it is, and not another thing" is to preclude an understanding and explanation of the very questions that interest us. Explanations are invariably in terms of correlations, as of colors with light waves. Maybe such explanations will prove finally unsuccessful, for color no less than for the "good," but to arrest investigation at the beginning on the grounds of a first-degree "fallacy" is not only to beg the question but, more seriously, "to block the path of inquiry." It would be to assume a seamless experience exempt from problems and difficulties, a completely careless holiday world where there is only "having" and no "understanding." Fortunately or unfortunately, this is not so. Everything may be what it is, but it is inevitably connected with other things, too. Were this not true, difficulties could never be overcome, nor would there even be anything to talk about.

Now, it would be less than fair not to point out that much of the preceding argument would be acceptable to the Moore approach, at least that part which suggests there are things to understand about, say, a color other than its sheer quality. The real problem is whether value is a quality. That issue cannot be fully met until a little later in the discussion (pp. 467–468).

Value and the Sense of "Oughtness"

One differentiating feature (*differentia*) of "value" has already been indicated, at least of the kind of value that is of concern here, ethical or moral value. This feature—that of "desirability"—has been pointed up by distinguishing "moral" from "felicity" values, the latter deriving from the happiness or pleasure inherent in the satisfaction of wants.[8] The reason for the separation is clear. It makes sense to talk about a "bad" pleasure or an "undeserved" happiness. As has been brilliantly documented by the economist Kenneth Galbraith, human "wants" can be artificially and cynically created, as by advertising.[9] The satisfaction of just any want does not necessarily establish the basis for a moral value.

A "moral" or "ethical" value is designed to distinguish between the "desired" and the "desirable," between the "wanted" and what "should" be wanted. There is no dispute here. The dispute arises when the basis for the distinction is assessed. To revert to well-worn language, the *differentia* of "desirability" is indeed a necessary condition for a definition of "value," but it is by no means a sufficient condition. And even if a necessary condition, the meaning of this particular *differentia*, especially when it appears as an "ought," needs to be explored to see if it is, as many insist, inexplicable. In such an exploration the distinction between the terms "good" and "right" may be noticed. The "good" may refer to something like a human aspiration or striving, to goals; it would then be teleological, referring to an end, as in Aristotle's conception of "happiness" and in John Stuart Mill's, though so different in content. Self-sacrifice or service to others would equally be "goods." "Right" carries the connotation of law or duty; it is a classic notion, going back to the Hebrews and the Stoics, and it occupies a central position in the ethical theories of Kant and in

---

[8] Cf. Bertram Morris, *Philosophical Aspects of Culture* (Yellow Springs, Ohio: Antioch Press, 1961), pp. 73–79.
[9] In *The Affluent Society* (Boston: Houghton Mifflin, 1948).

those of recent British theorists like Ross, Ewing, and others. The use of "intuition" and "fittingness" and a "sense of obligation" are new and sophisticated names for old ways of thinking. A still older way and name is "conscience."

It has been argued that the characteristic feel of "oughtness," so necessary for ethical judgment, attaches itself more easily to "right" than to "good." We can always ask whether we "ought" to do what is "good" and still be able to make sense, but less so, it is alleged, with "Ought we do what is the right thing?" Undoubtedly, different approaches to ethics are suggested by these various terms—"good" for the purposive approach, "right" for the command-and-duty sanctions, and perhaps "virtue" to connote approval—but it would seem to be a matter of taste to assert that the sense of obligation adheres more easily to one than to the other. In any event, the problem here is that of the nature of "oughtness."

To take off from a previous discussion, like "good," "ought" may also be regarded as polyguous. Not in the same way, since it would be difficult to discover the actual referent for the word. But "ought" *implies* (to use Edwards' phrasing) a variety of sanctions and calls upon reasons as diverse as those which would support "good" or "nice." Consider the justifications a Roman Catholic would use in contending that birth control "ought" to be opposed with those a secular social scientist would use in arguing that it "ought" to be recommended; or the reasons put forward by a conscientious objector set alongside those of a believer in the deterrence of war through armed strength—both employing "ought" language. The implications, without which that language would simply have no meaning, are as observably different as the colors of the spectrum. The "oughts" differ as much among themselves as do the facts appealed to. Whether it uses the language of "good" or "ought," the moral situation is an open one, and only arbitrarily can it be compressed into a single mold. For "ought" can be based on the will of God, or upon the class struggle, or the necessity to solve problems and alleviate misery, or upon manifest destiny or simply the obligation to keep up with one's neighbors. To insist that these are all the same experience is to succumb to a kind of verbal hypnosis.

It will be said, however, that this misses the point. "Different reasons" may be exploited as justifications, but the sense of obligation remains a simple and unexplained phenomenon, itself quite autonomous of the reasons given. The very least that can be said of this is that sheer feeling has been given a strength it certainly does not warrant, and that to insist upon the complete insularity of such feeling or intuition is to revert to a kind of primitivism. For it can be argued that "conscience" or whatever other term acts as its up-to-date surrogate, stands for an experience which has an evident natural history and which introduces no break into that history.

The issue here is not whether the sense of "oughtness" or "obligation" is phenomenological and thus inexpressible in other terms, much less whether it is to be "reduced" to something other than what it is. To look upon "oughtness" as "natural" is neither to deny its unique quality nor to approach it with a "nothing but" attitude: colors are a special experience but they are not, therefore, nonnatural in some esoteric sense. As was suggested before, to "explain" color is not to explain it away; to talk about the physiology of perception or the principles of optics is to introduce certain correlations without which color can, it is true, remain perversely inexplicable. Nonnaturalism would appear to exploit such perverseness, to insist that "ought" is isolated and hence cannot be discussed further without inviting a fallacy. This is the issue with "oughtness," not its uniqueness but the contention that it is fundamentally disconnected from anything else.

The "anything else" will, of course, vary as different sciences are consulted. But that man and all his works—including that luminous sense of obligation—are part of a biological and social continuum which, if not completely without breaks, certainly discloses no theoretically irreparable rupture, would seem to be an assumption necessitated by the very appearance of intelligence in the evolutionary process. To take evolution seriously (and one might wonder how else it could be taken) is to acknowledge such a continuity, and to question the actual meaning of nonnaturalism, as it was the burden of Part III of this volume to show.

Our present concern is with the unique sense of "oughtness" and whether it is connected with other things, such as its possible natural origin and development. At the risk of committing the "genetic" fallacy, that, of assuming that we have fully explained a phenomenon by describing its origins, it certainly can be argued that the knowledge of conditions out of which arose an ethical animal possessing a "moral sense" or "conscience" or whatever other term may be used, does shed a great deal of light on that which has come to be. It might also be argued that the originating conditions are not entirely in the past either, since at least social or cultural evolution is by no means over, nor perhaps even biological evolution.

This, of course, has been but a bare mention of a challenging point of view, one that is philosophically unorthodox. Basic to such an approach, however different may be the genetic agencies invoked, is the hypothesis that the sheer feeling of obligation or of "oughtness" is a transparent one: shining through it is some accountable process that has reached a burning focus here in man's consciousness. The undoubtedly precious sense of obligation can be regarded not as an isolated phenomenon but as relational and involving much beyond its own sense of immediacy.

Another Approach to Value

One element of a definition of value has already been indicated—that of "desirability." The point of the last few pages has been to resist the claim that such an element must be accounted for in a nonnatural way. Desirability represents, however, only one of several psychological states or processes, albeit a very important one. It is what is called the "affective" element, that which excites emotion. There are, as we have seen, theories of value such as the so-called "emotive," which exclude all but the affective element.

Even if it is an inescapable element, desirability or something similar of an emotive character is not enough for the purposes of definition. Other aspects of value need to be considered. There is, for instance, what is called the "conative" factor in the human make-up, that which exerts effort and which selects. Impulse and emotion, much less sentiment, may not exercise the active and selective choice—so necessary an element in any complete description of value. It should be added that cultural and historical factors are also involved in such a description, for axiology must include the record of man's long-range choices. To be sure, this does not remove us in any way from what is "desirable," since human preferences are not values unless or until they are justified. As was said before, fictitious choice may well prove to be a disvalue. But preferences have to be more than mere verbalisms; it is easy to say we prefer serious music and educational television when, as a matter of fact, we spend our time with the jukebox, the Western, and the soap opera. The desirable needs to operate so as truly to influence selection. It is of course possible that we may be prevented from acting out our choices by economic, psychological, or other blocks. Also, we may lie sometimes as much by our actions as by our words. Nevertheless, one element of a visible description of value would have to include the factor of seriously intended action.

Third, there is the cognitive element as a necessary part of a complete value situation. For one thing, "value" is an "idea" or "conception." Foresight is involved and with it an intelligible pattern of response, so that value cannot be exclusively emotive or conative. It functions also as an item of discourse, appearing as a rule or goal or principle. As an inescapable part of such an item, good reasons play a conspicuous role in any adequate description of what is intended by value. For even if value be regarded as simply expressing what I approve or indicating the imposition of an imperative, there still will be found some good and sufficient reason for the liking or the imperative. The reason may be implicit, but without it the brute arbitrariness of likings or commands would be such as to preclude meaning as well as discussion.

For example, if I approve of x's qualities, the approval does not itself establish that x possesses such qualities. To approve of x, or to exhort others to follow me in my approval, or to command (if and when one has the power to do so) that other men should act as does x—all these "moral" claims are without serious foundation or justification unless reasons are given and unless these reasons rest on a truth claim, a factual claim.

These three elements of a definition of value—the emotive, the conative, and the cognitive—have been put together by the late Clyde Kluckhohn, noted American anthropologist, to give us the following: "Value is a *conception*, implicit or explicit, distinctive of an individual or characteristic of a group, *of the desirable which influences the selection* from available modes, means, and ends of action."[10] Although lacking the flair found in the more celebrated philosophic definitions, it is a forthright and accurate compilation of what needs to be present in a working definition of "value." However, the definition still leaves us with an undefined element, the all-important "the desirable." Can anything further be said about this?

The name of John Dewey, among others, has been associated with a major attempt to take the preternatural quality out of "desirable" and "ought," and to define "value" so as to make it amenable to scientific inquiry.[11] Although this approach to what is at the very heart of value may today represent a minority opinion among value theorists, it is no silent or chastened minority, and there is even some evidence that in these days of continuing crisis it may be gaining adherents. It is an approach which attempts to cut someplace in the middle between two contrasting theories of value. One of them is that of traditional absolutism or rationalism, which regards value as fixed and given and as known by some special sense or faculty of man; the other reflects the attitude which identifies value with immediate likings, enjoyments, or interests, and which, more likely than not, emphasizes the emotive aspect and language of value. Neither of these extremes allows any place for the exercise of intelligence and judgment, and this omission would seem to be serious, since it prevents us from either understanding or implementing values.

Take the belief that any immediate liking or enjoyment or approval is *ipso facto* a value. That there are such likings and prizings, what now can be called *goods*, is indubitable; and that many, if not all, of these are inexpressible and unanalyzable may also be the case. But that enjoyment ceases to be a datum and becomes a problem is equally indubitable. Immediate likings and approvals, even imperatives, come into conflict with other things and even among themselves. It would be embarrassing to give illustrations, so familiar and poignant to all of us is this conflict. What we want, or like, or approve, or even would like to command, may do no more than set up a difficulty. For likings and "goods" are what they are—unreflective and noncognitive experiences, even if they may be

---

[10] Found in Talcott Parsons and Edward A. Shils, *Toward a General Theory of Social Action* (Cambridge: Harvard, 1951), p. 394. (Our italics.)

[11] Cf. Dewey's *Quest for Certainty* (New York, Minton, Balch, 1929; also Capricorn paperback), chap. X; his monograph, *A Theory of Valuation* (Encyclopaedia of Unified Science, Vol. II, No. 4. Chicago: University of Chicago Press, 1939). See also a volume based on his general thesis: *Value: A Co-operative Inquiry*, ed. by R. Lepley (New York: Columbia, 1949).

unutterably precious. But a "value," it can be said, is something else. It is the result of a judgment, however simple. "Value," so the present argument asserts, can be looked upon as a noun established by the verb or action of *evaluating*. It comes into being when the immediately enjoyed object or process becomes suspect, when it begins to cloy, when some other object of enjoyment competes for recognition. For instance, when a liking for popular music has to meet the competition of the symphony orchestra, as on television or on the radio, a problem arises. And when a problem arises, another dimension would seem to be introduced.

Whether "value" should be used for this other dimension may be a minor matter; but it is not a minor matter to distinguish between mere likings and those which make a claim upon our conduct; it is not a minor matter to separate the *de facto* from the *de jure*. This is what the whole issue is about. Evaluation is here being understood as a search for the connections between things, between the direct lauding or celebration of what we like and the conditions which make possible their manifestation and enjoyment. There can be no theorizing about immediate enjoyments, but there can—indeed, there must be—about the choices among them.

To put it another way: The "desirable" (the *de jure*) is that which has to do with the ends or purposes of human effort. It is what "will illuminate and guide the activities of men." To be sure, one might ask whether all ends or purposes are desirable, and the answer would have to be "No." Does not this then mean that "desirability" is still something opaque and beyond the ordinary activities of men? But notice the words "illuminate" and "guide." What is suggested here is that man is constantly being confronted with a choice between different kinds of "goods." He has to make a decision. If he were not in this situation, there would be no problem and therefore nothing to discuss. Man would revel, or perhaps wallow, in a bath of undiscriminated "likings." As with a replete oyster in its bed, he would live in a world empty of values (valuations). But this is a travesty. The human situation, to employ a phrase which has become somewhat pretentious in recent literature, is one in which enjoyments compete and decisions must be made.

The argument here is that the preferences in which intelligent decision does (or can) play a decisive part are different from those which are uncritically and casually made. The meaning of casual and criticized enjoyment is not the same; illuminated and guided purposes are different from obscure and random ones; and the word "value" can be reserved for those enjoyments which have partaken in some measure of intelligence, criticism, light, and direction. As Dewey puts it: "We may indeed enjoy the goods the gods of fortune send us, but we should recognize them for what they are, not asserting them to be good and righteous altogether." To be good altogether, an experience needs to include control of the causal conditions which enter into it as well as celebration of the final happy results. It needs to be more than luck or magic. This something more would make it "desirable," a value. In short, the point of view being outlined here is that the "desirable" rests on knowledge. People *ought* to desire what they *would* desire if they knew enough. To be sure, this is an unattainable ideal but it may help to indicate the suggested difference between "desired" and "desirable."

"Desirable" also gives the sense of making a claim on future action. "It is in effect a judgment that the thing 'will do.'" It involves a prediction. For example, one might say, "If I do x, then y will follow rather than z; and y will be preferable, at least in the present context." Thus, if I am gracious to others, the chances are good that I shall receive in turn a kindly reaction rather than ill-humor. Now, there are two parts to this prediction. The first is clearly an empirical matter: y will or will not follow if x—I shall (or shall not) elicit a kindly reaction in others if I act graciously. The second is a matter of foresight plus appraisal, elevating y over z and giving it a priority—it is better to be treated in a kindly fashion than with ill-humor. Is it this kind of appraisal, this assessment of ends, which is to be the meaning of desirable? And does such assessment in turn depend simply upon an unempirical liking or approval, quite different from the way we judge the success of means?

Since science is the enterprise supposedly limited to means, to instrumentalities; whereas values, it is held, have to do with ends, with what is regarded as intrinsic, it may be appropriate now to redirect the discussion of values and the desirable to another context. Above all, the question must be faced whether value is of such a nature as to permit its being handled by social science. Perhaps this question may provide a setting for the many problems that have been raised here and for others which will have occurred to any sensitive reader.

Selected Readings

Adams, E. M., *Ethical Naturalism and the Modern World View*, Chapel Hill: University of North Carolina Press, 1960.

Baier, K., *The Moral Point of View*, Ithaca: Cornell, 1958. (Also Random House paperback.)

Hall, E. W., *Modern Science and Human Values*, Princeton, N.J.: Van Nostrand, 1956.

Hare, R. M., *The Language of Morals*, London: Oxford, 1954. (Also Galaxy paperback.)

Köhler, W., *The Place of Value in a World of Facts*, New York: Liveright, 1938. (Also Meridian paperback.)

Margenau, H., *Open Vistas*, New Haven: Yale, 1961. (Paperback.)
Northrop, F. S. C., *The Logic of the Sciences and the Humanities*, New York: Macmillan, 1947. (Meridian paperback.)
Pepper, S. C., *Ethics*, New York: Appleton, 1960.
Stevenson, C. L., *Ethics and Language*, New Haven: Yale, 1944. (Paperback.)
Toulmin, S., *Reason in Ethics*, Cambridge at the University Press, 1950. (Paperback.)

CHAPTER 28

The Scientific Status
of
the Behavioral Studies

Before the questions raised in the preceding discussions can be met, it would seem necessary to ask whether the affairs of men can indeed be handled "scientifically." Folklore would seem to challenge that possibility, and on this score folklore would find itself in alliance with much of philosophy and science.

It will be remembered that in earlier chapters we have used "science" to refer to a method, and have suggested that to employ the term in an unqualified and, as it were, ceremonial sense is to court the dangers of transforming science itself into folklore. These earlier discussions also tried to pinpoint the meaning of scientific method, particularly in the context of the rise of mathematics and the physical sciences in the seventeenth century and of the subsequent development of other sciences, especially biology in the nineteenth century. It was also noted that "scientific method" does not constitute a master plan or a single model, and if the phrase does indeed suggest such a plan or model, then it can lead only to oversimplification. For, as in any inquiry, the procedures of science are reformulated in the course of inquiry, and they change as the subject matter changes.

Are these procedures generous enough to stretch beyond the physical and biological world? Is there, indeed, a science of man and society? May we speak of the social *sciences* or only of the social *studies*? The issue is a crucial one and it has occasioned a highly illuminating debate. Certainly it has provided one of the more exciting chapters in the philosophy of science.

What is at issue here is far more than commonplaces about the greater complexity of social phenomena and the impossibility of putting individuals and societies into test tubes. To be sure, no responsible writer would wish to ignore or minimize the problems posed by the complexity of man and society—all the more so since in the early history of the social sciences there was a tendency to oversimplify. Nor would serious students of society deny that their problem is immeasurably complicated by their inability to create the laboratory version of, say, Huxley's *Brave New World* to see what would in fact happen to the hapless members of such a society. But the problems here are problems connected with differences of *degree*—degrees of complexity and degrees of precision. Even if the proposition "Capital punishment fails to deter" cannot be confirmed as precisely as the proposition "Heated objects expand," significant confirmation is nevertheless attainable.

Much more serious are a number of considerations which suggest differences in the data and methods of the behavioral disciplines rendering them *inherently unamenable* to scientific treatment. Social phenomena are said to be different in *kind* from the data studied by the natural sciences. The first of these considerations is embraced under what has come to be known as the "sociology of knowledge."

Sociology of Knowledge

Even though Karl Mannheim may not be called the father of the sociology of knowledge[1] (a title which belongs more properly to Karl Marx), the term is inseparably associated with his name. In his now classic *Ideology and Utopia*,[2] Mannheim sought to show how thought is rooted in action and in group existence. Not unlike the American instrumentalists referred to in Part III (of whom Europeans rarely take cognizance) he wrote that "It is the impulse to act which first makes the objects of the world accessible to the acting subject, and it may be further that it is

---

[1] In this country the phrase also refers to a straightforward branch of sociology, dealing with studies of public opinion, mass communication, the growth patterns of significant social concepts, all of which are handled by appropriate techniques which do not necessarily rest upon any particular philosophy of history.

[2] Trans. by Wirth and Shils (New York: Harcourt, Brace & World, 1936). See also his *Man and Society in an Age of Reconstruction* trans. by Shils (New York: Harcourt Brace & World, 1940).

this factor which determines the selection of those elements of reality which enter into thought." (P. 4.) But men do not act, in particular they do not *think*, as solitary individuals.

Mannheim's general thesis, in summary fashion, is this:

(1)   History and social science can never be completely objective since they represent the cultural bias, the perspective, of the historian or the social scientist. "Ideology" is the term which denotes the complex of social ideas resulting from such perspectives.

(2)   But Mannheim was no skeptic. He recognized that a class of "intellectuals" might escape its perspective and appreciate ideas that are "situationally transcendent." "Utopian" is the term he uses for such ideas, ideas which do not necessarily fit in with any particular economic or political interest and which point the way to a better society. It is only when intellectuals, by understanding ideologies alien to their own, can free themselves from their own bias that a new "liberalism" can emerge.

(3)   Such an intellectual role is already played by the natural scientists and the mathematicians, who, because of their subject matter, can transcend, or at least discount, any particular social perspective.

Whether the social scientist can indeed do what the natural scientist is alleged to do is the issue, of course, around which swirls much of the controversy that Mannheim's provocative work has set into motion. The criticism has centered on the vulnerability of Mannheim's logic and terminology; and although the criticism has been acute and, in certain respects unanswerable,[3] it must first be made clear that the Mannheim approach fitted in with some of the great movements in social philosophy. One of them was Marxism.[4] Another was the work of Max Weber, one of the giants of sociological theory, who emphasized the dominance of the social institution and the way it functioned to set the pattern for man's behavior. Related to such an approach was the influential French sociological school of Durkheim and Lévy-Bruhl, except that here the moral and noneconomic aspects of group control were underscored. Other more contemporary

---

[3] Samples of this critical approach will be found in Robert K. Merton, *Social Structure and Social Theory*, rev. ed. (Glencoe: Free Press, 1957), chaps. 7 and 8; Ernest Nagel in *Readings in the Philosophy of Science*, ed. by Feigl & Brodbeck (New York: Appleton-Century-Crofts, 1953), pp. 694–695; Charles Frankel, *The Case for Modern Man* (New York: Harper & Row, 1955), chap. 7; Jacques J. Maquet, *The Sociology of Knowledge* (Boston: Beacon Press, 1951), Part I; F. S. C. Northrop, *Ideological Difference and World Order* (New Haven: Yale, 1949), chaps. 17 and 19; and A. Melden in *Civilization*, ed. by V. Lenzen (Berkeley: University of California Press, 1959), pp. 121–146.

[4] See pp. 386–391 for a discussion of Marxism. It should be noted, however, that although Mannheim was greatly influenced by the class analysis of Marx, he did proceed to criticize a "vulgar" and "dogmatic" Marxism, for example in this passage: "By these [social] groups we mean not merely classes, as a dogmatic type of Marxism would have it, but also generations, status groups, sects, occupational groups, schools, etc." (*Ideology and Utopia*, p. 248.)

positions which seem to gear in with the Mannheim thesis are: the increasing concern in anthropology with culture-bound perception as it is focussed on other cultures and on our own; the corresponding concern in psychology and psychoanalysis with self-knowledge as a means to increased objectivity; and the important, if criticized, theory of Sapir and Whorf that language itself is a determiner of what we see and how we judge— cultures using Indo-European languages will necessarily be different from other cultures, it is held, in the ways in which they perceive the world.

Our particular concern with Mannheim's arguments is to raise the question whether he has undermined the very possibility of social science, since one of the major claims of any enterprise which uses "science" is that it objectively reports what is true. Of course, even in physical science there is what is now recognized as "observer interference," a recognition stemming not only from relativity and quantum theory but also from some very recent studies of the relationships between the human anatomy and the forms taken by scientific observations and laws. The philosopher of science, Philip Frank, is now talking about "sociology of science."[5]

Sociology of knowledge, in the Mannheimian sense, could not well appear until men were willing to agree that "truth" as well as "error" was socially conditioned. Men have always accused their opponents of class bias of various kinds (this was Marx's own use of "ideology"), but it is only when we are sophisticated enough to realize the possibility of our own beliefs being a function of certain social arrangements that a philosophy of history like this could be seriously entertained. Not that "sophisticated" necessarily connotes "modern"—the gist of Mannheim's philosophy is found throughout the history of ideas and can be dated back at least to the Greek Sophists of the time of Pericles. Now, as the statement of a general and rather vague relation between ideas and their inevitable social setting, sociology of knowledge would seem to have a strong prima facie appeal. Actually, since the work of Freud as well as of Marx, modern man has tended to go overboard and to attribute not simply his defects to his surroundings and his parents but even, if he is broadminded, his virtues.

---

[5] Confirmation of this would seem to come from the distinguished physicist, Schrödinger: ". . . There is a tendency to forget that all science is bound up with human culture in general, and that scientific findings, even those which at the moment appear to be the most advanced and esoteric and difficult to grasp, are meaningless outside their cultural context. A theoretical science, unaware that those of its concepts and words that have a grip on the educated community and become part and parcel of the general world picture—a theoretical science, I say, where this is forgotten, and where the initiated continue musing to each other in terms that are, at best, understood by a small group of fellow-travellers, will necessarily be cut off from the rest of cultural mankind; in the long run it is bound to atrophy and ossify." (*British Journal of Philosophy of Science*, Vol. 3, No. 109; 1952); quoted by Percy Bridgman in *Determinism and Freedom, in the Age of Modern Science*, ed. by Sidney Hook (New York: New York University Press, 1958), p. 68.

Above all, his "reason" has seemed to succumb to being a mere reflex of early toilet training or of economic stratification. But it is when critics inquire about the *precise* relationship between class and ideas, for instance, that the difficulties begin to intrude.

Mannheim himself was not too helpful here, especially when he agreed to "leave the meaning of 'determination' open."[6] Therefore, the question necessarily presents itself: How specifically do the ideas of men "correspond' with the all-embracing social setting? Is the correspondence genuinely causal (waiving, for the moment, any further comment on "genuinely causal"), or something less demanding? If so, what? It should be added that these are not simply rhetorical questions directed to a possible chink in Mannheim's armor. On the contrary, detailed empirical investigation can be devised, and has long since been implemented, to determine the particular ways in which science is or is not affected by its perspective. A contention such as Mannheim's, plausible as it may be, cannot stand or fall on the ground of a warm or cool feeling about it. The relationship between ideas and their cultural setting can be established or discounted only on the ground of evidence, and this Mannheim has not provided. To be sure, we already are swept into a vortex, because sociology of knowledge, at least in its more iconoclastic moments, will call attention to the fact that the social scientist who is making these "empirical," and by its connotations, "objective," studies is himself the victim of some particular perspective. The logic of this argument will be returned to immediately.

Our present complaint is that Mannheim is guilty of an imprecise vocabulary. Other examples might be added. In some places Mannheim employs "knowledge" as if it embraced all the characteristic activities of man, activities which, of course, are socially determined; yet elsewhere he clearly exempts from subjectivity or relativism the "formal" knowledge of logic and of the exact sciences. The basis for this distinction is never made clear. Again, he tends sometimes to use "perspective" invidiously as equivalent to "incorrect," which would be counter to the very thesis of sociology of knowledge. It introduces, moreover, still another criticism: The very fact that we can detect bias, shows that we are capable of discounting it.

There is a nice logical predicament here. Is the sociologist of knowledge himself trapped in a perspective? If he is, then his very theory must bear the stamp of relativism, and so cannot be legitimately proposed as an objective generalization; if he is not, then other social scientists, too, may be exempt from a partial and distorted point of view, and the theory loses

---

[6] Cf. Merton, *op. cit.*, p. 255. The term Mannheim most frequently uses to stand for the relationship between ideas and their social nexus is *Entsprechung* or "correspondence," but the various usages of the term hover between out-and-out causal linkage, harmony, the focus of attention, in sympathy with the interest of; and this list is by no means complete. (Cf. Maquet, *op. cit.*, pp. 31–32.)

its applicability as a general formula. This kind of dilemma is part of the problem of the definition of a logical class or a set. Is such a class or set to be defined as including itself or not? For example, on an otherwise blank sheet of paper this sentence is written. "Every sentence on this page is false." Here is a genuine paradox.[7] If the sentence is true, it is false; and if false, true. There is no escape, for the class here clearly includes itself, unless we specifically exempt the sentence itself from the conclusion. But this would make the illustration meaningless.

The problem here is as old as that of Epimenides the Cretan, who said, "All Cretans are liars." Like the above paradox, this, too, is a self-refuting proposition, since Epimenides was a Cretan and therefore a liar; so his statement is not true and not all Cretans are liars. We go round and round. Yet what Epimenides clearly meant was that Cretans, in general, were not to be trusted, not that every last one of them lied upon every occasion. In terms of this particular warning, the class does not include all members of it, for example, Epimenides himself. Even though, technically, a proposition like this is self-refuting, its clear and ordinary meaning is to the effect that the statement is not to be tarred with its own brush. Consider certain classic examples: David Hume warned his readers against the blandishments of reason, yet he himself shrewdly used reason to make his point. The same with Henri Bergson: Despite his elevation of intuition over analysis, much of his work is a model of analytical reasoning. Are Hume and Bergson to be regarded as simply being hoist with their own petards?

Now let us reconsider Karl Mannheim. The judgment that the historian and the social scientist are the victims of perspective, and the judgment that they know this to be the case, cannot both stand together, it is alleged. One or the other must give over. Yet, surely, this is a rather cheap triumph, slick rather than persuasive. It is the kind of logical riposte that may truly be regarded as immature. For, to put it rather inelegantly, we have to give the philosopher a break. When he says "All men are liars," "All reason is suspect," even "There is no appeal beyond ordinary language"—when his own language is cultivated Oxonian, we must understand that his particular statement needs to be exempted from his own formula. (After all, Marx himself was a bourgeois and Mannheim a social theorist.) If we do not understand this, there is no point in reading him. The argument that a man always tends to refute himself when he proposes general observations like these is more facile than compelling.

What is vulnerable about the Mannheim thesis is rather that, like some other familiar theories, it presents a single-cause explanation and thus overstates its case. Writers such as Mannheim or Marx or Freud, to mention only a few of the more distinguished names, seem to be saying

---

[7] For students interested in logic, it may be mentioned that Bertrand Russell's celebrated theory of types is an attempt to dispose of this kind of paradox.

"All A is——," when what they mean, and undoubtedly could justify, is rather that "Some A is——," or even "Most A is ——." These latter statements, however, are not so dramatic, and might seem too modest to qualify as a philosophy of history or as an all-embracing theory of human behavior. Indeed, what has actually happened, in the case of Mannheim, for example, is that the more modest statement of his claim has tended to stimulate significant research, especially in the area of culture-bound perceptions; but this is a far cry from the literal and more pretentious thesis that the presence of a social perspective precludes the possibility of a science of society.

Such a thesis ignores the facts of scientific practice. Scientific knowledge, like any other, is inescapably selective and fallible, but to conclude that there can therefore be no reliable knowledge is to make an unscientific demand for omniscience. There *are* established devices for discounting bias, whether it be sociological, psychological, or even statistical. These self-correcting procedures have been built into the very structure of science. To argue that, nevertheless, there is no *certain* way of completely discounting bias, if only in an instrument, is unexceptionable but idle. To take it seriously would be, again, to block the path of inquiry. In short, "objectivity" is not impossible to achieve operationally; nor is the possibility of objectivity dependent solely on erecting a grandiose perspective of perspectives. "Objectivity" is a working technique which even the social sciences have well learned to employ. "Sociology of knowledge" is not a death warrant for social science; it may instead be an invitation to a more precise and more specific study of the conditions of inquiry.

There Are No Social Laws

A second basic difference between natural and social science is presumed to lie in the fact that, since historical and social phenomena are unique and nonrecurrent, whereas scientific laws are of the nature of universal statements, there can be no true laws—and therefore no genuine science —of social behavior. One of the defining criteria of scientific method, the subsuming of data under laws, regards this matter of generalizing or of abstraction as crucial. For example, were chemical elements x, y, and z to produce compound m on Mondays, Wednesdays, and Fridays, compound n on Tuesdays, Thursdays, and Saturdays, but never anything on Sundays, and if each month the sequence tended to vary, there would simply be no science of chemistry. Even if a statistical account of these reactions were to be plotted carefully and we found ourselves with a full record of a series of particular events, we might be able to publish some interesting distribution tables, but the absence of discoverable regularities and therefore of the possibility of prediction of effects, would preclude the development of what we understand as science.

At this point we need to distinguish between history and the social sciences. The relation between them is thorny, and the discipline of history can just as easily be assigned to the humanities as to the behavioral studies. (However, some recent books have suggested that history can ignore the findings of sociology, or even of psychiatry, only at a calculated risk).[8] The issue here may be illustrated by the simple observation that the historian is interested, say, in the Massacre of St. Bartholomew rather than in massacres at large; and his invoking of general social laws, if any, would be aimed at illuminating some particular event. Furthermore, history is cumulative. For example, the Russian revolutionaries were *aware* of what the French revolutionaries had done. This is as important as noting that while the missiles fired in the French and Russian revolutions described the same parabolic trajectories, the social "explosions" they detonated were quite different from each other.

It is not necessary here to develop the particular problems of history vis-à-vis the social sciences. Nor can there be any serious questioning of the undoubted uniqueness of the historical and, possibly, the social event. But it would be only shortsighted to deny to such events *any* traffic with universals. The behavior of crowds as compared with that of individuals; the influence of the years of infancy upon personality; the effects of a lowering of the interest rate or of the price of gold—these phenomena clearly approach the nature of law-like statements.

In a converse manner, physics has come to deal more and more with "groups" of events, for example, the statistical approach in dealing with quantum behavior, and the substitution of high probability equations for the regular uniformities of classical physics. If one employs the technical and somewhat dated terms "ideographic" (applying to what is unique), and "nomothetic" (what is repeatable and therefore predictable), then it might be argued that no science is purely one or the other. The distinguished logician and philosopher of science, Ernest Nagel, has called this particular distinction between ideographic and nomethetic oversimplified. For, in the homely words of Professor Adolph Grünbaum, "Things are tough all over." That is to say, there is no watertight insulation between theoretical and experimental science on the one hand, and comparative and historical science on the other. This does not mean that the two flow together; only that the unqualified separation of the "lawful" and the "lawless" is unjustified.

Generality and abstraction are indeed difficult to achieve in the social

---

8 Compare, for example, *American History and the Social Sciences*, ed. by Edward N. Saveth (New York: Free Press, 1965); and *Sociology and History: Theory and Research*, ed. by Werner J. Cahnman and Alvin Boskoff (New York: Free Press, 1965). See also J. H. Randall's "History and the Social Sciences," in *Readings in the Philosophy of Science*, ed. by P. P. Wiener (New York: Scribner's, 1953), espec. pp. 315–318.

disciplines but they cannot be ruled out in an a priori manner as impossible. There is a similar general pattern that may apply to the scientific enterprise, but all the details of that pattern do not have to be duplicated in every area. In social science, for instance, the patterns would have to be intricate and complex, dealing chiefly with interrelationships of a holistic or *Gestalt* character—which means relationships concerned with whole units and not simply with fragments. But this is also the case elsewhere. Albert Einstein and Leopold Infeld in their book, *The Evolution of Physics*, argue that the concept of "field" is of the highest significance in physics, for example, a field of force such as a magnetic or gravitational field. For in a field (a "social" situation), physical "particles" act differently: some of them may even be said to be constituted by the field. An electron outside the orbit of an atom acts differently from one in the orbit, although "outside" and "inside" in this connection are slippery concepts. It would be equally difficult to speak of individual persons apart from or outside the group to which they belong. The question here is not whether one type of science is borrowing from another, but whether it is possible to lay down a rigid separation between the unique and the repeatable so that one of them is and the other is not admitted into the precincts of science. The answer would appear to be negative.

One of the difficulties in this whole matter of the relation between natural and social science is that the early social sciences, as might have been expected, tended to ape, in a literal fashion, the regnant ideals of natural science—at least of the philosophers of natural science—of the late nineteenth and early twentieth centuries. These ideals were generally oriented toward postivism, mechanism, and "unity of science"—the last, prominent in the work of men like Otto Neurath and the early Rudolph Carnap. These two insisted that all science had to be adapted, at least linguistically, to the structure of physical science. The trouble was, as Professor Lewis Beck has carefully pointed out,[9] that social science was engaged in copying a natural science whose reductionistic bias was already becoming obsolete. This has always been a problem for the social scientist, how to respond to a prestigious idea in its ascendancy. At one time all science, natural or social, had to be mechanical like Newton's, or, at a later time, evolutionary like Darwin's. The same is true today in the use of the almost universal terms "field" and "axiomatics" (the study of the basic assumptions of any discipline), and in the desperate attempts to force every study into mathematical form. The issue, like that in the preceding paragraph, is to avoid a strong disjunction between "either-or." Social science cannot slavishly follow natural science; nor can natural

---

[9] "The Natural Science Ideals in the Social Sciences," *Scientific Monthly*, Vol. 68 (1949), pp. 386–394.

science, in which the criteria of scientific method are so clearly etched, be ignored. Furthermore, natural science in turn may adopt, and has adopted, concepts and techniques of the social disciplines. If some forms of social analysis are not particularly amenable to mathematical formulation, still, attention must be called to the increasingly important place of mathematics in social science, perhaps most prominently displayed in the comparatively new disciplines of econometrics and anthropometrics. There are a number of institutes for the mathematical study of social science, and particular attention is being paid by mathematicians, logicians, and economists to the mathematics of choice and decision.

Social Theory is More like Philosophy

A third alleged disqualification of the social field from scientific pretensions is found, among other shrewd arguments, in the work of an English philosopher, Peter Winch,[10] which may serve almost as a paradigm for an entire position. His contention is that social theory is—or should be—allied with philosophy instead of with the sciences. To understand this contention we must first be clear as to what he means by "philosophy." Winch espouses the contemporary Anglo-American interpretation of philosophy as the explicator of "meaning," the meaning of anything. The function of philosophy, to put it differently, is to make intelligible whatever it touches, which certainly includes the realm of social phenomena. It is not the complexity of these phenomena, together with their intransigent behavior, that remove them from the domain of science, but the sticky problem of what is meant by concepts like "social," "organic," "free," "unique," and the like. What counts as meaningful human or social behavior must first be established before any problem of methodology can arise, and the discipline which establishes such meanings and therefore has logical precedence, according to Winch and many others, is philosophy.

To take trivial and well-worn examples: "How many hairs must be missing before a man is counted as bald?" "How many grains make a heap?" Unless we understand the principles behind such deceptively simple questions we are in danger of falling into false analogy, the bane of much of social science. For instance, to compare a hurt cat with a damaged tree, or to see a fundamental similarity between a dog learning a trick and a man learning to understand—these are the traps an unphilosophical and therefore imprecise social theory falls into at its beginning, before any particular methodology is introduced.

At least this is Winch's position, as are the last two examples. He would

---

[10] *The Idea of a Social Science* (New York: Humanities Press, 1958).

undoubtedly feel that talk of bees or ants comprising a "society," or of computer machines correcting their own "mistakes" and even developing "neuroses," would be still more serious errors, as serious as to regard man as no more than a data-producing animal. And yet learning theory in physiology and psychology has developed into a powerful science and the analogies found within the patterns of mammalian learning are far from "literary" or fanciful. Experimentation with rats certainly does not exhaust the field of psychology, but to ignore the striking parallels between human and infrahuman behavior is scarcely more tenable than to explain away all human conduct as simply maze-solving. In the same way, the analogies between brains and computers are hardly to be considered as science fiction. Some of the most exacting work in all biological science is to be found in the increased knowledge of cortical functioning, knowledge which is definitely connected with that of electronic circuits.[11] In other words, the arguments against the false analogy are not always or necessarily stronger or less false than the analogy itself.

The gist of Winch's argument is that the basic concepts of the field of human behavior, or of any other field, are—or should be—determined by the enterprise of philosophy and not by that of science. (The word "enterprise" must be stressed, for the actual analysts or determiners of meaning are not necessarily the professional practitioners of philosophy.) For science is a science of "something" and the determiners of that "something" need to be outside the ambit of science, if only for this particular purpose of determining limits. Once a field is established, the function of science is then to contrive and use a methodology. The meaning of "prayer," for example, is determined not by sociology or psychology but by religion, or, more accurately, the philosophy of religion.

Another point made by Winch is to insist that social affairs are more of the order of the humanities than of the sciences; and in this contention he is joined by the distinguished English anthropologist, E. E. Evans-Pritchard and by a number of American anthropologists such as the late Robert Redfield. One reason given for this contention is that social relations are less like a collision of mechanical forces (and even less like a parallelogram) than they are like the exchange of ideas in a conversation. This is why, it is claimed, *significant* predictions in social science are impossible and mechanical prediction trivial or irrelevant. To predict a poem would be to write it, and to predict an invention would be to make it. Something like insight or intuition would be necessary here and this is supposedly outside the jurisdiction of science.

---

11 See, for example, *The Brain as a Computer,* by F. H. George (New York: Oxford, 1961); and D. E. Woolridge, *The Machinery of the Brain* (New York: McGraw-Hill, 1963).

How are we to appraise this whole argument? It is an argument which, in its ramifications, goes far beyond the limit of Winch's book. It really cannot be fully judged solely in the present context, but something can be said here. That clarity and intelligibility of concepts in any field is of paramount concern is almost axiomatic; without this there is really nothing to begin with. And that philosophy ever since Socrates has had an especial and peculiar concern with meaning and definition is equally unexceptionable; but is it a sufficient concern, at least for science?

Take the conception, widely accepted, that the subject matter of social science must be regarded as organismic or synthetic, that, to put it simply, its whole is more than a sum of its parts. (See Part III, pp. 353–358, 363.) It may well be that this is a necessary condition for legitimate research in the life sciences, and it may even be that acceptance of such a condition is a useful prophylaxis against the reductionism implicit in false analogies and mechanical models. But, even so, the conception carries us very little forward in devising an acceptable scientific technique. Now, on this point Winch would certainly agree, since he regards science as dealing with technique rather than with meaning. But to bifurcate the enterprise of science in this fashion is awkward at best; and, at worst, it would rightfully be regarded by the practising scientist as one more example of philosophic impertinence. The practising scientist would certainly point out that the meaning of his discipline and of its vocabulary cannot be imposed *ab extra* nor its adequacy judged *ab extra* but must derive from the very subject matter under inquiry. To say that the meaning of prayer, for example, cannot be defined by a social psychologist qua social psychologist, or that if he defines it sympathetically he would not be doing science, is to beg the question; an advance definition is formulated on the basis of something like intuition and the whole case is thereby prejudged.

Charles Peirce pointed out that the prime fallacy of intuitionism, as of any other form of immediate knowledge, is the contention that before we can learn, something must already be known, and known, preferably, for certain. This goes against the entire history of inquiry, for inquiry builds upon whatever prior beliefs or conjectures may be available. To be sure, this available material, even as a starting point for inquiry, is carefully scrutinized and refined; but it does not have to be certain any more than the final results of inquiry have to be certain: fallibility is canonical for scientific method. However, it is far from canonical to exclude by antecedent definition any area from scientific investigation; in Peirce's celebrated phrase, this would be "to block the path of inquiry."

Another reason for denying scientific status to the study of society is based on the assertion that because man possesses free will and free will represents a breach of causal law, generalizations of a scientific nature cannot be made about man. If generalizations were made, man, it is supposed, would be turned into a dehumanized, predictable animal. He would become merely a "thing" to be manipulated and exploited. Only such enterprises as religion, philosophy, literature and the arts are capable of gaining an insight into what is truly "human" rather than infrahuman in man's experience. This approach, welcome as it is for paying tribute to the humane studies, shows a failure to understand the nature of science.

This problem of determinism and freedom is so important that the following chapter will be devoted to it. However, two points may be noted here. First, it is quite possible that freedom involves no breach in the universal operation of causality, so that generalizations having the character of scientific laws may be formulated concerning all behavior, including that area of behavior in which man makes free choices. Many contemporary philosophers have taken this position. Second, even if freedom does imply a contracausal position, as some have argued, the area of human behavior in which such exercise of freedom occurs is admittedly very constricted—limited to those infrequent occasions in which we are confronted by a true moral dilemma—and hence irrelevant to the great body of behavior. Here, in such behavior, the social sciences, may prove entirely relevant. But these issues will be explored presently.

The Scientific Status of Behavioral Studies

We turn now to a contrasting approach. This is that social science, if not a branch of natural science, is closely related to it. There are a number of variations on this theme. For one thing, there is the flat statement that since natural science is the very model of science, any discipline that claims to be scientific must perforce claim also to be a natural science. This position is taken by many social scientists, but in most cases certain qualifications are added. For example, one familiar addendum is that the claim does not necessarily mean a mechanistic or "behavioristic" interpretation of social relationships. Such a qualification, to illustrate, is made by the influential British anthropologist, S. F. Nadel.[12]

When a social scientist holds that anthropology, or any other social study, is a natural science, he by no means also holds that it necessarily follows any single model such as that found useful in the physical sciences. He suggests instead, that social science must follow the general canons of scientific procedure, which theoretically apply to any universe of discourse. As a matter of fact, Nadel makes this quite explicit when he observes that "society" is a concept not subject to complete analysis, since the smallest "atomic" isolate, the individual, would still have to be considered as functioning in a social situation and as meaningless without it.

---

[12] In *The Foundations of Social Anthropology* (Glencoe: Free Press, 1953).

In short, to say anthropology, or any other social study, is a natural science is not at the same time to accept a completely analytical or mechanical view of either natural or social science.

This matter of analysis should be pursued a little further, since it may be a stumbling block in the attempt to certify social science. One of the major differences between natural and social science has long been said to be the impossibility of identifying stable units of analysis in social science similar to those found in the life and physical sciences. Almost any concept of natural science which comes to mind can serve as an example, an example of that which is uniform, repetitious, and ubiquitous: elements, chemical substances, enzymes, chromosomes, neurons, to go no further. These are the constants, the very categories, that make controlled manipulation possible. It has been argued, as was noted a few pages back, that social science can lay claim to no such constants. It has also been argued that when units of analysis have been proposed in the social sciences, they have been imposed upon the data rather than derived from the data. For instance, when intelligence testing first became prominent in the years following World War I, "intelligence" was regarded as a kind of fixed quality which then was to be tested in various ways, chiefly in terms of verbal ability, arithmetical insight, power to see analogies, and so on. In recent years, however, "intelligence" has come to be defined as "that which intelligence tests test." Even if this sounds circular, it is looked upon as a more sophisticated approach, because the unit of analysis now depends upon the data and can therefore serve its purpose, say, in the psychology of learning or in college placement, with more accuracy and fruitfulness.

Much of recent theoretical work in the various social sciences has been directed toward the search for units of analysis which are derived from empirical data and in this way better grounded than some of the traditional concepts like "the state," "society," or "the individual." There are, for example, in anthropology and sociology concepts like "culture" (Kroeber and many others); "function" or "functional analysis" (Weber, Kluckhohn, and others); "institutional analysis" (Merton); "social action" (Parsons); "social structure" (Radcliffe-Brown); also, "personality" in psychology; "decision-making" in political science; "games-analysis" in economics and elsewhere; in structural linguistics the "phonemes" (basic sound patterns) and general syntax, which seem to fit any language; and "general systems analysis" in all the social sciences. In each of these suggestions, a major consideration has been that the units of analysis—and, of course, there are many others—are matters for investigation instead of something taken for granted in advance of investigation.

Now, these illustrations are but a bare, undeveloped mention, the purpose of which is to indicate one direction taken by social science in line with the general march of natural science. Another direction is the so-called "behavioral" approach, which in the period since World War II has occupied a prominent if not a pre-emptive place in contemporary social science, particularly in political research. A credo of the behavorial position, that is, a statement of its assumptions and objectives, would go something like this: a search for regularities in social behavior, regularities verging on the law-like statements demanded by scientific method; an emphasis on verification, specifically verification of the consequences deduced from hypotheses; a development of self-conscious and refined techniques of investigation; a desire to systematize and integrate the whole area of social science; and the divorce of values from empirical research, or, in political language, the strict separation of judgments of policy from those matters undergoing "scientific" examination. It will be evident that this orientation is a major effort to bring social science into conformity with the procedures of natural science.

Concluding Remarks

The efforts to tie social and natural science closely together still require modesty and caution.[13] For one thing, there is a general lack in the social sciences of synthesizing and overarching hypotheses, "overarching" in the sense in which Newton's laws embraced those of Kepler and Galileo. Yet, in order to be fair, one should take into account the youth of social science. Newton came at the end, not at the beginning of the first Scientific Revolution. What social science needs and is getting at this state of its development, as Robert Merton, the American sociologist has said, is hypotheses in the "middle range." Until these are available and until methods of investigation are more firmly established, it would be premature to demand grand hypotheses with a cosmic sweep.

A related point has to do with the testing of hypotheses. In natural science it has usually been possible to test hypotheses one after the other, whereas in social science every hypothesis seems to involve collateral ones —generalizations about individuals point to social situations, and, conversely, theories in the social field are inescapably intertwined with those based on the nature of the individual. Yet it need only be remarked again that "Things are tough all over." Even in contemporary physical theory whole families of hypotheses need to be handled together, as in the relation of wave mechanics to quantum mechanics, and of cosmogony to nuclear physics.

And now, the important question: Must the social sciences avoid judg-

---

[13] Note the important treatment in Henry Margenau's *Ethics and Science* (Princeton: Van Nostrand, 1964), espec. chaps. 1, 2, and 7.

ments of value? We have already noticed several times that the general enterprise of science seems overtly and with a kind of public parade of purity, to eschew any commerce with values. The claim, in the social as well as the natural field, is for objectivity and neutrality, and this claim is not restricted to positivists or behavioralists only, but appears—or let us say "appeared," because there seems to be some evidence of a change of heart—to be a central pillar of the whole scientific structure. However, this claim is subject to certain serious reservations.

We are beginning to see that the social sciences, by their very nature, cannot be entirely value-free. This has nothing to do with "moralizing" or even "social welfare." But basic concepts like "social" itself, or "primitive," "normal," "pathological," even "culture," inevitably carry with them evaluative judgments. Indeed, a social institution, by its very nature, has normative connotations, since it implies purposive functioning and standardized modes of behavior. This may seem too pat although it would not be an easy argument to contravene. More to the point, perhaps, is that scientific method itself, even in its purest natural expression, is not entirely value-free, and many scientists have come to acknowledge this, if only in recognizing that there are "good" and "bad" solutions to problems. This is not a play on words any more than it would be to recognize that the objective and disinterested pursuit of truth is itself a high priority "good." Qualities like disinterestedness, publicity, and sharing of results, universalism, an organized skepticism—these, the very mores of the scientific enterprise, are accepted in great part on moral, even aesthetic grounds. "Scientific method . . . represents nothing less than the good manners of the mind," states Jerome Wiesner, the late President Kennedy's Special Assistant for Science and Technology.

But above all is the matter of selectivity. The analysis of the problem, the selection of the variables, the experimental design are all dependent upon the choices of the scientist, so that, as the American social psychologist, Hadley Cantril, shows (and his observation has been commonly adopted among scientists), scientific "objectivity" refers to the accepted rules of empirical research only *after* the above decisions have been made. In those decisions a number of executive scientific values play their part, such as the ones suggested above, to which could be added parsimony or economy of assumptions, elegance, fruitfulness, and many others. To neglect decisions like these would be to remove much of the force and appeal of the scientific venture.

The issue may be put another way. The scientist is not impressed by just any old fact. Not everything is taken into account. Certain data are accepted, others are rejected, still more ignored. As with his choice of what he feels to be significant problems, so with the scientist's choice of significant data: more accurately, those data are significant that are selected. It is not to much to say that data (facts) are those objects and events which the scientist has agreed to choose as important. The facts of chemistry are not the facts of the everyday world—acids and bases are "facts" for chemistry, hard and soft are "facts" for the everyday world. But neither are the facts of everyday common sense entirely unselective: many allegedly nonfactual things are omitted—dreams, hallucinations, ghosts, even neuroses. They are omitted because, in an admittedly arbitrary manner, they are judged to be not entirely relevant, and need not be reckoned with as sticks and stones and rain have to be reckoned with. In a similar way, the facts of American history will probably not include your Aunt Minnie. But her facts, too, are limited and determined by what she must take into account as important to her. In this way the gap between facts and values begins to diminish. Facts themselves become a kind of value because of this act of preference, an act which effectively prevents the layman or the scientist from being completely neutral, much less indifferent.

This point must not be caricatured. It scarcely implies travesties such as that of the scientist loading his dice or preferring alkalies to acids because, for aesthetic or political reasons, he does not want his litmus paper to turn pink. If terms like "objective" and "critical" are appropriate to scientific method, as they surely are, their meaning goes beyond mere not-taking-for-granted or impatience-to-be-shown. They are not synonyms for indifference or neutrality, but, instead, turn upon the scientific ability to select, to choose between alternatives, to say "yes" here and "no" there. And to choose is to establish or to employ a set of norms. Scientific objectivity is not equivalent to not-giving-a-damn. That it demands the discounting of personal prejudice is elementary and unexceptionable, but to take this as assumed should not reduce it to triviality. Objectivity becomes trivial when it becomes neuter.

From the historical view, it can also be argued that scientific method itself is one of the greatest of human values, a rather young and fresh one at that. Much of it is as young as the middle class and the New World and the national states of Europe. The revolution which propelled it into life saw also the birth of the great trading cities, and the rise of new theories of business and government, not to mention the rebirth of the humane arts themselves. Its method throughout is the product of historical processes, the end result of social decisions, some of them involving bare economic choices, others resting upon the most precious and intimate of human reasonings, but all of them deeply involved with evaluations. Natural science had to win its privileged position. Social science is in the process of winning its own. Man has decided, at least in certain areas, to solve his problems through the use of intelligent control, free inquiry, and self-correcting instruments. Can these values of scientific inquiry themselves be applied to other values? Let us postpone a response to that question for a while.

In a way, of course, the whole present discussion has been somewhat gratuitous. For social science is here, undoubtedly to stay. To argue whether it should give over to philosophy, or that it is vitiated at the start by indelible relativism, or that it is or is not like natural science, or that the human animal and its social arrangements can never under any circumstances be handled by scientific techniques—all this may remind us that it was once demonstrated on the strictest aerodynamical principles that a bumblebee could not fly. True, the social sciences are young and their subject matter is extraordinarily complex, so it is scarcely unexpected that a firm consensus among economists or psychologists or among political and social experts has not been achieved; although we must not allow an observation like this to blind us to the large and conspicuous areas of agreement that are found among social scientists. Social scientists are now very self-conscious about their methodology, and this is a sign of growing maturity in any discipline; they are also willing to extend their investigations as far as they will go, reaching into some of the most fragile and intimate of human relationships, and this is a sign of prospect and adventure, entailing not a little risk.

Having said this, we must, nevertheless, not minimize the prodigious hurdles a fully developed social science will have to overcome. Our institutions sometimes seem geared to prescientific and nonscientific attitudes, and these institutions include education as well as politics and the press. The entrenched habit throughout is to approach social issues in a polemical vein, or, at best, through "discussion." Too often this means, as Barbara Wooton, the English economist, has lamented, merely the parade of two contrasting errors; or, if that is too strong, the flat presentation of all-out "solutions" instead of the investigation of comparative strengths and weaknesses. "Socialism" and "capitalism" for example, are something to be for or against, not handled in the way hypotheses or theories in science are intended to be handled; and both the "fors" and the "againsts" are equally culpable. Discussion is too often of "isms"—a highly suspect suffix—carried on in an imprecise language and with a maximum of overgeneralization.

It may be argued, of course, that no other attitude could have been expected in a field as new, vested, and as complicated as that of social issues. The trouble is that a decision to this effect seems already to have been made, and made on a priori grounds without having been subjected to any serious investigation. Indeed, such an attitude has itself become a conspicuous item of the folklore, seemingly uninfluenced and sometimes even reinforced by the march of social science. So, the problem of the amenability of social affairs to scientific method is a real one; whether it is soluble is another question.

Selected Readings

Braybrooke, D., ed., *Philosophical Problems in the Social Sciences*, New York: Macmillan, 1965. (Paperback.)

Brown, Robt., *Explanation in Social Science*, London: Aldine Press, 1963.

Durkheim, E., *The Rules of Sociological Method*, Glencoe: The Free Press, 1950. (Friendship Press paperback.)

Frank, P., ed., *The Validation of Scientific Theories*, New York: Collier, 1961. (Paperback.)

Gibson, Q., *The Logic of Social Inquiry*, New York: The Humanities Press, 1960.

Jarvie, I. C., *The Revolution in Anthropology*, New York: The Humanities Press, 1964.

Kaplan, A., *The Conduct of Inquiry*, San Francisco: Chandler Publishing Co., 1964.

Kaufmann, F., *Methodology in the Social Sciences*, New York: The Humanities Press, 1958.

Lerner, D., ed., *The Human Meaning of the Social Sciences*, Gloucester: Peter Smith, Publisher, 1960. (Meridian paperback.)

Merton, R., *Social Theory and Social Structure*, rev. ed., Glencoe: Free Press, 1957.

Natanson, M. ed., *Philosophy of the Social Sciences*, New York: Random House, 1963.

Rex, J., *Key Problems in Sociological Theory*, New York: The Humanities Press, 1961.

Rose, A., *Theory and Method in the Social Sciences*, Minneapolis: University of Minnesota Press, 1954.

Weber, Max, *The Methodology of the Social Sciences*, Glencoe: Free Press, 1949.

CHAPTER 29

Freedom
and
Determinism

One of the many hurdles faced by the growing sciences of man is that, if finally successful, these sciences will have turned man—it is said—into a calculable machine, or, if one prefers, into something resembling a completely conditioned rat. His precious freedom will have evaporated. Belief in human freedom is a central tenet of the accepted wisdom about man. Moreover, few beliefs are more important than this, and few have attracted more attention among laymen as well as among philosophers. Our whole attitude toward crime and punishment, for example, or toward the problems of unemployment and the needy, may well be influenced by the way the issue of freedom is resolved. The problem is not merely academic; it moves quite beyond the tensions between science and the folklore.

Despite—or because of—this concern, the meaning of terms like "freedom," "free will," "determinism," "cause," "law," "compulsion," "responsibility," and the like has been blurred almost beyond repair; one of the major contributions of modern analytical philosophy has been to attempt to sharpen some of these concepts into usable form. Even so, the sharpness of a tool does not guarantee that it will cut at the right place. It is by no means radical to suggest that a mass of material could be amputated from the great body of "free will" discussion without any noticeable loss. Yet the literature on the subject seems, if anything, to be increasing.[1]

The Prima Facie Arguments

If a statistical summation were possible, it would be pretty certain that on this matter of freedom the split between layman and scientist would be pronounced. Theologians would, in general, incline toward the "free will" taken for granted by the so-called average man. However, the lines are by no means clearly drawn. Although most laymen seem to believe in free will, many are persuaded, for one reason or the other, that all of man's actions are completely determined. And while most scientists appear to be on the side of determinism, what with the varying interpretations of the "uncertainty" principles in modern physics, the line-up is by no means solid. Nevertheless, our rough polarization still holds.

What has convinced the ordinary man that he is "free"—in some as yet unspecified way—is undoubtedly the experience of doing what he wants to do. If he wishes to come or to go, to get up or remain down, to eat or not, he proceeds as he wills to proceed. He does not feel constrained or compelled by any force not of his own volition. And this is a strong prima facie ("at first appearance") argument. To use a technical term, he is "phenomenologically" free, which means simply that his immediate experience is what he judges by. It is undeniable that he does feel free. To say, "But you are not really free, you only think so," will not usually impress him. And were our hypothetical layman to go on and immerse himself in certain streams of contemporary thought he should find ultra-sophisticated justification for his own untutored intuitions. The phenomenological strain in modern existentialism (see pp. 440–442) is all to the effect of certifying the appeal of direct experience, which stands impressively as a testimony to some deep and significant aspect of our being. But even without going so far, the ordinary man will see little reason to discount what is palpably obvious and uncomplicated—his sense of free decision and the confirmed efficacy of it.

He could go further and support his position by presenting its contrast, for he never feels that he is free in all ways. Freedom has its limits. It is limited when there are no alternatives between which he can choose, or

---

[1] A few selected titles, chiefly of modern works, may be helpful to the student: *Determinism and Freedom in the Age of Modern Science*, ed. by Sidney Hook (New York: New York University Press, 1958); *Freedom and Responsibility*, ed. by Herbert Morris (Stanford: Stanford University Press), 1961; *Free Will*, ed. by J. Walsh and S. Morgenbesser (New York: Prentice-Hall, 1962); *The Idea of Freedom*, Mortimer J. Adler, 2 vols. (New York: Garden City, 1958–1961).

at least no viable alternatives. He does not feel free to choose to be a six-footer when, as an adult, he has stopped at five feet, seven inches. He does not feel free to become young again, much as he might like to. He does not even feel free to drive (being an American) on the left-hand side of the road, or to park next to a fire hydrant. True, here he could still make physical choices leading to catastrophe of varying degree; nevertheless, he *feels* constrained by the law that curtails his options. To put aside the testimony of his own luminous insights, whether of freedom or constraint, would make no sense to our protagonist.

The trouble is that insights are not all the same. Even if the feeling of freedom is common to men, at least to men of modern Western culture (as we believe it to be), it is certainly not universal even in that context. There is also the immediate conviction of fatalism. The intuition that all is somehow set down from eternity and written out specifically in the stars or in the cards, that in war there is a bullet with one's name on it, that premonitions of disaster testify to prearrangement of disaster ("disaster" = against the stars), that do what we will we are fated to have our lucky or unfortunate days, that, in short, ". . . the first morning of creation wrote / What the last dawn of reckoning shall read"—all this is not confined, say, to a Muslim culture or (theologically) to a Calvinist one. There seems to be prima facie phenomenological evidence which tends to contravene the more buoyant feeling of freedom, and in some cultures it is *this* feeling that buttresses the folklore. And even where this is not true, as in our own culture, there is still manifest, if only on occasion, the uneasy and somehow desperate intuition that nothing makes any difference. It may even be that we sometimes want to "escape from freedom" and its anxieties and to rest in willessness.

"Prima facie," we have said, means "at first appearance," and our initial interpretation of it has been that of the *feeling* of freedom. But the phrase also means, as in law, a case so directly established by the evidence that unless rebutted it must stand. Now, the conventional wisdom by no means relies on intuition exclusively. There is a logic to freedom, especially in the moral dimension, which also needs to be presented. For example, were men unfree, what would be the meaning of ethical judgment, of reward and punishment, of the feeling of regret? Further, does not the whole structure of the law rest upon the foundation of human responsibility; were men compelled to act in a completely predictable way, how could they be considered responsible? This, it is said, is not simply a matter of inner persuasion, it is a logical entailment: no control over action, then no responsibility, hence no law or morals.

Before we attempt to clarify some of these terms, we might first attend to an allegedly prima facie argument to precisely the opposite effect. The trouble is, again, that just as intuitions are not all inclined in the same direction, neither are the "first appearances" of argument, that is, those that give a case its initial strength. Consider this familiar argument—one deriving its strength from science—as making such a prima facie case: No event —short of miracles—is uncaused. Or, less stringently, there is a reason why anything happens. The human being is no exception to the domain of universal causation. For example, every individual is completely the product of his heredity and his environment; indeed, what else is there? His acts all come at the end of a long chain of causal connections and no link in that chain can be missing. This position is not quite that of fatalism. Nevertheless, it does imply that any specific act, since it cannot be uncaused, is, according to the principle of sufficient reason, what it is and clearly could not have been otherwise. The principle of sufficient reason admits of no gaps, at least not on theoretical grounds.

Accordingly, any specific act of an individual, however it be judged, is the end product of all that went before. If it be murder, well, his genes or his upbringing or the social background of his formative years or the emotional boiling over which concluded a predictable sequence of inescapable events—these, severally, or alone, are true "causes" of the act, for which act, therefore, the individual person cannot be held responsible. He is the creature of circumstance, of a world he never made.

The same causal-chain argument can be applied as well to the praiseworthy act. Temperament and ability (inherited) plus early training and education (acquired) have conspired to bring about the hero or the genius. He can rightfully take no credit. And if he still *feels* himself culpable or laudable, if he feels free of these causal compulsions, a Spinoza will point out to him the delusion and suggest that a stone thrown into the air and satisying all the points of its preordained parabolic trajectory would feel—if suddenly made self-conscious—that it was flying through the air with the greatest of voluntary ease and coming to rest precisely where it intended to come down. The stone would be mistaken. And so are we.

When two prima facie and seemingly compelling positions collide, it may be suspected that the terms being used need some measure of renovation. The first task of philosophers, or of scientists turned philosophers, has been directed to this end.

Toward a Clarification of Terms

If one could hit upon a single concept for separating, if not the sheep from the goats, at least the folklore and common sense from a more sophisticated approach, it might be that of "causal law." Common sense understands causality largely in terms of what Aristotle called the "efficient cause," that which truly "effects," which "brings out," as the sculptor "causes" the existence of a statue by his efficacious work. When event A causes event B, there is, as it were, something in A, some agency, some power or force, that literally coerces B into existence. If A is a moving billiard ball and B the ball that is hit, then the force in the first is somehow transmitted to the second, causing it to move, and move in a specific way. When I pick up a heavy object and transfer it, I exercise a compelling energy upon the object and actually push it around; and, moreover, I can experience myself exercising such effective power. Contrariwise, when I in turn am pushed around, at least literally, I can clearly feel myself being "effected," being "caused" to move. Events do not happen without a cause, and "cause" appears to denote physical, mechanical compulsion. Other causal connections, not so obviously mechanical, are regarded analogically.

"Law" is another word that has overpowering common-sense connotations, despite its respectable position in the vocabulary of science. The "law of gravitation" seems to suggest a coercive power which brooks no exception. It tends to resemble a statutory or constitutional "law," violation of which demands punishment.[2] In sum, "law" seems to frustrate human will, as when we half-seriously complain that everything we like is illegal, immoral, or fattening.

These unquestionably popular and sensible notions of "cause" and "law" are in flat contradiction with the burden of nearly all modern philosophy and science, and we may expand "modern" now to include the days of David Hume in the eighteenth century. His classic analysis of causality is one of the great moments of philosophy, and it has become almost canonical despite the fact that it flies clearly in the face of common sense. Hume argued that causality is a purely empirical phenomenon, one of sequential order, not one of logical necessity. That is to say, when billiard ball A hits billiard ball B, we merely notice that B moves in an appropriate manner. We observe no "effective" force between them, and the physicist knows of none either. All we, or anyone else, know is that the contact between the two spheres is followed by a certain further movement and by a realigned position of the two objects. When this happens sufficiently without exception, we expect the same phenomenon to recur —and we are not disappointed. The meaning of causality is thus one of sequence not consequence; we cannot legitimately say that B moved

---

[2] As an aside, it may be pointed out that "natural law" derives from Roman Stoic philosophy. In that context it had much relevance, for the Stoic metaphysic postulated an intelligent and well-ordered universe remarkably like the Roman Empire. Indeed, Roman Law was the reflection of Natural Law—perhaps the reverse. In any case, the law of nature had all the attributes of the law of the state: it was compelling, required obedience, and it was "good." And it might be added that the phrases "scientific law" and "law of nature" have never quite emancipated themselves from their juridical and political antecedents.

because it was struck by A, at least if we mean by "because" some necessary connection between the two events. All we can say is that experience has disclosed a certain connection which *we expect* will happen again. The compulsion, if any, is upon our ideas and not upon the objects. We form a habit of anticipation—in modern language, we have become "conditioned"—so that event A will be seen to require event B; but this is an expectation, a psychological impulsion, therefore, and not a physical compulsion. Thus, should we protest, say, that it is the parallelogram of forces which enables us to predict the vector line of the second billiard ball, we will be cautioned to remember that the parallelogram itself is but the memento of our experiences; it is ex post facto and tells us no more than that this is the way motions have been fused and that we can expect the same. Similarly with the expression that "potential" has been changed into "kinetic" energy—these are but symbols putting our experience into usable form. Why it should be this way, and whether it must be this way —these are irrelevant questions which go far beyond the permissible evidence. At least, according to Hume.

For this analysis, and similar ones, Hume has come to be regarded as the father of modern positivism, the view—as we have seen before—that our knowledge, including that of science, deals only with the phenomena of our experience and not with the "real" world itself. But even scientists who reject this position are still Hume's heirs. For scientific laws are now almost universally regarded as *descriptions* of what happens, not *prescriptions* of what has to happen. Or, putting it differently, a law is an hypothesis stating that *if* certain conditions hold, *then* other conditions will also.[3] The law of falling bodies is such an hypothetical statement. Based upon descriptions of past events, those descriptions having been put into simple mathematical form, this particular law states that *if* a body is falling freely, *then* its rate of acceleration will be such-and-such. The law does not report that any particular body is now falling, or when it will fall if it is not, or even that there are any falling bodies at all, much less that some mysterious power compels bodies to travel at the rate of $1/2gt^2$. Nor do Kepler's laws of planetary motion push the heavenly bodies around, or make it licit to push them. They are, once more, descriptions of what paths the satellites of the sun actually do take. Even a scientist like Einstein, who finally rejected positivism and felt that the universe was indeed causally determined, still deprecated the mechanical concept of forces operating compulsively upon bodies. A force, for Einstein and for physicists in general, was a particular mathematical aspect of a field. "Gravitation," for example, does not pull the earth around the sun in a rope-like yo-heave-ho manner. The relation

---

[3] An incisive treatment of this particular point of view will be found in Chapter 6 of *Knowledge and Society* by California Associates in Philosophy (New York: Appleton-Century, 1938).

of earth to its star is established by a calculable "deformation" within a force field; the relation is not one of stress and strain but, in a very general way, one of "statistics."

Natural laws are now regarded as high probability equations, as statistical accountings of observed happenings. Even if now orthodox, this interpretation is certainly not what we should call an item of common sense. Common sense is very persuasive when, as in the experience of astronauts, the *g force* is felt and felt compellingly. But "feeling" is not entirely trustworthy, and its analogue, the push-and-pull concept of cause and of law, is consistently[4] rejected in recent science and philosophy.

But the topic is determinism and freedom. How are they to be handled, at least in the *un*conventional wisdom? "Determinism" seems clearly to be a matter of predictability, of predictability by means of law, so that *if x* is in a state *a*, then it is highly probable that, under certain specified conditions, *x* will move on to state *b*. Thus, iron will expand if sufficiently heated. Is iron then "unfree"? Is it "compelled" to expand? Here is the nub of the problem. Folklore as well as common sense equates freedom with *in*determinism, and compulsion and constraint with causation. However, we have tried to suggest that "law" is descriptive and hypothetical, not compulsive in some unspecified, analogical sense; and that determinism implies predictability on the basis of law. Moreover, where hypothesis, law, and predictability are inadequate (for example, to decide what is the very next word I shall utter), then the concept of "determinism" simply does not apply. To be sure, we can still insist, on what can only be called metaphysical grounds, that there are adequate laws to explain every last phenomenon "if only we knew enough." Now, "If we knew enough we would know enough," is clearly a tautology and does not move us far forward. The real problem is on what grounds we make the assumption that everything is really determined even though this cannot be justified on the basis of extant knowledge. This assumption is palpably metaphysical, or logical, or, in certain cases, even political; in any event, it rests upon what must be considered parascientific grounds, such as that of the principle of sufficient reason or that of universal causation. These are undoubtedly impressive grounds, but they evidently are not in the same category with such simple predictions as that iron will expand if sufficiently heated. The following section will develop this point further.

It has already been suggested that "freedom" is equated in the folk-

---

[4] Consistently but not entirely. A. N. Whitehead, most brilliant of recent metaphysicians, has a completely different approach to causality, one which installs this relationship as primary, as a basic nexus that makes even the perceptual connection between minds and objects secondary. No one can plausibly deny that there is a discrepancy here that has given a certain poignancy to the whole subject; nevertheless, the judgment made above—that causal laws are standardized descriptions which apply hypothetically to recurrent phenomena—still represents the prevailing scientific attitude.

lore with the absence of "determinism." But if the above analysis has any merit, then this too, must be—and has been—amended. As a beginning we might recognize that the terms "free" and "freely" are not absent from the scientist's vocabulary. He uses them to mark out, as it were, the difference between "internal" and "external" causation. For instance, one speaks of the velocity of light in "free" space or of a "freely" moving planet or a "freely" falling body. On the contrary, when light travels through a refracting medium like water, glass, or even air, it is not free, since "outside" forces act upon it. If a planet is deflected from its elliptical path by, say, a hitherto undiscovered planet (as was the case when Neptune and, later, Pluto were found) then, to the degree of deflection from its orbit, the satellite is likewise not moving freely. Nor is a rock in an avalanche. Thus, even when dealing with inanimate objects, it is no contradiction to say that a planet or a photon moves freely and yet is determined—"determined," meaning, it will be remembered, no more (or no less) than that reliable predictions can be made about the position of the planet or the velocity of the photon on the basis of empirically determined laws.

Although analogies are always suspect, if only slightly, we might proceed in the same manner with animate and, more appropriately, self-conscious objects like human beings. They, too, are subject to "internal" and "external" pressures, for example, to being "determined" by their own wishes and purposes, or being "determined" by the opposed wishes and purposes of other individuals or by the obdurate and faceless powers of the world. In the first case there would be no necessary contradiction, it can be argued, between "freedom" and "determinism," since one's actions depended upon causes of one's own contriving. And to be self-determined is not to be unfree. In the second case, there is clearly coercion and compulsion (as well as "determinism") since alien forces are involved. "Freedom," thus, it can be said, is opposed to "compulsion" not to "determinism." But any acute reader will notice at once that we have moved beyond a simple attempt to clarify terms to a conclusion which, to say the least, is controversial. For one is almost constrained to point out that our own desires, motives, and intentions may themselves be the unconscious product of forces over which we have no control, so that once more we are deluded. And where, then, does "responsibility" enter?

These are questions that will be considered shortly. Meanwhile it is useful to examine several versions of the "metaphysical" aspect of the issue, the view that there is something in the universe (which may or may not be revealed to science) that makes things and events *really* and *completely* determined, or not.

Determinism and the Nature of Things

It was William James who made one of the most eloquent and persuasive attempts to force the discussion of freedom and determinism into the realm of metaphysics. In this he saw eye-to-eye with his contemporary, Charles Peirce. In a celebrated essay, "The Dilemma of Determinism," James, like Peirce, anticipated the recent discussion of "uncertainty" in physics by flatly putting forth the case for a chance or random element in the universe (see pp. 499–504). For him, there was a clear-cut cosmological disjunction: the world was completely determined down to its very last moment and item, or it was not. The former view he called "hard" determinism and, although he rejected it, he confessed it had a healthy and straightforward, if wrongheaded, appeal, one which he could respect. What he did not respect, since it was no more than a "quagmire of evasion," was what he termed "soft" determinism—which, it must be confessed, is what the preceding pages of the present discussion have been leading up to. In James' words:

Nowadays, we have a *soft* determinism which abhors harsh words, and, repudiating fatality, necessity, and even predetermination, says that its real name is freedom; for freedom is only necessity understood, and bondage to the highest is identical with true freedom.[5]

James might well have been thinking of John Stuart Mill, and the British followers of Hegel, as "soft" determinists, not to mention earlier thinkers like Thomas Hobbes and David Hume. Were he alive today, he could have added a great number of others, including A. J. Ayer, C. L. Stevenson, and John Dewey (at least in part).

Because of what he regarded as the confusions of "soft" determinism, James excludes the word "freedom" from his treatment, replacing it by "indeterminism." This, he feels, is not a psychological concept, it involves no casuistry, and is perfectly unambiguous. It proposes an hypothesis as to the way things really are, a forecast of cosmic weather. Here is James' statement of a fundamental dichotomy:

[Determinism] professes that those parts of the universe already laid down absolutely appoint and decree what the other parts shall be. The future has no ambiguous possibilities hidden in its womb: the part we call the present is compatible with only one totality. Any other future complement than the one fixed from eternity is impossible. The whole is in each and every part, and welds it with the rest into an absolute unity, an iron block, in which there can be no equivocation or shadow of turning. . . .

Indeterminism, on the contrary, says that the parts have a certain amount of loose play on one another, so that the laying down of one of them does

---

[5] Found in the collection of essays entitled *The Will to Believe and Other Essays* (New York: Longmans Green, 1927), p. 149.

not necessarily determine what the others shall be. It admits that possibilities may be in excess of actualities, and that things not yet revealed to our knowledge may really in themselves be ambiguous. Of two alternative futures which we conceive, both may now be really possible, and the one becomes impossible only at the very moment when the other excludes it by becoming real itself. Indeterminism thus denies the world to be one unbending unit of fact. It says there is a certain ultimate pluralism in it; and, so saying, it corroborates our ordinary unsophisticated view of things.[6]

The intention at this point is not to develop the full Jamesian position; it is rather to indicate that the espousal of one or the other of these alternatives, as they are delineated in his vivid words, may finally depend on one's taste in universes. James himself recognizes this when he admits that neither science nor "the facts" can decide the issue. Decision rests pragmatically on what we postulate as rational, as moral, or even as aesthetic; also upon whether we are "tough" or "tender-minded." For James, a pluralistic, restless, wide-open universe has all the appeal missing from an iron-block world.

James also has an argument based on the morality of regret, which goes something like this: If the world is indeed completely determined, then one does whatever one is "fated" to do. To regret what one—or anyone else—has done or failed to do is a gratuitous and superfluous luxury; worse than that, it actually compounds the evil. Yet we *do* suffer the pangs of remorse. As a radical empiricist and highminded man James could not easily have ignored or deprecated such pangs: they are phenomenologically compelling and morally important. He would rather have suspected what he considered the factitious appeal of all-out determinism. But the interest here is in the "metaphysics" of determinism-indeterminism, and James, along with Peirce, anticipated what has now become a high priority item in recent cosmology, that is, the Uncertainty Principle.

This principle, also known as the Heisenberg Principle, goes back to 1927. It can be simply stated—at least, outside the precincts of physics. The position and velocity of a fundamental "particle" like an electron cannot be determined together; if we know more and more accurately the position, we know less and less about the velocity, and vice versa. In the words of the American physicist, the late Percy Bridgman, "There is a correlation between the fuzziness of a position measurement and the fuzziness of a velocity measurement such that when one fuzziness becomes less the other becomes greater in proportion."[7] The problem is essentially restated in the so-called complementarity principle of the late Niels

---

[6] *Ibid.*, pp. 150–151. Note also the earlier discussion of novelty: see Part III, pp. 318–322.

[7] In *Determinism and Freedom*, ed. by Sidney Hook (New York: Collier Books, 1961), p. 61. (This book first published by New York University Press, 1958).

Bohr. Putting this also in the most simple form, there seems to be an indeterminism apparent in the behavior (or at least as reflected in our knowledge of the behavior) of the so-called "particles," which are the fundamental constituents of energy and matter. For in order to describe the behavior of these particles, we can choose either a space-time frame of reference or we can choose a causal one, that is, a "deterministic" one in the classical sense. But we cannot have both. The reason is that the very act of observing the particles introduces changes; it is not a transparent act. Photons of light directed, say, at electrons tend to deflect them out of their paths so that we cannot observe them, so to speak, in their naked or innocent state.

Now, common sense, if apprised of such a scandalous situation, might be expected—despite its predilection for free will—to argue that, if we knew enough, both the position and velocity of the electron could be determined, and that, contrary to Bohr, causality and space-time location cannot "really" be opposed to one another. Common sense has a naïve confidence in the capacity of science, especially physical science, to give us certain truth. Thus, the various statements of the uncertainty principle can be attributed only to our ignorance. "In reality" things are one way or the other. However, common sense would not jibe with the opinion of most present-day physicists. The "orthodox" opinion is to the effect that we cannot legitimately go beyond the experimental evidence and that the evidence consistently brings us to an impasse. (This orthodox interpretation is called the "Copenhagen," referring to Bohr's native city.) Even Einstein and Planck, although refusing to believe that "God plays dice," were unable to counter such evidence. But there has been no diminution in the attempts to soften or change entirely the "orthodox" position: among the distinguished names involved in these attempts are those of de Broglie, Schrödinger, Margenau, Bohm, and Bunge.[8]

This excursion into the rarefied atmosphere of physics is in no way out of order, since it brings us face-to-face with the problem under discussion. Is the fact that there is firm evidence for particle-indeterminism an *epistemological* or a *metaphysical* matter? That is to say, does it result only from the limitations of the instruments through which we observe these phenomena, or has it uncovered—as James and Peirce would have hoped (and Heisenberg himself asserted)—an area of basic

---

[8] The efforts of some of the unorthodox have been to insist on the existence of "concealed parameters," i.e., certain constant quantities which up to now have eluded the equations and apparatus of the experimenters. It would seem that this is a doubtful and somewhat desperate approach, and one that has been severely handled by a number of distinguished mathematicians, especially the late J. von Neumann. Nevertheless, it can not be denied, on a priori grounds, that hidden and still unrevealed factors bearing on the issue may yet come to light.

contingency in the universe, of "objective" indeterminism? This is a rhetorical question because no imminent answer can be expected. And in the absence of scientifically respectable answers our wishes and preferences seem to take over, sometimes even our politics.[9] The desire for a friendly and comfortable universe may sway us, or maybe for a universe that has not yet made up its mind what to do. These, however, are extrascientific interests and tend to direct the path of physics into "philosophy," not always a welcome direction.

But has all this really anything to do with man's "free will"? The answer must be "Yes and no." A number of outstanding physicists (Compton, Eddington, Jeans, *et al.*) have seriously believed that if there is "really" an irreducible unpredictability at the root of things, a kind of surd, then the human animal, itself made up of myriads and myriads of elemental particles, may well manifest the indelible property of its constituent elements and enjoy a freedom that is not merely phenomenological but a testimony also to the revelations of the new physics. This argument has had hard sledding.[10] Niels Bohr, for example, was completely unimpressed. "I should like to emphasize," he wrote, "that considerations of the kind here mentioned are entirely opposed to any attempt of seeking new possibilities for a spiritual influence in the behavior of matter. . . . For instance, it is impossible, from our standpoint to attach an unambiguous meaning to the view sometimes expressed that the probability of the occurrence of certain atomic processes in the body might be under the direct influence of the will."[11] The phenomena reported by quantum mechanics, as Bohr intimates, would be of use to a free-will psychology only if there were major evidence that neurological activity is triggered, in any significant way, by a single photon of energy, and there is no such evidence. Of more moment, however, in this whole debate is the problem of probability and the theory of large numbers.

Let us venture an analogy. An insurance company can predict with uncanny accuracy how many men aged fifty will die in any given year. Actuarial science is a highly refined branch of mathematics and allows the insurance company to set its premium rates at certain critical figures which, although leaving little margin, successfully discount almost any

---

[9] The problem is compounded by the fact that some of the "unorthodox" physicists (i.e., those who resist the Copenhagen interpretation) are also dialectical materialists —the case with Bohm, for instance—which introduces a political-*cum*-metaphysical variation.

[10] See, for example, Susan Stebbing's *Physics and the Philosophers* (New York: Dover, 1958), first published in 1937. Perhaps the best case for the free-will position is to be found in Arthur Compton's Terry Lectures, *The Freedom of Man* (New Haven: Yale, 1935).

[11] *Atomic Physics and Human Knowledge* (New York: Wiley, 1958), p. 11. Quoted by Adolph Grünbaum in "Science and Man," *Perspectives in Biology and Medicine*, Vol. V, No. 4 (Summer 1962), p. 501.

known catastrophe (possibly short of nuclear annihilation). **But can the almost omniscient insurance company foretell whether John Jones, aged fifty, will die this year?** Hardly. So far as the life insurance statistician is concerned the fate of a single individual is irrelevant. But the average longevity of the group is decisive. Now, how does one proceed from the indeterminate knowledge of the individual to the determinate knowledge of a class or set of individuals? At what critical point does indeterminism merge into determinism? To a statistician these may seem naïve questions, since his interest is in "populations," and each "population" has its own critical figure where predictions become significant. Yet even a noted scientist like Percy Bridgman could raise the same question:

. . . There are laws of statistical behavior, although there are not laws for individual events. But how can this be? How can individual events, each of which is completely haphazard, combine into regular aggregates unless there is some factor of control over their combination into aggregates, and what kind of control can there be over a haphazard event?[12]

Even if Bridgman raised these questions he himself would have been extremely loath to challenge the statistical probability character of physical laws. For example, Bertrand Russell, among others, has suggested that since gas molecules enjoy a perfectly random motion, there is a mathematical possibility (highly unlikely) that a kettle of water put on to boil may find all its agitated molecules suddenly congregating in the spout and all going in the same direction. Entropy will have happened in this small system and the water will be frozen as hard as the best-tempered steel. But Bridgman was unimpressed: "This may be conceded to be a rigorous consequence of the mathematics, but to me it is utterly incredible as a statement of physical fact." Indeed, he would rather doubt the deliverance of his senses—if such a surprising event were to appear—than accept the logic of the situation, a striking example of how science and common sense can come into conflict with each other even in the same person. In short, although the motion of any single gas molecule may be entirely unpredictable, the billions of billions of molecules in a kettle of water seem to be completely determined.

Yet this does not answer our question. For it still may be urged that "in reality" things are completely, not probably, one way or the other. Is a probability equation itself "real"? (For the physics student: Is the *psi* function of Max Born anything more than a convention?) Of course, terms like "real" and "reality" cry aloud for some linguistic analysis despite the fact (or because of it?) that the terms have "undergone a surprising renascence in the usage of physicists after a period of conscious abstention" (Bridgman). The trouble is that "reality" for many, is a value-term, needing to be followed by something like "Hear! Hear!" or loud cheers.

---

12 Hook, *op. cit.*, p. 63.

There is still another response to our present question—the question, whether probability statements reflect anything more than systematic caution. This response is associated with the name of Charles Peirce, himself a giant in the mathematics of probability. He admitted that "determinism" is a matter of predictability, probability, and large numbers, but he thereby excluded the whole concept from the *individual* event. More accurately, he restricted probability (what his friend, Justice Holmes, was to call "bettability") to propositions or statements about an event; it cannot apply to the existential event itself. Take the simple case of tossing a true coin. In the long run—the very long run, as a matter of fact—the chances are even that a head will turn up. But the actual event, this particular toss of the coin, certainly cannot be represented by the fraction ½. It is 1 or 0. That is, either a head will surely turn up, or it will not. Probability applies to a run of events, not to a single event. (From this can be developed a frequency theory of probability, such as is found in Keynes and others.) In Peirce's own words: "An individual inference must be either true or false, and can show no effect of probability; and, therefore, in reference to a single case considered in itself, probability can have no meaning . . . It follows that there can be no sense in reasoning in an isolated case, at all."[13] Peirce's conclusion is that there are indeed random, chance (tychistic) events in the universe and that these are surely real. In effect, everything is possible, but some things are more probable than others, and it is with the latter that science is concerned. However, the world, for him, does ultimately grow together and form "cosmic habits"—but that is quite another story.

It seems, then, we are back to William James, and that our needs and our tastes may finally have to decide what we choose as "real." And on this score, it must be confessed, science has little if any advantage over the folklore. Those scientists, for example, who have chosen all-out metaphysical determinism have had to tilt against the combined findings of experimental physics. Those who have opted for "free will" have had to torture the evidence to sustain their position. In both cases the grounds for the choices have been, more likely than not, extrascientific. They have been emotional, metaphysical, socio-political, or logical, the differences between them depending very often on the degree of frankness of the chooser. In other words, it seems almost as if scientists tended to turn philosophers in their attempts to reconcile folklore and common sense with science.

This is not meant to be a cynical observation. It is meant to suggest that the problem of moral responsibility—which is the incandescent edge

[13] *Collected Papers of Charles Sanders Peirce*, ed. by Charles Hartshorne and Paul Weiss (Cambridge: Harvard, 1932), Vol. II, Chap. 6 ("The Doctrine of Chances"), par. 652, p. 395. Found also in the volume of selections, *Chance, Love and Logic*, ed. by M. R. Cohen (New York: Harcourt, Brace & World, 1923), pp. 69–70.

of this whole business—cannot very well wait for its solution until all the evidence on the Uncertainty Principle is verified, collated, and, above all, interpreted. One cannot resist noticing that "the nature of things" is a poor criterion for holding individual *x* responsible for event *a*.

Concluding Remarks

A discussion of the problem of freedom and determinism cannot help being frustrating. For one thing, the problem as customarily stated seems to point in the direction of final and polarized answers between which one might be expected to choose with confidence, whereas the discussion almost unavoidably forces upon us qualifications and amendments which tend to remove the sharpness and replace it with apparent fuzziness. Moreover, we seem constantly to be confronting differences in taste or mood or temperament, such as the "tough-mindedness" and "tender-mindedness" described by William James. Nevertheless, some concluding remarks are in order, even if they exemplify what James called contemptuously "soft determinism."

In the first part of this discussion several distinctions were stressed: The concept of "determinism" was held to be not the same as the concept of "compulsion." Instead, "determinism" was seen to be a function of "predictability," although the two are not identical. Certainly determinism is not identical with *universal* and *mechanical* predictability. Further, it was suggested that "determinism" and "fatalism" were different concepts. "Fatalism" has been most clearly a theological term (as in Islam) which usually—although not always—specifies a predetermined and divinely-known destiny, fixed and ineluctable, for every individual. Sometimes the extremely "hard" determinist sounds as if this is what he meant, as when he holds that as individuals we can do nothing to change our established fates. But true "fatalism" seems to go even further than this and imply that there is, as it were, a "book" in which is written down the destiny of every man. Perhaps "if he knew enough" such a "book" would indeed be revealed to the all-out determinist. Finally, it was proposed earlier that "self-determinism" could not be regarded as incompatible with freedom, since the causal force would be, at least in part, within the individual's control. But here is where the issue seems to be joined.

The hard determinist—the adjective needs to be retained because the position being suggested here is intended also to be a "deterministic" one—will argue that our own desires and ends, those which we think help to make us self-determined, are themselves but the resultant outcome of a long series of conditions both innate and environmental that have joined to compel an individual to do just what he does do and to think that this is what he means to do. As succinct a statement as any is that of John Hospers:

The mother blames her daughter for choosing the wrong men as candidates for husbands; but though the daughter thinks she is choosing freely and spends a considerable amount of time "deciding" among them, the identification with her sick father, resulting from Oedipal fantasies in early childhood, prevents her from caring for any but sick men, twenty and thirty years older than herself. Blaming her is beside the point; she cannot help it, and she cannot change it.[14]

This is, of course, the argument used so effectively by the late Clarence Darrow, the noted criminal lawyer. It is the thesis of Meyer Levin's *Compulsion*, the story of the celebrated Leopold and Loeb case in which Darrow was counsel for the defense. The argument, in sum, is simply that a man cannot be held responsible, legally or morally, for his acts, since he could not have done otherwise.[15]

Now, let us admit—insist, to be more precise—that man's behavior is certainly part of a chain of sociopsychological events and, further, that the notion of causal discontinuity is a difficult one to maintain or even to understand. Let us also agree that in an unspecified number of his actions and characteristics man is "coerced" and not simply "caused" by this past—possibly the girl with the Oedipus complex, clearly the man who has lost a leg. But at this point a line needs to be drawn, and the terms "coerced" or "compelled" may suggest where to draw it.

Were a knife placed in a person's hand and overwhelming physical power exerted upon him, against his best efforts, by another person or persons so as to force him to plunge the weapon into a victim's defenseless back, "compulsion" would evidently be present and responsi-

---

[14] *Determinism and Freedom, op. cit.,* pp. 126–127.

[15] The complicated problem of legal responsibility has been focused in recent years on the so-called "Durham Rule" and its attempted overthrow, or at least mitigation, of the early "M'Naghten Rule." The latter, propounded in 1843, has dominated both English and American jurisprudence. It emphasized the rational capacities of man and excused from criminal responsibility only those individuals who at the time of the crime were "laboring under such a defect of reason, from diseases of the mind, as not to know" what they were doing. The inability to distinguish between right and wrong, or the presence of "irresistible impulse," was about as far as what its opponents call the retributive school of justice was prepared to go in recognizing the force of mitigating circumstances.

In 1954, in *Durham v. U. S.,* Judge David L. Bazelon held that the M'Naghten Rule was unjust, and made a ruling which not only resulted in a distinctly broadened definition of insanity—at least in the District of Columbia—but also stimulated a great deal of legal and social discussion. Most psychiatrists and social scientists have felt that the M'Naghten rule worked to exclude medical evidence and that it tended to make the penal system one of retaliation and revenge instead of being devoted, as they felt, to protection and rehabilitation. On the other hand, there are those who feel that Durham has hopelessly confounded the meaning of responsibility. Dean Jacques Barzun also wonders about the victims of the criminal: "Those who pay their way and do *not* stab their friends" are seen only as bourgeois and uninteresting. A good summary of these controversies will be found in *Contemporary Moral Issues,* ed. by Harry Girvetz (San Francisco: Wadsworth, 1963), pp. 80–105.

bility absent, at least for the holder of the knife. Here is a model of compulsion, the physical coercing of undesired acts, or the physical and literal thwarting of desired action.

Suppose now a knife were placed at a person's back and he was ordered, on pain of being stabbed, to perform a criminal act, say, a robbery or an assault. Would he be compelled, too? Is the teller in a bank *compelled* to hand over money to a robber who threatens him with a gun? To change the example, what about an intelligence or counterintelligence officer who is being tortured to reveal his country's secrets; or, to complicate it further, what if he be given Sodium Pentothal, the drug which so relaxes his inhibitions that the truth almost spills out of him? This last case would clearly be a matter of compulsion. But in the case of the bank teller or of the tortured spy, "compulsion" is a difficult word to use since, however unpleasant the alternative, it is not physically impossible to refuse the demand.

Nevertheless, in these cases the agent would not ordinarily be held liable for his actions. Although *under the given conditions* he chose to give over the money or to reveal the information, the alternatives were so unequal that, for all legal or moral purposes, the teller or the tortured officer would probably be held to have acted under compulsion. To be sure, here is where "casuistry" would enter—that is, efforts to solve doubtful cases of moral responsibility, as in the various categories under "homicide" and "manslaughter." For instance, is a man to be exonerated for spying if he proved that his family in a foreign country were being held as hostage for his espionage and would be seriously harmed if he failed to act accordingly? But we must not let details and, at times, clearly unanswerable questions obscure the following points:

(1) A cause does not necessarily compel; at least, this is the modern interpretation of "cause."

(2) Consequently, determinism (a matter of cause, of predictability) is not the same as compulsion.

(3) To insist still that "cause *does* compel" may be termed "mechanistic" as opposed to "scientific" determinism.

(4) To be free, therefore, is not incompatible with (scientific) determinism.

(5) For freedom can be understood to mean that my acts are determined, if only in part, by my own desires.

Many are content to stop here. We are free, they say, when we are able to realize our desires. A more sophisticated version would be that we are free when, in addition to being able to act on our own desires, we *know* as many of the facts about the consequences of our desires as are available to us in the circumstances, so that (1) we know what our desires really are, and (2) we act in such a way that a lesser desire is not permitted to interfere with a stronger one.

Nothing complicated is involved here, as a couple of examples will help to show. Thus I may train for law in preference to teaching because of the promise of a better livelihood but be ignorant of certain other available facts which would persuade me otherwise if I took the pains to acquaint myself with them; for example, the freedom provided by teaching to pursue other interests for three months of the year, or the freedom from the political pressures of clients with whose views I may be out of sympathy, and so on. Or, again, I might become active in politics without knowing that it conflicts with writing, which I actually find I prefer. Clearly, freedom in the sense thus far defined is, alas, a function of judgment, prudence, intelligence, perseverance in the quest for facts, although clearly, also, the facts are never *all* in and one cannot wait indefinitely before acting. The rash, impetuous person is, nevertheless, less free, even if he gets what he wants, than the person who knows the consequences (and even the antecedents) of what he is doing. Such an account of freedom certainly offers no breach of causal continuity.

But if the account of freedom ends at this point its vulnerability is patent. For if the ability to achieve what one desires without impediments or restraints is the test of freedom, animals may be said to be as free on occasion as we are, even though, to be sure, we can hardly say that they have a *sense* of being free. Such a sense of being free is, of course, a significant aspect of the whole phenomenon. We have it, seemingly, because we are able to imagine a contrary state of affairs —that is, we are able to project ourselves into a situation in which we are being restrained and in which we are not gratifying our desires.

Such an approach, however, is vulnerable at still another point. What about our desires and the sense of choosing freely among them? May not the desires themselves be determined and the sense of free choice only an illusion? Therefore, what about the sense of *responsibility* and the moral categories of praise and blame which flow from it? This may seem the same old impasse. But—to change the figure—perhaps the focus can become sharper. Let us suggest an argument based on one of Professor Sidney Hook's. An infant crawling about upsets a candle and sets fire to a house. No problem of responsibility here, at any rate for the infant. A man heavily insures a house, sets fire to it with no consideration for its inmates. Is he responsible? Perhaps he is a pyromaniac (however, we said he heavily insured the house beforehand), or he was enamored of a fire wagon at an early age. This is not idle levity; it is intended to suggest that if responsibility is assigned to the arsonist and not to the infant—as is surely so—the distinction rests on a convergence of elements, elements understandably of unequal weight, such as:

(1) The ordinary meaning of "responsibility," which confidently ascribes it in one case and not in the other.

(2) The immediate, intuitive corroboration of such a distinction.

(3) The "pragmatic" necessity of making differential ascriptions of responsibility for the purposes of social life, a point that even "hard" determinists like John Hospers and Paul Edwards have accepted.

(4) All of these can be summarized by saying that we hold a person to be responsible for his acts, or the contrary, to the degree in which he can exercise choice within the range of his abilities and powers. To stretch these limits to 100 or to shrink them to 0, as hard indeterminism or hard determinism seem to suggest—at least in their more exaggerated and sentimental moments—would make impossible any kind of intelligible social order. We simply have to recognize the presence, as well as the absence, of "extenuating circumstances," to use the language of the law courts.

This brings us back to the point made above where we proposed drawing a line between "caused" and "compelled." That line would appear to be set by the degree to which man's volitions prove to be one of the deciding factors in bringing about subsequent events, and this degree will shift, depending as it does upon the range of his abilities and powers. To say, on theoretical and admittedly a priori grounds, that *none* of man's volitions play a determining part in subsequent events would be as meaningless as to say that his volitions depend not at all upon antecedent events. Both extremes fly in the face of common sense and the empirically-established observations set out in the preceding paragraph, and would seem to substitute dogma for inquiry.

It will be granted that this kind of "compromise" permits of no all-out conclusions and no relaxing in the warm comfort of an absolute answer, but uncertainty is part of man's situation. The freedom-determinism issue is not a white-black one; we may be permitted to say that man is determined but that he is not necessarily unfree or irresponsible on that account. As Professor Hook says:

It is not true that everything that happens to us is like "being struck down by a dread disease" [as the "hard" determinist believes]. The treatment and cure of disease—to use an illustration that can serve as a moral paradigm for the whole human situation—would never have begun unless we believed that some things that were did not have to be, that they could be different, and that *we* could make them different. And what we can make different we are responsible for.[16]

The last sentence will suggest that responsibility *requires* determinism, although "hard" determinists would reject this. For "what we can make different" depends upon our powers and these flow from our training and our innate capacities. To use a stodgy academic illustration: The readers of this book (should they be college students) might possibly be

---

[16] *Determinism and Freedom, op. cit.,* p. 192.

called upon in an examination to demonstrate their progress in getting introduced to philosophy. Would they be so called upon—held responsible—if they had not been exposed to a teacher and to the reading required by him? It would be senseless to hold a person responsible for knowledge he had in no way been able to acquire. An undetermined responsibility would seem calculated to bring about, at the very least, a nervous breakdown; while a determinism which allows no place for responsibility would be most congenial to nerveless robots.

As has been noted before, there is a current widespread myth to the effect that the efforts of social science to understand the human animal must lead to something like "predictable man"—a kind of inhuman, completely manipulable machine. Such a misconception could apply only to the conclusions of the most adamantine of hard determinists. It would not apply to "scientific" determinism, and certainly not to the approach of physical science, which, as was noted earlier, affords no justification for flintiness in this area. Indeed, the conclusions being drawn here might suggest that the bearings of science upon the problem of determinism be so construed as to provide a place for the free choice of common sense without doing violence to science. Thus, the specter of man-becoming-automaton because of the researches of social science might give way to the really important questions: Just what is the range of man's abilities and powers? Does that range extend far enough to include his values? Does it extend far enough to relate moral responsibility not only to good will but to knowledge and inquiry as well?

Selected Readings

Bergson, H., *Time and Free Will*, trans. by Pogson, London: G. Allen, 1910.
Farrer, A. M., *The Freedom of the Will*, New York: Scribner's, 1960.
Hare, R. M., *Freedom and Reason*, London: Oxford 1963. (Also Galaxy paperback, 1965.)
Melden, A. I., *Free Action*, New York: Humanities Press, 1961.
Munn, A. M., *Free Will and Determinism*, Toronto: University of Toronto Press, 1961.
(See also books mentioned on p. 491.)

CHAPTER 30

Science and Value

A Minimum Contribution of Science to Value

Before beginning a discussion of science and value we may recall two points made earlier. One was the insistence that science, above all, meant a method; that the method although rigorous, was a broad one and not circumscribed by any single range of material; and that scientific techniques were themselves not entirely neutral or value-free. A corollary was that social science could be considered without apology as a branch of science. The second point was concerned with the allegedly total separation of fact from value. It was suggested that in terms of language, common sense, logic, as well as the very behavior of science, the attempt to provide complete insulation between these two realms was not consistently effective.

None of this need blur the distinction between fact and value. But to insist that things are different—even if we say *"vive la différence"*—is not also to insist that there can be no commerce between them; on the contrary. Men and women are different. . . . Furthermore, there is no intention here to urge that the data and methods of social science lead irresistibly and logically to values, nor that the sciences are designed to handle value. The definition of "value" is not being overlooked, nor is its essential yet troublesome element, "the desirable." But having acknowledged this, one must also go on to insist that there is a great deal more to say about the possible contribution of science to value.

For example, the history of ethics is studded with the quest for ultimates such as The Good or The Right. In this quest, the philosopher has characteristically sought for an immediate and direct answer. This may have come most economically by way of intuition, or, more slowly through an exercise in logic, and, occasionally, it came from what is claimed to be empirical evidence. But whatever the method, the hallmark of much of moral philosophy has often been overgeneralization. Take the familiar case of the supposed conflict between altruism and self-interest. Either side of the dispute can be espoused; there is a logic in the contrasting appeals, often the actions of men are appealed to as testimony for one side or the other. But suppose we learn that there are entire cultures, such as the Navaho, in which there is no such conflict between egoism and altruism, that, in fact, the issue itself is almost incomprehensible. Should this have any bearing on the question?

It would seem, if only to renovate some of the hackneyed and trivial "examples" of ethical speculation and to remove the professorial approach, that the wealth of new material, available as it is from cultural anthropology, would be welcome to the philosopher.[1] After all, it is no heresy to suggest that we now have information on human conduct that was not available to G. E. Moore, although it would be unorthodox to aver that such information had bearing upon the *judging* of human conduct. Few philosophers would cavil at the efforts of anthropologists and sociologists to discover what men actually do hold desirable in different cultures and subcultures; but most philosophers would draw the line, as has been stated so often, at going from what men do or have done or even will do, to what they ought to do. As C. D. Broad has said, statistics is irrelevant to ethics.

The question, then, is this: How wide (or narrow) are the precincts of the "ought" (ends), and how wide (or narrow) are those of science (means)? Or, in a different and perhaps more appropriate figure, how permeable is the region of "ought" and "desirable" to the activities of scientific knowledge? One answer has already been given (pp. 453–455), which was to the effect of making the realm of values and ends completely

---

[1] Some samples of the growing literature in this area are: A. MacBeath, *Experiments in Living* (London: Macmillan, 1952); R. B. Brandt, *Hopi Ethics* (Chicago: University of Chicago Press, 1954); John Ladd, *The Structure of a Moral Code*, a discussion of Navaho ethics (Cambridge: Harvard, 1957); Charles Morris, *Varieties of Human Value* (Chicago: University of Chicago Press, 1956); A. Edel and M. Edel, *Anthropology and Ethics* (Springfield, Ill.: Charles C. Thomas, 1959). See also Ethel Albert, "A Classification of Values," *American Anthropologist* (April 1956), pp. 221–248; and a symposium, "The Roots of Value," in the *Antioch Review* Vol. XVII, No. 4 (Winter, 1957–58), espec. the statements by Ethel Albert, Victor Ayoub, and Clifford Geertz.

impervious and nonnatural. A contrasting answer has already been suggested. Let us develop it further.

A minimum statement of such a contrasting answer would be along these lines: Social science cannot replace ethics but it can help to make ethics more relevant to the actual conduct of men in their varied cultures. It can supply the information from which can emerge ethical hypotheses more creative and more imaginative than the parochial and somewhat academic hypotheses on which the changes have been rung so long. The stilted and sheltered quality of much of contemporary ethical speculation has been recognized even by English analytical philosophers.

In addition to suggesting new hypotheses, the social sciences might make the standard generalizations of ethics more fruitful. Since anthropologists, for instance, deal with the workings of human values in specific and documented situations, it is more than likely that they can supply evidence which would support or fail to support some of the larger generalizations of ethical philosophy, such as those of egoism, or of hedonism, or of unselfishness. It would appear as a sensible demand, not that generalization be suspended, but that it be appraisable by something other than intuition or intuition's surrogates. It would also seem plausible that the structure of ethical theory, now almost solely dependent upon logical or phenomenological foundations, might find new analytical formulations implicit in an empirical study of values.[2]

The word "minimum" has been used here to describe a position which would be sympathetically considered even by those who contend that science cannot contribute in any constitutive way to an understanding of value. For example, that science may present all possible alternative ends to choose from but cannot itself make the choice among them, that it can clarify and implement goals but never set them, would be the position of the well-known mathematician and philosopher, John G. Kemeny.[3] A slightly different attitude is found in the political theorist, Arnold Brecht,[4] who believes that scientific method can be used to handle values and even to assert the superiority of some of them, but only up to the point where demonstration and proof is attempted. These are logical matters, he insists, and here science cannot encroach. The barrier between fact and value still remains high.

---

[2] For suggestions of such new analytical procedures, the following might prove helpful: *The Peoples of Ramah: A Comparative Study of Value Systems*, ed. by E. Z. Vogt and J. M. Roberts (forthcoming); A. Edel, *Science and the Structure of Ethics*, *Encyclopaedia of Unified Science*, Vol. II, No. 3 (Chicago: University of Chicago Press, 1961) and *Method in Ethical Theory* (New York: Humanities Press, 1963); and E. Albert, " 'First Principles' in Logic and Ethics," *Bucknell Review*, Vol. VIII, No. 3 (March 1958).

[3] *A Philosopher Looks at Science* (Princeton, N. J.: Van Nostrand, 1959).

[4] *Political Theory* (Princeton, N. J.: Princeton, 1959).

Ends and Means

If there is any possibility of overcoming that barrier, something beyond a minimum role for science vis-à-vis value needs to be considered. And in both philosophy and the sciences there are those[5] who are prepared to give a larger role to science and intelligent inquiry. A discussion of such a point of view may profitably begin with the means-ends problem; "problem" because the two are supposed ordinarily to inhabit entirely different universes and, like fact and value, to remain permanently segregated. Of course, even if this were true, it would still make a world of difference just where the line between ends and means were to be drawn. Although segregated, ends could be pushed back so as almost to be out of view, and most attention given to means; or the line could move forward. This would be simply another pictorialization of the supposed tug of war between philosophy and science.

It can certainly be argued that means are never "merely" means nor ends superlatively and aloofly set off by themselves. For one thing, the two are logically bound together in the same way as are cause and effect. A means without a foreseen end is not simply Philistine drudgery; it is blind and dismembered and not a means to anything. Ends, like consequences and effects, cannot be independent entities; they are literally "meaningless" without the interposition of something else, unapproachable ideals which lose their sense along with their possibility of being realized. Take some unimpeachable and final end, say, love, or the consummation of aesthetic or religious experience. Such an end is not simply lauded by those who claim it to be final and intrinsic; it has to be made effectual and meaningful; discriminations must be recognized, relations need to be discovered or improved. Without these connections, the most honorable end becomes as trivial as our most irresponsible daydream: we wish to be a great musician—but not to practice; to be a world-famous scientist—but without mathematical training; to lose weight—without dieting. These may be juvenile and even innocent ways of passing time in our heads, but they surely provide no paradigm for value theory!

The term "end" is by no means self-explanatory, for it means several things. There is, for instance, the simple meaning of a limit, the stop or *terminus* of an action. This may be only a pun, yet some of the difficulties of the notion of "final end" or "end-in-itself" might be removed if this temporal or periodic sense were taken seriously. For the processes of nature do start and stop. Some of these beginnings and endings favor man, others do not. The rhythms of nature are what they are: to man

---

[5] Some of the representatives of this approach are John Dewey, Sidney Hook, Abraham Edel, Clyde Kluckhohn, J. Bronowski, Charles Morris, and Abraham Maslow.

they can be beneficial, neutral, or malign. To regard all natural processes as exclusively good, bad, or indifferent is to make the world center on man in a kind of latter-day medievalism. But to regard man, living in a world not made for him but also not made to thwart him in some conspiratorial fashion, as choosing among the events around him in order to survive and grow, is to discover why some natural endings become ends-in-view and others endings-to-be-rejected. But, it will be said, what about "to survive and grow"—is not this an end-in-itself, final and intrinsic, a "value" unaffected by anything else?

A naturalistic ethic will undoubtedly give the highest marks to survival and healthy growth, but it will question the meaning even of these as ends-in-themselves. Consider, for instance, "health." A physician in treating a patient, following Dewey's illustration, "forms ends-in-view . . . on the ground of what his examination discloses is the 'matter' or 'trouble' with the patient. . . . But he does not have an idea of health as an absolute end-in-itself, an absolute good by which to determine what to do. . . . There is no need to deny that a general and abstract conception of health finally develops. But it is the outcome of a great number of definite, empirical inquiries, not an a priori preconditioning 'standard' for carrying on inquiries."[6]

According to this interpreation, ends or values (the desirable) emerge as the consequences of specific procedures; they are not something absolute and grandly out of context, which is what "absolute" seems to imply. Ends like "health" or "growth" or even "happiness" are not final in the sense of being unamendable and disconnected from or unaffected by the various ways in which alone they can be realized. Ends may be reappraised when the means are scrutinized: "wealth" may be put aside as just involving too much trouble to get it, or it may conflict with some other end-in-view, just as physical "health" will vary from person to person and may even be rejected entirely as by a writer who chooses to create at any risk. To be operative, ends must be in the closest mutual relationship to means, without which they remain not merely abstract but frustrating as well. A process, in fact, seems to be going on; parts of that process stand out now as ends and now as means. An end, however majestic it may be, becomes a means when it points to something beyond itself; and a means stands as an end until it is reached and surpassed. The two tend to change places. This is brought about by the dynamic logic of the transaction, just as sellers are not always sellers but also buyers.

Again, an objection: Ends cannot forever be potential means. Unless at least one end is intrinsic, that is, not an instrumentality to something else,

---

6 *Theory of Valuation, International Encyclopaedia of Unified Science,* Vol. II, No. 4 (Chicago: University of Chicago Press, 1939), p. 46.

the whole serial process is left swimming in vacancy. The student is familiar with the classic Aristotelian argument for a final end (Part I, pp. 135–137). Nearly everything is wanted for the sake of something else. To use a current example, one is in college, ostensibly to graduate. To what end? Perhaps to get a husband or wife. Or to proceed to a graduate or professional school. To what end? To be married and a parent, and/or a lawyer, physician, physicist. For what purpose? To make money, to be a success, be loved, help your fellow man, please your parents. Why? Well, in the Aristotelian canon, something must be the reason (the final cause) for all this. Aristotle, it will be remembered, called it "happiness"—at least, that is the usual translation of his *eudaimonia*, which means literally "good spirited," or "well-souled." This, then, is what is wanted for its own sake, and for the sake of which all else is wanted. True, such "happiness"—which, for Aristotle, is to be found in thought and contemplation —may change as circumstances change, and so in that measure can be said to be relative; nevertheless, it is a final end, not itself a means to an end. Such a final end might possibly be plural, although this would involve the logical issue of the relationship among several finalities. Aristotle himself recognized a number of "secondary goods," on a level lower, however, than that of happiness. The trouble with a *single* end for all men is that it ignores the differences among men, and that, if it were precisely defined and pressed, it would begin to border on fanaticism.

What about this argument? Perhaps the reader may be asked if he indeed directs his life in this Aristotelian fashion. Does he rise each morning, gird up his loins as it were, and say resolutely: "I'm going to be happy?" Do all our problems in this area of value-decision get pushed back to the more overpowering ultimates? Or is it not the case that we are constantly running in the middle lane between frantic improvisation and the final realities, so that what we "ought" to do is usually a matter of practical judgment in which, *if* this particular action is taken, *then* some predicted result should follow. The urgencies of the situation, as Professor Sidney Hook has put it, dominate, and not some far-off ideal. Suppose the problem of contemplated suicide is involved. Few persons considering committing suicide have ever been reached by general arguments concerning the "value of life." Only by the suggestion of specific conditions and possibilities, like William James' "wait for the next mail," could they be influenced. For "the value of life," in a laudatory sense, is precisely what would fail to move the prospective self-killer. It remains outside the ambit of his immediate interests—or disinterests; it is not operational or meaningful.

To be less dramatic, do not the average man's value transactions also constitute a continuous flow, usually uninterrupted by the invoking of ultimates; and is not any one of us able to corroborate this? Indeed, ends-in-themselves seem somehow strident and melodramatic. "Success is in itself pompous and not very attractive; health is a little too ruddy; peace is ascetic like a will-less Madonna in the rose garden; and even amiability seems a little empty-headed."[7] Instead of such finalities we appear to be confronted, in a sense, by a series of mountain ranges, all needing to be climbed. There seems to be no last range, but when we get tired of climbing, it has been said, then we die.

The phrase "if-then" was used above. This suggests a hypothetical approach, that moral propositions can be treated like provisional claims. The words "practical judgment" were also used, and these, like "hypotheses," indicate the possibility of empirical confirmation. Take the cry of "Help!" by a man in peril. This may simply be an ejaculation like a reflex action; and, according to a prestigious contemporary theory, it may also be understood as indicating that the distressed man does not like the situation in which he finds himself. But the exclamation is, of course, much more than this. It is a call for *help*, which means (1) that the condition appears to be beyond the unaided control of the man in trouble; and (2) that the cry is expectant: aid will come, or might come. Both of these statements are clearly confirmable or disconfirmable. "Help!" turns into an empirical proposition, not a mere ejaculation. The cry is now a sign or a symbol, it becomes "significant." It is no longer simply an expressed wish for a more desirable condition. It makes a claim, it is cognitive, and can be handled intelligently, even "scientifically"—should, say, the distressed man be an astronaut in a space capsule which has missed its target area.

These last illustrations may seem somewhat afield. This is not so if the whole preceding anatomy of the ends-means and value-fact situation is kept in view. That situation seems to be a "practical" one, in the sense, first of all, that some difficulty needs to be overcome. The situation seems also to be one in which the gap between ends and means narrows and in which the two may even change places; at the same time, ends-in-view tend to supersede intrinsic ends, or ends-out-of-relationship, especially in a crisis situation. The man in the water crying "Help!" wants out. This is his immediate end-in-view. For him to be considering something like "life," "happiness," or even "survival," would be somewhat literary, almost whimsical, although when he is rescued and at leisure, these larger and more embracing ends-in-view may well take over. Finally, according to this particular analysis, the value-situation is empirical, in that certain consequences are expected to follow from the hypotheses proposed to meet the initial difficulty. And those consequences will or will not be verified.

---

[7] Bertram Morris, *Philosophical Aspects of Culture* (Yellow Springs, Ohio: Antioch, 1961), p. 114.

How far can an analysis like this be carried? Can the sense of "ought-ness" or "obligation" be accommodated to it, assuming that such a sense is a natural one possessing a natural history? Suppose we try to illustrate this proposed if-then aspect of the evaluation process by the all-too-familiar problem nowadays of whether we *ought* to go on a diet of some kind—low-fat, low-sugar, salt-free, low-cholesterol, not to mention no nicotine, no alcohol, and the rest. The problem is clearly one in which there is an "if" clause (if you want to be slim, avoid coronary trouble and high blood pressure, and perhaps live longer and more soundly) followed by its consequent (then you *should* refrain from eating this or that). Words like "should" and "ought," as has been seen, have a tendency to block, even to paralyze, discussion. Yet these terms, at least according to the present interpretation, have a clear role to play, just as they do in any hypothetical argument: They connect judgments about an antecedent and conditional state with those dealing with a predictable and consequent state. If x, then y.

"But why *should* I be slim, healthy, long-lived—or enjoy my food?" However, even if I am forced back by such questions to something like "happi-ness" or "duty" or, possibly, "the will of God," the analysis would still seem to hold: *if* I want to be happy, etc, then I *should* do thus and so. Moreover, both the "if" and the "then" clauses need to have empirical content. I would have to be able to know, for one thing, when I am happy, or there is no point in striving for happiness; and, for another, I would have to be able to assess the steps which got me to that favored position.

Suppose we now ask, "Why *ought* I be happy? or "Why *ought* I sur-vive," even "Why *ought* I obey the will of God?" Grammatically, these are legitimate questions. Yet what kind of answer would satisfy them? Could not any answer at all be met with the same devastating rejoinder? Devastating—but not very meaningful. A question that no answer would satisfy is not a real question. An impregnable sense of fittingness or obliga-tion, ordinarily intuitive in character, is used to block any inquiry into human conduct; yet this itself but continues the game, which any number can play, since I can always proceed to ask: "Why *ought* I follow my intuition?"

There have been many expressions of the moral quest for certainty. The intuitive approach is one of them. In recent years, this quest has ex-ploited the term "wisdom," which in much present-day writing, journalis-tic as well as the more pretentious, is set over against mere "knowledge." This itself is no problem. The problem arises when "wisdom" is under-stood to carry an aura very close to that of "intuition" itself. The merely knowledgeable man, it is said, is all too often unwise, even derelict, about his personal affairs. The great scientist may be a moral idiot. Which no-body can deny. But if "wisdom" has a manageable meaning and is not simply a reverential accolade, then it surely can mean nothing more—or nothing less—than *relevant* knowledge, knowledge sufficient to meet the question being raised, knowledge applied to the conduct of life. Surely wisdom is not opposed to knowledge. The knowledge of the amoral scientist—if such there be—is simply lacking, or is not being addressed to the appropriate problems, or it is fragmentary and not usefully put together, or functions differently on different levels. If wisdom means knowledge that is adequate, relevant, and synthesized, there is no particular issue. It is when the word seems to connote, as it does so often, that *no* knowledge is relevant to moral affairs, that obscurantism seems to be introduced. When "wisdom" alone is pertinent to such affairs, then we have reached the point of no return.

To anticipate an objection, the contention here is not that the word "knowledge" means but a single thing. No one can deny that we get a great deal of knowledge about men from Shakespeare or Dostoevski, or that many items of the sciences of man may prove to be mere curiosities and quite irrelevant to great issues. But to set literature over against science as if they were competitors in knowledge, and thus to widen the rift between the two cultures, can be of help nowhere.[8] It would seem designed only to preserve the quest for certainty in morals, a quest, it can be argued, that may well prove to be the greatest barrier to understanding morals.

On the other hand, it can also be argued that without such certainty the quest for values is meaningless. The growth of scientific knowledge, it might be added, pushes to the conclusion that values are only relative; something else, therefore, is needed to certify their absolute nature.

Value: Absolute or Relative?

Certain problems undoubtedly go back to man's earliest speculations. This may be true of the familiar and provocative idea that my own beliefs and actions, and those of my group are—or should be—the approved and universal way of doing things. If there are problems of this almost primeval nature, not much can be said about their origins. But when such problems first appeared in ancient Greece, they could without too much distortion be laid to the impact of new learning upon the on-going mores. Such an interpretation would be most apt for the Sophists, from the little we know of them, for they self-consciously and belligerently attacked the "old-fashioned" ways in the light of their more "advanced" knowledge. The problem, as was noted earlier (pp. 71–77), is whether to regard the work of the Sophists, who were primarily teachers, rhetoricians, and polemicists, as "science" or as something else. The contemporary philosopher, Karl

---

[8] On this point, see the late Aldous Huxley's last book, *Literature and Science* (New York: Harper & Row, 1963).

Popper, feels that "the beginning of social science goes back at least to the generation of Protagoras and the Sophists," who challenged "the strong inclination to regard the peculiarities of our social environment as if they were 'natural' "[9]

Whatever the case for the development of ancient problems like these in the shock of new knowledge upon the standardized beliefs, there would seem to be little question that they have been restated and rethought as they felt the exploding impact of recent science. This was true with the problem of freedom and determinism, and the case is even clearer with the problem of values as absolute or relative. Here anthropology has been a major source of conflict.

To call standards or values "absolute" is to hold that they are not contained within the boundaries of any given social order. No particular culture or historical epoch could make lying right, justice wrong, or legitimize the moral confusion of love with hate, or kindness with cruelty; for these moral predicates depend upon no special context. Indeed "absolute" could be defined—albeit with prejudice—as that which has no context, an impossible situation to come upon. Absolute values must stand on their own—splendid, isolated, and carrying clear and unmistakable marks of recognition. To know them, therefore, would seem to require a device such as intuition, that is, an immediate awareness plus a sense of conviction. In the history of ethics this approach to value is ordinarily known as a "rational" approach—one of the many uses of an overburdened word—"rational," because it rests its case on what is felt to be rockbottom and axiomatic, from which less certain truths may be deduced.

There is, thus, a logic to be invoked, since it is held that the existence of relatives entails at least one existent which is not relative and without which "relative" would forfeit its meaning. Even the Einsteinian system, although it sees little meaning in absolute frames of reference for motion, mass, or time, still relies on c, the absolute (unchanging) velocity of light in free space, upon which depend the relativity equations. To the skeptic's doubt of the very meaning of absolutes, the believer will aver, like Plato, that without the firm foundation of an unchanging and uncontaminated essence, nothing else has meaning or even existence: Unless we know what "equality" is, how can we ever know whether line a equals line b? And if we had no similar basis in ethics, here, too, everything would be swimming in vacancy. Fortunately, man does possess the standard equipment, according to the ethical rationalist, without which he would simply not be a man, and that equipment includes apparatus for grasping the moral ultimates.

Is the belief in such finalities indeed a part of our established wisdom?

[9] *The Open Society and Its Enemies* (London: Routledge, 1945), Vol. I, p. 58.

Do men feel, in general, not only that they possess such immediate judgments on moral matters—which may be called conscience or revelation—but also that such ability testifies to the undoubted existence of standards independent of any given society yet somehow underpinning all of them—standards such as natural law? This is a cherished and widely-held notion, but it runs up against the supposedly more "sophisticated" and "scientific" approach known as "cultural relativism." And yet the feeling that "there is nothing either good or bad but thinking makes it so" is also often met, especially among college youth, although the few opinion surveys on this difficult matter seem to indicate that commitments to the absolutistic idea tends to prevail. The trouble is, however, that very few know precisely what they mean by "absolute," nor do they see how in their own conduct they tend to ignore their own assumptions. Max Lerner, an acute observer of American culture, has summed up the matter succinctly by observing that "despite the spread of relativism in many areas of American thought, it did not triumph in the sphere of morality. As each of the generations came of age, it did not discard the idea of enduring moral values but was skeptical as to whether the values it inherited were those it could live by."[10]

Cultural Relativism

Like so many other ideas, that of "cultural relativism" is traceable as far back as we please to go. For example, the historian Herodotus was struck by the wealth of un-Greek and "barbarian" practices that he came upon in his travels and inquiries, not all of them stupid or outrageous. In fact, he confessed to approve much of the strange behavior he had discovered, and was forced to acknowledge that "Custom is king," that morals vary with geography. His account of what men thought good to eat, to love, and how to eat or to love or to bury or to fight, is, much of it, as interesting and as "modern" as what we expect to find reported by a contemporary anthropologist. The same is true of the sardonic comments of the Greek Sophists, and of the iconoclastic essays of the great Montaigne, packed as they are with a fund of information, and misinformation, about "sauvages" and "canniballes." Indeed, the Utopian literature of the seventeenth century stemmed in large part from the Age of Exploration and its revelations of a New World, not simply of gold and land and sun but of "noble redmen" with their unspoiled, "natural" folkways putting to shame the effete and decadent practices of Paris, London, or Lisbon. Whatever the merits of such a contrast, there is little doubt of a collision between the seemingly absolute, Christian, and civilized mores of a dominant Europe and the fresh and innocent practices of "Indians," or of the result-

---

[10] *America as a Civilization* (New York: Simon and Schuster, 1957), p. 76.

ing transvaluation of values—at any rate the values of the literary and enlightened in their more literary and enlightened moments.

The development of anthropology, beginning in mid-nineteeth century, has justified the insights of a long line of relativists with an abundance of now familiar illustration. We have learned that there is almost nothing right or wrong in one culture that is not totally reversed in another, nothing so unspeakable or unprintable for, say, Americans, which has not been made the object of religious worship elsewhere. We send our grandparents to St. Petersburg, Florida, if we can; we do not kill them and eat their hearts so as to get their virtue. Ruth Benedict, in her widely read *Patterns of Culture*, has provided a mountain of convincing evidence on such cultural divergences. The challenge of cultural relativism, however, is not in the mere recitation of cultural oddities: this is a descriptive matter which no one could challenge. What is debatable is the normative judgment which asserts that "The customs of one culture are as good as those of any other." This judgment is the heart of the doctrine and is exemplified in the work of the late Melville Herskovits,[11] somewhat less belligerently in Ruth Benedict, as well as in the writings of a great number, possibly the majority, of contemporary anthropologists.

It would be difficult to question the importance of such an approach. It is a prophylaxis against intolerance and a healthy corrective for "that sort of man," as Jeremy Bentham describes him, "who speaks out and says, I am of the number of the elect; now God himself takes care to inform the elect what is right. . . . If, therefore, a man wants to know what is right he has nothing to do but to come to me."[12] This man whom Bentham is satirizing has unconsciously elevated his own values to an absolute and universal position; he is guilty of "ethnocentrism," that is, the parochial worship of one's own mores, whether of the in-group, the tribe, the nation, or even of a whole culture. On the other hand, what cultural relativism emphasizes is the comprehension and sympathetic acceptance of different cultural values, those of the other fellow; it accords a dignity to every culture, even the preliterate and most simple (to use "primitive" might imply a derogation). Relativism thus tends to provide the basis for mutual understanding, and acts to remove one of the basic causes for intolerance, prejudice, and possibly of war itself. On this level, the level of countering bias and establishing a sophistication in dealing with Strangers and Outsiders, the proponents of cultural relativism have done real service. They rest their case upon well-authenticated and fully documented studies of how "other" people live and (as even with Herodotus and Montaigne) how sensibly. Absolute standards come now to be seen as no more than one's own practice writ large.

---

[11] See espec. his *Man and His Works* (New York: Knopf, 1948).
[12] *Principles of Morals and Legislation* (Oxford at the Clarendon Press), pp. 17–20.

Why then is cultural relativism not as persuasive a doctrine as it was a decade or two ago, and why is the word "sophistication" no longer unquestionably reserved for it? One reason certainly has been historical and political, the spread of communism and fascism. When the murder of six million Jews and the liquidation of whole classes and nations were exempted from moral judgment by an approach like this (and Professor Herskovits, for one, was driven to this extreme), something seemed to be lacking. When moral judgment is suspended on any culture, our own or an alien one, the implicit assumption is that all cultures are of equal moral worth, that they are all "genuine" cultures. But this is a position without a contrast. For it seems to say that any existent totality of social institutions adds up to a culture, and that it is meaningless to talk of malfunctioning, destructive or self-stultifying cultures. It would seem nothing short of desperation to assert that this is true, that cultures cannot be ranged from the genuine to the spurious.[13] It would be curious if judgment could be made on all things except culture itself. Certainly not even the most adamant relativist could object to immanent criticism, that from inside a culture—Ruth Benedict, for instance, was quite critical of middle-class American culture. Yet such criticism could scarcely be expected to remain entirely intramural.

We shall be warned, however, that judgments can be made only on the basis of our own culture ("ethnocentrism") and are inapplicable beyond it. This presents a logical problem. Most exponents of cultural relativism would appear to regard tolerance and appreciation of other points of view as "good." Is this itself not a culturally determined value? For there are many cultures which do not find tolerance admirable. To celebrate moral equality among cultures would seem to demand as a jumping-off place a society where what could only be called "cosmopolitan" values were highly rated. Yet such values are found only in some cultures. If consistent, the relativist would have to admit that tolerance was "bad" in an authoritarian culture, and, if stubbornly consistent, that free intelligent inquiry was simply the luxury of certain social orders and could not legitimately be made the model for all. The circularity of this is apparent.

But is the believer in "genuine" cultures any better off? Are not concepts like "harmony," "balance," "vitality," and "integrity," as it has been said, simply those held highly by certain cultures, such, possibly as our own—although hardly by everyone in it. In short, is not man irretrievably culture-bound? These questions may recall the earlier discussion of sociology of

---

[13] This is the language of the distinguished anthropologist, Edward Sapir, as quoted by Professor Bertram Morris, with "genuine" suggesting criteria like "harmony," "balance," "vitality," "integrity," and so on; Morris, *Philosophical Aspects of Culture*, *op. cit.*, chap. I.

knowledge (pp. 475–477), and the comment would be the same: The "logic" of the situation need not be pushed to the extreme which makes discourse impossible. Both the cultural relativist and his critic need to be extricated from a possibly self-destructive position if only to allow them to make their respective cases. Even Karl Mannheim allowed his "intellectuals" to break out of their "ideologies," and perhaps the cultural anthropologist may be granted some advantage over a witch doctor.

This suggests perhaps a more serious criticism of cultural relativity, one coming from anthropologists themselves as well as from outside the field. It is charged that the fascination with "culture," particularly with the simpler cultures, has tempted social scientists to accept these simpler ways of doing things as a kind of norm, thereby putting the scientific observer and the practitioner of ritual and magic on the same level. Preliterate folklore and the primitive ceremonial have been upgraded to the point where moral agnosticism plus uncritical praise of sheer primitivism may well be an abiding consequence in anthropology. At least such is the severe opinion of an American economist, C. E. Ayres.[14] He is joined in this general point of view by a number of anthropologists who feel that anthropology has become increasingly timid and wary, afraid of making any value judgments whatsoever. This moral timidity is a possible reaction from the ill-fated evolutionary approach of the nineteenth century which thought to find a progressive development in the history of cultures. Because this attempt to apply evolutionary principles where apparently they did not belong proved to be misguided, comparative studies of culture have been under a cloud until very recently.

It was suggested some pages back that cultural relativity is not quite as persuasive or "sophisticated" a theory as it was a few years ago. Perhaps the major reason for this has come from anthropology itself with its increasing interest in the hypothesis of transcultural values and in the research studies turned in this direction, like the Ramah Project of Harvard University. Some of the eminent names involved are those of the late Clyde Kluckhohn, Ralph Linton, George Lundberg, G. P. Murdock, among others.[15] Almost forty years ago John Dewey was suggesting the basis for this kind of research in "the psychological uniformity of human

---

[14] Expressed in his recent *Toward a Reasonable Society* (Austin: University of Texas Press, 1962) and in the earlier *Theory of Economic Progress* (Chapel Hill: University of North Carolina Press, 1944).

[15] A good review of the present status of cultural relativity may be found in an article by R. D. Lakin, "Morality in Anthropological Perspective," in *The Antioch Review*, Vol. XXI, No. 4 (1961), pp. 422–440. Another convenient summary may be found in a symposium of three articles in the *Journal of Philosophy*, Nov. 10, 1955, particularly that of Professor Kluckhohn, "Cultural Relativity: *Sic et Non*," pp. 663–677. See also an article in the same periodical by Carl Wellman, "The Ethical Implications of Cultural Relativity," Vol. LX, No. 7 (March 28, 1963); and a collection of articles in *The Monist* Vol. 47, No. 4 (Summer, 1963).

nature with respect to basic *needs*. . . . There are certain conditions which must be met in order that any form of human association may be maintained. . . . In consequence the extreme statement sometimes made about the relativity of morals cannot be maintained."[16]

This approach is being increasingly explored, and although the question is still very much in debate, it would not be inaccurate to say that the hypothesis of universal needs and capacities serving to provide a broad outline for a general, cross-cultural morality is one which is now seriously entertained. Professor Kluckhohn maintained that "Cultural differences are compatible with identity in value," and in several places he proceeded to illustrate the claim.[17] He shows, for instance, that no culture has accepted in-group suffering or cruelty as an end-in-itself, and that even the application of cruelty to the out-group is regarded as a matter of means, not of ends. Just so, no culture has failed to memorialize death. In addition, each culture seems to distinguish between normal and pathological members of the group, the criteria being determined by such things as ability to associate with others or to exercise communion with the natural world. Such similarities, and there are a number of others, led Kluckhohn to say: "It seems increasingly clear and increasingly important that some values, perhaps entirely of a broad and general nature, transcend cultural differences."[18] There may even be large temperamental similarities among men, independent of culture. In a study of such similarities, Professor Charles Morris, also impressed by "the orderliness and structure in the domain of value," has gone so far as to identify some five common "ways of life" that seem to cut across culture.[19]

It must be realized, however, that even if anthropological research continues to disclose wide likenesses among cultures, the basic issues may well remain untouched. For one thing, are such similarities *good?* All that the projects have done, it will be said, is to describe certain interesting and possibly common practices, which is clearly not to judge them. Even if pressed to admit that there are necessary conditions of survival found everywhere, the critic of this whole "universalistic" approach to value will argue that no one has yet demonstrated that survival itself is a good. He will insist on separating values from facts.

On a less formidable level, another type of criticism points to the

---

[16] From a chapter, "Anthropology and Ethics," in *The Social Sciences*, ed. by Ogburn and Goldenweiser (Boston: Houghton Mifflin, 1927), pp. 34–35.

[17] See especially his "Values and Value-Orientation" in *Toward a General Theory of Action*, ed. by Talcott Parsons and Edward A. Shils (Cambridge: Harvard, 1951); and also his chapter on anthropology in *What Is Science?* ed. by J. R. Newman (New York: Simon and Schuster, 1955), espec. pp. 343–345.

[18] *Toward a General Theory of Action*, p. 417.

[19] Cf. his *Varieties of Human Value* (Chicago: University of Chicago Press, 1956). Those five ways he calls, Buddhist, Dionysian, Promethean, Apollonian, and Christian.

truistic nature of the hypothesis under discussion. Certainly men are all alike in being alive, in having common wants as animals and common behavior patterns as social animals, but these are so general, not to say commonplace, that they can afford no discriminating criteria for purposes of evaluation. "Life" is not something which can be judged good or bad, but only the specific ways in which it is manifested. That all men have to eat is a trivial observation; what and how they eat—and these would appear to be culturally determined—is alone of interest or significance. And the same with all other "basic needs." Value discussion has to concern itself with specific means as well as with abstract and empty ends.

What conclusions may be drawn from this discussion of cultural relativism—conclusions, that is, bearing upon the problem of values as absolute or relative?

One would seem to be this: Even if anthropologists do come around to accepting some form of cross-cultural values, this would afford no necessary comfort to the believer in *absolute* value. "Universal" is the term preferred and not simply as a matter of taste. As was noted before, "absolute" carries with it connotations of a clearly nonverifiable and changeless character, as, for example, in the traditional version of absolute natural rights. These connotations would be distinctly uncongenial to a scientific approach.[20]

Next, does the hypothesis of cross-cultural values throw some doubt on the split which imputes "absolute" to conventional belief and "relative" to scientific? To some degree, yes. As previously noted, cultural relativism in its ascendancy provided a sophisticated, empirical refutation of the existence of absolute or even of universal standards; at the very least, it stood in opposition to an uncritical cultural chauvinism. If this theory has indeed undergone amendment and has been partially relaxed, then the folklore may not be as sharply divergent from science on this count as formerly. However, the point made above must be repeated: The uncritical and customary acceptance of universal values on the basis of intuition or revelation is an entirely different matter from the patient and self-corrective investigations which characterize the sciences of man. The scientific method of approach to universal values—if such could ever be agreed upon—is totally different from that of uncritical common sense.

Third, does the softening of cultural relativism, if it is softening, also help to remove at least one interdict on any scientific attempt to handle

---

[20] Cf. Herskovits, *Man and His Works, op. cit.*, p. 76, where he writes: "It is essential, in considering cultural relativism, that we differentiate absolute from universal. *Absolutes* are fixed, and, in so far as convention is concerned, are not admitted to have variations, to differ from culture to culture, from epoch to epoch. *Universals*, on the other hand, are those least common denominators to be extracted, indirectly, from comprehension of the range of variation which all phenomena of the natural or cultural world manifest."

value? The interdict imposed here, as also by sociology of knowledge, is that values are so relative to a culture, or to a social perspective, that they can only be described and never evaluated. Any mitigation of such a negative attitude would be an exciting stimulus to many philosophers and scientists to reinvestigate the claims of those who still cling to the hope of universal values. The possibility of the existence and discovery of values that may spill over cultural boundaries has motivated the search for some basis of intercultural, or even intracultural, agreement, so desperately needed in these days of crisis.[21] Although this may well be an exciting stimulus to some philosophers and scientists, it runs flatly counter to the dominant concerns of contemporary ethical theory.

Can Science Provide Values?

Among the dominant contentions of contemporary ethical theory is the firm persuasion that the endeavors of science can be directed only to the determining of means and never of ends or values. Science, it is held, cannot generate or justify value. So that even if the gap between fact and value could be systematically reduced, the test of whether values were indeed impervious to the ordinary procedures of empirical knowledge and of intelligent inquiry would be this: the ability of science to make a creative and constitutive contribution to the realm of ends or values. To be sure, the very possibility of such a contribution can be ruled out on a priori principles, as we have already seen, but however respectable the auspices of such an exclusion, logically it is no more than a simple begging of the question at issue.

Less than a short generation ago, few scientists would have responded to a challenge like this. That is no longer true. In increasing numbers, social scientists, psychologists, and biologists have been prepared to select among the profusion of human values and to validate the selection. This is still not an engagement with the question whether values can be derived from, or created by, science, but that possibility is also being discussed. This response on the part of scientists rests, of course, upon the framework of a naturalistic ethic. Upon a number of occasions in this section of the book, it has been noted that a sincere and obdurate insistence that values must be forever beyond the range of inquiry and that in truth they present entirely unanswerable problems, unless they be adopted into a nonnaturalistic and intuitive dimension—that this kind of attitude simply must be bypassed.

Within the framework of a naturalistic ethic, human survival must be

---

[21] See, for example, an important article by the English psychologist, R. E. Money-Kyrle, "Towards a Common Aim," *British Journal of Medical Psychology*, Vol. XX, pp. 105–118.

a necessary condition for any judgment about good or bad. True, it has been proposed by more than one contemporary moralist that there is no possible way of deciding that human survival is indeed desirable. This is a dramatic and iconoclastic position and, when presented with flourish and panache, it is exciting in a macabre fashion and is sure to appeal to the self-styled nonconformist. But with all its seeming sophistication, it is a position no more meaningful than one which would raise the question whether it is desirable for an organism to ingest. By definition organisms have end-directed activities, leading to survival, health, growth, and reproduction. So do cultures, although they are not organisms. Now, if a human organism suddenly contends that it prefers to develop in an abnormal manner, unhealthy and short-lived, the biologist could only respond that it would be flying in the face of the natural processes. If the reply is, "So what?" then no adequate answer is available, for the question has jumped into an orbit where almost any answer would be judged unsatisfactory by the questioner. It is the same case as the suicide's. The English philosopher, A. C. Ewing, has asserted it is not illogical to say that the whole course of evolution has itself been harmful. But such an argument can be made only if man were to be regarded as outside nature and judging it, a characteristic assumption of nonnaturalism. "If harmfulness is to be assessed entirely from the point of view of the products of evolution [one of them, of course, being man] and without bringing in any exterior, non-evolutionary point of reference, it is I think illogical (in the sense of being a contradiction in terms) to suppose that the whole evolutionary process is harmful."[22] Man is part of the evolutionary continuum. As such, he can make significant intramural judgments about himself and about other parts of the continuum. But to put him suddenly on the outside of the whole process is to testify that the hard lesson of biological continuity has not been learned.

"Survival" is a shorthand symbol standing for the imperative that any organism, including the human, must satisfy its basic needs. There would seem to be little question that at least a naturalistic interpretation of what is desirable and valuable for man would have to *start*— but by no means *finish*—with such an imperative. The relation between needs and values is, however, a very complicated one, since need-satisfaction provides only a potential, a necessary background, out of which various value patterns may emerge. Moreover, there is still no clearly established inventory of human needs; nor is there a consensus as to whether they are entirely flexible, being satisfied (as early behaviorism believed) in many different ways, or whether (as later behaviorists like Tolman and Hull held) they express a few really fixed and primary innate

---

[22] C. H. Waddington in *The Ethical Animal* (New York: Atheneum, 1961), p. 78.

drives.[23] In addition, and of most importance, a normative issue is already present in any attempt to rate the various needs. Even if a purely egalitarian attitude were taken and all human wants (implausibly) were judged to be of the same rank—so that the power drives and the various forms of acquisitive self-expression were given equal weight with the urges toward affection, cooperation, and the relaxing of tension—this, too, would obviously be a value judgment.

What has been happening is that this particular nettle (the appraisal of needs) has been firmly grasped by a number of scientists, and whether or not the sting has been less sharp because of that, at least the plant has not been conscientiously avoided as some kind of magic mandrake. It is being proposed that scientific knowledge come along as an ally in the inevitable making of value decisions, and not by default leave it all to intuition and charisma. Not that these two sources have to differ. Both Christian saint and tough-minded psychiatrist are in agreement when they insist that love is better than hate, that one "ought" to love rather than hate. (Perhaps both of them might also offer to qualify, and admit that "evil" things—the devil, Hitler—might merit hate.) Both saint and scientist may, in addition, have based their conclusions on what cannot be denied to be knowledge. But when a Karl Menninger, among others, demonstrates in detail the relation of mental health to the outgoing activities of what he does not hesitate to call "love," and the contrary pathological tendencies involved in withdrawal and cruelty, it can be argued that experimental and verifiable knowledge about man and his relationships to others is helping in some cases to justify, and elsewhere even to establish, norms of conduct.

Menninger[24] was but one of an increasing number of psychologists, psychiatrists, and social scientists who now believe that among the functions of science is the necessity to throw as much light as possible on the human options, not only as a matter of describing them but also in the hope of making a selection among them. Men like Sullivan, Cantril, Fromm, Maslow, Money-Kyrle, Parsons, Shils, Kardiner, Bronowski,[25] and many

[23] On this whole problem, see the anthropologist Dorothy Lee in "Are Basic Needs Ultimate?" *J. of Abnormal and Soc. Psy.* (Vol. XLIII, 1948, pp. 391–395).

[24] The work referred to here is *Love Against Hate* (New York: Harcourt, Brace & World, 1942).

[25] Among the works referred to in this connection are the following: Kurt Goldstein, *Human Nature in the Light of Psychopathology* (Cambridge: Harvard, 1940); Weston La Barre, *The Human Animal* (Chicago: University of Chicago Press, 1954); Abram Kardiner, *The Psychological Frontiers of Society* (New York: Columbia, 1945); Karen Horney, *Neurosis and Human Growth* (New York: Norton, 1950); Erich Fromm, *Man for Himself* (New York: Rinehart, 1947); R. E. Money-Kyrle, *Psychoanalysis and Politics* (London: Duckworth, 1951); J. Bronowski, "Science and Human Values," *The Nation* (Vol. 183, No. 26, Dec. 29, 1956); Hadley Cantril, *The Why of Man's Existence* (New York: Macmillan, 1950); H. S. Sullivan, *The Interpersonal Theory of Psychiatry*, ed by Perry and Gawel (New York: Norton, 1953); P. Mullahy, *A Study*

others have been bold enough to include values as a deliberate part of their work; and a number of them have been still bolder and have proposed that their study of human nature—both in its individual and cultural aspects as well as in its conscious and unconscious—has led them to indicate the way human nature "ought" to operate. Although there are inevitable differences in what they see as a healthy human nature (which they regard as the goal of any value system) still there is surprising agreement among them. Whether it be "self-actualization," "positive freedom," "relief from tension and anxiety," "dynamism," "creative interchange," "human dignity," "total personality," or something else (all of them inadequately and almost caricaturishly denoted in a bare list like this and even by the naked labels themselves), the source of values appears to lie in an integrated experience where problems do not fester but are resolved.

"Basic needs" are not confined to the physiological, and "survival" includes much more than merely to live. Indeed, man must live if he is to live well, but until he lives well—developing his curiosity, widening his horizons, exploiting his capacities for intellectual growth, keeping sharp and alert his sensitivity to beauty, cherishing his communion with others —he still has not satisfied his most characteristic wants. Professor A. H. Maslow, summarizing the "new knowledge" about values, remarks that among the scientists represented in his symposium,[26] and they include celebrated names in many fields of inquiry, there is almost unanimity on the imperative of "decentering" for a healthy and desirable life. This refers to the seeking and achieving of affection, warmth, union with others in various ways—in general, the socializing of man without which he becomes truncated and impoverished. Such a recommendation is not simply hortatory in the sense that man is being urged to consider his fellow men with charity; the social factor is being singled out as a main contribution to a sound and rich life.

The reason for this is clear. Whether or not the contentions of George

---

of *Interpersonal Relations* (New York: Hermitage, 1949); Talcott Parsons and Edward A. Shils, *Toward a General Theory of Action* (Cambridge: Harvard, 1951); G. W. Allport, "Scientific Models and Human Morals," *Psychological Review*, Vol. 54, No. 4 (July, 1947); Richard Rudner, "The Scientist qua Scientist Makes Value Judgments," *Philosophy of Science*, Vol. 20: pp. 1–6; C. West Chuchman, "Science and Decision Making," *Philosophy of Science*, Vol. 23; pp. 247–249. In addition, there also needs to be mentioned the new mathematical work being done (especially at Stanford University under the direction of Patrick Suppes) in the calculus of human choices, an enterprise attracting the attention not only of economists and mathematicians but also of mathematically trained professional philosophers.

[26] *New Knowledge in Human Value* (New York: Harper & Row, 1959). Some of these scientists are men like Th. Dobzhansky, L. von Bertalanffy, H. Margenau, J. Bronowski, P. A. Sorokin, and G. W. Allport. They represent, of course, differing points of view on this matter of values and science. See also Maslow's recent books, *Toward a Psychology of Being* (Princeton, N. J.: Princeton, 1962), and *Religions, Values and Peak-Experiences* (Columbus: Ohio State University Press, 1964).

Mead about the social nature of mind, self, and consciousness be accepted,[27] it would appear that the "moral self" is the product of interpersonal forces, of the obligations arising from the give-and-take among the members of even the simplest community. No more than "mind" is the *cause* of communication, is "conscience" the *cause* of morality. The argument here is that just as mind and self are the fruits of communion among evolving organisms, so is the moral sense an attribute of evolving social organisms when they reach a particular level, as in man. Indeed, to be accountable to others and to one's (social) self establishes the very conditions for moral experience. The moral questions need not be exclusively those of defining "good" or "right," as they are in one segment of contemporary ethics, or of introverted soliloquizing, as they are in another, but rather of specifying the conditions for cooperation among men. "Social" would seem to be a prerequisite for existence itself, and not merely for human existence.[28] In the case of man, a radically isolated individual simply does not exist. "To exist" suggests "to exist in or along with"; for man "to exist" implies "to exist in a culture."

This may seem a travesty to the outsider. Like certain existentialists today, he would feel that to present value as predominantly social in nature is no more than a bourgeois manifestation of frightened "togetherness." Even the reducing of tensions and anxiety may well be acting in bad faith; the individual, alone and absurd, must turn within himself and become, not an organization man, but one cherishing his solitude and apartness. But are not total outsiders as mythical as Adam or as Robinson Crusoe— at least, a "biological" Crusoe, that is, one born all alone on his island (a difficult feat for a mammal) and who had met no one at all until Friday came along? A deliberate outsider like Thoreau was a highly socialized person before he went to Walden Pond, and what he saw there was seen through the eyes of a sophisticated Massachusetts citizen. Man cannot define himself in a vacuum.

The present emphasis on the social grounding of values and on the possibility of exploiting scientific resources in validating them, should not be misinterpreted to mean that only the prosaic and, as it were, "groupy" values are available to naturalism. The outsider and the existentialist have no monopoly on the tragic or the dramatic. There is tragedy implicit in the whole problematic set-up, which is so fundamental to the approach that has been outlined in the preceding pages: for when *a* is chosen, *b* must be rejected, and, if *a* and *b* are true rivals, the dilemma is almost a definition of the tragic situation. The insistence that determina-

---

[27] See above, pp. 376–377.

[28] As A. N. Whitehead and others have insisted, relatedness is a basic trait of the world at all levels; it would seem to be a fundamental category of explanation. Nothing in nature, it can be argued, is totally independent.

tion of the "desirable," in contrast to the "desired," derives from the element of knowledge, is another gateway to tragedy, since knowledge is rarely of an all-or-nothing character, and therefore the unacceptable "desired" remains a viable and poignant possibility. In a world such as the one man encounters, no philosophy has an exclusive claim upon pathos. Moreover, it must be recalled that "values"—at least according to the present approach—emerge only when there are real and live options, genuine difficulties; the "valuable" by no means encompasses each and every human condition. There are immediate experiences that are part of everyman's portion, benign and unexpected consummations which are no less precious for being what they are, optionless and uncontrived. No philosophy can or does ignore such experiences.

What is being argued here is that the moral imperative be looked for in the discoverable nature of man. That the nature of man is no mystery, that it was as well known to Saint Augustine as to Sigmund Freud, simply does not hold. For new dimensions of man *are* being revealed, a fact that must be taken into account. What is being asked now is that these new dimensions of the organic and social structures of man, unconscious as well as conscious, be enlisted in the search for moral sanctions. It is not important at the moment whether the scientists mentioned above are correct in the norms they are suggesting; it is important that they are willing to give us norms of any kind, based not on an inner sense or revelation but on meticulous clinical and experimental research, subject to the normal, self-corrective processes of scientific method. Here is an attempt to cut the Gordian knot.

Although the myth does not suggest it, there may be other knots. The hard one, to be sure, is that already encountered—the one which securely ties science outside the field of value altogether. Even if this one be loosened, another remains to fasten science to the task of choosing among values but never letting it free to create them. This confinement has been challenged by a number of scientists, perhaps most persistently by J. Bronowski.[29] He contends, first of all, that the special activity of present-day civilization is that of science. Now, science's findings may be regarded as neutral or value-free or possibly as evil, but not, he insists, its methods and its general attitude. That attitude is one which, above all, seeks a warranted answer to its questions. If the phrase "search for truth" be substituted, then this must be regarded as a prime value implicit in the very nature of scientific endeavor, or, more broadly, in the nature of intelligence itself. In this search, other "values" are not only involved but in a measure constituted, for example, independence, originality, the

---

[29] In addition to his article cited above, see also *Science and Human Value* (New York: Messner, 1956).

importance of dissent, the spirit of tentativeness, and the insistence upon being shown. For Bronowski, these are precious values which, if not actually created by the scientific temper, are certainly justified by it. Therefore, to complain that "science" is employed by dictators (fascist or communist) to bring about unworthy ends or that "science" is to be blamed for "The Bomb," is to misuse terms in a serious way. Scientific method must be "democratic," meaning by that: publicity of results, international co-operation, objective verification of findings, independence of political, ideological, national, or racial domination—in short, reliance on the over-reaching "value" that "facts" cannot be contravened. This is an attitude that "ought" to have the highest priority in any system of values, ac-cording to the approach being outlined here. It is an approach intended to lift science from a merely instrumentalist position—the justifying of already-accepted goals—to a constitutive or generative one in which science dares, or, more accurately, is constrained, to propose a number of ends-in-view as worthy of moral consideration on any level.

Among the most dominant of such ends-in-view, at least according to this maximum interpretation of the contribution of social science to value, is that men need, above all, to understand themselves and their surround-ings through the use of free intelligent inquiry. What gives such a con-tention its high priority for some scientists is that it does not separate ends from means, but suggests instead that operations and methods are them-selves of prime concern and desirable on their own account as well as for what they effect. It suggests also that a concern with method and technique might serve to give more substance to the admittedly laudable yet often empty and abstract goods like "peace," "health," "freedom," "survival," and the rest. These quickly can become platitudes, merely ceremonial and legendary, fit for celebration but about which nothing more is said. But to say more and to go beyond the rites of celebration would seem to require information in addition to good will and analytical acumen.

Even with the most unexceptionable ends—"life," "health," "the general welfare"—we cannot, to use the words of Professor William Dennes, "fore-close on the relevance of knowledge." For any kind of reportable experi-ence may prove pertinent. All three of these "goods" just mentioned might well be affected by the next government report on pesticides, nico-tine, or the hallucinatory drugs. The most plebian and routine knowledge may serve to clarify and possibly change already established ends as well as help men to realize them. It seems pretty evident that our energies need not all be spent in reaffirming the moral verities; in fact, to pay attention to noble words alone may lead to vacuity at one extreme or fanaticism at the other. But to concentrate on the manageable and the reachable is at the same time to put a premium on human intelligence.

Selected Readings

Albert, Ethel, and Clyde Kluckhohn, A *Selected Bibliography on Values, Esthetics, and Ethics in the Behavorial Sciences and Philosophy, 1920–1958*, Glencoe, Ill.: The Free Press, 1959.

Edel, A., *Method in Ethical Theory*, Indianapolis: Bobbs-Merrill, 1963.

Edel, A., *Ethical Judgment: The Use of Science in Ethics*, Glencoe, Ill.: The Free Press, 1955. (Friendship Press paperback.)

Gellner, Ernest, *Thought and Change*, Chicago: University of Chicago, 1965.

Hartmann, N., *Ethics*, trans. by Coit, New York: Macmillan, 1932.

Hobhouse, L. I., *Morals in Evolution*, New York: Holt, Rinehart & Winston, 1915.

Margenau, H., *Ethics and Science*, Princeton: Van Nostrand, 1964.

Olson, Robert G. *The Morality of Self-Interest*, New York: Harcourt, Brace & World (Harbinger paperback), 1965.

Schoeck, H., and J. W. Wiggins, eds., *Scientism and Values*, Princeton: Van Nostrand, 1960.

Waddington, C. H., *The Ethical Animal*, New York: Atheneum, 1961.

Westermarck, E. V., *Ethical Relativity*, New York: Harcourt, Brace & World, 1932.

Epilogue

To compare Part I of this volume with Part IV is to encounter a kind of glorious paradox: in its Greek dawn, science had first to be freed from the realm of value so that, amplified and mature, it might be enlisted today at its high noon in the quest for more meaningful values. This is true not only of science as a generalized method, but of the knowledge it now gives us about the nature of man and society. And yet that free intelligent inquiry with which science is identified is by no means the same as philosophy. It is therefore appropriate, in conclusion, to restate the central role of philosophy as this role has been interpreted in the foregoing pages. To do so is in a sense to present a "philosophy of philosophy," a major preoccupation of philosophers in the twentieth century. Three interpretations of the role of philosophy have been suggested in the preceding discussions even if they have not always been explicitly formulated:

1. Historically, most philosophers have thought of philosophy as the way to achieve absolute truth about ultimate reality. Many have thought of themselves as providing such revelations. As we have seen, few philosophers today share this aspiration. Nor is such a role for philosophy defended here.

2. Today, as Part IV has emphasized, many, if not most, philosophers in the English-speaking world have taken the opposite position that philosophy has been concerned with pseudo-problems; that it has no disclosures

to make about the nature of things that are not better made by the scientific disciplines; that, above all, it has no suprascientific truths to reveal; and that it must content itself with the quest for *clarity* as a substitute for the quest for *certainty*. Hence, the vogue of language analysis in the last several decades, for it is language that confuses us, involves us in false problems, leads us astray. If, as Wittgenstein said in the famous phrase already quoted, the puzzles of philosophy merely reflect the "bewitchment of our intelligence by language," it is with the clarification of language, either everyday language ("ordinary English") or the language of science, that philosophy must concern itself.

3. The interpretation assumed here is that, while many of the problems of philosophy do stem from verbal confusions which philosophers must exercise themselves to dispel, other problems have deeper *psychological* and *cultural* origins, and no amount of language analysis will solve them. Second, while the quest for certainty and truth in some absolute sense is indeed visionary and chimerical, philosophy can provide understanding and explanation of a kind not yielded by the sciences as such. Contrary to Wittgenstein's observation that philosophy is "not a body of propositions, but to make propositions clear," it has been assumed here that philosophy is *both*; except that the propositions of philosophy are *neither* timeless truths nor explanations of the kind provided by the several sciences.

Explanation and understanding are achieved differently in different areas of human interest—in different problematic areas, the pragmatist might say. As we have seen, even within the area of the sciences different types of explanation are used. Do we not have in philosophy in the broadest sense still another way, a culminating and inclusive way, of providing explanation and achieving understanding? Clearly, one does not expect truth in the sense in which one finds it in the physical or biological sciences or even the science of society. Perhaps instead of truth and falsity we should speak here of adequacy and inadequacy. Those philosophies have been adequate which have been successful in resolving the major tensions of their time, especially where such tensions are produced by the rival cognitive claims of science, common sense, and the received wisdom. Along with the received wisdom one should no doubt mention also the great visions and intuitions of inspired and gifted men. Some of these claims and the tensions resulting from them are peculiar to a particular epoch, and the philosophies pertinent to them are therefore ephemeral and have only an historical interest. But other competing claims are recurrent and persistent for we are, after all, cultural descendants of the Greeks and not arrivals from another planet. To that extent the philosophies in which such claims are reconciled are of enduring interest and importance; the understanding such philosophies provide is as relevant today as it was yesterday.

Even though such "understanding" cannot be verified as we verify the cognitive claim of a hypothesis in science, we have agreed in the foregoing pages with Morris Raphael Cohen, one of the revered philosophers of the first decades of this century, when he wrote that "To introduce order and consistency into our vision, to remove pleasing but illusory plausibilities by contrasting various views with their possible alternatives, and to judge critically all pretended proofs in the light of the most rigorously logical rules of evidence, is the indispensable task of any serious philosophy."[1] Surely the understanding arrived at by this kind of effort is the most important one of all. If nature, because it includes man, contains facts and values, stubborn preconceptions and great visions, routine acceptance of what is and creative insight, then philosophy as well as science is required, if nature is to be fully understood.

Those who come to philosophy for the first time should find an answer in this approach to their two most common complaints. They are often troubled by what seems to them to be the remoteness, abstractness and artificiality of the problems to which they are expected to address themselves. The determination of philosophers to face such problems seems to them arbitrary and gratuitous. The assumption in these pages that the major problems of philosophy are precipitated by the inevitable clash in our kind of society between new knowledge and accepted belief should make such problems appear as real and urgent as they in fact are.

Newcomers to philosophy are also understandably troubled by the variety of philosophical standpoints. They want answers. After all, the philosophers they are asked to study sought answers—and in most cases thought that they had found them.

Perhaps "answers" is misleading. Students expect a consensus among philosophers concerning the issues with which philosophers deal comparable to the agreement that prevails among scientists concerning the main corpus of their science. Such a consensus among experts would suggest—at least so the novice would argue—some approximation to truth, that is, an "answer." Again, as they learn that philosophical speculation has a long history, students expect to find cumulative knowledge not unlike what they find in biology or astronomy. Instead they learn that, while a physicist may ignore Archimedes, a philosopher who was ignorant of Plato would not be taken seriously. The issue involves distinctions between cumulative and noncumulative knowledge which cannot be explored here. It is raised in order to stress the predicament of the student who finds nothing comparable to the progress with which the advance of the natural sciences has familiarized him. What has a discipline, in which the most authoritative spokesmen are unable to achieve even approximate agreement, or to advance greatly the solution of problems that were posed more than

[1] M. R. Cohen, *Reason and Nature*, 2nd ed. (Glencoe, Ill.: Free Press, 1953), p. ix.

2000 years ago, to offer him? If the experts are unable to agree, how is he, a novice, to choose among them? Such perplexities may well prompt the student, as they have many of his teachers, to dismiss the traditional concerns of philosophy as mere word play.

However, if one accepts the role of philosophy defended in this volume, it becomes possible to make sense of the multiplicity of philosophical standpoints. For these are now seen as rooted in problems and predicaments that vary as the content of knowledge and experience varies. On the other hand, difference tends to overshadow agreement. Diverse philosophical standpoints often have much in common—as much in common as Socrates with Bertrand Russell or Archimedes with Albert Einstein. The distance between fifth-century B.C. Athens and twentieth-century Cambridge, between Archimedes' Syracuse and Einstein's Princeton may be great, but surely all these men rejected Morris Raphael Cohen's "pleasing but illusory plausibilities," surely their scorn of "pretended proofs" and passion for "rigorously logical rules of evidence" make them members of the same great community. That is why the history of philosophy has enduring value for us and why there is so much of the history of philosophy in the foregoing pages.

INDEX